Placenames of Georgia

PLACENAMES

OF GEORGIA

Essays of John H. Goff

edited by
Francis Lee Utley and Marion R. Hemperley

University of Georgia Press
Athens

Paperback edition, 2007
© 1975 by the University of Georgia Press
Athens, Georgia 30602
www.ugapress.org

All rights reserved
Designed by Gary Core
Printed digitally in the United States of America

The Library of Congress has cataloged the hardcover edition
of this book as follows:
Library of Congress Cataloging-in-Publication Data
Goff, John H. (John Hedges), 1899–1967.
Placenames of Georgia : essays of John H. Goff / edited by
Francis Lee Utley and Marion R. Hemperley.
xxxviii, 495 p. : map (on lining papers) ; 24 cm.
Includes bibliographical references and index.
ISBN 0-8203-0342-9
1. Names, Geographical–Georgia. 2. Georgia–History, Local.
I. Title
F284 .G63   1975
917.58'003   73-88366

Paperback ISBN-13: 978-0-8203-3129-4
ISBN-10: 0-8203-3129-5

Contents

Abbreviations	xi
Preface, by Marion R. Hemperley	xiii
Introduction, by Francis Lee Utley	xvii

THE PARTICULAR

Short Studies of Georgia Placenames (1954–1964)

1. The Golden Groves 1
2. The Longstreets 3
3. The Barkcamp Districts 6
4. Oak Cane Branch 9
5. Upatoi Creek 10
6. The Stalkinghead Creeks 13
7. Great Coat Branch 16
8. Penholoway Creek 17
9. Attapulgus 21
10. Mars Hill 26
11. Withlacoochee and Willacoochee 27
12. Aucilla River 31
13. Plains (and Plains of Dura) 35
14. Tobesofkee and Rocky Creeks 37
15. Hachasofkee and Sofkee Creeks 40
16. Echeconnee Creek 43
17. Mulberry, Ossahatchie, and Sowhatchee Creeks 44
18. Bad and Worse Creeks, No Man's Friend Pond, The Troublesome Creeks, Devil's Cove, Tearbritches and Rough Creeks, Hell's Half Acre, The Bad Prong of Ten-Mile, Lordamercy Cove, and Useless Bay 46
19. Canoochee River 48
20. Oostanaula and Eastanollee 49
21. Tukpafka, Punk Creek, Pink Creek, Rotten Wood Creek, and New Yorka 50

22. Yellow Dirt Creek 54
23. Ball Ground and Ball Play Creek 55
24. Chattooga (and Guinekelokee) 58
25. Teloga Creek 61
26. The Cherokee Town of Quanasee 62
27. Hiwassee and Hiawassee 67
28. The "Dividings," the Hiwassee Trail, Timpson Creek, Racepath Creek 73
29. The Great Pine Barrens 81
30. Towaliga River 90
31. Four Killer Creek (Spanish Pete's Old Place, Some Settlements of the Cherokee Downing Family, Cedar Creek, Vickery Creek) 93
32. Unawatti Creek, the Flat Creeks, Level Creek, Pataula Creek 95
32-A. Unawatti Creek 98
33. Young Deer Creek (Two Mile, Four Mile, and Six Mile Creeks of Forsyth County) 101
34. Tussahaw Creek 103
35. Bolivar and Ypsilanti 104
36. Long Swamp Creek 105
37. Lazer ("Lizer") Creek 107
38. Paramore Hill (and Scull Creek) 109
39. Rincon (and Some Other Spanish Names) 112
41. [sic]. Po' Biddy Crossroads 113
40. Egypt (and Egypt Hollow) 114
41. Some "Coined" Names: Adsboro, Arco, Arcola, Ausmac, Bidawee, Captolo, Cenchat, Centralhatchee, Elko, Hopeulikit, Muckafoonee, Neyami, Ochlawilla, Oredell, Penhoopee, Rockalo, Rockmart, Subligna, Tennga, Villanow, etc. 116
42. Stitchihatchie or Tickeehatchee Creek, and Whitley Branch 126
43. Gopher Town ("Go' Town") and Goat Town 128
44. Iron Hill (and a former "Deer Lick") 128
45. Social Circle, Society Hill, Social Hill, Merry Hill, Fancy Hill, Fancy Bluff, Fancy Hall, Jolly (and Fashion) 130
46. Bloody Branch (and Bloody Creek) 133
47. Salacoa Creek 135
48. Sumach and Holly Creeks 137
49. Possumtrot Branch 138
50. Big Bend and the Panhandles 139
51. Okefenokee 140
52. The "Sixes" Places: Sixes Old Town, Sixes District, Sixes Creek, Sixes Mine, Sixes Trail, Sutalee (and Satolah) 142
53. Catoosa 147
54. No Business Creek 149
55. Yonah Mountain and Sillycook Mountain 151
56. Ochillee Creek and Halloca Creek 152
57. Schatulga 155

Contents / vii

58. Gardi and Guard Jam Bluff 155
59. Fort Buffington 157
60. Lost Town Creek and Shut-In Creek 158
61. Waleska 159
62. Buzzard Flopper (or Buzzard Flapper) Creek 160
63. Jekyll Island 161
64. Panola, Panola Shoals, Panola Road, South River, Cotton River, Reeves Creek and Upton Creek 165
65. Silco 169
66. Standing Boy Creek, End Creek, East and West End Creeks, and Heifer-Horn Creeks 170
67. Roaring Creek (Formerly the Chissehulcuh) 174
68. Cataula (and Mulberry Creek) 175
69. Mountain Creek and House Creek 177
70. Laingkat 178
71. Cuttingbone Creek 179
72. Cohelee or Cahelee Creek 181
73. The Rock Landing 183
74. Wahoo Island, Wahoo River, the Wahoo Creeks, Wahoo District, Barbour Island, and Barbour Island River 185
75. Lewis Creek 189
76. Fishing Creek in Baldwin County 191
77. Oakfuskee Creek 192
78. Toms Shoals (Toms Fords, Toms Path, Chehaw Path, Tuskio-Micco Path, Popes Ferry and Road, Wallers Ferry and Road, Booths Ferry and Road, Calhouns Ferry, Grays Road, the Otaulganene or Islands Ford of Flint River, the Sulenojuhnene Fords, the Creek Town of Buzzard Roost, Hootens Ferry, Cantelows Ferry, Trices Ferry and Smuteyes Trail) 193
79. Anneewakee Creek 214
80. The Intrenchment Creeks 216
81. Eastahatchee, Now Sanborn Creek 220
82. Breastworks Branch (A Camp Site of Andrew Jackson's Men and an Old Fortification in Upper Wilcox County) 221
83. Walnut Creek (Formerly the Oakchuncoolgau) 226
84. Christmas Branch 229
85. Tallahassee Creek (Formerly the Osketochee) 230
86. Five Mile Creek (Formerly the Saoxomoha) 232
87. Alapaha River, Alapaha Creek, Little Alapaha River, Grand Bay Creek or Little River (Formerly the Alapahoochee), the Town of Alapaha, and the Indian Settlement of Alapaha Talofa 234
88. Yahoola Creek 243
89. The Milksick Coves 245
90. Pears or Perry Creek 247
91. Pine Log Creek, Pine Log Mountain, and the Former Cherokee Town of Pine Log in Bartow County 249
92. Marbury Creek 254

93. Haynes Creek (and Cornish Creek) 255
94. The Red Hills Region (and an Early Description of Parts of Macon, Peach, Crawford and Bibb Counties) 258
95. Sweetwater Creek (of Crawford County) 265
96. The Big Savannah, Savannah District, Savannah School, Dougherty, Palmers Creek, Russells Creek (Originally Child Toaters Creek) Proctors Creek, Bags Branch, Baggs Creek, Wicked Creek, Toto Creek, Dukes Creek (and the Former Cherokee Town of Tensawattee) 267
97. Betty Creek, Mud or Estatoah Creek, (and the Former Cherokee Settlement of Eastertoy) 277
98. Rossville 280
99. Spring Bluff 281
100. Sardis or Sardins Creek (Formerly Sartains Creek) 283
101. Spoil Cane Creek 284
102. Fodder Creek 285
103. Sopes Creek and Soap Creek 286
104. Fulsams Creek (Formerly Folsoms Creek) 288
105. Black Creek (Formerly the Weelustie) and Iric Creek 290
106. Cowpen Creek (Originally Jones Cowpen Creek) 291
107. Alecks Creek, Aleck Island, Doctortown, Doctors Creek, Old Doc Slough, Sansavilla Bluffs, the Williamsburg Reserve, the Dead Town of St. Savilla or Williamsburg, Fort Defense, Williams Fort (and the Indian Settlements of Santa Sevilla and St. Iagos Town) 293
108. Beards Bluff, Beards Creek, Fort James Bluff, Five Mile Creek, Ten Mile Creek, Boundaries of the Creek Land Cession of 1773, Oglethorpe Bluff (and Mount Venture) 302
109. Amicalola Creek, Amicalola Falls (and the Former Cherokee Community of Bread Town) 313
110. Sterling Creek 315
111. Pocataligo 316
112. Muckalee Creek and Some of Its Tributaries 319
113. The Tobler Creeks and the Poor Robin Places 324
114. Ossabaw Island, Wassaw Island, Wassaw Sound, the Warsaw Places, and Cumberland Island, Formerly Wiso 329
115. Suomi 333

Unnumbered Short Studies

Old Chattahoochee Town: An Early Muskogee Indian Settlement (1953) 335
Hog Crawl Creek (1954) 339
The Creek Village of Cooccohapofe on Flint River (1961) 341
An "Indian Fort" on Flint River (1963) 344

THE GENERAL

    Retracing the Old Federal Road (1950) 349
    Wolf Pens and Wolf Pits (1953) 361
    Ty Ty as a Geographic Name (1954) 363
    The Poley Bridge Creeks (1954) 367
    The Beaverdam Creeks (1954) 370
    The Buffalo in Georgia (1957) 379
    Some Old Road Names in Georgia (1957) 388
    The Devils Half Acre (1959) 399
    The Poor Mouthing Placenames (1959) 406
    The Derivations of Creek Indian Placenames (1961) 416
    Pronunciations of Georgia Placenames, Part I (1963) 437
    Pronunciations of Georgia Placenames, Part II 441
    Pronunciations of Georgia Placenames, Part III 445
    The Rising Fawns (1963) 448
    The Hurricane Placenames in Georgia (1964) 459
    Our Changing Placenames (1964?) 470

Index   481

Abbreviations

EUQ   *Emory University Quarterly*
GM   *Georgia Magazine*
GMNL *Georgia Mineral Newsletter*
GR   *Georgia Review*
IJAL *International Journal of American Linguistics*

Preface

JOHN H. GOFF'S delightful and informative sketches on Georgia placenames were first published as a series in the *Georgia Mineral Newsletter*, a publication of the Georgia Geological Survey in Atlanta. The *Newsletter*, which has since ceased publication, saw only limited distribution within the state to specialists in only one of the fields that have a direct interest in Professor Goff's subject matter. Now, with the republication of Goff's sketches, along with some of his longer essays on placenames, scholars as well as the general public will have access to these very valuable and interesting contributions to Georgia's history and local color.

On the face of it, Professor Goff, who was an economist specializing in transportation and industrial economics, was an unlikely author for these placename sketches. And indeed, his work in onomastics was a hobby and not his profession; but for Goff, as for many of us, his hobby was not entirely unrelated to his professional interests. In fact, his work in placenaming had grown out of his curiosity about and research in the history of early transportation in the Southeast. From a study of the routes of such economically important roads as the Lower Creek Trading Path and the Old Federal Road it was only a small step to investigating the history of these old roads, and from there to a full-fledged curiosity about the naming of towns and villages along the state's roads and waterways (which, we must remember, formed a crucial part of the transportation network of colonial and post-Revolutionary Georgia).

It is easy to imagine that John Goff's placename hobby eventually became a consuming interest. His writing style, so unlike the jargon-choked scholar's, is clearly that of a writer who enjoys what he is doing. Onomastics, especially American onomastics with its characteristic emphasis on history rather than on etymology and its ability to discover in our recent history the actual process of naming a place

(European placenames, we must remember, are much older and must therefore be approached more by a purely linguistic analysis), is one of the livelier of the linguistic arts and sciences, of interest to quite a wide range of students and scholars. Goff's essays will assist the folklorist, the cartographer, the historian, the student of Indian history and lore, the archivist, the geographer, the anthropologist—amateur and professional alike.

Professor Goff's approach to placename study was thoroughly American in that it was basically historical. He searched for over thirty-five years for primary source material for his sketches and essays in Georgia's original land grants, plats of survey, and maps. In addition, he travelled to surrounding states and to Washington, D.C., Chicago, and London to find the material he needed to track given names to their sources.

In addition to the placename writings collected in this book John H. Goff was the author of many articles on local history of the Southeast. He was the author, coauthor, or director of several published reports on transportation and industrial economics. Goff was especially interested in the economic history of the early Southeast and wrote many papers in that field. His testimony played an influential part in the appraisal of Creek Nation lands in southern Georgia and southeastern Alabama in the suit which resulted in the federal government's paying over $3.5 million to the Creeks for territory which they claimed had been underestimated at the time of the treaties.

A native Southerner born in Kentucky, John Goff moved to Georgia when he was in his teens. He graduated from Oglethorpe University in 1919 and soon thereafter attended several schools in Europe: the universities of Paris and Strasbourg and the Centro de Cursos Historicos in Madrid. In 1929 he received his Ph.D. from the Georgetown University School of Foreign Service. Goff taught at a number of colleges and universities, including Mississippi State College, Starkeville; Georgia Institute of Technology, Atlanta; Armstrong College, Berkeley, California; Auburn University, Auburn, Alabama; and Emory University, Atlanta. He was Acting Dean of the School of Business Administration at the latter institution upon his retirement in 1959.

In 1936–1939, and again in 1942–1944, Professor Goff went on leave from Auburn University to serve as Director of the Transportation and Industrial Economics Division of the Tennessee Valley Authority. He served as consulting economist for the TVA in Alabama and for the Bonneville Power Company, Portland, Oregon. During

World War II, Goff was Chief Economist and Director of Research for the United States Transportation Board of Investigation and Research, Washington, D.C., under President Roosevelt.

Some months before Professor Goff's untimely death on September 7, 1967, he presented his entire collection of maps, notes, and prints to the Georgia Surveyor General Department of the Office of the Secretary of State, Atlanta. This large collection is on file in that department for the use of historians, anthropologists, and geographers interested in research in the southeastern United States.

MARION R. HEMPERLEY

Introduction

CONNOISSEURS of placename study have long known John Goff's short studies as one of the most informative and charming contributions to the study of toponymy. Hence they have bewailed its burial in a periodical, the *Georgia Mineral Newsletter*, thoroughly reputable among mineralogists but more or less inaccessible to the humanists who study onomastics. These studies deserve to be brought together with other scattered articles, in the *Georgia Review*, the *Emory University Quarterly*, and the *Georgia Magazine*, which help to broaden the scope of the short studies and to draw Goff's finely drawn particulars into the realm of the universal. It is both revealing and exciting to see how an amateur of language and history, a professor of business administration, was able in the fifties and early sixties to lay down an approach to placenames which serious scholars can admire and gentle readers enjoy. This editor was therefore honored when the University of Georgia Press asked him to join with an old friend of Goff's, Marion Hemperley of the Surveyor General Department of the State of Georgia, in bringing these essays to a wider public.

Your editor must admit that in undertaking such a task he violates the letter if not the spirit of his own canons of placename study, for he has long claimed that the student of local names should cultivate four major disciplines: linguistics, history, geography, and folklore.[1] Though he can claim some experience with the universals of linguistics and folklore and their local applications, he is no professional historian or geographer, and above all he is ignorant of the particulars of a state famed for its sense of community and local pride. He is not even a native Georgian. His grandfather fought for the North in the War Between the States, but Theodore Utley was safely in Andersonville Prison when Sherman made his devastating march through Georgia. Your editor counts, then, on Goff's intensive knowledge of the local history and geography which are the eternal correctives of the brash theorist, and likewise on his coeditor, who comes from the precious local scene. Goff's studies, reprinted here with a minimum of correction and editorial annotation, can stand tall and easily support our fourfold criteria. Indeed, on the stimulus of Goff, we may add a fifth canon: the "psychology" of naming.

Linguistics has generally been thought to be the primary disciplinary component of toponymy. In Europe, where onomastics has its proper place in academic curricula, it is classed with linguistics and with the study of the national language which it adorns. Yet, like many a subfield of the study of how men speak, onomastics stresses lexical data and is only secondarily interested in syntactical systems. Hence it achieves status in scientific rosters and world congresses but not in American linguistic departments; it has been scanted in the universities and relegated to the amateur. The best we can say is that an occasional professor of English or geography manages a little exposure to his graduate students. Abroad it is central to the study of the Indo-European and Finno-Ugric language families, and in England and France it is one of the strongest supports of the early history of these countries, with their Celtic, Germanic, and Latin origins. Unfortunately the American onomastician has a special problem: the languages he needs to solve his puzzles are American Indian, and the vocabularies of these widely diverse families are buried in obscure publications and in manuscripts at the Smithsonian. Rarely can he depend on expert authorities, for many of the collectors of Indian word lists are (or were) as amateur as he is. Ever since the Middle Ages derived *Noah* from *Bacchus*, etymologies have been a risky occupation. Today lexicographers have massive data and yet often disagree, though the best of them follow the axiom that if an etymology is to be respected, it must be itself respectful both to phonetic and to semantic laws. Many typonymic etyma in the United States must be based on guesswork, for only on the basis of a succession of equations between "English" names and Indian words can one base a word history, which will be largely the product of trial and error, with slow elimination of the wild or impossible.

On the whole Goff's guesses are good ones; he understands the competition between Iroquoian Cherokee and Muskogean Creek, the languages of the two major groups who had settled Georgia before the white man came, and he continually measures the potential etymon against Cherokee and Creek spheres of influence (see Nos. 20, 24, 56: Oostanaula, Chattooga, Ochillee). A systematic study of such names, if it is ever possible, might help to write the unwritten history of these tribes, just as Anglo-Saxon historians can fix the areas of Celtic, Norman, and Scandinavian settlement by isoglosses based on placenames. This kind of close work must be left to more comprehensive surveys, such as that planned for the American Placename Survey by Z. J. Farkas and Claude Britt of Georgia Southern College. Yet there are ventures in the direction of unwritten Indian history in Goff: Aneewakee Creek, Bloody Branch, and the Rock Landing, for instance (Nos. 79, 46, 73). Goff does not seem to have seen a pair of essays on Georgia Indian names by William A. Read, a pioneer student who also studied aboriginal names in Louisiana, Alabama, and Florida.[2] I have used Read extensively in the notes: often he confirms Goff's argument and sometimes his data unconsciously queries it (see Chokee in Read; Goff's "Derivations" and Towaliga, No. 30). Many times Goff has the advantage of information far beyond Read's range, from history and geography as well as linguistics.

Moving to another linguistic stratum, we find Goff explaining the mysteries of Indian and pioneer phonetics with reasonable clarity and accuracy. Perhaps a linguist, with his established IPA or Trager-Smith alphabets, could explain the Hitchiti voiceless *l*, here spelled *thl*, somewhat more simply by noting that the *th* is simply a sign of the fortis breathing demanded when a consonant is unvoiced. But it is just possible that that "simplicity," which appeals in its precision to the student long-grounded in phonetic patterning, vowel charts, and acoustic phonetics, may be obscure to the general reader. I have noticed that sometimes it is so to undergraduates. Goff's occasional excursions into a phonetic process, notably that very thorny one which consists of the transformation of a word from one linguistic system to another, may be simpler than that of the student of distinctive features. In his article on pronunciations Goff discusses a few crucial points: the Anglicization of foreign names—Wien /viyn/ to Vienna, Taliaferro to the very local Tolliver; the shift of dialects—Northern Albany /'ol bə niy/ to /ol 'bey niy/; the folk-etymologization of Guardi to Guard-eye and of Ty Ty to Tighteye (with close to open juncture); the deceptive orthographies, masking more authentic Indian sounds, of Towaliga /tay 'lay giy/, Upatoi /'yuw pə toy/, Sawhatchee Creek /say 'hæc iy/, and Pogo's swamp Okefenokee /"ow kiy fiy 'now kiy/. He discusses the suppression of an Indian *a* in Cherokee Tuckaseeking, now pronounced /'tʌk siy kiŋ/, its pioneer restressing to an /iy/ is Chickamauga /"cik iy 'mo giy/, and its gradated unstressing and syncope in Pallachucola /"pæ l ə 'cuk la/. He notes the free variation between /'skre vən/, /'skriy vən/, and /'skray vən/ in Screven County, a linguistic feature which can only be fully witnessed on the local ground. Sometimes the variation is introduced by newcomers, as when DeKalb /də 'Kæb/ becomes the swanky /diy 'kolb/. When Goff explains that Spanish Villa Rica /'viy ya 'riy ka/ has become /'vi lə 'ri kə/ his equation of Villa with "fill 'er" will confuse the Northerner, who is not used to attempts to demonstrate the loss of *r* in Southern speech; the same reader has trouble with Joel Chandler Harris's *Brer Rabbit*. Just as Ohio's Wooster /'wuw stər/ is a respelling of Massachusetts' Worcester /'wu stər/ or /'wu stə/, which has introduced a new spelling pronunciation in its turn, so Georgia's Gloster does the same for England's Gloucester, but it is closer than Ohio's, for both are /'glo stə/, and only the spelling is changed. Berkeley in Madison County, like the name of the newsworthy university town in California, is Americanized to /'bər kliy/ or /'bʌ kliy/, though the philosopher of appearance was George /'bar kliy/. When Goff says that Aragon sounds like "Arrow' gun" or "Arrer' gun" (his accents follow the syllable, whereas ours precede in common linguistic practice) he baffles the outlander who does not know that for a Georgian both *ow* and *er* are ways of writing the unstressed mid-central /ə/ or "schwa" vowel. No doubt Goff would have said /'win də/ for window; my dialect has /'win "dow/. Mauk, he says, is pronounced either "Mock" or "Mawk"; a linguist would say that the sound hovers between a low-mid unrounded and a low-back rounded vowel.

"The Derivations of Creek Placenames" pays closer attention to clashes of phonemic pattern between Creek and English. Goff says there were only eight vowel sounds in Creek; he does not tell us whether there was, as in English, a system of complex and simple vowels—*meet* /miyt/ versus *mitt* /mit/, or whether they were all simple—*mitt* /mit/ versus *met* /met/. In any event the sound system was simpler than that in English, and it is therefore not surprising that there was difficulty in conforming English sounds and spellings to the sounds of unwritten Creek. The lack of the meet-mitt contrast in the high-front area, for instance, is notorious; it inhibits the native Spaniard speaking English from using the common words beach and sheet. Upatoi is a modern spelling of an earlier *apata -i*, probably "covering"; it involves a confusion of an older Creek /a/ as in otter with the English /ʌ/, the low-central vowel with the mid-central stressed vowel. To compound the problem, one modern pronunciation is /'yuw pə toy/, a "spelling-pronunciation," since initial *u* is often pronounced with a /y/ glide as in union, united, universal. Your editor suffers from these same equations in his surname: properly /'ʌt liy/, he commonly hears /'yuw tliy/ from those who don't know him, and one year he was honored at a reception in Venice by being taken for the British Prime Minister Clement Atlee, which the Italians pronounced /'at liy/. Thus in Georgia the common generic term for creek, *hachee*, which should be /'hʌ ciy/, is now universally /'hæ ciy/. Muskoki, the linguistic family, becomes Muskogee, with a voicing of the intervocalic *k*, a lenis form of the fortis,³ as in German /'ba ris/ for Paris, French /'pa riy/ with an uvular *r*, English /'pæ ris/.

The Creek broad *a* or *ä*, as in father and psalm, must be spelled according to Goff with an *au* or *aw* to keep it from becoming an /æ/ as in cat. Sometimes even an *ar* is called in, and *achitohto*, corn-crib is written as Archibookta, in a state where a Northerner's *arch*, /arc/ would be pronounced /ac/. One recalls William Faulkner's *The Reivers*, where Uncle Parsham, a wise and gentle old Negro, is called Uncle Possum. Creek probably made a distinction between /š/ as in shin (Chemolley); /c/ as in chin (Echo, properly /'iy kow/ but by analogy with the English word echo /'e kow/); and the palatal and guttural spirants /ç/ /χ/ as in German *ich* and *ach*, Scottish *loch*. Hence *hachi*, creek, stream, was originally *hahchi* /'haχ ciy/ but the sound, now impossible in English though common in Old English *draht*, draught, and in Middle English (Chaucer's *The droghte of March hath perced to the roote*), is in these Georgia names either dropped completely or converted to a /k/. Creek even had a /j/ as in *judge* which is rendered by this same ambiguous English *ch*; *Chulapocca* is recorded also as Tulapocca and Julapocca. The alternation Withlacoochee / Willacoochee represents English despair at spelling and pronouncing the voiceless *l*, common enough in Welsh and in Old English (Lloyd, Llewellyn; hlaf, meaning loaf). In one case the *thl* represents some kind of approximation, and the *ll* represents complete absorption into the English voiced /l/. To say that there is no voiceless *l* in modern English is untrue; there is no intervocalic, initial, or final voiceless *l*, but after another voiceless consonant like the voiceless *th* (as in thin; father contains the voiced *th*) the *l* is easily unvoiced. Hence *Withlacoochee*. Since many early Georgians were brought by Oglethorpe from the London area, there is something to be said for Goff's description of the added /h/ in Hiawassee (Cherokee *ayuhwasi*) and Hightower (Etowah) as Cockneyisms, but one would be happy to know from the field the way in which the Indians pronounced these initial vowels, to see whether there was any trace of initial aspiration (Nos. 27, 26). If the Cockney explanation holds, one might also cite a Lazer which becomes Lizer (No. 27). One recalls the common pronunciation in Australia of the country's name: /"o 'stray lyə/. Such explanations as we have given demonstrate that Goff's linguistics is sound enough, though it might have been a little clearer to the linguist if the phonetic alphabet had been used. Many present readers may disagree.

A true placename dictionary, which of course Goff's short studies make no pretense of being, should contain phonetic transcriptions made in the field on the basis of what local inhabitants say, since they are the proper authorities for the sound of their local names. Often this may seem a work of supererogation, since common names like Barnes and Cooper and Ohio need no glossing as /barnz/, /kuw pər/, and /ow 'hay ow/. Or do they? What of Georgia, where they are /banz/, /'ku pə/, or southern Ohio, where the state is /ə 'hay ə/? Goff may leave the full task of transcriptions to the Georgia Survey under Farkas and Britt; he does provide us with occasional interesting free variations. Jekyll Island, for instance, named after General Oglethorpe's eighteenth-century patron Sir John Jekyll, is normally /'je kəl/, but coastal people call it /'jey kəl/, a conservative historical pronunciation (No. 63). More important, Goff collects all the early spellings of a name, which leads him closer to the admittedly adequate recorders, whose records may nevertheless in their variety help to solve the puzzle of an Indian name: Upatoi, Canoochee, Hightower, Ochillee, and a host of others (Nos. 5, 19, 26, 56). He deserves special credit for his extensive use of the diaries and letters of the eighteenth-century traveller Colonel Benjamin Hawkins (see, for instance, No. 94). Like the famous Ohioan Zeisberger among the Delaware Indians, Hawkins recorded the words by syllables. This has two advantages: it avoids the temptation to create smoothed English consonant clusters, and as a result it does not obscure the possible boundaries between "words" or morphemes, making it easier to break the name down if there is a compound etymology. So the well-known Okefenokee Swamp (No. 51) was recorded as O-ke-fin-o-cau and E-cun-fin-o-cau, which supports Goff's interpretation as quivering earth rather than trembling water.

As elsewhere, folk-etymologizing or the conversion of an unfamiliar name to a familiar word in the host language, is an abounding process in Georgia. Centralhatchee is such a conversion of an older Sundalhatchee, perch creek (No. 41). Hightower is a transformation of a Cherokee placename Itawa or Etowah, which may be Cherokee *etawaha*, deadwood, or a borrowing from Creek *italwa*, town (Nos. 26-27). Stalkinghead Creek memorializes the use of a deer's head for creeping up on a favorite Indian prey, but it occasionally is converted to Stocking Head (No. 6). Penholoway Creek would mean Turkey Creek, but Goff argues that it should be rather Finhalloway, high footlog creek; in this event the confusion would have taken place between two Indian names rather than between an Indian name and an English adaptation (No. 8). Sillycook appears to be a somewhat facetious conversion of Saligugi, turtle (No. 55); Cuttingbone is a far cry from Crittington (No. 71). With the transfer of Great Coat Branch to Grey Coat Branch the adaptation takes place in English, as the older word for overcoat lost currency among Georgians (No. 7). Alecks Creek suggests a nickname for Alexander to us today, but it appears to be rather the name of a Cusseta chief whose name in the native idiom meant doctor (No. 107).

One of the most interesting of these folk etymologies is treated in Goff's article on the various Ty Tys. He argues a kind of reverse process where the name for a crowded brush thicket, tighteye, becomes the name of the brush, ty ty. Just what has happened is uncertain. Lorenzo Turner believed that the Ty Tys in coastal South Carolina came from a Gullah Negro personal name 'titi /'tiy tiy/, which has African antecedents. He also provides potential African etyma for a number of other names common to Georgia and South Carolina, and usually thought to be Indian in origin: Wassaw (see No. 114), which he derives from Twi *wasau,* "a district, tribe and dialect of the Gold Coast," Wando (No. 74) from Herero $wan_1\ do_2$, trousers, and Wahoo (No. 74) from Yoruba $wa_3\ hu_1$, to trill the voice. This raises the old problem of Indian versus African origins for elements of Deep South folklore and folk naming; we cite it to indicate that there are always further horizons of investigation in onomastics.[4] As a further footnote to Ty Ty we cannot neglect the unforgettable old rascal, paterfamilias, and treasure hunter in Erskine Caldwell's *God's Little Acre* (1933), which is set in the Georgia mill area, and which seems to recall the poor-mouthing names which Goff discusses with such zest (No. 18, "The Devil's Half Acre"). Caldwell was born in White Oak in Coweta County, Georgia. Goff knew both Caldwell's novel *Tobacco Road* and a true road by that name ("Some Old Road Names in Georgia"); the latter was simply a road which carried one of the state's staple products to market. It was a "rolling road" over which tobacco was transported in oaken hogsheads, from Grovetown west of Augusta through Fort Gordon to east of Gracewood. Ty Ty was a Gullah personal name and a Georgia placename; Caldwell as usual catches the smell of earth.

Linguistics, as we see, carries us into the realms of meaning. One of the most important such realms is history, and our second major component in placename study is history. This is especially true in a land where naming is a dramatic event which can often be pinpointed in the records. Thus George Stewart's informative *Names on the Land* is described on the title page as "A Historical Account of Place-Naming in the United States" rather than a study of placenames alone. Goff, close to the records and imbued with a love of his native state, has Stewart's dynamic view of placenaming, reinforced by his own intimate knowledge of the local scene. He decides that Golden Grove, which might have been thought to be a mere descriptive name of "the autumnal splendor of a given forest" (No. 1), may actually owe its name to Royalist Bishop Jeremy Taylor's prayer-book, itself named after a seat of the Earls of Carbery, where Jeremy took refuge during England's Civil War. I myself suspect that New Yorka (No. 21), the name of a Creek settlement, represents some kind of folk etymology, but no satisfactory Indian etymology has been found, and Goff's knowledge of the historic occasion when representative Creeks went to New York to sign a treaty (an ironically appropriate place, considering the notorious Manhattan Island purchase by the Dutch) shakes my cautious reserve. If he is right, it would be an almost unique example of the Indian's accepting a white man's name for his own settlement, though we might remember the common name for the Lenni Lenape, Delaware, with its origin in the name of a Norman-descended nobleman.

Popular etymology may obscure history, and only accurate knowledge will reveal the truth. So Daniel O'Cain's Branch, clearly attested by a petition of December 7, 1762 (No. 4), becomes Oak Cane Branch, flaunting unknown flora. This demonstration of how a careful use of the records can provide a historical demonstration to confront the linguist and the puzzle-solver is a testimony to historical method. I have noticed a similar case in England, where Hamsey in Sussex, explained by a competent linguist as Old English *hammes ēg*, island or marshy land in the bed of a river, turned out on close study of the local charters to reflect the *hām* or home of the Norman owner, Geoffrey de Say.[5] Some history is relatively transparent; one need not be a rigorous historian to understand the early sentiment which named Georgia towns Ypsilanti (also in Michigan) and Bolivar (also Ohio, West Virginia, Tennessee, and Oregon), but one may suspect that other Revolutionary heroes will not become American eponyms. We may probably expect no Georgian Leningrad, Castroville, or Che-town. There are several Spanish strata, most notably names from the early explorers and conquistadores, like Rincon (No. 39) and possibly Ca Lera (No. 41), or from the Mexican War, an event which placed a Rio Grande /'ray ow "grænd/ so far north as Ohio. A systematic study of American placenames from Spanish sources outside the Southwest is badly needed; it could be one of the major results of a national computerized survey. Fredonia and the Elkos and Arkos and Arcolas would also have their history clarified by such a wide-scale study (No. 41)—the first is a name for the United States which has survived only as the name of towns and cities, and the last three are extremely common names for railway stations which may reflect a company name (the L company, the R or Railway Company?). We could do with a careful plotting of the whole series on a map, with dates of naming, and some evidence of the persons bestowing the name. I have my own theory, unsupported except by the collocation of Arco and Elko, that they may be mystic remnants of Royal Arch Masons and the Benevolent and Protective Order of Elks. We need the dates and the personalities.

On the more prosaic side, Goff's use of the archival records is efficient, a model for students, as we may see in the consultation of the Rossville platbooks (No. 98). Oglethorpe Bluff (No. 108) brings us back to the realm of reconstructive and half-written history, as do the puzzling ascriptions of Breastworks Branch (No. 82) and the Intrenchment creeks (No. 80). The last two names reflect warfare, and Goff's essays are models of cautious but ingenious historical speculation. So far as I know, his valuable suggestion for the use of aerial photography, so useful in England and the Holy Land for archeological reconstruction, has never been carried out; Americans gladly contribute to the study of problems of the kind abroad, but not at home. There is a similar kind of reconstruction in the hurricane names which Goff studies, since the paths of destruction of these tropical winds, which still harass us with their now intensely media-watched and meteorologically recorded feminine names, provide evidence for both natural history and human history.

Our third discipline, geography, is closely allied with history; the hurricane names are a sample. In America our best professional onomasticians are on the staff of the United States Board of Geographic names and the Department of the Interior. Though their basic task is the establishment of standard names for the Post Office Department and the like, the best practitioners like Donald Orth and Merideth Burrill have always combined a deep allegiance to the historical and geographical disciplines. A notable example is Orth's *Dictionary of Alaska Place Names* (Washington: U.S. Government Printing Office, 1967). The placename dictionary should, though few of them do, adopt from the gazetteer a strict locationing by means of latitude and longitude or, if one is dealing with lost towns and places, make the gap in our knowledge clear. For the longitude and latitude grids Goff substitutes his close work with maps and platbooks. His special talent is for the tracing of old Indian trails and pioneer roads. One suspects that his whole fascination with placenames might have derived from an early article he wrote in 1950, "Retracing the Old Federal Road," an account of "an historic highway that once joined Georgia and Tennessee across the Cherokee Nation." He had apparently travelled a part of the road long before Emory University gave him a grant to retrace the vanishing pathway, which the Cherokee ceded to the federal government in 1805, and which played an important part in wars with Creeks and Seminoles. Goff follows the trail with meticulous care, and by this method solves many problems of naming and calls attention to a milestone in the now fantastically crisscrossed federal "defense" system of highways which dominates travel today.

One of the earliest of the short studies (No. 2) is about the Longstreets, where Goff demonstrates the geographical nature of their naming, which we might be tempted to assign to one of Lee's major lieutenants. Another fine essay on trails is keyed to the name Hiwassee (Nos. 27–28). Fascinating also is Toms Shoals (No. 78), where Goff traces a long trail with many names attesting to an old Indian guide (Samuel Thomas?) and reconstructs its past both by his fieldwork and by his use of Benjamin Hawkins's "Viatory," written by an explorer who worked for Thomas Jefferson. In a sense Goff is a reincarnation of Hawkins, whom he follows both in the library and on the spot. The Poor Robin names (No. 113) may likewise commemorate an indispensable early guide. Geography tells us many things in these retracings, of the generic turned particular, The Dividings, which derive their name from an important fork in a trail or road (No. 28), or The Great Pine Barrens (No. 29), where we learn the meaning of a "desert forest" and witness the exploitation of the wilderness which both William Faulkner and Thomas Wolfe have described with so much concern, long before ecology became a subject that concerned both rebellious youth and respectable age. The remnants of these "piney woods" still exist in the Gulf states; they support a famous vocational school for blacks in Mississippi, and they still are famed for summer resorts, since the pines and the lack of pools keep down the mosquitoes and malaria. Joel Chandler Harris used to write about them.

History can be found in the books and the archives, but geography demands a view of the scene.[6] Goff did plenty with the library and maproom (he even sent to Ann Arbor for a Georgia map—No. 4). If the historian can correct the too-ingenious linguist, the geographer acquainted with the spot itself can do even more. One clue to the meaning of Attapulgus is the actual presence of a dogwood grove (No. 9). Henry Gannett, whose early and enthusiastic but often careless work has made him the target of many later students, was very happy to find that a Creek *sofki* meant hominy or corn meal, and he consequently created the ad hoc legend that Tobesofkee was so named because "An Indian spilled or lost his sofkee while crossing the stream" (No. 14). Though the function of the *Tobe* element is still in doubt (Read thinks it a wooden ladle), the comparison of Hatchasofkee and Sofkee Creeks strengthens the idea that the *sofkee* meant deep, a point testable by Goff's observation. Being on the spot helped also in the case of Oostanaula and Eastanollee (No. 20), where the presence of shoals and Hawkins's early testimony justifies interpreting the names as "shoaly" rather than as Read's "ford" or Toomey's "white man," the last a desperate Cherokee etymon in avowedly Creek territory. In view of the dispute about the name of Savannah, from the Shawnee or "Savannah" Indians or from the Spanish word *sabena* for treeless plain (No. 96), geography steps in to inform us that there are plenty of actual damp savanna(h)s in Georgia, where T. S. Eliot's Hippopotamus might have relaxed. The Cherokee name for such treeless plains was *ayuhwasi*, preserved as Hiwassee or Hiawassee (No. 27). The argument will probably never be settled completely, but the geographical evidence makes us lean to some kind of reinforcement theory, where Shawnee becomes Savannah because of the presence of such Spanish-named plains.

Similarly unsettling is Long Swamp Creek, apparently a translation from the Cherokee, but lacking anything very swampy in the vicinity. The testimony of Goff's eyes suggests that the *igati* original, which could mean either swamp or thicket, must have been mistranslated; the present name should be Long Thicket Creek (No. 36). Goff kept after a name like a hound on the trail; Unawatti Creek is a good example (Nos. 32 and 32a). In his first article he rightly calls it a flat creek, that is a shallow and slow-running stream useless as a millsite; his census of flat creeks throughout the state is valuable. Yet the name, with no sure etymon, still bothered him, and he finally found a platbook which listed it as "Yone Water Creek," which despite the folk etymology of water can be traced back to a Yonawattee or Old Bear. Apparently the term was applied to this stream and to the Bear Creek into which it now flows; probably the Indians made no distinction between the main stream and the tributary. Systematic work with both the records and the site thus paid off. Another example of the value of local knowledge is the name *hill* or *mountain*. Often puzzling to the onomastician at a distance, who looks at reports of distance above sea-level,[7] such names become understandable at the source, where one experiences the vista from a proper vantage-point. Though Paramore Hill (No. 38) is only 270 feet above sea-level it "is distinctive because its western slope is a steep face that drops precipitously almost to the edge of the river, permitting an open and rare view over the Ogeechee Swamp and its moss-draped trees below."

Under geographical expertise should be placed a knowledge not only of the topography but also of the local flora and fauna. The gopher of Sinclair Lewis's Gopher Prairie is a rodent, but the gopher of Georgia's Gopher Town is a burrowing land turtle (No. 43). The exact species of bear grass or silk grass which lies behind Salacoa Creek could use a Darwin as well as a Goff (No. 47). The Indian settlement of Cooccohapofe on Flint River seems to mean "by the cane brake," and a huge expanse of cane was attested by Hawkins (see the article "Cooccohapofe"). Knowing the locality enables Goff to get drama out of every word, as with Deer Lick and Iron Hill (No. 44). Knowing the thickets of Gardi–Guardeye and Ty Ty–Tighteye (No. 58, "Ty Ty") does not solve all the puzzles, but it serves to put them clearly before us. A close look at the traveller Hawkins helps to untangle the evidence about Sweetwater Creek (No. 95). The essays on Buffalo and Beaver dams teach us more about Georgia fauna, but that on "The Rising Fawns" is on Cherokee personal names and not on a deer haven.

Many a literal-minded student of placenaming, when he has learned to be careful with his etymologies and to check his history in the records and his geography on the spot, prides himself for his acumen in denying the local stories of how the town was named and forgets that folklore is one of the sciences of man, deserving as much respect and care as the other three disciplines. Of course it is part of the task to ascertain the true story, if that is obtainable, but the tales the inhabitants tell are as fascinating to the student of culture and personality as the positive and prosaic facts themselves. Folk etymology must be tested by linguistics, but its products are themselves part of the fun. Legends are the unwritten philosophical history of mankind. And folk life, the practical and attractive technology of people not caught up in a mechanized and urban civilization, is fast becoming at least an emotional salvation for men today, as they begin to wonder if the towering civilization they have built with much mind but little spirit is on the verge of self-destruction. Northern Georgia has just produced a best-seller, which college youth buy in droves as they yearn toward the less-settled places: Eliot Wigginton's *The Foxfire Book* (Garden City, 1972), a folklorist's supplement to *The Last Whole Earth Catalogue*.

Folk life is well treated by Goff; he does not merely explain a place-name with an obscure allusion to a major feature in pioneer life-style, but he teaches us fully about the material culture behind the name. Thus he reveals a whole milieu in his account of the Barkcamps and Crawl-Ins of Burke and Hall counties (Number 3) and describes in detail these outposts for minding cattle and temporary shacks for lumbermen, supplanted later by crawl-ins, rude log cabins which kept out the bears, panthers, and wolves. Or he points to the stalkingheads which helped the Indians to make deer decoys of themselves (No. 6), or the deertraps which gave a name to Echeconnee (No. 16). The staple crop, tobacco, did not only name a road, but it also caused an exotic importation from Sumatra, Laingkat in Decatur County, named from a special kind of wrapper tobacco planted in that region from Deli in Lankat province in Sumatra (No. 70). Anneewakee Creek memorializes a Cherokee family which raised cattle: *ani* for clan and *wakee* from Spanish *vaca* for cow. The cow was not native to America, but an import. The use of rock moss, a slimy substance which may have provided salt for animals and hence attracted them to deertraps (Nos. 83, 16) reveals one aspect of Indian cattle-breeding and hunting; in Goff's discussion of Walnut Creek, formerly Oakchuncoolgau, the folk life is good even if the linguistics seems a little shaky. The eating of some flora was dangerous for the cattle and for the human beings who drank their milk. The Milksick Coves reveal a striking aspect of folk medicine (No. 89); Goff need not have been so disparaging about "some old folk-tale or superstition." The Cowpens (No. 106) and the Wolfpens ("The Wolfpens") and the Hog Crawls ("Hog Crawl Creek") all represent stockades or corrals which provided safety for cattle from the intruder and safe prison for the intruder when he was captured. Spoil Cane Creek (No. 101) probably denotes an area where the cattle grazer had to be warned not to stop, since the forage was overgrazed; Dead Sleep Creek is probably a hyperbolic name for what was simply a sleeping stop along the trail. The Tobler creeks (No. 113) may all owe their names to illicit rumrunners, a significant aspect of folk life in some areas.

Folk religion manifests itself in Biblical names like Sardis and Smyrna, Plains of Dura, and Mars Hill (Nos. 100, 13, 10). Plainly the pioneers, even if some of them came from the urban ghettoes, knew their Bible. The red man's religion is reflected in a host of colorful names. Ball Ground and Ball Play Creek memorialize the ritual games and dances of the Cherokees and Creeks (No. 23). Four Killer and Sixes are testimonies to the grimmer game of war: the numbers are like notches on a gun or scalps on the belt (Nos. 31, 52). Possibly Alapaha recalls a ceremonial Bear House (No. 87); Yahoola is the cry at a "black drink" rite, perhaps even of the god who inspires both the drink and the cry (No. 88). Buzzard Flopper Creek may owe its name to a ritual dance (No. 62). Weelustie, the old name for Black Creek, meant West Water (No. 105). Since there is nothing particularly black about the water, it may perhaps be equated with west, since the Creeks equated the cardinal points with colors.

Goff records a few legends; more could probably have been mined from the rich collections of Cherokee and Southeastern myths by Mooney and Swanton. There is a romantic Indian legend from George White about a Catawba maiden called Hiwassee, "the pretty fawn," and a Cherokee youth called Notley; it flies in the face of the proper etymon savannah for Hiwassee (No. 27) as the lovers flew from the faces of their parents. Towaliga River (No. 30) is reported to owe its name "roasted scalps" to a pause Indians made to dry fresh scalps taken from the whites. Catoosa, explained by the Cherokees who have migrated to Oklahoma, is said to mean People of the Light, but it probably meant something less romantic, possibly wind—the name remains a puzzle (No. 53). Pocataligo (No. 111), in local pronunciation /"pow kiy 'tæl iy gow/, is said to go back to an old Negro's advice on how to deal with a balky mule: "poke 'e tail 'e go"; in another account the same words are used to make an obstinate turtle open his shell. This is of the vintage of the explanation for Wisconsin's Sheboygan, said to be the remark of a philoprogenitive old Indian at a trading post. One final story deserves quotation. The clerk of the Superior Court at Talbotton swears he was present at the naming of Po' Biddy Crossroads (the first No. 41):

Some thirty odd years ago, . . . a group was having dinner . . . with fried chicken being the main dish. When one guest took the last piece of chicken, the women serving exclaimed: "There goes the last of the po' biddy!" When

Introduction / xxxi

sometime later a man who lived at the Crossroads came to the Courthouse to register a trade name for a filling station he was building, he chose the name which has remained ever since.

Goff's charming essays on "Bad and Worse Creeks" (No. 18), "Social Circle" (No. 45), "The Devil's Half Acre," and "The Poor Mouthing Place Names" suggest a fifth discipline to add to the canonical four: psychology. The four disciplines we have been discussing are all disciplines with methods which may have to be adapted to the field of onomastics but which remain rigorous within the professional frame: the linguistics must be not only ingenious but accurate, as accurate as possible with dead and dying languages, like Creek and Cherokee, which have not been too scientifically recorded. The history must be generally meaningful and locally sound, based on the careful and systematic use of platbooks, court records, travels, and reports. The geography must localize a place with the precision of a gazetteer and demonstrate knowledge of the trails, the topography, the flora and fauna. Folk life and folk history must be treated with the same caution in recording as written history, since it reveals the worship, the humor, and the speculative mind of man in his non-technological surroundings. All of these tasks Goff accomplishes, through an intimate knowledge of the local scene and a respect for the people who have inhabited it and thought about its origins. He lives up to the codes of the disciplines as he combines them for the interdisciplinary needs of toponymy.

We use the term *psychology*, however, in a sense which would satisfy neither a behaviorist who plunges into the comparison of mice and men, nor a psychoanalyst who plunges into the abysses which swallow our little egos. Instead we use the term in the popular sense of why men act as they do, with popular surface explanations. In this area Goff is a master in revealing the whimsies of the pioneer mind at play with names. Simply to mention some of the names is to feel their point, their prickle: Bad and Worse Creeks, No Man's Friend Pond, Tearbritches, Hell's Half Acre, the Bad Prong of Ten-Miles, Lordamercy Cove, Useless Bay, Devil's Elbow, Devil's Trash Pile, Devil's Drag Out (where it is hard to float logs), Big and Little Hell Sluice, Hell Gap, Little Hell Landing (a hell of a place to land), the River Styx (which is not the Sticks!), Hades, Horse Heaven Hills, Hardscrabble (a neighbor to Hopewell), Poverty Creek, Hunger and Hardship creeks, Pinch Gut Creek, Pull-Tight, Lickskillet, Blue John Creek (from the dialectal name for skimmed milk), Buttermilk Shoals and

Bottoms, Bonny Clabbers Bluff (cottage cheese), Scuffle Bluff, Scrougetown, Cracker's Neck, Barefoot (folk-etymologized to Barefoot), Tuckahoe (from "Indian Bread," a poor substitute for a regular diet), Mangy Branch, Trouble Creek, Rocky Comfort Creek, No Business Creek, Frog Bottom, Possum Trot, Peckerwood District, Scantville, and a host of other poor-mouthing names.

Against these we may place the names which show high and boastful spirits: Social Circle, Merry Hill, Fancy Bluff, New Yorka, Jolly, Fashion, A One, New Hope, Ideal, Prosperity, Cornucopia, Eureka, Zenith, Blackacre, and Paradise—all names for the American Eden. A later group, of the kind which summer people bestow on their homes, is often a whimsy gone sour: Bidawee, Happy Hollow, Hopeulikit, and Lake Shangri La (No. 41). D. H. Lawrence was repelled by similar names for Australian beach bungalows (*Kangaroo*):

Somers had been watching these names. He had passed "Elite," and "Tres Bon" and "The Angels Roost" and "The Better 'Ole." He rather hoped for one of the Australian names, Wallaby or Wagga-Wagga. When he had looked at the house and agreed to take it for three months, it had been dusk, and he had not noticed the name. He hoped it would not be U-An-Me, or even Stella Maris.[8]

It turned out to be Torestin, which for a moment looked foreign and safe, until his wife deciphered it as To-Rest-In.

Some coined names are less whimsical, though they are not always more beautiful. The bulk of them commemorate a corporation or a town straddling a state line: Adsboro (from adze), Muckafoonee (from Muckalee and Kinchafoonee), Ellen N (L & N Railroad), Arcola, Arco, Tennga (Tennessee and Georgia), Alaga (Alabama and Georgia). Ausmac joins the surnames Ausley and McCaskill, and Subligna is said to be a translation of Underwood. If so, our amateur Latinist was doubly wrong, for the proper singular accusative is *lignum*. But even if the number were correct the word would be wrong, for *lignum* is harvested wood, lumber, whereas the English surname is referring to wood(s) or forest, which would properly be *silva*. Pioneers in the field need their dictionaries, especially when they want to be exuberant or whimsical.

One task of a rigorously pursued discipline is to tell us what we don't know as well as what we do. Many of the names remain puzzles, and perhaps Goff, seeking for a dramatic solution to please his reader, is occasionally too anxious to solve the unsolvable problem. Examples are Ty Ty, Oakfuskee (No. 77, which takes no account of the common Creek *Oc-* for water because *-fuskee* is in doubt), and Scull Creek (No. 38, that there might have been a man named Scull is possible, but as a guess to replace the more likely "skull" we need the records). In Salacoa, Read has plausible alternatives (No. 47). More properly, Goff gives up on Eastertoy (No. 97), though an explanation is possible. Scholars, anxious to make brilliant discoveries, often push their cases too far; it is better to admit one's ignorance, for that may give the signal to another man, possessed of a different bag of tricks, to try his hand at the solution. Goff usually avoids these dangers, but occasionally he fails, as with Yahoola (No. 88), where he is too hasty to dismiss Mooney's ritual knowledge and too rigorous in applying the Creek-Cherokee differentiation which he had often ignored in time of need elsewhere.

There remain many puzzles still: Tussahaw (No. 34), Sutalee and Satolah (No. 52), the Social Circles (No. 45), No Business Creek (No. 54), Standing Boy Creek (No. 66), the Shoals in Toms Shoals (No. 78), Muckalee (No. 112), and so forth. Goff's work on Indian personal names in Numbers 96 and 109 and "The Rising Fawns" is excellent, but it illustrates one problem never quite solved in placename study. Since personal names often lie behind placenames, we seem to be getting somewhere when we identify the person with the name. One suspects, from the number of Indian chiefs brought in to explain American placenames which otherwise would have no explanation, that there were many more chiefs than Indians. Of course it is not the task of a student of Georgia names to explain that General James Oglethorpe probably got his name from Odkell's thorp or village,[9] or to go further and explain where the Norse Odkell got his name. This can become a game of infinite regression. But if the name is that of an "Indian chief" one would like the student, armed with what word lists he is lucky enough to have at hand, to do what he can with the personal as well as with the placename. Goff does his best; that is all any of us can do. We must leave it for others to work out more fully the nature of Soaps or Sopes Creek (No. 103), Standing Boy Creek (No. 66), Child Toaters Creek (No. 96), Cuttingbone Creek (No. 71), to name a few. An American placename survey will reduce to a system the gathering of Cherokee and Muskogean dictionaries, published and unpublished, for the solution of the names of Georgia and its neighboring states—one state may, indeed, provide a clue which another state lacks.

Goff of course has only skimmed the cream off the mass of Georgia names, and much more than "blue john" and "bonny clabber" remains. Looking at a casual list of Georgia towns and topographical features, we find a hundred more interesting names remaining to be tackled. I have not moved from my desk to guess at or solve those which follow. There are more Biblical names, and in each case we should like to know why the particular one has been chosen: Aaron, Benevolence (surely religious in origin), Bethlehem, Cyrene, Hephzibah, Herod, Ruth, Shiloh, Smyrna, Sparta. Is Herod a poor-mouthing name, for instance? And does Simon of Cyrene, who helped Jesus carry the cross, reflect the possibility that the saint might have been a black man? There are the literary names: Abbottsford and Rowena (which recall the Southern cult of Sir Walter Scott), Arp (Bill Arp the humorist?), Byron, Dixie (which came first: the town, or the Manhattan Island slaveowner, or the Mason and Dixon line, or the Ohioan Dan Emmett song?), Lanier, Nankipooh (a thing of shreds and patches?), Rydal (Wordsworth's Rydal Mount?). Upper state New York had more classical naming, but Georgia has its Agricola, Americus, Camilla, Campania, Cassandra, Clito, Cornelia, and Sparta, all plausible enough in a state where the plantation owners called their favorite slaves Pompey or Caesar. What are on the surface personal names of settlers or their sisters, cousins, and aunts abound, but they deserve a story true or fictitious which is unknown to me: Acworth, Adgateville, Baconton, Bemiss, Blackshear, Blun and Blundale, Bronwood, Chamblee, Doverel, Esom Hill, Faceville, Flippen, Huching (a form of Hutchins?), Jimps (?), Lee Pope (this strange combination of the southern Robert E. Lee and the northern John Pope must be an ironic coincidence, unless John Pope became a Georgian hero because he lost the battle of Second Manassas in 1862), Lizella, Louvale (?), Menlo (an Irish personal name), Meldrim (a Scottish personal name, as in Sir David Lyndsay's *Squire Meldrum*), Mize (?), Morven (?), Munnerlyn (?), Nunez (from the Spanish era?), Uvalda (the Texas Uvalde, where Cactus Jack Garner lived a long life, is a Spanish personal name), and Winokur (?). Is Rhine, like Cornish, from a person or a place? What tie does Bolingbroke have with Shakespeare's Henry IV? Is it one more of these royal names in the wilderness, like Dauphin, or is it another literary allusion?

Some placenames are famous because famous people later have borne them: Bogart (Humphrey—the word can mean a bogey-man or bugaboo), Ringgold (Lardner—he was born in Michigan, so one presumes both he and the Georgia town got their names from Major Samuel Ringgold, first American officer killed in the Mexican War), Tallulah Falls (which gave their name we know to Tallulah Bankhead,

Introduction / xxxv

the Broadway actress), and Kennesaw Mountain (an Indian puzzle preserved in the forename of a famous jurist, Kennesaw Mountain Landis). Other placenames come from the person himself; Calhoun (a good Southern neighbor from the Carolinas), Carnegie (steel mill or library?), De Soto (named by the Spaniards or by the schoolteachers?), Epworth (the town from which John Wesley, who spent so much time in Georgia, came), and Tuscaloosa (from Black Warrior, a Choctaw chieftain in Alabama). Descriptive names make one wish one could check the scene on the spot: Chalybeate Springs (what else besides iron is in these waters?), Deepstep, Dewey Rose, Doerun, Double Branches, Grovania (generic grove or personal Grove?), Persimmon, Pineora, Racepond, Relay, Resaca (old river channel, stream with undertow, or memory of an American victory in the Mexican War at Resaca de la Palma?), The Rock (a splendid generic become specific), and so on. The systematic linguistic check I am sure will some time be made will help with some of the following names: Acree, Allatoona, Alpharetta (one of those strange Southern girl's names for the first daughter?), Amboy (Algonquin, at home in New Jersey, but what is it doing in Georgia?), Aska (I'll bet there's a folk-etymological story about it), Auraria, Cohutta, Cusseta, Dacula (has a vampire lost his *r*?), Dahlonega, Ellijay, Elmodel, Eton (who was the plantation schoolboy who named it?), Flovilla, Frolona, Hahira, Ila, Inaha, Lexsy, Manassas (famous name without an etymon?), Mauk, Mesena, Molena (Spanish *molina*, mill?), Musella, Mystic (in New England an Algonquin name, folk-etymologized), Nacoochee, Ogeechee (related to the tribal Uchee?), Ohoopee, Padena, Penia, Poulan, Pridgen, Surrency, the often-sung Suwanee (Cherokee, meaning unknown), Talmo, Unadilla, Valona, Wenona. Finally, there are the whimsical names, or those with a special intention smiling through: Between (what?), Box Springs (surely someone has sensed the ambiguity, although the modern aid to comfort in bed may have come after the Springs were named), Climax (to what?), Dames Ferry (did the Lord of the Manor have to swim?), Eldorendo (is the misspelling of El Dorado intentional or not?), Elmodel (probably named too early to involve a bad pun on motel, a modern invention; a hybrid on model?), Enigma (which is just what it is to your editor), Experiment, Gratis, Headlight, Philomath, Zenith (Sinclair Lewis in Georgia?).

No editor or reader will object because Goff's dramatic style and terminal illness kept many of these problems unsolved. They are cited here as a sample of the many challenges awaiting a systematic survey of Georgian and of American placenames, with combination both of xxxvi / Introduction

close work in the field by the polymath who combines linguistics, history, geography, folklore and psychology, and of sophisticated computerized information banks, which can quickly tell us of the names elsewhere which may help to determine migration patterns of naming and the solutions to numerous problems where the data in one state is not enough. To Goff we owe one of the finest beginnings in the United States, where all state surveys are still beginnings, and the essays to form a book far-ranging, full of interdisciplinary vision, and charming for the reader.

In editing these articles two systems of arrangement have been combined, chronology of publication and the polarity of the particular and the general. Overlap is inevitable, and there is a double chronology, for the short studies, which should retain their numerical integrity for ease in reference, then of a few particular studies which appeared separately, and finally of the general studies in which Goff tried to group his particulars and draw conclusions from them. In the short studies we have even preserved two articles numbered 41 without renumbering them, to avoid a dislocation throughout; we have been similarly thrifty in renumbering footnotes when an editorial addition was needed. Thus there are actually 116 short studies, rather than 115. The element of the general enters some of these shorter studies, as with "Bad and Worse Creeks" (No. 18), "Some 'Coined' Names" (No. 41), "Social Circle" (No. 45), "Toms Shoals" (No. 78) and a few others, yet the general nature of this basic series dwells at the needed length for one name or one phenomenon.

Except in the final paper, hitherto unpublished, we have rarely tampered with Goff's style, except to correct silently a few misprints and an occasional obvious error. In some of this process we have been guided by marginal notes in Goff's copies, which represent afterthoughts of his own. A stern formalist might object to Goff's colloquialism, most of it a search for verbal variation where repetition of concept was inescapable: "tab," for instance, and "moniker." Goff knew what he was doing.

We have made no attempt to check the archives further for geographical and historical detail, a task which would be formidable and which probably would result in only a few minor corrections. Nor has there been any attempt to proceed with fieldwork on the names, new and old, to secure some kind of phonetic representation, for the task would again be immense and a blow to the pleasant informality of the book for the non-specialist. The taste of phonetics we have given in the introduction is quite enough. The greatest advantage to this gathering of Goff's placename work, apart from making the book convenient for the non-specialist, is to provide a take-off point and easy source of reference for the Georgia Survey promised for the American Bicentennial of 1976. What changes further research make necessary can there be incorporated without pedantry or fussiness.

Marion Hemperley has provided the account of Goff's life and the index, and he has also read this introduction with the eye of an archivist and a Georgian. FLU, editor of the text, has kept his comments to this introduction and to a few footnotes, labelled with his name. These notes do not represent wide research, but only some occasional speculation, aided by three important studies which were either unknown to or too late for Professor Goff:

William A. Read, "Indian Stream-Names in Georgia," *International Journal of American Linguistics* 15 (1949): 128-32; 16 (1950): 203-207.

George Stewart, *Names on the Land* (New York: Random, 1945).

George Stewart, *American Place Names* (New York: Oxford University Press, 1970).

FRANCIS LEE UTLEY
The Ohio State University
September 29, 1972

NOTES

1. See Francis Lee Utley, "The Linguistic Component of Onomastics," *Names* 11 (1963): 145-76; "A Survey of American Place Names," *Proceedings of the Ninth International Congress of Onomastic Sciences*, ed. J. McN. Dodgson (Louvain, 1969), pp. 455-63; "Mountain Nomenclature in the United States," *Disputationes ad Montium Vocabula*, ed. H. H. Hornung (Wien, 1972), 3:34-35; "Onomastic Variety in the High Sierra," *Names* 20 (1972): 73-82; review of *The Place-Names of Birsay*, by Hugh Marwick and W. F. H. Nicolaisen (Aberdeen, 1970), in *Names* 19 (1971): 47-50.

2. For Read's bibliography see Richard B. Sealock and Pauline A. Seely, *Bibliography of Place-Name Literature: United States and Canada*, 2nd ed. (Chicago: American Library Association, 1967), Nos. 353-54, 597-98, 1072-74, 1101, 1486-88, 1765, and see the end of this introduction.

3. It is not certain what Goff means by "the true Muskogean tongue" as contrasted to Creek. Muskogean is the name of a Gulf language family which includes the extant Creek, Choctaw, Chickasaw, and Hitchiti, as well as the dead or dying Natchez, Tunica, and Apalachee. See Mary R. Haas, "A Proto-Gulf Word for *Water*," *IJAL* 16 (1950): 71.

4. Lorenzo Turner, *Africanisms in the Gullah Dialect* (New York: Arno Press, 1969), p. 307.

5. Utley, *Names* 11 (1963): 156.
6. "Onomastic Variety," *Names* 20 (1972): 73-82.
7. "Mountain Nomenclature, " p. 39.
8. *Kangaroo* (London, 1950 [1963]), p. 5.
9. Eilert Ekwall, *The Concise Oxford Dictionary of English Place-Names,* 4th ed. (Oxford: Clarendon Press, 1964), p. 349.

The Particular

Short Studies of Georgia Placenames (1954–1964)

No. 1
The Golden Groves

Among the many unusual appellations which have appeared as Georgia placenames is the interesting label Golden Grove. This name has been used here in at least three instances, although the only spot actually retaining the full title today is the Golden Grove bend and bar on the Altamaha River, in Toombs County, a mile or so downstream from the bridge on today's U.S. Highway 1.[1] A better-known remnant of the designation, however, can be found in the present Grove Creek of Oglethorpe County, which rises northwest of Lexington and flows north into the South Fork of Broad River. Few persons of that section seem aware of the fact that the first land surveys of their area, dated in the 1780's, marked this stream Golden Grove Creek.[2] Apparently the original term was considered too long, and perhaps too ornate, because the name was being shortened to prosaic Grove Creek as early as 1801.[3]

It was not possible to learn how long the Golden Grove bend on the Altamaha has borne its designation since old maps and records do not mention the place. Perhaps early rivermen operating boats to Indian trading posts near the junction of the Ocmulgee and Oconee long ago gave the name to the site.

The earliest mention of a Golden Grove in the Georgia *Colonial Records* appears in connection with a grant in 1748 of 500 acres to William Hester of North Carolina.[4] Hester's petition to the Georgia colonial authorities for land he desired mentions the place as "Poplar Springs," located on the south side of the River Midway in what would be today's Liberty County. Seemingly Hester promptly applied the name Golden Grove to his new property, because a few months later Thomas Goldsmith, a lieutenant in Oglethorpe's regiment, petitioned for 500 acres on the north side of the Midway, opposite the lands of William Hester that were known as the Golden Grove.[5] And a short time afterward, John Bennet asked for and received 100 acres, also on the north side and about a mile above the Golden Grove.[6]

The shortening of Golden Grove Creek to Grove Creek in Oglethorpe County may raise a question in the reader's mind about the origin of the name Grove Creek in Banks County. This stream, which heads near Belton and flows southeastwardly across the lower part of the county to join Hudson River thence into the Broad, seemingly has always been known to white people as Grove Creek. It is listed by that title in early land plats for original Franklin County. Its designation apparently is derived from an area that was called the Grove, and which was situated along the creek between what are now Homer and Maysville. Banks County does have a Golden Hill District, but no evidence could be turned up which linked this appellation to the name of the creek.

In reflecting upon the origin of the name Golden Grove it is easy to think that the autumnal splendor of a given forest or grove naturally suggested these words as a proper designation for such a beautiful spot. This conclusion would especially seem logical for a region like Georgia that has colorful fall trees, or for South Carolina which also used the name Golden Grove.[7] But Jamaica, a tropical island,[8] has a Golden Grove too, although it does not have the climate which causes brilliant autumn leaves. Actually there is good reason to believe that this interesting appellation was an immigrant to the New World, being brought here indirectly, probably from Wales. Several places in Britain bear the name Golden Grove.[9] The best known of these spots and the one that is most likely to have furnished the name to America is located on the Towy River,[10] a mile or so to the southwest of Llandilo in Carmarthenshire, Wales. This Golden Grove, a former seat of the Earls of Carbery, is especially significant because during England's Civil War, in the mid-seventeenth century, the noted theologian and writer Bishop Jeremy Taylor, a Royalist sympathizer, took refuge here with the Earl of Carbery. During his stay Taylor wrote some of his most eloquent works; and in tribute to his protector and patron, his "Manual of Daily Prayers and Litanies" was entitled *Golden Grove*. It is reasonable to believe that this widely read work had much to do with spreading the name to other places in England and eventually to America.

—*GMNL* 7(1954): 87

NOTES

1. The Golden Grove Bend is not listed on many charts. The spot is best remembered by old-timers along that stretch of the Altamaha as the Golden Grove Bar, for a formation that juts out into the river at the tip of the bend. Hudgin's *Map of Toombs County Georgia* (Atlanta, 1913) shows the place under this last designation.

2. Land of John Crutchfield, Wilkes County, survey of 1784, Headrights Platbook H, p. 253; land of John Colly, Wilkes County, survey of 1785, Platbook CC, p. 107; land of Glascock and Hith, Wilkes County, survey of 1785, Platbook H, p. 59, Land Records of Georgia, Surveyor General Department, Atlanta.

3. Land of Henry Brooks, Oglethorpe County, survey of 1801, Platbook VV, p. 42.

4. Allen D. Candler, *The Colonial Records of Georgia* (Atlanta: Franklin, 1904-1916), 6:219.

5. *Ibid.*, p. 233.

6. *Ibid.*, p. 392.

7. See "Golden Grove Cr.," in the "Greenville District" (1820), Robert Mills, *Atlas of the State of South Carolina*, new facsimile ed., by Lucy H. Bostick and Fant H. Thornley (Columbia, 1938). This South Carolina watercourse, like the stream in Oglethorpe County, Georgia, is now called Grove Creek.

8. Eastern end of the island; cf. map of the West Indies, *National Geographic Magazine*, March, 1954.

9. John Bartholomew, ed., *Survey Gazetteer of the British Isles*, 7th ed. (Edinburgh: Bartholomew & Sons, 1927), p. 295.

The sites listed in this source are: (1) Golden Grove, seat of the Earl of Cawdor [formerly of the Earls of Carbery] on R. Teifi [sic] 2¾ mi., S.W., of Llandilo, Carmarthenshire; (2) Golden Grove, seat, N. R. Yorks, Hawsker with Stainsacre par.; (3) Golden Grove, seat, 4 mi., N.E., Rhuddlan, Flintshire; (4) Golden Grove, seat, Offaly Co., 2 mi., N.W., Rosecrea; and (5) Golden Grove Inn, near Chertsey, W. Surrey.

10. Bartholomew, *Survey Gazetteer*, erred in placing this Golden Grove on the River Teifi instead of on the Towy. The latter flows southward through the center of Carmarthenshire and the former westward along the boundary of Carmarthen and Cardigan.

No. 2
The Longstreets

> O earth, what changes hast thou seen!
> There where the long street roars, hath been
> The stillness of the central sea. . . .
>
> Tennyson, *In Memoriam*, CXXIII

Some of Georgia's most distinctive geographic names rarely, if ever, appear on maps. An interesting illustration of this point can be found in the name Longstreet, an expression once used here to designate a rural stretch of highway which was relatively well-bordered with homes and other buildings. The state still has two old ways that retain this unique appellation, although these thoroughfares are now sometimes referred to as Longstreet Roads.

One of these routes is in southeastern Elbert County, stretching along today's Georgia 72, between Bethel Church and Bethlehem Church Crossroads; and, while the designation was originally used for just this strip, the name today has been extended to the whole community through which the road passes. In fact, the section at present is officially called the Longstreet District, or Georgia Militia District No. 190.

The other Longstreet is in northern Bleckley County. It remains as a segment of an early noted stage and postal route known as the Old Milledgeville—Hawkinsville Road that led from the former capital via Jeffersonville and today's Coley Station to Hawkinsville and from there on to southwest Georgia and west Florida. The Longstreet portion of this thoroughfare begins on the Twiggs-Bleckley line and runs some four miles southwestward past Longstreet Methodist Church to Old Evergreen Church Crossroads, located three miles to the north of Cochran. Apparently the stretch has borne its name for a century and a half.[1]

In these days the use of street in connection with a rural road strikes one as a curiosity, because the term according to our way of thinking is distinctly urban in significance, so much so that names like Worth Street, Wall Street, LaSalle Street, Peachtree Street, or The Street are symbolic of metropolitan commercial centers. But this view arises from the fact that over the years street has continually evolved in both its spelling and application. Webster's *New International Dictionary of the English Language* shows that the word comes from the Medieval English *strete*, which was derived from the Anglo-Saxon *stræt*, that in turn came from the Low Latin *strata*, meaning a paved way. Thus as the early English employed the term, it was applied to a thoroughfare that passed through both the countryside and towns. Even today the English still use street in connection with certain country roads as well as in urban sections.

It should be added, however, that when the expression Longstreet was used in Georgia a century and a half ago, the word did not here denote a paved thoroughfare.

In connection with a discussion of the Longstreets, it might be of interest to the reader to consider also the subject of placenames with contrary meanings. Georgia's rich variety of appellations offers numbers of such opposite words: Gratis as against Grab All; Welcome versus Shakerag; Cotton Hill versus Poverty Hill; Richland versus Lick Skillet; and so on. Each of these pairs of names had opposite implications in the pioneer way of thinking.

The point to this digression is that Longstreet too had its antonyms. Since that word referred to a strip of highway which passed through a populated area, there were also names for routes which traversed lonesome, empty sections. The simplest word with an opposite meaning to Longstreet was Stretch. This expression, of course, can mean several things, but the way old-timers used it in this particular sense, the term signified a long segment of road that was sparsely settled or devoid of homes. An early route bearing such a name was the Eighteen Mile Stretch from what is now Sycamore to Tifton. This old way coincided closely with the course of today's U.S. 41, one of the state's main arterial routes, and a way that is now heavily settled. A hundred years ago, however, no one lived on this long reach.[2]

A much more intriguing antonym than Stretch for Longstreet, however, is the Dark Entry of Camden County. This interesting name, that seemingly dates back to colonial days, applies to an old road which runs northwestward from St. Marys, passing several miles to the north of today's Georgia 40. Some two and a half miles northeast of Kingsland, to the east of U.S. 17 and on the south side of Crooked River, it forks. The left turn is a remnant of a former noted trading path to the Creek Indians of west Georgia and central Alabama; the right fork, leading on through Seals, to Jeffersonton and Owen's Old Ferry on the Satilla, is a former stage and postal route which once linked St. Marys on the southeast corner of the country with the rest of the nation. The Dark Entry proper stretches from the outskirts of St. Marys through some ten miles of dense pine woods to the road fork just mentioned. Apparently few people have ever lived on the road. It is a lonesome route to this very day.[3]

—*GMNL* 7(1954): 88

NOTES

1. An interesting discussion of this Longstreet can be found on pp. 72-77 of *History of Pulaski County Georgia*, compiled by the Hawkinsville chapter of the D.A.R., and published by the Walter W. Brown Publishing Co., Atlanta, 1935. Bleckley County was once a part of Pulaski.

2. William P. Fleming, *Crisp County, Georgia* (Cordele: Ham Printing Co., 1932), p. 48.

3. [No doubt Goff's local knowledge of the Long Streets, preserving an Old English relic name of the Roman paved strata, is sound, and the age of the Bleckley Longstreet is convincing. Yet one would enjoy a sure disclaimer of connection with the great Confederate general James L. Longstreet. Though born in Virginia, he held posts in Georgia after the War Between the States. Mention of the Elbert County Military District suggests homage to the General. *FLU.*]

No. 3
The Barkcamp Districts

Georgia has at least two communities that are known as Barkcamp[1] districts. One of these sections is in lower Burke County, on the north side of the Ogeechee River and immediately to the west of the Jenkins boundary line; the other is in northwest Hall County in the area about Price, to the south of Murrayville.

The Barkcamp District of Burke is one of the early communities of Georgia. The area, which stretches along a little stream called Barkcamp Creek, has borne its name for around 200 years, a span which actually outdates the period in which the first permanent settlers started moving into the section subsequent to its cession by the Indians in the 1763 Treaty of Augusta. The main center of the district is Barkcamp Crossroads, a community that lies to the west of the creek and some six miles above Midville. This particular vicinity is so old the people thereabouts are prone to think of it as the place which gave rise to the name. The spot, in fact, does have a long history and it was one of the earliest post offices of Georgia.[2] But documentary evidence points to another location as the probable site of the original Barkcamp. This place is 3 miles to the southeast of the present crossroads, on the east side of Barkcamp Creek and just below the bridge on the Midville-Birdsville road.

With respect to this spot and the name Barkcamp, colonial land grant records dated in the 1760's and 1770's mention the area as "Case's Old Place,"[3] "William Case's Old Settlement,"[4] and "Case's Camp."[5] The term Old in these references gives the impression that Case had occupied the place prior to the time in which the regular settlers came to take up lands that had been formally granted to them by the Colony of Georgia subsequent to the treaty in 1763. Before that date the western boundary for the province was indefinite, so the authorities had not given grants in this area beyond the vicinity of present Millen, to the east of the Barkcamp District. Presumably, therefore, Case was a trespasser on Indian lands. It is not clear what he was doing in the region because his nominal home was on the south side of Briar Creek to the east and well within the territory which had been settled by the white people.[6] Case was interested in cattle-raising,[7] and the use of Settlement in connection with his activities leaves the thought that he may have established his "camp" as a wilderness outpost for minding cattle. It was common for backcountry cattlemen to let their animals range at large regardless of ownership of grazing grounds, Indian or otherwise; but it was also customary to set up a central eating and resting place in the general browsing area for watching the stock.

The Barkcamp area of Hall County is old, but apparently far less so than the community in Burke County. The exact site which gave rise to the designation is not shown on modern maps although the name is perpetuated in the Barkcamp District or Georgia Militia District No. 569.[8] The original location, according to an 1869 map, was in lot 53 of District 10 of Hall County.[9] This point was a little to the northwest of today's Price, and on the west side of Georgia Highway No. 136. Not much is known about the history of the site, but people in the vicinity say it was once a place where travellers going to and from the mountains stopped to camp. For protection from the weather, someone erected at the spot a hut of slabs from a nearby sawmill. Such a building, however, was not like a true pioneers' barkcamp, but was more of a crude shanty which is usually known around Georgia as a "slab camp."[10] It is common to find such structures as sheds or shacks at "Peckerwood" sawmill sites.

Fortunately we know what the original barkcamps were like because people continued to use them long after colonial days. Within recent decades even, they were still being constructed in remote sections of the mountain counties as camping places for cattlemen and hunters. A genuine barkcamp resembled the familiar lean-to. It consisted of a shoulder-high framework of stakes and poles, with a roof and sidings of bark, usually from small pine trees. The covering was surprisingly effective in keeping out rain, when the bark was properly placed, with every other strip being inverted or cupped downward over the upturned edges of adjoining lengths. The Indians are said to have taught white people how to make these structures, and it is easy to accept this version of the camp's origin because the red people are known to have made extensive use of bark in their buildings, especially for roofing.

The open face of the barkcamp permitted the use of a fire to warm the occupants. But this exposed front was also a disadvantage when the wilderness abounded with bears, "tigers" (panthers), wolves, and even skulking human enemies. Perhaps this shortcoming was the factor which encouraged some people to build in lieu of the barkcamp a more secure, pen-like hut called a "crawl-in." Again we know what these structures were like because they too were being erected not so long ago in the Georgia mountains. Crawl-ins were miniature, unchinked log cabins that were made of stout saplings. The structures, without doors, windows, or chimneys, had a bark roof. It was easy for the occupant to move a part of this covering, bank the bottom with a good bed of leaves and crawl in for a comfortable rest. Seemingly such structures were once fairly common in the frontier woods, but they did not leave an imprint on our place names as did the barkcamp.

—GMNL 7(1954): 124-25

NOTES

1. In early records the designation is usually found as "Bark Camp"; current references tend to make the expression a single-word name.

2. *American State Papers*, VII. Post Office Department, list of Georgia Post Offices for 1828, p. 205.

3. Allen D. Candler, *Colonial Records of Georgia* (Atlanta: Franklin, 1904-1916), 9: 411, petition of Thomas Wimberley, Sept. 3, 1765. The land mentioned was on the "north" side of Barkcamp Creek, adjoining the lower line of Jethro Rowntree. The latter's property was 3 miles up the creek from the Ogeechee; cf. *Colonial Records of Georgia* 9: 410, petitions of Kendred Braswell and Robert Braswell, Sept. 3, 1765.

4. *Ibid.*, p. 678, renewal of petition by Wimberley, dated Nov. 4, 1766. His first request received approval of the Provincial Council but he could not raise the survey fee within the stipulated time.

5. *Ibid.* 11: 40, petition of Manoah Yarborough, May 1, 1770.

6. *Ibid.* 8: 123, petition of William Case, Sept. 4, 1759. He requested 100 acres on the south side of Briar Creek where he had been settled for three years.

7. *Ibid.* 9: 184-85, petition of William Case to purchase 200 acres on Ogeechee for the "Conveniency of settling stock of cattle," June 5, 1764. The request was refused. Perhaps Case had been forced by authorities to move from his "settlement" on Barkcamp Creek.

8. The highway map of Hall County, Georgia, State Highway Board, 1940, shows the boundaries of Georgia Militia District, No. 569, the Barkcamp District.

9. B. W. Frobel, map of Hall County, 1869, original in the Land Records of Georgia, Surveyor General Department, Atlanta; a 1951 *Map of Hall County* (Gainesville, Ga.) by Georgia D. Newton of Gainesville, Ga., does not show the site.

10. Georgia has a stream called Slab Camp Creek in south Oconee County, below Elder Crossroads; cf. *Athens, S.E. Quad. Ga.*, preliminary compilation, 1946, topographical map, U.S. Geological Survey.

No. 4
Oak Cane Branch

In Jenkins County, on the north side of the Ogeechee River, two miles southeast of Millen, there is a small creek which the people thereabout call Oak Cane Branch. Indeed, the stream is even reported on a topographical map under that label.[1] Such an odd designation intrigues a placename hunter and is sure to set off mulling and searching to ascertain the significance of the tab. But the derivation in this instance was easy, because Savery's Map of 1769 provides the clue which unlocks the original meaning of the name.[2] On his chart, the stream is marked "Ocain's Branch." By referring to the colonial land records of Georgia, it was found that Daniel O'Cain, on December 7, 1762, filed a petition with the provincial authorities for a grant of 300 acres in St. George Parish, on the north side of the Ogeechee, at Millen four miles below Buckhead Creek.[3] O'Cain's request was approved, but for some reason, he failed to take up the land within the stipulated time. On July 5, 1763, therefore, he renewed his petition for the same area.[4] Again it was approved, and on November 6, 1764 the governor formally signed the warrant for the property.[5]

On the basis of these official sources then, it is plain that the little stream derived its name from the pioneer Daniel O'Cain. Somewhere along the way in the intervening period of nearly 200 years, the designation got converted into the outwardly enigmatic Oak Cane Branch.

—*GMNL* 7(1954): 126

NOTES

1. *Millen Quadrangle—Georgia*, topographical map of the U.S. Geological Survey, ed. of 1920.

2. Sam'l Savery, D.S., "Sketch [Chart] of the Boundary Line between the Province of Georgia and the Creek Nation," 1769, original in the William L. Clements Library, Ann Arbor, Mich.

3. Allen D. Candler, *Colonial Records of Georgia* (Atlanta: Franklin, 1904-1916), 8: 773-74. Buckhead Creek, a north-bank tributary of the Ogeechee, is a little to the west of Millen.

4. *Ibid.* 9: 64.

5. *Ibid.*, p. 240.

No. 5
Upatoi Creek

The Indian placenames that Georgia has retained among its geographic designations are usually easy to pronounce, and even the uninitiated on reading these appellations for the first time can make a fair effort at saying most of them in the way which has come to be accepted as proper by people who are familiar with the names. But occasionally there are difficulties in this respect, and one may muff a seemingly simple tab. Such an elusive name can be found in Upatoi, the title of a large creek that heads in Harris, Talbot, and Marion, and flows southwestward as the common boundary between Muscogee and Chattahoochee counties to enter the Chattahoochee River a few miles below Columbus.

Upatoi is a plain word on its face, but should it be pronounced: "Upp a toy" or "Oop a toy" or "Yoo pa toy"?

The long-time residents who live along the stream use "Yoo pa toy," and say, as far as they know, the name has always been pronounced in that fashion. Now, ordinarily old timers are acceptable authorities on an Indian word. Their version of a given term may not retain the subtleties of the true redskin form, but at least they are usually able to give a faithful reproduction of a name as it first appeared in the white man's early records. With respect to Upatoi, however, such is not the case. Somehow over the years there has been a change in this word because originally it was not spelled in a way which would suggest its present pronunciation: "Yoo pa toy." Furthermore, the appellation was not initially used to designate the main creek which now bears the name, but as the title of an Indian community situated in the forks of the stream between present Kendall Creek and Tar River in extreme eastern Muscogee County.

Colonel Benjamin Hawkins visited this Indian site in the late 1790's and called the locality "Au-put-tau-e."[1] *The Handbook of American Indians* does not list the place as "Au-put-tau-e," but notes it as "Apatoi" and states that it was the name of an Indian village, probably located on the site of present Upatoi,[2] a station on the Central of Georgia Railroad, in eastern Muscogee County. This version of the appellation was apparently supplied by Gatschet, who mentions the word as "Apata-i" and says that it refers to a sheet-like covering, from the Muscogee *apatayäs*, I cover.[3] This authority does not make it clear, however, in what precise sense the term was applied as a proper name.

The word Upatoi seemingly began to emerge in the early part of the past century, prior to 1826. In that year the surveyors of original Muscogee County caught the name in transition from the older form to the word which we know today, because the big stream now called Upatoi Creek was marked "Upatoy River" by one district surveyor.[4] A surveyor in an adjoining district, however, entitled the stream "Opatoy Creek."[5] And with respect to present Kendall Creek, a tributary which flowed past the Indian settlement, one man labels that fork "Opotahway,"[6] while another marks its waters "Upatoy Creek."[7]

As noted, the main stream which is now known as Upatoi Creek did not originally bear that name. In Indian days it was called Hatcheethlucco,[8] or Big Creek. In fact, some early reliable sources refer to it by that English Title.[9] With a little more usage, perhaps that denomination might have become permanent for the stream and thereby permitted it to join the rather large number of Big Creeks which can be found around Georgia.

In conclusion, it might be of interest to venture beyond the subject of placename derivations and add some summary comments on "Au-put-tau-e."[10] Beginning about 1790, the village was founded as a satellite settlement of Cusseta Town, a main Lower Creek center which was located on the Chattahoochee River at the site of present Lawson Field of the Fort Benning Reservation. The little outpost is of more than passing interest because its establishment came at a time in which the Indians under the impact of the white man and his ways were leaving their traditional central towns and "settling out" in surrounding areas to take up farming and stock-raising. The place had a population of 43 gun men (warriors) in 1797 and Colonel Hawkins states they enjoyed the best characters among the Lower Creek Indians. He also notes that they would not admit neighbors unless they agreed to fence their holdings. At this village Hawkins, as Indian agent, introduced the plow in 1797, perhaps the very first plow to be used in western Georgia, and in that year sent a farmer to tend a crop of corn and show the Indians how to prepare their fields in the white man's way. Tussekiah Mico (the Warrior King of the Cussetas), a leader much respected by Hawkins, was the headman of this unique Indian community. Prior to its settlement, so this chief told Hawkins, the area had been the "beloved bear ground" of the Indians and had been reserved for hunting those animals as long as it was of value for that purpose.[11]

—GMNL 7(1954): 126-28

NOTES

1. Benjamin Hawkins, *A Sketch of the Creek Country in the Years 1798 and 1799*. Collections of the Georgia Historical Society, Vol. 3, pt. 1 (Savannah, 1848), p. 59.

2. Bulletin 30, Bureau of American Ethnology (Washington, D.C., 1910), pt. 1, p. 69. The suggested location in this source is incorrect. As stated in the text, the site was in extreme eastern Muscogee County. Col. Hawkins says the settlement was 20 miles from the Chattahoochee "in" the forks of "Hatchee thlucco" [present Upatoi, Kendall, and Tar River creeks]. Cf. Hawkins, *Creek Country*, pp. 59-60. Upatoi station is only 15 miles from the river and is located to the west of the forks referred to.

3. Albert S. Gatschet, *A Migration Legend of the Creek Indians* (Philadelphia: G. Brinton, 1884), 1: 128.

4. District 6 of Muscogee County, survey of 1826, Winfield Wright, D.S., Platbook LLLL, lots 95, 96, 98, *passim*, Land Records of Georgia, Surveyor General Department, Atlanta.

5. District 9 of Muscogee County, survey of 1826, John Townsend, D.S., Platbook LLLL, lots 240, 242.

6. District 10 of Muscogee County, survey of 1826, James Whatley, Platbook LLLL, lots 225, 226, 234, 251, *passim*.

7. District 17 of Muscogee County, survey of 1827, Wm. Mason, D.S., Platbook MMMM, lots 127, 133, 155, *passim*.

8. *Letters of Benjamin Hawkins, 1796-1806*, Collections of the Georgia Historical Society, Vol. 9 (Savannah, 1916), pp. 54 and 69. On the last page he writes "Hatcheethlocco"; Hawkins, *Creek Country*, p. 59. Here he uses "Hatchee thlucco"; and Eleazer Early, *Map of the State of Georgia, 1818*.

9. Map of District 7, original Muscogee County, survey of 1827, Norman McRaeny, D.S.; and District 10 of Muscogee County, survey of 1826, James Whatley, D.S., Platbook LLLL, lots 12, 23, 48, 124, 228, *passim*. This last source was also cited in connection with Opotahway Creek; see note 6. These plats show present Upatoi as Big Creek and Opotahway, which is today's Kendall Creek.

10. These comments are from Benjamin Hawkins, *Letters*, pp. 69–71; and his *Creek Country*, pp. 59-60.

11. [Read, *IJAL* 16 (1950): 207, suggests for Upatoi *apata-i*, a covering of any kind, or *apatana*, bullfrog. Stewart, *American Place Names*, p. 505, adduces a Muskogean (Creek) word meaning "last, farthest off(?)." *FLU.*]

No. 6
The Stalkinghead Creeks

The tenacity of placenames is a striking feature of geographic appellations. Once a designation has been applied to a particular spot or area, or to some physical object like a stream, it is generally prone to continue in permanent usage. But there are hundreds of names in Georgia, and as one might expect there have been changes in numbers of them over the years. Many of these shifts were apparently arbitrary because no good reasons can be found to explain why they occurred. On the other hand it is sometimes possible to trace changes and to follow the evolution of a given name from one form to another, even through a transition in which an appellation is modified so drastically that the word we know today bears an entirely different connotation from the original designation.

This sort of change has been especially pronounced for original names whose significance was not generally grasped by people; or for terms which may have once been understood but whose meanings were somehow lost with the passage of time, thereby leading people of later days to convert the names into forms that have no relation to the earlier names.

An interesting example to illustrate one of these name evolutions can be found in the tab Stocking (or Stockin) Creek, a designation which is borne by a small stream that arises a mile or so to the northeast of St. Clair in Burke County and flows northward to join Brushy Creek immediately above the latter's mouth on Briar Creek.[1]

Now, Stocking Creek would not be an unusual name in itself because Georgia has several streams which bear the label of some sort of clothing or vestment, viz.: Hat Creek, Red Cap Swamp, and so on. In the case of Stocking Creek, however, that title was not the stream's original designation. When the little waterway first entered the provincial records in 1766, it was unmistakedly called "Stalking head Branch." In that year Evan Lewis petitioned the colonial authorities for 150 acres in St. George Parish, on Briar Creek where Stalking head Branch emptied into the larger stream.[2] He received the grant, and a plat for the land can be found in the official land records of Georgia in the state's Surveyor General Department.[3] But a distortion of the original name started with this listing, because the clerk or surveyor who entered the plat in the platbook wrote "Stalknay Head Branch" instead of Stalking Head.[4] This version of the name apparently persisted, because years later the water course was mentioned as Stalkney Head Branch.[5] But the original term was Stalking Head because in 1769 Robert Pior (sic) petitioned for 200 acres at the head of a stream by that name in St. George Parish.[6] On the other hand, we get another version of the name, and a forerunner of the present-day appellation through a 1772 petition of Richard Shepherd who asked for 100 acres on "Stockin head branch" in St. George.[7]

The deviations Stalknay Head, Stalkney Head, and Stockin head plainly imply that significance of the expression Stalkinghead was not understood by some people. The first two forms appear to be mere efforts at the name, where as Stockin head seemingly represented an attempt to convert the expression into the then familiar stocking cap, a head covering that was once much used, especially by seamen and sailors.

As for the original name, Stalking head, one is warranted in concluding that the term actually referred to a real stalkinghead, a deceiving device that was worn by hunters for slipping up on prey. In this case, the expression probably pertained to the skinned head and shoulders of a buck deer used for approaching within shooting distance of wary game. And too, the name was probably Indian in origin, because it is common knowledge that primitive peoples make use of such camouflage in hunting. This conclusion seems reasonable in view of the fact that some of the whites apparently did not understand the appellation and were not familiar with the stalkinghead. If the expression were borrowed from the Indians, however, it is not clear though why the English translation was used instead of the red man's form. Perhaps the latter was difficult to pronounce. In any case, it is not unusual here to find placenames that were converted from the aboriginal. Georgia has many such renditions in its geographic appellations. These translations, of course, offer fruitful opportunities for this series of placename studies and in time it is hoped they will be discussed.

In addition to the Stocking Creek of Burke, we have in northeast Candler County a Stocking Head Branch which rises in the upper central part of the county, to the east of Union School Crossroads, and flows southward to join the left side of Fifteen Mile Creek about a mile and a half to the northeast of Metter.[8] The stream has long borne its name, even on some land plats dated in 1837.[9] There is no evidence, though, to show that it was called Stalkinghead prior to that time. One plat dated in 1818, however, mentions the stream as "Stawkinghead."[10] This early variant leaves the strong suggestion that the original expression may actually have been stalkinghead and not stocking head, the denomination which has long been used. This conclusion is supported by the pronunciation of *stalking* in our idiom. It would be fairly commonplace in this section to hear that word pronounced "stawking."

In contrast to these names there is still a third Stalkinghead Creek whose name seemingly has never suffered from distortion. This large stream arises in southwest Jasper County, to the west of Adgateville, and flows southward across parts of Jasper and Jones to join Falling Creek on its right side in upper Jones.[11] The waterway apparently bore its title in Indian days, because one of the first surveyors of this section noted the same as "Stalking head Creek" on his land plats in 1807 when he laid off the area, after it had been ceded by the red people.[12]

—*GMNL* 7(1954): 163-64

NOTES

1. Stocking Creek is shown and named on *General Highway Map of Burke County Georgia*, State Highway Department of Georgia, 1952.

2. Petition of Evan Lewis, July, 1766, in Allen D. Candler, *Colonial Records of Georgia* (Atlanta: Franklin, 1904-1916), 9: 557. Lewis requested land on Briar Creek at the "mouth" of a stream called "Stalking head Branch." Today Stocking Creek empties into Brushy immediately above its juncture with Briar. From the point where Brushy and Stocking join, however, the stream threads out into a swamp. On this basis, then Lewis was probably justified in saying at the "mouth" on Briar Creek.

3. Land of Evan Lewis, St. Georges Parish, survey of 1766, on "Stalknay Head Branch," Platbook C, p. 143, Land Records of Georgia, Surveyor General Department, Atlanta.

4. *Idem.*

5. Land of Elijah Johnson, Burke County, survey of 1818, Platbook YY, p. 195.

6. Petition of Robert Pior, St. George Parish, Oct., 1769, in Candler, *Colonial Records of Georgia*, 10: 886.

7. Petition of Richard Shepherd, St. George Parish, March, 1772, in Candler, *Colonial Records of Georgia*, 12: 235.

8. This stream can be found on the map of Candler County, Georgia, State Highway Department of Georgia, 1945.

9. Land of James Holloway, Bullock County (now Candler), survey of 1837, Platbook AC, p. 339; and land of Richard Kirkland, Bullock County (now Candler), survey of 1837, Platbook AC, p. 340.

10. Land of William Bird, Bullock County (now Candler), survey of 1818, Platbook HHHH, p. 153.

11. The stream is named and shown on the map of Jasper County, Georgia, State Highway Board of Georgia, 1939. It is shown but not named on the same agency's *Jones County Georgia*, ed. of 1940.

12. District 12 of original Baldwin County (now parts of Jones and Jasper), R. De Jernatte, D.S., survey of 1807, Platbook RR, lots 88, 89, *passim*.

No. 7
Great Coat Branch

In lower Jefferson County there is a small creek which arises to the northeast of Bartow and flows southward to join Williamson Swamp Creek about midway between Bartow and Wadley. Many people in the vicinity call this stream Gray Coat Branch. But here, as in the case of the Stocking Creek discussed above, there has been a conversion of a name, because on a land plat dated in 1801 the same little waterway is labelled "Great Coat Branch."[1] This switching of names can be attributed to the fact that people generally no longer understand the significance of the expression *great coat* and have been led to adopt an appellation that is more meaningful in the light of present clothing styles. Today gray coats of one kind or another are commonplace, whereas great coats have long since given way to overcoats or top coats except in the military field where some officers still wear great coats.

It is not known how Great Coat Branch first received the tab and it is sheer conjecture to guess at the origin. One ventures to suggest, though, that the expression may have been humorous in nature, a quality that is characteristic of many of our geographic appellations. Perhaps the designation arose because some individual fell into the stream while wearing his great coat and had to scramble out under embarrassing circumstances. Pioneer people considered such incidents extremely funny and were prone to remember them. They might well have applied the name to the branch after such an event.

—*GMNL* 7(1954): 164

NOTE

1. Land of David Duglas (sic), Jefferson County, survey of 1801, Platbook II, p. 197, Land Records of Georgia, Surveyor General Department, Atlanta.

No. 8
Penholoway Creek

Penholoway Creek arises in some large "bays" of lower Wayne County and flows in a northerly direction to join the Altamaha River to the southeast of Jesup.[1] The stream is of more than passing interest to Georgia because it was one of the key points on the "Big Survey," colonial Georgia's first large-scale survey that was made to establish the boundary between the province and the Creek Indian Nation subsequent to the Treaty of Augusta in 1763.[2] Actually there seem to have been two surveys to lay out this line: The first, in 1766, apparently incompletely made because of a dispute about the correct course between the Indians and the whites who were marking the boundary;[3] and the second in 1768 to "inspect" and complete the first line.[4]

On its face, Penholoway would be an interesting word. The distinctiveness of the name, however, lies in the fact that for nearly 200 years people have differed on both the spelling and the meaning of the term. Few other appellations can equal it in this respect, and even now, perhaps, there are readers who are questioning the form of the name that is being used here. But be that as it may, some version of the tab was needed to start this discussion. Penholoway was chosen because that spelling presents the name as it is often employed today. Indeed, as will be seen, the writer believes another version of the word should be used to reflect more accurately the original Indian form.

After the limits between the whites and the red people were decided, references to the creek began to appear in the records. Usually it is called "Finn Halloway,"[5] "Fin halloway,"[6] or "Finhalloway."[7] The first written reference to a meaning of the name appears in a talk of Governor James Wright to the Indians in the summer of 1768. He mentions the name as "Penholloway or Turkie Creek."[8] The Indian name used here is interesting because the spelling is like that which is now in common usage. Furthermore the element *pen* in the name does indicate that the word had some meaning which involved turkey. At the time this communication was written the Governor also prepared a small chart which shows the juncture of the Altamaha and "Penholloway or Turkie Creek."[9] This little sketch apparently was the first map on which the creek was noted. A month or so later Wright mentioned the name again but this time he wrote it "Phenholloway or Turkey Creek."[10]

Another early reference to the name can be found in the works of J. G. W. De Brahm who spells the word "Phennohaloway" and adds a footnote saying that the name is a Creek Indian word signifying "a Turkey."[11] This comment is interesting because De Brahm, a surveyor general of Georgia, is credited by one authority as being the surveyor who ran the original boundary.[12] De Brahm does give a table of field notes for the survey but he does not actually say that he laid off the line.[13]

The best early map showing and naming the creek was Samuel Savery's chart of 1769, which that survey prepared after he was employed in 1768 to resurvey the original boundary and make some adjustments which the Indians had agreed to.[14] Savery labels the waterway "Phaenehalloway," and in addition he shows and names the big "Phaenehalloway" swamps in which the stream heads and terminates. He depicts too, the Alachua Trail crossing on the creek, since he followed a considerable stretch of that route toward the St. Marys where the line ended. The field notes which De Brahm cites also mention this trail at the creek as the "Latchokowae Path."[15] These references to the Indian thoroughfare should be noted because the crossing point on the creek was the probable site that gave rise to the name Penholoway, or more properly Finhaloway.

One other early version of the name should be noted. In the 1773 Treaty of Augusta the boundary line of 1763 is mentioned and the stream is labelled "Phinhotoway Creek."[16] This spelling, however, very probably was due to an error in transcription. In early orthography it is sometimes difficult to distinguish between an *l* and a *t*.

In the years following these early references, the stream generally was called Finholoway or Finholloway. As before, though, other spellings were offered for the name. Two of these variants can be found on the land plats for the official survey of original Wayne County in 1805. Here, in plats for the same land district, the designation is spelled both "Phinholloway"[17] and "Pinholloway."[18] Adiel

Sherwood in his *Gazetteer* of 1829 mentions a creek named "Pin Holloway," but curiously he does not attempt to locate the stream.[19] He adds that the appellation is from *pinaway*, a turkey, and *holloway*, high up, and states that the name was derived from a turkey being shot out of a high tree by an Indian on the bank of the creek. Presumably he was referring to Penholoway Creek because there is no other water course by that name in Georgia.

In maps of recent years the stream is usually listed as Penholoway or Penholloway Creek. But the early version still hangs on. In a topographical map dated 1943 the lower part of the waterway is labelled "Phin Holloway River," and the great swamp that stretches from its mouth upstream along the Altamaha is called "Phin Holloway Swamp."[20] This version of the name, of course, is reminiscent of that used nearly two centuries ago. Interestingly enough, however, on the topographical sheet for the adjoining area to the west the swamp and the creek are marked "Penholoway."[21]

So much for the various spellings of the name; attention should now be turned to its meaning. It is plain that early people were mistaken in the interpretation of the words Finhalloway, Phenholloway, etc., and that they confused the Creek word *fina*, meaning a footlog, with *pinewa*, a turkey. Furthermore, no one apparently except Sherwood paid any attention to the significant element *holoway* in the name. This form is from *halwa*, or *halwi*, meaning high. Thus the original Indian appellation meant high footlog, referring to a passage over a stream. The name had no connection whatsoever with turkey except by misinterpretation. We can be certain of this appraisal of the meaning. Albert Gatschet an authority on Creek names supports the conclusion by saying *fin' halui* means high footlog.[22] Furthermore there is today a stream called Fenholoway River in Florida, and Professor William Read in his study of Florida placenames translates that appellation as high footlog.[23] The name certainly concerned a footlog because in an 1818 report by one of Andrew Jackson's officers this Fenholoway stream is referred to as "Slippery Log Creek."[24]

As has been previously noted, the footlog, or rather high footlog, that gave rise to the name Finhaloway (now Penholoway) was very probably the crossing point on that creek for the noted Alachua Path running from the Altamaha into Florida. This crossing was several miles above the mouth of the stream, in a narrow part of the creek's swamp, at a bluff on the north side. The spot would be almost exactly on a line drawn from Odessa in Wayne County to the MacFishery Landing, on Old River at the edge of the big Penholoway swamp. A woods road still leads to this crossing on both sides of the creek and presumably it is a remnant of the old trail.

It might be of interest to close this sketch with a digression: Georgia has numbers of Turkey creeks. One of them still retains a modified form of the Indian word *pinewa* for turkey. It is called Pennahatchee,[25] and can be found in western Dooly County where it arises eastward of Vienna and flows westward to join Turkey Creek near Drayton, thence into Flint River, just above Georgia Highway 27.[26] In Indian days Turkey Creek (the larger of the two streams) was also called Penhatchee or Pennahatchee.[27]

—*GMNL* 8(1955): 22-24

NOTES

1. Map of Wayne County, Georgia, State Highway Board, 1938. The stream heads in the southeast corner of the county in Penholloway Bay. It is joined on the left by Little Penholloway, that in turn arises in a swampy area to the east of Screven. From the point where the creek and Altamaha join a wide, wild area called Penholloway Swamp stretches up the main river for 10 miles or so to the vicinity of Doctortown.

2. The "Big Survey" began at the head of Williams Creek near today's Barnett on the Warren-Taliaferro line, thence southeast to Brier Creek, thence westward to Ogeechee River and down it to Scull's Bluff, now Paramore's Hill, thence southwest to the Altamaha at the mouth of Penholoway, thence southwest to the upper St. Marys River.

3. "Talk" of Gov. James Wright to the Indians, Sept. 5, 1768, in Allen D. Candler, *Colonial Records of Georgia* (Atlanta: Franklin, 1904-1916), 10: 576-77.

4. *Ibid.* 15: 162-63, 402-404. Savery, the surveyor, said he was employed to "inspect" and run the boundary; he claimed pay at a resurveying rate of 21 shillings a day.

5. *Ibid.* 9: 508-509; a land petition dated April 1, 1766.

6. *Ibid.* 10: 775.

7. *Ibid.*, pp. 690, 823, 857, 964, 982, and 11: 55, 134.

8. Manuscript volume of the Colonial Records of the State of Georgia, arranged in the Georgia Department of Archives and History, Atlanta, 37: 347.

9. *Ibid.*, p. 351. The map in this source is a penciled sketch; the original is in the British Public Records Office, London.

10. "Talk" of Gov. Wright, Sept., 1768, *Colonial Records of Georgia*, 10: 576.

11. John Gerar William De Brahm, *History of the Province of Georgia* (Wormsloe, 1849), p. 31.

12. Charles C. Royce, *Indian Land Cessions in the United States*, 18th Annual Report of the Bureau of American Ethnology, pt. 2, p. 637.

13. De Brahm, *History*, p. 34.

14. Samuel Savery, "Sketch of the Boundary Line Between the Province of Georgia and the Creek Nation," 1769, original in the William L. Clements Library, Ann Arbor, Mich.

15. De Brahm, *History*, p. 34.

16. Robert and George Watkins, *A Digest of the Laws of the State of Georgia* (Philadelphia, 1800), p. 764.

17. District 3 of Wayne County, survey of 1805, Abner Davis, D.S., Platbook GG, lots 86, 112, 113, *passim*, Land Records of Georgia, Surveyor General Department, Atlanta.

18. *Ibid.*, lots 84, 85, 87, 115, *passim*.

19. Adiel Sherwood, *A Gazetteer of the State of Georgia*, 2nd ed. (Philadelphia, 1829), p. 100.

20. *Ludowici Quadrangle*, by the Corps of Engineers, U.S. Army, 2nd ed., 1943 (1st ed., 1920, prepared by the U.S. Geological Survey).

21. *Georgia-Jesup Quadrangle*, U.S. Geological Survey, ed. 1918, reprinted 1943.

22. Albert S. Gatschet, *A Migration Legend of the Creek Indians* (Philadelphia, 1884), 1: 130. He says the name applied to a town of the Lower Creeks or Seminoles (*sic*). This place was reported in the Creek census of 1832 ("Census of the Creek Nation, East," *Emigration of Indians*, Senate Doc. 512, 23rd Cong., 1st Sess., 4: 359). This settlement is said to have been located just to the south of the present village of Hatchechubbee in Russell County, Alabama, on a stream that is still called High Log Creek.

23. William A. Read, *Florida Place Names of Indian Origin and Seminole Personal Names*, Louisiana State University Studies No. 11 (Baton Rouge, 1934), p. 10. This Fenholoway stream arises in upper central Taylor County, Florida, and flows directly to the Gulf, passing a few miles to the west of Perry. A village named Fenholoway is just off U.S. 27, some 6 miles southeast of Perry.

24. Captain Hugh Young, "A Topographical Memoir on East and West Florida with Itineraries of General Jackson's Army, 1818" (with Introduction and annotations by Mark F. Boyd and Gerald M. Ponton), *Florida Historical Quarterly* 13, no. 1(July, 1934), pt. 1, p. 45; and no. 3 (Jan., 1935), pt. 2, pp. 146-47.

25. The Creek Indians often dropped the ultimate and even the penultimate syllable of the first word used in composing a name. Thus the name became (in frontier orthography) Pennahatchee or Penhatchee and not Pinewahatchee. Likewise, high log was *finhalwa* and not *finahalwa*. But *finhalwa* on the other hand was awkward for white people. It will be noted in every case of the English names cited for the creek that the word contained an extra syllable, being spelled *holoway* instead of *holway*.

26. Map of Dooly County, Georgia, State Highway Board, 1939.

27. [Goff's argument for "high foot log" is confirmed by Read, *IJAL*, 15 (1949): 203. *FLU.*]

No. 9
Attapulgus

The word Attapulgus can be found four times as a Georgia placename, and in each case in the same area of southeast Decatur County: (1) Big Attapulgus Creek which heads near Climax and flows southward; (2) Little Attapulgus Creek that arises near Fowlstown[1] and runs southeastwardly to join the above stream just below the Georgia-Florida line; (3) Attapulgus, a town which lies between these two waterways; and (4) Attapulgus District, or Georgia Militia District No. 694, which embodies generally the area of the town and the lower reaches of the creeks listed above.[2]

At a glance Attapulgus has the appearance of a Latin word,[3] but actually it has an Indian origin and a very interesting background at that, because the term is a rare remnant to remind us of an early practice that the whites once had of referring to an Indian town or community in a plural sense. Thus according to this custom, instead of calling a place known as Eufaula by that correct singular form, some people would refer to the settlement as the Eufaulees, or as the Ufallahs, Eufaulies, and so on.

The name Attapulgus had just such an origin. It grew from a small Lower Creek or Seminole village that is variously referred to in the singular as Taphulgee, Tophulga, Topkegalga, Topkélaké, Tuphulga, etc.[4] The place, which was initially located somewhere in extreme lower Decatur County, came into prominence at the beginning of the Indian troubles that led to Andrew Jackson's campaign against the Seminoles in 1818.

The appellation can first be found in the plural form as "Atlapalgas,"[5] in an 1817 power of attorney issued by some Indian chiefs to Alexander Arbuthnot, an alleged British agent operating in Florida.[6] Some months later, in January of 1818, the settlement was again named in the plural when it was referred to by Lieutenant-Colonel M. Arbuckle, the American commander of Fort Scott on Flint River. He wrote Andrew Jackson that his troops had visited "Allapulges,"[7] about 14 miles southeast of that outpost, and had found the place abandoned.[8]

The town was next noted in a plural form by Captain Hugh Young of Jackson's staff as "Attapulgas."[9] He says the place was settled on a fine body of land on Little River, and that it had about 25 warriors. He adds the chief of the settlement was a rogue and that the people with few exceptions were perfidious and unfriendly to the whites. The Little River which he mentions is a translation of Withlacoochee, the name by which the stream had long been known.[10] The Big and Little Attapulgus creeks mentioned above and the present Willacoochee Creek of lower Decatur County were upper tributaries of this river. In Florida, where the stream joins the Ochlocknee it is still called Little River.

One should note that Young was probably not referring to the original village in Decatur County, but to a new settlement the Indians had made lower down on Little River in Spanish territory, somewhere about the present crossing of U.S. 90 over that stream. It will be remembered that Colonel Arbuckle found the first site abandoned with the people and all of their stock gone. This officer does not say that he destroyed the place but there is a strong presumption that he did so because his troops on the previous day had burned the Fowltown village, a neighboring settlement.

The present spelling Attapulgus apparently arose shortly after the troubles with the Seminoles and subsequent to Jackson's campaign in the area. In the 1820 official survey of district 20 of original Early County, now part of Decatur, Big Attapulgus Creek appears under that same spelling as does Little Attapulgus.[11] In the survey for the adjoining land district 19, in the same year the headwaters of the larger stream are also marked "Waters of Attapulgus."[12] In the survey of 1819 for district 22, to the south of district 20, however, the surveyor was apparently not familiar with the name Attapulgus (or Attapulgas, or Attapulges) because he labels Big Attapulgus "Big Sandy Creek" and Little Attapulgus "Porter's Creek."[13]

Years after these early references the name is turned back to its more accurate singular form by Orr and Whitner in their 1859 survey of the Georgia-Florida boundary line. In a lineal "Development" of the boundary which appears at the bottom of an official Georgia map about the disputed boundary these surveyors mark the large stream "Big Attapulgee" and the small creek "Little Attapulgee."[14] On the map proper, curiously enough, the Big Attapulgus and Little Attapulgus are not named. Here the label Attapulgus is reserved for present Willacoochee Creek that lies westward of the two former streams and flows parallel with them to join the Little River of Florida that has been mentioned.

This point is significant because the village of Attapulgus was probably located on the Willacoochee and not on one of the two creeks that presently bear the name Attapulgus. This conclusion is reasonable in view of the fact that Colonel Arbuckle said the settlement was about 14 miles southeast of Fort Scott, which was on the west side of Flint River, in a bend, some two miles airline to the northwest of the present village of Recovery in Decatur County. The nearest spot on one of the Attapulgus creeks southeastward from the fort would have been something like 18 to 20 miles. One concludes then that the village was on present Willacoochee Creek, at the point where the Faceville-Bettstown-Taylors School-Attapulgus road now crosses that stream. This site is 14 miles southeast of the old fort and is just inside of Georgia. The place is almost certain to have been in this state because Arbuckle was probably very careful not to get over into Spanish territory. (He was to leave that move to Old Hickory a short time later). Even though the exact boundary was uncertain, Arbuckle must have known its approximate location because it ran from the juncture of the Chattahoochee and the Flint not far to the west.

Before turning to the meaning of the word Attapulgus, one other point should be developed about the location of the settlement. When the people of the original village fled prior to the visit of the American troops in early 1818, Colonel Arbuckle conjectured that the occupants had removed to or beyond the Ochlocknee, to the east. Very probably, though, as previously stated, they had moved farther down, into Spanish Florida, and settled on Little River near where U.S. 90 now crosses, because in an 1823 report a settlement called "Taphulga" is mentioned in the *American State Papers* as being 30 miles east of the Appalachicola River and one mile north of the "Forbes Purchase."[15] This location would place the community about the site noted above. Another 1823 reference mentions a "Topulgee Village" in the same general area.[16]

Let us now turn to the meaning of Attapulgus. The *Handbook of American Indians* says the word is from the Creek *atap' halgi*, signifying dogwood grove. It is thus derived from *atap' ha*, dogwood, plus the collective suffix *ulga* or *algi*, meaning in this case a grove. The forms *ulga* and *algi* explain why the frontier American names were sometimes spelled Attapulgas and Attapulges. The *g* in *algi* is hard, therefore, the *ge* in Attapulges should be pronounced hard as in Ocmulgee. These derivations do not explain, though, how the modern word came to be spelled Attapulgus. Seemingly this form was derived from the surveyors of districts 19 and 20 of original Early who incorrectly rendered the name on their official land plats, although they did retain and thus perpetuated the plural form of the appellation.

The present plural spelling once misled Albert Gatschet in an interpretation of the name. In his *A Migration Legend of the Creek Indians*, issued in 1884, he says Attapulgus is from *itu-pulga*, meaning boring holes into wood to make a fire, from *itu*, wood, and *pulgas*, I bore.[17] In 1901, however, he changed his version to that which is now given by the *Handbook of American Indians*.[18] Possibly that last source was guided by the amended interpretation of Gatschet.

Perhaps the reader is wondering how Attapulgus is pronounced. In use it usually sounds about as it looks, although some old folks in the area where the name occurs may make it a bit like "Atteepulgus." The 1891 Cram's *Family Atlas of the World*, map of Georgia, gives a label much like this but spells it "Ateapulgus."[19]

—*GMNL* 8(1955): 25-26

NOTES

1. Present-day maps of Decatur County usually spell this word Fowlstown. The name commemorates an Indian village that was once located in the confines of the present county, probably on the east side of Flint River, in the vicinity of Four Mile Creek. In old records, this place is referred to in the singular as Fowltown.

2. These streams and places are all shown on the map of Decatur County, Georgia, State Highway Board, 1939.

3. Georgia has used many Latin words in its placenames, e.g., Loco, Auraria, Gratis, Agricola, Subligna, Alto, Ludowici, Tranquilla, etc.

4. *Handbook of American Indians*, Bureau of American Ethnology Bulletin 30, pt. 1, p. 115.

5. This name seemingly suffered an error in transcription; it was difficult to distinguish between a *t* and an *l* in early orthography.

6. *American State Papers, Documents, Legislative and Executive, of the Congress of the United States*, Class V. Military Affairs (Washington, D.C., 1832), 1: 727.

7. Attapulges was probably intended; see note 5.

8. *American State Papers*, p. 695.

9. Captain Hugh Young, "A Topographical Memoir on East and West Florida with Itineraries of General Jackson's Army, 1818," with Introduction and annotations by Mark F. Boyd and Gerald M. Ponton, *Florida Historical Quarterly* 8, no. 2 (Oct., 1934): pt. 1, p. 86.

10. Joseph Purcell, "A Map of the Road from Pensacola to St. Augustine in East Florida," 1778, Hulbert's Crown Collection of Photographs of American Maps, Series III, 2: 110, copy in the Ayer Collection, Newberry Library, Chicago. Purcell spells the name Weethlakutchee. Eleazer Early in his *Map of the State of Georgia*, 1818, shows the stream as Wethlacoochee.

11. District 20 of original Early County, survey of 1820, John Wood, D.S., Platbook EEE, Land Records of Georgia, Surveyor General Department, Atlanta. Big Attapulgus is named in lots 7, 53, *passim*, and Little Attapulgus in lots 102, 103, *passim*.

12. District 19 of Early County, survey of 1820, Lemuel Grisham, D.S., Platbook EEE, lots 21, 22, 23.

13. District 22 of Early County, survey of 1819, Chas. Phillips, D.S., Platbook EEE. Shows Porter's Creek in lots 15, 16, 48, Big Sandy Creek in lots 18, 47, 82.

14. William Phillips, C.E., *Map of the Boundary Line of Georgia and Florida*, compiled from original surveys of Georgia and field notes of survey by Orr and Whitney [their survey was 1859; see Bulletin 817], printed by S. G. McLendon, Secretary of State of Georgia (Atlanta, 1923).

15. *American State Papers*, Class II. Indian Affairs, 2: 439.

16. Mark F. Boyd, "The First American Road in Florida," *Florida Historical Quarterly* 14, no. 2 (Oct., 1935), pt. 1, letter from Jesup to Burch, dated St. Augustine, Dec. 1, 1823, pp. 92-99, 95.

17. Albert S. Gatschet, *A Migration Legend of the Creek Indians* (Philadelphia: Brinton, 1884), 1: 71.

18. Albert S. Gatschet, "Towns and Villages of the Creek Confederacy in the XVIII and XIC Centuries," *Publications of the Alabama Historical Society*, Miscellaneous Collections, 1901, 1: 393.

19. [Goff's Attapulgus argument is confirmed by Read, *IJAL* 16 (1950): 205. *FLU.*]

No. 10
Mars Hill

When the Apostle Paul stood in the Court of the Areopagus on Mars Hill in the year A.D. 51 and gave his moving interpretation of God to the idolatrous Athenians,[1] he perpetuated in the Scriptures a name that was eventually to find much usage in America. For instance, Georgia alone employs the appellation Mars Hill at least five times. As one might suppose the name was originally used for church sites. In certain cases, however, in Georgia and elsewhere, the designation has been extended from these meeting house places to adjacent crossroads or to surrounding communities. In some states the name has been applied even to villages and towns.[2]

The Mars Hill sites and localities of Georgia are:

1. Mars Hill Church in north Oconee County, some five miles to the west of Watkinsville. This noted point is apparently the oldest place in the state that bears the name. The community around the church has long been known as the Mars Hill District, and to the south on Barbers Creek, there is an early spot called the Mars Hill Factory or Mill site.

2. Mars Hill Church and Crossroads, on U.S. 19, four miles southwest of Cumming in Forsyth County.

3. Mars Hill, a church and road fork two miles to the south of Acworth in Cobb County.

4. Mars Hill Church, School, and Crossroads on Georgia 27 in eastern Dooly County, to the northeast of Vienna.

5. Mars Hill Church and Cemetery on Georgia 37, some two and one-half miles northwest of Edison in Calhoun County.

In addition to these sites there is a place in northeast Decatur County (to the east of Parker Crossroads, and very near the Grady line) which is shown on a county highway map of Decatur as the "Old Morris Hill Church."[3] Perhaps the cartographers were mistaken in this instance and the name really should have been Mars Hill.

—*GMNL* 8(1955): 26

NOTES

1. Acts 17: 22-30.
2. Mars Hill, Me., on the Bangor and Aroostook Railroad, near the Canadian line; Mars Hill, in Madison County, N.C.; and Mars Hill, Ind., a station on the Pennsylvania Railroad, to the southwest of Indianapolis.
3. Map of Decatur County, Georgia, State Highway Board, 1939.

No. 11
Withlacoochee and Willachoochee

When one studies a map of Georgia two interesting names that catch the eye are Withlacoochee and Willacoochee, the euphonious designations for two large streams in the southern part of the state. The Withlacoochee, speaking of it as a system, heads in Turner County to the west of Worth and flows in a southerly direction to enter Florida at a point almost due south of Valdosta. From here it continues southward to join the Suwannee near Ellaville on U.S. 90. The Willacoochee, the smaller of the two waterways, heads in Ben Hill County, in the area about Fitzgerald, and flows southward to join the Alapaha near the crossing of U.S. 82, westward of the little town of Willacoochee in Atkinson County.

Despite a difference in spelling, Withlacoochee and Willacoochee have a common Indian origin and both words originally meant the same thing: Little River. The two spellings are simply different versions by white people of the composite Creek word Withlacoochee (or Wethlocoochee), that in turn was derived from *wewa*, water + *thlucco* (or *thlocco*, or *thlocko*), big + the diminutive suffix, *oochee*,[1] little or small. Thus the basic Indian term had the curious literal English meaning of little big water. When white people of other years encountered the name, they adopted the Indian form or ignored the outward contradictions of big and little by taking the intent of the word and translating it into the easy Little River. As will be seen, the whites have retained both the Indian and translated forms in stream naming.

We can be certain that these names had the same origin, because a surveyor of district 5 of original Irwin County refers to the Willacoochee under several different spellings of that name, but in two places he also marks the stream "Withlacoochee" and "Withlockochee."[2] On the other hand, the surveyors for districts 6, 7, 8, and 9 of original Irwin refer to the Withlacoochee or its tributaries as "Weolockochee,"[3] "Welakochee,"[4] "Welucoche,"[5] "Willockoche,"[6] "Welockochee,"[7] and "Welockoochee."[8]

We also have other evidence to show that Withlacoochee and Willacoochee have the same origin. This proof can be found in the name of the Willacoochee Creek,[9] a stream that arises in southern Decatur County and flows southward into Florida to join Little River which in turn unites with the Ochlocknee to the south of Quincy. This Little River, and its important upper tributaries in Georgia, viz., Big Attapulgus, Little Attapulgus, and the present Willacoochee Creek, were once called Withlacoochee or some variant of the name. In fact, this waterway is seemingly the first stream in Georgia to bear the written Indian tab because Joseph Purcell mentions it in 1778 as "Weethlakutchee or Little Big Creek";[10] while Benjamin Hawkins about 1799 calls the same stream "Wethluc-coo-chee."[11]

In addition to the streams which have been discussed, we once had another Withlacoochee River in Georgia. This waterway is the present Little River which gathers its waters in Walton, Morgan, Newton, and Jasper and flows along the common boundary of Putnam and Baldwin to enter the west side of the Oconee to the north of Milledgeville.[12] Benjamin Hawkins makes it plain that this Little River was once called "Withlaccoochee"[13] or "Wethlucooche."[14]

Possibly the reader is wondering if the noted Little River that joins the Savannah above Clark Hill Dam was also once a Withlacoochee stream. No evidence could be found in this instance to show any relationship between Indian and white names. Perhaps this very old appellation is purely English in origin and was devised by the early settlers simply to differentiate Little River from the main Savannah. The name might be a translation of the Uchee words for Little River although no documentary evidence could be found that points to such an origin. This possibility exists however, because the Uchee

Indians once lived along the Savannah River in the area of its juncture with Little River.

In Cherokee County there is another Little River, a left-bank tributary of the Etowah. This name may once have been a Cherokee appellation, but no proof could be found that such was the case. Even in Indian days white people called the stream Little River.

Some special comments should be made about the first Withlacoochee which was discussed above. On the early surveys this stream and numbers of its tributaries can be found marked Withlacoochee or waters of Withlacoochee. Over the years, however, the affluents have been given definite names like Cat Creek, Mule Creek, Brushy Creek, Warrior Creek, etc. In the meantime, too, the major branches of the waterway have also received separate names. The main prong of the stream from a point near Worth in Turner County to a juncture with the river proper to the northwest of Valdosta is now called Little River. This fork on numbers of early maps is shown as the main Withlacoochee River.[15] On today's maps, though, the Withlacoochee proper is the east fork of the stream with headings in eastern Tift and upper Berrien counties.

For simplicity's sake the present-day spellings of Withlacoochee and Willacoochee have been mainly used in this sketch. Before these versions of the name were eventually formalized there were numbers of variations used in the spellings of the words. For instance, on old plats the Withlacoochee can be found as: Weth lock, oo, chee, Withlocoochee, Withlecoochee, Withloocoochee, and Withlucoochee, etc. While Willacoochee is listed in some plats as Welecoochee, Wilockoochee, Wilokoochee, Wilucoochee, Wilicoochee, Willicoochee and so on. The last two versions are interesting because in the area of the Willacoochee it is common today to hear the name pronounced "Williecoochee."

It is safe to say that neither Withlacoochee nor Willacoochee are now written in a way which would permit an accurate pronunciation of the original word. In fact, the only element in the words which a Creek might recognize would be the suffix *oochee*. Otherwise the names have been modified so much that an Indian would not understand the sounds which result when the words are pronounced.

The factor which caused the difficulty was the elusive character of the Creek *thlucco* for big. This word actually began with a voiceless *l* which we can not properly render with our orthography. In order to reproduce this surd letter in a Creek word, the early settlers sought to depict it variously by *hl, cl,* or *thl,* with the last combination being by far the most common. The subtle *thlucco*, therefore, caused trouble for the whites from the beginning, and ultimately led to distortions of the present names. We now write Withlacoochee and pronounce the word "With la coochee. But there was no "with" sound in the original form. Rather it was *wee*, not *wĭ*. The *th*, if it had value at all, should not have become a part of the first syllable, but should have gone with the following *l* to denote the voiceless *l*. Attaching the *th* to the initial syllable twisted the first syllable of *thlucco* into *la*, *lo* or *lu*, with a definitely voiced *l*.

In the above respects Willacoochee is the same as Withlacoochee, except that some surveyors instead of trying to indicate the voiceless *l* of the former with a *th*, merely wrote that surd letter as an English *l* or *ll*. In this case, the first syllable of *thlucco* also dwindled to *la*, *lo*, or *lu*, with a voiced *l*, while the remaining *c* of the word has become attached to the suffix *oochee*.[16]

—GMNL 8(1955): 78-79

NOTES

1. In using this diminutive suffix, it was customary to drop the final vowel or vowels of the preceding element and join its terminating consonants to the suffix thus: Withlucco—Withluccoochee, Muckalee—Muckaloochee, Suwannee—Suwannoochee, etc. Sometimes, apparently, only the *chee* of the suffix was used, e.g., Willocko(chee) and Welocko(chee). The last words are mentioned in the text.

2. District 5 of original Irwin County, survey of 1820, Thomas Johnson, D.S., Platbook GGG, Land Records of Georgia, Surveyor General Department, Atlanta. In lot 357 he wrote "Withlacoochee" and in lot 4 he marked the plat "near waters of Withlockochee."

3. District 6 of original Irwin County, survey of 1819, George W. Johnson, D.S., Platbook HHH, lot 205.

4. District 7 of original Irwin County, survey of 1819, A. Dobson, D.S., Platbook HHH, lot 107.

5. *Ibid.*, lot 108.

6. *Ibid.*, lot 220.

7. District 8 of original Irwin County, survey of 1820, Charles Smith, D.S., Platbook HHH, lots 27 and 28.

8. District 9 of original Irwin County, survey of 1820-1821, Thomas Glenn, D.S., Platbook HHH, lots 124, 292, 293, *passim*.

9. This stream is shown and named on several maps, but cf. map accompanying *Soil Survey of Decatur County, Georgia*, Series 1933, no. 24, U.S. Department of Agriculture, 1939.

10. Joseph Purcell, "A Map of the Road from Pensacola to St. Augustine in East Florida," 1778, Hulbert's Crown Collection of Photographs of American Maps, Series III, 2: 110, copy in the Ayer Collection, Newberry Library, Chicago. The map has also

been reproduced in 9 sections in the *Florida Historical Quarterly* 17, no. 1 (July, 1938): 15-25.

11. Benjamin Hawkins, *A Sketch of the Creek Country in the Years 1798 and 1799*, Collections of the Georgia Historical Society, Vol. 3, pt. 1 (Savannah, 1848), p. 84.

12. The lower reach of the Little River is now a part of Lake Sinclair, a water power reservoir.

13. *Letters of Benjamin Hawkins 1796-1806*, Collections of the Georgia Historical Society, Vol. 9 (Savannah, Ga., 1916), p. 274.

14. *Ibid.*, p. 278. He wrote "Little River (Wethlucooche)" and was unquestionably referring to the stream under discussion.

15. For examples, see S. Augustus Mitchell, *The Tourists' Pocket Map of the State of Georgia* (Philadelphia, 1836), H. S. Tanner, *Georgia and Alabama* (Philadelphia, 1825) (the stream is called "Withlacuchee"), and J. H. Young, *A New Map of the State of Georgia* (Philadelphia: DeSilver, 1856) (gives the name as "Withlochoochee").

16. [Goff's "little big river" is confirmed by Read, *IJAL* 16 (1950): 203. *FLU.*]

No. 12
Aucilla River

The Aucilla River heads in central Thomas County near Merrillville and runs southeastwardly to leave Georgia and enter Florida near the corner of Thomas and Brooks counties. After reaching the latter state it continues in a southerly direction to empty into Apalachee Bay to the east of St. Marks. Since such a small part of the waterway lies in this state, the stream is not well-known here and is not considered of particular importance to us. But for placename students the river's title is of interest because a good case can be made that it is the oldest native geographic name which white people use in connection with Georgia.

The word is derived from a Timucua Indian settlement which was once located in the general area of the Aucilla River bridge on U.S. 90 in Florida. DeSoto passed this community in 1539 and the chroniclers of his expedition mention the place as Agile, Axille, Aguile, and Ochile.[1]

When the Spaniards later took active possession of east Florida and began to develop it, they ultimately opened in the seventeenth century a chain of mission stations across the province from St. Augustine to the Apalachicola. One of these early missions was established at or in the vicinity of the original Indian site, and named San

Miguel de Asile. The place was in existence by 1655[2] and was mentioned again in 1675 by Bishop Calderón as San Miguel de Asyle.[3]

The spellings Asile and Asyle furnished the basis for the Anglicized form of the name which was to appear later. Colonel William B. Bull's map of 1738 lists the place as "Assille,"[4] while Joseph Purcell in his chart of 1778 marks the stream "Assilly River."[5] The present form of the name apparently began to emerge in the late 1790's because Benjamin Hawkins around that time refers to the river as "Aussille."[6] In 1819 when the State of Georgia made its original surveys of the area which embodies the headwaters of the river the surveyors labelled the stream "Ossilla"[7] and "Osilla."[8] In the years following this period the waterway is variously called "Aussilly,"[9] "Oseilla,"[10] "Ocilla,"[11] and "Aucilla."[12]

Thus the name in one version or another has been in continuous use for a remarkable span of time. The appellation began as the designation of an Indian town, but it is reasonable to conclude that the river also bore the same name from the earliest days because there are numbers of examples of streams being called after towns that stood on their banks: Chattahoochee, Coosa, Oconee, Tugalo, Uchee, Fowltown Creek, and so on.

Only one other indigenous geographic name which we use would be older than Aucilla and that term is Apalachee. Cabeza de Vaca mentions this word in his account of the Narvaez expedition of 1528, which followed a route across Florida that corresponded closely with the first segment of the later DeSoto journey.[13] Although Narvaez apparently did not visit what is now Georgia, he did reach the province of the Apalachee Indians and the town of Apalachee in the area of today's Tallahassee, Florida, and thus caused the name Apalachee to be introduced into print.

Now Georgia does use the word Apalachee as the name of a river in the east central part of the state.[14] But it is a mystery how the designation came to be applied there because the stream was a long way from the country of the Apalachee Indians in Florida. Furthermore, Tulapocca was the usual name that the Creek Indians applied to the river which we now call the Apalachee.[15] Perhaps the name Apalachee was brought to east Georgia by some Apalachee Indians that Colonel James Moore brought back to the Savannah River after his victorious raid against Spanish Florida in 1704. These Indians lived on the Savannah for a period in the areas about Augusta and Shell Bluff. Possibly they eventually migrated westward and settled on the present Apalachee in Georgia. But be that as it may, the term

Aucilla has continued all the while in usage in the section where the name was first found by the Spaniards in 1539.

Perhaps during the above discussion of Aucilla and Apalachee the reader has wondered about the names of other streams that DeSoto passed prior to reaching Aucilla, and especially about the Suwannee which the Spaniards crossed. They called this last waterway the River of the Deer. The present Suwannee has no connection with that name. As the Spaniards continued their journey they encountered and noted such names as Altamaha, Coosa, and Conasauga. But these appellations, of course, came after they had visited Aucilla and recorded the name.

There is no satisfactory explanation of the meaning of Aucilla. The word is a Timucua name, but knowledge of the language of those Indians is limited. The report of the committee on the DeSoto expedition mentions the Timucua word *aha*, acorn, as a possible origin but does not elaborate on the derivation.[16] Professor William Read in his study of Florida placenames considers Aucilla, although he does not attempt to interpret it. In fact he places the appellation under a category embodying names of unknown or dubious origin.[17]

Before closing attention should be given to Ocilla, the county seat of Irwin County. Mr. J. B. Clements in his history of this area concludes that Ocilla is derived from Oswitchee, an Indian town.[18] He goes on to say the place changed its name several times: Assile, Aglie, Axilla, Agulil, Ochile, and lastly Ocilla.[19] These names in the main, however, are the same as those reported by DeSoto's chroniclers for the original Aucilla. Oswitchee on the other hand was a well-known Lower Creek Indian town which was located in present Russell County, Alabama, in the big bend of the Chattahoochee, below Fort Mitchell. The Indians of this settlement, though, did live on Flint River before removing to the place on the Chattahoochee.[20] Thus they once inhabited the general area of original Irwin County.

Nonetheless one questions that Ocilla was derived from Oswitchee. The word is simply a long-established version of Aucilla, and since Ocilla is an attractive appellation, it is reasonable to believe someone in Irwin proposed the word as a good name for the town when the place was established.

In conclusion, it might be pointed out that Georgia has both an Ocilla and an Aucilla; the former is the county seat of Irwin and the latter is a little crossroads in southeast Thomas County. Phonetically the two names are the same.

—*GMNL* 8(1955): 79-80

NOTES

1. John R. Swanton, Chmn., *Final Report of the United States DeSoto Expedition Commission*, House Doc. 71, 76th Cong., 1st Sess. (1939), p. 56. The chronicler Ranjel called the place "Agile"; the Gentleman of Elvas wrote "Axille"; Biedma used "Aguile"; and Garcilaso de la Vega spelled the name "Ochile." The last writer did not actually accompany the DeSoto expedition but wrote from hearsay and documents.

2. Mark F. Boyd, "Spanish Mission Sites in Florida," *Florida Historical Quarterly* 17 (April, 1939): 254-80.

3. Lucy L. Wenhold, *A 17th Century Letter of Gabriel Diaz Vara Calderón, Describing the Indians and Missions of Florida*, Smithsonian Miscellaneous Collections 95: 8.

4. "Map of East and West Florida, South Carolina and Georgia, transmitted by Col. Bull (President and Commander in Chief of South Carolina) . . . to the Board of Trade, 25 May, 1738," from a photostatic copy in the Library of Congress, original in the British Colonial Office.

5. Joseph Purcell, "A Map of the Road from Pensacola to St. Augustine in East Florida," 1778, Hulbert's Crown Collection of Photographs of American Maps, Series III, 2: 110, copy in the Ayer Collection, Newberry Library, Chicago. This map has been reproduced in 9 sections by Mark F. Boyd, *Florida Historical Quarterly* 17 (July, 1938): 15-25.

6. Benjamin Hawkins, *A Sketch of the Creek Country in the Years 1798 and 1799*, Collections of the Georgia Historical Society, Vol. 3, pt. 1 (Savannah, 1848), p. 84.

7. District 13 of original Irwin County, survey of 1819, Platbook III, lot 147, Land Records of Georgia, Surveyor General Department, Atlanta.

8. District 14, original Irwin County, survey of 1819, Platbook III, lots 17, 29, 64, *passim*. In lot 16 the name is also spelled Ossilla.

9. H. S. Tanner, *Georgia and Alabama* (map) (Philadelphia, 1825).

10. J. Lee Williams, map of Florida in *The Territory of Florida* (Goodrich, N.Y., 1837).

11. David H. Burr, *Map of Florida Exhibiting the Post Offices, Post Roads, Canals, &c.* (circa 1836); and Williams Phillips, C.E., *Map of the Boundary Line of Georgia and Florida*, compiled circa 1870 from original surveys of Georgia and field notes of survey by Orr and Whitner in 1859, printed by S. G. McLendon, Secretary of State of Georgia (Atlanta, 1923).

12. Aucilla is now the generally accepted form of the name on maps for both Georgia and Florida.

13. Enrique de Veda, ed., "Naufragios de Alvar Nuñez Cabeza de Vaca y Relacción de la Jornada que hizo a la Florida con el Adelantado Pánfilo de Narvaez," *Biblioteca de Autores Españoles* (Madrid, 1931) 22: 521.

14. The Apalachee is the main upper western fork of the Oconee. It arises near Hog Mountain in north Gwinnett County and joins the Oconee just above the bridge of the Georgia Railroad in eastern Morgan County.

15. *Letters of Benjamin Hawkins 1796-1806*, Collections of the Georgia Historical Society, Vol. 9 (Savannah, Ga., 1916), pp. 242, 243, 257, 287. It should be noted that Hawkins in this source also mentions the stream as the "Appalatchee"—cf. p. 286.

16. *Final Report*, p. 60.

17. William A. Read, *Florida Place Names of Indian Origin and Seminole Personal Names*, Louisiana State University Studies No. 11 (Baton Rouge, 1934), p. 45.

18. J. B. Clements, *History of Irwin County* (Atlanta: Foote & Davies, 1932), p. 35.

19. *Ibid.*
20. Hawkins, *Sketch of the Creek Country*, p. 63. He spells the name "Oose-oo-che" and says the town at the site on the west side of the Chattahoochee in Alabama was established in 1794. He then adds the people once lived in Flint River. In another place Hawkins calls the Chattahoochee River settlement "Ooseuche"—cf. his *Letters*, p. 171. The name in Russell County, Ala., is perpetuated by a crossroads called Oswichee, which is near the location of the former Indian town.

No. 13
Plains (and Plains of Dura)

Plains, Georgia, is a small town in western Sumter County on the Seaboard Airline Railroad and the U.S. Highway No. 280. It is a pleasant place, located in the midst of an open and prosperous farming area that is noticeable for its relative levelness. A visitor to the town is prone to think of the name as quite descriptive of the location and to conclude that the community naturally derived its designation from the appearance of the surrounding country. But Plains has a more interesting and roundabout origin. Actually the name is drawn from a much older point called Plains of Dura which was located about a mile to the north of the present place, at a spot that is now a mere crossroads.

It is not known exactly when Plains of Dura was founded, but in all probability the time was the mid-1830's because the site was important enough to be designated as a post office in 1839, making it one of the first post offices in southwest Georgia.[1]

The old place bore a Biblical name and took title from the Plain of Dura near Babylon where Nebuchadnezzar erected a colossal golden image which he ordered his subjects to worship.[2] The reader will recall that Shadrach, Meshach, and Abednego were bound and thrown into the fiery furnace for their refusal to bow down before this idol.[3]

It should be noted, however, that the Biblical site was Plain of Dura, whereas the little place in Sumter County became Plains of Dura. The reason for the plural designation is a matter of conjecture, but that spelling was used from the beginning because it can be found on early maps. When the railroad came through the section some 60-odd years ago, the Plains part of the name was appropriated for a station that was established on the line. The present town, of course, developed around this railway point.

Some old people around Plains follow an interesting practice of referring to the place as "the Plains." The usage of this form by elderly persons leaves the thought that the custom may date back to the years in which Plains of Dura was a prominent spot in the community. Perhaps the original site was actually referred to with the definite article.

It might be of interest to add that the crossroads at Plains of Dura was the intersecting point for two early traces. One of these routes, Bond's Trail,[4] led southward from old Traveller's Rest, below Montezuma, on Flint River via Ellaville, Quebec (on Georgia 153 in Schley County), Concord Crossroads, Plains of Dura, Plains, and Paradox Church Crossroads in the southwest corner of Sumter. From there it crossed into extreme northwest Lee County and joined what is now the Edwards Station-Bodsford road, just to the east of Chokeeligee Creek. This last route, a former Indian path, ran along the eastside of Kinchafoonee Creek. To the south of its juncture with Bond's Trail, at a point about two miles northwest of today's Neyami, in Lee County, it forked with one branch leading southeastward through Neyami to the site of old Starkville,[5] thence eastward to Pindertown, a noted Indian crossing point on the Flint River. The other prong continued south along Kinchafoonee Creek to Kennards Settlement and Cowpen,[6] at the present bridge on Georgia 32.

The east-west route that crossed the Bond's Trail at Plains of Dura is now remembered as the Old Americus–Preston Road. It follows part of a former Indian thoroughfare that led from Hawkinsville westward past Drayton, the lower side of Americus, Plains of Dura, and Preston to former Creek Indian communities on the Chattahoochee. Between Hawkinsville and Flint River this path was called the Slosh-eye Trail. No evidence could be found, however, to show that this droll name was used for the route to the west of the Flint via the site of Plains of Dura.

—*GMNL* 8(1955): 80-81

NOTES

1. Records of Appointments of Postmasters—Georgia, 1827-1844, Records of the Post Office Department, Record Group 28, National Archives, microfilm copy in De-

partment of Archives and History, Atlanta. David W. Robinett was named postmaster on Aug. 17, 1839.

2. Daniel 3: 1.

3. *Ibid.* 3: 21-23.

4. This trail is also called Barnes' Trail. Many old people in the area through which it passes, however, insist the name should be Bond's. The *Map of Sumter County, Georgia* (Atlanta: Hudgins Co., *circa* 1910) shows the correct course of the route in that county but names it Boyd's Trail. This version is not remembered by elderly citizens of Sumter, Schley, and Lee.

5. Starkville was the county seat of Lee before the coming of the railroad. It was located on the west side of Muckalee Creek, several miles eastward of present Leesburg. Across the Muckalee from Starkville was the site of a Chehaw Indian town.

6. Kennards Settlement and Cowpen was a noted center of southwest Georgia in the Indian days. The place was established by two prominent half-breed brothers, Jack and William Kennard. Both men were Lower Creek chiefs. Their descendants, now known as Canards, continue to be leading citizens of the Creek Indians in Oklahoma.

No. 14
Tobesofkee and Rocky Creeks

Tobesofkee Creek heads on the lower edge of Barnesville in Lamar County and flows across Monroe and Bibb to unite with the Ocmulgee some ten miles below Macon. Not far above this juncture with the river, to the north of the little town of Sofkee, it is joined on the east by Rocky Creek. These streams have carried their names for a long period of time, apparently even for a span that outdates the founding of Georgia. Since the two waterways lay across the course of the famous Lower Creek Trading Path from Charleston to the Indians of today's western Georgia and eastern Alabama, English-speaking traders must have become familiar with the streams about 250 years ago.

One of the first maps to give an intimation of the creeks is Henry Popple's chart of 1733.[1] In the general area of the present Tobesofkee he shows a stream named "Togosohatchee R." that is joined on the left by "Octohatchee R." He also depicts and names in the same locality the present Echeconnee Creek. This last waterway, however, is shown to the east of the Togosohatchee, whereas it is actually situated to the west of our Tobesofkee. Since there is no other large creek or small river on the west side of the Ocmulgee in this general section, there are grounds for believing Popple got his streams reversed, putting Togosohatchee (Tobesofkee) in the position of the

Echeconnee and vice versa. The fact that he shows no big stream between the Echeconnee and the Ocmulgee supports this view, because the intermediate Tobesofkee is a considerably larger stream than the Echeconnee and logically would not have been left out of the chart.

Many years after the date of the Popple map, William Bartram in 1776 mentions the creek as "Tobosochte,"[2] and a little later William DeBrahm refers to it as "Tobosophskee."[3] The present form of the name began to emerge about the 1790's when Benjamin Hawkins spells it "Tobosaufkee,"[4] "Tobe saufe ke,"[5] and "Tobesauke."[6] John Dutton on his 1814 map makes the stream "Tobofuskee,"[7] and Eleazer Early in his fine chart of 1818 calls it "Tobe saufkee."[8] H. S. Tanner, however, in his 1825 map of Georgia and Alabama switches the name to "Chupee Creek."[9] This version was later used by some other cartographers, but in the main the original word in one spelling or another was continued until it finally became accepted as Tobesofkee.

It should be noted in passing that both Bartram[10] and DeBrahm[11] mention a *Little* Tobesofkee Creek, but do not refer to the Echeconnee. The latter writer was probably reporting from hearsay, although Bartram passed through the area where the streams lie and states that he crossed a "Great" and "Little Tobosochte." This account leaves the impression that his Little Tobosochte may actually have been the Echeconnee, because beyond the former, he adds his party camped beside the Sweetwater which is a west-bank tributary of that stream. Now, there is a Little Tobesofkee but it is in Monroe County, much to the north of the old trading path which Bartram travelled and plainly he did not cross that waterway. This analysis then leads to the conclusion that the Echeconnee was sometimes known as the Little Tobesofkee.

The meaning of Tobesofkee is uncertain, although on its face it contains the Muscogee or Creek word *sofki*, meaning hominy. This version though is an offhand translation because the term *sofki*, or *sofkee*, can be found in connection with a number of Creek foodstuffs that were prepared with maize: hominy, corn meal, parched corn, corn flour, a kind of gruel, and even the forerunner of our grits.

Henry Gannett says the word is from *sofkee*, dish of meal and *tobe*, I have lost, being so named because an Indian spilled or lost his *sofkee* while crossing the stream.[12] This explanation may be correct, but it is open to doubt. For one thing the early first element in the appellation was often *Tobo* or *Toba* and not *Tobe*. Furthermore, the original designation may not have contained the word *sofki* at all, as evidenced by the names which were first mentioned above: Togosohatchee, Tobosochte, Tobofuskee and Tobesauke. These forms contain elements having various meanings which bear no apparent relation to *sofkee* or hominy. Without more information then, it would be mere speculation to attempt to translate Tobesofkee. Eventually let us hope that some acceptable source such as an early trader's journal or diary will turn up to give an adequate explanation of this old and interesting name.

The Rocky Creek which was mentioned is not named as such on the Popple map of 1733, although it may be the "Octohatchee" which he shows uniting with the "Togosohatchee." Bartram, however, mentions the stream and calls it "Stony Creek."[13] Hawkins in the same paragraph referred to it in 1797 as both "Rockey" and "Stoney" Creek.[14] These versions leave the intimation that both Bartram and Hawkins were giving the English translation of an Indian name which would have been Chattohachi, from the Muscogee *chatto*, rock or stone + *hachi*, stream.

Literally, of course, the name would have been simply Stone Creek or Rock Creek, but apparently it was the practice of the backlanders to use Stony and Rocky in converting this sort of name.[15]

—GMNL 8(1955): 122-23

NOTES

1. Henry Popple, "A Map of the British Empire in America . . . ," sheet 10 (London, 1733), photostatic copy from the Library of Congress. It might be noted in connection with this source that Popple shows but does not name these streams on an earlier map, entitled "A Map of the English and French Possessions on the Continent of North America" (1727), MS in the British Museum, photostatic copy in the Library of Congress.

2. William Bartram, *Travels Through North and South Carolina, Georgia, East and West Florida* (Dublin, 1793), p. 380.

3. John Gerar William DeBrahm, *History of the Province of Georgia* (Wormsloe, 1849), p. 31.

4. *Letters of Benjamin Hawkins, 1796-1806*. Collections of the Georgia Historical Society, Vol. 9 (Savannah, Ga., 1916), p. 88. The date of this note was Feb. 22, 1797.

5. "A Viatory or Journal of distances and observations," trip from Flint River to Ocmulgee, June, 1800, MS in the Library of Congress. He notes the stream was "fine for fish."

6. *Ibid.*, trip "From Col. Hawkins at Flint River to Ocmulgee old fields," *circa* 1801.

7. John Dutton, "The State of Georgia" (1814), photostatic copy in the Library of Congress, original in the British Museum.

8. Eleazer Early, *Map of the State of Georgia* (Savannah and Philadelphia, 1818).

9. H. S. Tanner, *Georgia and Alabama* (map) (Philadelphia, 1825).
10. Bartram, *Travels*, p. 380.
11. DeBrahm, *History*, p. 31.
12. Henry Gannett, *The Origin of Certain Place Names in the United States*, 2nd ed., U.S. Geological Survey, House Doc. 399, 58th Cong., 3d Sess. (1905), p. 301.
13. Bartram, *Travels*, p. 379.
14. Hawkins, *Letters*, p. 88.
15. [Read, *IJAL* 15 (1949): 132 says "Tobesofkee means *sofky stirrer*—from Creek atapa stirrer probably a wooden ladle; and safki *corn gruel*." Like Goff, he rejects the Gannett etymon. See No. 15. *FLU.*]

No. 15
Hachasofkee and Sofkee Creeks

In addition to the Tobesofkee, there are two other Georgia stream names that contain the form *sofkee* or *sofka;* Hachasofkee Creek, which arises to the east of Talbotton and flows north to join Flint River above Prattsburg in Talbot County; and Sofkee Creek that begins above Millers Crossroads, below Whigham in Grady County and runs eastward to enter Tired Creek, to the south of Cairo.

The Hachasofkee appears under one spelling or another in the 1826-1827 original surveys for what is now Talbot County: "Hatchasaufka,"[1] "Hatchesaufka,"[2] "Hachasofka,"[3] "Hatchesaufkee,"[4] "Hatchasofka,"[5] and so on. The name undoubtedly means Deep Creek in Muscogee, from *hachi*, stream or creek + the adjective *soofka* or *sufki*, meaning deep. The position of the modifiers *saufka*, *sofka*, or *saufkee* in the above names substantiates this translation. The name could not have been intended for Hominy Creek, because to have had that meaning the elements would have been reversed, thus: *sofkihachi*, or in the Anglicized form, sofkeehatchee. There is, of course, a distortion in the name through a conversion of *sufki* or *soofka* into *sofkee*, the word for hominy, but this is a small shift considering other twists which pioneer whites gave to Indian appellations. Perhaps familiarity with the well-known term for hominy led people to change the word in this instance.

Benjamin Hawkins offers an alternate and older name for the Hachasofkee. In a listing made about 1797 of the principal west-bank tributaries of Flint River from the Flat Shoals[6] down river to the vicinity of today's Bainbridge, he names the affluents and gives the distances between them.[7] At approximately the right spot for the mouth of Hachasofkee Creek, he notes a stream called "Aupiogee."[8] Now interestingly enough some official land plats for the first survey of Talbot show parts of the present Hachasofkee as "Ahapioka" or "Ahhapioka."[9] There is enough resemblance between these designations and the name given by Hawkins to warrant the conclusion that the Hachasofkee was also once known as Aupiogee, Ahapioka, or Ahhapioka. This point should be of more than passing interest to students of early geography and Indian matters, because in his listing of the Flint's tributaries, Hawkins discloses some original stream names that had not previously appeared in other writings, and also furnishes certain significant comments about Indian sites and fords on that river. Unfortunately, however, the distances Hawkins gives are difficult to follow with precision. The more, therefore, researchers can verify with other sources and pinpoint the exact streams which he names, the more we can learn about the definite locations of the various places mentioned by him.

It might be of interest to note that Georgia once had another Hachasofkee. This stream was the present Whitewater Creek of lower Heard and western Troup, which enters the right side of the Chattahoochee just above the Atlantic Coast Line Railroad bridge to the west of LaGrange. Benjamin Hawkins crossed this stream in October, 1798, and labelled it "Hatche soof, kee" or "deep Creek."[10]

To return to the Sofkee Creek in Grady County, it should be mentioned that the stream has carried the tab·at least since 1820, when the official surveys were made of the area in which it lies. But the surveyor merely wrote the name "Sofka Cr."[11] This listing leaves the appellation in an uncertain status. On its face the designation means Hominy Creek. If, however, this Sofka represented a conversion of *sufki* or *soofka* into *sofka*, the name signifies deep, with the word *hachi* or *hatchee*, for creek, being understood.

In conclusion, it should be pointed out that Carroll County has an old waterway called Hominy Creek (an east-bank tributary of the Little Tallapoosa) which arises to the south of Hickory Level. In the Indian days the stream might have been a Sofkeehatchee. We may never know about this little matter, though, because the surveyor of District 6 of original Carroll in 1827 failed to name the creek on his land plats.[12]

—*GMNL* 8(1955): 123-24

NOTES

1. District 24 of original Muscogee County, survey of 1826, Platbook NNNN, lots 31, 32; and District 16, original Muscogee County, survey of 1827, Platbook MMMM, lots 224, 246, 258, Land Records of Georgia, Surveyor General Department, Atlanta.
2. District 24, Platbook NNNN, lot 71.
3. *Ibid.*, lots 34, 48. The stream named here is today's Potters Creek, a tributary of the present Hachasofkee.
4. District 16, Platbook MMMM, lot 284.
5. District 15, survey of 1827, *ibid.*, lots 209, 210, 211
6. The Flat Shoals of Flint River lie between Pike and Meriwether, to the southwest of Concord in the former county. The noted Oakfuskee Path or Upper Creek Trading Path crossed the river there; cf. "Some Major Indian Trading Paths Across the Georgia Piedmont," *Georgia Mineral Newsletter* 6 (1953): 122ff.
7. *Letters of Benjamin Hawkins, 1796–1806*, Collections of the Georgia Historical Society, Vol. 9 (Savannah, Ga., 1916), p. 172.
8. *Ibid.*
9. District 24 of original Muscogee County (now parts of Talbot and Taylor counties), Platbook NNNN. The stream is called "Ahapioka" in lot 4 and "Ahhapioka" in lots 34 and 35. These names apply within this land district to the main Hachasofkee above its juncture with today's Potters Creek, which joins the former on its east side to the west of Prattsburg. In these plats, the Hachasofkee began at the head of what is now Potters Creek and flowed to the Flint, with the present creek being treated as a tributary. In adjoining districts, however (save in District 23), the main stream is properly called Hachasofkee or some variant of that name—cf. notes 1-5. In District 23, Platbook NNNN, the surveyor apparently was not familiar with the names Hachasofkee or Ahapioka, because he labelled the stream "Upland Creek" (cf. lot 258). In lot 254, interestingly enough, he marks the waterway "Hupland." The Cockney *h* as manifested in this spelling was once common in Georgia stream names, although it was rare to see the form as late as 1826, the date of the survey of District 23.

The meaning of Aupiogee or Ahapioka is not certain. The last apparently contains the Creek word *aha* or *ahau*, meaning potato. The stream reaches Flint River about one-half mile below the mouth of Potato Creek on the east or Upson County side of the river. Potato Creek in Indian days was called Auhau—cf. Eleazer Early's "Map of the State of Georgia" (1818). Perhaps the *pioka* element in Ahapioka denoted some sort of relationship or location with respect to the Upson County Potato Creek.

10. Benjamin Hawkins, "A Viatory or Journal of distances and observations," trip to Etaw-Woh (Etowah), beginning Oct. 5, 1798, MS in the Library of Congress.
11. District 19, original Early County, survey of 1820, Platbook EEE, lots 191, 193, 194, 195, 197, 198, *passim*. This source shows Sofkee Creek joining Turkey Creek in lot 199, not far above the latter's juncture with Tired Creek. This depiction is at variance with modern maps that show the Sofkee entering Tired Creek directly; cf., for example, *Grady County, Georgia* (State Highway Board, 1939).
12. District 6, original Carroll County, survey of 1827, Platbook OOOO. [Stewart, *American Place Names*, pp. 194, 452, 485 takes all the *sofkee* elements in this and the preceding article to be *sofkee*, deep root; there is no mention of hominy. *FLU.*]

No. 16
Echeconnee Creek

Echeconnee (pronounced "Eechyconny") is one of Georgia's oldest geographic names, and since the appellation was mentioned in connection with Tobesofkee above it properly should be discussed in conjunction with the little essay on that creek.

The stream heads at the corners of Lamar, Upson, and Monroe and runs parallel with the Tobesofkee to join the Ocmulgee some miles to the east of the little town of Echeconnee in Peach County. For a considerable part of its course, the waterway forms a common boundary between Bibb on one hand, with Crawford, Peach, and Houston counties on the other. Henry Popple in his map of 1733 shows the Creek as "Itcheecono."[1] Bartram and DeBrahm do not mention the stream,[2] but it appears in later sources under such spellings as: "Icho-conno,"[3] "Echeconno,"[4] "Echeconnee,"[5] etc. The official Georgia surveys of the area mark it "Itchocunno,"[6] "Ichiconna,"[7] "Ichocunno,"[8] "Echconna,"[9] and so on. Benjamin Hawkins mentions the stream in one place as "Itchocunnau"[10] and in another as "Itchocunnah."[11] He makes the interesting comment that the name means deer trap, and was so called because Indians hid on the banks at shoally places to ambush deer which resorted to such spots to feed on a slimy vegetation known as "moss" that grows on rocks in shoals.[12]

In its simplest form Echeconnee is derived from the Creek *echo*, deer (pronounced "ee echo") + *conna*, trap. In view of the fact however that the element *itchee* or *eche* has appeared so long and so often in the different versions of the name, this part may actually have been derived from *itchi*, the Hitchiti word for deer. There is a similarity between *echo* and *itchi* because Hitchiti is a Muskogean dialect that is closely kin to the Creek.

Apparently the final *ee* in the present spelling of Echeconnee can be attributed to backcountry white people who were prone to change a final *a, au, ah, o,* and even an *er* into *ee*, thus: Augusta into "Augustee," Georgia to "Georgee," beaver to "beavee," Echeconna to "Echeconnee," and so on in great profusion.[13]

—*GMNL* 8(1955): 124-25

NOTES

1. Henry Popple, "A Map of the British Empire in America . . . ," sheet 10 (London, 1733), photostatic copy from the Library of Congress.
2. These writers apparently referred to the Echeconnee as the Little Tobesofkee—see the comments about this point in item No. 14 above.
3. Eleazer Early, *Map of the State of Georgia* (Savannah and Philadelphia, 1818).
4. S. Augustus Mitchell, *The Tourists' Pocket Map of the State of Georgia* (Philadelphia, 1836).
5. J. H. Young, *A New Map of the State of Georgia* (Philadelphia, 1856).
6. District 3 of original Houston County (now parts of Bibb and Crawford), survey of 1821, Platbook TTT, lots 74, 90, 92, *passim*, Land Records of Georgia, Surveyor General Department, Atlanta.
7. District 7 of Houston County (now Bibb), survey of 1821, *ibid.*, lots 95, 96.
8. *Ibid.*, lots 57, 59.
9. *Ibid.*, lot 58.
10. Benjamin Hawkins, "A Viatory or Journal of distances and observations," trip from Flint River to Ocmulgee, June, 1800, MS in the Library of Congress. He adds a note that the stream was "good for fish."
11. *Letters of Benjamin Hawkins, 1796-1806*, Collections of the Georgia Historical Society, Vol. 9 (Savannah, Ga., 1916), p. 88.
12. *Ibid.*
13. [Read, *IJAL* 15 (1949): 129 says "from *icho deer* and *kunhi trap*. The Indians bent down small trees so as to form traps for deer. See *deer trap*" in *Dictionary of American English* 2: 740. This *kunhi* form makes the "Augustee" explanation unnecessary, though Goff's conjecture is plausible in view of the pioneer "Indiany" and "Lucindy, Cindy," and the related hyperurbanisms "Missoura, Cincinnata." For a similar hyperurbanism see "Catoosa," in this series, No. 53. *FLU.*]

No. 17
Mulberry, Ossahatchie, and Sowhatchee Creeks

Mulberry Creek gathers its waters in eastern Harris County and flows westward to join the Chattahoochee River a short distance below Bartlett's Ferry Dam. The designation is of Indian origin because Benjamin Hawkins mentioned the stream in the 1790's as "Ketale"[1] and "Ketalee" creek.[2] This name is derived from the Muscogee *ke*, mulberry + *tali* or *tale*, meaning withered or dead. The exact implication of the appellation is not known because the English name for the stream has always been simply Mulberry Creek. A village and community called Mulberry Grove, located on the south side of the stream to the west of Cataula, intimates that the mulberry tree was once common in the vicinity of the creek.

Ossahatchie (or Osahatchee) Creek, a tributary of the Mulberry, heads to the south of Waverly Hall in Harris and enters the main creek just above the bridge on U.S. 27. This name means Pokeweed (or Pokeberry plant) Creek, being derived from the Muscogee *osa,* pokeweed + *hachi,* a waterway or stream.

The original land surveys for the area in which the stream lies label it "Osauhatchee,"[3] "Ossohatchee,"[4] "Osouhatchee,"[5] "Osohatchee,"[6] and "Osawhatchee."[7] These various early spellings of Ossahatchie suggest an explanation for Sowhatchee, or Sawhatchee, [8] a large tributary of the Chattahoochee River, in Early County. This name may also have once been another Osahachi or Pokeweed Creek because backcountry white people (and seemingly even the Indians) sometimes dropped the first syllable of an Indian name, thus making words like Amuckalee into 'Muckalee, Alapaha into 'Lapaha, Emuckfaw into 'Muckfaw, etc. In the Early County name the *o* in *Osahachi* might well have been dropped and the word slurred into 'Sawhatchee, or 'Sowhatchee.

To the south of Ossahatchie Creek, on alternate U.S. 27, or Georgia 85, there is a village called Ossahatchie. This place in pioneer days was known as Lowes and was a well-known stop on the noted Old Alabama Road running from Indian Springs to Coweta Falls, later Columbus.[9]

—*GMNL* 8(1955): 125

NOTES

1. Benjamin Hawkins, *A Sketch of the Creek Country in the Years 1798 and 1799,* Collections of the Georgia Historical Society, Vol. 3, pt. 1 (Savannah, 1848), p. 55. He spelled the name "Ke-ta-le."
2. *Letters of Benjamin Hawkins, 1796-1806,* Collections of the Georgia Historical Society, Vol. 9 (Savannah, Ga., 1916), p. 61.
3. District 18 of original Muscogee County (now Harris), survey of 1827, James Pace, D.S., Platbook MMMM, lots 188, 196, 200, 216, Land Records of Georgia, Surveyor General Department, Atlanta.
4. *Ibid.,* lots 190, 198, 217, 244.
5. *Ibid.,* lots 197, 199, 218, 233.
6. *Ibid.,* lot 234.
7. *Ibid.,* lot 247.
8. The name can be found under both of these spellings—*The Geologic Map of Georgia,* for example, published in 1939 by the Georgia Division of Mines, Mining and

Geology uses "Sowhatchee"; the *Map of Early County, Georgia,* by the State Highway Board, 1938, marks the stream "Sawhatchee." On the basis of pronunciations used in the area of the creek, either form could be correct.

9. [Read, *IJAL* 15 (1949): 131-32, confirms Goff's etymon of Ossahatchie, but derives Sowhatchee from "Hitchiti sawi *raccoon* and hahchi *creek.*" *FLU.*]

No. 18
Bad and Worse Creeks, No Man's Friend Pond, The Troublesome Creeks, Devil's Cove, Tearbritches and Rough Creeks, Hell's Half Acre, The Bad Prong of Ten-Mile, Lordamercy Cove, and Useless Bay

The old-timer was often given to a tedious repetition of many geographic names, like Dry Creek, Poplar Springs, Caney Creek, Pine Level, and Turkey Creek; but when he really had a good incentive for thinking up an intriguing designation, he could display a gift for coining an interesting appellation. This talent was manifested in a number of ways, but perhaps it is best illustrated in the pioneer's flair for whimsical terms that applied to areas which were laborious and fatiguing to penetrate or cross. No doubt the difficulties of moving about in rugged or dense localities furnished the motive for devising the diversity of waggish tabs which can be found in connection with such places.

The names in the heading above by no means represent a complete listing of all such designations that can be found in Georgia, but they do illustrate well this particular phase of placenaming.

The appellations shown are old. Some of them appeared on the very first maps and land plats of the areas in which they can be found. They serve to remind us that though the backwoodsman has disappeared from our midst, his sense of the droll continues about us in the placenames which he left.

Bad Creek and Worse Creek lie in extreme lower Rabun County. They head on the eastern slope of Rocky Mountain, to the north of Tallulah Falls, and flow parallel with each other through a rugged area to enter the Chattooga River in lot 36 of the 4th District of Rabun, almost due east of the Tallulah Gorge. People who have travelled along these waterways say their names are quite descriptive of the streams in question.

No Man's Friend Pond is a dense woody and swampy area that lies to the southwest of Adel in Cook County. The area is not a pond in the conventional understanding of that word; rather it is more of a bay, a low swampy section that is heavily forested. The place is reputed to be so thick that a person can easily get lost in it.

There are several Troublesome or Trouble creeks in Georgia. One of these, and seemingly the oldest stream bearing the name, arises on the eastern outskirts of Lexington in Oglethorpe County and flows east to join Long Creek. The stream is now usually referred to simply as Trouble Creek. In former years, however, it was also known as Troublesome Creek. Another Troublesome Creek begins on the east side of U.S. 41, at Highland Mills above Griffin, and flows northeast to join Towaliga Creek in upper Spalding County. In former years there was a little Troublesome Creek that entered the Alapaha River above Statenville in Echols County. The name, however, has disappeared from present-day maps and it is not known if the designation is remembered by people who live in the area.

The Devil's Cove is a narrow, rough little valley that lies a mile or so to the southwest of Estelle, in Walker County.

Tearbritches Creek[1] heads on the north side of Little Bald Mountain, just inside of Murray County from the Fannin line, and runs northward to join the Conasauga River at the Murray-Fannin boundary. Arising in the same general area, Rough Creek parallels Tearbritches, to the west, and enters the Conasauga a mile or so downriver, in Murray County.

Hell's Half Acre is a dense thicket and wooded area that is situated to the north of the Barkcamp community and to the east of Magruder in lower Burke County. The name is merely a backwoodsy figure of speech because the place is far larger than a half-acre. The spot is so thick hunters of the locality say a dog can not pass through it.

The Bad Prong is a western affluent of Ten-Mile Creek in southeast Candler County.

Lordamercy Cove is a deep, steep-sloped little valley that heads on the north side of the Blue Ridge at the Union-White County line, to the northeast of Tesnatee Gap. The branch which drains from it is an extreme upper tip of the Right Fork of Nottely River in Union County. The noted Appalachian Trail down the Blue Ridge skirts the southeast rim of Lordamercy Cove.

Useless Bay is a large, swampy, wooded area, to the northwest of Homerville, in Clinch County. One informant when asked about the origin of the name said it was so-called because "Hit's hard to git about in, and ain't fit fer nuthin."

—GMNL 8(1955): 158

NOTES

1. [For non-Americans it should be explained that *tear* is /ter/ and not /tiyr/, and that *britches*, which can be torn, is a common American spelling and pronunciation of *breeches*. *FLU*.]

No. 19
Canoochee River

The Canoochee is one of the state's noted streams, since, like the Savannah and Ogeechee, it is closely connected with the history of colonial Georgia. The spelling of the name has now been formalized into Canoochee. But over the long years it can be found written many ways: Canouchie, Conoche, Conoochee, Connochee, Canouchee, Coonoche, Coonnoochie, and so on.

Albert Gatschet suggests that Canoochee is from the Creek *ikano'dshi*, meaning graves are there.[1] The author, however, believes the name is more likely to be derived from 'Kanoochee meaning simply Little Ground, from *ikana*, (pronounced "ee kun a") ground or land + the diminutive suffix *oochee*, little.

Why the Indians might have referred to the stream as Little Ground is not known. Perhaps it flowed past a particular area that bore such a tab. One can be certain though that the Creeks used this sort of name. For instance, Benjamin Hawkins mentions an area (along the southside of Upatoi Creek, to the east of Ochillee, and within the present Fort Benning Reservation) as the "Ecun, hut, coo, chee," meaning the Little White Ground.[2]

—GMNL 8(1955): 158-59

NOTES

1. Albert S. Gatschet, *A Migration Legend of the Creek Indians*, (Philadelphia: Brinton, 1884), 1: 63.
2. Benjamin Hawkins, "A Viatory or Journal of distances and observations," trip from Cussetuh to Fort Wilkinson, starting Dec. 6, 1797, MS in the Library of Congress. [Read, *IJAL* 15 (1949): 129, cites both a Bryan County river and a creek by the name of Canoochee, and derives it from "a country or province which Vandera transcribes as Canosi." Read tends to agree with Gatschet and remarks, "In Creek the expressive term for the dead is ikan odjalgi land owners." *FLU.*]

No. 20
Oostanaula and Eastanollee

The Oostanaula River of northwest Georgia is one of the state's finest waterways. The Cherokee name which the stream bears is a pleasing designation in any one of the various renditions in which it can be found: Oustanale, Estanola, Oustanalee, Oostanaula, Ustanali, Oostinawley, etc. The last form listed represents a good approximation of the everyday current pronunciation of the name. Benjamin Hawkins in 1798 spelled the word "Oos, te, nau, leh" and said that it signified shoal or shoally.[1] Thus the appellation Oostanaula River is equivalent to the English Shoal or Shoally River.

Northeast Georgia has a stream that has variously been called over the years: Estanola, Eastanolee, Eastanola, Eastanolla, and so on. Present-day maps usually spell the word Eastanollee. The stream arises on the lower side of Toccoa in Stephens County and flows southeastward to enter the Tugalo River in Franklin County, just below the Stephens line.

Despite a difference in spelling Oostanaula and Eastanollee have a common Cherokee background, and both words refer to shoals, shoally places, or barriers in streams.

Noxon Toomey in writing of Eastanolle says the name is from the Muskogee word "isti nol-li," meaning white man.[2] This interpretation seems without merit. For one thing, white man in Muskogee is *istehátke* or *istehutke*, and not *istinolli*. Furthermore, Eastanollee Creek was definitely within Cherokee country and would hardly have borne a Creek or Muskogee name.[3]

—GMNL 8(1955): 159

NOTES

1. "A Viatory or Journal of distances and observations," trip to Etowah, commencing Oct. 5, 1798, MS in the Library of Congress.
2. Noxon Toomey, *Proper Names from the Muskhogean Languages,* Hervas Laboratories of American Linguistics, Bulletin 3 (St. Louis, 1917), p. 8.
3. [Stewart, *American Place Names,* p. 345, connects Oostanaula with Cherokee "place-of-rocks-across-stream," i.e., a ford. A geographical check would help resolve the issue. *FLU.*]

No. 21
Tukpafka, Punk Creek, Pink Creek, Rotten Wood Creek, and New Yorka

In a discussion of Muskogee Indian settlements, Benjamin Hawkins mentions a place called "New-Yau-Cau," which was located on the south side of the Tallapoosa River in what is now northern Tallapoosa County, Alabama.[1] He goes on to say that the settlement was named for New York.[2] Presumably this designation was adopted by the town after the Creek Indian chiefs visited New York City in 1790 to negotiate a treaty with the United States. Hawkins further adds that the people of this community once lived at "Tote-pauf-cau" or "Spunk-knot" on the Chattahoochee River and that they removed to the Tallapoosa in 1777.[3]

John R. Swanton[4] and Albert S. Gatschet[5] both mention Hawkins' Tote-pauf-cau but they correct the name to Tukpafka. The last writer in his discussion says the term signifies punky wood, spunk, rotten wood, or tinder,[6] meaning a material also called "punk" which white people and Indians secured from the woody parts of trees for use in starting fires.

Neither of these authorities on the Creeks, however, undertook to locate with precision the original site of Tukpafka on the Chattahoochee. And the band removed from that stream so long ago that no early map showing the river depicts the exact location of the settlement. This omission leaves a little gap in the knowledge of the Creek

Indian town sites on the upper Chattahoochee because, with the exception of Tukpafka, the approximate locations of the other communities are known to Indian students of this area.

The writer has studied this matter and feels that the location of the former town can be narrowed to one of two possible sites. One of these spots is near or at the mouth of present Pink Creek in upper Heard County, on the west side of the Chattahoochee, at the beginning of a big bend in the river, and some three miles airline to the northeast of the village of Centralhatchee. Now interestingly enough, this Pink Creek, which is also known locally as Miller Creek,[7] was called Punk Creek on some land plats for original Carroll County made in 1827.[8] Since the name is unusual, there is reason to believe that the surveyors in this instance merely took the Indian name Tukpafkaháchi and translated it into the simpler English term, Punk Creek.

Now, ordinarily these official surveys would be good documentary support for concluding that the town of Tukpafka was located at or close to the mouth of Punk Creek, or present Pink Creek. There is a complexity in the matter, however, because Cobb County has a Rotten Wood Creek that is also an old name and also a tributary of the Chattahoochee. On the basis of Gatschet's translation of Tukpafka this stream may also have once been known as Tukpafkaháchi; and the former village may have been at its mouth, which is about a mile above the bridge on U.S. 41, or Georgia 3-E, and to the northeast of today's Vinings in Cobb County.

These two possible locations for Tukpafka still leave the exact site in doubt, but it is reasonable to believe that the settlement was on the Chattahoochee at or near the mouth of one of the creeks mentioned. The writer favors the site on Punk Creek or Pink Creek in Heard County, but he has no evidence for this choice other than a similarity between Hawkins' "Spunk-knot" and "Punk." Maybe there were two Tukpafkas, one in Heard County and another in Cobb. But this point is only a conjecture; there is no documentary evidence available to suggest that there were two towns on the Chattahoochee with the name.

In considering this matter, other students may contend the Rotten Wood stream of Cobb could not have been derived from a Muskogee name because the area involved was in Cherokee territory. As a matter of fact, however, the section was only a part of the Cherokee lands for a relatively short time before those Indians removed to the West. Historically speaking, until the Creeks and Cherokees agreed upon a new southern boundary to begin at Buzzard Roost Island on the Chattahoochee[9] and run westward to the Coosa, the Muskogees claimed as far up the river as the Old Suwanee Trail, now the Shakerag Road, or present boundary between Fulton and Forsyth counties. Rotten Wood Creek, therefore, was well within traditional Creek lands.

Benjamin Hawkins had a chance to settle this little question about the location of Tukpafka, but apparently he was unaware of the opportunity. In a trip up the west side of the Chattahoochee in 1798 he noted the names of most of the streams which he crossed. When he reached the area of what seems to be Pink or Punk Creek, he labelled the stream "Nucus oe, sum, gau, The Bears Hiding Place."[10] Perhaps if the site of Tukpafka were at the mouth of the creek, the town had been abandoned so long, Hawkins's guides failed to mention the name to him. On this trip, Hawkins gradually veered away from the Chattahoochee as he moved northward and seemingly did not travel parallel with the river as far up as Rotten Wood Creek. He, therefore, had no chance to cross and note the stream.

In conclusion, it might not be going too far afield from Georgia placenames to return to the subject of Hawkins's "New-Yau-Cau." At least the settlement was located in a general territory claimed by Georgia at the time Hawkins wrote about the town. This community can be found in old records under a number of spellings: New York, New Yorka, Niuyaka, New Yaucaw, New Yauger, Nuyaka, New Youka, Nuoquaco, Newquacaw, etc. The name is one of the most singular of all Indian designations because it involved the adoption by the red people of a white man's name for one of their towns. There are numerous instances, of course, in which white people appropriated Indian names, but New Yorka was the single exception on the other hand, at least in this part of the country.

New Yorka in post-Revolutionary years was a considerable place. It was one of the Oakfuskee settlements of the Upper Creeks. For a time it was the home of the noted White Lieutenant, an able and respected chief who was long friendly to the whites.

The town was located on the left side of the Tallapoosa, across the river from the battle site of Horse Shoe Bend where Andrew Jackson defeated the Creeks in the spring of 1814. Prior to this fight, however, in December of 1813, New Yorka and its 85 houses had been destroyed in a little-remembered but daring raid by a small army of Georgians under the command of General David Adams.

The site of New Yorka is now a large but nondescript corn field. About two miles to the south of the old place, at a road fork, there is a little meeting house called the New Yorka Church, but seemingly the people who live thereabouts are unaware of how the church derived its odd name.

—*GMNL* 8(1955): 159-60

NOTES

1. Benjamin Hawkins, *A Sketch of the Creek Country in the Years 1798 and 1799* (Americus, Ga.: Americus Book Co., 1938), p. 44.

2. *Ibid.*

3. *Ibid.* This source says 1777, but John R. Swanton notes that Hawkins's original manuscript in the Library of Congress reads "after the year 1777"—cf. his *Early History of the Creek Indians,* Bulletin 73 of the Bureau of American Ethnology (Washington, D.C., 1922), p. 249, n. 6.

4. John R. Swanton, *The Indian Tribes of North America,* Bulletin 145, Bureau of American Ethnology (Washington, D.C., 1952), p. 162. In this source Swanton states the place was in Heard County, Ga.

5. Albert S. Gatschet, *A Migration Legend of the Creek Indians* (Philadelphia: Brinton, 1884), 1: 148.

6. *Ibid.*

7. According to John Whatley of Bowdon, Ga. The author is indebted to Mr. Whatley for much valuable information about early names and sites in the area of Heard and Carroll counties.

8. District 4 of original Carroll County, survey of 1827, Sihon House, D.S., Platbook OOOO, lots 189, 191, 194, Land Records of Georgia, Surveyor General Department, Atlanta. Punk Creek actually enters the Chattahoochee in lot 193 of this district. Lot 193 is not given in this platbook, but on the plat for lot 194 the stream is shown entering the river in the area which would be in lot 193.

9. Buzzard Roost Island is in the Chattahoochee River, opposite the beginning point for the present boundary of Cobb and Douglas counties. The name is derived from a Creek Indian village that once stood on the Chattahoochee at the island.

10. Benjamin Hawkins, "A Viatory or Journal of distances and observations," trip to Etowah, starting Oct. 5, 1798, MS in the Library of Congress.

No. 22
Yellow Dirt Creek

Some miles above the mouth of Pink (or Punk) Creek, in extreme northeast Heard County, the Chattahoochee is joined by a stream called Yellow Dirt Creek. This tributary, which gathers its waters in south central Carroll County, was called "Yellow Land Creek" on the 1827 survey plats for District 4 of original Carroll.[1] The exact significance of the name is not known. Perhaps the stream flowed past an area or bed of yellow earth that gave rise to the designation. Anyhow the two versions of the appellation leave the strong impression that the name is a translated Creek Indian title. If the original label was Yellow Land Creek, as shown by the first survey of the area, the stream in Muskogee would have been IkánlanihácI, from *ikána*, land or ground + *lani*, yellow, + *háchi*, a stream. It is possible that this name will turn up someday in an old record which will show the appellation in a slightly different and more Anglicized version, like Ecunlahnihatchee, or Econlauneehachee, etc. If the real Indian name, however, actually signified Yellow Dirt Creek, as the present-day listing suggests, the Muskogee designation would have been Fokelanihách from *foke*, dirt, earth, or clay, + *lani*, yellow + *háchi*, a waterway or stream.

The element *háchi* in these Creek names involves a matter which properly should have been discussed prior to this time because the word has been mentioned in previous sketches of the series. *Háchi* is not pronounced like its familiar Anglicized counterparts hachee, hatchee, hachie, etc. Rather it should be pronounced "hutchee." The á in *háchi* is similar to the *a* in the English words about and around. Actually the *a* in this case resembles our English *u* in words like nut, cut, rut, jut, and so on. This explanation may be news to some people, since the form *hatchee* is commonplace in Southeastern names. Nonetheless, individuals who are familiar with the Muskogee tongue are positive that the correct expression is *háchi* or "hutchee." The writer himself would be reluctant to accept this true Creek form, if he had not been reassured by people who know the proper way of pronouncing the word. However, in going over scores of old land plats, maps, charts, sketches, etc., pertaining to this area, the author does not remember a single case of *háchi* being rendered as *hutchee*—it was always *hatchee, hachie, hachee, hatchie, hassee*, etc.[2]

—*GMNL* 8(1955): 160

NOTES

1. District 4 of original Carroll County, Sihon House, D.S., Platbook OOOO, lots 65, 66, 95, 97, 98, 135, 157, *passim,* Land Records of Georgia, Surveyor General Department, Atlanta.
2. [/a/ in American English *top,* British English *half,* the low central vowel without lip rounding, and /ʌ, ə/, the mid central (stressed) vowel in American *nut,* and the first (unstressed) syllable of *about* are easily confused. It is not clear which of the last pair (stressed or unstressed) Goff is discussing. The *-hatchie, -hachee* forms are Anglicized with a low front vowel /æ/, adjacent to but not the same as the low central and the mid central vowels. *FLU.*]

No. 23
Ball Ground and Ball Play Creek

In Georgia's galaxy of interesting geographic names three designations which constantly attract the attention of people from other sections are Rising Fawn, Ty Ty, and Ball Ground. Indeed, it is fair to say that Georgians themselves regard these appellations as being among the unique placenames of the state and anyone here who might be called upon to list the most distinctive tabs of Georgia would almost surely include these titles in such a compilation. Rising Fawn, the translated name of a noted Cherokee chief, will receive attention in these little essays at a later date. Ty Ty has already been treated in the *Mineral News Letter.*[1] This article will discuss Ball Ground and its kindred expression Ball Play Creek.

As a background for understanding the significance of the names, it should be noted that the Cherokees (and other tribes in this region) were extremely fond of playing a type of ball that resembles lacrosse. The game was played on a level, grassy meadow and involved two teams that sought to score by throwing a small ball with stick-like rackets toward goals located at the ends of the field. There was much rivalry between different towns and even different tribes in these contests. The game ranked next to war as a manly occupation and was attended with considerable ceremony prior to play. A part of this ritual called for the players to plunge into a creek seven times before a game commenced.[2] For this reason the ball grounds were customarily opened beside streams. This locational influence no doubt gave rise to the name Ball Play Creek, which will be discussed.

Since there was so much interest in this widely played game every significant settlement or community had its ball ground or ball play flat. It is not surprising then, in view of the tenacity of placenames, that we still retain among our geographic appellations words which commemorate these former ball-playing sites. But curiously enough, to be a bit contradictory, these spots are found in the old Cherokee country. The Creeks were fond of playing the game, but for some reason we did not retain the name in areas of Georgia which were occupied by the Muskogees and their affiliated tribes.

The best-known place that perpetuates the name is the town of Ball Ground in northeast Cherokee County.[3] This community grew up as a station on the Louisville and Nashville Railroad. In all probability though, there was not originally a ball field at the site of the town, but the name was adopted from a nearby ball ground on a stream in the vicinity.

In addition to the town of this name, there is a little crossroads called Ball Ground in southern Murray County. This name has an official status because the surrounding area, Georgia Militia District No. 1807, is known as the Ball Ground District.

There were Ball Play creeks as well as Ball Grounds. In fact, the former name is the older of the two designations, since Lieutenant Henry Timberlake shows a Ball Play Creek in his report of a 1762 visit to the Overhill Cherokees on the Little Tennessee River in East Tennessee.[4] This stream is presently referred to by the people of Monroe County, Tennessee, as Toqua Creek.[5] Not far away, however, as a tributary of Tellico River, there is another small waterway that even now is called Ball Play Creek.[6]

Georgia also has one of these Ball Play creeks. It is located in eastern Lumpkin County, where it flows into the left side of the Chestatee River, to the east of Dahlonega.[7]

In District 8, Section 2 of original Cherokee County, in what is now Fannin County, there was once another Ball Play Creek which entered the east side of Toccoa River.[8] This name though was changed, and it is now difficult to identify exactly the stream which once bore the designation. Apparently it was present Hemptown Creek, which enters the Toccoa near Mineral Bluff.

Just over the Tennessee line, not far to the northeast of Tennga, Georgia, on U.S. 411, there is still another Ball Play Creek which is a right-bank tributary of the Conasauga River that arises in this state but curves into Tennessee before swinging back into Georgia.

Since Ball Play Creek has been mentioned in connection with Tennessee, it might also be added that Alabama uses the appellation. Not far over the Georgia line, to the west of Floyd and Polk counties, in eastern Etowah County, Alabama, there is a Ball Play Creek and a Ball Play crossroads. These places are in a big bend of the Coosa, to the east of Turkey Town. Even nearer to Georgia, in Cherokee County, Alabama, is a community called Ball Flat. These places were all near the old Cherokee-Creek boundary, but the names are probably derived from the Indians.

In northwest Pickens County, where the Old Federal Road through the Cherokee Nation crosses Talking Rock Creek, there is an early fording spot called the Ball Creek Ford.[9] This name is derived from a little stream that joins Talking Rock at the site. Perhaps this waterway was once a Ball Play Creek with the word *play* being understood as a part of the designation.

In eastern Forsyth County, flowing southeastward to join the Chattahoochee, is a stream that is now called Ball Ridge Creek. This waterway though is not one of the Ball Play creeks. On the earliest official map of this section it was marked Baldridge Creek.[10] In the intermediate years between the first surveys of the area and the present it became Bald Ridge Creek. Some people in the area insist this form was the original name. This belief no doubt led to the use of the tab Little Ridge Creek for one of the tributaries of the main stream. Nonetheless, this writer is prone to believe that the original form was Baldridge and that it was derived from a prominent Cherokee family which bore that English name and which probably lived on the stream.

—GMNL 9(1956): 32-33

NOTES

1. John H. Goff, "Ty Ty as a Geographic Name," *Georgia Mineral Newsletter* 7 (1954): 36-38.

2. Numbers of writers discuss the Cherokee ball play; a good source to consult is William Harlen Gilbert's *The Eastern Cherokees*, Bureau of American Ethnology Anthropological Papers, No. 23 (Washington, D.C., 1943), pp. 318, 337-38. [As among the Central American Indian civilizations, Cherokee ball play was an important ritual and dance occasion. For an extensive account of it see Frank G. Speck, Leonard Broom, and Wild West Long, *Cherokee Dance and Drama* (Berkeley and Los Angeles: University of California Press, 1951), pp. 55-70. *FLU.*]

3. The area about the town of Ball Ground is also called Georgia Militia District No. 1032, the Ball Ground District.

4. "A Draught [Map] of the Cherokee Country" in the *Memoirs of Lieut. Timberlake* (London, 1765).

5. *A Map of Monroe County Tennessee*, compiled by Sehorn and Kennedy, Engrs. (Knoxville, 1934).

6. *Ibid.*

7. *Dahlonega Quadrangle*, topographical map by the U.S. Geological Survey (1903; reprinted 1951).

8. John Bethune, Surveyor General of Georgia, *A Map of that part of Georgia Occupied by the Cherokee Indians* (Milledgeville, 1831).

9. In this particular area the Old Federal Road across the Cherokee country followed today's Ga. 156.

10. Bethune map.

No. 24
Chattooga (and Guinekelokee)

The name Chattooga can be found several times in the placenames of Georgia:

1. Chattooga River that arises in southwest Jackson County, North Carolina, and reaches Georgia at the northeast corner of the state, where the stream then starts serving as a common boundary with South Carolina till it unites with the Tallulah River to make the Tugalo;

2. Chatuge Reservoir of the Hiwassee River on the Georgia–North Carolina line;

3. Chattooga River that heads on the edge of LaFayette in Walker County and flows southwestward into Cherokee County, Alabama, where it joins Little River, thence into the Coosa;

4. Chattooga Church Crossroads in southern Walker County;

5. Chattooga County, which occupies part of a former Chattooga District of the Cherokee Indians; and

6. Chattoogaville, a well-populated community in lower Chattooga County, near the Alabama line. This locality occupies the approximate area of a Cherokee settlement known as Chattooga Village.[1] The present-day place seemingly takes its name from the Indian town and thereby illustrates the interesting placenaming practice of joining a Latin-derived suffix to an aboriginal appellation.

The name Chattooga seemingly was initially derived from an early Cherokee town which once stood on the South Carolina side of the first river named above, near the mouth of Warwoman Creek of Rabun County, Georgia, and to the east of Clayton.[2] We know little about the place except its location. Apparently the site was abandoned at an early date, probably in 1760, because it lay on the route of two British armies that invaded the Cherokee Country in 1760 and 1761. Perhaps the town was even destroyed and burned by the first of these forces. Anyhow, when William Bartram in 1776 and Benjamin Hawkins in 1796 passed the spot they did not mention the place, although the former noted some ruins in the area.[3]

The name Chattooga is a simple word, but over the years people have spelled it in a diversity of ways: Chattooga, Chatooga, Chatuga, Chattugie, Chattoogee, Chatugee, Chatugy, Chatugui, Chatugi, and Chatuge. There is no formalized version of the appellation, although Chattooga is coming more and more to have that status. In the sections where the name occurs it is common to hear it pronounced "Chattoogee," "Chatugee" and so on. In this rendition the *g* is always hard, as in the *g* of Gillespie. Thus the *gee* element of Chatugee is not pronounced *"jee,"* but must take the sound of *gee* as found in the word Ocmulgee.

In common with numbers of Cherokee names, the exact meaning of Chattooga is not now known. If early white people had understood the significance of the name, they might long since have converted it into some English equivalent. Such conversions were a common practice in the Georgia area of the old Cherokee country, as is evidenced by names like Brass Town, Warwoman, Dirtseller, Cut Cane, Young Deer, Noonday, White Path, and so on in great profusion. Some actual Cherokee names that were retained can be translated, like Yonah (bear), Oostanaula (shoals), Hiawassee (savanna), etc., but numbers of the Cherokee terms, especially for towns and communities, can not be readily explained.

With respect to the meaning of Chattooga, James Mooney gives the Cherokee spelling as Tsatú gĭ, but says the word is possibly of foreign origin, meaning borrowed from some other tribe.[4] At one point he intimates the word might be Creek.[5] Now, the name can be found in areas that were once claimed by the Creeks, as in the case of the Chattooga River section of northwest Georgia; but to the lay student of Indian matters the appellation only occurs in what was known as Cherokee country. This is true for South Carolina,[6] North Carolina,[7] Georgia, Tennessee,[8] and northeast Alabama. If this fairly common name actually were Creek, it is strange that it can not be found in other regions which those Indians definitely occupied over a long period.[9]

In concluding this sketch an interesting point should be made about a tributary of the Chattooga in eastern Rabun County, which is now called the West Chattooga River. In contrast to most of the other waterways around the fringes of the state, this stream flows *into* Georgia and not out of it. This prong of the river arises in lower Macon County, North Carolina. Its headwaters unite into a stream that becomes known as Overflow Creek, which in turn becomes the West Chattooga River mentioned above. Interestingly enough, when the Georgia surveyors first laid off Rabun County in 1820, this fork's name did not contain the element Chattooga. It was then called "Guinekelokee,"[10] "Guineekeloke,"[11] and "Guinekelochee."[12] The meaning of this interesting term is not known. Perhaps it signifies Overflow Creek; or maybe West Fork, which as noted are the present designations of the waterway.

—GMNL 9(1956): 33-34

NOTES

1. John Bethune, Surveyor General of Georgia, *A Map of that part of Georgia Occupied by the Cherokee Indians* (Milledgeville, 1831).

2. Several maps show the town of Chattooga in the area indicated. Two good ones to consult are: George Hunter's representation of the Cherokee Nation based on a map of Col. [John] Herbert, May 21, 1730, photostat from the Library of Congress; the name here is spelled Chattuga. And, "Map of East and West Florida, South Carolina and Georgia, transmitted by Col. [William] Bull (President and Commander in Chief of South Carolina) with his representations to the Board of Trade, 25 May 1738," photostatic copy from the Library of Congress, original in the Library of the British Colonial Office. This chart spells the word Chatugee.

3. Mark Van Doren, ed., *The Travels of William Bartram* (New York: Dover, 1928), p. 275.

4. James Mooney, *Myths of the Cherokee*, Nineteenth Annual Report of the Bureau of American Ethnology, 1897-98, (n.p., n.d.), pt. 1, p. 536.

5. *Ibid.*, p. 383.

6. In addition to the Chattooga River which serves as a part of the boundary between South Carolina and Georgia, the former state has a Chattooga Ridge that runs parallel with the river from the North Carolina line to a point opposite the north corner of Stephens County, Ga., on the Tugalo River.

7. In addition to the designation Chattooga River, North Carolina uses the name Chattooga in the Chattooga Cliffs of southwest Jackson County and in the Chattooga

Ridge also in the southwest part of the same county. These places apparently derive their names from the river which flows near them.

8. Tennessee had the tab Chattooga at an early date in the name of a settlement situated near Great Tellico which was located at or about today's Tellico Plains in southeast Tennessee. Cf. map of the Cherokee country and parts of South Carolina, copied by George Hunter, Surveyor General of South Carolina, from a map prepared by Capt. George Haig, 1751, photostat in the Library of Congress. The map marks the place "Chatugy" but in a marginal listing of the settlements the name is marked "Chatuga."

9. [Read, *IJAL*, 16 (1950): 204, cites for Chattooga Sweanton's conjecture, "fall of rocks," with a Creek and not a Cherokee origin. *FLU.*]

10. District 3 of original Rabun County, survey of 1820, H. Rousseau, D. S., Platbook PPP, lots 54, 99, 27, *passim*, Land Records of Georgia, Surveyor General Department, Atlanta.

11. *Ibid.*, lot 95.

12. *Ibid.*, lot 55.

No. 25
Teloga Creek

Teloga Creek heads about a village called Chelsea, above Menlo, in western Chattooga County, and flows northeastward to join the Chattooga River near Trion. Although the stream is in former Cherokee Country, the name is apparently of Muskogee origin. This could well be, because the Creeks or Muskogees once claimed the area in which the waterway lies. The name signifies Pea Creek, being derived from the Muskogee *telogi*, pea, + *háchi* (pronounced "hutchee"), a stream. The designation can be found in other sections which were occupied by the Creek Indians, viz. in the present Pea River of South Alabama, which was once called Tellaugue hatche,[1] and in a west-bank tributary of the Ocklockney River in Liberty County, Florida. The last stream is now marked as Telogia Creek. In former years, however, it appeared on various maps as "Tologie,"[2] "Tellokee,"[3] etc. These last versions phonetically are very similar to the Georgia Teloga that is pronounced "Telogee" by many old people in Chattooga County.

The pea involved in these old names is what pioneer people called the turkey pea or partridge weed. The plant was prized for its grazing qualities in the wilderness days when grass was scarcer than it is now. We even commemorate the plant in English forms, as in Pea Ridge on which Buena Vista stands in Marion County, and in Peavine

Creek and Peavine Ridge of Walker and Catoosa counties. Another such moniker can be found in Peabottom Cove at the head of Brasstown Creek in Union County.

—*GMNL* 9(1956): 34

NOTES

1. Benjamin Hawkins, "A Viatory or Journal of distances and observations," "Rout to Pensacola 16 April 1799," MS in the Library of Congress. Hawkins crossed the upper waters of the river and refers to the stream both as "Pea Creek" and as "Tellaugue Hatche."
2. David H. Burr, "Map of Florida Exhibiting the Post Offices, Post Roads, Canals, Rail Roads &c.," *circa* 1834, Land Records of Florida, Office of the Commissioner of Agriculture, Tallahassee, Fla.
3. "Georgia," *Finley's General Atlas* (Philadelphia, 1823).

No. 26
The Cherokee Town of Quanasee

Among the important early towns of the Cherokees there was a place which old charts and records mention variously as Quanasee, Quanassee, Quanassie, Quanessee, etc. Some good, but rather generalized eighteenth-century maps show this community on the south side of the upper waters of a stream called Eufasee or Euforsee, which is our Hiwassee River. Henry Popple's map of 1733 depicts the spot as "Quanessee an Eng. Factory,"[1] meaning an English trading post. Colonel William Bull on his map of 1738 also marks the place "Quanessee" and likewise refers to it as an "Engl. Factory."[2] William Bartram notes the settlement under the name "Quanuse" in his 1776 list of major Cherokee towns,[3] but he does not give the location except in a most general fashion.

Now interestingly enough, and in contrast to the situations of many other Cherokee centers, we seem to have lost account of the site of Quanasee. Students of Indian matters either disagree on the whereabouts of the place, or say that they do not know the location. Among those who state the site is unknown is John R. Swanton, a recognized authority on Southern Indians.[4] *The Handbook of American*

Indians[5] offers no discussion of Quanasee, although under the spelling "Quanusee" it does mention the name as a synonym for a town called Tlanusiyi. James Mooney in *Myths of the Cherokee* omits treatment of Quanasee, but mentions Tlanusiyi, and says it was located at what is now Murphy, North Carolina.[6] One gathers from reading Mooney that he does not actually intend to say Quanasee and Tlanusiyi were the same places. He gives some Anglicized synonyms for Tlanusiyi, but only one of these words, "Quoneashee,"[7] bears any particular resemblance to Quanasee. As a leading scholar on the Cherokees, Mooney must have been aware of Quanasee, but apparently he chose not to discuss it in the *Myths*, either because he was not familiar with the location or because the place bore no particular relationship to matters treated in that work.

The author has studied the question of the location of Quanasee and concluded that it was on the left bank of the Hiwassee River, in today's Towns County, Georgia, somewhere between the old Macedonia Church site, near U.S. 76, and the mouth of Bell Creek.

Colonel Benjamin Hawkins provides the evidence which leads to this conclusion in an account of a trip from the home of General Andrew Pickens, in upper South Carolina, to the Tellico Blockhouse, on the Little Tennessee River in East Tennessee.[8] In the company of General Pickens, two surveyors, an officer and two dragoons,[9] a guide, and presumably some packhorsemen, Hawkins commenced this journey on March 23, 1797.

On the night of March 24 the group camped on the Chattooga River near the mouth of Warwoman Creek of today's Rabun County, Georgia. The next day the party travelled up this creek to its head, thence past present Clayton, "west" to the source of Scott Creek, which was then considered as "Sticcoa" Creek. On the course of what is now U.S. 76, they crossed a divide and reached today's Timpson Creek. The group turned northwest up this stream for a distance; then after climbing a rugged ridge, they descended to what we call Persimmon Creek. In the neighborhood of present Blalock Crossroads the party camped on the night of the 25th.

The next day, March 26, the travellers crossed the Persimmon and after following a westward course for a bit crossed a large creek called Oloktah. That stream was the upper Tallulah River. This conclusion seems correct because the upper Tallulah on the original 1820 surveys of Rabun County was called "Uluftey,"[10] "Ulufty,"[11] and "Uluftoy."[12] There is enough resemblance between the last form and Oloktah to warrant the belief that the two designations were simply different versions of the same name.

Across the Oloktah the party bore northwest and followed a tributary stream to reach a passage over the Blue Ridge. This waterway seemingly was today's Plumorchard Creek and the point at which they crossed the ridge was Tom Coward Gap, in Towns County, below the corner of Rabun and Towns.[13] Hawkins's description of the journey fits this course, and furthermore, a main trading path to the Valley towns and Overhill settlements of the Cherokees followed this route.[14]

Over the Blue Ridge the travellers came to the "western waters," in this case, the headwaters of what is now Little Hightower Creek, in northeast Towns County. They continued down this stream, following a trail that ran on the right bank or north side of the creek. The present-day road down the valley seemingly follows substantially the same course.

Soon the stream which was being followed was joined on the left (south side) by a creek which the guide called "Etowwah." Hawkins makes a particular note that it came into the juncture "nearly at right angles." This waterway seems to have been the Swallow Creek of today. Apparently in those days it was considered the head prong of the Hightower.

This name Etowwah is the main clue which enables Hawkins's account to throw light on the location of Quanasee because it confirms his course. By mentioning Etowwah, the Colonel tells the party's whereabouts, since in Georgia, the Anglicized equivalent of this name is Hightower. There is abundant proof that the two designations are alternate names. The well-known Etowah River, for instance, which arises in Lumpkin County and flows westward to join the Coosa, is even now commonly called the Hightower by many old people of Lumpkin, Dawson, and Forsyth counties. Furthermore, in the northwest area of Lumpkin where the Etowah arises, the section is named the Hightower District, or Georgia Militia District No. 1252. In western Forsyth County, on the east side of the Etowah, a crossroads on the route of the Old Federal Road is now called Hightower. And, a main branch of the noted upper Indian trading route from Augusta that led to the Etowah River settlements of the Cherokees was named the Hightower Trail.[15]

Thus when Hawkins notes the name Etowwah he shows that the group was travelling down the present Hightower Creek of today's eastern Towns County. He also verifies that the party was following the old trading route which led down this same stream.

The travellers continued along the creek and soon the country begins to open out a bit. Then Hawkins starts mentioning the "river," which means they had reached the Hiwassee. The party was somewhere in the vicinity of the present town of Hiawassee and now ready to camp for the night of the 26th.

For a wilderness trip in a mountainous country, Hawkins and his fellow travellers had come a long way on this day. Many years ago the author travelled a substantial part of the same route on foot and even in the days of roads, he was hard pushed to walk in one day from the Tallulah River to the area of Presley.

The party encamped by the Hiwassee, and Hawkins notes that above the site there was a point in the stream where the river curved around from a southeast to a northwest course. The probable stopping place was below the mouth of Shake Rag Branch (to the south of Hiawassee) and in an area that is now flooded by the Chatuge Reservoir.

The Colonel goes on to say the former site of Quanasee was on the left (south) side of the river. He notes that nothing then remained of the settlement save open flats which were once the corn fields of the old place. He does not positively state the former town was opposite the encampment, but he leaves the clear implication that it was in the vicinity, over the river.

Thus one concludes Quanasee was in the area to which the party was traced. It was certainly not at the site of Murphy because the travellers could not reasonably have reached that locality in one day. The old town may have been near the mouth of Bell Creek. But more than likely, this writer believes, it was just to the south of the town of Hiawassee, in what are now inundated bottom lands.

Colonel Hawkins gives no further details about Quanasee except to comment that the place was the residence for many years of an Irish trader named "Cornelias Daughtertu," or more properly, Cornelius Dougherty. Since this interesting individual was closely connected with Quanasee, this sketch would not be complete without a few words about him. He was one of the most noted early Irish settlers to reside among either the Cherokees or the Creeks. John Haywood says he probably came to the Cherokees about 1690.[16] He states the trader was reputed to be 120 years of age when he died in 1788.[17] If these statements were correct, and if Dougherty had actually originally settled at Quanasee, he would probably have been the first English-speaking white person to dwell in what is now Georgia. Judge Samuel Cole Williams, however, questions the 1690 date, by stating that Dougherty claimed in an affidavit made at Charleston that he did not go to the Cherokee Nation till 1719.[18] But even so, this last date would still make him one of the first of the Cherokee Indian countrymen.

Dougherty, according to the records, became the progenitor of a Cherokee family. In this connection, perhaps it will not be too much of a digression from locating Quanasee's site to mention a little crossroad called Dougherty in southeast Dawson County, on Georgia 53. The spot is situated at the eastern end of the Big Savannah, a beautiful, fertile area that stretches for some miles down the north side of the Etowah River. Old people in the community say the name Dougherty has long been connected with the area, and that the designation was used there when the first regular settlers came to set up homes along the valley. If this tradition is true, maybe one of Cornelius Dougherty's descendants furnished the name, in which case, it should be classed with Vann, Ross, Vickery, Rogers, Pettit, Taylor, McNair, and other Cherokee-English family names that were left in the former Cherokee country.

—*GMNL* 9(1956): 34-36

NOTES

1. "A Map of the British Empire in America with the French and Spanish settlements adjacent thereto," engraved by Willm. Henry Toms, London, 1733, photostatic copy from the Library of Congress. With reference to the location of Quanasee as developed in the text, it is significant to note that the town is placed just below the juncture of the two upper heads of the "Euphasé R." These sources are the upper Hiwassee River and today's Hightower Creek. [A marginal note queries the Eufasee-Euforsee citation. Is the query Goff's? Here and in *Short Studies* No. 27 he spells the pair Euphasee, Eufasée. *FLU.*]

2. "Map of East and West Florida, South Carolina and Georgia, transmitted by Col. [William] Bull (President and Commander in Chief of South Carolina) with his representation to the Board of Trade, 25 May 1738," from a photostatic copy in the Library of Congress, original in the Library of the British Colonial Office. This map also places the town below the two head forks mentioned in n. 1, but farther down the Hiwassee.

3. *Travels through North and South Carolina, East and West Florida* (Philadelphia, 1791), pt. 3, ch. 3, p. 371.

4. *The Indian Tribes of North America*, Bureau of American Ethnology, Bulletin 145 (Washington, D.C., 1952), p. 220.

5. Frederick Webb Hodge, *Handbook of American Indians*, Bureau of American Ethnology, Bulletin 30 (Washington, D.C., 1919), p. 1125.

6. James Mooney, *Myths of the Cherokee*, Nineteenth Annual Report of the Bureau of American Ethnology, 1897-98, (n.p., n.d.) pt. 1, p. 535.

7. *Ibid.*

8. *Letters of Benjamin Hawkins, 1796–1806*, Collections of the Georgia Historical Society, Vol. 9 (Savannah, Ga., 1916), pp. 105ff.

9. The officer, a "Lieutenant Mossley" [sic] and the two dragoons turned back at Persimmon Creek. *Ibid.*, p. 107.

10. District 1 of original Rabun County, survey of 1820, John G. Pittman, D.S., Platbook 000, lot 36, Land Records of Georgia, Surveyor General Department, Atlanta.

11. *Ibid.*, lot 15.

12. *Ibid.*, lots 14, 16, 25, 26, 35, *passim.*

13. An excellent map of use in retracing this journey is *Chattahoochee National Forest—Georgia* (1954), prepared by the U.S. Forest Service.

14. There were several trails over the Blue Ridge to the Valley towns and Overhill settlements, but the two main ways were the Unicoi path and the route which Hawkins followed. Segments of these two significant routes are shown on John Bethune's *A Map of that part of Georgia Occupied by the Cherokee Indians* (Milledgeville, 1831).

15. The Hightower Trail spurred from a prong of the Upper Trading Path on the west side of the Apalachee River, in Morgan County. It ran thence to a ford on the Chattahoochee just below today's U.S. 19, thence to the Etowah River in the area of the present crossing of U.S. 41. Early Gwinnett and present DeKalb County were laid off along this trail. Its course is well remembered by many people. [Read, *IJAL* 16 (1950): 205, cited a Cherokee *Itawá*, the name of several towns, perhaps a loan word from the Creek *italwa*, town, or possibly from Cherokee *etawaha*, deadwood. *FLU.*]

16. John Haywood, *The Natural and Aboriginal History of Tennessee* (Nashville: George Wilson, 1823), p. 233.

17. *Ibid.*

18. *Dawn of the Tennessee Valley* (Johnson City: Watauga Press, 1937), pp. 70-71.

No. 27
Hiwassee and Hiawassee

Hiwassee and Hiawassee are two of Georgia's most beautiful geographic names. The two words basically have a common Cherokee origin, but find different present-day applications. The form Hiawassee is the official spelling for the county seat of Towns County; while Hiwassee is the long-established designation for a fine river which heads on the north side of the Blue Ridge in the same county and flows out of Georgia, across extreme western North Carolina to enter the Tennessee River to the south of Dayton, Tennessee.

Despite the slight difference in spelling, both names are customarily pronounced "High wah see." And, as has been noted, both have the same background, being derived from the Cherokee word *ayuhwasi*, signifying savanna or rather savannah, to give the spelling which has long been used in Georgia and other parts of the Southeast. The expression savannah applied either to a grassy meadow-like place, or to a level, fertile, open area (usually a valley) that was covered with a thick expanse of reed or switch cane. This translation has good support.[1] The fanciful explanation of Hiwassee or Hiawassee which is given in a romantic Indian legend about a Catawba maiden called Hiwassee or the Pretty Fawn, and a Cherokee youth named Notley is without substance.[2] One is reluctant, of course, to offer the prosaic meaning of meadow or canebrake in lieu of an interesting story but the change is desirable for a correct understanding of these old and interesting names.

Under one application or another, and under various spellings, the designation Hiwassee has been in usage for a remarkable span of time. Initially the word can be found in connection with two settlements in the Old Cherokee Nation. Both of these communities were on the river which we now call the Hiwassee, but which in early English records was also known as Quannessee,[3] Euphasee,[4] Euphasé[5] and so on, for other towns that were once situated along the banks of the stream.

One of the Cherokee spots named Hiwassee was on the north side of the river in today's Polk County, Tennessee, in the vicinity of the bridge on today's U.S. 411. The place eventually became known as the Savannah Ford, for a noted crossing at that point. This last name is still remembered by some old people now living in the area of the former town.

The other early settlement (and probably the oldest of the two places) was situated at the juncture of the Hiwassee River and Peachtree Creek, in North Carolina to the east of present Murphy. This place seemingly was visited by DeSoto in 1540 and was mentioned by his Chroniclers as "Guaxule," "Guasuli," and "Guasili."[6] Students of the Spaniards' journey across the Southeast have held varying ideas about the location of the site which bore these names, but John R. Swanton, who served as chairman of a governmental committee appointed to study and retrace DeSoto's route, believes the names refer to this second Hiwassee town.[7] This conclusion is based on the similarity of the names, especially of Guasili, with Hiwassee. At first glance, one might see little relationship in the words. In the case of

Guasili, however, if the *li* element is taken from the word and it is then pronounced "wah see" in the Spanish fashion, the resulting sound is similar to our present-day Hiwassee. In fact, it is identical phonetically with one later American version of that appellation.[8]

The Indian guide who supplied the Guaxule, Guasuli, or Guasili for the Spaniards apparently slurred the first syllables of Ayuhwasi and added the locative suffix *li* or *le*. Such a locational ending was common in Cherokee geographic designations, although the usual locatives employed by those Indians were *hi* and *yi*. The committee report on the DeSoto expedition explains the exceptional *li* by saying the guide may have been a Muskogee Indian who used that ending in lieu of one of the customary Cherokee terms.[9]

In later English and American records the name Hiwassee appears without the initial *h* of today under several spellings: "Iwassee,"[10] "Iwasee,"[11] "Owassa,"[12] and "Aiwassee."[13] In numbers of early sources though the word can also be found spelled with the *h*, which is now an accepted part of the appellation: "Hywassee,"[14] "Hewassee,"[15] "Haywassee,"[16] "Hiwassee,"[17] "High Wassee,"[18] "Highwassee,"[19] and so on. The last form is fairly common on old charts. Two other versions using the *h* are George Haig's "Hyowassy," mentioned in 1751,[20] and Benjamin Hawkins's "Heia Wassea," which was noted in 1798.[21] These renditions are especially interesting because they are reminders of the original Cherokee Ayuhwasi and because they resemble the name which the Towns County people later adopted for their county seat.

The Cherokee Ayuhwasi and some of the early English renditions of Hiwassee make it plain that the original name was not spelled with an *h* at the beginning of the word. This point leaves the implication that that letter was supplied by the Indian country English-speaking whites in the form of what we now call the Cockney *h*. This conclusion seems correct because in colonial years, when we were closer to the British, it was fairly common to use an initial *h* with geographic names beginning with a vowel. Some examples which may interest the reader were "Hogeechey," or "Howgeechu," for Ogeechee; "Hocony" for Oconee; "Hockmulgi"—Ocmulgee; "Hohoope"—Ohoopee; "Hoositchi"—Osotchi (Oswichee); "Hallatomahaw"—Altamaha; "Hughnaky"—Unaka; "Hughphala" for Ufala (Eufaula); and so on. Indeed in rare instances the use of an *h* in such a manner was continued long after the Revolution. For example, a surveyor of ceded Creek lands, in 1826, referred to a stream called Upland Creek as "Hupland";[22] while a surveyor of original Cherokee County, in 1832, noted a waterway that must have properly been named Oostanaula or Oustanauli as "Houstanaula Cr."[23]

The retention of an initial *h* in the modern, formalized spellings of Hiwassee and Hiawassee then is one of the unique little aspects of Georgia placenames. Only one other geographic appellation seems to fall into this same category, and that exception can be found in the word Hightower, which is an Anglicized alternate for Etowah, or Itawa, to give a closer aboriginal version. In Lumpkin, Dawson, and Forsyth counties the Etowah River is still commonly spoken of as the Hightower, and in eastern Towns County, one of the upper tributaries of the Hiwassee River is known as Hightower Creek. Benjamin Hawkins once referred to a main branch of that stream as the "Etowwah."[24]

There are two other Hiwassee names which have been used in Georgia and which perhaps properly should have been mentioned prior to this time. One of these tabs involves present Hiwassee Gap in the Blue Ridge, on the Rabun-Towns line, below Dicks Gap on U.S. 76. Presumably this pass was named for a trail that once led over the ridge to the Cherokee towns along the Hiwassee River. In another case, the present Plumorchard Creek of western Rabun County was once called Highwassee[25] or Hiwassee Creek.[26] The stream, no doubt, derived that name from a main trading route called the Hiwassee Trail which led across present Rabun and Towns to the Cherokee settlements on the Hiwassee River and to the Overhill centers in present east Tennessee. This significant thoroughfare and its connections will be discussed in the following essay.

—*GMNL* 9(1956), 75-77

NOTES

1. James Mooney, *Myths of the Cherokee*, Nineteenth Annual Report of the Bureau of American Ethnology, 1897–98 (n.p., n.d.), pt. 1, pp. 416, 512.
2. This legend was reproduced by George White; cf. his *Historical Collections of Georgia* (New York, 1854), pp. 660-61.
3. Map of the Cherokee country and parts of South Carolina copied by George Hunter, surveyor general of South Carolina, from a map prepared by Captain George Haig, 1751, photostat in the Library of Congress. The stream is labelled "Quannesee River." With respect to this last name, see No. 26 above.
4. "Map of East and West Florida, South Carolina, and Georgia, transmitted by Col. William Bull . . . to the Board of Trade, 25 May 1738," photostatic copy from the Library of Congress, original in the British Colonial Office.

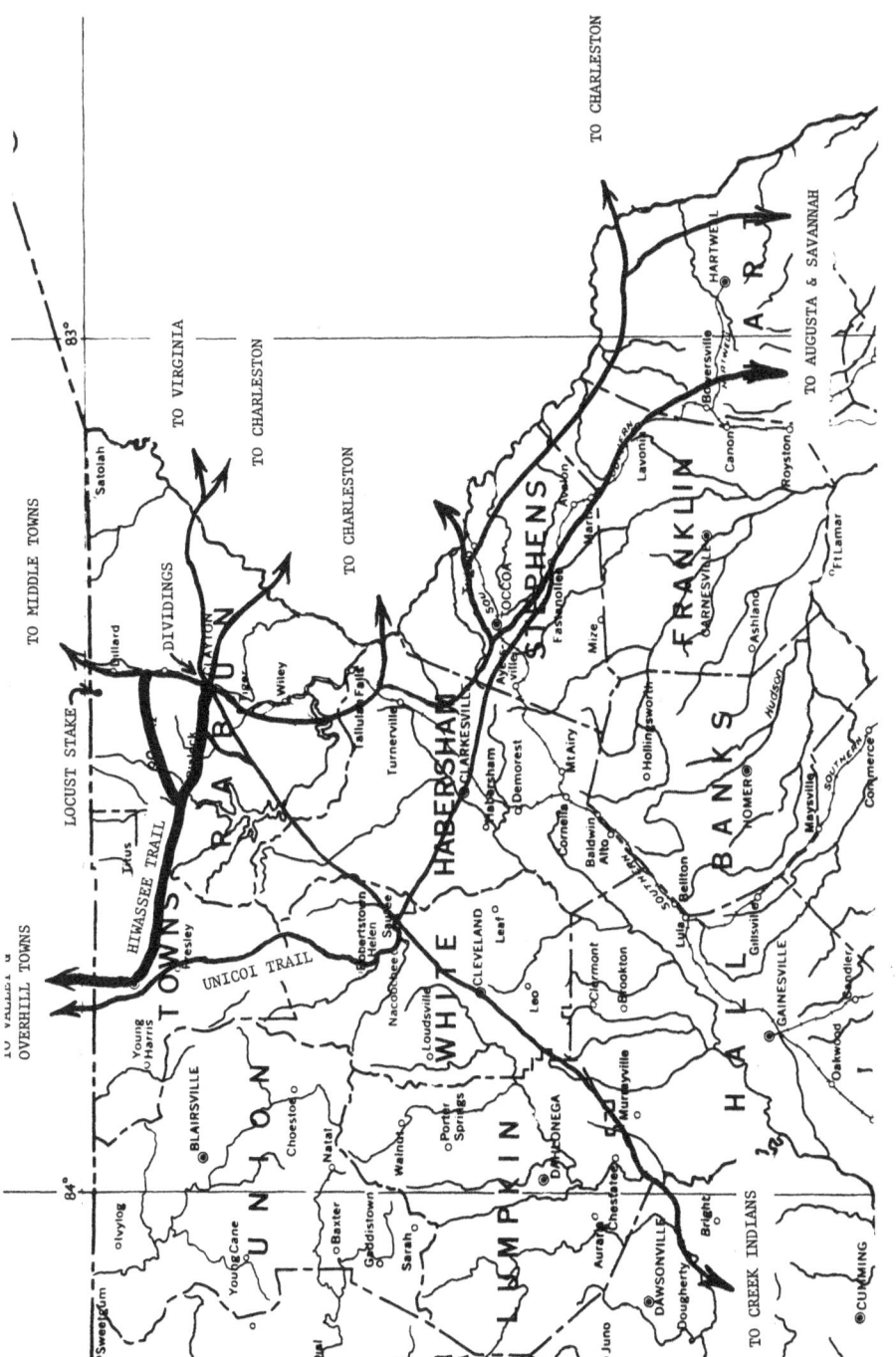

The Hiwassee Trail and its connections

72 / Placenames of Georgia

5. Henry Popple, "A Map of the British Empire in America, with the French and Spanish settlements adjacent thereto," engraved by William Henry Toms, London, 1733, Sheet 10, photostatic copy from the Library of Congress.

6. *Final Report of the United States De Soto Expedition Commission*, House Doc. 71, 76th Cong., 1st Sess. (Washington, D.C., 1939), p. 57. The chroniclers Garcilaso de la Vega and the Gentleman of Elvas wrote the name "Guaxule"; Biedma reported it as "Guasuli"; while Ranjel wrote "Guasili." The last writer was De Soto's secretary. For his account see "Relation of Ranjel," *Narratives of the Career of Hernando de Soto . . .* , ed. Edward Gaylord Bourne (New York: Allerton Book Co., 1922), 2: 49 ff. (106).

7. John R. Swanton, *The Indians of the Southeastern United States*, Bureau of American Ethnology Bulletin 137 (Washington, D.C., 1946), p. 31; and *The Indian Tribes of North America*, Bureau of American Ethnology Bulletin 145 (Washington, D.C., 1952), p. 217. Dr. Swanton was chairman of the governmental committee appointed to retrace the DeSoto journey; see also the *Final Report* of that committee, pp. 50, 54, 189, and 201-202.

8. Map of the 18th District, 1st Section of Cherokee County (now Towns), July 7, 1832, Joseph Byers, D.S., original in Land Records of Georgia, Surveyor General Department, Atlanta. The surveyor originally marked the stream "Wassee River." Someone later made the name "Highwassee."

9. *Final Report*, pp. 201-202. The report says the actual ending may have been the Catawba ri, which was transposed by a Muskogee interpreter into li. The Muskogees, lacking the r in their language, were prone to convert the letter into an l.

10. Map, George Hunter's representation of the Cherokee Nation based on a map of Col. [John] Herbert, May 21, 1730, photostat from the Library of Congress.

11. Newton D. Mereness, ed., "Colonel Chicken's Journal to the Cherokees, 1725," *Travels in the American Colonies* (New York: McMillan, 1916), p. 115.

12. Mooney, *Myths of the Cherokee*, p. 512. He attributes this spelling to Lanman.

13. John Gerar William De Brahm, *History of the Province of Georgia* (Wormsloe, 1849), p. 18, note c, and p. 54. De Brahm, a Dutchman and surveyor general of Georgia, here uses the continental dipthong ai in place of the i or ay of the English and colonial Americans.

14. "A Map of the Southern Indian District, 1764," author not known, photostatic copy in the Georgia Historical Society (Savannah), original in the Library of the British Museum.

15. John R. Swanton, *Early History of the Creek Indians and Their Neighbors*, Bureau of American Ethnology Bulletin 73 (Washington D.C., 1922), plate 7, reproduction of part of the Purcell map, *circa* 1770. Marks the river "Hewasse." Benjamin Hawkins mentioned the stream as "Hewossa"; see *Letters of Benjamin Hawkins, 1796-1806*, Collections of the Georgia Historical Society, Vol. 9 (Savannah, 1916), p. 109.

16. Swanton, *Early History*, plate 7. Mentions one of the towns as "Haywassee"; the river is marked "Hewasse"—see n. 15.

17. William Bartram, *Travels Through North and South Carolina, Georgia, East and West Florida* (London: Johnson, 1792), p. 371.

18. John Dutton, "The State of Georgia," 1814, photostat from the Library of Congress, original in the Library of the British Museum.

19. John Bethune, Surveyor General of Georgia, *A Map of that part of Georgia Occupied by the Cherokee Indians* (Milledgeville, 1831).

20. Hunter's reproduction of George Haig's map shows a town as "Hyowassy or Euforce" on the "Quannessee River."

21. Benjamin Hawkins, "A Viatory or Journal of distances and observations," trip to Etowah, commencing Oct. 5, 1798, MS in the Library of Congress. The name here referred to the river.

22. District 23 of original Muscogee County (now a part of Talbot), Platbook NNNN, lot 254, Land Records of Georgia.

23. Map of District 22, Section 2, of Cherokee County, survey of 1832, Andrew Lawson, D.S. The stream indicated was on the edges of Districts 22 and 14 of Section 2. Seemingly the waterway was the present Shoal Creek of today's northwest Cherokee County. *Oostanaula* means shoal or shoaly; see No. 20, "Oostanaula and Eastanollee" above.

24. Hawkins, *Letters*, p. 108.

25. District 1 of original Rabun County, survey of 1820, John G. Pittman, D.S., Platbook OOO, lots 35, 49, 69, 70, 90, *passim*.

26. *Ibid.*, lot 67.

No. 28.
The "Dividings," the Hiwassee Trail, Timpson Creek, Racepath Creek

Contrary to a common belief, the interior of Georgia in early days was not a trackless wilderness. Indeed there is substantial proof to show the region in those times was fairly well-threaded with a network of aboriginal ways. Because of this fact (and just as is the case with the modern highway complex) there were important junctures where the forest routes converged or diverged. One of the most significant of these Indian-country intersections was a point called the Dividings, located at present Clayton in today's Rabun County. This interesting place is depicted in a general fashion on several early maps, but it is also shown fairly accurately by the Haig or Hunter chart of 1751.[1] William Bartram also mentions the spot. He passed there in 1776 while on a visit to the Cherokees, and although he does not call it the Dividings, he does state the "road" to the Cherokees forked there.[2] Benjamin Hawkins, in 1796 and 1797, actually refers to the intersection as the "dividings";[3] and the Eleazer Early map of 1818 also mentions the place under the same name.[4] The original and official surveys of Rabun County, made in 1820, failed to name the crossways, but they show that it was in lot 21 of District 2 of Rabun,[5] a location which places it in the city limits of Clayton, near the center of town.

Although this intersection was both a trail-crossing as well as a converging point, one concludes by reason of the name Dividings that it was primarily thought of as a branching place for routes that fanned out to diverse and remote points. In fact, the intersection was what we later came to know as a five points.

One of the routes leading from or to the Dividings, and the most important thoroughfare concerned with the juncture, was the Warwoman Road, which ran eastward through Saddle Gap and down Warwoman Creek to a ford on the Chattooga River located just above the mouth of the creek, thence over the Oconee Mountain of South Carolina to a fork where the route branched to Virginia and Charleston.

Another but less well-defined trail led southeastward from the Clayton area toward South Carolina, approximately along the course of today's U.S. 76. A strip of this path is shown on Henry Mouzon's map of 1777[6] passing the Cherokee village of "Chicherohe," a name which even now is retained in the Chechero District of southeast Rabun County.[7]

Still a third fork, and a very significant way, led northward from the Dividings to the important Middle Cherokee settlements that centered present Franklin, North Carolina. This thoroughfare ran along the course of today's U.S. 23 and 441 past present Mountain City, through Rabun Gap or the Pass Over (as old-timers called it), to the headwaters of the Little Tennessee River. Going north, at Rabun Gap the trail veered right from today's U.S. 23 and 441, down the east side of the river to a point about three-quarters of a mile south of Dillard where it forded the Tennessee at a present bridge, above the mouth of Darnell Creek, thence to rejoin the modern road for a stretch just above Dillard, thence back over the river again and into North Carolina along the right bank as the stream enters that state. A considerable segment of this trail later became known to the pioneer people of Rabun County as the Locust Stake Road.[8]

A fourth route stemming from the Dividings ran southward along the course of U.S. 23-441, to a point a mile and a half below Clayton,[9] where it forked with one branch leading along the west side of the present Tallulah Falls Railroad, past Tiger and Bovard, thence nearly directly south, running over the high hills to the west of Wiley and Lakemont to Cranes Old Ford on the Tallulah River, near the Dobbs summer home on Lake Rabun. Below the river this route also forked. One prong bore southeastward to a crossing on the Tugalo just below the juncture of the Tallulah and Chattooga rivers. This trail apparently was an alternate way to the lower Cherokee towns of upper

South Carolina and another route to Charleston. The other branch continued southward to the vicinity of Toccoa. This turn was a way to Augusta and Savannah, and, of course, offered connections to Charleston. This route also coincided substantially as far as Toccoa with the lower segment of the thoroughfare which the early white settlers called the Locust Stake Road.[10]

Back at the first forking of this trail running south from the Dividings, to the south of Clayton, a second path bore southwest down U.S. 23-441 for about a mile, then veered past the southeast base of Tiger Mountain, thence across the Tallulah River to Nacoochee Valley, thence to Cherokee towns along the Etowah River in northwest Georgia. From there it continued on to the Upper Creek Indians of Alabama. Benjamin Hawkins travelled this way in 1796 while on a journey through the Creek and Cherokee country, and his description of the trip fits the known segments of the trail which can now be found on maps.

The last route which stemmed from the Dividings was the Hiwassee Trail, the central subject of this sketch. It was a main way over the Blue Ridge Mountains of Georgia to the Valley towns of the Cherokees in extreme upper Georgia and North Carolina and to the Overhill settlements of those Indians in east Tennessee.

Beginning at the Dividings, this route led west up an easy valley, almost exactly on the course of today's U.S. 76, to the head of Scott Creek.[11] Thence, after crossing a low divide, it reached Timpson Creek and turned up this stream for about a mile, then bore northwest over a high ridge to reach Racepath Creek, an affluent of Persimmon Creek in western Rabun County.[12] From the turn off at U.S. 76 on Timpson Creek, to the Persimmon, the route still remains as a rough mountain path which is known locally as the Racepath Trail.

The Hiwassee way crossed the Persimmon below the juncture of the two streams, then veered west to reach a ford on Tallulah River, situated downstream from the mouth of Plumorchard Creek, at the western edge of lot 25 of District 1 of Rabun.[13] A present-day road crosses near the same spot. The old trail next bore west on a course that is now abandoned, then turned up a present mountain road to the Plumorchard community on the eastern slope of the Blue Ridge in extreme western Rabun. Thence the path led west through the Tom Coward Gap in the Blue Ridge.

To the west of the ridge, in that part of Towns County which lies in former Cherokee County, the original surveys do not show the Hiwassee Trail. One early official map depicts a strip of it but only in a general fashion.[14] Benjamin Hawkins, however, used the route in 1797, and from his account, one can pick out with reasonable accuracy the remainder of the course to the North Carolina line.[15]

From Tom Coward Gap, on a rough path that remains, the Hiwassee Trail dropped from the Blue Ridge to join what is presently the course of U.S. 76 in eastern Towns County at a little spot bearing the droll moniker Barefoot, or maybe originally Bearfoot. From this point it continued along what is now No. 76 to Visage,[16] thence down the north side of Hightower Creek to the Hiwassee River. At the bridge on 76 near the Old Macedonia Church site, the Hiwassee path intersected a branch of the Unicoi Trail, later Unicoi Turnpike, the first vehicular way of this part of Georgia. This thoroughfare was also another noted route to the Cherokees of western North Carolina and east Tennessee. Beginning at the Tugalo River to the east of Toccoa (and with important connections from Augusta in the vicinity of Toccoa Falls), it passed above today's Clarkesville, through Nacoochee Valley, and over the Blue Ridge at the Unicoi Gap to the Hiwassee River. Just below that stream, to the north of Presley in Towns County, it forked into alternate paralleling ways.[17] One branch continued down the left bank of the river while the other turn crossed to the north side where it was joined by the Hiwassee Trail.

The united routes continued down the Hiwassee past the present town of Hiawassee.[18] Below the North Carolina line, this leg of the Unicoi Path crossed back to the west side of the river, rejoined the other segment, and left this state running down the west bank of the Hiwassee.

No doubt some travellers who had reached this vicinity on the Hiwassee Trail followed that former course and went on to the destination Cherokee towns via the Unicoi route. Nonetheless there was also a way that continued down the river on the east bank, because Benjamin Hawkins followed such a route in 1797,[19] and since he had reached the area in question via the Hiwassee Trail, it is reasonable to suppose the thoroughfare he followed into North Carolina was the same path, particularly since it must have led on to the Cherokee town of Hiwassee which was located farther along at the juncture of Peachtree Creek and the Hiwassee River in North Carolina. From there the route apparently continued past other Valley settlements of the Cherokees, and in the vicinity of Murphy rejoined the Unicoi Trail, thence over the Unaka Mountains to the Overhill towns of east Tennessee.

Back in Rabun County there was a branch of the Hiwassee Trail that has not yet been mentioned. The fork which is shown and named in the original surveys for Rabun spurred from the route leading northward from the Dividings up U.S. 23-441 toward the Cherokee towns around Franklin, North Carolina. This branch of the Hiwassee route led westward from the way to North Carolina, beginning on the east side of the Little Tennessee River, below Blacks Creek, at the western edge of land lot 118 of District 2 of Rabun.[20] The forking place was in present fields, about two miles north of Rabun Gap (the "Pass over") and one mile southward of the Rabun Gap–Nacoochee Junior College. On a course now abandoned, the trail ran nearly west passing through the fields on the divide between Jerry Branch and the Little Tennessee. A half-mile beyond Rickman Creek at a road bend it entered the present Dillard–Keener Gap highway and continued west, over the Blue Ridge through Keener Gap. A mile and a half beyond this crossing, where today's road veers southwest, the Indian path kept on west, past the lower side of Howard Mountain to King's Chapel. Here it turned sharply southwestward past Buzzard Mountain to join the main Hiwassee Trail at the ford on Tallulah River.[21]

This branch of the Hiwassee Trail apparently was a well-established route from the Middle Cherokee settlements around Franklin to the Valley communities of north Georgia and western North Carolina. It was a circuitous but comparatively easy way to connect the areas in question. A more direct east and west route between those settlements would have had to traverse a succession of formidable mountains.

There is an indirect connection from the Dividings that should be mentioned. This was a spur of the Hiwassee Trail that led down Timpson Creek. When the latter route reached this stream, coming from the Dividings, it bore northwest up the creek. At this turn, though, there was another trail that continued westward down Timpson Creek toward the Tallulah River. The original surveys do not show this fork but Hawkins mentioned it.[22] The exact destination of the path is not known. It may have been merely a hunting trail that led to the mountains, or it may have run westward to join the Unicoi route over the Blue Ridge. Very probably, however, it curved down the Tallulah and joined the way through Nacoochee Valley that has been mentioned.

The Hiwassee Trail was a rugged thoroughfare and Benjamin Hawkins complained of it on that score. In fact, he complained more about it than any other route which he travelled and mentioned in records that we retain. Nonetheless, considering the terrain traversed, it followed a good course, and it was probably less laborious to travel than any other way over the Blue Ridge to the Valley towns except perhaps for the Unicoi Path. The Hiwassee Trail was relatively more direct than today's U.S. 76. The route of the latter may suit white people of today, but judging with a modern eye, a wilderness path along the same course would have been rough indeed, especially for a trader's packhorse train. The old Hiwassee Trail had difficult, steep spots too, but it was less winding.

Perhaps it should be pointed out that scholars interested in the routes of the DeSoto journey seemingly have not spotted the Hiwassee thoroughfare as one of the possible ways which the Spaniards might have taken over the Blue Ridge. A number of students of that expedition agree the explorers passed through the general area in which the path lay, but none of them apparently considered the route followed by the Hiwassee way as a segment of the Spanish journey.[23] This point could well receive further study. The Hiwassee Trail (and its connection up Warwoman Creek) was a natural passage, considering topographic conditions of the area, and should not be overlooked as a possible way for the Spaniards to have used.

With respect to the stream names listed in the title of this sketch, today's Timpson Creek was originally Timson, according to the 1820 surveys of Rabun.[24] This designation was apparently derived from a Cherokee family by that name. Emmet Starr, quoting Walter N. Wyeth, says a Cherokee named John Timson was the first convert in 1823 of the Baptist missionaries to the Cherokees.[25] Since the Hiwassee Trail led from the Dividings along a part of the creek to the area of the Valley Town Church, the first of the Baptist missions, there is a hint that the Timsons may once have lived along the thoroughfare, beside the stream that bears their name.

Racepath Creek is one of the unusual geographic appellations of Georgia. Its exact derivation is not known. Some people believe the name may have arisen from a mill race that was once constructed along the stream. Possibly, however, in a way that is not now clear, the expression originally referred to the Hiwassee route. Anyhow, as was noted, a remnant of that thoroughfare is now called the Racepath Trail.

One final point about the Hiwassee Trail merits mention. Running east and west through the center of Clayton there is a principal street called Savannah Street. At the western edge of the town, this thoroughfare, as U.S. 76, becomes the Hiwassee Road. Now, today's

No. 76 does lead from Clayton over the Blue Ridge to the town of Hiwassee, and, as has been noted, it coincides closely with substantial segments of the former Hiwassee Trail. But people are now prone to believe that 76 is called the Hiwassee Road because it goes to the present place of that name and that the designation is relatively modern. The chances, are, however, the appellation is actually old and that it harks back to the days when English-speaking people first travelled this way over two centuries ago. Savannah Street may simply be another name for the same route, because, as has been shown in the sketch No. 27 above, Savannah is the English equivalent of the Cherokee Hiwassee.

—*GMNL* 9(1956): 77-80

NOTES

1. Map of the Cherokee country and parts of South Carolina, copied by George Hunter, surveyor general of South Carolina, from a map prepared by Capt. George Haig, 1751, photostat in the Library of Congress.

2. William Bartram, *Travels Through North and South Carolina, Georgia, East and West Florida* (London: Johnson, 1792), p. 343. He says the "road" forked: to the left led the trail to the Overhill towns; Bartram took the right turn, i.e., the way northward through Rabun Gap, toward Franklin.

3. *Letters of Benjamin Hawkins, 1796-1806*, Collections of the Georgia Historical Society, Vol. 9 (Savannah, 1916), pp. 16, 106. On p. 107 he also refers to the place as the "dividing."

4. Eleazer Early, *Map of the State of Georgia* (Savannah and Philadelphia, 1818).

5. District 2 of original Rabun County, survey of 1820, Hiram Glazier, D.S., Platbook 000, Land Records of Georgia, Surveyor General Department, Atlanta.

6. Henry Mouzon and others, "An Accurate Map of North and South Carolina with Their Indian Frontiers," Paris, 1777, photostat from the Library of Congress.

7. Mouzon's "Chicherohe" is now customarily spelled Chechero and pronounced "Chur che ro" or "Cher chee ro." The *he* element of the older name is the Cherokee locative suffix *hi*, signifying a site, place, or spot. For a modern translated name that contains this form, see Spring Place in Murray County. The author intends to write on Chechero in a forthcoming issue of the *Mineral Newsletter*.

8. The Locust Stake Road was the first north and south vehicular route of Rabun County and extreme northeast Georgia. It followed much of the Indian ways which ran up and down in the area, except at the northern end and in the vicinity of Wiley and Lakemont. Seemingly, the road led past these last places, whereas the Indian path went over the hills to the west. Both courses, however, converged on Cranes Ford to cross the Tallulah. At the upper end, the road apparently began at the North Carolina line on the west side of the Little Tennessee, while the Cherokee trail used the opposite bank.

The Locust Stake Road is said to have derived its name from a locust stake which once marked the Georgia-North Carolina boundary where the thoroughfare began.

80 / Placenames of Georgia

The spot on a modern map is noted as Locust Post; cf. *Chattahoochee National Forest—Georgia* (1954), prepared by the Forest Service of the U.S. Department of Agriculture.

9. The District 2 survey of original Rabun made in 1820 does not show a trail leading southward from the Dividings. However, the plats for District 5 on the south depict significant stretches of the paths' branches that are mentioned in the text. One can be sure a trail ran south from the Dividings, because Benjamin Hawkins followed it in 1796; see his *Letters*, p. 16.

10. From the vicinity of Toccoa southward to Augusta the first main connection of the Locust Stake route was the Red Hollow Road, that led to the Broad River, and next, the Petersburg Road which ran from that stream into Augusta.

11. District 2 of original Rabun, cited above: westward from Clayton, the order of the lots through which the trail ran is as follows: 21, 20, 19, 18, 17, 13, and 14. At the last lot the trail dipped into lot 56 of District 5 of Rabun, then turned northwest into District 1. The Hiwassee Path is not shown or named in the plat in District 5, but due to the narrowness of the valley here it is certain to have run a short distance in lot 56 of that district.

12. District 1 of original Rabun County, survey of 1820, John G. Pittman, D.S., Platbook 000. With the exception of lots 19, 49, and 50 the route is shown completely. It ran thus: 1, 2, 18, 17 (NW corner), 24 (crosses Persimmon Creek), 25 (crosses "Uluftoy," now Tallulah River), 26, 27, 34, 47, 33, 32, and 31. It ran into District 18, Section 1, of original Cherokee County in the southwest corner of lot 50.

13. The ford was in a bend of the Tallulah, or "Uluftoy," just inside of lot 25, to the southwest of Buzzard Mountain.

14. John Bethune, Surveyor General of Georgia, *A Map of that part of Georgia Occupied by the Cherokee Indians* (Milledgeville, 1831).

15. Hawkins, *Letters*, pp. 107-110.

16. This interesting name is derived from an early settler named William Visage, according to Dr. A. J. Ritchie; see his *Sketches of Rabun County History* (1948), p. 208.

17. This branching of the Unicoi way is shown on "A Map of the 18th District 1st Section" in James F. Smith's *The Cherokee Land Lottery* (New York: Harper, 1938).

18. Trails described in this article are plotted upon a standard base map of Georgia prepared by the U.S. Geological Survey. In spite of the great care exercised by these cartographers they have inadvertently misspelled the name of the town Hiawassee.

19. Hawkins, *Letters*, entries for March 27 and 28, 1797, pp. 108-109.

20. District 2 of original Rabun County, cited above.

21. District 1, *ibid.*

22. Hawkins, *Letters*, p. 107.

23. There are many discussions of the De Soto trip, but a good source with maps and references is the *Final Report of the United States DeSoto Expedition Commission*, House Doc. 71, 76th Cong., 1st Sess. (Washington, D.C., 1939).

24. District 1 of original Rabun, cited above, lots 2, 19, and 20; and District 5 of Rabun, survey of 1820, William Davis, D.S., lot 57.

25. Emmet Starr, *Early History of the Cherokees* (Oklahoma City, Okla., 1917), p. 76.

No. 29
The Great Pine Barrens

One of the most interesting geographic features of this country in its primeval state was a vast pine forest that swept in a great crescent from the lower Chesapeake Bay to the Mississippi River. This belt of trees was approximately 1,000 miles long and from 60 to 200 miles wide. It ranged over the eastern portions of Virginia and the Carolinas, and, in its widest part, spread over upper Florida and lower Georgia, Alabama, and Mississippi. The immense pineland occupied a substantial part of what is known today as the Atlantic-Gulf Coastal Plain, an area that is characterized along the coastal margins by flat sandy lands and inland by gently rolling sandy or sand-clay hills that gradually rise to merge with the higher country of the interior.

Some eight or ten species of the so-called yellow or pitch pines composed this pineland, the most important types of which were the short-leaf, loblolly, slash, and long-leaf pines. The last variety, the most distinctive of the trees, tended to favor the lower or more southerly parts of the belt. By means of deep tap roots and a moist climate these pines were able to flourish in the relatively infertile sandy soils of the sun-drenched Coastal Plain.

In their virgin state the pines did not grow thickly, but were scattered about with considerable intervening space between the trees. The trunks of the original stands rose like superb shafts to a height of 50 to 70 feet before the first spreading branches were reached. These great arms then stretched out and often touched the boughs of neighboring trees, thus forming a canopy for the ground below. This covert, in conjunction with the indifferent soil, caused the pinelands to be singularly lacking in underbrush, thereby permitting the view, over great reaches, to fade into a wall of arboreal columns. Possibly the only place left in the country today where one could find comparable vistas would be in the great ponderosa pine forests on the eastern slopes of the Cascade Mountains in our Pacific Northwest.

The first whites to traverse the expansive pines and leave a record were the chroniclers of De Soto. They mentioned the pinelands numbers of times and referred to a part of them, in probably what is now middle south Georgia, as being a "desert." During the three centuries following the Spaniards' expedition this term was to be used many times in referring to the great pine belt. Even William Bartram, the noted botanist, who made a tour through the Southern colonies just prior to the Revolution, wrote of the pine woods, paradoxically, as "desert forests," and noted that birds were not numerous there. Much later, in the middle of the last century when Richard Cuyler and a group of Savannah citizens were trying to promote a railroad from that place to the Gulf of Mexico, via what are now the flourishing Georgia cities of Waycross, Valdosta, Quitman, and Thomasville, the area to be served by the proposed road was hooted at as Cuyler's Desert.

While the pinelands were often referred to over the years as deserts, and occasionally as sandy wastes, in time they became known generally from one end of the belt to the other as the pine barrens, or simply, in the vernacular of early settlers, as "pine barr'ns."

As time passed, roads were cut across the pine belt by the early settlers, who, as will be seen, were principally interested in pushing on to the higher and more fertile regions beyond. With the opening of these roads greater numbers of people traversed the forests and more writers recorded their impressions of the immense woods. These reports nearly always reflect the same reaction, by harping upon the themes of interminable pines, the sterile soil, and the monotonous levelness of the barrens. Today one can well imagine that a trip through the region was tedious, considering the slowness and difficulties of early travel. Certainly a journey lengthwise of the forest from Norfolk to New Orleans, for example, might well have taxed the hardiest and most patient traveller. Furthermore, a person making such a trip would have gathered an odd idea of the southeastern part of the country, if he did not know by hearsay or personal experience that the region was endowed with mountains, plateaus, and valleys as well as with a seemingly boundless forest of pines.

American travellers across the belt were in the main phlegmatic in their comments on the pinelands. Apparently most of them seemed to know what to expect before visiting the region, and they dismissed the barrens with customary comments on the sterility of the country and the tediousness of travel through the forest.

The reactions of foreign visitors, on the other hand, tended to be much more distinctive, since the great pinelands were totally unlike anything known to western Europeans.

The comments of English visitors are especially interesting and descriptive. Captain Basil Hall, a British naval officer, in his *Travels in North America* left an unusually effective impression of the forest as it was in 1828. In describing the stems of the tall pines between Charleston and Savannah, he wrote: "The eye was bewildered in a mass of columns receding far back, and diminishing in the perspective to mere threads, till they were lost in the gloom. The ground was everywhere perfectly flat, and the trees rose from it in a direction so exactly perpendicular, and so entirely without lower branches, that an air of architectural symmetry was imparted to the forest, by no means unlike that of some gothic cathedrals."

Later, en route to Macon, Georgia, he noted: "Our road, on the 22d of March—if road it ought to be called—lay through the heart of the forest, our course being pointed out solely by blazes, or slices, cut as guiding marks on the sides of the trees. It was really like navigating by means of the stars over the trackless ocean!"

Curiously enough, Captain Hall did not tire quickly of the vast and lonely barrens. After explaining that he and his family must have travelled at least 500 miles in the South, by carriage, he continued:

"I don't know exactly what was the cause, but it was a long time before I got quite tired of the scenery of these pine barrens.[1] There was something, I thought, very graceful in the millions upon millions of tall and slender columns, growing up in solitude, not crowded upon one another, but gradually appearing to come closer and closer together, till they formed a compact mass beyond which nothing could be seen." He goes on to say, however, "These regions will probably be left for ages in neglect."

The reaction of Charles Joseph Latrobe, another Englishman, to the tiresomeness of plodding through the sand-bed roads of the pinelands was more like that of most observers. This writer made a circuit of the lower South in 1833 as far down as Florida. By the time he reached St. Marks in that state, he reports in *The Rambler in North America* that he had seen enough of the monotonous level of the longleaf pine barrens to produce "complete satiety." Unhappily for Latrobe, this satiation was reached half-way around his tour; he still faced the long return across the virgin pine regions of south Georgia! On the other hand, another Britisher, Sir Charles Lyell in his *Travels in North America*, in 1841 found the pine barrens interesting *because* of their uniformity and monotony.

Fanny Kemble, the English actress who married a Georgia planter and resided in the winter of 1838-1839 at a plantation on the Altamaha River, left a striking but overdrawn picture of the great forest. Endowed with a lively imagination, an acid pen, and obsessed by a dislike of her sojourn in Georgia, she describes an excursion into the pines in her *Journal of a Residence on a Georgian Plantation*:

The road was a deep, wearisome sandy track, stretching wearisomely into the wearisome pine forest—a species of wilderness more oppressive a thousand times to the senses and imagination than any extent of monotonous prairie, barren steppe, or boundless desert can be; for the horizon there at least invites and detains the eye, suggesting beyond its limit possible change; the lights, and shadows, and enchanting colors of the sky afford some variety in their movement and change, and the reflections of their tints; while in this hideous and apparently boundless pine barren you are deprived alike of horizon before you and heaven above you.

Miss Kemble goes on to comment upon the blue-green expanse under the dark green umbrella formed by the pines' foliage. But, curiously enough, neither she nor other early observers of the pines make mention of the purplish tinge which is so noticeable in the bark of present-day pine trees. A number of the writers, however, were as much impressed by the sighing and murmuring of the yellow pines as are the people of today. For instance, Levasseur, who accompanied LaFayette to the United States and reported on the trip in his *Lafayette en Amérique, en 1824 et 1825*, in speaking of Macon said:

She has sprung up as if by magic in the middle of the forests. It is a civilized point lost in the still immense domain of the first children of America.[2] Within a league of there we are in the bosom of the virgin forests; the tops of these old trees, which seem to measure the age of the world, sway over our heads; the wind stirs them with that murmur in turn low and sharp which M. de Chateaubriand calls the voice of the desert.

Sir Charles Lyell was affected in much the same way as Levasseur, stating in his *A Second Visit to the United States of America*, during 1846, that the sound of the wind in the "long-leaved" pines reminded him of waves breaking on a distant seashore, and that it was agreeable to hear it swelling gradually and then dying away as the breeze rose and fell.[3]

Many of the early accounts of the great pine belt leave the notion that the pines stretched in unbroken array across the region. As one early account stated it, "There was nothing but pines." This same impression may also be gathered from some of the original and official surveys of south Georgia lands after they were acquired from the Indians. In mapping these areas the surveyors were required to write on the different land lots the types of trees growing thereon. On their maps often the only trees named over wide areas were: pines, pines, pines.

This impression of a complete continuity of the forest is not correct, however, since the reaches of pines were often interspersed with other types of vegetation. Occasionally, and especially back from the coasts, there were areas, often gentle rises, which the pioneers came to know as hummocks, hommocs, hommocks, hammacks, or hammocks. On such spots hardwoods grew, and since their presence was an indication of a soil change for the better over the sandy pinelands, the hammocks were early sought for homesteads by those who settled in the pine woods.

Then too, here and there, the somber pines were occasionally enlivened by open glades or natural meadows which the pioneers called savannahs. Such spots were relatively low and moist, and were consequently avoided by the pines. But native grasses grew lushly in such localities, and they were much frequented by deer and the settlers' stock.

There were also low spongy areas scattered through the forest which the pioneers named bay galls. These spots, which were quite common in Georgia, Alabama, and Mississippi, were left by the pines to myrtles, small bay trees, and gallberry bushes.

In addition to these breaks in the great pines, numerous streams, some of them quite large rivers, traversed the pinelands. Here the pines gave way to dense canebrakes and thick swamp forests of hardwoods and cypress.

With the exception of the narrower and older portions of the forest in Virginia and the Carolinas, the great pine belt was settled relatively slowly. The soils of the pinelands proper were infertile when compared with those of the rich bottomlands along the rivers, or with the lands of the Piedmont plateau beyond the barrens. As a rule then the settlers sought sites for farms or plantations in the river-bottoms of the Coastal Plain or pushed on to the higher hardwood lands across the pine belt. There were those who appreciated the value of the great pines for timber and naval stores, but transportation facilities were poor, and the forest seemed so endless and the supply of trees so inexhaustible that few dared to predict the great future which was eventually to materialize for the region.

Chief among the first who did settle in the pine barrens were stockmen, who ranged their cattle on the wiregrass which grew among the trees as well as on the savannahs and extensive brakes of reed cane that were found here and there in the forest. Occasionally, too, a farmer who did not object to the solitude of the pine wilderness would carve out a home for himself and family among the pines.

When he settled in a hammock area, he prospered in a limited fashion, but if he selected a spot out in the barrens, he was likely to have only a meagre livelihood and an humble economic status. In early years the people who made this last choice were called pinelanders. Later they became known generally as piney woods folks, although in Georgia and upper Florida they were often referred to as crackers.

Around the beginning of the last century and up to the time of the War Between the States, parts of the pine barrens developed economic importance as places of refuge from the seasonal diseases which beset the coastal cities and the lowcountry towns and plantations. With the onset of summer, the sickly season, town residents who could afford it removed to the sandy regions of the pine barrens. Likewise, the rich planters of the fertile lowlands along the rivers and coast found it healthier to migrate with their families to temporary summer abodes or resorts amid the pines, leaving plantation operations in charge of overseers. In turn, with the advent of the cool weather in the fall, these groups would then venture back to their permanent homes.

In Georgia such places were referred to as the sand hills, the desert, or the piney woods.

By experience the seasonal migrants had learned that the pine barren areas were more salubrious than the lowcountry, but they did not understand why. They speculated much on the reasons for the difference and advanced several theories to explain the superior healthfulness of the pines.

The chief reasons offered to explain the salubrity of the barrens rested upon a belief in the purity and elasticity of the air among the pines as contrasted with the atmosphere of the marshy and swampy sections surrounding the lowcountry homes. It was commonly held, for instance, that the low areas produced dangerous exhalations which bore miasmatic fevers. It was also thought that the heavier foliage of the hardwoods in the swampland sections held down these contagious vapors sufficiently long for them to afflict the people residing in the lowland communities. On the other hand, the same pernicious gases rising among the towering pines were able to dissipate their noxious effluvium without serious risks to dwellers in such areas. Others argued, however, that the healthfulness of the pines should be attributed to resinous particles from the pine needles, which purified the air of the pinelands by increasing the amount of oxygen in the atmosphere, thereby divesting it of any infectious material or virulence which it might bear for human beings. There were still others who insisted that the very sterility of the soil in the barrens rendered it incapable of generating vapors which were uncongenial to the human body or noxious for respiration.

Such explanations as these disclose serious misapprehensions under which intelligent people used to labor. Today with our knowledge of the nature of contaminated water and understanding of the transmission of malaria and yellow fever by mosquitoes, the answers to the questions which puzzled those folk seem elemental. The simple explanation of the superiority of the barrens as far as mosquitoes were concerned lay in the fact that the sandy soils of the pinelands soaked up the rain and minimized the dangers of mosquito-breeding in stagnant waters.

Many of the spots of seasonal refuge, or "summering places" as they were known, became famous, and a stay at one of them was considered a delightful social experience, comparable to a present seasonal sojourn at the seashore or in the mountains.

Certain sections of the sand-hill area along the Great Fall Line Belt where the Coastal Plain and Piedmont Plateau meet were particularly noted as healthy summering places. Especially was this true for the area north and west of Augusta, Georgia. Grovetown, sixteen miles from that place, was such a spot, and so were Bon Air and Bel Air which were nearer. Not far from Bel Air was Sahara, a name which reminds one again of the use of the term desert in connection with the piney woods section. And, interestingly enough, the words Bon Air and Bel Air take on a different connotation from that which we would give them today when one recalls the old beliefs about contaminated atmosphere being the cause of the malarious and bilious season.

Walthourville in Georgia was another prominent summering place. It was used by rich planters from the area around Riceboro. Summerville, South Carolina, was likewise a notable refuge spot in the barrens for Charlestonians. Summertown, in Emanuel County, Georgia, was also a well-known resort for Georgia plantation and coastal families, and Salubrity, northwest of Tallahassee, was a similar asylum in Florida. There were still other but lesser-known places. They bore names like Pine Retreat, Pine Bowery, Pine Head, Pine Ridge, Pine Rest, etc. Today we should be prone to think of such appellations as merely the result of prosaic, backwoodsy placenaming, but terms such as these were once deliberately selected to carry appeal to would-be summer residents, just as nowadays resort names like Highlands and Little Switzerland are dangled before the public to attract those who would flee oppressive summer heat.

Summering places in the pines have long since lost their importance, although the Mississippi Gulf Coast may be cited as an exception. In that area, because of the absence of sand dunes, the pine barrens once came right down to the beach, and visitors sought refuge there to avoid the risks of fevers in New Orleans, Mobile, and other cities. Nowadays, however, the section is frequented by summer visitors who come to enjoy the Gulf breezes, with never a thought of avoiding pestilential vapors back home.

Curiously enough, in the change of things over the years, some areas which were once prominent summering places for escaping low-country afflictions have evolved into well-known winter resorts. This change is particularly notable for points in the Carolinas and in the sections around Augusta.

The eventual development of the pine barren region came with a rush. It took the magic of the railroad, as in so many other instances of American economic growth, to unlock the potentials of the great pinelands. Such a vast reservoir of trees was a paradise for lumbermen and naval stores operators when they were assisted by means of cheap transportation in exploiting the forest. The railroad gradually threaded the region following the War Between the States, and by the 1890's, the section, especially in Georgia, Alabama, and Mississippi, began to boom. It became the chief naval stores–producing region of the world, and by the turn of the century was the leading lumbering belt of the nation. Towns sprang up overnight. In this rush the expression "pine barrens" was quickly forgotten. One Floridian said the name was all wrong anyway, because he thought the term was a corruption of "pine bearing," an expression which was more descriptive of the true potentialities of the area.

But exploitation of the pines was swift, ruthless, and wasteful. By 1910 there were beginning to be ghost communities here and there when sawmills closed down and moved their activities elsewhere, leaving thousands of acres of cutover lands in the recent scene of their operations. It was out of this exigency, however, that the region began to develop the prosperous agriculture for which it is noted today. The soil, which had for so long been considered poor and mean, proved remarkably productive in many localities when farmed with the aid of mixed fertilizers. The land was generally level and easily worked and the climate was favorable to a variety of crops. In these developments, however, there was relatively little effort to raise cotton, because, with the exception of the famous sea-island variety along the coastal fringes of Georgia and Florida, the staple had never thrived in the sandy areas of the pines. Rather the people turned to melons, cane for making syrup, vegetables, fruits, nuts, tobacco, peanuts, and eventually a variety of new products which ranged from cut flowers to tung nuts.

The livestock industry also went through a regeneration, with scrubby piney woods horned cattle giving way to better stock. At the same time improved types of hogs were substituted for the once ubiquitous razorbacks and pine rooters.

In the meantime, however, the pines were coming back. Fortunately for the region, the trees reproduce easily and grow fast if given an opportunity. With this great advantage the pinelands were able to retain a place as an important lumber and turpentine-producing section. In the last two decades a big new industry, the pulp and paper business, has settled in the area to offer further outlets for the forest resources of the region in the form of pulpwood.

Thus we find the section which was formerly known as the great barrens. Today it is a prosperous region sprinkled with thriving communities and pretty towns. Few people living there nowadays have heard the name and would be reluctant to believe that it was ever applied to their locality. Here and there one may yet encounter infertile spots, and a few stretches of the country are still monotonous to ride through, but one no longer thinks of the pinelands as either a desert or barren.

—*GMNL* 9(1956): 105-108; reprinted from *EUQ* 5(March 1949)

NOTES

1. Hall's reaction in this case is interesting, and is analogous to that of present-day people who view America's Great Plains or the desert sections of the western United States for the first time. They too find themselves fascinated by such scenery, and will often stare for hours at the landscape from train windows without knowing exactly the cause.

2. It is interesting to note that a century later, the Americans themselves were to regard another variety of trees—the huge sequoias of California—as the *premiers enfants* of America.

3. On a visit to the South during his second trip to America, Lyell, who was a keen observer, took the occasion while waiting during a change from a stagecoach to train at Chehaw, Macon County, Alabama, to measure the stumps of some newly felled virgin pines. One stump was 2 feet 5 inches in diameter 3 feet from the ground. On it he counted 120 rings of annual growth. A second stump with 260 rings was only two

inches greater in diameter. A third with 180 rings was 2 feet across, and the stump of a fourth fallen giant measured 4 feet through and showed 320 growth rings. The height of the trees varied from 70 to 120 feet. He added the comment that no such trees would be seen by posterity after the clearing of the country, except where they happened to be preserved for ornamental purposes.

No. 30
Towaliga River

> But their memory liveth on your hills
> Their baptism on your shore,
> Your everlasting rivers speak
> Their dialect of yore.
>
> Lydia H. Sigourney, *Indian Names*

In connection with essay No. 5 of this series on Upatoi Creek,[1] it was pointed out that most of Georgia's Indian placenames are fairly easy to pronounce properly, or at least, easy to say in the forms which have become accepted by present-day people. But there are exceptions on this score, and sometimes a word is not sounded in accordance with its written spelling. The most deceptive Indian name of all in this respect is Towaliga, which is the designation of a small river that rises in southern Henry County near Hampton and flows southeastward across Henry, Spalding, Butts, and Monroe to enter the west side of the Ocmulgee above the little town of Juliette. On its way to this union, the stream is joined by a considerable creek called the Little Towaliga that begins to the north of Barnesville in Lamar County.

In addition to its use in connection with these streams, the name in the vicinity of the waterways is also applied to some church and old school sites. And too, the tab can be found in the designation of a crossroads and community along the river in western Butts County. It also occurs as Towalaga in the name of a railroad station in northeast Spalding County. It is fairly common today to find the appellation spelled in this manner, and the version occurs in old records. It is reasonable to believe, however, that Towaliga is the correct form. Indeed the *liga* ending must be used if the term is to be meaningfully translated.

Old-timers who live in the area of the Towaliga employ one of four slightly different pronunciations for the appellation. Some people say "Tyé wee laǵ gee," while others may use "Tyé wee lyé gee." On the other hand there are some individuals who slur the word and say either "Tyé ee laǵ gee" or "Tyé ee lyé gee." The "tye" sound apparently has long been used and probably occurred in the original word. J. G. W. DeBrahm, a colonial surveyor general of Georgia, mentioned the name as "Taiwalagaw."[2] In this instance he simply used the dipthong *ai* to gain the *y* sound shown here by *tye*.

There are subtleties in the spoken word that are hard to capture precisely, even with the international phonetic system. The second syllable *wee* or *ee* is only lightly sounded. And too, the final syllable has a hard *g* sound. It is not pronounced "jee" but must be "gee," as in Ocmulgee and Gillespie. DeBrahm may have used the ending *gaw* to emphasize this hard *g*.

It is probably natural for the uninitiated on reading the printed name Towaliga to pronounce the word in such a way that the *Towa* element will rhyme with sour or with thrower. It is also natural to turn the form *liga* into "leega."

The differences in the written and spoken versions of Towaliga and Towalaga pose difficulties in translating the expression. On its face, present-day Creeks say the written word signifies in, about, or among trees, or at a place where a specific grove of trees is located. This version would be derived from the Muskogee *éto*, trees + the locative *liga*, signifying a place, site, location, spot, roost, etc. This explanation assumes the *éto* got converted into *étow* + an *a* to make *etowa*, and that the initial *e* of the latter was slurred and eventually dropped entirely.

Another interpretation that can be advanced to explain the written form of Towaliga holds the expression simply refers to an old place or spot, from the Creek *towé*, old + the locative *liga*. The usual Muskogee terms for old were *hasi* (or "hassee") and *achula* (or "'chula"), but *towé* also signified old, especially with reference to some particular spot.

The long-standing *tye* sound in the spoken word makes it unlikely that these versions correctly interpret the expression.

Adiel Sherwood offered an explanation of Towaliga which furnishes an inkling for the most logical interpretation of the spoken version of the name. In the 1829 edition of his *Gazetteer*, he spelled the word "Towelaggee" and said it was derived from "Tow-elaggie" meaning "roasted scalps."[3] The name arose, he stated, because some

Indians once stopped beside the stream to roast [cure] some fresh scalps which they had taken from the whites and which were spoiling because of the hot weather. Sherwood got his words garbled but the designation actually could have arisen from this gruesome episode, because there was a Creek word *tiwa* meaning hair, which was used in place of the usual term *ecauhalpee*, signifying headskin, or scalp. It is difficult to see, however, where he got the *elaggie* for roasted, unless he was offering a badly distorted form of *eckopeta*, to roast.

Now, Tiwaliga literally means hair place or spot, with no reference to roasting, curing, or drying. Since *tiwa*,[4] however, was used to signify scalp, it is reasonable to conclude that the old Creeks looked on some spot along the river as the "scalp place," meaning in its full implied sense, the site where the party stopped to dry scalps.

There actually was a Muskogee village of Towaliga which is mentioned as "Towaleges" in a 1715 list of Creek settlements.[5] The location of this community is conjectural. It may have been situated at or near the mouth of the stream on the Ocmulgee. This location would be a good guess because it was fairly common to name a creek after a town that stood at the juncture of the stream with a main river. Another possible site was in the Towaliga District of western Butts County, near Glens Bridge over the Towaliga River. This section offered several good spots along the stream for an Indian village. Furthermore, the famous Upper Creek trading path, or Oakfuskee path, from Charleston and Augusta to the Creek Indians crossed the river a short distance upstream from the bridge. If the Indians did stop to dry their scalps at this site and thus gave rise to the name, perhaps the party was travelling the Oakfuskee path, because it was a war trail whereas the paralleling main Lower Creek route to the south was a "white path" or peaceful thoroughfare.[6]

—GMNL 9(1956): 136-137

NOTES

1. *Georgia Mineral Newsletter* 7 (1954): 126-28.
2. *History of the Province of Georgia* (Wormsloe, 1849), p. 31.
3. *A Gazetteer of the State of Georgia*, 2nd ed. (Philadelphia, 1829), p. 100.
4. Albert S. Gatschet indicates that *tiwa* was a foreign word (borrowed from some other Indian language?); see his *A Migration Legend of the Creek Indians* (Philadelphia: Brinton, 1884), 1:213.
5. Appendix to "A Journal from Carolina in 1715," *Yearbook* (City of Charleston, S.C., 1894), p. 354. The plural form Towaleges, which is used in this source, was once

fairly common in referring to Creek Indian towns. Coweta, for instance, might have been referred to as the Cowetas. The present-day Attapulgus is a remnant of this practice—see item No. 9 of this series.

6. [Read, 15 (1949): 132, doubts the "scalp" etymon and prefers Creek *tawa*, summit, and *laiga*, place. *FLU*.]

No. 31
Four Killer Creek (Spanish Pete's Old Place, Some Settlements of the Cherokee Downing Family, Cedar Creek, Vickery Creek)

In upper Fulton County, lying almost midway between Roswell and Alpharetta, there is a little stream that bears the intriguing name Four Killer Creek. The waterway arises a couple of miles or so to the west of the last-named town and flows southward to join today's Big Creek above the Old Lebanon Mills site, to the northeast of Roswell.

This unusual appellation is derived from a prominent Cherokee called Four Killer who once lived at the head of the stream which bears his name. The official 1832 surveys of original Cherokee County show that his settlement was in lots 477 and 513 of Land District 1, Section 2 of Cherokee, which is now a part of Fulton.[1]

Four Killer in turn derived the English version of his name from the Cherokee Nunggihtehe ("Nankeeteehee") which literally means Four Killer from *nunggih* (or "nankee") four + the suffix *tehe* (or "teehee"), a war title signifying killer. The Cherokees were obviously proud of the designation and apparently as a man vanquished one enemy after another, his rank could be moved up accordingly. Thus there were various gradations of killers: One Killer (Saquohtehe); Two Killer (Taleetehe); Three Killer (Tsawitehe); Five Killer (Hiskeetehe); and Six Killer (Sutaleetehe). Presumably, of course, there could have been killers of higher ranks, but this observer has never noted the title beyond the sixth gradation. In view of the fact that a Two Killer was a sufficiently prominent individual to be a signatory to an important treaty,[2] one can reasonably conclude that the Four Killer who gave his name to our little stream was a considerable personage.

It might be added that the title *tehe*, or "teehee," was used in ways other than with cardinal numbers. For example, there seem to have been First Killers as well as One Killers. Perhaps the former designated the first man who slew an enemy on a war expedition. Then too, there were names like Path Killer, Chickasaw Killer, Tuskega [Tuskeegeé] Killer, White Man Killer, and so on. The last individual must have been audacious indeed to show up around white people with such a title. But his name can be found affixed to the Cherokee treaty of 1817.[3] Path Killer or "Ne, no, hut, ta, hee" was a distinguished chief who signed the treaty of 1805.[4] One assumes that Chickasaw Killer, or Chickasawtehe, was a particularly distinctive rank, because a Chickasaw brave was usually a formidable warrior himself and was not easily vanquished. Chickasaw Killer's name is signed to the Cherokee treaty of 1791.[5]

In writing these little placename essays, there is usually a temptation to digress from the main subject in the heading. This shortcoming arises from the fact that in gathering material for a study one often sees in the records or on the old maps interesting bits of information which he thinks some fellow student may like to know. For instance, from the map for Land District 1, Section 2 of original Cherokee County (now upper Fulton), it was noted that other interesting individuals lived near the site of Four Killer's old home.[6] One of these was Spanish Pete, who resided in lot 916, just to the east of Big Creek (on the present Kimball Bridge Road), some two and a quarter miles southeast of today's Alpharetta. And too, there was a James Downing that maintained a settlement, with clearings, in lots 554, 555, 596; and a William Downing who had a place in lots 553 and 554.[7] These men were Cherokee neighbors of Four Killer because they lived about a mile to the southeast, near or on present U.S. 19. Presumably these Downings were members of a well-known family of that name which had resided among the Cherokees since post-Revolutionary days. Colonel Benjamin Hawkins mentioned some of the Downings and spoke of their good character.[8] Indeed, after the removal to the West, the family continued to be counted among the leaders of the Cherokees.

It might be of interest to add that the stream now called Big Creek was called Cedar Creek in the Cherokee days, and the main right bank tributary of Four Killer Creek was called Caney Creek. The old map shows and notes extensive cane brakes along the stream in lots 434, 443, 444, 471, and 472.[9] Perhaps this section was the area in which Four Killer grazed his stock, because in wilderness days, cane was the chief browsing plant for cattle and horses.

The upper headwaters of Big Creek (formerly Cedar Creek) is called Vickery Creek. It derives the name from a Cherokee family of that name, which lived in the area at the head of the stream, in present western Forsyth County.

In conclusion, it should be mentioned that other tribes also used the title killer. For example, there was a prominent Creek chief named Chekilli, or Cherokee Killer.[10] This name, of course, indicated that the distinctiveness of the killing business worked both ways.

—GMNL 9(1956): 137-38

NOTES

1. Map of District 1 (Gold), survey of 1832, N. C. Barnett, D.S., Land Records of Georgia, Surveyor General Department, Atlanta.

2. Richard Peters, ed., *The Public Statutes at Large of the United States of America* (Boston: Little, Brown, 1856), "Indian Treaties," 7: 42—signatories to the treaty of Holston, 1791.

3. *Ibid.*, p. 160, Treaty of Cherokee Agency.

4. *Ibid.*, p. 94, Treaty of Tellico.

5. *Ibid.*, p. 42, Treaty of Holston.

6. Map of District 1, cited above.

7. *Ibid.*

8. *Letters of Benjamin Hawkins, 1796-1806*, Collections of the Georgia Historical Society, Vol. 9 (Savannah, Ga., 1916), p. 15, entry for Nov. 24, 1796. The Downings originally lived around Pine Log, to the north of the Etowah River.

9. Map of District 1.

10. Chekilli was a prominent Creek chief at the time of the foundation of Georgia. In English orthography the name was properly Chelokeeilitchee. *Ilitchee* (or *ilitci*) was the Muscogee equivalent of the Cherokee *tehe*. The early whites slurred the name into Chekilli, or some very similar form.

No. 32
Unawatti Creek, the Flat Creeks, Level Creek, Pataula Creek

Unawatti Creek begins on the western edge of Lavonia in Franklin County and flows southwestward to join another stream called Bear Creek, thence into the north fork of Broad River. The word *Unawatti* is Cherokee and signifies a shallow running stream or creek.[1] In pioneer terminology the English expression for the same type of waterway was flat creek. Such a designation was commonplace because old streams called flat creeks can be found in various parts of Georgia.

With respect to both the terms *unawatti* and flat creek it is important to note that a waterway bearing the label should contain moving water. If the stream were one in which water only flowed intermittently or seasonally the white people called the stream a dry creek. Or, if the water did not flow at all (or only moved during a flood), the stream was labelled a deadwater creek, slough, or "lake." In the earliest years in the lowcountry area of Georgia such a stream might even have been called a lagoon.

In the pioneer view the tab Flat Creek was quite descriptive because the name was intended to differentiate this sort of stream from other categories of waterways. The expression for instance carried the opposite connotation of streams bearing designations like Swift Creek, Falling Creek, and Tumbling Creek. A flat creek from the physical nature of the water course usually did not provide a good mill site, or sufficient water supply for such an installation. On the other hand, the expression falling creek denoted the opposite condition.

In one or two instances the name Level Creek appears on Georgia maps. This appellation was a synonym for flat creek and had the same meaning as the latter name. In northwest Gwinnett County there is a Level Creek which is an east-bank tributary of the Chattahoochee.

Streams bearing the name Flat Creek can be found in the counties named below. It will be noticed that the waterways are well-distributed around the state.

1. Fannin—the creek begins just inside the eastern Gilmer line and flows into Fannin to enter the Toccoa River.

2. Gilmer—the stream arises in the western area and joins the Coosawattee River.

3. Fayette—heads northeast of Tyrone and runs south into Line Creek.

4. Walton—Big and Little Flat creeks unite and drain into the Alcovy at the Newton-Walton line.

5. Spalding—the creek, a small stream, begins in southwest area and joins Flint River.

6. Miller—begins in the northwest region of the county and joins Aycocks Creek to the west of Colquitt.

7. Clay—begins in the southwest and joins Colomokee Creek.

8. Berrien—there are two Flat creeks in this county; one begins in the north central section, joins Hog Creek, thence into the east side of the Willacoochee. The other stream arises some miles above Nashville and also enters the Willacoochee on the east.

9. Montgomery—creek commences northwest of Mt. Vernon and empties into the Oconee.

10. Emanuel—the waterway enters the left side of the Canoochee, above Georgia Highway 26.

11. Meriwether-Troup—the stream begins in the western part of the first county and joins Yellowjacket Creek in upper Troup.

12. Houston—starts on the edge of Peach County and flows east to unite with Big Indian Creek to the south of Perry.

13. Twiggs—Flat Creek begins in the north central part and enters the Ocmulgee below Adams Park.

14. Hall—the stream commences on the southwest edge of Gainesville and unites with the Chattahoochee near Browns Bridge.

15. White—the creek heads to the east of Cleveland and flows south to join White Creek, thence into the Chattahoochee.

16. Rabun—in the northwest part of the county, a small Flat Creek or Branch flows west to join the upper Tallulah River, just inside extreme northeast Towns County.

17. Dawson—a Flat Creek heads to the east of Dawsonville and flows westward to join Shoal Creek, thence into the Etowah River.

Perhaps it should be noted that Flat creeks are not the same as Flat Shoals creeks. The names of the latter imply that each of the streams has one or more flat shoally areas whose firm, hard bottoms offer good fording sites. Except at these particular crossing points, the waterways may be deep and swift, and not flat or shallow. Some streams, of course, can have flat shoals fording sites without being called by that name. For instance, the most famous Flat Shoals of the state are on Flint River, to the southwest of Concord in Pike County. The noted colonial Upper Creek trading path, or Oakfuskee trail, crossed the Flint at those important shoals. The Flat Shoals creeks and the Flat Shoals fording points provide interesting subjects for later discussions in this series of studies.

In view of the fact that several of the Flat creeks mentioned above, in Fannin, Gilmer, Rabun, etc., are in former Cherokee country, these streams may once have borne the Cherokee designation unawatti, which was translated by the white people to Flat Creek. It was fairly common for early surveyors and pioneer citizens to convert Indian names. We may never know about these cases, though, because the white people readily made use of Flat Creek themselves and were quite willing to apply their own appellation in appropriate instances.

In the region occupied by Creek Indians there is no stream name containing the Muskogee term *tapiksi,* or "tapeksee," signifying flat. It should be added, however, that the word Pataula might have that meaning. This name is applied to a large stream that arises in eastern Stewart County and flows across Randolph, Quitman, and Clay to enter the Chattahoochee above Fort Gaines. Pataula can not be found in Creek language word lists, but the name is similar to the Choctaw *patala,* meaning flat. Those Indians did not live in Georgia, but in the southwest part of the state, where the Hitchitees and Seminoles resided, there are some unusual names which resemble Choctaw forms more than the pure Muskogee. Pataula may have been a dialectal word which was akin to the Choctaw. This point, however, is merely a suggestion. There is a possibility that Pataula is of remote Spanish-Indian origin and that its real significance in no way contains a meaning that could be interpreted as signifying flat, shallow, or level.

—*GMNL* 9(1956): 138-39

NOTES

1. The writer wishes to express his appreciation to the following persons for assistance in interpreting *unawatti*: Mrs. Mary Smith Witcher of Tulsa, Oklahoma, who had prominent Cherokee forebears in Georgia; Mr. L. R. Gourd and Mrs. E. M. Bowers of Tahlequah, Oklahoma; Mr. Dave Sunday of Locust Grove, Oklahoma; Mr. Calvin Turner of Hominy, Oklahoma, and Mr. Bill Hoge of the *Tulsa Sunday World.*

No. 32-A
Unawatti Creek

Beginning with this issue and from time to time hereafter, supplemental statements will be offered to present additional information on some of the placename sketches that have already appeared in the series or to modify the explanations of certain names. For convenience, these added comments will be numbered according to the particular prior sketches to which they relate with the added letter *A* after the number.

An appellation that should be reconsidered is Unawatti Creek which was discussed in Sketch No. 32. In that presentation an incorrect explanation was given for the meaning of Unawatti due to the fact that the word is a garbled version of a name whose real significance was not learned until additional early records containing information pertaining to the word were available.

The Unawatti, which is locally pronounced "Yoo na wä teé," arises in Franklin County to the west of Lavonia and flows southward to join Bear Creek, thence into the east side of the North Fork of Broad River. The name under the spelling Unawatti or closely related versions has long appeared on maps. The writer studied the word for a considerable time and being unable to derive a satisfactory explanation for it, wrote some Oklahoma Cherokees to inquire about its meaning. Certain well-qualified informants replied that the term *unawatti* referred to a shallow, slow-moving body of water—meaning a type of waterway that is known in this state as a flat creek. On this basis then, the creek was included in Sketch No. 32 which mainly concerns Georgia's Flat creeks.

The informants no doubt gave a correct explanation of *unawatti* under that spelling. They had no way of knowing the word had been garbled over the years and that it was derived from a form which originally had nothing to do with a flat creek or a slow-moving stream.

The real significance of Unawatti was discovered some months ago in the early platbooks of Franklin County which have now been deposited in the Georgia Surveyor General Department. In going through these documents, one noticed the plat for a 1789 survey for land of Hugh Hay.[1] This property was on "Yone Water Creek" of the North Fork of Broad River. The name and location, of course, caught the eye and set off a search for similar references to the stream. Sufficient evidence turned up in the records to show that the present Unawatti was originally listed as the Yonawatte, Yonawattee, etc. These early names signify "old bear," from the Cherokee *yanuhweti*, which was composed in turn from *yanuh*, bear plus *weti*, old. *Yanuh* is harder to pronounce properly than appears. The frontier white people usually turned it into "Yona" or "Yonah," as found in the name Mount Yonah. But these renditions are not correct because the old Cherokees did not use a letter that is the equivalent of our long *o*, such as found in "Yonah" or "Yona." The *a* of *yanuh* had a sound that falls between an *o* and *aw*. The best example which approximates the correct sound can be found in the spoken version of the word Cherokee. In pronouncing this expression few people say "Cherókee." Nearly everybody says "Cherakee," and sounds the *o* of the written word as if it were an *a* like that occurring in the English expression all.

In addition to the difficulties with the *a* of *yanuh*, the early citizens also had trouble with the *uh* ending of the word which had a sound something like *u* in cut and jut. Apparently as evidenced by "Yone," "Yona," "Yonah," or even by "Una," the white people could not capture the proper sound of the syllable in accordance with the correct pronunciation used by the Cherokees.

No doubt the difficulties of pronouncing Yanuhweti caused the expression eventually to be turned into Unawatti, although for a period the name was originally listed as beginning with a *Y*. It was mentioned as "Yona Wattoe" in 1792[2] and as "Yeonuwattee" in 1801.[3] By the time B. W. Frobel prepared his official map of Franklin, in 1869, however, the name had turned into Unawattie.[4] This version in time became the Unawatti that is used today.

No information could be turned up to explain why the stream was referred to as the Yanuhweti or Old Bear Creek. Perhaps it was named for some Cherokee by that name who once lived on the waterway when the tribe occupied the section before the area was ceded by the Indians to Georgia in 1784. A signatory to the 1799 Treaty of Holston River is listed as Yonewatleh or Bear at Home.[5] This man may have been the Indian who gave the Georgia creek its name but the translation of Unawatti into Old Bear would seem to make such a derivation doubtful.[6]

It will be recalled the Unawatti is now a tributary of Bear Creek. The early maps and records, though, make it clear the Indian designation originally applied to the whole stream. At some period over the years the south prong and lower part of the waterway became known as Bear Creek, while the label Unawatti was retained for the north fork. Perhaps it may strike the reader as a curious situation for a stream's name to be split into an English version for one segment of the waterway and into an aboriginal designation for the other portion of the same stream. This practice, however, has been followed a number of times in Georgia. For example, in Dooly County, there is a large tributary of the Flint which has two main branches. One of these is called Turkey Creek, while the other is known as the Pennahatchee, from *pinawa*, turkey, plus *hachi*, a stream. In Indian days, the whole waterway was the Pennahatchee. And again, in south central Georgia, there is a Little River that joins the Withlacoochee River to the northwest of Valdosta. Now, Withlacoochee, freely translated, means Little River—from *wiwa*, water + *thlako*, big + the diminutive, *uchi* or "oochee," little. During the early years the entire stream was known as the Withlacoochee. In time, though, the English designation Little River was applied to the western fork.

—*GMNL* 15(1962): 100-101

NOTES

1. Land of Hugh Hay, 500 acres, survey of 1789, platbooks for original Franklin County, Vol. 1, 1784-1798, Land Records of Georgia, Surveyor General Department, Atlanta.
2. "A Map of the Defensive plan of the Western Frontier," August, 1792, MS in the map collection of the library, University of Georgia, Athens.
3. Land of David Northington, original Franklin County, survey of 1801, Platbook R, p. 14.
4. "Map of Franklin County 1869," B. W. Frobel, made by the authority of the state, Land Records of Georgia.
5. Richard Peters, ed., "Indian Treaties," *The Public Statutes at Large of the United States of America* (Boston, 1856), 7: 42.
6. [The Una-, Yonah-, and Yanah- malic variation looks like an original Cherokee /ya/ gradated to /yə/ because stress is on final syllable of the word, and then restressed to /yo/ and /yu/. *FLU.*]

No. 33
Young Deer Creek (Two Mile, Four Mile, and Six Mile Creeks of Forsyth County)

The early white people were prone to a tedious repetition of names like Buck Creek, Beaverdam Creek, Sand Creek, Pine Ridge, Sandy Springs, etc., but when they chose to give an interesting turn to a name, they were quite capable of doing so. This ability is well illustrated in the translations of Indian personal names such as Little Carpenter, Hanging Maw, Gun Merchant, Devil's Landlord, Mad Bear, and so on in great variety. But the frontiersmen could also give a pleasing twist to geographic names which they translated from the Indian. For example, Talking Rock Creek is a more inviting name than Echo Rock Creek; Noonday Creek, than Midday Creek; and so on.

One of these interesting turns to a geographic name can be found in the designation Young Deer Creek,[1] a stream that arises in eastern Forsyth County, to the northeast of Cumming, and flows southward to enter the Chattahoochee. Now, Young Deer was probably a personal Cherokee name, borne by an individual who lived on the stream. The appellation in Cherokee would have been *ahwi-agina,* signifying fawn. Instead of making the name simply Fawn Creek, however, the white people chose to use the literal meaning by translating the tab into the interesting form Young Deer Creek.

Not far to the east of Young Deer Creek, between it and the Chattahoochee, are three streams that should be noted while we are in this vicinity of Georgia. These waterways are Two Mile Creek, Four Mile Creek, and Six Mile Creek. The streams roughly parallel each other, but join just before entering the Chattahoochee.

The little waterways derive their names from the fact that, going west from the Chattahoochee, they measure distance along the former Middle Cherokee trading path from Augusta. This thoroughfare after 1805 became the Federal Road, the first vehicular way across the Cherokee country between Georgia and Tennessee. This route crossed the Chattahoochee at Vann's Ferry, located about a mile and a half below today's Browns Bridge on Georgia 141.

Before the establishment of the ferry and the vehicular route, the trading path crossed at Goddards Old Ford, at the site of Browns Bridge. From either crossing, the distance to the creeks mentioned was still approximately two miles, four miles, and six miles.

—*GMNL* 9(1956): 139

NOTE

1. Young Deer Creek bore its name in the Indian days; cf. John Bethune, Surveyor General of Georgia, *A Map of that part of Georgia Occupied by the Cherokee Indians* (Milledgeville, 1831).

No. 34
Tussahaw Creek

Some of the most interesting Indian names of Georgia have such obscure backgrounds that we may never be able to translate them properly. This condition arises from the fact that often no intimations can be found of the meanings in available word lists and dictionaries of the Indians who once lived in these parts. In other instances, the white people who originally noted certain indigenous names apparently garbled them so badly they can not now be correlated with any definite Indian forms. For these reasons one often has to guess at the probable meanings of Indian names or make incomplete explanations of them. A good word to illustrate the situation can be found in the name of Tussahaw Creek, which commences just below McDonough in Henry County and flows southeastwardly to enter Jackson's Lake of the Ocmulgee River, in northeast Butts County.

Some people with a knowledge of Creek believe the name Tussahaw signifies ability to inflict pain on you; or do direct pain to you, such as shooting at you; or as a bee, wasp, or scorpion stinging you. Mr. Acee Blue Eagle, the distinguished Indian artist of Okmulgee, Oklahoma, who had Creek forebears that once lived in this region,[1] believes the word may have been intended to signify something like warrior shooting at you. In view of the fact that the *tussa* element in the name is the same as the root of the Muskogee words *tassakaya, tasikaia,* ("tussakaya," "tussikiah") and *tastanagi* (or "tustunuggee," "tustanuggee"), meaning warrior, this explanation may represent the correct meaning of Tussahaw.

Some people living along the creek pronounce the name "Tusseehaw." This verison is of long standing, because one of the surveyors of original Henry County, in 1821, labelled the stream Tussy Haw.

—*GMNL* 9(1956): 139-40

NOTE

1. The author is indebted to Mr. Acee Blue Eagle for valuable information on a number of Georgia names of Muskogee origin. He is a descendant of William McIntosh, the noted Creek chief.

No. 35
Bolivar and Ypsilanti

The recent Hungarian revolt brings to mind an interesting feature of American placenaming. The people of this country are prone to be admirers of revolutionary heroes in other nations and have willingly adopted the names of such leaders as designations for towns and villages. For instance, the *United States Official Postal Guide* (Part I), lists two Kossuths (one in Mississippi and another in Pennsylvania) which commemorate the Hungarian patriot Lajos Kossuth who led a revolution against Austria in 1848. And Simon Bolivar, the great South American leader, is honored by a sizable list of United States localities. Not all of the places bearing his name have attained status as towns and cities, although the *Postal Guide* gives six Bolivars that are now post offices: in Missouri, New York, Ohio, Pennsylvania, Tennessee, and West Virginia. In addition to these points, *The Official Guide of the Railways of the United States* also notes other spots: in Indiana, Illinois, and Georgia. Old maps show more places with the name. New York even had two Bolivars at one time.

Georgia's Bolivar is a little station on the Louisville and Nashville Railroad, above Rydal, in northeast Bartow County.

Another foreign hero's name which is used in America is Ypsilanti, for Demetrios Ypsilanti, the Greek patriot who led the Grecian movement for independence from Turkey during the early part of the last century. There are at least three Ypsilantis in the United States: one, a substantial city in Michigan; a town in North Dakota on the Northern Pacific Railway, located to the south of Jamestown; and a crossroads in northeast Talbot County, Georgia. Our Ypsilanti is some nine miles to the northeast of Talbotton (via Po' Biddy Crossroads), and four miles northwest of Prattsburg. The place is old and was once an early post office. It is still a substantial community where four roads meet. None of these ways, however, is a major thoroughfare, and few outsiders have an occasion or opportunity to visit this spot with such an unusual name.

It might be of interest to add that the people of Talbot County pronounce Ypsilanti in accordance with the word's proper pronunciation as shown by gazetteers and encyclopedias. This is actually unusual because Americans commonly give a distinctive twist to a foreign name by pronouncing it differently from the original term. Indeed, Bolivar, which seems so easy, is a good example of this practice. Most

Americans say "Bŏl'i ver" (or "Bŏl'i vuh" in the South), whereas the correct Spanish form is "Bō leé var".

Bolivar and Ypsilanti, as in the case of so many other places about the state, by the turn of fate have remained little spots; perhaps they will always be destined for such a status. But one can not be sure on this score. Sometimes fate, after ignoring a village for years and years, will swing about suddenly and make the community grow. Doctortown on the Altamaha in Wayne County and Conley, with its big supply depot, are instances of such swift changes. More recently, Barrettsville in southwest Dawson County has experienced a reawakening. Barrettsville was once a well-known point on one of the noted old emigrant routes across Georgia to the West. Then for upward of a century it became a mere crossroads. In recent months, however, the community has received new attention by finding itself on the fringe of an atomic research development.

—*GMNL* 10(1957): 32

No. 36
Long Swamp Creek

Long Swamp Creek heads on the lower side of Burnt Mountain in extreme northeast Pickens County and flows southward, passing near Jasper, Tate, and Nelson to enter the Etowah River some three miles to the southeast of Ball Ground. The name is old and represents a translation from the Cherokee. One of the first written references to the stream was made by Colonel Marinus Willet in 1790 when he passed through the area and noted the Cherokee settlement of Long Swamp, located near the juncture with the Etowah. He referred to the town as "Long Swamp or Neueconoheta."[1] Colonel Benjamin Hawkins, the Indian agent, crossed the creek in late 1796 and mentioned it as "Looccunna heat (Long Swamp)."[2] He noted that the town bearing the name was on the west side of the stream, and also left the impression that the place was near the union with the Etowah. Apparently the settlement had been abandoned by 1796 because Hawkins spoke of "remains" and added there were some peach trees standing at the site as well as old cotton and corn stalks.[3]

Both Willet and Hawkins garbled the Cherokee expression for Long Swamp with their respective versions of "Neueconoheta" and "Looccunna heat." Both names, however, undoubtedly embody the Cherokee *gunahita,* signifying long. The fact that they began this modifier with a *c* instead of a *g* was not unusual. It was fairly common for early white people to convert the *g* of a Cherokee name into a *k* or hard *c*. Unless there is a Cherokee word for swamp that has been lost, Willet and Hawkins also failed to catch the proper form in the *Neue* and the *Looc* which they used. The correct Cherokee expression for swamp (or thicket) is *igati.*

Available Cherokee word lists do not give the exact Indian way of saying Long Swamp, but one surmises that it was something like Gatigunahita, from *igati,* swamp or thicket, plus *gunahita,* long. Thus, in the fashion of many Cherokee (and Muskogee) names, the word was probably a compound form, with the modifier following and joined to the noun.

It is difficult today to see why Long Swamp Creek should have been called by that name. The stream is big and deep, but its margins do not impress one as being particularly swampy—certainly not in the sense in which one finds wide, dense swamps along the fringes of many creeks of comparable size on the Coastal Plain. Since *igati* can mean either swamp or thicket, it is possible the Cherokees thought of the stream as Long Thicket Creek, whereas the white people merely translated the name as Long Swamp.

—*GMNL* 10(1957): 32-33

NOTES

1. William M. Willet, ed., *A Narrative of the Military Actions of Colonel Marinus Willet* (Carville, New York, 1831), p. 98.

2. *Letters of Benjamin Hawkins, 1796-1806,* Collections of the Georgia Historical Society, Vol. 9 (Savannah, 1916), p. 18.

3. *Ibid.*

No. 37
Lazer ("Lizer") Creek

On several occasions in these little essays reference has been made to the enduring quality of placenames. The great majority of appellations used in this state are original designations that have clung with remarkable persistence to the localities, sites, mountains, streams, etc., to which they were originally applied. But there have been changes in geographic words. Sometimes these shifts were abrupt and arbitrary because people at certain places wanted to adopt new names. The substitution of Commerce for Harmony Grove and of Winder for Jug Tavern are cases in hand. But in addition to these abruptly changed words, there are numbers of names that have gone through slow, evolutionary alterations in which the spelling, pronunciation, and even the meaning are modified. This sort of change is exemplified by Stalkinghead Creek which became Stockinghead[1] and Great Coat Branch which has been shifted to Gray Coat.[2]

Now, since some words have actually evolved, the question may logically be asked: Are there any names that are currently undergoing changes into other forms? This question can be answered affirmatively. There are several appellations which are presently changing. A good example can be found in Lazer Creek, which arises on the lower side of Pine Mountain, where Harris and Talbot corner, and flows across the latter county to enter the right side of Flint River, to the northeast of Talbotton. More and more, people are dropping the old word Lazer and referring to the stream as Lizer. The new form in fact is beginning to appear in print. Since Lizer is a curious expression and meaningless on its face, it is reasonable to believe evolution of the word will continue until some day it will wind up as Liza.

It should be emphasized that Lazer was the original name used by surveyors when what is now Talbot was first officially surveyed and laid off in 1826-1827, after the acquisition of the region from the Creek Indians. The appellation has also appeared under that same spelling in several reliable early maps prepared subsequent to the above dates.

The meaning of Lazer is not known, and this fact is possibly the influence which is causing a change in the name. People are prone to alter an appellation when they do not understand it. Lazer may be an Indian word, although such an origin is doubtful. In fact, Colonel Benjamin Hawkins in 1797 gave "Authlucco" as the Muskogee designation for the waterway.[3] Authlucco probably signifies Big Potato Creek,[4] with the word creek being understood as a part of the name. This assumption rests on the premise that the word comes from the first syllable of *aha* (or "Auhau"), potato, + the augmentative suffix *thlucco*, big.

Lazer may be a corruption of the *thlucco* element in the Muskogee name, but this would be a tenuous assumption at best. *Thlucco* was difficult for the white people to pronounce and it can be found in various garbled forms, like "thlocko," "lika," "hlocko," "lacco," etc. None of these renditions, however, contains a z as is found in Lazer. Since original surveyors used Lazer and seemed to be familiar with the stream's title, one ventures to suggest that Lazer was the surname of some Indian country white man who lived in the vicinity of the waterway and gave his name to it.

—*GMNL* 10(1957): 33

NOTES

1. For a discussion of Stalkinghead and Stockinghead, see item no. 6, above.
2. For a sketch of Great Coat Branch, see *ibid.*
3. *Letters of Benjamin Hawkins, 1796-1806,* Collections of the Georgia Historical Society, Vol. 9 (Savannah, 1916), p. 172.
4. Downstream from the mouth of Lazer Creek, on the Upson County side, the Flint is joined by a stream that is now called Potato Creek. The name is a translation from the Muskogee. And, just below the mouth of this Potato Creek, the Flint is joined on the right or Talbot County side by Hachasofkee Creek. In Indian days this last stream was known as the Aupiogee, Ahapioka, or Ahhapioka. These last names also seem to contain the Muskogee *aha,* or "auhau," signifying potato. (For a discussion of these names, see item no. 15, above.)

The names Au'hlucco, Potato Creek, Aupiogee, and Ahapioka imply that some variety of the Indian potato was once common along the streams named.

Georgia has numbers of Potato creeks and places. The author intends to write about them in some future issue of the *Newsletter.*

No. 38
Paramore Hill (and Scull Creek)

Georgia has many geographic designations containing the word hill. One of the oldest and most interesting names in this group is Paramore Hill, a high, sandy ridge that stretches for a mile or so down the east bank of the Ogeechee River in lower Jenkins County, to the south of Millen. The summit of the hill is some 270 feet above sea level. This height is not appreciably greater than that of some other rises in the general locality, but Paramore Hill is distinctive because its western slope is a steep face that drops precipitously almost to the edge of the river, permitting an open and rare view over the Ogeechee Swamp and its moss-draped trees below. Except from an aircraft or forestry watchtower, or possibly from some big bluffs on the lower Savannah or Altamaha, it would not be possible to find a comparable scene anywhere else in Georgia.

This sharp declivity in earlier years caused the eminence to be referred to as a bluff and not as a hill. In colonial times, the spot was one of several Indian Bluffs along the Ogeechee. Then it became known as Scull's Bluff, presumably for a colonial [man or] family by that name.[1] This early designation is still reflected in Scull or Scull's Creek[2] that empties into the west side of the Ogeechee, opposite the lower end of the bluff.

The first person to receive a colonial land grant on what is now Paramore Hill was Eison Roberts, who petitioned for 200 acres on Scull's Bluff in 1765.[3] The request was granted in that year,[4] and Samuel Savery shows Roberts's home site on the north end of the hill in his map of 1769.[5] Interestingly enough, this cartographer put a Cockney *h* on Eison's name and made it "Hyson" or "Heison."[6] Savery also notes that a "Philip Sherril" had a place on the lower, or south end of the bluff.[7] It is not clear how Scull's name was originally connected with the spot. He may have been a squatter who lived across the river, by the creek which still bears his name. If this were the case, however, he was living on Indian lands.

Still later the ridge became Paramore's Bluff for some member of a family bearing that surname. The early land records of Georgia do not indicate that a Paramore was granted land at the hill, but they do show that numbers of Parramores or Paramores received post-Revolutionary grants in Effingham, Burke, Screven, and Bulloch.[8] These early counties are the areas surrounding the hill. Presumably one of the Paramores bought property at the place and caused his name to be attached to it. When the Central of Georgia Railway was constructed in the 1830's, it passed along the eastern base of the ridge. Eventually one of its stations was designated as Paramore Hill, and under this form the name has endured for over a century. It might be added that old people around about pronounce the word "Perrymore." This version, and the form Perrimore, are of long standing because they can be found in the early land records.[9]

Paramore Hill is significant to the geographic history of Georgia in several respects. For one thing, a noted trading path from Charleston via Mt. Pleasant on the Savannah River to the Creek Indians crossed the Ogeechee at the bluff. Over the river, this route forked. One branch, the Canouchee Path, led southwestward to trading posts at the forks of the Ocmulgee and Oconee. Another prong turned up the Ogeechee for a distance, then bore westward to the Rock Landing on the Oconee, situated a few miles below present Milledgeville. From there it went on to the Lower Creeks of western Georgia and eastern Alabama. General Oglethorpe very probably crossed the Ogeechee at the bluff and followed this last way in 1739 on his journey to treat with the Indians at Coweta Town on the Alabama side of the Chattahoochee, a few miles below present Columbus.

When St. Philip's Parish was created, its eastern line ran up the Ogeechee to the crossing of this trail. Thus Paramore Hill was located at one of the corners of that parish.

And finally, Paramore Hill or Scull's Bluff was important because the site marked a key point on the "Big Survey," which was made in the 1760's to delineate the boundary between Georgia and Creek Indians. This line came down the Ogeechee from the area of the Shoals of Ogeechee, and opposite the lower end of the bluff, continued on a direct course to the mouth of Penholoway Creek on the Altamaha,[10] thence to the St. Marys River in today's lower Charlton County.

It is not now possible to locate the exact old fording site of the trading path that crossed the Ogeechee at Paramore Hill. Apparently improvements made on the river in later years to facilitate navigation changed the stream. One surmises from a reading of old records that the ford was located toward the lower end of the bluff.

Apparently Paramore Hill was once a favored spot for the Indians, judging by the numerous pieces of pots, flints, and stone artifacts that can be found in the fields on the crest. This evidence is especially pronounced in the area about the present forestry watchtower located there. But the place was a peculiar site for Indians because it was far above a water supply. Ordinarily the red people of this section preferred a flat, sandy location immediately beside a stream, but high enough not to overflow with an ordinary flood. Unless there were once springs on the side of the bluff, one can be sure the Indians who stopped on the hill had a stiff climb in bringing up water. Perhaps these people did not live permanently on the top, but merely camped there occasionally in coming and going.

One final point should be made about Paramore Hill: The famous Louisville-Savannah Road crossed the full length of the ridge from north to south. This noted way was one of the early main thoroughfares of the state of Georgia. Before this route was opened as a road, it was called the Ogeechee Trail. After Louisville was made the capital in 1795, it then became the Capitol Road. Today, however, the route is remembered simply as the Old Louisville–Savannah Road.[11]

—*GMNL* 10(1957): 33-34

NOTES

1. Sam'l Savery, D.S., "Sketch [Chart] of the Boundary Line between the Province of Georgia and the Creek Nation," 1769, William L. Clements Library, Ann Arbor, Mich.

2. Georgia also has a Scull Shoal Creek, which arises in the vicinity of Danielsville in Madison County and enters the right side of Broad River.

3. Allen D. Candler, ed., *The Colonial Records of Georgia* (Atlanta: Franklin, 1904-1916), 9: 265.

4. *Ibid.*

5. Savery map.

6. *Ibid.* The map is slightly mutilated under Roberts's first name; only a "H——son" remains.

7. *Ibid.*

8. Index to Headrights, Grants, in Land Records of Georgia, Surveyor General Department, Atlanta. The name is variously spelled Parramore, Paramore, Parrimore, Parrymore, etc.

9. *Ibid.*

10. For a discussion of Penholoway Creek, see sketch no. 8, above.

11. [The apostrophe in Scull's Creek may indicate a folk etymology, but if it is traditional it suggests a personal name rather than a human skull accompanying the Paramore Hill artifacts. According to Stewart, *American Place Names*, p. 447, skulls often give names to places in the West, but rarely in the East. *FLU.*]

No. 39
Rincon (and Some Other Spanish Names)

In common with many states, Georgia has shown a propensity for using Spanish words in geographic naming. We have a substantial number of such designations scattered about the state. Indeed, along the coast there are Spanish names that have been retained from the remote years in which the Spaniards occupied that area: St. Catherine, St. Simon, Sapelo, and St. Marys. Then we have Spanish forms that commemorate sites and battles which were connected with the Mexican war: Palo Alto, Laredo, Montezuma, Resaca, Buena Vista, etc. And, in accordance with our American proclivity to name places after foreign cities, we have a Seville, Montevideo, Cordova, and Toledo.[1] But the largest group in this general category consists of Spanish words that were adopted because the people apparently liked the names: Alta Vista, Rio, Eldorado, Colon,[2] Aragon, Villa Rica, Sante Fe (or "Santa Fee"), and so on. Included in this group would be some possible Spanish names, or pseudo names, like Pavo, Condor, Sonoraville, Elmodel, Eldorendo, Vacuna, Ryo, Bermuda, Anguilla, and Belle Vista.[3]

All of these appellations are interesting and they certainly merit eventual treatment in these little sketches. Perhaps several essays will be needed to discuss and locate them in the way they deserve.

The Spanish name which is singled out for discussion here is Rincon, a town on the Seaboard Airline Railroad in lower Effingham County. Residents of the community are not sure how they got the tab, although the consensus is that the railway people supplied the designation when a station was established at the site after the line was built around the early 1890's.

Although the people do not know who first applied Rincon to the community they do have a good idea of the word's meaning since they say it was intended to signify a little nook, or hiding place. This explanation is a good rendition of the Spanish meaning, although the term also can be used to denote a corner or place of secrecy. If the person originally thinking up the name, however, had actually wanted to say *little* nook or *little* hiding place, he could have proposed Rinconcillo or Rinconcito.[4] It is just as well perhaps that one of these last diminutive forms was not used because the citizens have had enough difficulty with Rincon!

The pretty Spanish word *retiro* conceivably could have been suggested in lieu of Rincon because the former has about the same significance as the latter, plus the added meaning of retreat. In fact, the Americans have used the word retreat in their own placenaming, like Retreat, or Rural Retreat, Pine Retreat, etc. Upper South Carolina even had an old place called Bachelors' Retreat. But something must have happened to the bachelors who dwelt there because ultimately the name became simply Retreat.

The people of Rincon pronounce the word "Rink'on," or sometimes even "Rink'kon." This pronunciation shifts the accent from the original form, because in Spanish the name is "Rin cōn'"; or "Reen coné," to give an Anglicized version of the sound.

—*GMNL* 10(1957): 34-35

NOTES

1. In the case of two words in this particular list, Georgia used the English versions and not the true Spanish forms: in Spain Seville is Sevilla and Cordova is Cordoba.
2. Colon is the Spanish version for Columbus.
3. This name is a hybrid expression, consisting of the French *belle* and the Spanish *vista*. The correct designations in each language, respectively, would have been Belle Vue and Bella Vista. Belle Vista is a little place on U.S. 25-341 in northwest Glynn County.

Names like Belle View, Belvue, Beauvoir, Beaulieu, etc., were once popular in the Southeast as designations for plantations and county seats.

4. The diminutive suffixes *(c)illo* and *(c)ito* used in these words are reminiscent of the Muskogee diminutive *oochee*, which is found in Georgia names: Suwanoochee (Little Suwannee), Muckaloochee (Little Muckalee), etc.

No. 41 [*sic*]
Po' Biddy Crossroads

Speculation on the meaning of an enigmatic placename is an interesting though often fruitless diversion. Without some evidence to give an inkling as to the significance of an unusual appellation it is rare for one to think through and hit upon a correct interpretation of such a name. When one does eventually learn the meaning of a baffling term, it is interesting to compare the real explanation with the results of the cogitating that went on before the true sense could eventually be developed by research in records or by inquiry.

The writer has had many experiences in the speculative and theoretical approaches to placename analysis, but usually with surprising results when the final interpretation of a given word came out.

One of these experiences involves a community called Po' Biddy Crossroads, located three miles to the east of Talbotton, on U.S. 80 or Georgia 22. This designation, which certainly ranks with the singular names of Georgia, was long an incentive for much mulling and even an occasional personal inquiry, but always without satisfactory results until Mr. R. H. Callier, Clerk of the Superior Court at Talbotton, was encountered. Since he was present at the incident that gave rise to the name, he was able to give an account of the origin.

Some thirty odd years ago, according to Mr. Callier, a group was having dinner in what is now Po' Biddy, with fried chicken being the main dish. When one guest took the last piece of chicken, the women serving exclaimed, "There goes the last of the po' biddy!" Much joking and joshing ensued as a result of the remark, but some time later when a man who lived at the crossroads came to the courthouse to register a trade name for a filling station he proposed to erect at the place, he chose the name Po' Biddy, and the community has borne the moniker ever since that time.

For the reader who is not familiar with the Georgia vernacular, the woman was referring to a poor little chicken, presumably a frying-size bird that may have been a pet. She did not, of course, mean biddy in the sense of a baby chick.

—*GMNL* 10(1957): 35

No. 40
Egypt (and Egypt Hollow)

Behold, I have heard that there is corn in Egypt

Genesis 42:2.

America more than any of the nations of the New World has shown a willingness to adopt names of older countries, continents, and cities. Georgia alone could offer numerous illustrations in this respect:

Rome, Cairo, Athens, Lisbon, Vienna, Amsterdam, Damascus, Geneva, Madras, Berlin, Tunis, Hahira, Bremen, Turin, Scotland, Mt. Asia, Ceylon, Mecca, Africa, Natal, and so on.[1] An interesting particular example of the practice can be found in the community called Egypt, which is located in northwest Effingham County on the Central of Georgia Railway. The name is old and people living thereabouts say the tab was derived from a notable corn-raising ability which the section once enjoyed. Thus seemingly because this capacity compared favorably with that of Egypt, the place was called Egypt.

The corn raised around Georgia's Egypt, of course, was Indian corn or maize. The Biblical term corn used in connection with ancient Egypt was simply a generic term signifying grain.

In addition to the Egypt of Effingham, there is an Egypt Hollow in Dade County. This little valley lies between Tatum Mountain on the east and Murphy Mountain on the west, and its stream drains northward into Running Water Creek[2] in lower Marion County, Tennessee.

It is not known how Egypt Hollow got its name, and it is mere speculation to guess at the origin. One ventures to say the tab may have been intended for a bit of humor. This conjecture is based on the fact that many hollows bear waggish and whimsical monikers. Maybe the valley was actually regarded as being poor and the name Egypt in this case was a satirical term to convey the opposite connotation to the farming conditions that prevailed in the area about the Egypt in Effingham County.

—*GMNL* 10(1957): 35

NOTES

1. In the cases of some of these names it is interesting to note the English spellings for the words were adopted here. Thus Rome, Lisbon, Vienna, Geneva, and Turin were used, and not Roma, Lisboa, Wien, Geneve, and Torino. Some of the names in the list, of course, are the same as those used in the country in which the original cities are found, e.g., Amsterdam, Berlin, and Bremen.

2. Running Water Creek is a descriptive designation that means exactly what it says. The antonym for the expression is Dry Creek. Georgia has many Dry creeks. In early years, a synonym for a Running Water stream was Watery Creek or Watery Fork.

No. 41
Some "Coined" Names: Adsboro, Arco, Arcola, Ausmac, Bidawee, Captolo, Cenchat, Centralhatchee, Elko, Hopeulikit, Muckafoonee, Neyami, Ochlawilla, Oredell, Penhoopee, Rockalo, Rockmart, Subligna, Tennga, Villanow, etc.

Georgia in common with many states is dotted here and there with appellations which properly can be referred to as coined names, that is, designations which have been deliberately improvised for application to sites, communities, or streams. The roster of such names in this state is surprisingly long, so much so in fact, that no attempt will be made to list all of the tabs which are used here. Nor will an effort be made to analyze and interpret each of the words which are to be noted in the present sketch.[1] Indeed, the writer has been unable to determine the significance of some of the terms; and the information about several of those mentioned herein is based on tradition or hearsay which may be open to question in some instances.

In addition to some contrived names that have been omitted, the author wishes also to defer certain unusual words for later essays. One of these singular designations is Atlanta. This unique name is probably the ranking improvised appellation of the nation and as such should be discussed separately. Another invented word which will be deferred till a later time is Fredonia. This expression (one of the country's oldest coined words) was originally thought up in the early 1800's as a proposed national name for Americans and America. There are numbers of Fredonia places around the United States. Georgia alone has several such spots, and because of the age and unusual nature of the word it will be treated by itself.[2] Valdosta could perhaps be regarded as a coined name, but it too will be presently omitted and held for a discussion with several interesting place words that were connected with the life of George Troup, one of Georgia's most prominent governors.

Some other designations have been omitted as not being true coined names. Marble Hill and Tiptop, for instance, are such expressions. They lack the synthetic quality of contrived tabs. Then too, names like Smithsonia, Indianola, Pineora, Rockdale, Pinehurst, etc., are being left out, because, while they have some of the attributes of coined appellations, they more logically belong in other categories.

Pinehurst, for example, would be more meaningful if treated with words containing pine or hurst. And Rockdale should properly be discussed with expressions containing the term dale.

One generalization should be made about coined names before taking up the list to be discussed: the improvised words are mainly of relatively recent vintage when compared to the great body of Georgia geographic names. Most of the place words used here hark back to the formative years of the state and are as a consequence heavily imbued with the pioneers' spirit, outlook, and sense of values. The contrast between the old and new names is sometimes pronounced and this difference can be made pointed by merely listing a few very modern coined expressions that are among the last names to be placed on Georgia maps: Bidawee, Happy Hollow, Hopeulikit, and Lake Shangri-La. Even a cursory knowledge of older placenames should be sufficient to convince one that earlier people would rarely, if ever, have invented such monikers. The old-timers at their worst in placenaming were obtuse and rustic but not inane.

To return to the coined names which will be discussed, it is interesting to note that they have one common characteristic with most sizable bodies of placenames: they can in the main be catalogued and subdivided into different categories. In this paper there will not be many words mentioned in each of the classes, but nonetheless the pattern is there.

One group of coined names involves railway stations. Railroad people, apparently under compulsion to provide numerous labels for their many little stations, have shown a general propensity for improvising names. A good example from the Georgia list is Cenchat, a village in the Chattanooga valley of Walker County. At this place a former branch of the Central of Georgia crossed a road now called the Tennessee, Alabama, and Georgia. The original chartered name of the last line, however, was Chattanooga Southern Railroad. And at the point where it formed a junction with the Central a station called Cenchat was established.[4]

Another interesting station name is Elko, on the Southern Railway in lower Houston County. For some reason which the writer has not been able to discover, this tab is a favored name for railroad folk. The *Official Guide of the Railways* lists six Elkos in the United States and one in the Canadian Province of British Columbia. Another such term is Arcola, the designation of a village in southeast Bulloch County, below Brooklet. But interestingly enough, Georgia's Arcola is not now on a railroad line. Originally though, it was established on the

118 / Placenames of Georgia

old Savannah and Statesboro which has long since been abandoned. Around the nation the *Railway Guide* shows there are ten railroad points called Arcola: in Illinois, Indiana, Kansas, Louisiana, Minnesota, Mississippi, Pennsylvania, Texas, West Virginia, and Wyoming. There is also a similar place in Saskatchewan. Another railway name that is similar to Arcola is Arco, a point on the Atlantic Coast Line at the edge of Brunswick. The *Railway Guide* lists three other Arcos: in Idaho, Minnesota, and Tennessee. Still another railroad tab is Reka, on the Seaboard Airline, between Pembroke and Groveland in Bryan County.

One interesting railroad coined designation apparently has been dropped. This word was Ellen N, on the west side of Atlanta, near the present yards of the Nashville, Chattanooga, and St. Louis Railway. This name, no doubt, was derived from L & N, the common abbreviation for the Louisville and Nashville Railroad.

Although it only contains two words, one category of the coined names can properly be labelled the state border group. This class embodies Tennga, a village on U.S. 411, at the Tennessee-Georgia line in Murray County. Another such place is Alaga, a station on the Atlantic Coast Line in Houston County, Alabama. While the site is actually in Alabama, it should be mentioned because it is just over the Chattahoochee from Georgia and because it contains the abbreviation of this state as a component.

Georgia only has these two names, but is is quite common to find improvised terms around the country along state boundaries. The national list is substantial, in fact. Some states have even contrived several such labels, especially in cases in which the names of adjoining states are suitable to synthesizing. Colorado and its neighbors afford good examples. Along their borders, one finds words like: Cokan, Kanorado, Kanado, Wycolo, Ucolo, etc. Although Tennga and Alaga are pleasing words, Georgia does not lend itself well to blending with names like North Carolina, South Carolina, and Florida. Thus we are happily not afflicted with concoctions like Nocaga, Gasoca, and Gafla; or like Ganoca, Socaga, and Flaga.

Before leaving Tennga, a point should be made about the pronunciation of that word. It is not an old name relatively, but elderly people thereabouts call it "Tenngee." In this instance the g is hard, and thus the final syllable is sounded like the *gee* of Ocmulgee and not like the *gee* of gee whiz. This method of saying Tennga no doubt stems from the long-established colloquial practice of making a final *ga* into a *gee* with a hard *g*, thus: "Chattanoogee," "Chattoogee,"

"Telogee" and "Conasaugee." It should be emphasized that the people are not distorting these particular names; they are merely pronouncing them in the way that was handed down from the Indians. It is interesting to see though, that they transferred the familiar pronunciation to a relative newcomer like Tennga.

Of the numerous coined names in Georgia, only one expression appears to fall into a category which could be labelled humorous. This is a decided contrast to the relatively large group of amusing and whimsical appellations which can be found among the older conventional placenames of the state. The exception among the coined words is Adsboro. It is not applied to a village as the label implies, but to a community, Georgia Militia District No. 282, located to the south of Rutledge, in western Morgan County.

Adsboro on its face seems to be a surname plus the suffix *boro*. But according to elderly people who live in the community, it actually is an improvised designation which should properly be spelled Adzboro. The moniker arose many years ago, say these informants, from an incident in which a man shaping a timber with an adz hit himself in the knee. The episode no doubt was painful to the victim, but there was something funny about the affair which caused the people to commemorate it with the droll Adz or Adsboro.

Seemingly the largest group of coined words has arisen from a play on personal names, or from joining together syllables from such words. Subligna, the name of a little place in northeast Chattooga County, is an example of the former practice. This name is said to be a latinized form of Underwood, being derived from *sub*, under, and *ligna* (sic), wood.

Names devised with syllables from proper names are much more common. One of these is Ausmac, on the Seaboard Airline Railroad in northwest Decatur County. This word (pronounced "Ossmack") was derived from the surnames of two men called Ausley and McCaskill who carried on large turpentining operations in the vicinity of the place. When a station was opened at the site, its label was devised from the family names of these partners.[5]

Another such composed word can be found in Neyami, a small place on the Central of Georgia and U.S. 19 in upper Lee County. There has been much debate about the origin of the name. At a glance it seems to be Indian, but it does not actually fit into this category. A widely repeated version of the appellation holds that it was coined because the point lies halfway between New York and Miami. For a long time the writer accepted that explanation, although he was always puzzled over a route whereby Neyami could have been midway between the two cities mentioned. Mr. Frank Sheffield of Americus furnished a much more logical and acceptable explanation of the term.[6] He stated until the late 1920's the site of Neyami was called Adams Station. At that period, three men, a Mr. Newton, a Mr. Yancy, and a Mr. Milner, bought up a large plantation in the vicinity with the view of cutting it up for sale in small tracts. These men created a new tab for the place by taking the first two letters of their respective names to make up the present Neyami.

Another south Georgia town that is said to have been contrived from a personal name is Nahunta, the county seat of Brantley County. This name like Neyami has the air of an Indian word. Indeed, the writer believes it *is* Indian but seemingly he is the only one who holds that view. Nahunta is commonly said to have originated because a man named N. A. Hunter once owned a sawmill at the place which was served by a rail siding. The train crews began referring to the place as "N. A. Hunter's," and gradually this expression evolved into Nahunta and was applied to the whole community which had previously been called Victoria. This version may be correct, but it is open to doubt. There is some reason for believing the name was brought to Georgia by North Carolina turpentine and lumber people, who hailed from a village called Nahunta that lies between Raleigh and Goldsboro, N.C. This place in turn derives its name from a large nearby swamp called Nahunta. The name has been in use since colonial days and is seemingly of Tuscarora Indian origin. Since it is known that numbers of North Carolinians immigrated to lower Georgia to engage in lumbering and turpentining, there are grounds for believing some of them came from the Nahunta of that state and brought the name with them.[7]

A word that has the appearance of being improvised from a personal name is FDR, the designation for a school site in middle Seminole County. The letters offhand give the impression of representing the well-known initials of President Franklin D. Roosevelt. Actually, however, the tab arose from a combination of the initials of three names in a consolidation of schools.[8] These schools were formerly at Fairchild, Desser, and Reynoldsville in Seminole County. When the three institutions were merged into one operation, a name was developed for the new site by taking the first letter of each of the older places.

A considerable number of fish ponds and lakes in recent years have been given coined designations that seem to be made up from personal names. Ca Lera Lake in southeast Cobb County is a good illustration of such terms.[9]

It may surprise the reader to learn that several coined designations have actually been created from Indian names. The best known fabrication in this respect is Muckafoonee, a large stream that enters Flint River on the upper side of Albany. The appellation plainly represents a merging of elements from Muckalee and Kinchafoonee, the names for two big creeks that unite not far above Albany to form the Muckafoonee. The latter word has been in use for years, although historically the lower end of the united streams was formerly regarded as the Kinchafoonee because it is larger than the Muckalee.

Muckafoonee is purely a white man's improvisation. It has no meaning in the Muskogee language. There are explanations, however, for the component names that were used to make it up. Colonel Benjamin Hawkins mentioned Muckalee and said it meant "pour upon me."[10] This interpretation has been questioned by students of the Creek tongue. But these individuals themselves have confused the matter by offering some rather far-fetched substitute explanations. One writer contended the word is the same as the Cherokee Amicolola, as found in the name of the beautiful falls in upper Dawson County. In contrast to Muckalee, Kinchafoonee is easier to explain. It means mortar bone (i.e., pestle, or pounding block) from the Muskogee *kitcho*, mortar, plus *funi* (or "foonee"), bone. One can be positive of this translation, although it may leave the reader wondering how the initial element got turned from Kitcho into Kincha, or rather "Kinchee," to say the form as it is actually pronounced by hundreds of people. The transmutation was unquestionably made to get a smoother word. *Kitchofuni* is simply not as euphonious as Kinchafoonee or Kincheefoonee.[11] The switch brings out the point that in numbers of cases early white people slightly changed some Indian words to achieve a more pleasing sound. This smoothing process was carried out with both Muskogee and Cherokee terms.

Another improvised Indian name is Penhoopee, an old school site and former station on the Georgia and Florida Railroad, located to the southwest of Oak Park in Emanuel County. The exact connotation or intended meaning is not known. The spot is not far from the Ohoopee River and seemingly contains elements of that name. Despite the fact, however, that the Ohoopee, or 'Hoopee, is one of Georgia's oldest Indian terms, the significance of the name is not clear. The *pen* element in Penhoopee may be an English form, or it may be from the Muskogee *pinewa*, meaning turkey. We find a portion of the latter word in Pennahatchee Creek in southern Dooly County. This last name signifies Turkey Stream Creek.

One of the most singular Indians words in Georgia may be a coined term. This name is Ochlawilla, the designation for a church in extreme southeast Brooks County, near the Florida line. The name is unusual because it seemingly is the only indigenous word in the state that now retains the Hitchitee form *okla*,[12] signifying people, or even town. The *willa* element of the expression perhaps was borrowed from the nearby Withlacoochee River. Basically this last Creek name is identical in origin with that of Willacoochee, another Georgia stream in Irwin County. As has been brought out elsewhere in these sketches the Withlacoochee in early years was also referred to as the Willacoochee.[13] Withlacoochee and Willacoochee both signify Little River. Perhaps, then, Ochlawilla was intended to mean something like Little River People, or Little Riverians, or Little River Town. This assumption, however, is tenuous. Most likely the name was simply coined by the people who applied it to provide an attractive Indian expression for their church. The writer has never encountered anyone who could give a good explanation of the origin of Ochlawilla. The word is so intriguing, further effort will be made to ascertain the meaning or intended significance of the word, and if these attempts are successful, the results will be reported in these sketches.

Centralhatchee, the name of a village and creek in northern Heard County, is a possible coined, pseudo-Indian word. It would properly fall into this category if it were a hybrid expression, consisting of the English *"central,"* plus the Muskogee *håchi* (or "hatchee") meaning a stream. The waterway was not listed as Centralhatchee by the original surveyors who laid off the area of present Heard in 1827, so presumably the tab was devised after that time. There is a possibility that the word is not actually an invented form but a garbled Indian name. It may be derived from the Muskogee *sundal*, perch, plus *håchi*. In this case, of course, it would have meant Perch Creek. What is even more likely, however, the "Central" element is an English translation of the Muskogee *chåbba* (or "chubbuh") signifying middle, halfway, central, or intermediate. The full Muskogee designation for the stream would have been *håchichåbå* (or "hatcheechubbuh," "hatcheechubbee," and so on), signifying Middle Creek, or in this instance Central Creek. The white people who thought up the name might well have translated *chåbå* as "Central" and attached it to the Indian *hatchee*. In doing so, however, it should be noted they switched the

Some Coined Names / 123

position of the modifier to place it properly according to the English language.[14]

Since this periodical is primarily published for the benefit of the geologists and mining people, it might interest the readers from those fields to know that there are some coined words which pertain to their areas. One of these is Oredell, an iron-ore shipping point on the Southern Railway in northwest Polk County. Rockalo in northwest Heard is another such name; and Flexatile, on U.S. 411 in Bartow County is possibly another. The most important name by far in this group, however, is Rockmart in eastern Polk County.

There are some improvised names that can not be easily categorized. One interesting appellation in this respect is Adel, the county seat of Cook County. The word is said to be derived from the middle portion of Philadelphia. The writer is not positive that this derivation is correct, but he has been assured by people who should know that such is the case.[15]

On the basis of one authority, Villanow, a village in southeast Walker County, is another coined word. According to James Alfred Sartain, historian of Walker County, the term was proposed by a Mrs. Constantine Woods at the time when a name was needed for a prospective post office which was to be established at the site. Since the place was then no longer a mere hamlet but a village, Mrs. Woods suggested that the community be called Villanow. This proposal was accepted and the designation has been used since that time.

On the other hand, another version of the origin of Villanow holds that the appellation is not a made-up term at all, but that it came from Jane Porter's novel *Thaddeus of Warsaw*,[16] wherein Villanow was the title of a magnificent palace on the banks of the Vistula and the favorite residence of King John Sobieski of Poland. The writer does not know which of these explanations is correct. Jane Porter's book was widely read a century ago, at the time Villanow's name was adopted here. Perhaps, while Mrs. Woods proposed the word, she was actually influenced by the name used in the novel.

As indicated in the beginning, this sketch by no means intended to exhaust the roster of coined names in Georgia. There is still a substantial number which could have been mentioned. Most of these words have been omitted in the discussion because no explanations could be developed for them or inklings obtained to throw light on their meanings. Possibly it will be of interest to list a few of these remaining names to let the reader know about them and their locations:

Captolo, an old community in lower Screven County.
Cliponreka, an old school site in northeast Bulloch.
Clopine, on Georgia 7, in extreme southeast Peach County, between Fort Valley and Perry.
Imlac, on the Atlantic Coast Line, in eastern Meriwether.
Persico, on Georgia 85, in southeast Meriwether, between Woodbury and Manchester.
Posco, in Polk County, near the Bartow line.
Saco, a crossroads in eastern Mitchell.
Slygo, a cove and ridge in Dade County.

The last two names are interesting because they can be found elsewhere in the United States. *The Official Guide of the Railways* shows there are five Sacos in the country that are railroad stations: in Alabama, California, Minnesota, Montana, and Pennsylvania. Seemingly the word, like some of those previously mentioned, has been a favored designation in station-naming. Curiously enough, though, Georgia's Saco is not on a rail line. The same source does not list any Slygo stations but does show three Sligos: in Alabama, Colorado, and Pennsylvania. Apparently Georgia spells such words with a *y* instead of an *i*; for instance, Clyo in Effingham County is written with a *y*, whereas in other states the word is spelled Clio.[17]

—*GMNL* 10(1957): 56-59

NOTES

1. The places which are discussed can be found in the following sources: maps and schedules of *The Official Guide of the Railways;* topographical sheets for Georgia of the U.S. Geological Survey; county road maps issued by the Georgia Highway Department; map of Georgia issued by the U.S. Geological Survey, edition of 1933, reprinted 1944; *Geologic Map of Georgia,* 1939, by the Georgia Department of Mines, Mining and Geology; soil maps that have been prepared for many Georgia counties by the U.S. Department of Agriculture in cooperation with the State College of Agriculture; and the series of various county maps, published *circa* 1910, by the Hudgins Company of Atlanta.

2. [Fredonia exists all over the United States, and clearly goes back to the coinage of Dr. Samuel Latham Mitchell of New York in 1803 of "freedom" plus the simulated Latin suffix *-ia.* It has been a common source for folk etymological stories: Fredonia in Kentucky is said to have been a prophecy of abolition made around 1830 and applied to a black girl, Free Donia; whereas in Arizona "free doña" is explained as a Spanish hybrid applied to Mormon wives escaping governmental persecution across the Utah line. As a town name the first Fredonia was presumably that of New York. See Allen Walker Read, "Proposed Names for the United States," a paper read at the Modern Language Association, Dec. 28, 1937 (from a typescript in FLU's possession generously provided by Professor Read); see also FLU, "A Survey of American Place-Names,"

Proceedings of the Ninth International Congress of Onomastic Sciences, ed. J. M. Dodgson (Louvain, 1969), pp. 455-63. *FLU.*]

3. Bidawee is the name of a fish pond in McDuffie County, to the east of Thomson. Happy Hollow is the name of a crossroads in the same county, located in the southwest part, at the juncture of Briar and Sweetwater creeks. This community in post-Revolutionary years was the site of a noted place called the Sweetwater Iron Works. Hopeulikit is a point in upper Bulloch County. Lake Shangri-La is a fishing pond in Clayton County, located a mile or so to the north of Clayton.

4. Letter dated June 7, 1957, from Mr. H. G. Edmondson of Ringgold. Mr. Edmondson is General Agent in Chattanooga for the N. C. & St. L. Railway. The author is much indebted to him for information about other placenames in northwest Georgia.

5. Mr. Frank Jones of Bainbridge. Mr. Jones is well informed about the history and geography of southwest Georgia. The writer on numbers of occasions has benefited from Mr. Jones's wide knowledge of his region.

6. Letter to the author, July 3, 1956.

7. [Stewart, *American Place Names*, p. 316, agrees on the borrowing of the Georgia Nahunta from the North Carolina swamp, and derives it with a query from a Tuscarora (Iroquoian) word for tall trees. William S. Powell, *The North Carolina Gazetteer* (Chapel Hill: University of North Carolina Press, 1968), p. 344, thinks the name comes from Tuscarora *kahunshe wakena*, black creek. We still seem to be in the realm of guesswork. *FLU.*]

8. Letter dated May 23, 1957, from Mr. N. P. Malcolm, Superintendent of Seminole County Schools, Donalsonville. [One would like to see more of this letter, to see whether FDR was applied to the school so early that it was impossible to have at least a reinforcement from Franklin D. Roosevelt's political career, which began as early as 1920. One is suspicious of information conveyed as late as 1957, though not necessarily of the conveyer. The somewhat striking shift of stature of President Roosevelt in Southern eyes during his long term in office may have played a part in shifting the explanation of the school name. One would expect some tendency to honor the most famous patron of the Warm Springs Foundation in Georgia. If the name comes from the three consolidated schools, as the letter states, it may well have been reinforced by the notable eponym at some time in its career. *FLU.*]

9. [The derivation of Ca Lera Lake from a personal name is queried (by Goff?) in the margin of our copy, and by both editorial readers. Stewart, *American Place Names*, p. 71, derives an Oklahoma Calera from a personal name Cali, and an Alabama Calera from the Spanish word for lime-kiln. Was there a lime-kiln at the Georgia lake? *FLU.*]

10. Benjamin Hawkins, *A Sketch of the Creek Country In the Years 1798 and 1799* (Americus, Ga.: Americus Book Co., 1938), p. 61.

11. *Kitchofuni* could have referred either to a pestle or to a pounding block. The Creeks employed both objects. The former was made of stone and used to pulverize or grind materials like paint pigments; while the latter was a fairly heavy device of wood that was used with a hollowed log to pound maize into meal and grits.

12. *Okla* is also the Choctaw word for people. It is here attributed to the Hitchitees because they lived in the area of Ochlawilla and because there were some similarities between their language and the Choctaw tongue. The former Indians resided in South Georgia, whereas the Choctaws were not inhabitants of this state.

The state of Oklahoma contains the *okla* form but the word in this instance is Choctaw, signifying red people, from *okla* people, plus *huma* or *homa*, red. Georgia uses

126 / Placenames of Georgia

oklahoma, but only as an imported name, e.g., Oklahoma, a street and railroad station in Waycross.

13. See sketch no. 11, "Withlacoochee and Willacoochee," above.

14. [Read, *IJAL* 15 (1949): 132, confirms the derivation of Centralhatchee from Creek *sandalakwa*, perch (a fish); it should be Sundalhatchee. A clear case of folk etymology. Read says nothing about the *chabba*, middle, possibility. *FLU*.]

15. [The derivation of Adel from Philadelphia seems rather far-fetched. Oregon's Adel is from a woman's name; Iowa's Adell is probably "a dell." See Stewart, *American Place Names*, p. 3. *FLU*.]

16. [Goff refers to Sartain's *History of Walker County, Georgia* (Dalton: A. J. Showalter Co., 1932), 1: 279, for the Woods naming, and to Jane Porter, *Thaddeus of Warsaw* (Philadelphia: Lippincott, 1878), pp. 21, 25, 39. Stewart, *American Place Names*, p. 512, believes Villanow to be a blend of "villa-now" with the Porter character; he appears to be merging Goff's two explanations. *FLU*.]

17. Stewart, *American Place Names*, p. 416, mentions a Saco in Maine and another in New Hampshire from Algonquin "river-mouth, outlet of stream." We would not expect an Algonquin etymon in this region. Slygo may well be from the Irish town of Sligo. The *-co* words, Goff is implying, suggest a corporation or "company" name. A marginal note adds "Silko in Camden" County to the group. But see No. 65. *FLU*.]

No. 42
Stitchihatchie or Tickeehatchee Creek, and Whitley Branch

Stitchihatchie Creek arises on the edge of Chester in northern Dodge County and flows east through Laurens, past Dexter, to enter Rocky Creek to the southwest of Dublin. This name is undoubtedly of Creek Indian origin because it contains the word *hatchie* (a variant of *hâchi*) which signifies a stream in that language. The *stitchi* element, however, was long a puzzle and stumbling block in determining the significance of the appellation because no satisfactory explanation for *stitchi* could be derived from available Muskogee or Creek word lists.

Eventually, though, the little problem was solved by consulting the early land plats for Wilkinson County, from which Dodge and Laurens were created. These plats were prepared from the official surveys made in 1806-1807, after the area in question had been acquired from the Creeks. These records show that the Stitchihatchie was not originally known by that designation but was called Tickehachee[1] or Tickee hatchee.[2] Somehow over the years these earlier forms were garbled and this shift turned the name into a version which could not be fully translated.

Tickehachee and Tickee hatchee, though, are meaningful and are easy to interpret. They can be translated into Crossing Creek, or Fording Creek, or maybe simply Ford Creek, from the Muskogee *tiken*, a crossing or a fording point, plus *hâchi*, a stream. Presumably the waterway was so named because it was crossed by some prominent trail of the redskins.

We should not leave Stitchihatchie Creek without a word about its present main tributary, Whitley Branch. This little affluent also underwent a change in name. On the original 1806 survey of District 18 of Wilkinson[3] (now Laurens), it was marked Miller's Branch, and seemingly was named for James Miller, one of the chain carriers who assisted Thomas Cooper, the surveyor, in laying off the district. This naming of wilderness streams after chain bearers was a fairly common practice of the district surveyors, especially in the areas from central Georgia westward to the Chattahoochee. Although Miller's Branch has been dropped in favor of Whitley Branch, numbers of these English family names are still retained by the streams to which they were originally applied by the surveyors. These appellations offer interesting possibilities for these sketches and in time some of them will be discussed.

It is not known when the name Whitley Branch was substituted for Miller's Branch.[4]

—*GMNL* 10(1957): 59

NOTES

1. District 18, Wilkinson County, survey of 1820, Thomas Cooper, D.S., Platbook KK, Land Records of Georgia, Surveyor General Department, Atlanta. The stream is labelled "Tickehachee" in land lots 4, 6, 7, 8, 9, 22, 23, *passim*.

2. District 19, Wilkinson County, survey of 1807, H. Walton, D.S., Platbook LL. The creek is marked "Tickee hatchee" in lots 7, 24, 25, 36, *passim*.

3. District 18, Wilkinson County, lots 88, 93, 97, 123, *passim*.

4. [Read derives Stitchihatchie from Creek *isti*, man, and *chati*, red, i.e., red Indian, with *hachi* for creek. Tickeehachi is Creek *atiki*, border; cp. Alabama's Talladega, border town. Here the folk etymologizing occurs between two Indian names, as with English Welsh rabbit, rewritten as Welsh rarebit. *FLU*.]

No. 43
Gopher Town ("Go' Town") and Goat Town

Gopher Town, or "Go' Town" as the place is sometimes called, is a crossroads on Georgia 39, below Donalsonville in central Seminole County. According to a good informant,[1] the name was derived from the fact that an enormous gopher was once killed in the vicinity and its dried shell hung over the door of the community store. The term gopher in this case does not refer to any of the various species of western rodents, but to a burrowing land turtle *(Xerobates polyphemus)*, which can be found on the lower Coastal Plain. The creatures are sometimes caught and their flesh used as food.

Goat Town is the name of a store and road intersection, located on the west side of Deepstep in northwest Washington County. The store owner at the site once kept a large flock of goats in a nearby pasture. Sometimes the animals would escape and block the roads, much to the vexation of vehicle drivers. Some local wag then started calling the store Goat Town and the name has endured.[2]

—*GMNL* 10(1957): 59-60

NOTES

1. Letter to the author, dated May 23, 1957, from Mr. N. P. Malcom, Superintendent of Seminole County Schools.
2. Letter from Mr. Hillard Veal of Deepstep, dated June 5, 1957.

No. 44
Iron Hill (and a former "Deer Lick")

In laying off the various land acquisitions of the state of Georgia, the original surveyors were customarily directed to note and record the names and courses of streams, location of trails, and such other matters as might seem to be worth mentioning. The surveyors responded to this mandate with varying degrees of completeness and exactness. One district surveyor who arouses particular admiration for his keen observations and faithfulness in reporting what he saw was Levin

Wailes who had charge of surveying District 2 of original Baldwin County in the surveys of 1804.[1] The writer is not able or qualified to pass upon the accuracy with which Wailes ran the courses and boundaries of his district and land lots, but from the standpoint of detail about physical objects he left us one of the finest records for historical geography that can be found in the old land documents of this state.

Carefully noted, for example, were all of the streams, shoally places, and even the sites of head springs. In one instance, in lot 304 of District 2, he named and depicted a "Deer Lick." This notation constitutes a rare reference to such a spot in the early official land records of Georgia. At another place in lots 447 and 457, he outlined a "Rock about one mile in circumference." This large outcrop was in today's Putnam County, on the west side of the Oconee, and nearly opposite the point where the present boundary between Greene and Hancock reaches the east side of the river.

Perhaps the most interesting place which Wailes portrayed was Iron Hill. He showed the formation on the edges of lots 41 and 42 of District 2 and named it in both lots. The site of this hill is in present northwest Baldwin County, to the south of Little River and very near today's boundary between Jones and Baldwin counties.

Two other Georgia places bearing the name Iron Hill are: (1) a crossroads located about three miles southwest of Dearing in McDuffie County, on a divide between Headstall and Fort creeks; and (2) a church and road intersection situated to the north of Acworth, on Georgia 293, in southeast Bartow County, just above the Cobb line.

—*GMNL* 10(1957): 60

NOTE

1. District 2, Baldwin County, survey of 1804, Levin Wailes, D.S., Platbook EE, Land Records of Georgia, Surveyor General Department, Atlanta.

No. 45
Social Circle, Society Hill, Social Hill, Merry Hill, Fancy Hill, Fancy Bluff, Fancy Hall, Jolly (and Fashion)

One of Georgia's most widely known placenames is borne by Social Circle, a town in lower Walton County. The name is one of a category of kindred appellations, but Social Circle is by far the best-known designation in the group because it appears on most maps of the state and is also listed in the *United States Official Postal Guide* and in *The Official Guide of the Railways*. These listings permit an easy spotting by placename students. Furthermore, Social Circle was once much publicized by a Supreme Court case of some sixty-odd years ago when the town became the center of a freight-rate controversy of national importance in which some railroads challenged a finding of the then relatively new Interstate Commerce Commission.[1] The court's decision in this instance indirectly gave rise to another challenge of the commission's powers,[2] with the result that Social Circle's name was much mentioned and repeated across the country for a period of years.

Social Circle is a pioneer community that was founded in the 1820's at an intersection of two former Indian country thoroughfares[3]—the Hightower Trail that led westward from the Apalachee River to Cherokee settlements on the Etowah River; and the "Rogue Road" which ran southward through Walton County along, or close along, today's Georgia 11. At a point a little below Social Circle it connected with a path to a crossing on the Ocmulgee River below present Jackson Lake, thence southwestward to Coweta Falls, now Columbus.

The exact manner in which Social Circle received its name is not known. Tradition holds that a group of people met at the place and, aided by stimulation from a keg or bottle, decided to name the convivial spot Social Circle. This explanation could well be correct, but there is a possibility that the name was simply brought from Bulloch County and applied to the place in Walton because Eleazer Early's map of 1818 shows an older Social Circle in the former county.[4] This earlier place was possibly in existence for a considerable period before Walton County was opened for settlement in 1820 because an 1807 land plat for Bulloch County shows a route marked "Road to the Circle."[5]

The listing of a Social Circle in Bulloch on an 1818 map demonstrates then that the designation has been known in Georgia for many years. Indeed, as noted, the appellation belongs in a category of names that has long been used in Georgia and other states. Here and there, for instance, across the country one can find similar names on maps or in records: Alabama, Society Hill; Arkansas, Fancy Hill; Connecticut, Long Society; Kansas, Fancy Creek; Kentucky, Fancy Farm and Quality Valley; Maryland, Society Hill; New York, Cream Street, Fancy and Fancy Hill; Ohio, Socialville; and in Pennsylvania, Society Hill and Social Hall. South Carolina uses this type of name in at least three instances: she has a Society Hill, that is as well-known as Georgia's Social Circle; and in addition, U.S. 78 through St. George, South Carolina, is locally known as Society Street; while in the older part of Charleston ("above" Broad Street!) there is still another Society Street.

But back to Georgia, this state apparently has used a longer list of these names than any other area, and this bent commenced in colonial years. For example, the earliest such designation that could be located was "Merry hill spring branch," which was mentioned in 1766 as being on the north [east] side of the Great Ogeechee.[6] Apparently the name has long since disappeared and it is not possible to identify the stream today. Another such name that has disappeared was Social Hill, which is shown on an 1852 map of Georgia.[7] This place was located to the north of present Alpharetta, above Cooper Sandy Creek, between Old Bethany Church and Fields Crossroads.

Most of the Georgia names in this category, however, are still in use. There is a Society Hill Church and community in eastern Crawford County, below Deep Creek, and some nine miles southeast of Roberta. There are at least three *fancy* places in the state. One of these is Fancy Bluff, a community that is located across from Brunswick, between South Brunswick River and the Little Satilla. A stream, Fancy Bluff Creek, skirts the edge of the bluff and connects the two rivers mentioned. Fancy Bluff is an old place and was important enough to be named a post office in 1830, with John Anderson as the postmaster.[8] Another such place is Fancy Hall, located on a rise along the north bank of the Midway River in lower Bryan County. The spot is nearly opposite the site of Old Sunbury in Liberty County. And finally, there is a Fancy Hill on U.S. 411 in Murray County, above Crandall.

Two final appellations which should be mentioned in connection with the *social* and *fancy* names are Jolly, a village on the Southern

Railway in northwest Pike County; and Fashion, a crossroads point in Murray County, to the northwest of Eton and to the southwest of Crandall. According to Miss Lizzie R. Mitchell, the former name was adopted in 1886 when the railroad was being built through the point which became Jolly.[9] The railway people asked the citizens of the community to propose a name for the new place. Several individuals offered possible designations, but a newcomer to the area, a laborer, noting the good humor of the people in the locality, suggested Jolly as a name and this proposal was adopted.[10] No explanation can be offered about the origin of Fashion, but the tab is an interesting name and one ventures a guess that it properly belongs in the category of the *social* and *fancy* names.

—*GMNL* 11(1958): 31-32

NOTES

1. *C.N.O. & T.P. Railway Co.* v. *I.C.C.*, 162 U.S. 184 (1896), the Social Circle Case.
2. *I.C.C.* v. *C.N.O. & T.P. Railway Co.*, 167 U.S. 479 (1897), the Maximum Rate Case.
3. The writer wishes to express his appreciation to Mrs. Robert S. Sams of Monroe, Ga., for information about Social Circle and other placenames of Walton County.
4. Eleazer Early, *Map of the State of Georgia* (Savannah and Philadelphia, 1818); Social Circle is shown a slight distance to the east of Statesboro.
5. Land of Nicholas Aneiaux, Bulloch County, survey of 1807, Platbook WW, p. 61, Land Records of Georgia, Surveyor General Department, Atlanta.
6. Allen D. Candler, *Colonial Records of Georgia* (Atlanta: Franklin, 1904-1916), 9: 632, petition of James Bowey to the Council, meeting of Sept. 2, 1766.
7. Wm. G. Bonner, *Pocket Map of the State of Georgia* (Milledgeville, 1852).
8. Record of the Post Office Department—Record Group 28, Records of Appointments of Post Masters—1827-1844, microfilm copy from the National Archives in the Georgia Department of Archives and History.
9. Lizzie R. Mitchell, comp., *"History of Pike County Georgia, 1822-1932"* (scrapbook, 1933), pp. 94-95, on file in Georgia Department of Archives and History, 975.8 (Pike).
10. *Ibid.*, p. 95.

No. 46
Bloody Branch (Bloody Creek)

The Bloody Branch is a small stream that arises a few miles to the northwest of Burnt Fort in Charlton County and flows southward to join the right side of Great Satilla River a short distance below the old fort site.[1] The name is one of the rarest designations in the state because it seems to be the only remaining appellation which commemorates an Indian massacre on the frontiers of Georgia. There are numbers of places here where Indian attacks are known to have occurred, such as Greensboro, Traders Hill, Kettle Creek, and so on, but the names of these places are peaceful enough on their faces and contain no inkling that the localities were once the terrifying scenes of depredations by marauding bands of red warriors. A trail crossing on Bloody Branch, however, was the setting of an incident which shocked people so that the event (if not the particulars of the affair) are remembered to this day. The site is some two miles west of Burnt Fort, at almost exactly the same spot where present Georgia 252 now crosses Bloody Branch.[2]

Several stories which differ as to details have been offered to explain how Bloody Branch received its name, but a sworn deposition in the Georgia Department of Archives and History tells in simple words about the event which gave rise to the name.[3] This document, dated Cumberland Island, November 7, 1802, was filed by a Mrs. Elizabeth Turner as a claim against the Creek Indians for property losses that were sustained in the incident. At the time, in March, 1794, Mrs. Turner was then the wife of James Keene, and apparently, she, her husband and four children, with their stock and personal effects were moving to a new location. According to the statement, when the party reached the stream which became the Bloody Branch, a group of twenty Indians suddenly attacked them, killed Keene and one child, and seized all of the property consisting of some 20-25 head of cattle, five horses, and a wagon.

The deposition specifically states that the stream where the incident occurred had since come to be known as the Bloody Branch.[4]

Mrs. Turner does not say how she and the remaining children got out of their predicament. Presumably the Indians fled with their loot and escaped into the safety of nearby Spanish Florida. The trail which the Keenes were following had several connections to crossings on the St. Marys River to the south. One of these incidentally, was the

Ghost Hole Ford, which is located a little over a mile above present Moniac in lower Charlton County. This spot is also said to have derived its name from a frontier killing. People living thereabouts say the incident involved a stage coach hold-up in which the driver was shot. It is possible that the affair also involved Indians, because the Seminoles hung out in the area until the 1830's. Anyhow, the citizens aroundabout say the Ghost Hole Ford is a haunted site and that after nightfall one can hear shots, screams, and the wild threshing of frightened horses at the old place. The Ghost Hole Ford is a good subject for further treatment in these sketches and the author plans to write more about it when he gets around to the "Boogery" names, of which there is a profusion in Georgia.

In addition to the Bloody Branch, Georgia also once had a Bloody Creek, which is shown in a 1793 land plot as a tributary of the north fork of the Oconee River, in old Franklin County.[5] The name has long since disappeared and the stream which once bore the title cannot now be identified. No details have yet been turned up to indicate how the creek received the name.

—GMNL 11(1958): 32-33

NOTES

1. The writer wishes to express his appreciation to Mrs. Mary Givins Bryan, Director of the Georgia Department of Archives; to Miss Beatrice Lang of Woodbine, Ga.; and to Mr. Perry Barber of Harriet Bluff, Camden County, for information about the Bloody Branch.

2. A land plat dated June, 1794, names Bloody Branch and shows the trail and crossing where the Indian murder must have taken place. The route is virtually identical in course with today's Georgia 252. Cf. land of Randolph McGillis, Platbook CC, p. 383, Land Records of Georgia, Surveyor General Department, Atlanta.

3. "Indian Depredations" (manuscript), 4: 51, Department of Archives and History.

4. *Ibid.* [Marginal notes suggest that Keene should be Greene. *FLU.*]

5. Land of Malichi Jones, Franklin County, survey of 1793, Platbook CC, p. 160.

No. 47
Salacoa Creek

Salacoa Creek heads on the slopes of Rich Mountain in southwest Pickens County and flows in a westerly direction across Cherokee, Bartow, and Gordon to enter the Coosawattee River to the north of Red Bud in the last-named county. Much of the stream's upper course traverses a rugged region except in northern Cherokee where its margins widen into an interesting mountain-locked area called Salacoa Valley.

The name, pronounced "Sallacoee," or "Sallycoee" by many old people, is of Cherokee origin and signifies silk grass place or bear grass place. Other meanings, such as greasy corn and great corn have been advanced to explain the name,[1] but one can be sure of the interpretation given above, although there is doubt about the scientific designation of the actual plant that gave rise to the name. In October of 1798 Colonel Benjamin Hawkins travelled along the stream and mentioned it several times in his "Viatory," a log which he kept of his journeys in the Indian country. He called the creek the "Sa, le, quo, heh—Silke grass."[2]

James Mooney, the noted Cherokee scholar, also mentions the Salacoa. He spells it "Sălikwâ'yĭ" and notes that the name means bear grass, which he attributes to the *Eryngium* family.[3]

Now, in pioneer terminology silk grass and bear grass were often used as alternate terms to designate a number of fibrous plants. The best-known vegetation which bore (and in fact still bears) the dual name is the *Yucca filamentosa*. Mooney's classification of his bear grass as an *Eryngium*, on the other hand, indicates that the Salacoa did not receive its name from the *Y. filamentosa*. The next best possibility perhaps is the *Eryngium yuccaefolium*, or buttonsnake root, which is sometimes also called bear grass. This last plant, however, is offered merely as a suggestion—the matter of pinning down the exact vegetation which gave rise to the name should properly be left to some botanist who might be interested in the botanical origin of placenames. One ventures to suggest, though, that Salacoa probably referred to the leaves and not to the root of the particular silk grass or bear grass plant which was involved.

In the Cherokee version of Salacoa offered by Hawkins and Mooney, it is interesting to note that the former used the Cherokee locative suffix *hĭ*, a place, in the "heh" of his "Sa, le, quo, heh"; while the latter employed *yĭ*, another suffix that also signifies place. In the present-day pronunciations by old folks these locatives come out in the *ee* of "Sallacoee" or "Sallycoee." In translating the *hĭ* or *yĭ*, which were customarily attached to Cherokee placenames, the white people mostly converted the forms into the English word town; Brasstown, Cedartown, Frogtown, Hemptown, Squirreltown, Fightingtown, etc. So far as the writer can recall, the only case in Georgia in which a Cherokee locative was properly carried over into English is to be found in the name Spring Place in Murray County.

There was a Cherokee village named Salacoa, but some uncertainty has prevailed about its location. Mooney indicates it was on Salacoa Creek in Gordon County;[4] while John R. Swanton says it was probably in the Salacoa Community of northern Cherokee County.[5] Colonel Hawkins does not tell of the exact site of the place but he apparently supports Mooney as to the general location of the settlement. On October 14, 1798, he skirted the lower part of Salacoa Creek and passed a path to the village. He next made a note: "Sa, le, quo, heh to our right."[6] If this comment refers to the village, the spot was somewhere on the lower reaches of the creek, probably in Gordon County, because at the time of the notation Hawkins was nearing the Coosawattee River.

On some maps Salacoa is often spelled Sallacoa. This form is not supported by the original term. Hawkins, in fact, makes it plain the name should not be spelled with the *ll*. In his first notation of the name, he wrote "Sal, la, quo, a," but marked out this version and substituted "Sa, le, quo, heh."[7]

—*GMNL* 11(1958): 33-34

NOTES

1. Apparently these explanations were suggested by the fact that the Cherokee word for corn, *selu*, resembles the first elements of Salacoa.

2. Benjamin Hawkins, "A Viatory or Journal of distances and observations," MS in the Library of Congress. Trip to Etaw Woh (Etowah), beginning Oct. 5, 1798, entries for Oct. 14, 16, and 18. The last two marginal entries were made after he passed the vicinity of Salacoa Creek. Seemingly the notations were double reminders to him not to forget that "Sa, le, quo, heh" meant silk grass.

3. James Mooney, *Myths of the Cherokees*, Nineteenth Annual Report of the Bureau of American Ethnology, 1897-98 (n.p., n.d.), pt. 1, p. 530.

4. *Ibid.*

5. John R. Swanton, *The Indian Tribes of North America*, Bureau of American Ethnology Bulletin 145 (Washington, D.C., 1952), p. 220.

6. Hawkins, "Viatory," entry for Oct. 14, 1798.
7. *Ibid.* [Read, *IJAL* 16 (1950) gives equal weight to Cherokee *salikwayi* or *selikwayi*, with the meanings bear-grass or small green snake, to Cherokee *selu-egwa*, big corn, and to Cherokee *kusawetiyi*, old Creek Indian place. *FLU.*]

No. 48
Sumach and Holly Creeks

On the trip in 1798 in which Colonel Benjamin Hawkins noted Salacoa Creek he also mentioned the present Holly and Sumach (or Sumac) creeks of today's Murray County. Interestingly enough he gave Cherokee words for the streams and thus shows us that the names are actually translated versions of the Indian designations for these tributaries of the Conasauga River.

On October 16, 1798, he crossed Holly Creek at or near today's bridge on Georgia 225, above the present crossroads of Holley, and commented in a marginal note in the "Viatory" that the stream was called "Oose, tus te."[1] He added there was a great deal of holly on the right bank, and in the text of the account stated there were hollies and beeches on the north (right) side of the creek.[2]

Hawkins continued his journey and on the next day crossed the "Shewmake."[3] On the margin of the page he added a scratched version of the stream's Cherokee name.[4] The word he wrote seems to be "qual, lo, kia, ica, ie." He may have intended it, however, to be "qual, lo, kea, ica, ia." Anyhow he added the name meant "litterally, big Shoemak stream." His name does seem to contain in garbled form the Cherokee term *egawa* for big, but one can not readily see in his version of the Cherokee word *keyung* (or *uwe yûñi*) signifying stream.

—*GMNL* 11(1958): 34

NOTES

1. Benjamin Hawkins, "A Viatory or Journal of distances and observations," MS in the Library of Congress. Trip to Etaw woh (Etowah), beginning Oct. 5, 1798; entry for Oct. 16.
2. *Ibid.*
3. *Ibid.*, entry for Oct. 17.
4. *Ibid.*

No. 49
Possumtrot Branch

The Estelle Quadrangle depicts a Possumtrot Branch in Walker County, to the northwest of LaFayette.[1] The little stream arises in a cove between Shinbone Ridge and Pigeon Mountain and drains south to join Duck Creek near Marsh Crossing, in the upper part of Burnt Mill Valley. The listing in this instance is unique, because, while possum trot sites are common in many parts of Georgia, it is rare to find the name on a map. Indeed, as far as the writer can recall, the Estelle sheet is the only modern Georgia chart which shows such a place.

The name Possum Trot stems from the formative years and has long been used in Georgia for designating nondescript localities, usually inconspicuous little crossroads points. The expression is intended to be a bit derogatory in its connotation and in present terminology means approximately the same thing as our hole-in-the-road. The latter term would not have been very meaningful to the old-timer because in his days nearly every road was full of holes and no place could have been particularly disparaged by calling it a hole-in-the-road. Possum Trot was more derisive because the term did not refer to a gait or movement of the animals but rather to a remote spot where possums formed regular trails, i.e., trots, in travelling to and fro.

Perhaps the expression is also known in other parts of the country as Possum Track. One of Walt Disney's comic films showed a railroad station bearing that name.

—*GMNL* 11(1958): 34

NOTE

1. *Estelle Quadrangle,* edition of 1947, prepared by the Maps and Surveys Division of the Tennessee Valley Authority, distributed by the U.S. Geological Survey.

No. 50
Big Bend and the Panhandles

In studying lists of American geographic designations one is struck by the fact that states often make use of the same names. For instance, two of the best known tabs of Texas are Big Bend and Panhandle. Georgia uses these same names, although one must admit in advance that our places with these designations are not as big as those of Texas. The Big Bend of this state is found in lower Charlton County and is formed by the St. Marys River which heads on the southeast edge of the Okefenokee and flows south, then east and then north before turning eastward again toward the Atlantic. With respect to Panhandle, Georgia has at least three areas that carry this designation:

1. An elongated strip of southeast Warren County, lying between Brier Creek on the east, Jefferson County on the south, and Glascock County on the west. This section is officially known as Georgia Militia District No. 150, or the Panhandle;[1]

2. The extreme southwestern tip of Clayton County, bordering Flint River on the west, Henry County on the east, and Spalding on the south. This area is also officially known as the Panhandle, or Georgia Militia District No. 538;[2] and,

3. A section of upper Taylor County, lying to the northeast of Butler. The name in this instance apparently arises from the fact that Militia District No. 768 of Taylor has the approximate shape of a pan with a handle that hangs down as a narrow strip between two other militia districts, No. 741 to the east and 757 to the west and south.[3]

—GMNL 11(1958): 34-35

NOTES

1. *Warren County Georgia* (State Highway Board of Georgia, 1939).
2. *Clayton County Georgia* (State Highway Board of Georgia, 1940).
3. *Taylor County Georgia* (State Highway Board of Georgia, 1940). [These Panhandles are clearly "map-names," bestowed not because of visible geography but because new settlers moved by the map. Compare Long Island, and possibly Oregon, in Stewart, *Names on the Land*, pp. 69, 153. FLU.]

140 / Placenames of Georgia

No. 51
Okefenokee

Some of Georgia's most unusual placenames—Prairie, Territory, House, The Pocket, Jackson's Folly, etc.—are used in connection with the noted Okefenokee Swamp. These appellations offer interesting possibilities for this series of sketches and in time it is hoped they can be discussed. In this little essay attention will be confined to the word Okefenokee because all too commonly that distinctive name is subject to flowery misinterpretations such as land of the trembling earth, land of quivering ground, and so on. Now, because of the physical conditions prevailing in the expansive swamp, the area properly at times has been referred to in Indian words that mean both trembling earth and trembling water. The designation Okefenokee which we have formally adopted, however, translates into the last expression and does not contain an aboriginal element that signifies earth or land. Okefenokee simply and literally means water trembling from the Hitchitee *oke* (or "oki," "okih," "oka," etc.), water, and *finoca*, trembling, quivering, or shaking.

The name is here attributed to the Hitchitees because these members of the Creek Confederacy lived in south Georgia, the section in which the swamp lies. The Hitchitees spoke a dialect which differed in many respects from the true Muskogee tongue, and this difference is exemplified by their word *oke* for water. The same form is found in such other Hitchitee-derived appellations as Ocmulgee, Okapilco, and Okeewalkee. The Muskogee term for water was *wewa*, which can be found in Creek names like Wehadkee, Withlacoochee, Willacoochee, and so on. Apparently the word *finoca* for trembling or quivering was the same in each language.

In the early records it is common to see the name of the swamp spelled in aboriginal words that contain elements signifying both earth and water. For instance, Samuel Savery, a colonial surveyor and one of the first cartographers to mention the place, marked the swamp "Ekanphaenoka" on his map of 1769.[1] He noted the name meant "the Terrible Ground" and that the Indians claimed the swamp was inhabited by a race of Immortals called "Este Fatchasicko."[2] Savery's version of the name may have connoted terrible ground to the Indians, but on its face it means earth trembling, from *ikana* (or akana, ecunna, econna, akona, etc.), signifying earth, land, or ground, and *phaenoka* for trembling. The latter is merely a variant of *finoca* which in turn has become our present *fenokee.*

Colonel Benjamin Hawkins makes it clear that the trembling water and trembling earth forms were former alternative names. At one place he mentioned the swamp as "Okefinacau (quivering water)," and as "Akinfinocau (quivering earth)."[3] In another source he noted the first designation as "O-ke-fin-o-cau," and the second as "E-cun-fin-o-cau," from "E-cun-nau," earth, and "Fin-o-cau," quivering.[4] He goes on to add after the last remark that the quivering water name was most common among the Creeks. The comment is interesting because this is the version which we retain in modernized form, although we have confused its meaning by attributing an incorrect interpretation to it.

The United States Geographic Board adopted Okefenokee as the official spelling of the word,[5] and the Geological Survey follows this version in its maps. This is a pleasing rendition, although one could justifiably argue that Okefinokee would be closer to the original Indian expression.

Before we formalized the name into Okefenokee, there were many variants of the appellation. In a study of maps and accounts showing the word Albert Hazen Wright found 77 different spellings in 192 sources.[6] His list of names, covering the period from 1763 to 1921, contains a diversity of forms like: Owaquephenogaw, Oquafanoka, Eokenfonoghka, Oofunooka, Okeefernokee, and so on in great variety. This roster contains terms that can be translated into both the trembling water and quivering earth renditions of the name, with a predominance of the former.

Curiously enough, some people who live around the fringes of the swamp, and especially on the Florida side, employ unusual pronunciations of the name. They pronounce it "Okeefeenoak," or "Oakfeenoak." In addition to marking a departure from the generally accepted way of saying the word, these versions also ignore the euphonic and poetic qualities of such a beautiful expression as *Okefenokee.*[7]

GMNL 11(1958): 54-56

NOTES

1. "Sketch [Chart] of the Boundary Line between the Province of Georgia and the Creek Nation," 1769, original in the William L. Clements Library, Ann Arbor, Mich.

2. This interesting Muskogee expression is easy to translate, and literally it has exactly the opposite meaning of "immortal" in the common understanding of that English word. To correct "Este Fatchasicko" a bit, it would be *iste fâchesiko* (pronounced "eastie futchieseeko"), from *iste*, people, *fâche*, right, honest, or righteous, plus the negative form *siko*. Thus the name referred to people who were not correct or who deviated from the accepted. In the white man's way of thinking immortals are imperishable worthy figures. If Savery's "Este Fatchasicko," however, merely refers to beings who were not subject to death, the designation possibly could be construed as signifying immortal. It might be noted that even now there are individuals who believe spirits inhabit the Okefenokee. The swamp has a Bugaboo Island which these people insist is infested with "hants." (See Folkston Quadrangle [U.S. Geological Survey, 1942]).

3. *Letters of Benjamin Hawkins, 1796-1806*, Collections of the Georgia Historical Society, Vol. 9 (Savannah, 1916), p. 85. The comment was dated Feb. 18, 1797.

4. *A Sketch of the Creek Country in the Years 1798 and 1799*, Collections of the Georgia Historical Society, Vol. 3, pt. 1 (Savannah, 1848), p. 21.

5. *Decisions of the United States Geographic Board, July, 1913, to July, 1914* (Washington, D.C., 1914), p. 25.

6. A. H. Wright, "The Okefenokee Swamp—Its History and Cartography," *Our Georgia-Florida Frontier* (Ithaca, N.Y., 1945), pt. 1, pp. 4-7.

7. [The annotator has deleted Ocmulgee from the list in paragraph two. This is not in accordance with Read, *IJAL*, XVI (1950), 206, who derives Ocmulgee from Hitchiti *Oki* "water" and *mulgis* "it is boiling or bubbling," describing a kind of Indian Springs. *FLU.*]

No. 52
The "Sixes" Places: Sixes Old Town, Sixes District, Sixes Creek, Sixes Mine, Sixes Trail, Sutalee (and Satolah)

In Cherokee County's fascinating diversity of geographic names, three appellations that stand out are designations containing the word Sixes: *Sixes District*, or Georgia Militia District No. 1279, in the southwest part of the county; and *Sixes Creek*, which in turn was the site of the old *Sixes Gold Mine*. This former mine, situated some six miles southwest of Canton, began operations around 1831 and was one of the most noted gold-producing spots in Georgia. George White, writing in 1849, said at that period the workings had yielded $200,000 of the metal.[1] These mines were on *Sixes Branch* now called *Downing Branch* on lots 212 and 221.

These *Sixes* places derived their names from a former Cherokee settlement called *Sixes Old Town*, that was located at the juncture of the Etowah and Little River.[2] Usually maps depicting the place show it within the forks of these streams. One early official chart, however, indicates that a part of the town was on the north bank of the Etowah, opposite the main community.[3]

The site of Sixes Town is now covered by the waters of Allatoona Dam, but before this inundation the place was a pretty area of open fields, and was a part of the old original Joseph E. Brown plantation.

Not much is known about the locality—when it was founded or how it derived the name. White says 400 Indians resided in the town in 1833, and that the headman at this date was a chief named Stop.[4] The place was not an ancient Cherokee settlement, but use of the word *old* in connection with the community implies that the town had been in existence for some time when it began to be noted in the records of the 1820's and 1830's. Colonel Marinus Willet did not mention the place when he travelled through the area in 1790; nor did Colonel Benjamin Hawkins comment on it, although he journeyed through the section in 1796. These travellers came down the Etowah, but in the neighborhood of today's Canton veered away from the river to visit the Cherokee Village of Pine Log in present northeast Bartow County. They thus passed to the north of Sixes Town, and even if it existed at that time, they did not see the settlement.

There is scant documentary information to explain how the name Sixes arose, and significance of the term will have to remain largely in the conjectural stage until more evidence turns up on the subject. One can be reasonably sure, though, that the appellation is Cherokee and that it was derived from the word *sutali*, or "sutalee," meaning six. The last form is still retained in a little crossroad called Sutallee, located in the western part of Cherokee County above the Etowah, and a few miles to the northwest of the site of Sixes Old Town. Sutallee is an old community and for a considerable period was a post office.[5]

The occurrence of Sixes in the English possessive form in old records suggests that the designation applied to some prominent individual who may have been the headman of the community when it was founded. This implication in turn furnishes a clue to the possible meaning, because the Cherokees used numerals with a noun suffix title *tehe*, or "tehee," signifying killer, to indicate various gradations in a rank which those Indians used. Thus there were names like Two Killer, Three Killer, Four Killer, and so on. The title, however, was not necessarily always used in connection with a number, because there were also prominent men with such names as Path Killer, Night Killer, Creek Killer, and Chickasaw Killer.

Six Killer was a name of particular importance, not only because of its war-attainment implications, but also because the designation had a mythological meaning among the old Cherokees. James Mooney says the priests of this tribe sometimes referred to the sun or the moon as Sutalidihi or Six Killer.[6] The significance of this usage has been lost.

It might be of interest to add that the Cherokees continued to use the killer names in the West. The designations apparently have long since lost their war or ceremonial significance, and have been turned into family surnames in the English fashion. The census of the Five Civilized Tribes published in 1907, for instance, shows many killers of various kinds among the western Cherokees at that date.[7] There were more Six Killers in the listing than in any other grouping within the category. The point emphasizes again the importance of the name, but also indicates a weakness in the analysis above which tried to interpret Sixes in terms of the noted rank. Since *tehe* was an important adjunct of the name, it would seem that the title *killer* would have always been used in connection with the Sixes' name, if the designation applied to an individual and if he were really entitled to be called Sutaleetehe, or Six Killer. Perhaps white men, through a lack of understanding of the Indian order, simply called the man Six, without the important titular form. This omission could have occurred, because the whites did sometimes shorten the names of red leaders, among both the Cherokees and the Creeks.

In addition to the Sutallee in Cherokee County, there is also a little post office called *Satolah* in eastern Rabun County. The spot in fact is the most northeasterly community in Georgia. The place derives its tab from a nearby mountain named *Satolah*, but pronounced "Suh toó lah."[8] The significance of the appellation is not known; it may or may not be a variant of Sutalee. No evidence has been found which indicates that the suffix *tehe* has ever been used with Satolah. If such a combination could be found, the name, of course, would be translated as Six Killer.

In concluding this sketch mention should be made of *Sixes Trail* which is shown on the 1832 survey for land District 1, Section 2 of the original Cherokee County, now upper Fulton.[9] The path proper began at a trail intersection located at the present Old Lebanon Church site, on U.S. 19 above Roswell. To the south and east of that spot it

The "Sixes" Places / 145

had several connections to crossings on the Chattahoochee. Some of these passages were early ferrying points. The most important natural crossing place, however, was the Island Ford at the lower end of the shoals and islands, above the mouth of Big Creek and some two miles to the southeast of Roswell. The path which forded the Chattahoochee at this point had an easy connection with the Hightower Trail which was the most noted east-west aboriginal thoroughfare of this section of the state.[10]

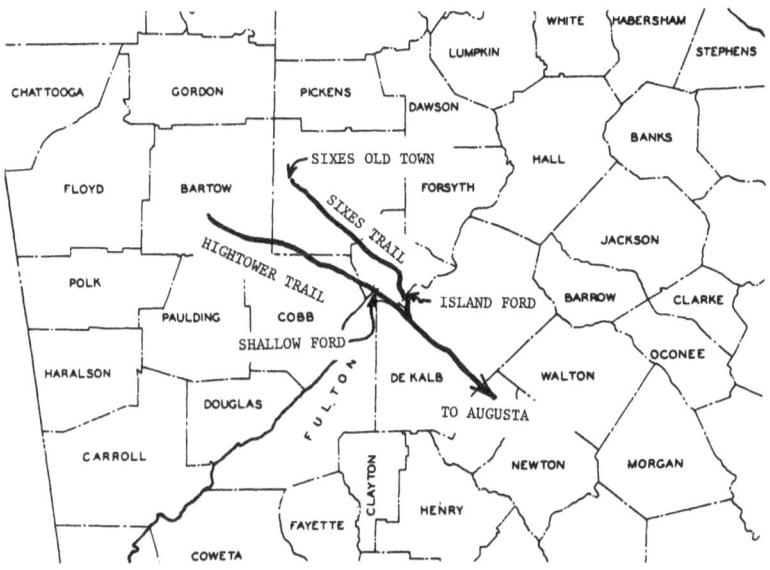

Sixes Trail and Hightower Trail

At Lebanon Church, on a course now abandoned, the Sixes Trail led northwestward on a route that roughly paralleled for a distance the present Crossville Road, which was called the *Alabama Road* in Indian days. The path to Sixes crossed today's Roswell-Crabapple Road where the Strickland Road now spurs off, then paralleled and finally crossed the Chaffin Road. It is shown leaving District 1 in the northeast corner of lot 314.[11] The surveyor for District 2 above did not name or mark the trace, but by placing a straight edge on a map between Lebanon Church and the site of Sixes settlement, one can be reasonably certain of the remainder of the course. The path continued northwest, passing to the east and north of present Mountain Park to intersect today's Cox Road, which in fact may be a remnant of the trail. It ran along this road, over Little River, thence on to Sixes Old Town via Toonigh and Cherokee Crossroads.

For those readers who read Sketch No. 31 on Four Killer Creek,[12] it might be of interest to add that Sixes Trail ran about a mile and a half to the south of Four Killer's old home place in lots 477 and 513 of District 1, Section 2. The site was in north Fulton County, to the west of today's Alpharetta, and on the west side of the stream that still commemorates *Four Killer's* name.

—*GMNL* 11(1958): 56-57

NOTES

1. George White, *Statistics of the State of Georgia* (Savannah, 1849), p. 178.

2. An official chart which shows Sixes Town is *A Map of that part of Georgia Occupied by the Cherokee Indians,* by John Bethune, surveyor general of Georgia (Milledgeville, 1831).

3. John Coffee, "Sketch [chart] of the Disputed country between the State of Georgia and the Cherokee Nation," *circa* 1830, original in the National Archives, Washington, D.C.

4. George White, *Historical Collections of Georgia* (New York, 1854), p. 390.

5. In the *United States Official Postal Guide,* No. 1 (Oct., 1874), the place is called Sutalla; in the *Guide* for 1890 it is listed as Sutallee.

6. James Mooney, *Myths of the Cherokee,* Nineteenth Annual Report of the Bureau of American Ethnology, 1897-98 (n.p., n.d.), pt. 1, pp. 257, 528. In one place (p. 257) the author says the priests called the sun Sutalidihi; while in the other comment (p. 528) he states the moon in the sacred formulas of the Cherokees was referred to as Sutalidihi, or Six Killer. It is not known whether Mooney made a slip in this instance, or if he intended to say the expression was used in referring to both the moon and the sun.

7. "Index to the Final Rolls of Citizens and Freedmen of the Five Civilized Tribes in Indian Territory," 1907, copy in the Bureau of Indian Affairs, Washington, D.C.

8. The writer is indebted to Mrs. A. J. Dillard of Dillard, Ga., for information on Satolah.

9. "Map of District I (Gold), 2nd Section of Cherokee County, October 27, 1832," N. C. Barnett, D.S., Records of the Surveyor General Department, Atlanta.

10. For a map and discussion of the Hightower Trail, see John H. Goff, "Some Major Indian Trading Paths Across the Georgia Piedmont," *Georgia Mineral Newsletter* 6 (1953): 122ff.

11. "Map of District 1, 2nd Section, Cherokee County."

12. *Georgia Mineral Newsletter* 9 (1956): 137-38. [No. 31, above.]

No. 53
Catoosa

This Cherokee name is found in the designations of Catoosa County of northwest Georgia, on the Tennessee line; and in an old community in the eastern part of that county called *Catoosa Springs.* A small stream that drains the last locality is known as *Catoosa Springs Branch.* In addition to these places, there was also an early spot called *Catoosa,* which was formerly located between Amicalola in Lumpkin County and Cartecay in Gilmer.[1] The place does not appear on modern maps and it is not known if the name is still remembered by elderly people of the section.

The Cherokee word for Catoosa was *gatusĭ,* or "gahdoosi," signifying or referring to a hill, small mountain, or even a mound.[2] Fundamentally the term was an adjective employed to describe a place or locality of higher elevation than the surrounding vicinity.[3] Presumably, the name was used in connection with the Catoosa County section because of a series of ridges and small mountains that slope across the area from the northeast to the southwest.

In Catoosa County some old people pronounce the name "Catoosee," and thus preserve a form that is fairly close to the original Cherokee word. The switch from Gatusi to Catoosee was not a great change relatively compared to the garbling which many Indian names experienced from the white man. The substitution of the C for the G of Gatusi was a fairly common practice because the pioneer white people often changed a Cherokee *g* to a hard *c* or *k.* The use of *a* for the terminating *ĭ* of Gatusi represented an attempt at refinement of the name and seemingly arose because the transcribers were not certain of the correct written form that should have been used in spelling the word. In their own spoken language they often employed a final *ee* in words that properly terminated in *a:* "Augustee" for Augusta; "Georgee" for Georgia, and so on. Thus in writing down a word which ended with the Indian *ĭ* (or "ee" sound), as in the case of Gatusi and numbers of other Cherokee names, the whites were prone to convert the *ĭ* to an *a* to make sure that it was correctly spelled in accordance with what they conceived to be the proper literary form. The result in this instance gave rise to our present Catoosa instead of Catoosee.

Catoosa is a simple designation, but analysis of the word illustrates well the difficulties and pitfalls which one encounters in trying to determine the meanings of Georgia placenames of Indian origin. The first plausible meaning for the word was found in a listing of Cherokee terms prepared by Benjamin Hawkins for Thomas Jefferson.[4] In this group, Hawkins mentions the word "Ca, too, se" and states that it means wind. On the basis of such a good authority as Colonel Hawkins, one would ordinarily have been safe in assuming his "Ca, too, se" was the same as our Catoosa, particularly in view of the fact that old people in the county still say "Catoosee." Furthermore, Catoosa County has a stream with the long-established name of *Hurricane Creek*. This last designation suggested there was a possible relation between the word "Ca, too, se" for wind and the name of the waterway. But further study of the matter disclosed that Hawkins's version of "Ca, too, se" could not be substantiated, because the usual Cherokee word for wind is *unauli* (or "unawle," "unawleh," etc.), and the expression for whirlwind or hurricane is *akalugi*.

After this conflicting information developed, no further inkling of the meaning of Catoosa was encountered until receipt of the Oklahoma Semi-Centennial edition of *The Tulsa Tribune* of May 30, 1957. In this issue an item from the Oklahoma town of Catoosa says that place derived its name from a Cherokee word Gi-tu-zi, meaning People of the Light, for a clan of that name which formerly met on a hill to the west of the town. This explanation seemed a bit pretentious because one has learned that present-day people often tend to be rhetorical and fanciful in their explanations of Indian placenames.

Hesitancy to accept People of the Light as a proper interpretation of Catoosa led to correspondence with Oklahoma friends about the meaning of the word. These individuals are of Cherokee descent and have a good knowledge of the traditions and language of those Indians. They furnished the explanation which was given and cited at the beginning of the sketch.

After a satisfactory interpretation of the word had been received, it was concluded that the writer of the news item from Catoosa, Oklahoma, missed the point about the origin of his community's name. Instead of being named for the Cherokee band that met there, the place probably derived its title from the hill near the town where those people gathered.

—*GMNL* 11(1958): 57-58

NOTES

1. J. H. Young, *A New Map of the State of Georgia* (Philadelphia: Desilver, 1856).
2. The writer wishes to express his appreciation to the following for assistance in developing the meaning of Catoosa: Mrs. Mary Smith Witcher of Tulsa, Okla.; Mrs. Elizabeth Smith of Muskogee; Mrs. Lula G. Bowers and Mr. Louis Gourd of Tahlequah; and Mr. W. E. Sunday of Claremore, Okla.
3. Mr. Louis Gourd of Tahlequah, Okla.
4. "A Comparative Vocabulary of the Muskogee or Creek, Chickasaw, Chocktaw and Cherokee languages . . . by the late Col. Benj. Hawkins to Mr. Jefferson," original in the American Philosophical Society Library, Philadelphia.

No. 54
No Business Creek

No Business Creek arises near Snellville and flows southward through lower Gwinnett County to join the left side of Yellow River in extreme eastern DeKalb County. The name first appeared in the records when it was mentioned in the land plats of the 1819 survey for District 4 of original Walton County.[1] In the same year, however, the surveyor of District 6 of Gwinnett was apparently not acquainted with the name because he merely marked the stream "Waters of Yellow River."[2] Two years later, when District 16 of Henry County (now parts of DeKalb, Rockdale, and Newton) was laid off, the surveyor was familiar with the stream because he noted the name on one of his plats.[3]

The writer has known of No Business Creek for years, but he still lacks a good explanation for this unusual designation. Old people who lived near the stream used to offer two different interpretations of the name. Both of these versions concerned the noted Hightower Trail which crossed the lower extremity of the creek at what is now a fishing lake.

One of these traditional accounts went thus: The former ford of the Hightower Trail on the creek was difficult and dangerous when the stream was in flood; and people learned they had no business trying to cross the stream under such risky conditions, thus giving rise to the expression *No Business Creek*. The explanation may be correct; but if it is, the origin of the tab goes back to the days of Indian country travel, because as stated above some original surveyors noted the name when the area was being surveyed shortly after acquisition of the lands from the Creeks.

The other account of the name involves a strip of the former Hightower Path over a steep, red hill that begins on the west side of the old fording point and extends about a mile from the creek to a point near the Rock Bridge where the old trace crossed the *Yellow River*. In former years, so this version went, the hill was exceedingly difficult for a vehicle to negotiate, and one had to work like nobody's business to get over the place, especially in rainy times. This explanation seems to be an afterthought, because the label No Business was applied before wagons began to follow the Hightower Trail in the early 1820's. Furthermore, the expression nobody's business would not necessarily have turned into No Business.

No Business Creek is one of the distinctive names of Georgia and for a long time the writer thought it was the only such moniker in the country until he found a North Business Creek listed in Henry Gannett's *Gazetteer of Virginia*.[4] This discovery led to some searching which turned up a second No Business Creek, in Morgan County, Alabama, northwest of Hartselle.[5] This find in turn raised a question about Gannett's North Business Creek; perhaps he had made a slip by interpreting No as No., an abbreviation of north. Apparently there was such an error, because a reliable Virginia map disclosed that the correct designation is No Business and not North Business Creek.[6] Further study may show the name is also employed in other sections. But be that as it may, usage of the expression in such widely separated areas as Virginia, Georgia, and Alabama implies that old-timers were generally familiar with the appellation.

—*GMNL* 11(1958): 58-59

NOTES

1. District 4, Walton County, survey of 1819, E. L. Thomas, D.S., Platbook MMM, land lots 321, 333, 345, 347, 349, *passim*, Land Records of Georgia, Surveyor General Department, Atlanta.

2. District 6, Gwinnett County, survey of 1819, Joseph T. Cunningham, D.S., Platbook MMM, lots 3, 4, 15, 16, *passim*.

3. District 16, Henry County, survey of 1821, James White, D.S. Platbook CCCC. The creek is named in lot 255 at the Hightower Trail and is shown entering Yellow River at lot 226.

4. Henry Gannett, *Gazetteer of Virginia*, Bulletin 232 of the U.S. Geological Survey (Washington, D.C., 1904), p. 109.

5. *Hartselle Quadrangle: Alabama, Morgan County,* Tennessee Valley Authority, Maps and Survey Branch (1951; distributed by U.S. Geological Survey). The stream is a west-branch tributary of Flint Creek.

6. *State of Virginia* (U.S. Geological Survey, edition of 1957). The waterway arises in western Giles County and flows west to join Kimberling Creek, in Bland County, Va.

No. 55
Yonah Mountain and Sillycook Mountain

Yonah Mountain is situated in upper White County, a few miles northeast of Cleveland.[1] The name is derived from the Cherokee word *yanu* (or "yonuh," "yonung," "yawnung," etc.) signifying bear. The designation is apt, because from a distance, and especially from the south, the eminence does have the shape of a bear.

James Mooney says the proper Cherokee name for the mountain was "Gadalú lŭ," but he adds the meaning of the term was not known.[2] This point suggests the interesting thought that white people actually gave the mountain its present name but used a Cherokee word in doing so. Colonel Benjamin Hawkins passed the area of Yonah in 1796, and while he left an interesting description of the mountain, he did not offer a name for it.[3]

Sillycook Mountain lies about 11 miles to the northeast of Mt. Yonah, in northern Habersham County, near the Rabun line. On its face, Sillycook seems to be a waggish, backwoodsy name, but one can be virtually certain that it is of Cherokee origin, being derived from *saligugi,* or "saliguga," signifying turtle. Thus in English the designation means Turtle Mountain, presumably because of the shape of the formation. This interpretation is supported by the fact that a Cherokee settlement called *Turtle Town,* on the North Carolina-Tennessee boundary near the Georgia line, was also referred to as Sillikokeh in an official map.[4]

The reader may wonder at the convolutions that turned Saligugi into Sillikokeh and Sillycook, but the change was not great compared to some mutations to which Cherokee words were subjected. The most decided shift in deriving Sillycook involved a conversion of the *a* of Saligugi to an *i,* and a dropping of the final *i.* The *g*'s of the word were also converted to a hard *c* and a *k.* But as noted above in the sketch on Catoosa, the latter substitutions were fairly common in the

Cherokee names which the whites adopted. The dropping of the final vowel was justifiable, because otherwise the name might have ended up in the preposterous anglicized form Sillycookee.

—*GMNL* 11(1958): 59

NOTES

1. Both Mt. Yonah and Sillycook Mountain are shown on the *Dahlonega Quadrangle* (edition of 1903, reprinted 1951, U.S. Geological Survey).
2. James Mooney, *Myths of the Cherokees*, Nineteenth Annual Report of the Bureau of American Ethnology, 1897-98 (n.p.,n.d.), pt. 1, p. 518.
3. *Letters of Benjamin Hawkins*, Collections of the Georgia Historical Society, Vol. 9 (Savannah, 1916), p. 17, entry for Nov. 27, 1796.
4. "Map of part of the Cherokee Territory situated among the Mountains of N. Georgia and Tennessee from surveys under the direction of W. G. Williams, Capt. U.S. Topl. Engrs. in 1837 and 1838 . . . ," original in Record Group 77, Records of the Office of the Chief of Engineers, National Archives, Washington, D.C.

No. 56
Ochillee Creek and Halloca Creek

Ochillee Creek arises near Glen Alta in extreme western Marion County and flows across Chattahoochee County, through the Fort Benning Reservation, to join Upatoi Creek southeast of Columbus. On its way it passes a little railroad station that is also called *Ochillee.* The name is of interest because the present spelling does not follow the form which appeared in the first records that mention the stream and this shift has misled students who sought to translate the word. Colonel Benjamin Hawkins crossed the creek in 1797 and referred to it as the *"Nochillehatche."*[1] Eleazer Early's map of 1818 lists the waterway as the *"Nochillee,"*[2] and one of the original surveyors of the section in 1826 used substantially the same version on his plats.[3] At some period in the intervening years the word was changed to the present Ochillee. On its face *Ochillee* seems easy to translate because it appears to be a Muskogee term that signifies Dead Hickory, from *ochi,* or "ochee," hickory, and *ili,* or "ēlē," dead. This derivation, of course, could not be the true explanation of the early name since the first element of the original expression was *noch* and not *och. Noch* is from the initial syllable of the Muskogee word *nochka,* meaning sleep. Literally, then, the earlier name meant dead asleep from *noch,* sleep, plus *ili,* dead, and Hawkins's *"Nochillehatche"* thus signified Dead Asleep Creek. It is to be doubted, however, that the Creeks intended the word to have such a literal meaning. More than likely, one ventures to guess, the expression was intended to signify Sleeping Creek, or by implication, Camping Creek. This explanation could well be correct because the stream lay athwart the main strand of the famous Lower Creek Trading Path from Charleston and Augusta to the Creek towns along the middle Chattahoochee, and along the lower Tallapoosa, in present Alabama. Colonel Hawkins was travelling this route when he recorded the name *Nochillehatche.* His account lends a bit of support to the explanation of the appellation which was given above because on this journey he pitched camp near the stream on the night of December 6, 1797.[4]

Halloca Creek, an upper tributary of the Ochillee, arises to the north of the village of Ida Vesper in eastern Chattahoochee County and drains southwestward to join the main stream to the north of the present-day town of Cusseta. The name is old because the original surveyor of the area in 1826 encountered the word and recorded it on his plats and maps as "Hallokee,"[5] "Hallockee,"[6] and "Hallookee."[7] The first form, Hallokee, is identical phonetically with the current pronunciation used by many old people in Chattahoochee County.

The name *Halloca* is intriguing, because, while it is found in the heart of the old Lower Creek country, it seemingly is not of Muskogee origin. Students of Georgia Indian placenames have generally considered the word as being derived from the Choctaw expression *haloka,* signifying beloved, sacred, or dear. The occurrence of the name in Georgia, far from the Choctaws of Mississippi, is indeed a puzzle, so much so in fact, this writer initially assumed the expression might actually have been Hitchitee and not Choctaw. This assumption seemed reasonable because there are many similarities between Hitchitee and Choctaw words. Furthermore, a band of the Hitchitees once dwelt on the lower side of present Chattahoochee County, in an area not far from Halloca Creek. This possible origin was dismissed, however, because the Hitchitee term for beloved is *hola'hti,* or "holahta," and there is little chance that Halloca or Hallokee is a garbled version of that word. An explanation for the appellation was then sought in other directions. Colonel Benjamin Hawkins furnishes the best inkling which may explain why the name came to be applied in Georgia. In his letters he mentions a former Chickasaw village that was once located near the Lower Creek town of Cusseta,[8] which in turn was situated on the Chattahoochee River at the site of the air field at the western end of today's Fort Benning Reservation. The Chickasaw settlement was to the east of the Creek town, somewhere about the present headquarters area of the fort and not far from Halloca Creek. Now, the Chickasaws mainly resided in northwest Alabama, northeast Mississippi, and western Tennessee, but on several occasions small bands of them moved eastward and resided among the Creeks. Apparently the settlement near old Cusseta Town was made by one of these migrant groups. The significant reason for these comments lies in the fact that the Chickasaw and Choctaw languages are identical in most instances. *Haloka* is one of the words that is common to both tribes. And thus while placename students have usually considered the word as being Choctaw, it was probably Chickasaw and was brought here by those Indians and applied to the Halloca Creek locality.

We shall probably never know exactly how Halloca Creek, the beloved stream, received its name. But one can be sure the Indians used such expressions because Colonel Hawkins in writing about the upper stretches of Upatoi Creek (to the north of the Halloca) says the Lower Creeks once looked upon the area as a "beloved bear ground" which was reserved for hunting those animals.[9] Perhaps in a way that is not clear to us, the Creeks allowed the Chickasaws to have some sort of "beloved" section or reserve in the area along the Halloca.[10]

—*GMNL* 11(1958): 131-32

NOTES

1. "Viatory or Journal of distances and observations," trip from Cusseta Town to Fort Wilkinson, beginning Dec. 6, 1797, MS in Library of Congress.

2. *Map of the State of Georgia.*

3. District 6, Muscogee County (now Chattahoochee), survey of 1826, Winfield Wright, D.S., Platbook LLLL, Land Records of Georgia, Surveyor General Department, Atlanta. In lots 19 and 189 the stream is marked "Nochille"; in lots 44, 76, and 86 it is listed as "Nochillee"; in lots 106 and 119 as "Nochile"; in lot 166 as "Nochilla"; and in lot 188 it is labelled "Nochillio."

4. Hawkins, "Viatory."

5. District 6, Muscogee, lots 7 and 8.

6. *Ibid.*, lots 25 and 56.

7. *Ibid.*, lots 74, 75, and 86.

8. *Letters of Benjamin Hawkins,* Collections of the Georgia Historical Society, Vol. 9 (Savannah, 1916), p. 55.

9. *Ibid.*, p. 70.

10. [Read, *IJAL* 15 (1949): 131, sticks to "dead hickory" for Ochillee. Goff has done better homework, tracing the name to its earlier form. The loss of an initial *n* may be "false division," as in Spanish *naranja* and English orange, preceded by the article an. Here the original Creek name may have been commonly spoken in English with a locative preposition like in or on. *FLU.*]

No. 57
Schatulga

Schatulga is a Muscogee County village located on U.S. 80, some nine miles to the east of Columbus. The name appears to be a Creek Indian word that signifies crawfishes, perhaps signifying in an implied sense "crawfishes place." It is derived from the first element of the word *sakcho*, or "saktcho," crawfish, plus the plural-forming collective suffix, *algi*, or "ulga." The "scha" of the Anglicized form was probably adopted by the whites because the *s* of *sakcho* was sounded like an *sh*. This *sh* for an *s* was common in Hitchitee words and apparently sometimes also occurred in Creek terms.

—*GMNL* 11(1958): 132

No. 58
Gardi and Guard Jam Bluff

Gardi (pronounced Gar dī) is a small town on the Southern Railway and U.S. Highway 25-341 in northern Wayne County. The name gives a first impression of being of foreign origin, like *Lodi* in western Coweta County and *Paoli* in lower Madison. But *Gardi* is a frontier name and is thoroughly indigenous to the Georgia scene. One can be virtually certain that it was derived from the expression guard-eye, a tab which was originally applied to a small creek and swamp in the vicinity of the present town. The name of the stream and swamp was in use by the middle 1790's because it was mentioned on two land plats of that period.[1] Presumably the name arose because people crossing the thick swamp had to guard the eyes from swishing limbs and thorny bushes.

Gardi's origin brings to mind the derivation of Ty Ty. The latter, one can be sure, is a version of Tight-eye, referring to a thick, bushy place that was difficult to see through. Ty Ty has already been discussed in the *Georgia Mineral Newsletter.*[2]

Georgia's navigable rivers are lined with an array of unique names which were left by old rivermen who once plied the streams with their poleboats, rafts, and steamboats. One interesting example which belongs in this category can be found in Guard Jam Bluff, located in lower Laurens County, on the east side of the Oconee River, some five miles above Mercers Creek which marks the Treutlen County line. The little bluff is in a bend where the current swings against the eastern shore and undercuts the bank, causing an overhang in the soil at the top of the bluff. Such a situation was dangerous for craft that allowed themselves to be caught in the sweep and forced against the bank because in trying to fend a vessel away the crew ran the risk of precipitating a cave-in. This exigency, one can be reasonably certain, caused the name *Guard Jam Bluff* to be attached to the site by early poleboatmen. The meaning and significance of the appellation will be clear if a few details are given about the operation of a poleboat. As the name implies, such a craft was poled or pushed by a crew with long poles. These men acted under the command of a patroon, or captain, who guided the vessel and gave orders on the handling of the boat. In many stretches, due to deepness of the water or swiftness of the current, the crew had to forego poles and resort to boathooks to pull themselves along by catching overhanging trees or by pushing against the bank at the waterline. The former operation was called hooking and the latter jamming. Since both activities involved working close to shore, it is understandable that a patroon would not want his crewmen to jam an unstable, overhanging bank for fear of causing a cave-in which would overwhelm his craft. Guard Jam Bluff was one of these dangerous spots which received its name because the rivermen were careful to guard against jamming the bank at that point.

—*GMNL* 11(1958): 132

NOTES

1. Land of George Calley, Glynn County (now part of Wayne), survey of 1795, Platbook BB, p. 136, Land Records of Georgia, Survey General Department, Atlanta; and land of James Powell, survey of 1796, Platbook CC, p. 410.
2. See below, pp. 363-66. At the time this article was written, the writer was not positive that Ty Ty is derived from the expression Tight-eye. Since then, however, he has seen numbers of references in old plats and in surveyors' field notes which make it plain that the name originally was Tight-eye.

No. 59
Fort Buffington

Fort Buffington is a village in the eastern part of Cherokee County, some four miles from Canton, on Georgia Highway 20. The community dates from the 1830's and derives its name from the fact that it was established as a stockade, or "fort," for concentrating the Cherokees when these Indians were removed to the West in 1838. There were a number of such stockades in Georgia, but Fort Buffington is the only place which still retains the word fort in its name. A manuscript map by a Lieutenant Keyes shows the location of the various concentration points in Georgia and in neighboring states of North Carolina, Tennessee, and Alabama.[1] It will be noted that the last state also retains one of the fort names in present Fort Payne. Fort Barrow, located in Tennessee, some miles north of Tennga, Georgia, is now simply referred to as Old Fort.

One can not be sure who furnished the name for Fort Buffington, but it was probably named for Joshua Buffington, a prominent mixed-blood Cherokee who lived near Blackburn's old ferry, in present Forsyth County, on the Etowah River.[2] He had extensive holdings at this place and at another place on the Etowah.[3]

—*GMNL* 12(1959): 63

NOTES

1. "View of Posts and distances in the Cherokee Nation: To illustrate major general Scott's operation in 1838," MS in the National Archives, Record Group 75, Map

CA 96. The writer is indebted to Mrs. Mary Jewett of the Georgia Historical Commission for his copy of the map.

2. "Census of the Cherokees in the limits of Georgia in 1835" (the "Henderson Roll"), p. 46, Record Group 75, National Archives.

3. "Valuations made in 1836 [of Cherokee properties in Lumpkin and Forsyth counties, Ga.] by agents Hutchins, Shaw and Kellogg," item no. 9, Record Group 75, Records of the Bureau of Indian Affairs, National Archives.

No. 60
Lost Town Creek and Shut-in Creek

Lost Town Creek arises on the eastern slopes of Pine Log Mountain, in western Cherokee County, and flows southward to join the right side of Shoal Creek, to the southwest of Waleska.[1] Two spurs of Pine Log Mountain roughly parallel the stream, but not far above its juncture with Shoal Creek these prongs curve inward and nearly come together. As a result, Lost Town Creek's little valley is almost locked in by mountains. This detached location, one can be reasonably sure, gave rise to the use of the word Lost in connection with the name. It has long been the practice in Georgia[2] and in numbers of other states to speak of a remote or isolated area, stream, lake, or mountains as "lost."

Lost Town Creek received its designation in the Indian days because it is mentioned in records concerning the Cherokees in the National Archives.[3] In fact, it is fairly certain that the name is of Cherokee origin. The use of the English word Town in the appellation is a plain clue that such is the case. The name very probably was derived from the Cherokee *tsudá yê lûñ yĭ*, which refers to a detached or isolated place. This aboriginal designation, however, was so difficult for white people to pronounce, it is reasonable to conclude that they turned the name into the easy Lost Town. The suffix *yi* at the end of Tsudayelunyi explains the use of the word Town in connection with the name. This locative form simply signified place, but in many instances the early whites translated it into town.

It might be added that a small tributary of Lost Town Creek is named *Shut-in Creek*. It originates on the western spur that surrounds the west side of the Lost Town valley and joins the main stream on the right side.

—*GMNL* 11(1958): 63

NOTES

1. For a good map showing Lost Town Creek, see the *Waleska Quadrangle* (U.S. Geological Survey, edition of 1950).
2. Some interesting Lost places in Georgia are: Lost Mountain in Cobb County, to the west of Marietta; Lost Creek in Mitchell, Colquitt, and Thomas counties; and Lost Branch near the head of Jacks River in Fannin County.
3. "Valuations [of Cherokee Indian properties] in Cobb, Cherokee and Gilmer counties, Georgia in 1836 by Agents Yancy and Worley," Record Group 75, Records of the Bureau of Indian Affairs, National Archives.

No. 61
Waleska

Waleska is a town on Georgia 140, in northwestern Cherokee County. The place, commonly called "Waleskee" by the people thereabouts, was first settled in 1835 by Lewis W. Reinhardt and his family.[1] At that time the Cherokees still lived in the area and when they were removed a few years later, Mr. and Mrs. Reinhardt named their settlement for Warluskee, a Cherokee girl whose family lived in the area and who had to leave with the other Indians at the time of the Removal.[2]

Now, interestingly enough, Warluskee was probably not the girl's given name but was her surname, because the Cherokee census of 1835 discloses that an Indian named Walaska lived with his fullblood family on Shoal Creek,[3] not far westward of the present town of Waleska. This document shows there were six members of this family and four of them were females, two of whom were listed as weavers and two as spinners. It might be added, too, that the census shows one member of the group could read Cherokee. Perhaps this individual was the girl for whom Waleska is named.

—*GMNL* 12(1959): 63-65

NOTES

1. Lloyd G. Marlin, *The History of Cherokee County* (Atlanta: Walter W. Brown Publishing Co., 1932), p. 49.
2. *Ibid.*, p. 132.
3. "Census of Cherokees in the limits of Georgia in 1835" (the "Henderson Roll"), Record Group 75, Records of the Bureau of Indian Affairs, National Archives.

No. 62
Buzzard Flopper (or Buzzard Flapper) Creek

One of the most unusual geographic appellations of Georgia is found in the name *Buzzard Flopper Creek* of eastern Cherokee County. This stream arises near the upper edge of Lathamtown and flows northward to join Smithwick Creek, thence into Etowah River to the south of Ball Ground. No explanation could be found to explain this curious moniker but one can be virtually certain that it is of Indian origin because the 1835 census of the Cherokees lists a Buzzard Flapper as living on the waters of Etowah River.[1] In another place, records relating to the Georgia Cherokees mention a Buzzard Flopper on the Hightower River."[2] Presumably this reference is to the same man, because Hightower is a pioneer Anglicized version of Etowah. The conflict in the spelling of the name leaves one wondering which version is correct. The matter becomes more complicated by reason of the fact that a second Buzzard Flapper was mentioned in 1836 as living on Gum Log Creek in original Union County.[3] The 1835 Cherokee census, on the other hand names a Flopper as a resident of Cartecay Creek.[4] If this fellow were a Buzzard "Flopper," his name, of course, would be the same as the present Cherokee County version. Perhaps some white people translated the word as Flapper while others used Flopper. In any case, occurrence of the name Buzzard Flapper in widely separated areas intimates the name was probably well-known to the Cherokees. The tab may strike us today as intended for a bit of drollery, but if the true meaning could be ascertained, the expression might prove to be serious in nature. It might, for instance, have been a ceremonial title that was used in some rite or dance.

—*GMNL* 12(1959): 65

NOTES

1. "Census of Cherokees in the limits of Georgia in 1835," p. 38, Record Group 75, Records of the Bureau of Indian Affairs, National Archives.
2. "Valuations [of Cherokee Indian properties] in Cobb, Cherokee and Gilmer counties, Georgia," made in 1836 by Agents Yancey and Worley, item 3, Record Group 75.
3. "Valuations" of Cherokee properties made in 1836 by Agents Hutchins, Shaw and Kellogg, item 75, Record Group 75.
4. "Census of Cherokees," p. 41.

No. 63
Jekyll Island

Jekyll Island, the smallest of the Golden Isles of the Georgia coast, was acquired by the state in 1947. It has been made a Georgia state park and is now being rapidly developed into a spot that is inviting in every way—with beautiful beaches, fine drives, splendid trees, and attractive facilities for visitors. Much has been written about this lovely island but this information is readily available and need not be summarized here. This sketch will be confined to a bit of geography and a discussion of the placenames which the island has borne in its long and interesting history.

Jekyll Island bears one of the oldest English-derived appellations in Georgia. It was named by General Oglethorpe himself in January of 1734,[1] in honor of Sir Joseph Jekyll, a distinguished lawyer and statesman who undoubtedly played a part in the establishment of the colony. Jekyll was born in 1663, the son of John Jekyll of London.[2] He was admitted to the bar in 1687,[3] knighted by George I in 1700,[4] and named Master of Rolls in 1717.[5] As a long-time member of Parliament he was in an influential place to support and advance plans for the foundation of the province. And, after the establishment of Georgia, as Master of Rolls, he was in a position to keep in close touch with developments here because the Georgia charter provided that the holder of this office was one of the officials who were to receive mandatory written reports on the progress that was being made.[6]

Both Sir Joseph and his wife contributed financially to the establishment of the new colony. The former gave £500 for this purpose while Lady Jekyll contributed £100.[7] Oglethorpe was not unmindful of this interest and support and on his first trip southward from the Savannah area he honored the benefactor by naming an island for him.

On a later visit to the south in 1738 the General wrote Sir Joseph that he was at the island and reminded him that it had been named in his honor.[8] Jekyll never received this letter because he died on August 19, 1738, and was buried at Rolls Chapel.[9]

When Oglethorpe named the island in early 1734 on his trip down the coast, he was actually beyond the southern limits set for the colony in the original charter. This document provided that the lower boundary was to be the Altamaha River.[10] Since Oglethorpe, however, realized that the islands below this stream were essential to the protection of the colony, he reconnoitered them and ordered the construction of fortified points at various strategic places on them. The wisdom of this course was to be amply sustained in a few years.

The Spanish names for the island were Gualdaquini,[11] Gualequini,[12] and Obaldaquini.[13] Before Oglethorpe applied Jekyll to the place, the English used garbled versions of the Spanish names. For instance, the John Herbert map of the coast in 1725 mentions the inlet between St. Simons and present Jekyll as *"Wallegony Bay."*[14] An early Spanish chart shows the same passage as *"Barra de guadalquini."*[15] The latter word plainly represents another version of the Spanish name for the island. The corrupted English designation continued for some time after Oglethorpe renamed the place because the noted Bull map of 1738 refers to the island as *"Wollegany."*[16]

The French called the island *He de la Somme.*[17] This appellation was applied by early explorers and should not be attributed to the French families who acquired the island in the 1790's and some of whose descendants continued to own it for nearly a century thereafter.

The least certain of the early names for Jekyll is its aboriginal designation. This name is commonly mentioned as *Ospo*, a word that apparently is of Guale origin, because those Indians lived on the stretch of the coast where Jekyll lies. The linking of *Ospo* with the island, however, is open to question, since the writers do not say how they determined that it applied to Jekyll. John R. Swanton discusses Indian appellations along the Georgia coast in his scholarly study on the Creek Indians, but he does not identify *Jekyll* as *Ospo*. On the contrary, he connects it with a town called *Espogue*, which was located on the mainland,[18] perhaps at the head of Doboy Sound which lies between Sapelo Island and the mainland. Espogue must have been in the area indicated because the Spanish chart mentioned above shows the Barra de Espoga in the proper location for the present Doboy Sound.[19] It is possible of course, that Swanton erred in identifying *Ospo* with *Espogue*. Maybe the two places were different and the former was farther south, on the mainland, or on lower St. Simon, or actually on Jekyll. One is not sure of the matter.

When present-day backlanders come down to visit their island, they are surprised to hear coastal people pronounce the name "Jay'kul." Away from the coast the word is conventionally pronounced "Jekk'ul." One does not know if the coastal version has its roots in the colonial years. The inlanders, however, can find some support for their pronunciation in Thomas's *Universal Pronouncing Dictionary*, in which the name is listed as "Jek'yll."[20] Sir Joseph and his wife had no survivors, but there are other families of the name in England and it is assumed Thomas gives the correct pronunciation as used in Britain.

In old records the name is variously mentioned as Jeckel, Jeekel, Jekyll, Jekil and *Jekyl*. The last form is common and seemingly has led some people to assume the word was properly spelled in that fashion and that modern people have added an extra *l* to it. The present Jekyll, however, is the correct form and this spelling can also be found in early sources. When Oglethorpe, for instance, wrote Sir Joseph in 1738 reminding him that the island bore his name, the General spelled the name *"Jekyll."*

Some comments about the ancillary use of Jekyll in the waters about the island will perhaps be of interest to geographers. The segment of the Intracoastal Waterway leading southward from Brunswick River through the salt marshes that border the upper western part of the island is called Jekyll Creek. Farther along where the passage widens considerably, the waterway takes on the name Jekyll River. And still farther south, in the area opposite the mouth of the Little Satilla River and the southwest end of the island, and just above St. Andrew Sound, the name *Jekyll Sound* is applied. In the early years, this designation was reserved for the inlet now called *St. Simons Sound*, which lies to the north between Jekyll and St. Simons Island.[21] The English were much impressed with the relatively deep water and fine natural advantages of this first Jekyll Sound. It was referred to as one of the best entries south of Virginia.[22] One deponent pointed out that a ship could sail from the bar at Jekyll Sound and in twenty-four hours run into the Gulf Stream, where the "Spanish Galleons" passed.[23]

In addition to its use in connection with *Jekyll Island*, the name Jekyll was also once applied to a section of Savannah. A post-Revolutionary plat shows a Jekyl Tithing Derby Ward in that place.[24]

In conclusion there is one note to add about the island. At a meeting of the Provincial Council on March 25, 1765, a law was passed which declared "That the island of Jekyl shall from henceforth be and forever continue a part of the parish of St. James."[25] The finality of this statute, of course, was to be nullified later by the American Revolution.

—*GMNL* 13(1960): 35-36

NOTES

1. Charles C. Jones, *The History of Georgia* (Boston: Houghton, Mifflin, 1883), 1: 163.
2. Sidney Lee, ed., *Dictionary of National Biography* (New York: Macmillan, 1892), 29: 287.
3. *Ibid.*
4. *Ibid.*
5. *Ibid.*, p. 288.
6. Allen D. Candler, ed., *Colonial Records of Georgia* (Atlanta: Franklin, 1904-1916), 1: 11-26 (17), "Charter of the Colony."
7. *Ibid.*, p. 122.
8. Oglethorpe to Sir Jos. Jekyll, Jekyll Sound, Sept. 17, 1738, "Letters from General Oglethorpe," *Collections of the Georgia Historical Society*, Vol. 3 (Savannah, 1873), pp. 48-49.
9. Sidney Lee, ed., *DNB*, 29: 288
10. Candler, ed., *Colonial Records of Georgia*, 1: 18.
11. John R. Swanton, *Early History of the Creek Indians and Their Neighbors*, Bulletin 73, Bureau of American Ethnology (Washington, D.C., 1922), p. 41.
12. *Ibid.*, p. 51.
13. *Ibid.*
14. In Herbert, "A New Map of His Majesty's Flourishing Province of South Carolina . . .," 1725, DeRenne Collection, Library of the University of Georgia, Athens.
15. "Mapa de la Ysla de la Florida," Madrid, Ministry of War [1683?], MS in Library of Congress.
16. "Chart . . . transmitted by Col. [William] Bull (President & Commander in Chief of South Carolina) with his Representation to the Board of Trade," May, 1738, MS in the Library of Congress.
17. Swanton, *Early History of the Creek Indians*, p. 51.
18. *Ibid.*, pp. 51, 82.
19. "Mapa de la Ysla de la Florida."
20. Joseph Thomas, *Universal Pronouncing Dictionary of Biography and Mythology*, 4th ed. (Philadelphia: Lippincott, 1915), p. 1379.
21. Candler, ed., *Colonial Records of Georgia*, 4: 669.

22. *Ibid.*
23. *Ibid.*, 3: 420.
24. Re-recording in 1812 of a 1794 plat showing the waterfront at Savannah, Platbook M, Land Records of Georgia, Surveyor General Department, Atlanta.
25. Candler, ed., *Colonial Records of Georgia,* 18: 690-91.

No. 64
Panola, Panola Shoals, Panola Road, South River, Cotton River, Reeves Creek, and Upton Creek

Panola is the designation of a community in lower DeKalb County and along the upper fringe of Henry, on both sides of South River, in the area about Georgia 155, the Decatur-McDonough highway. At the point where No. 155 crosses the river there is a rocky, shoally stretch which has long been known as Panola Shoals. Within the community there are two specific points which have borne the name *Panola.* One of these is a little road intersection on Georgia 212, on the north side of the river, downstream from the shoals and about a quarter of a mile east of Georgia 155. The second spot is another road intersection, lying at the edge of Henry County. At this site a dirt road leads southwestward from highway 155 in the direction of Jonesboro. The route is of significance to this sketch because it is known as the *Panola Road.* In the original 1821 surveys it was labelled *Strawns Road.*[1] By linking it with other known Indian country thoroughfares it can be traced to the area of Newnan where it joined the main McIntosh Trail, one of the early east-west traces of western Georgia and eastern Alabama.

No precise information could be found to explain how the Panola places received their names. The word *Panola* is not mentioned in the field notes, plats, or land district map of the first surveyor who laid off the locality in 1821, after the area had been acquired from the Creeks. This omission indicates that the name came into use after the date of the survey. Perhaps so, but such an omission does not necessarily prove the designation was not known in 1821, because on occasion Indian names for places and streams had a way of continuing in use even though the first surveyors of the sections where the tabs applied missed or ignored them.

Panola is an Indian word that has also been widely adopted across the country as a placename: in Alabama, Illinois, Michigan, Mississippi, Oklahoma, and Texas. Perhaps it was used in Georgia because of its pleasing qualities, and particularly at a time when the community needed a name for a post office. Maybe the word was borrowed from the last named state. In the formative years of Texas, Georgians were much interested in the Lone Star State. They adopted the word Texas for place names and even now retain these appellations in the Georgia geographic nomenclature. But be that as it may, there is some evidence which suggests another derivation of the name *Panola* as used in DeKalb County.

Despite the presence of the name in former Creek country of Georgia, the word is not of Muskogee origin. It is derived from the Choctaw language and signifies cotton.[2] The latter Indians lived far from Georgia, in western Alabama, and in Mississippi, and it is very improbable that they themselves would have left the name here. More than likely then, if *Panola* were originally applied by Indians it was left by the Creeks who had borrowed the term from the Choctaws. This borrowing could well have taken place because cotton is not a native of these parts and the old Creeks had no name for it. The Choctaws were logical Indians to provide a term for the plant because they lived near the Mississippi Valley where there was an early interest in cotton raising and because their language was the chief basis of an interesting *lingua franca* which was used by other Southeastern tribes as a common tongue for communicating with each other. Thus it would have been logical for the Creeks to borrow a word for cotton from their neighbors the Choctaws.

To advance further this suggestion about the origin of Panola, it should be mentioned that a large creek called *Cotton River* arises just to the south of the Panola community and flows across Henry County to join South River. One upper tributary of this stream commences on the lower side of the Panola Road that has been noted. Three different surveyors mentioned Cotton River in the original surveys of old Henry County.[3] The fact that these men knew the name indicates it was well known, even though the area being laid off was wilderness country that had only recently been ceded by the Indians. It should be noted the surveyors applied an English name to the waterway; they did not make it Panolahatchee, the Muskogee equivalent of *Cotton River*.

Whoever named Cotton River must have had a good reason for choosing this particular appellation, a point which implies someone may have been raising cotton in the locality of the stream. Such an activity very probably would not have been carried on by the Creeks because there is little evidence to show that these Indians were concerned with raising the staple. More than likely if it were being grown, it was planted by white people. Now interestingly enough, one of the surveyors found at least two white men settled on the waters of Cotton River. One of these was a man named Upton, who had a home on the south side of Panther Creek, near its junction with a stream now called *Upton Creek,* but which the surveyor labelled *Prairy Creek.*[4] The site was to the north of Stockbridge, near the western boundary of Henry County, upstream from the bridge of the Southern Railway over the present Upton Creek. The other settler was named Reeves. He had a place (in lot 32 of District 12) on a stream marked *Reeves Creek,* a tributary of Cotton River.[5] This man's settlement was to the southward of Stockbridge. The present Reeves Creek still commemorates his name.

If Upton and Reeves had white families they were certainly "intruders" (squatters) on Indian lands. Perhaps they had married into the Creeks and were permitted to reside in the Nation. Both men lived near the eastern fringe of the Creek country, removed from any significant Indian town. This fact intimates they were farmers or cattlemen and not traders. Indeed, the surveyor showed that Upson had a field near his house.[6] In view of the interest that had developed in cotton by the 1820's it is reasonable to believe the men were raising the crop. The Creeks were jealous of their lands, and it is hard to believe the settlements and activities of Upton and Reeves would have escaped their attention. If the men were growing cotton, the Indians might have noted the fact and named the area Panolahatchee which the white people changed to Cotton River, although somehow the word *Panola* remained in the area and was later attached to the DeKalb County community.

Perhaps we shall never know the truth about the matter. Maybe there was no relationship between *Panola, Cotton River,* and the possible farming activities of Upton and Reeves. But presence of the two names and the two settlers was an unusual coincidence even if the combination had no bearing on the origin of the name *Panola.*

The introduction of South River in this sketch was largely a matter of convenience because of its connection with the word *Panola.* The name merits more than a cursory discussion, but it properly should be treated in a sketch on Yellow River, to which it is tributary. People commonly assume South River received the name because it is the main south prong of the former stream. In the wilderness days, though, it may have been considered as the extreme upper south branch of the Ocmulgee. Indeed, one old surveyor actually marked the river "*South Fork of Ocmulgee.*"[7] This labelling was correct in a sense but only by indirection, because it had to join with Yellow River which in turn united with the Alcovy to form the stream that we call the Ocmulgee.

The use of the word South in the river's name is an interesting feature of the designation because it offers an insight into pioneer indications of direction. For some reason which is not entirely clear, the early citizens sometimes used the word south to denote a direction which we would label west. The best examples of the practice appear in colonial records wherein the right banks of the Savannah and the Great Ogeechee are referred to as the south sides. Coming down the Atlantic coast, the lower sides of these streams, in the areas immediately adjacent to their mouths, properly should have been referred to as south sides. But this should not have been the reason, according to present thinking, for applying south to the west banks of the rivers, back in the interior where the streams were running nearly due south. South River appears to be an example of this pioneer manner of indicating direction. More than likely, present-day people would have designated the stream as West River or as West Fork. But there are other interesting aspects of the name, and as has been noted, these matters will be discussed in an article on the Yellow River.

—GMNL 13(1960): 36-37

NOTES

1. District 12, Henry County, survey of 1821, Benjamin Fontaine, D.S., Platbook BBBB, lots 48, 49, 81, *passim*, Land Records of Georgia, Surveyor General Department, Atlanta.

2. The Choctaw word for cotton is also listed as *ponola*. White people, and seemingly also Creeks, have used the form *panola*.

3. Benjamin Fontaine in District 12 of Henry; W. L. Mitchell, D.S., District 11, Henry County, survey of 1821, Platbook BBBB; and James Watson, D.S., District 6 of Henry, survey of 1821, Platbook AAAA.

4. Plats for District 12, Henry County. Upton's house was in the northeast corner of lot 103.

5. *Ibid.* Lot 32 shows "Reeves House & Spring," but no clearing.

6. *Ibid.* The "Field" was about half in lot 103 and half in 102, on the north-south line that divides the two lots.

7. "Map of District 15 of Henry County," survey of 1821, John Kell, D.S., Land Records of Georgia.

No. 65
Silco

Since considerable conjecture and some argument were resorted to in discussing the origin of Panola in Sketch No. 64 above, this sort of approach might as well be continued with respect to Silco, another word of possible Indian derivation. Silco is the name of a community on Georgia 110 in western Camden County, located to the south of the Great Satilla, not quite halfway between that stream and the St. Marys River to the south. The appellation apparently has been in use for a considerable time. It has the earmarks of a coined word and was considered for discussion with other artificial designations that were treated in Sketch No. 41. Eventually it may turn out that Silco is actually a coined name. The place was once a center of important turpentining operations and the word may have been devised from the concern which carried on these activities, with the *sil* element representing a part of some proper name and the *co* standing for the abbreviation of company. Such a derivation, however, could not be verified at this time and this circumstance leaves the thought the name may have had another origin. Perhaps it is derived from the Creek word *silkosi*, meaning narrows or narrow place. This might well have been the case, because the Silco community lies in the relatively narrow strip of land which separates the Satilla from the St. Marys. A glance at a map will show there are big bends in the rivers at this point and that the two streams swing within five miles of each other in the area of the village. Farther westward a bit from the place, the distance across is even shorter. In times of floods, the Satilla backs water into the wide marginal swamp on its south side and nearly severs the land passage between Camden and Charlton counties. Such contingencies, of course, could have seriously affected travel on the Indian routes and early white man's traces that once crossed the neck. It is easy to believe the Indians referred to the area as Silkosi, narrow place, and that the white people adopted and continued the designation in the modified form of Silco.

—*GMNL* 13(1960): 37-38

No. 66
Standing Boy Creek, End Creek, East and West End Creeks, and Heiferhorn Creek

Standing Boy Creek arises near Ellerslie in lower Harris County and flows southwesterly to join the Chattahoochee River in northwest Muscogee County. Colonel Benjamin Hawkins first mentioned the stream in the late 1790's. In one place he lists it as "Chusethlocco,"[1] and in another as "Chussethlucco."[2] In the former he states there was an Indian village called "Itatchee Uscaw (head of a creek)" located about four miles up the stream from the river.[3] In the second source he notes the name of the settlement as "Hat-che Uxau (head of a creek)" but locates it up the "Ke-ta-le,"[4] a stream to the north of Standing Boy and which is now called Mulberry Creek. This last location by Hawkins was in error, because the village was actually on today's Standing Boy, somewhere about the juncture of that stream and the present Douglas Creek, near the point where the latter is crossed by Georgia 103. The settlement was certain to have been up Standing Boy, because as will be seen below, the designation Hatche Uxau was eventually turned into End Creek, a name that applied to the main stream while the expression Standing Boy was limited to the waterway we now call Heiferhorn Creek.

Chusethlocco or Chussethlucco do not translate into Standing Boy, although Colonel Hawkins may have intended his names to have that approximate meaning. The *thlocco* and *thlucco* forms used by him are plainly intended for the augmentative suffix *thlåko*, which the Muskogees used with nouns to signify big or large. The use of *chuse* and *chusse*, however, complicates interpretation of the name. If the latter were the real form, which is doubted, the word would be translated into Big Buckskin, from *chusse*, buckskin or leather, plus the suffix *thlåko*, big. "Chuse" on the other hand might be interpreted as *chuse*, young thing, or as *chusi*, younger brother, with the complete expressions meaning respectively big young thing and big younger brother. Despite these curious English derivations, Hawkins was reasonably close to Standing Boy with his "Chuse," if not with "Chusse." Today, even we may refer to a sturdy boy baby who is able to stand as a big little thing or as a big little fellow. Nevertheless the name Chusethlocco does not literally signify Standing Boy. In Muskogee the precise word for this expression is *chiponusihuili*, from *chiponusi*, boy, plus *huili*, standing. As will be seen shortly, forms similar to this last Creek name can be found in later records that refer to the stream. Hawkins had not been in the Creek country very long as Indian agent when he recorded his names and was perhaps not yet familiar enough with the language to select the exact Indian wording for the stream's name. There is a chance, of course, that the creek was once called Chusethlocco, and later Chiponusihuili, or Standing Boy.

When the area in which the creek lies was first surveyed there was confusion between surveyors about the name. Willis P. Baker, surveyor of the 8th District of Muscogee apparently did not know the Indian designation for the stream because he labelled it Mountain Creek,[5] an English designation that was descriptive of the waterway. On the other hand Augustus Crawford, surveyor for the adjoining 19th District, mentions the creek as "Cheepounhuiltee or Standing Boy" on his district map[6] [and as "Chepounhuiltee" in his field notes].[7] It is important to state that he confined this name to the waterway which is now called Heiferhorn Creek. This stream commences in lower Harris County, to the south of Cataula, and joins our Standing Boy Creek just to the west of Georgia 103, in northwest Muscogee. In these records the present Standing Boy is listed as the "Hatchauxa" in the field notes[8] and as "Hatchee Uxa or End Creek" on the map of the 19th District.[9] The Hatchee Uxa was clearly drawn from the Indian village Hat-che Uxau mentioned by Hawkins. This name is derived from the Muskogee *háchiuksa*, signifying at the head of or at the end of a stream.

The designation End Creek for the main strand of today's Standing Boy endured for some time. The major upper branches of the waterway were once even labelled East End Creek and West End Creek. The use of End Creek continued at least till 1869 because an official map of Harris shows the name at that date.[10] Following this period, however, the appellation became obsolete and the name Standing Boy was transferred to the main stream from the beginning to its mouth.

Heiferhorn apparently is a relatively new name that has taken the place of Surveyor Crawford's Cheepounhuiltee, or Standing Boy. No reason could be found to explain how the tab Heiferhorn came to be employed in connection with the creek. People of other years often made use of names like Hog Jaw, Bear Skull, Cow head, Mule Jaw, Possum Snout, Buck head, and so on. Apparently Heiferhorn belongs in this rustic category, although the exact reason for using the name has been forgotten.

This sketch should not end without some additional discussion of the term Standing as used in Standing Boy Creek. The Indians (and seemingly the early whites) were fond of the word in their placenames, as is evidenced by designations like Standing Boy, Standing Peachtree, Standing Rock, and so on. It should be noted, however, that we use the English versions of these names and not the Indian. The reason for this, one may safely conclude, can be attributed to the difficulty of pronouncing the Muskogee word *huili* for standing. Surveyor Crawford, it will be recalled, wrote the term as "huiltee," and it is fairly common to find it as "weethly." But neither of these renditions is correct. The difficulty with *huili* arises from the fact that it contains the voiceless *l*, a surd letter which we do not have in English, although it occurs frequently in Creek words and to a lesser extent in Cherokee names. Some well-known Creek appellations which originally contained the letter are Withlacoochee, Willacoochee, and Lannahassee. And those who read Sketch No. 60 of this series on Lost Town Creek will remember that the Cherokee equivalent for this name is Tsudaye 'lunyi signifying an isolated or detached place, and that the white people probably did not retain this Cherokee name for the creek and its mountain-ringed valley because they could not pronounce the word.

Various devices have been used by students to signify the surd *l*: '*l*, *tl'*, *cl*, *hl*, *thl*, and even *thr*. But with the exception of *hl*, these forms at best are no more than signals to caution that the letter is unusual. Save for the *hl*, they will not assist in pronouncing the letter. The *thr* is very deceiving because it has no *l* sound whatever, and as far as Muskogee names are concerned it introduces the letter *r* which those Indians did not have. The most commonly used of the devices is the *thl*, but why it came to be employed is not known. Perhaps because English words containing *thl* are so rare some one concluded there would be no confusion if Indian words with the voiceless *l* were spelled with *thl*. But the combination misleads by causing such names to be pronounced with a *th* although this sound does not actually occur in the names. The case of Withlacoochee, a river in south Georgia, is a good example. This word properly does not carry a *th* sound, but some one put a *thl* in the name over a century ago and it has been pronounced "Withlacoochee" ever since.[11] Interestingly enough, the Anglo-Saxons employed the voiceless *l* and the Welsh even now retain the letter in numbers of words. Perhaps the reader who is interested in Indian names would like to experiment a bit to learn the nature of the curious letter. Before attempting this, however, one should pronounce some common English words such as the following: like, lap, lock, lick, and lack. It will be noticed that the *l* is definitely voiced in each word. Now place the tip of the tongue firmly against the fore palate and pronounce these Anglo-Saxon words: *hlid*, (lid), *hleap*, (leap), *hlaf*, (loaf), and *hlinc*, (a rising ground or hill, which is retained in our link, as in golf link). Next take a Welsh name like Lloyd, and pronounce it as "Hloyd." It will be noted that the aspirated *h* spills the breath along edges of the tongue, while the tip pressed against the palate keeps the *l* from being voiced as it would be in the English pronunciation of Lloyd. Next turn to some Muskogee words like "Wēhlacoochee" (for Withlacoochee), "hláko" (for the *thláko* mentioned above which should come out "hlucko" because of the obscure *a* in the word), and "huihli" (wee'hlee) for the *huili* in *chiponusihuili* (for standing boy). After a bit of practice with the above rather simple words and the development of some proficiency in pronouncing the voiceless *l*, one may want to attempt more difficult forms. A good one to try is Thlathlothlakupka[12] which contains three voiceless elels and should be attempted as "Hlahlohlakuffka." This word which is the early Creek name for St. Marys River has been reported in old records to mean rotten fish.

Perhaps, one may decide after several tongue-straining attempts at "Hlahlohlakuffka" that St. Marys is a pretty name and that we can get along well enough with it without attempting to recall and pronounce its forgotten, malodorous aboriginal designation. Perhaps too, one may conclude the frontier white people were sensible when they converted Pakanahuili into Standing Peachtree, Chatohuili into Standing Rock, and Chiponusihuili into Standing Boy.

—*GMNL* 13(1960): 38-39

NOTES

1. *Letters of Benjamin Hawkins, 1796-1806*, Collections of the Georgia Historical Society, Vol. 9 (Savannah, 1916), p. 61.
2. *A Sketch of the Creek Country in the Years 1798 and 1799* (Americus, Ga.: Americus Book Co., 1938), p. 52.
3. *Letters*, p. 61.
4. *Creek Country*, p. 52.
5. Survey of 1826, Platbook LLLL, lot 104, Land Records of Georgia, Surveyor General Department, Atlanta.
6. "Map of District 19 of Muscogee," survey of 1827, Land Records of Georgia.
7. "Field Notes," District 19, Muscogee.

8. *Ibid.*

9. "Map of District 19."

10. B. W. Frobel, "Map of Harris County," 1869, made by authority of the state, MS in Land Records of Georgia.

11. [See Sketch no. 11, above.]

12. Different versions of this name can be found in various records. The form cited is from Samuel Savery's chart showing the boundary between Georgia and the Creek Nation, 1769, original in the William L. Clements Library, Ann Arbor, Mich. The name appears to be a dialectical expression and not a true Muskogee form. The *thlathlo* element means fish, but *thlakupka* is not the customary expression for rotten. The correct word in Muskogee is *likwi* or "lekwe." If the *kuphka* element of this word is a real Creek term, it is derived from *ogufki* meaning muddy, in which case the name signifies muddy fish instead of rotten fish.

No. 67
Roaring Creek (Formerly the Chissehulcuh)

At the same time Benjamin Hawkins listed the Chusethlocco, which is presently labelled Standing Boy Creek, he also mentioned a stream called the "Chisse Hulkuha"[1] or "Chisse-hul-cuh."[2] This waterway, now known as Roaring Creek, enters the Chattahoochee about halfway between Columbus and the Standing Boy. The designation Roaring Creek was first applied in 1826 by Willis P. Baker, the surveyor who laid off original District No. 8 of Muscogee County.[3] One can be certain the name is not a translation of Chisse-hul-cuh because Roaring Creek in Muskogee would be Wewokihachi. Baker did not seem to be familiar with Indian nomenclature because he used English names on his map except for the Chattahoochee which borders the western side of the district. Very probably he applied the name Roaring Creek to the stream because it made a roaring sound as it flowed its rocky course to the river.

One can not be positive of the meaning of Hawkins's Chisse hulkuha and Chisse-hul-cuh. The second element of the former expression is certainly garbled and can be dismissed as far as this analysis is concerned. On its face Chisse-hul-cuh may have meant Crawling Rat, from *chissi*, rat and *hálki*, crawling. This derivation, however, does not sound like a Muskogee placename. More than likely one believes the appellation was intended to mean Rats Creek, from *chissi*, rat, plus the plural-forming suffix *álgi,* "ulgee," or "ulga," with the word *háchi* for stream being understood as a part of the name.

—*GMNL* 13 (1960): 39-40

NOTES

1. *Letters of Benjamin Hawkins, 1796-1806,* Collections of the Georgia Historical Society, Vol. 9 (Savannah, 1916), p. 61.
2. *A Sketch of the Creek Country in the Years 1798 and 1799* (Americus, Ga.: Americus Book Co., 1938), p. 52.
3. "Map of District 8 of Muscogee," survey of 1826, Land Records of Georgia, Surveyor General Department, Atlanta.

No. 68
Cataula (and Mulberry Creek)

Cataula is the name of a village in lower Harris County, on the Central of Georgia Railway and U.S. Highway 27. The area surrounding the place is also known officially as the Cataula District for Georgia Militia District No. 696. Since there are some 1,800 militia districts in Georgia, the relatively low 696 indicates the Cataula community is comparatively old.

Cataula is derived from the Muskogee word *kĭtáli,* or "ke tä'lee," signifying withered or dead mulberry. Presumably the name referred to a locality where there were once some deadened trees of this species. A likely spot for the site is a crossroads located five miles west of today's Cataula, and which has long been known as Mulberry Grove. This last community lies a short distance to the south of Mulberry Creek which perpetuates in English a part of the aboriginal name. One can be certain of this point since Colonel Hawkins mentioned the stream in 1797 as the "Ketalee."[1] In the years between that date and the first surveys of Muscogee County in 1826-1827 the stream began to take on its present name, because one district surveyor referred to it as the "Cataulee,"[2] two others mentioned it as the "Cau tau lee or Mulberry,"[3] while a fourth merely listed the waterway as "Mulberry Creek."[4]

The present village and community undoubtedly adopted the name of the stream, but when the word was taken over it was "corrected" by changing the final ĭ, or "ee," of the Indian version to an *a*. This practice was followed numbers of times in the adoption of Georgia placenames of Indian origin. The "refinements" were made apparently because people feared they would adopt a backwoods colloquialism if they used a word ending with a short *i* or "ee" sound. Frontiersmen regularly terminated many words with this sound, such as "beavee" for beaver, "Georgee" for Georgia, "Augustee" for Augusta, and so on. Many Indian words actually ended with the ĭ (or "ee") and it was a mistake to change the letters to an *a*. Even now there are old folk around Cataula who say "Cataulee" and no doubt leave the impression on some modern people that they are giving a rustic turn to the name when as a matter of fact they are using an ending which has been handed down from Indian days.

Cataula is a good word to illustrate the garbling of an Indian term into a hard-to-identify name. The kĭ got turned into "ca" and the broad *a* of *tä* was shifted to "au." The *ä* in Indian words has been particularly hard to retain in present-day appellations. Usually it has been converted into "aw," "au," or "ah." On occasion though it has become "ar," as in "Armuchee" for the Cherokee Amutsi. In other instances the *ä* has become *o*, as found in the English words dock, lock, etc. For instance, our Ochlocknee River derived its name from the Hitchitee Okĭläkni, meaning water yellow. And finally, the letter has at times been changed into another type of *a*. This shift is illustrated by the first *a* of Chattahoochee that has now taken on the sound of *a* in fat. In the original word the "Chatta" element was *chä'tö*, signifying stone or rock.

—*GMNL* 13(1960): 40

NOTES

1. *Letters of Benjamin Hawkins,* Collections of the Georgia Historical Society, Vol. 9 (Savannah, 1916), p. 61.

2. "Map of District 18 of Muscogee," survey of 1827, James Pace, D.S., Land Records of Georgia, Surveyor General Department, Atlanta.

3. "Map of District 19 of Muscogee," survey of 1827, Augustus Crawford, D.S.; "Map of District 22 of Muscogee," Alfred M. Horton, D.S., Land Records of Georgia.

4. "Map of District 17 of Muscogee," survey of 1827, William Mason, D.S., Land Records of Georgia.

No. 69
Mountain Creek and House Creek

While we are in western Georgia discussing names in Muscogee and Harris counties there are two other waterways that merit mentioning. One of these is Mountain Creek, a big stream of Harris County that begins at the Pine Mountain State Park near Chipley and runs westward to the Chattahoochee. When Benjamin Hawkins mentioned the streams referred to in the sketches above he noted there was a large creek upriver from the Mulberry but he did not give it a name. The original surveyor for the area in 1827 applied the name Mountain Creek which we still retain.[1] No doubt he used this designation because it flows from Pine Mountain. In fact, he mentioned Pine Mountain and thus shows this appellation was in use at that date.

Upstream on the Chattahoochee from Mountain Creek there is an interesting waterway called House Creek. On the first survey of the section in 1827 it was labelled "Old House Creek."[2] The same designation was reaffirmed a year later in another official survey of islands in the Chattahoochee.[3] Somewhere in the intervening years, people dropped the Old in the name and simply called the stream House Creek.

The location of the house which gave rise to the original name is a matter of pure conjecture. It could have been on the creek to the north of Whitesville, near the bridge on Georgia 219, because an Indian path leading to the Chattahoochee crossed the creek at that point. Maybe the old house was at the mouth of the creek. This part of the Chattahoochee was an important crossing place for Creek trails, and it is possible the house was a hut or place of refuge for travellers who came and went at one of these crossings.

—*GMNL* 13(1960): 40

NOTES

1. "Map of District 20 in the 2nd Section," (District 20 of original Muscogee County), survey of 1827, John G. Bostick, D.S., Land Records of Georgia, Surveyor General Department, Atlanta.
2. *Ibid.*
3. "Islands and Reserves," Platbook EEEE, p. 27, Island No. 13 in the Chattahoochee River, 1828, Thomas Mitchell, Surveyor, Land Records of Georgia.

No. 70
Laingkat

At various times in these sketches mention has been made of the American proclivity for borrowing the names of foreign countries, areas, and cities. This state has followed the national bent and thus Georgia has an abundance of designations like Budapest, Hahira, Cuba, Madras, Warsaw, Ceylon, Turin, Donegal, Amsterdam, and so on. An interesting appellation which belongs in this grouping is Laingkat, a station and community on the Seaboard Airline Railroad in southeastern Decatur County, below Attapulgus and near the Florida line. It is difficult to learn exactly why many of these foreign names were borrowed for use in Georgia, but such is not the case with Laingkat. Mr. Frank S. Jones of Bainbridge says the place was named about sixty years ago when a man called Upson came to Decatur County from New York State and established a farm near the station to raise a Sumatran tobacco.[1] He named his place Deli Laing-Kat and this designation remains today in the shortened version Laingkat. Mr. Upson no doubt called his farm after the port of Deli, and the Province of Langkat on the northeast coast of the island of Sumatra, in the area about the present city of Medan. This region is noted for a distinctive variety of Sumatran tobacco that is used for cigar wrappers. It might be added too, that Decatur County and northwest Florida in the section around Havana have also developed distinction as producers of wrapper tobacco.

In addition to being a placename of foreign origin, Laingkat also belongs in a category of names that denote some sort of economic activity. Thus it properly falls into a group that includes such appellations as Lumber City, Pecan City, Rockmart, Cement, Tarboro, Stevens Pottery, Fruitland, Traders Hill, and so on in an interesting variety.

Since Laingkat is a foreign word, some people have trouble in pronouncing it. "Lan'cat" is a common local version of the name. This pronunciation apparently has been in use for a considerable period because a 1927 map lists the name as "Landcat."[2]

—*GMNL* 13(1960): 40-41

NOTES

1. Letter to the author, dated July 3, 1959.
2. W. M. Arline, C.E., *Map of Decatur County Georgia 1927* (Bainbridge).

No. 71
Cuttingbone Creek

Cuttingbone Creek commences eastward of Bovard, on U.S. 23-441 in Rabun County and flows eastward to join Chechero Creek not far above the juncture of the latter with the Chattooga River. Analysis of the name presented interesting possibilities for consideration. On the first approach it was assumed that the expression might be a translated version of the Cherokee word for scratcher. This might have been a correct explanation because those Indians "scratched" young warriors and ball players to lend strength and make them valorous. The ceremony involved cutting the player or brave lightly with a wolf bone, turkey bone, or rattlesnake teeth arranged in a sort of comb. Presumably briars were also sometimes used for this purpose because the Cherokee name for the ceremonial scratching device was *kanuga*, a word which embodies the term for briar. Since bone was used, however, it was reasoned that the frontier whites might simply have translated the expression as cuttingbone, and thus given rise to the name in connection with the creek because ball grounds where players were scratched were customarily located beside streams.

Another meaning considered for cuttingbone was the possibility that the name might have been a backwoodsy expression which was intended to signify something like cut shin. The stream flows through a relatively rugged terrain and pioneer people sometimes referred to a rough, rocky area as a cut shin place. This speculation about the name received support from the fact that some people who live aroundabout the stream refer to it as Cut'bone. Also the original surveyor who surveyed the district in 1820 named two streams which he encountered in the survey Bad Creek and Worse Creek.[1] These monikers imply a rustic sense of humor that easily could have led to the application of Cuttingbone Creek to a neighboring stream in the same land district.

But interestingly enough, a look at the surveyor's records discloses that he marked the stream "Crittingtons Creek"[2] or "Crittentons Creek"[3] and not as Cuttingbone. This name throws an entirely new, but nonetheless interesting light on the derivation of the name. The field notes of the survey do not list a Crittenton as a member of the surveying team which indicates that the creek was not named for any individual in the party. The use of Crittingtons or Crittentons in the possessive plainly signifies that some one by that named lived, or had lived at one time, along the waterway. If he resided in the locality at the time of the survey, he had no business being there because the lands being surveyed were to be distributed by lottery to Georgia citizens who would become the rightful owners. More than likely, one believes, Crittenton was an Indian country white man, or mixed blood, who resided among the Cherokees and removed farther westward into Georgia with these Indians after the cession of the Rabun County area by the Cherokees in 1819.

It might be added that the surname Crittenden or Crittenton became a common English family name among the Cherokees before the final removal of these Indians to the West in 1838. And even now, in Oklahoma, there are Cherokees who bear this name. It is reasonable to conclude that some member of this family once resided on the creek when the Cherokees inhabited Rabun County. Perhaps this individual was the progenitor of the Cherokee family.

But back to Cuttingbone Creek and its derivation: as curious as the change may have been, it seems probable that the appellation is merely a distortion of Crittington or Crittenton and that the word never had any connection with the Cherokee scratching device or with the barking of shins in the rocky areas about the stream.[4]

—*GMNL* 13(1960): 41

NOTES

1. "District 4 of Rabun County," survey of 1820, Joseph S. Loving, D.S., Platbook PPP, Land Records of Georgia, Surveyor General Department, Atlanta.

2. "Map of District 4 of Rabun," survey of 1820, Joseph Loving, Land Records of Georgia.

3. "Field Notes" for the survey of District 4 of Rabun, Joseph Loving, Land Records of Georgia.

4. [Stewart, *American Placenames*, p. 124, accepts the Crittington explanation, with bad handwriting and folk etymology both contributing to the evolution to Cuttingbone. He says nothing about Goff's "cutshin," but one is reminded of "the rocks and

branch water of Cutshin" in Leonard Roberts' excellent book of Kentucky folktales, *Up Cutshin and Down Greasy* (Lexington: University of Kentucky Press, 1959), p. 37. *FLU.*]

No. 72
Cohelee or Cahelee Creek

In addition to simple translations of Indian placenames into English, it is common in Georgia geographic nomenclature to find appellations that have been radically changed from aboriginal forms into white man's tabs that have no relation to the original Indian designations. On occasion, however, the reverse of this situation has taken place. There are some names that were listed by the first white people in English but which later reverted to, or were converted to, Indian words. It is reasonable to think that the majority of these shifts were reversions to the original Indian names because place designations are tenacious and they are not easily forgotten. An interesting example of this switching back can be found in the name of Cohelee or Cahelee Creek, that arises west of Blakely in Early County and flows southwestward to join the Chattahoochee a short distance above the bridge on the Dothan Division of the Central of Georgia Railway.

The stream was labelled "Big Creek" by the first surveyor who surveyed this part of Early County in 1820.[1] Later the stream became known for a long period as the Cohelee, and it is now referred to as Cahelee. One assumes that these related versions reflect the original Indian name that somehow survived and was continued in use after the area was settled by white people.

Cohelee or Cahelee might have been derived from the Creek words *koha*, cane plus *huili*, standing, signifying Standing Cane. More than likely, however, the name is from *koha*, cane, and *hili*, meaning good, excellent, nice or pretty. The word *háchi*, "hatchee," for stream or creek is understood as a part of the name. This last derivation is probably the correct one because if Cohelee had signified standing cane the name would logically have turned into something like Coweelee, since *huili* the word for standing is pronounced approximately like "weelee." Furthermore, Good Cane Creek is a bit more meaningful than Standing Cane Creek. Cane was the chief browse plant in frontier days and a stream with good cane along its margin would have been a distinct asset to either Indian country stock raisers or to the early white cattlemen.

Benjamin Hawkins reported on a word which resembles Cohelee. He states that "Co-hal-le-wau-gee"[2] (Kohaliwagi) was the fourteenth of the physic plants used by the old Creek medicine men in making up a potion that these Indians drank as a purifying drink at their annual Busk or Green Corn Dance, that was held toward the end of summer after the corn began to ripen. The expression means soft or limber young cane. A Cohelee or good cane place, of course, might have been an area where suitable "Co-hal-le-wau-gee" could be gathered.

J. Clarence Simpson in his study of Florida placenames mentions a Cahellahatchee as the obsolete designation of a stream at the head of St. Marks River in Florida.[3] This Seminole name may be another version of the Cohelee (or Kohili) used in Georgia. Indeed, for all we know, the Florida place may have been named by Indians who removed from the Cohelee Creek section of Georgia following the cession of the Early County area, at the treaty of Fort Jackson in 1814.

In making up the name Cohelee, it will be noted the second syllable of *koha* was dropped. In compounding Creek words it was common to omit one or more syllables of the component forms.

The *l* in the Kohili which probably gave rise to Cohelee or Cahelee is a voiceless *l*, a surd letter which we do not have in English. The aboriginal form was pronounced "Kohee'hlee." This word is more difficult to say than appears, and it is easy to believe the first Early County settlers were quite willing to adopt the simpler Cohelee.

—*GMNL* 13(1960): 41-42

NOTES

1. District 28 of Early County, survey of 1820, Robert Kennedy, D.S., Platbook FFF, lots 350, 370, 413, 415, *passim*, Land Records of Georgia, Surveyor General Department, Atlanta.

2. *A Sketch of the Creek Country in the Years 1798 and 1799* (Americus: Americus Book Co., 1938), p. 72. This study was originally published as Vol. 3, pt. 1 of Collections of the Georgia Historical Society (Savannah, 1848).

3. J. Clarence Simpson, *A Provisional Gazetteer of Florida Place-Names of Indian Derivation*, ed. Mark F. Boyd, Special Publication No. 1, Florida Geological Survey (Tallahassee, 1956), p. 34. The name of the stream at present is Blue Spring.

No. 73
The Rock Landing

One of the best-known spots in the interior of Georgia during the Indian days and the post-Revolutionary years was a place called the Rock Landing. It was located on the east side of the Oconee River, some four miles below Milledgeville, and about a quarter of a mile downstream from the mouth of Buck Creek. The place primarily owed its importance to the fact that several significant trails converged on the site to cross the Oconee at this point. One of these routes was the main strand of the famous Lower Creek trading path, leading from Augusta via the Rock Landing and present Macon to the Indians of western Georgia and eastern Alabama. Except for the relative directness of the course via the Rock Landing, it is not clear why the paths should have gathered at this particular crossing. There was no good fording spot in the immediate area; and in fact the river was so deep at the Landing the traders and other travellers had to swim their horses and resort to canoes or rafts for carrying over their goods and personal effects. When David Taitt passed this way in 1772 he said the water was 20 feet deep at "the Landing" and his party had to use a canoe for getting across.[1] In his journey to the Mississippi, William Bartram visited the Rock Landing on the outward trip and apparently came back the same way.[2] On the return his group used a folding leather canoe to get across the Ocmulgee, and Bartram implies they got over the Oconee in the same way.[3]

The Creek settlement of Oconee Old Town was located just below the Rock Landing and the presence of this community may have been another reason why the trails led to this part of the river. Benjamin Hawkins says the Oconee River derived its name from this place.[4] The town was abandoned around 1715 when the inhabitants removed to the Chattahoochee River.

The Rock Landing is mentioned many times in early records, but so far as could be ascertained, the first document to locate the place with exactness is a 1784 land plat showing the property of Ruth Bonner.[5] This drawing names the Oconee, and along the river, just below a stream labelled "Beaver Creek" (the present Buck Creek), it is marked "Rock Landing." Twenty-five years later, because of a dispute about two ferries that were operating at a crossing above the mouth of Buck Creek, another plat was drawn of the Ruth Bonner property.[6] It was prepared in 1809 by Daniel Sturges, the state's surveyor general and one of the most competent of the pioneer surveyors of Georgia.

Dr. J. C. Bonner, of the Georgia State College for Women at Milledgeville, has made a study of the Rock Landing and has had the benefit of talking to old people along the Oconee about the place. He concluded the name applied to an area that stretched for approximately one-half to three-quarters of a mile on the river, below Buck Creek. The Sturges plat shows the *"Rock Landing Path"* leading to about the middle of the river frontage mentioned by Dr. Bonner. The point reached by this trail, one concludes, was the actual old crossing place and the probable site of the rock which gave rise to the community's name, the Rock Landing. The expression plainly implies there was some sort of rock or ledge at the crossing point. But interestingly enough, after three trips to the spot, and much walking up and down the river below Buck Creek, the writer was unable to find any such ledge or rock, even though one of the visits was made during a prolonged dry spell when the river was low. Perhaps the rock has long since been blasted out to improve navigation. A survey of the Oconee made in 1889 with the view of improving the river mention an Elephant Rock below Buck Creek and very close to the site reached by the old trail.[8] This rock may have been the formation which gave rise to the older name. In any case, there does not seem to be any Elephant Rock at the site today, and one presumes it was removed years ago to make the river safer for boats and rafts.

The Rock Landing today is a placid, detached place that has been turned into a modern cattle pasture, interspersed with strips of woods. One would never guess now that the spot was once served by one of the great arterial thoroughfares of the region. But curiously enough, even over a great span of time, the area still retains some of the air which pleased William Bartram when he visited the place in 1776. He mentioned the old Indian fields stretching along the banks charmingly diversified with groves of detached trees.[9] With the exception of a change from fields to pastures, this depiction of the scene coincides well with the impression which one receives today.

Before closing the sketch, it should be noted that there was another Rock Landing on the Oconee. The 1889 survey of the river which has been mentioned lists a "Rock Landing," below the mouth of Big Creek, on the east side of the river, upstream from Dublin.[10] The place was considerably below the other Rock Landing. Nothing could be learned about this spot and it is not known how long the appellation has been in use.

—*GMNL* 13(1960): 102-103

NOTES

1. Newton D. Mereness, "Journal of David Taitt," *Travels in the American Colonies* (New York: Macmillan, 1916), pp. 561-62.
2. William Bartram, *Travels Through North and South Carolina, Georgia, East and West Florida* (Dublin, 1793), pp. 377-78.
3. *Ibid.*, pp. 457-58.
4. Benjamin Hawkins, *A Sketch of the Creek Country in the Years 1798 and 1799* (Americus, Ga.: Americus Book Co., 1938), p. 62.
5. Plat for the land of Ruth Bonner, Washington County, 1784, Platbook B, p. 36, Land Records of Georgia, Surveyor General Department, Atlanta.
6. "Report of Daniel Sturges Esq., Surveyor General" relative to a caveat between Aaron McKinzie vs. James Thweatt, inserted in Platbook B, opposite p. 36, Land Records of Georgia. It should be noted the Sturges plat shows the property as 450 acres. The 1784 plat gives the land as containing only 400 acres.
7. J. C. Bonner, "Where is Rock Landing?" (manuscript), p. 5.
8. *Oconee River, Georgia*, House Doc. 211, 51st Cong., 1st Sess. (Washington, D.C., 1890), Sheet 1.
9. Bartram, *Travels*, p. 377.
10. *Oconee River*, Sheet 5.

No. 74
Wahoo Island, Wahoo River, the Wahoo Creeks, Wahoo District, Barbour Island, and Barbour Island River

The mere listing of Wahoo in the above title has probably already evoked a smile from the reader because of the common usage of the word to signify drivel, twaddle, or tommyrot. But apart from this seemingly modern slang meaning, Wahoo is a respectable term that has found usage in Georgia geographic nomenclature for over two centuries. The first time the appellation entered placename records was in 1760 in connection with a petition of John Barber to the governor and Provincial Council for a grant to some "Hammocks" on the lower side of South Newport River, in what is now McIntosh County.[1]

In his request, Barber was really seeking a confirmation of his rights to the lands, because he stated he had settled the place twenty years before with the permission of General Oglethorpe.[2] He added the interesting information that the Indians had known the site as the Wawhoo Islands.[3] The place, now called Wahoo Island, is to the east of U.S. 17, on the south bank of South Newport River and on the upper side of Wahoo River, a tidal stream that leads into the South Newport immediately above Sapelo Sound.[4] Just across the Wahoo River, to the south of the Wawhoo hammocks, is Barbour Island. It is bounded on the west by another tidal waterway called Barbour Island River, which also drains into Sapelo Sound at the mouth of Sapelo River. There is reason to believe this island and stream perpetuate John Barber's name because an application for land in the area filed in 1757 mentions the spot as Barber's Island.[5]

Another old Wahoo can be found in Wahoo Creek, which arises at the southwest edge of White County and flows across the southeast corner of Lumpkin, thence southward through Hall to join Little River a short distance above the latter's union with the Chattahoochee, to the north of Gainesville. This stream's name was first recorded by the surveyors of Districts 10 and 11 of Hall in the original survey of the section in 1820.[6] In the upper reaches of the waterway, in District 11, the surveyor also used the designations "East Wahoo," "Middle Fork of Wahoo," and "West Fork of Wahoo."[7] These last names are still employed by some people in Hall.

It should be mentioned that the surveyor of District 12 also used the name Wahoo in connection with the two main branches of Little River.[8] He referred to the present East Fork of the latter as "East Wahoo" and to the West Fork of Little River as "Middle Wahoo."

The surveyor in District 10 below did not adopt these names, apparently because he had already shown a Wahoo Creek in the western part of his survey. He simply listed the forks under the name *Little River*.

In view of the fact that two different surveyors employed the designation Wahoo in connection with the creek that still bears the tab, there is a basis for believing the name was already in use before the white man came to demarcate the area with his system of metes and bounds.

Before leaving this region to pass to a second Wahoo Creek in another part of the state, mention should be made of the Wahoo community in the southeast corner of Lumpkin County at the head of Wahoo Creek and in the area about Georgia 52, one of the Dahlonega-Gainesville roads. The section is old and is officially known as the Wahoo District, or Georgia Militia District No. 1051. For a considerable period the community once had a post office called Wahoo.

The other Wahoo Creek is in Coweta County. It arises northeastward of Newnan and flows west to join the Chattahoochee near the eastern edge of the McIntosh Reserve, and down river from Whitesburg in Carroll County. This stream's name was first recorded in 1826-1827 by the surveyors of Districts 4 and 5 of original Coweta.[9] One of these men, however, labelled the creek "Big Warhoo."[10] And again, since both men knew the name of the waterway and properly connected it on their maps, there are grounds for believing this designation was also in use, by Indian countrymen, if not by the Indians, before the time of the surveys.

Interestingly enough, *A Dictionary of American English* gives two different origins for the word Wahoo and both derivations are Indian, although each expression has a different application. In one instance the term is noted as being derived from the Dakota word *wanhu* ("wãhu"), for a shrub known as burning bush—*Evonymus atropurpureus;* and in the other, from the Creek word *ûhawhu,* for the cork or winged elm—*Ulmus racemosa* or *U. alata;* or, for any one of several other trees that produce a bark which can be made soft and pliable by soaking in water.

As far as the Georgia Wahoo names are concerned, one concludes the word was drawn from the Creek term, because those Indians lived here and because white people adopted the term long before they had any opportunity to borrow an expression from the Dakotas.

In view of the fact that the Muskogee generic name for elm is *táfoso* ("tuh fō'so)", it is reasonable to conclude that *ûhawhu* was a descriptive term applied to trees having the pliable bark. The word, however, may not actually have been a pure Muskogean expression. It may be derived from the language of some subtribe or group living in the area of the old Creek Confederacy. The name, for instance, might have been Guale, because those Indians once resided in the coastal section where Wahoo Island is found.

In any case, the tab Wahoo became well known among Georgia pioneers and early surveyors. The latter frequently employed the term in connection with trees that were used to mark the stations and corners along the courses of their surveys. The name was even carried into Cherokee country as is evidenced by the Wahoo names of Hall and Lumpkin counties. The Cherokee word for elm was *tsuwa-do-*

nah, but there is no evidence that the white people ever took over and used this name.

Webster's *International Dictionary* gives the preferred pronunciation of Wahoo as "*wä hōō'*." This version is not used in Georgia and if the word is actually derived from the Creek *ûhawhu,* that pronunciation was probably never employed here because it is unlikely that this expression would have been accented on the last syllable, even as a dialectical form of some Muskogean language. In this state the stress on Wahoo tends to be equally divided between both syllables, although some people may put slight emphasis on the *wä* element, or first syllable.

It should be noted that Wahoo is distinctive in that it is one of the relatively few Indian names that still retain the broad *a* in present-day usage. Mostly this letter has been converted to *au, ah, aw, ar* and even into other sounds in the Indian appellations that we retain. Indeed the earlier people had trouble with the vowel. It will be recalled that John Barber wrote Wahoo as "Wawhoo," while surveyor Dickerson of the 5th District of Coweta made it "Warhoo."

—GMNL 13(1960): 103-104

NOTES

1. Allen D. Candler, ed., *The Colonial Records of the State of Georgia* (Atlanta: Franklin, 1904-1916), 8: 260.
2. *Ibid.*
3. *Ibid.*
4. These places can be found on the topographical sheet *Sapelo Sound,* prepared by the U.S. Geological Survey, edition of 1954.
5. Candler, ed., *Colonial Records of Georgia,* 7:679-80, petition of Jacob Anderson.
6. District 10, William Triplett, D.S., Platbook NNN, lots 117, 120, 126, *passim;* and District 11, Francis Gideon, D.S., Platbook NNN, lots 37, 40, 42, 43, 50, *passim,* Land Records of Georgia, Surveyor General Department, Atlanta.
7. District 11, Platbook NNN.
8. District 12, Hall County, survey of 1820, Walter L. Campbell, D.S., Platbook NNN. East Wahoo is shown in lots 26, 27, 47, 48, *passim,* and Middle Wahoo in lots 2, 3, 4, 8, 9, *passim.*
9. Map of District 4 of the 4th Section (now part of Coweta), survey of 1827, Joel E. Mercer, D.S.; Map of District 5 of the 4th Section (now Coweta), survey of 1826, O. T. Dickerson, D.S., Land Records of Georgia.
10. Map of District 5.

No. 75
Lewis Creek

Lewis Creek heads at the right of way of the Seaboard Airline Railroad, southwest of Cox in McIntosh County, and flows roughly parallel to the Altamaha to enter the latter some three miles due west of Darien. The creek was named two hundred years ago for Samuel Lewis, Sr. Lewis arrived in the province a short time prior to 1758, with a wife and six children. In that year he applied to the governor and Colonial Council for a headright grant of 450 acres on a branch of the North Swamp of South Newport River.[1] This application was approved, but Lewis could not find that much available land in the area specified. The following year, he petitioned for 450 acres on the north side of the Altamaha, "near where Capt. McIntosh formerly kept a store."[2] This request was also granted and Lewis quickly found a suitable tract, because he took up land along the creek and caused his name to be attached to the stream since a plat dated 1759 shows the property bordering Lewis Creek.[3] Apparently some of Lewis's children were sons because in the following years old plats show lands for other Lewises in the area.

It is not known what Lewis expected to do with the property other than that he promised to cultivate it and improve it.[4] The land was in a low area, subject to overflow, and in a section that even today is regarded as one of the widest and wildest river swamps of the state. Presumably he planned to engage in rice raising and perhaps to exploit the timber because of the relatively good water transportation that was nearby.

It should be noted that the rising point for Lewis Creek applies to the present stream. In colonial years the creek was probably several miles longer. This was the case because a DeBrahm plat of the Fort Barrington area[5] some four miles farther up the Altamaha, shows a Lewis Lagoon leading off the river at the old trail crossing point on the Altamaha, near the lower end of the fort site.[6] This lagoon is now called Harpers Lake. By a series of sloughs and channels, its waters reach nearly to the Seaboard tracks, the beginning of Lewis Creek. The narrowness of the present gap makes it reasonably certain that the creek once ran all the way from Fort Barrington to the point near Darien.

Perhaps the most interesting note which can be made about Lewis Creek pertains to the discovery along its margins of the much talked about Lost Gordonia—the *Franklinia alatamaha*. John and William Bartram found the plant in the fall of 1765 on a trip southward from Savannah to Florida. Francis Harper states the discovery was made October 1, 1765, and that the probable point was 1.7 miles northwest of present Cox.[7] On this date, however, John Bartram's "Diary" of the trip says they missed the path and came out four miles below the fort,[8] where they made camp before continuing the next day to Barrington.[9] This notation leaves the impression that the *Franklinia* was found to the south of the fort, especially in view of the fact that Bartram said they discovered several curious shrubs on the date in question.[10] In this case, then the plant was found to the southwest of Cox, near the head of present Lewis Creek.

—*GMNL* 13(1960): 104-105

NOTES

1. Allen D. Candler, ed., *The Colonial Records of the State of Georgia* (Atlanta: Franklin, 1904-1916), 7: 798-99, minutes of the Council for Aug. 1, 1758.
2. *Ibid.*, p. 887, minutes for Feb. 6, 1759.
3. Platbook C, p. 159, Land Records of Georgia, Department of Archives and History, Altanta.
4. Candler, ed., *Colonial Records of Georgia*, p. 887.
5. Fort Barrington, one of Georgia's early outposts, was on the north side of the Altamaha, in the western part of present McIntosh County. It was to the north of today's Mt. Pleasant on U.S. 25-341, in Wayne County. The noted early trail from Georgia to Florida crossed the river at the place, and this factor was of prime importance in causing the fort to be built at this place.
6. W. G. deBrahm, "The Environs of Fort Barrington," surveyed about 1770, in Hulbert's Crown Collection of Photographs of American Maps, copy in the Ayer Collection of the Newberry Library, Chicago.
7. Francis Harper, *The Travels of William Bartram* (New Haven: Yale University Press, 1958), p. 337.
8. John Bartram, "Diary of a Journey Through Carolina, Georgia, and Florida, 1765-6," ed. Francis Harper, *Transactions of the American Philosophical Society*, N.S. 33, pt. 1: 31.
9. *Ibid.*
10. *Ibid.* The Bartrams did not name the plant at this time; apparently they thought it was a Gordonia. When it was later decided a new genus had been discovered, it was named Franklinia Altamaha for Benjamin Franklin; cf. Bartram, *Travels Through North and South Carolina, Georgia, East and West Florida* (Dublin, 1793), p. 465n.

No. 76
Fishing Creek in Baldwin County

A surprising number of Georgia placenames in English form are really translations of original Indian designations. In many instances it is easy to verify that these shifts have taken place from one language to another. In other cases, however, the English versions seem so appropriate and so commonplace in meaning that one would never learn the words could be traced back to the Indians except for strokes of luck that turned up obscure references which give clues as to the original versions of the names. A good example to illustrate the situation can be found in the name Fishing Creek, a stream that arises in eastern Jones County and flows across Baldwin to enter the Oconee just below Milledgeville. Now, one could easily conclude that the name was originally English and that it was probably adopted by the first white settlers subsequent to the settlement of the area following the initial survey of the land in 1804. But the name was Indian in the beginning and this fact is verified by a little reference in the *American State Papers,* wherein some Creek chiefs made recommendations about a suitable site for the establishment of a fort on Indian land, pursuant to a provision in the 1796 treaty of Colerain.[1] The chiefs suggested a high bluff on the west bank of the Oconee at a place which subsequently became the site of Fort Wilkinson. In order to identify the proposed spot, they mentioned that it was about a mile below old Fort Fidius (on the east side of the river), and three miles below "Thlock-laoso, or fishing creek, very valuable always, for fish, particularly for shad, in the Spring."[2] The transcriber who took down the statement of the chiefs garbled the Indian version of the name, but he could not be blamed for this because the expression involved two surd letters called voiceless els which we do not have in our language. He got the name sufficiently correct, however, for one to recognize the word as being intended for *thlathloasa* ("hlä hlō′ä′sä"), which freely in English signifies Fishing Creek, from *thlathlo* (or "hlahlo"), fish, plus the suffix *asa.* The last form is susceptible to different renditions, depending on the sense or connotation of the noun to which it is attached. Usually the expression signified runner, tracker, or chaser. Thus, for instance, when used in connection with the word *echo* ("eacho") for deer, the full expression would be *echoasa* and would mean literally deer tracker or deer chaser. The term could also be shifted to the gerundive forms of tracking, running, or chasing and, by implication, in the case of the Baldwin County name, into taking or catching. These little intricacies in the meanings of *asa*, coupled with the difficulty of pronouncing *thlathlo* correctly, obviously led the pioneer white people to convert the name into the simpler Fishing Creek and let it go at that.

—*GMNL* 13(1960): 105-106

NOTES

1. Colerain was on the St. Marys River, in southwest Camden County, southeastward of today's Folkston.
2. *American State Papers*, II. Indian Affairs 1: 611.

No. 77
Oakfuskee Creek

On occasion in these sketches mention has been made of the fact that some of Georgia's most unusual placenames rarely, if ever, appear on maps. Such appellations are sometimes used for generation after generation without being noted on charts. An interesting example can be found in the name of a small stream called Oakfuskee Creek, that arises a mile or so to the west of Concord in Pike County and enters Flint River a short distance upstream from the noted Flat Shoals. Oakfuskee is derived from the Muskogee *ak*, or "oc," signifying in, or down in, and *fáski*, or "fuskee," a point. Now, the creek actually joins the Flint at a sharp bend in the river, but it enters on the outside of the curve and not within the bend, which lies on the west side in Meriwether County. It is probable then that the stream did not receive its designation from any physical condition prevailing at the site of its union with the river. More than likely the creek derived its name from the fact that the famous Oakfuskee path skirted the fringes of the waterway on its way to the fording point at the Flat Shoals. This noted route, also known as the Upper Creek path, was one of the historic Indian trading routes of the country.[1] It was first used by the English about the turn of the eighteenth century from Charleston and the area of present Augusta via today's Dearing, Warrenton, Eatonton, Indian Springs, Griffin, and the Flat Shoals for reaching the Upper Creek towns on the Chattahoochee, Tallapoosa, and Coosa rivers. From points on the latter stream, it also had connections to the Choctaws and Chickasaws in what is now Mississippi. Its main course, however, led to the important Upper Creek town of Oakfuskee. This place was located in a bend on the west side of the Tallapoosa River in Dade County, Alabama. The situation one can be sure gave rise to the name Oakfuskee—in a point. If the assumption about the origin of the Oakfuskee Creek of Georgia is correct, the designation is the only surviving placename in this state which commemorates the famous trading route.

—*GMNL* 13(1960): 106

NOTE

1. For a discussion and retracing of this noted trail see John H. Goff, "The Path to Oakfuskee," *The Georgia Historical Quarterly,* for March, 1955, pp. 1-36; and June, 1955, pp. 152-71 (with map).

No. 78
Toms Shoals (Toms Fords, Toms Path, Chehaw Path, Tuskio-Micco Path, Popes Ferry and Road, Wallers Ferry and Road, Booths Ferry and Road, Calhouns Ferry, Grays Ferry Road, the Otaulganene or Islands Ford of Flint River, the Sulenojuhnene Fords, the Creek Town of Buzzard Roost, Hootens Ferry, Cantelows Ferry, Trices Ferry and Smuteyes Trail)

On the Oconee River, near the northeast corner of Milledgeville, at the mouth of a stream called Tobler Creek, there is a spot known as Toms Shoals. And, to the west, on the Ocmulgee, about a half-mile below Popes[1] Ferry in Monroe County, there is another place bearing the same name. It is significant to add that these second shallows are also located at the mouth of another Tobler Creek, which enters the

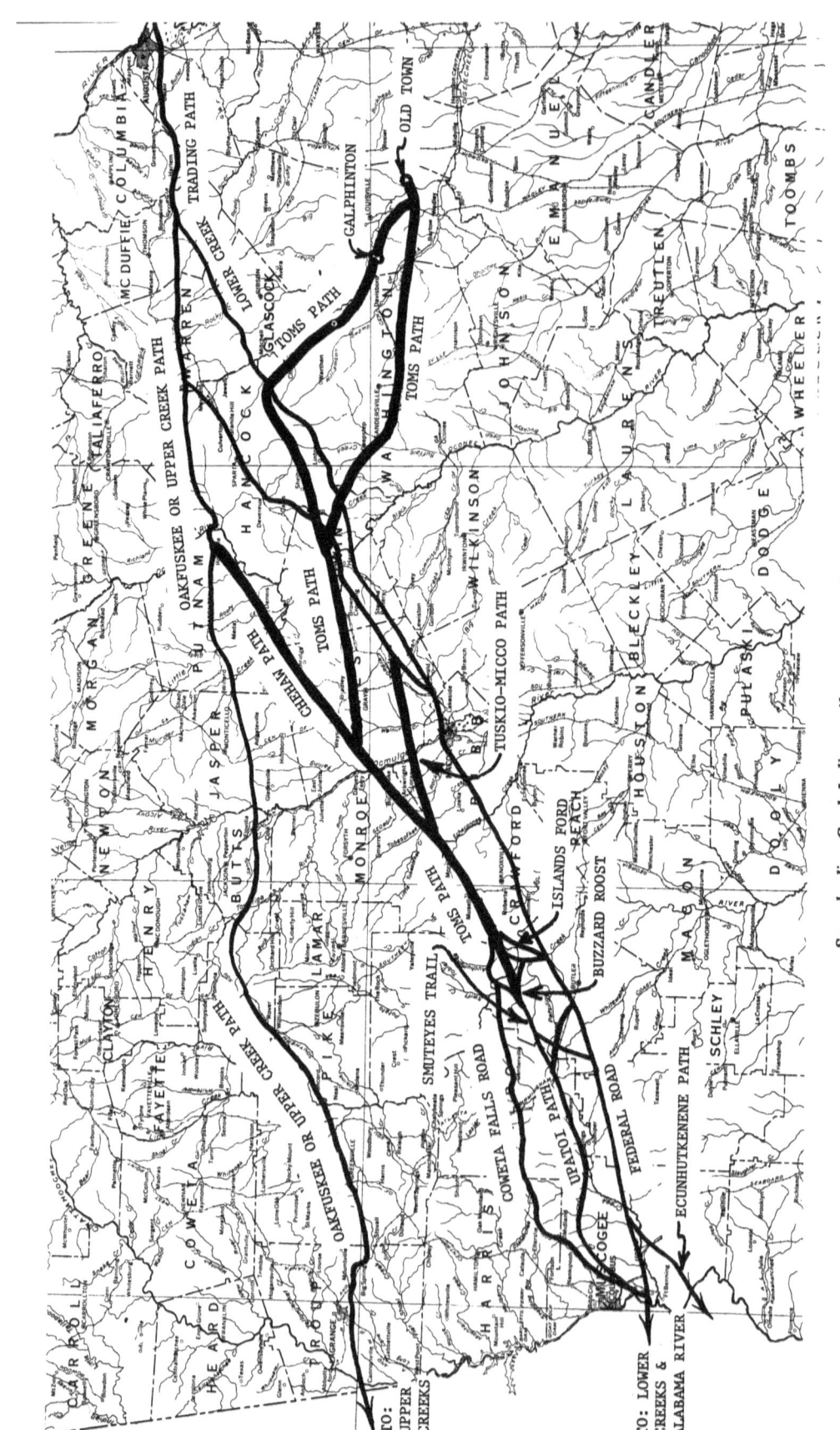

Some leading Creek Indian trails across central Georgia

Ocmulgee on the west or Monroe side. These two shoals are interesting because they derive their names from a noted Indian trail called Toms Path, which once crossed the Oconee and Ocmulgee at the sites indicated. This trace, a segment and alternate way of the famous Lower Creek trading route, spanned the region from the Ogeechee River section in Jefferson County to the middle Flint River areas of present Crawford and Upson counties, where it had a number of connections to important Lower Creek towns along the Chattahoochee in western Georgia and eastern Alabama. From these settlements there were also links leading on to the Upper Creeks on the Tallapoosa and Coosa rivers of central Alabama; and from these centers in turn, there were connecting trails to the Choctaws and Chickasaws of Mississippi.

The accompanying map[2] shows the course of Toms Path with some of its connecting routes and depicts its relationship to other notable traces to the Creeks across central Georgia.

As mentioned, Toms Path was a link and major alternate of the Lower Creek route. The latter was not a single thoroughfare as the name implies but rather a complexity of entwined, alternating ways and spurs that connected points on the Savannah River with the Indian centers mentioned above. The main strand of this braid was the Chelucconeneauhasse,[3] or Old Horse Path, which is commonly referred to as the Lower Creek Trading Path. This famous thoroughfare led westward from Augusta via the Rock Landing on the Oconee, present Macon on the Ocmulgee, and the site of the old Indian Agency on the Flint (in western Crawford County) to the Creek towns on the Chattahoochee below today's Columbus. It was one of the historic Indian trading routes of the country and was used by Carolina traders before the foundation of Georgia. The trail was remarkably straight, as can be seen by the map. This directness was possible only, however, because the traders and the packhorsemen who used the thoroughfare usually did not depend on fords for crossing big streams athwart the course but carried folding leather canoes, or resorted to other man-made devices such as improvised rafts, hideaway dugout canoes, or in later years, actual "flats" or ferries, for getting themselves and their goods across waterways like the Oconee and Ocmulgee. There were fords on these streams at or near the crossing points but they were not dependable or safe in times of high waters. The ferrying facilities permitted the traders to follow a straight course, but it should be noted that this directness compelled them to climb the relatively high, sandy, north and south dividing ridges that lay between the various rivers all the way to the Chattahoochee. The plodding of such a course with a heavily loaded pack train must have been extremely tedious for both man and animal.

Since early travellers to the Creeks usually journeyed in the company of traders, they generally followed this well-known trace and as a consequence mentioned it more in their writings than was the case for alternate ways such as Toms Path, or for the Tuskio-Micco trail which will be discussed.

Toms Path was more circuitous than the noted trading path, but a retracing of both ways leaves the impression on a modern observer that the former was deliberately laid out to take advantage of an easier course and especially of better fording sites on the Oconee, Ocmulgee, and Flint. Indeed, its advantages in these respects are so manifest, one may reasonably conclude that it was probably the main aboriginal route running east and west in this part of Georgia before packhorsemen and other travellers began to favor the way that became the Old Horse Path. Colonel Benjamin Hawkins states the latter route was the oldest trail to the Creeks but one ventures to state he was writing of the generalized Lower Creek route and not of a specific trail, because on occasion the Colonel made use of parts of the convenient Toms Path on his own journeys.

Owing to the naturalness of its course, Toms Path may have been the principal thoroughfare used by the first Carolina explorers and traders to reach the Ocheese towns that once stood on the Ocmulgee from present Macon to Juliette.[4] This suggestion applies to the way which the first English followed to reach the noted Ocmulgee Town on the east side of Macon because even in these days the main travelled route between the Milledgeville area and Macon is Georgia 22 which follows closely the Old Toms Path as far as Gray. In the vicinity of the latter point, in Indian days, as now, there was a route that led to the site of Ocmulgee Old Town and Fields.[5]

The course of Toms Path for the most part is fairly well outlined in old records, although with present information there must be assumptions or conjectures about important segments of the route and about its connections with certain other trails. The most difficult aspect of retracing the path concerns its eastern point or points of beginning. This situation arises from the fact that original maps and plats in the official land records of the state do not give a continuous picture of the trail in the headrights section lying to the east of the Oconee. Numbers of early plats of this area depict and name the trace under one name or another but often on a given chart the adjoining lands are marked "vacant," i.e., not yet granted or surveyed. These gaps make it impossible to trace the path with consistency from one property to another.

Despite these uncertainties, however, sufficient documentary evidence exists to show there were at least two eastern prongs of Toms Path leading to the Tom Shoals on the Oconee, at the northeast edge of Milledgeville. On the basis of the complexity of the Lower Creek route, it is reasonable to conclude there were also other segments of this route that converged on the same ford, or which had spurs that branched off to it. One such connection which is almost certain to have existed was a crossover from the Upper Creek Path to the Old Trading Path. This link began at the Ogeechee crossing of the former above Mayfield and led toward the Rock Landing via Sparta and Devereux.[6] In the vicinity of present Black Spring Church crossroads, to the east of Milledgeville, on Georgia 22, this route crossed one of the known forks of Toms Path. It would have been easy here to turn out of the crossover from the Upper Path into Toms trail.

Of the two ascertainable forks of Toms Path to the east of the Oconee, one branch seemingly began at Old Town, on the east side of the Ogeechee below Louisville and ran by Galphinton,[7] on the Ogeechee in western Jefferson County. It led up Williamson Swamp Creek,[8] and above the head of this stream, on the Washington-Hancock line (in the area where Georgia 15 now crosses from one county to another), it intersected and crossed the Lower Creek Trading Path[9] running east and west on what is now the county line. In the same vicinity it also intersected Lamars Trail,[10] leading southward out of today's Hancock County.

Lamars Trail is of interest because an unpublished, unofficial source states this thoroughfare was also known as "Old Toms Lower Trail."[11] No available official document mentions such a dual name for the Lamars route, although a Washington County plat dated 1787 does show a strip of Toms Path on the "south[west]side" of Williamson Swamp Creek,[12] on a course that could have coincided with the upper stretches of Lamars route in the vicinity of Warthen. Lamars Trail went on to the Oconee, to a crossing that later became well known as Balls Ferry. The course of the trace is shown on various old plats, but these listings do not use the word Toms in connection with the route.

It is conceded, though, that this Old Toms Lower Trail may have been an alternate way of Toms Path, that ran up the west side of Williamson Swamp Creek to unite at Warthen with Lamars Trail, thence to the point where Toms Path and Lamars trace intersected on the Washington-Hancock line.

From the intersection with the Trading Path and Lamars Trail, Toms Path bore off in a westerly direction toward the Oconee ford. Its exact course can not be identified with current roads, but early plats show strips of it on the upper waters of Buffalo Creek.[13] Another plat shows it in today's Baldwin County, just to the east of the ford on the Oconee.[14]

As can be seen from the map, this eastern prong of Toms Path curved. Indian trails were ordinarily not nearly so circuitous, and there must have been some good reason for such circuity. The most plausible reason for the roundaboutness was a desire to by-pass Williamson Swamp Creek, which was a formidable stream to cross in frontier days. In addition to difficult marginal swamps, the creek had some large beaver dam areas that were impassable.

The second prong of Toms Path forked from the Chickasaw Path on the east side of Buffalo Creek, below Deep Step in Washington County.[15] The Chickasaw trace led on to the Savannah River, but from the Oconee to the place where Toms Path branched off it seems closely identifiable with parts of the route which we now call the Upper Sandersville Road from Milledgeville to Sandersville.

After spurring from the Chickasaw trail, this Toms Path crossed Keg Creek on a southeasterly bearing. The next time it appears in the land records is on a plat showing the trace running along the upper side of Limestone Creek in southeast Washington, and leading to a crossing on Williamson Swamp Creek.[16] Its exact course between Keg Creek and this ford is not known, but one source mentions it in the area between Sandersville and Tennille,[17] a section which would have been on its logical course between the two streams mentioned.

Just where this prong led beyond Williamson Swamp Creek is not known. In all probability, however, it went on to Old Town, because when last shown it was headed toward that place. The site was long a trading point of note and it is reasonable to conclude the path ran the relatively short distance to reach the spot.

This second prong of Toms Path was the more direct of the two known forks, but interestingly enough, the circuitous first branch is the one which is most often shown in the plats.

But to return to the westward course of Toms Path, the trace crossed the Oconee near the mouth of Derisoes Creek,[18] which is now called Champion Creek. The crossing was known as Toms Ford and Colonel Hawkins labelled it a "good one."[19] Today the place seems wide and deep. Although the site is remembered as Toms Shoals, the crossing does not now seem particularly shoally. Perhaps since the time the place served as a ford, the channel has been deepened and widened in an effort to improve navigation.

Beyond the Oconee, the Toms route led west across Tobler Creek,[20] thence over a divide and up Fishing Creek Valley close along the way now followed by Georgia 22 to Gray.[21] At this place, it bore northwestward, passing four land lots to the north of Clinton, and led on to the fording point on the Ocmulgee—below Butlers Creek in Jones County,[22] and above Tobler Creek on the Monroe side. This crossing is the place which elderly people of the section remember as Toms Shoals. Today the old ford appears wide and formidable. One imagines that many a wilderness traveller must have entered such waters with a feeling of trepidation.

In connection with this ford, it is important to mention that Toms Path was joined on the right a short distance east of the crossing by a trail called the Chehaw Path.[23] The old way remains today in this area as a field and woods road leading down to the river from the Popes Ferry–Clinton highway.

In the Indian years the Chehaw Path was a crossover from the Oakfuskee or Upper Path to the Lower Creek way.[24] It branched from the former near the old Dejarnette place,[25] to the south of Rockville in southeast Putnam County, and not far to the west of the fording point of the Oakfuskee trail on the Oconee at the mouth of Shoulderbone Creek.

On a course now largely abandoned, the Chehaw Path led on a direct course to Toms Ford on the Ocmulgee, passing en route a bit to the south of present Wayside on Georgia 11.[26]

The path presumably was named for the Chehaw Indians of the Creek Confederacy. This band had towns on both the Chattahoochee and the Flint. One assumes the trail derived its name from the former settlements because it joined Toms Path which connected with the Chehaw places on the Chattahoochee. The Chehaw Path illustrates a curious and interesting aspect of Indian thoroughfares. For some reason, which is not now clear, different bands and tribes of Indians sometimes had their own routes for reaching the same general destinations. Thus there were Uchee paths, a Cusata Path, a Chickasaw Path, and so on leading in the direction of Augusta. The subject of differing routes for Indian groups is a fascinating topic which will receive later attention in this *Newsletter* series. Chehaw Creek (now commonly called Jenkins Branch) in southeast Putnam County is seemingly the sole remaining placename reminder of this former Indian thoroughfare.

Before continuing a tracing of Toms Path, it should be noted that some Lower Creek chiefs used an interesting name for the site of Toms Ford on the Ocmulgee. They referred to the place as Ochee Finnau.[27] The expression signifies hickory bridge or footlog, from *ochi*, hickory and *fina*, a crossing facility over a stream. Apparently the designation in this instance was intended for hickory footlog. One does not see, however, how the name could have been applicable to Toms Shoals because the place was far too wide for a footlog and there is scant chance that an actual bridge was erected at the site during Indian days. Moreover, hickory is heavy, decays rapidly, and would be unsuitable for use as a footlog. Or, perhaps in a way that is not now understood, Ochee Finnau was somehow connected with one of the early Ocheese towns on the Ocmulgee. Either side of the river at Toms Shoals could have served as the site for such a settlement.

Beyond the Ocmulgee, Toms Path led off southwestward toward fords on Flint River.[28] It followed fairly closely a present dirt road to the east side of Coloparchee Creek, crossing en route today's U.S. 41 a mile below Bolingbroke. Beyond the Coloparchee the route is now completely abandoned for a considerable stretch. The 1821 surveys of Monroe, however, give the former course and show the trace was joined on the left by a thoroughfare named Wallers Road,[29] leading from Wallers Ferry on the Ocmulgee, above the mouth of Beaverdam Creek.[30] It seemingly was not an Indian trail but a newly blazed wagon route.

To the west of Rocky Creek, Toms Path was also joined on the right by a spur of Popes Road,[31] coming from Popes Ferry on the Ocmulgee. This crossing was opened sometime prior to 1821 a short distance upstream from Toms Shoals.[32] The trace was a white man's road and there can be little doubt that it was "cut" and the ferry established to provide a by-pass around the Ocmulgee ford that was better suited to vehicular travel. Popes Ferry remained in use for several generations and only ceased operating in recent years.

Toms Path continued southwestward to the site of old Montpelier[33] in Monroe County, located just above the point where Crawford, Bibb, and Monroe corner. Here it left District 13 of Monroe and here its name Toms is last mentioned in the original survey records.[34] One can be sure the trail went on to the Flint, however, because a

1793 military order directed some Georgia troops to march to the place where Toms Path crossed that river.[35]

Just below the site of Montpelier there is some uncertainty about the precise course of the path due to discrepancies in presentations of the trace in the surveys of the four land districts which adjoin in this area.[36] But these differences are slight and it is plain the route entered Crawford in the northeast corner of the county.[37] It takes up again as a present-day way at the Hopewell Road near the former Montpelier Station on the now-abandoned Macon and Birmingham Railroad, and runs southwestward on an unbroken course across upper Crawford County, passing Hopewell Crossroads, the Ceres School site, and Hammock Grove. It passes a mile below today's Musella on U.S. 341.

Shortly after leaving the Montpelier Station, where the old trail is now intersected by Georgia 42, Toms Path was joined on the right by a trace coming from the northeast.[38] This connection was Booths Road leading from Zachariah Booth's ferry on the Ocmulgee, located below today's Juliette and above the mouth of Rum Creek.[39] The intersection could also have been another connection with the Popes Road because a second spur of the latter apparently joined the Booths route.[40] The name Booths Road is significant because farther along Flint River Toms trail was given this designation in the 1821 survey of District 1 of original Houston.

Beyond Hammock Grove where the present road along Toms Path intersects U.S. 80, there was a significant fork in the early route.[41] One branch continued along No. 80, while the other (on a course now abandoned) curved southward over Ulcohatchee Creek to a ford on Flint River,[42] [located just below the mouth of Auchumpkee Creek,][43] in extreme southwest Crawford County. This fork is mentioned in the first official survey as the Big Shoals Road.[44] One can be reasonably certain this designation was the eastbound name of a trail that connected with Toms Path and that the Big Shoals which gave rise to the name were at a crossing place on the Ocmulgee, above Macon, and not on Flint River at the point which was reached by the fork of Toms Path. This latter place was the noted Islands Ford of the Flint. Colonel Hawkins mentions it as the "Island's ford,"[45] but elsewhere he makes it plain the correct name was in the plural by giving the Creek designation as "Otaulganene,"[46] from *oti*, island, plus the plural-forming suffix *álgi*, or "ulga," plus the word *nini*, or "nene," signifying trail or path. Further evidence that the site was the Islands Ford can be found in the name applied by the first surveyor to the

Ulcohatchee and the lower stretch of Auchumpkee Creek. He marked the waterway "Autoolee Creek."[47] This designation is simply a garbled version of *otiálgi*, the Muscogee word for islands. The stream was so named, of course, because it emptied at some islands where the path crossed.

Hawkins referred to the Islands Ford site as "the second falls" of the Flint,[48] meaning apparently the second falls from the lower edge of the Fall Line Belt. The place at present consists of three islands,[49] interspersed between four lateral channels of the river. Hawkins states the place was a good crossing,[50] although he commented on the broken nature of the land on both sides of the ford.[51] The place today is sometimes referred to as Reeves Island and Shoals, for a family of the area. Of the three big fords that have been mentioned thus far—on the Oconee, Ocmulgee, and Flint—the Islands Ford impresses a modern observer as being the safest and easiest to cross.

Over Flint River, the original 1827 surveys of what is now Taylor County do not show in the immediate vicinity of the Islands Ford, the western connections of Toms Path, or the Big Shoals Road. One can be sure, though, that there were links with westward-leading paths to the Chattahoochee. One of these went to the Damascus School site on Georgia 263.[52] Another led upriver a half-mile to join the former Grays Ferry Road out to Five Points on U.S. 19; and still another mounted a steep hill along the south side of the river, through a peach orchard to the west of the Wainwright place,[53] and ran a short distance southward to Ficklins Mill, located at an old fording point on Patsiliga Creek. Here this connection joined the main line of the Old Horse Path and the Ecunhutkenene, or White Ground Path to the Chattahoochee. At this place, these united trails were exactly on the course of the 1805 Federal Road across the Creek Country, leading from Fort Hawkins on the Ocmulgee to the Alabama River above Mobile. It was the first white man's thoroughfare of western Georgia and the first vehicular route of this state leading directly west.[54]

Back in Crawford County, on today's U.S. 80, where the Big Shoals Road segment of Toms Path turned off to the Islands Ford, another prong of the Toms route continued west for a mile or so along the course of what is now No. 80 to a point beyond Hickory Grove crossroads where it veered sharply southwestward from 80, down a present little dirt road leading past the Olive Grove colored church (near the Crawford-Upson line), thence across Auchumpkee Creek into Upson County. This route was marked Booths Road on the first surveys of the area made in 1821.[55] The name (like the Big

Shoals Road) may have been an eastbound designation because the trace connected eastward to Booths Ferry on the Ocmulgee. If the road led westward to a ferry maintained by Booth on the Flint, no such facility is mentioned on the surveys and the Georgia statutes do not show that the state had empowered Booth to establish a crossing on that river.[56] For some mysterious reason the Booths Road fork of Toms Path was stopped abruptly on the surveyor's plats at the western edge of land lot 304 of District 1, just a fractional land lot short of Flint River. Since fording opportunities beyond the point where the road was last shown are not good, one concludes there must have been an early ferry to serve the trace, although the site of the crossing was not shown and the name of the operator not given. But be this as it may, in 1825, four years after the original surveys, Samuel Calhoun was authorized to open a public ferry,[57] at or very close to the point Booths Road would have reached had it continued directly ahead from the point where it was last depicted on the surveys. Calhouns Ferry was established at a strategic place, and some years later when the land west of the Flint was ceded by the Indians and surveyed, the surveys show several important traces gathering in, or radiating from the west-side landing. One of these was the Coweta Falls Road that ran to what is now Columbus, along the most northerly of the several paralleling routes that led to the Chattahoochee in this section of Georgia. Another connection was the Smuteyes Trail. This route actually began at Trices Ferry (located at the site of the present bridge on U.S. 80),[58] but it ran downriver a short distance to the approach to Calhouns Ferry, thence southward to intersect several main westward routes. One of these was the Upatoi Trail and another was the Federal Road. Much of the old Coweta Falls trace and the Smuteyes Trail still continue in use today.

Since Booths Road was a vehicular way and was probably used in conjunction with an early ferry located at or about the site of the later Calhouns Ferry, there still remains the matter of explaining where the predecessor trail and branch of the early Toms route got over Flint River. There must have been some fording point for the aboriginal path. This spot was located about three-quarters of a mile to the south of the point where the surveyor ended Booths Road, at the upper side of an island, now called Harris' Island, and located above the mouth of Auchumpkee Creek, something like a half-mile above the Islands Ford that was mentioned. Hawkins speaks of this second crossing as the "Sulenojuhnene ford."[59] The expression literally signifies Buzzard Roost trail and does not contain the Creek word for ford. The appellation is derived from a former town known as the Buzzard Roost that was located in the locality and which will be treated shortly. The route being discussed, however, was properly the *lower* Buzzard Roost ford and trail because there was another Sulenojuhnene and fording place *above* the town, upstream from the bridge on U.S. 80. This route will also be mentioned below.

Before leaving this part of the Flint, it should be mentioned that in later years there was a successor to Calhouns Ferry. This crossing, called Grays Ferry, was opened a bit downstream from the site of the earlier Calhouns Ferry and about a half-mile upriver from the lower Sulenojuhnene crossing. Grays Ferry has been abandoned for years but the spot merits mentioning because the former approaches to the landing on both sides of the river are still called Grays Ferry roads. The route of this name leading westward away from the crossing toward Five Points in upper Taylor seems to be an old and well-worn thoroughfare. It is in a proper position to have been the original aboriginal path leading to and from the lower Sulenojuhnene fording spot.

Once again back in Crawford County at Hickory Grove crossroads, where the early Booths Road turned from the course of present U.S. 80, there was a third fork in the old Toms route. This way continued west along the general course of No. 80 into Upson County. Instead of turning southward, however, to cross the Flint at the site of today's bridge on 80, it continued westward to the Nottingham place to a ford downstream from the mouth of Tobler or Swift Creek. The trail indicated is not shown by the first surveys of the area but it is certain to have existed along the approximate route described. The fording place was one of the best on Flint River and was the first good, natural crossing above the Sulenojuhnene and Islands Ford located near the mouth of Auchumpkee Creek. It was exactly in the right location to serve an early trace along U.S. 80 without deviation from a relatively direct course. The crossing must have been the level, shallow ford which is mentioned as being located "above" the Buzzard Roost town.[60]

Colonel Hawkins referred to this route as the "Left path crossing Flint River above Sulenojuh"[61] and confirms the existence of the ford at the site indicated because he once travelled that way on an eastbound trip.[62]

This third fork of Toms Path followed an easy course and when the white people settled the section after 1821, it quickly became a vehicular way. An early crossing called Hootens Ferry was established near the fording point.[63] This facility was later taken over by Louis Cantelow.[64] Nevertheless the name Hooten also continued to be connected with the ferry for a long time. A place named Hootenville developed on the trail at the intersection with what is now U.S. 80, and even today the community aroundabout continues to be known as the Hootenville District.

Beyond Flint River the third prong of the Toms route had easy connections westward via the Coweta Falls Road and the Smuteyes Trail.

In several instances mention has been made of the Creek settlement known as the Buzzard Roost or Sulenojuh. The Indian name does not translate literally into the English version but signifies "having buzzards." The correct expression for Buzzard Roost in Muskogee was *sulikagi*, from *suli*, buzzard, and *kagi*, a roosting place. This expression in a distorted form can be found in the designation of present Sylacauga, Alabama.

The Buzzard Roost of Flint River was an out-settlement of the Cussetas whose main center was on the east side of the Chattahoochee and below Upatoi Creek, in the Fort Benning Reservation. In the post-Revolutionary years, the Roost was the largest and most easterly settlement of the Creeks. It was a compact town of 70 gunmen (warriors) in 1787.[65] But in the spring of that year, the people quit the place after a Colonel Alexander killed seven of their townsmen near Shoulderbone Creek.[66] It will be recalled that Toms Path connected eastward toward the mouth of this stream by way of the Chehaw Path from the Toms Ford on the Ocmulgee.

The Buzzard Roost is shown on numbers of early maps of Georgia, and it is sometimes incorrectly placed on the east bank of the Flint. The settlement had some fields on that side and maybe a few of the people resided there, but Richard Thomas, Colonel Hawkins' clerk, makes it clear the town was on the west bank, because on a 1798 trip westward he mentions having to cross the river to reach the place.[67] The left or east bank in the area of the settlement is generally high and rough and would not have been a good location for an Indian town. The west-side fields of the Buzzard Roost extended three miles above the settlement. This area embodied the bottoms that stretch upstream from the lower Sulenojuhnene Ford to the mouth of Tobler or Swift Creek. The actual town house site or center of the community was near the south end of these fields, to the west of the point where Booths Road ended and near the west landing of the old Calhouns Ferry.

The site and name Buzzard Roost apparently has long since been forgotten by the people presently living in the locality. There is an area now called the Buzzard Roost located some miles down the Flint, on the east side, at the back of the Clay Hollis place, but this spot is so far from the old Roost there is little chance that it is in any way connected with the early name.

In a brief undated section of his "Viatory" (a log or journal of wilderness travels), Colonel Hawkins tells of a trip along a segment of Toms Path on a visit to Fort Wilkinson. He crossed the Flint at the upper Buzzard Roost ford[68] and travelled eastward toward the Ocmulgee. He did not go on to Toms Ford, below Popes Ferry, however, but somewhere took a right path leading to an Ocmulgee crossing which he labelled "Chaukeethlucco."[69] This expression means Big Shoals from the Muskogee *chanki*, shoals, plus *thláko*, big. It is not possible with information at hand to identify the exact location of this Big Shoals fording site, but very probably it was the shoally area upstream from the mouth of Savage or Sabbath Creek, in upper Bibb County, about seven miles above Macon, and at the lower end of a stretch that is now known as Taylors Shoals. No other spot on the Ocmulgee, from the area of Macon to these shoals, would properly qualify for the designation Big Shoals. Furthermore, it is certain there was an important Indian crossing near the mouth of Savage Creek because a trace called the Tuskio-Micco Path reached the east side of the Ocmulgee at this point.

The Tuskio-Micco Path, eastbound, began on the Ocmulgee at a place bearing the odd name of Mount Berrien & Burnet, in lot 192 of District 8 of original Baldwin County,[70] now a part of lower Jones. It led gently southeastward and below today's James, and to the west of Commissioners Creek,[71] joined an east-west thoroughfare that became known as the Garrison Road. The latter trace received this name because it was blazed as a wagon route to connect Fort Wilkinson on the Oconee and Fort Hawkins on the Ocmulgee. Today's Georgia 49 between Milledgeville and Macon follows closely the old course and still retains the name Garrison Road.

The Tuskio-Micco Path, one may reasonably assume, was named for Tussekiah Mico (*Tàsikayà Miko*), the Warrior King of the Cussetas, who lived during the late 1790's at the village of Upatoi, located in the forks of Upatoi Creek, in eastern Muscogee County.[72] He was a leading Lower Creek chief and Colonel Hawkins thought highly of him.[73] It was fairly common for trails leading to prominent Indians' home sites to be named after the respective leaders involved. Thus, since the Tuskio-Micco trace had a westward bearing and could easily have connected via Toms Path to the Upatoi village, it seems likely the trace was named for the chief of that place.

Unfortunately the district surveyors of original Monroe did not show a continuation of the Tuskio-Micco Path to the west of the Ocmulgee, or the full course of the route that Hawkins used to reach the Big Shoals. The survey for District 13 of Monroe, however, does depict some disconnected segments of an Indian trail in approximate locations to have been an extension of the Tuskio-Micco route. These fragments may have been portions of that trail, but if so, it is uncertain how or where it joined Toms Path. This survey was made in 1821, a considerable time after the surveys of old Baldwin County to the east of the Ocmulgee. Perhaps in the intervening time the Tussekiah's trace had lost its importance and the name of the chieftain forgotten.

Curiously enough, however, the surveyor of District 13 of Monroe actually did give some of the disconnected stretches of the Indian trail a name. In his field notes he marked it "Federal Road,"[74] a mislabelling which the man must have been aware of because the real Federal Road, the most important route of the whole region at the time, lay not far to the south. The surveyor probably intended to signify that the trail led on to connect with the Federal Road. It could have done this by curving southward to intersect the noted route, or by continuing westward to join Toms Path, thence to one of the Flint River crossings that were discussed, and from there down to the Federal Road. Evidence that this last way may have been followed to join the federal route can be found in the fact that another surveyor actually marked a section of Toms Path as the "Federal Road."[75]

We have wandered back and forth across a band of central Georgia, discussing pioneer sites and the intricacies of Indian trails without touching upon the origin of the name Toms as used in connection with the Toms Shoals and the old path. The derivation of the name, with present information, unfortunately, is as uncertain as were the locations of some wilderness routes that have been discussed. The main difficulties about the derivation arise from the fact that certain key records which might have helped in explaining the name are contradictory. Mostly the appellation is mentioned as Toms Path. It is also listed as "Old Toms Path,"[76] and as "Indian Tom's Path."[77] The last form, of course, plainly indicates the route was named for an Indian. This origin for the name receives support from an unofficial document pertaining to Washington County which states the trail was named for an Indian chief called Tom.[78] Other sources mention a well-known Cuseeta Indian courier named Tom,[79] but there is no indication that he ranked as a chief. He was the "squaw father in law" of Richard Thomas,[80] a clerk and assistant to Colonel Hawkins. This Tom resided at Cuseeta and died there in 1798.[81] It is possible in his service as a courier that he caused his name to be linked with the trail which became known as Toms Path.

In contrast with this possible Indian origin of the name there is evidence to indicate the trace was named for a white man called Samuel Thomas, who long served as a Creek interpreter.[82]

On two occasions the Toms route is marked "Sam Thomas' Path."[83] One document gives the name as "Thomas' Path,"[84] while a map mentions the Oconee crossing as "Thoms Ford."[85] This spelling intimates the appellation was closer to the name Thomas than to Toms.

A Samuel Thomas had some interest or connection with old Washington County, the section where the path began on the east, because he received a bounty grant of 278½ acres in that county in 1784 for his services in the Revolution.[86] There is no plat, though, in the state's land records to show that he exercised his rights and took up this grant.

It is possible that Samuel's real surname was Tomes and not Thomas. The *Colonial Records of Georgia* mention an Indian trader named "Sam Tomes."[87] If positive evidence could be turned up to show that Thomas and Tomes were the same man, there would be good grounds for concluding the path was named for him and not for an Indian.

In view of the close relationship of Toms Path to three successive Tobler Creeks, perhaps the reader has been wondering if the name of the trail could have been derived from some one named Tobler—a Tom Tobler. The documents and records consulted do not mention a person of that name but they disclosed much about a Creek Indian named Tobler, who evidently was a picturesque character and a grand rascal of the Georgia frontier. In several instances his name was connected directly with Toms Path but there is no evidence that he furnished the designation of the route.

In the next issue of the *Newsletter* there will be a discussion of the Tobler creeks and some other names of streams which were crossed by Toms Path. These appellations are among the most intriguing Indian names in the state. The Tobler creeks are of especial interest because they illustrate a singular feature of Georgia geography and nomenclature which seemingly is without an exact parallel in any other state.

—*GMNL* 13(1960): 129-38

NOTES

1. In Georgia geographic names it is the common practice to drop the apostrophe from well-established names that were originally in the possessive: St. Marys, Wrens, etc.

2. Many early maps and documents were consulted in preparing this chart. The route of Toms Path, the central theme of the sketch, was mainly taken from plats and maps in the land records of the Surveyor General Department, Atlanta. These documents consist of unpublished field notes, plats, maps, and numerous other records. References will be made to specific items as the paper progresses. This source will hereinafter be referred to as Land Records of Georgia.

The writer retraced Toms Path and related ways in the field and he wishes to express his gratitude to the Research Committee of Emory University for a grant which enabled him to trace these paths and numbers of other historic routes in Georgia and the Southeast.

Appreciation is due Dr. W. B. Warthen of Davisboro, Ga., and the late John Cain of Grange, Ga., for information about Toms Path.

The course of Toms Path on the map is correct, except for the eastern end where there had to be some speculation about the route. The Chehaw Path and Tuskio-Micco Path are correct according to official Land Records of Georgia.

With respect to the connections of Toms Path at Flint River, there was some conjecture in making the map, but it is believed the links shown were close on or identical with original traces that are known to have existed.

The spur of the Ecunhutkenene, or White Ground Path, shown branching from the Federal Road, is offered for reference. The precise route of this fork of that trail has been lost, but it followed the approximate course indicated.

3. In English, this interesting name literally means Deer big path old, from *echo*, deer, plus *thláko* (or "thlucco"), big, plus *nini*, path, plus *ahasi*, old. When the horse was introduced among the Creeks, those Indians lacked a name for the animal. They called it big deer, and this word remains today in the Muskogee language as *chelucco*, *cholokko*, etc.

4. The statement does not mean to imply that the Ocheese towns only extended up to the Ocmulgee as far as Juliette. Any of those settlements above that place would logically have been reached by the route that became the Oakfuskee Path or Upper Creek Trading Path and not by the trail that became Toms Path.

5. One surveyor referred to a segment of this spur as "Larkins Path." Map of District 8, Baldwin County (now Jones), survey of 1807, David Glenn, D.S., Land Records of Georgia.

6. A segment of this crossover is shown on a 1793 plat as the "Treaty [Trading?] Road," near present Culverton, to the east of Sparta. See Land of James Dawson, Washington County (now Hancock), Platbook CC, p. 477, Land Records of Georgia.

210 / Placenames of Georgia

7. Galphinton was on the south side of the Ogeechee, in western Jefferson County, some six or seven miles to the west of Louisville. George Galphin established the place as a trading post when he removed his store to the site from Old Town.

The exact location of Galphinton is not known, but the late John Cain of Jefferson County and Dr. W. B. Warthen of Davisboro place the site in the general area indicated above. These men were well informed on the background of this section of Georgia.

8. Land of John Watts, survey of 1786, Platbook I, p. 274; land of Elijah Padget, survey of 1787, *ibid.*, p. 318; and land of David Neal, survey of 1785, Platbook F, p. 400. All of these properties were in Washington County.

9. Land of Henry Graybill, Washington County, survey of 1786, Platbook O, p. 51.

10. *Ibid.*

11. Undated statement entitled "Warthen" [Georgia] in the possession of Mrs. C. Findlay Irwin of Sandersville, Ga. It was written by a son of Richard Warthen, probably by Macon Warthen. The former was a pioneer resident of the town of Warthen, in Washington County. The writer is indebted to Mr. Leon Hollingsworth of Decatur, Ga., for a transcript of the statement.

12. Land of Michael Dixon, Washington County, survey of 1787, Platbook A, p. 80, Washington County records, Sandersville. The author did not consult this document at the source, but used a transcript furnished by the late John Cain.

13. Land of Robert Walton, Washington County, survey of 1784, Platbook F, p. 422, Land Records of Georgia; land of Benjamin Griffin, Washington County, survey of 1785, Platbook O, p. 48.

14. Land of Ayers Holliday, Washington County (now Baldwin), survey of 1784, Platbook F, p. 155. The trail is shown running beside "derosos's Cr." [Derisows], now Champion Creek, which enters the east side of the Oconee, near the site of Toms Ford.

15. Land of Francis Tennill [*sic*], Washington County, survey of 1787, Platbook W, p. 30.

16. Land of Benjamin Scott, Washington County, survey of 1784, Platbook W, p. 5.

17. Minutes of the Inferior Court of Washington County, 1843-1863 (1854), p. 171, Ordinary's Office, Sandersville. The writer is indebted to the late John Cain for a transcript of this entry.

18. The name of this stream appears under various spellings in old records: "deresous," "Dorosous," "Deresows," "Derossows," "Derisoes," etc. No land plat shows a property owner by this name in the area of the creek. Perhaps the stream was named for James Darouzeaux, an old Indian countryman and well-known interpreter who resided for a long time among the Lower Creeks at Coweta, near today's Columbus.

19. *Letters of Benjamin Hawkins, 1796-1806*, Collections of the Georgia Historical Society, Vol. 9 (Savannah, 1916), 282.

20. Map of District 1, Baldwin County, survey of 1794, John Ragan, D.S., Land Records of Georgia. The path enters at "Tom's Foard," above Tobler Creek, at lot 341.

21. Map of District 9, Baldwin County (now Jones), survey of 1807, John L. Porter, D.S.; Map of District 8, Baldwin County, and Map of District 11, Baldwin County (now Jones), survey of 1807, William Watson, D.S.

22. Map of District 11, Baldwin County, lot 184.

23. *Ibid.*

24. For a study of the Upper Path, see John H. Goff, "The Path to Oakfuskee," *Georgia Historical Quarterly*, March, 1955, pp. 1-36 (with map); and June, 1955, pp. 152-71.

25. Map of District 2, Baldwin County (now part of Putnam), survey of 1805, Lewin Wailes, D.S., lot 432.

26. Map of District 11, Baldwin County. Wayside is in the southeast corner of lot 28; the trail passed below in lots 19 and 26.

27. Louise Frederick Hays, "Unpublished Letters of Timothy Barnard, 1784-1820," MS in Department of Archives and History, Atlanta, pp. 296-98, a communication from Chiefs of the Lower Towns to Col. Hawkins, dated Coweta, March 14, 1809, and interpreted by Timothy Barnard.

28. Map of District 13, Monroe County (now parts of Bibb and Monroe), survey of 1821, Isaac Welch, D.S., and Map of District 2, Houston County (now Crawford), survey of 1821, Samuel Watson, D.S.

29. Map of District 13, Monroe County, lot 129.

30. *Ibid.*, lot 319.

31. *Ibid.*, lot 109.

32. Although the site of Popes Ferry is shown on the 1821 survey for District 5 of Monroe, no authority had been granted by the state at that period to operate the facility as a public ferry. This right was not given until 1834 when Cullen Pope received the privilege. See *Acts of the General Assembly of the State of Georgia* (1834), pp. 127-28.

33. Montpelier Avenue of Macon and Montpelier Road of Bibb County apparently were named for this former place, because they led to it.

34. District 13, Monroe County, Platbook YYY, lot 2. It is here marked "Toms Road."

35. *American State Papers*, II. Indian Affairs 1:370, W. Urquhart to Gen. Twiggs. Augusta, June 11, 1793. This order was later countermanded and the movement did not take place.

36. The path is shown leaving the southwest corner of District 13 of Monroe, leading into the extreme southeast corner of District 12 of Monroe, headed for the Montpelier Station site in northeast Crawford. The trace, however, is not shown in District 12. See Map of District 12, Monroe County, survey of 1821, Thomas Baber, D.S.

37. Instead of entering District 2 of Houston (now Crawford) from District 12 of Monroe, above, the trail entered the former district on the northeast edge, at the boundary with District 3 of Houston (now parts of Crawford and Bibb). See Map of District 2, Houston County, survey of 1821, Samuel Watson, D.S., lot 136. The path is not shown on the map for District 3 of Houston.

The gap between the point where the trail ended in District 13 and the place where it began in District 2 is only the width of two or three land lots and one can be certain the route continued as described in the text.

38. Map of District 2, Houston County, lot 190. The "Booths Road" is not named in this district, nor is it shown in District 12 of Monroe, above, but from the course of the trace when last given in District 13 of Monroe, it is plain the route went on to join the Toms way at the place indicated.

39. Map of District 5, Monroe County, survey of 1821, Hugh G. Johnson, D.S., fractional lot 234. This ferry was in operation before it was authorized as a public facility. See *Acts of the General Assembly of the State of Georgia* (1821), p. 194, Act of Dec. 21, 1821.

40. This spur of Popes Road and Booths Road are depicted leaving District 13 very close together and apparently headed for a union just over in District 12 of Monroe. The plats and map for this latter district, however, show no roads. It has been assumed the intersection actually took place.

41. Plats for District 1, Houston County (now parts of Upson and Crawford), survey of 1821, Thomas J. Triplett, D.S., Platbook SSS, lot 133.

42. *Ibid.*, lot 268.

43. Ulcohatchee and Auchumpkee creeks unite a short distance from the Flint. The correct name of the stream after the juncture is a matter of question. People in Upson County commonly call it the Auchumpkee. Historically, perhaps it should rightly be the Ulcohatchee. The Auchumpkee locally is often referred to as the Oakchunk.

44. District 1, Houston County, Platbook SSS, lots 149, 150, 178, 190, *passim*.

45. Benjamin Hawkins, *A Sketch of the Creek Country in the Years 1798 and 1799* (Americus, Ga.: Americus Book Co., 1938), p. 60.

46. *Letters of Benjamin Hawkins*, p. 172.

47. District 1, Houston County, Platbook SSS, lots 31, 32, 91, 110, 150, *passim*.

48. *Sketch of the Creek Country*, p. 60.

49. Hawkins says there were two islands at the place in 1797. See *Letters*, p. 172. At present there are three islands; when water is high one of these apparently is severed to form a fourth.

50. *Letters of Benjamin Hawkins*, p. 172.

51. *Ibid.*

52. In 1797, on a trip from Cusseta to Fort Wilkinson, Benjamin Hawkins reached the Islands Ford on a course that corresponds closely with this strip of Ga. 263. See his "A Viatory or Journal of distances and observations," entry beginning Dec. 6, 1797, MS in the Library of Congress.

53. Evidence of this path over the hill still remains and some elderly people of the area say it is traditionally regarded as a former Indian trail.

54. For an essay on this Federal Road, see John H. Goff, "Excursion Along an Old Way to the West," *Georgia Review* 6 (Summer 1952): 189-202 (with map).

55. District 1, Houston County, Platbook SSS, lots 175, 219, 262, 263, *et passim*, to the western edge of lot 304.

56. The 1827 survey for District 24 of Muscogee (now parts of Taylor and Talbot) shows a "Booth's Ferry" on the Flint at that date, but this crossing was too far upstream to have had any connection with "Booths Road" under discussion in this paper.

57. William C. Dawson, *A Compilation of the Laws of the State of Georgia* (Milledgeville, 1831), Act of Dec. 24, 1825, p. 386.

58. *Ibid.*, Act of Dec. 22, 1827, pp. 394-95. In this act, William Trice was empowered to open a ferry at a place formerly known as Smutely's. This site was at the present crossing of U.S. 80.

59. *Letters of Benjamin Hawkins*, p. 172. Hawkins states here there was a small island to the right of the ford and a ridge of rocks to the left. This description is still apt. The rocks must have made this ford a dangerous crossing, especially for heavily loaded pack animals.

60. *Ibid.*

61. "Viatory," entry not dated, but covers a trip to Fort Wilkinson about 1800 via the "Left path [or upper] crossing Flint River above Sulenojuh."

62. *Ibid.*

63. Map of District 24, Muscogee County (now parts of Taylor and Talbot), survey of 1827, Sylvester Radney, D.S., edges of fractional lots 155 and 156.

64. *Acts of the General Assembly of the State of Georgia* (1834), Act of Dec. 22, 1834, pp. 130-31.

65. *Letters of Benjamin Hawkins*, p. 172.

66. *Ibid.*

67. *Ibid.*, p. 474, notes on a trip by Richard Thomas, from the Ocmulgee River, entry for Jan. 13, 1798.

68. "Viatory," "Left path crossing Flint River above Sulenojuh."

69. *Ibid.*

70. District 8, Baldwin County, survey of 1806, David Glenn, D.S., Platbook NN, and Map of District 8, Baldwin County. The former refers to the trail as "Tuskio-Micco Path" while the chart mentions the route as the "Tusco Meco Path."

71. District 6, Baldwin County, Platbook PP, lot 80.

72. For a discussion of Upatoi, see Sketch No. 5, above.

73. *Letters of Benjamin Hawkins*, pp. 69-71.

74. Field notes for District 13, Monroe County, survey of 1821, Isaac Welch, D.S.

75. District 2 of Houston (now Crawford), Platbook SSS, lot 9.

76. Land of David Neal, Platbook F, p. 399.

77. Land of Benjamin Griffin, Platbook O, p. 48.

78. Statement on "Warthen."

79. *Lettesr of Benjamin Hawkins*, pp. 472, 480.

80. *Ibid.*, p. 472.

81. *Ibid.*, p. 489.

82. Deposition of Jacob Moniac and Samuel Thomas, a sworn interpreter of the Lower Creeks, dated Oct. 31, 1774, *Georgia Gazette*, Supplement to No. 578, Nov. 2, 1774.

83. Land of Henry Graybill, Platbook O, p. 51; and land of Ayers Holliday, Platbook F, p. 155.

84. Land of Robert Walton, Platbook F, p. 422.

85. Map showing forts along middle Oconee River, *circa* 1793, no author, photostatic copy in the Surveyor General Department, Atlanta.

86. File of Samuel Thomas in Land Records of Georgia, Surveyor General Department. These records indicate he was recommended as being entitled to a land bounty by John Twiggs, on March 23, 1784, and that an application was received, granted, and entered, May 26, 1784.

87. Allen D. Candler, ed., *The Colonial Records of Georgia* (Atlanta: Franklin, 1904-1916), 6: 357.

No. 79
Anneewakee Creek

Anneewakee Creek in Douglas County arises to the south of Douglasville and runs southeastward to join the Chattahoochee River at a point downstream a bit and opposite the site of old Campbellton. The original surveyor of the area first reported the stream in 1827 as "Annawaka Creek."[1] Since the waterway lies in former Creek country, it was first assumed in the analysis of the name that it is of Muskogee origin, particularly in view of the fact that the *wakee* element of the expression might be construed as being from the Creek word *waki*, meaning prostrate or lying down. After much study, however, no meaningful Muskogean origin could be derived for the appellation. A well-qualified Creek informant in Oklahoma was asked about the word but he could not identify it as being from his language.

After receipt of this information, an explanation for the name was sought in other directions. More than likely it was finally concluded the expression is Cherokee and not Creek, and that it was derived from a Cherokee family name that is variously listed as Anne waky, Aunawaka, Ah na wu kies, Anny wagey, and so on. It is quite possible that some member of the family once lived on the stream and caused his name to be attached to it. The reader may be surprised to learn of a Cherokee name in Creek country, but sometime around 1815 the Cherokees thought they were going to be allowed to settle in Creek territory as far south as a line running through today's upper Heard County, and apparently some of the tribe started moving down into the contemplated new area at about that time. The 1818 Eleazer Early map of Georgia depicts this prospective boundary and is one of the few charts to show or mention it. This map was prepared by Daniel Sturges, one of the finest pioneer surveyors and a former surveyor general of Georgia. One can be certain he placed the contemplated line in the area where he understood it would be marked off by the Creeks and Cherokees.

In 1821, however, the two tribes agreed upon another line which was located considerably to the north of the boundary originally proposed. The new border began at Buzzard Roost Island on the Chattahoochee, where Douglas and Cobb counties now corner, and ran westward to the Coosa River in Alabama and passing not far above the head of Anneewakee Creek. This change in the line placed the Anneewakee in Creek territory and presumably if any Cherokee Anne wakys had settled there they removed above the final boundary but left their name behind them, just as the Creeks left some of their names in Cherokee country when they removed to the south of the frontier.

But to return to the origin of Anneewakee, the name seems to be derived from *ani,* a Cherokee animate prefix signifying clan, tribe, nation, people, or species, plus *waka,* cow or cattle. The latter term was borrowed from the Spaniards and is a Cherokee version of *vaca,* the Spanish word for cow.

Anneewakee did not signify cow clan because the Cherokees only had a small number of clans and these were of an ancient origin which outdated the introduction of the cow among the tribe. More than likely one thinks Anneewakee meant something like cow people or cattle people, or even cattleians, because the prefix *ani* was the equivalent of our suffix *ian,* as in Georgian, and the expression was applied because the family had taken up the raising of stock.

The analysis above is supported by the fact that the Creek Indians also used names that are analagous to *ani-waka.* In colonial years they had a chief who was known to the whites as the Cowkeeper; and in later years among the Seminoles there was a leader called Vacapuchassie, or cow master.

It might be of interest to add that the Table of Post Offices for the United States in 1851 discloses there was a post office called Annawaika in DeKalb County, Alabama. This area of that state was once occupied by Cherokees.

—*GMNL* 14(1961): 30

NOTE

1. District 1, original Carroll County, survey of 1827, F. G. Stewart, D.S., Platbook NNNN, land lots 12, 13, 22, 46, 76, *passim,* Land Records of Georgia, Surveyor General Department, Atlanta,

No. 80
The Intrenchment Creeks

Georgia has, or rather had until a few years ago, two Intrenchment creeks—one, an upper prong of South River that arises in Fulton County on the lower edge of Atlanta and flows southeastward to join the main stream just below Constitution, in southwest DeKalb County; and two, an east-bank tributary of the Chattahoochee, in western Hall County, to the northwest of Flowery Branch. The latter stream, known as Little Intrenchment Creek, has now been inundated by Lake Lanier, the Buford Dam Reservoir, and it seems likely the name is destined for oblivion.

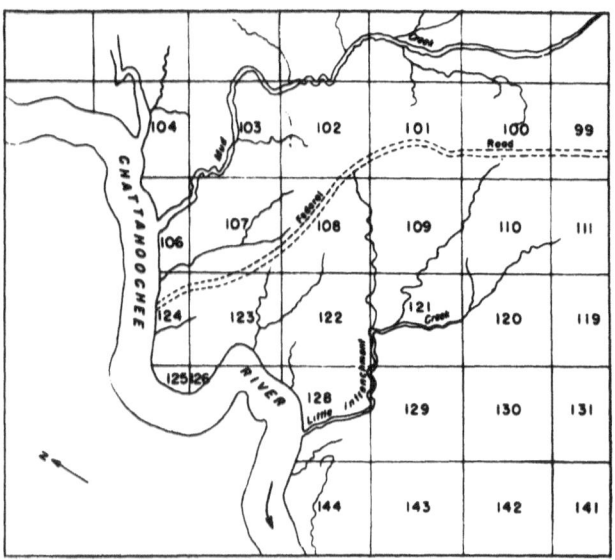

Tracing from a portion of the original map of district 8 of Hall County, showing the location of Little Intrenchment Creek

The names of these streams were both recorded by the original surveyors who laid off the areas where they lie.[1] Naturally enough, perhaps, people who live about the Intrenchment Creek of Fulton and DeKalb counties assume that waterway derived its name from some connection with the trenches that were dug around Atlanta during the War Between the States. As a matter of fact, however, the designation was known long before that period because it was listed by District Surveyor John Kell in 1821.[2]

In his field notes, map, and plats Kell does not give any intimation to show why the stream was called Intrenchment Creek. He may have named it for an Indian mound or mounds that stood along the waterway; or, he may have applied the name because of some trenches which the Indians had dug in quarrying soapstone in the vicinity of the stream. It is known that the red people did secure this mineral and make objects from it in sections about South River and its upper tributaries.

One clue intimates Intrenchment Creek may have derived its name from some sort of defensive structure. Mr. Wade H. Wright of the Georgia Power Company was reared on the lower side of South River, downstream from the mouth of the creek. He states on his father's farm there was a field which was traditionally known as the Fort Field because the Indians were said to have maintained a fort on the site.[3] The field was closer to the mouth of Sugar Creek than Intrenchment Creek but presence of a fort in the community suggests there may have been some connection with the latter stream that is not now clear.

With respect to Little Intrenchment Creek of Hall County, one can be sure the waterway derived its name from a breastwork or trench that once stretched across a bend of the Chattahoochee, lying upstream from the mouth of the creek. This structure was not shown on the map of the district surveyor,[4] but it is depicted by Thomas Mitchell on his map representing a survey of the Chattahoochee and its islands in 1828 as an "Old Intrenchment."[5] A tracing of a portion of that chart is being reproduced here to indicate the location of the intrenchment[6] The facility can be seen as a double line of dots beginning at a point below Winn's Ferry and running back from the river. Winn's Ferry was originally Vann's Ferry and was established in late 1804 or early 1805 by James Vann, a Cherokee, as a crossing point for the noted Federal Road which was opened to link Georgia and Tennessee across the Indian country.[7] Vann's Ferry was the oldest ferrying place on the upper Chattahoochee and the point merits noting because presence of the crossing and the Federal Road may have had something to do with construction of the intrenchment mentioned by Surveyor Mitchell.

Before the waters of Lake Lanier covered the place, the writer examined the area of the Old Intrenchment on several occasions. He could not find signs of a former trench but did conclude that the structure was designed to seal off a bend in the river and that it probably began about the southwest corner of lot 124 (the lot in

218 / Placenames of Georgia

which Winn's or Vann's Ferry was located) and ran eastward close along the lower boundaries of lots 124 and 123 to the southeast corner of the latter. A tracing of a portion of the original map of District 8 of Hall that is reproduced here will assist the reader in following the course indicated above. A stockade or trench along the line mentioned would have offered protection for a fine camping or cantonment site on a small flat-topped ridge that extended into the bend of the river, along the eastern boundaries 124 and 125.

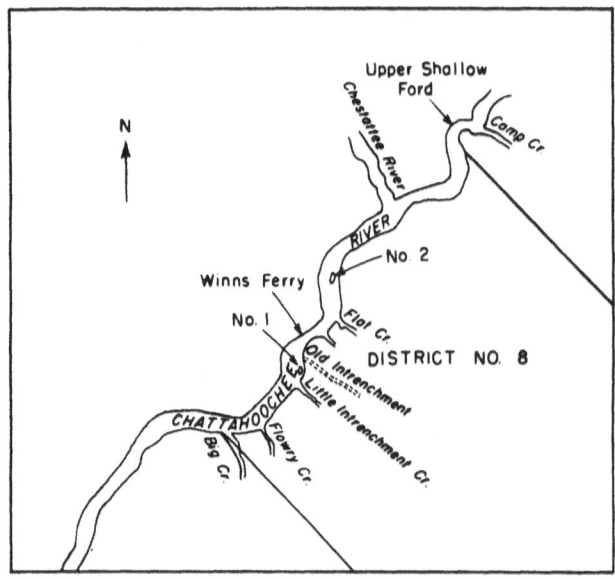

Tracing from original map of the Islands of the Chattahoochee River, 1828

The expression Little Intrenchment Creek implies there may also have been a Big Intrenchment Creek that failed to receive mention in the old records. If such a stream existed, it would, of course, have been located in the area of the Old Intrenchment. One strongly suspects there was such a creek in the form of a sluice or slough that once began about the southwest corner of lot 124 on the river and curved with the inside bend to rejoin the main channel at the eastern edge of lot 126. Surveyor Mitchell confirms the existence of such a slough in a plat showing an island off the tip of the bend in the Chattahoochee. He labelled the island "No. 1," meaning the first island of the river going upstream in the Hall County reaches. A tracing of this plat is reproduced here.

The sluice, or slough, separating the island from the mainland could well have been thought of as a creek (i.e., Big Intrenchment Creek) because it was actually much longer than indicated by Mitchell's plat and because it lay behind the Old Intrenchment which he showed on his map. This slough dried up with the passage of time, but later-day examination plainly disclosed that it began around the bend of the Chattahoochee approximately at the point where the Old Intrenchment commenced at the edge of the river.

No information was developed about the time or the reason for making the intrenchment that gave rise to Little Intrenchment Creek's name, and it is purely conjectural here to speculate on the question. It is possible the trench may go back to the days of the Spaniards. This suggestion is not as farfetched as it seems, because the Federal Road, a former middle path to the Cherokees, was one of the known early routes into the Indian country. And incidentally, a main prong of the trail passed near Fort Mountain in Murray County, with its much written-about "fortifications." Most likely, however, the Old Intrenchment was erected sometime after the opening of the Federal Road in 1805 as a camping place for troops that travelled the federal route or which may have been stationed along the east side of Chattahoochee to keep an eye on the Cherokees.

Although the site of the former intrenchment is now covered by water, students who are interested in the spot might still be able to find evidence of it in aerial photographs of the area which were made prior to the rise in the reservoir.

—*GMNL* 14(1961): 30-31

NOTES

1. Intrenchment Creek is listed on the Map of District 15 of Henry County, survey of 1821, John Kell, D.S.; and Little Intrenchment Creek is shown on Map of District 8 of Hall County, survey of 1820, James Meriwether, D.S., Land Records of Georgia, Surveyor General Department, Atlanta.

2. District 15, Henry County.

3. Letter to the author, dated April 20, 1959. Mr. Wright is now retired from the Georgia Power Co.

4. District 8, Hall County.

5. Islands of the Chattahoochee River, survey of 1828, Thomas Mitchell, Surveyor.

6. The writer wishes to express his appreciation to Mrs. Pat Bryant, Deputy Surveyor General, in charge of the records of the Surveyor General Department, for this tracing and the other tracing that accompanies this sketch.

7. For a discussion of the Old Federal Road, see "Retracing the Old Federal Road," below, pp. 349-60.

8. Survey of July 15, 1828, Thomas Mitchell, Surveyor, Platbook EEEE.

No. 81
Eastahatchee, Now Sanborn Creek

Eastahatchee is the obsolete name for present Sanborn Creek that commences near Faceville in extreme lower Decatur County and runs into the south side of the Jim Woodruff Reservoir at Flint River, to the north of Faceville. It is not known when the designation Sanborn was applied to the stream but the original surveyor of the district in 1819-1820 marked the creek as "Eastahatchee,"[1] "Easterhatche,"[2] and "Estahatchee"[3] in his plats. In the field notes for the survey he listed it as "Eastahachee."[4] Although the name occurred in a section that is commonly regarded as Hitchitee, it is of Muskogee origin, from *isti*, people, plus *hàchi*, or "hatchee," stream. If the designation were Hitchitee it would have been *Oklihahchi*, from *okli*, people or town, plus *hahchi*, stream. Since the Creek term *isti* was probably also intended to signify town in this instance it seems reasonable to assume the creek was named Eastahatchee because of a settlement or village along its banks or about its mouth on Flint River.

One does not have to worry about the switching of the final *i* of *isti* to an *a*. That substitution was conventional for early surveyors and white pioneers. This final *i* had a "ee" sound, but since the former citizens used the same sound at the end of a great variety of spoken English words, they usually sought to "correct" written Indian names by changing a terminating *i* to *a*. In the case of the initial *i* of the Indian word, the surveyor changed it to *ea* as in east. He could not well have shifted the first *i* to an *a* because this switch would have converted Easta into the meaningless Asta.

The surveyor in the adjoining land district to the east did not mark the creek as Eastahatchee but labelled its upper waters "Shell Creek."[5] Interestingly enough, this Shell Creek does not now join present Sanborn Creek, the former Eastahatchee, but drains directly into Flint River by a small stream that is presently marked Dry Creek. The latter now enters the Jim Woodruff Reservoir a short distance above the mouth of the Sanborn. The early surveys, however, show it united with the Eastahatchee before reaching the river.

—GMNL 14(1961): 31-32

NOTES

1. District 21, Early County, survey of 1819-1820, John S. Porter, D.S., Platbook EEE, lot 265, Land Records of Georgia, Surveyor General Department, Atlanta.
2. *Ibid.*, lot 266, where it reaches the Flint.
3. *Ibid.*, lots 284, 285, *passim.*
4. Field Notes, District 21, Early County, survey of 1819-1820, John S. Porter, D.S.
5. District 20, Early County, survey of 1820, John Wood, D.S., lots 351, 364, 365, 366, 385, *passim.*

No. 82
Breastworks Branch (A Camp Site of Andrew Jackson's Men and an Old Fortification in Upper Wilcox County)

Breastworks Branch (which is actually a small creek several miles in length) heads on the east side of Georgia 39, to the north of Blakely in Early County and flows southeastward to join Dry Creek to the east of the town. The stream's name is old, but curiously it is out of place because the breastworks that very probably gave rise to the name were located to the south of Blakely in lot 150 of District 28 of Early. The original surveyor of the section shows the stockade in this location on his district map[1] and on the plat for lot 150.[2] The exact location and form of the structure, which the surveyor marked "Breastworks," is shown on the original plat.[3]

The stockade was located on a small stream that drained into Breastworks Branch. One believes this little tributary was the original Breastworks Branch and that the name was eventually extended to the whole creek which circles above Blakely to the edge of Georgia 39. This conclusion is reasonable because the surveyor does not mention or show any other fortified site in the area of Breastworks Branch.

The "Breastwork" in lot 150 was located beside the Fort Scott Road, leading from Fort Gaines to Fort Scott. The latter place was situated on the west bank of Flint River some 14 miles by land southwest of today's Bainbridge. The fort was established in September of 1816 by federal troops of the Fourth Infantry, but was abandoned the following December.[4] It was re-occupied, however, in April or May of 1817 by a company of artillery, which was joined in December of that year by the Fourth and Seventh Infantry.[5] These men were joined shortly by considerable militia forces from Tennessee and Alabama. All of these troops were being gathered for an invasion of Spanish Florida in early 1818 under the command of Andrew Jackson.

Fort Scott in Georgia was the staging point for this dubious and dangerous expedition, and the first incursion was in the direction of the Spanish Fort at St. Marks and the Indian towns about today's Tallahassee, Florida, with an eventual thrust eastward toward the Suwannee River.

With the exception of Jackson and his staff, a company of Kentucky volunteers and some Georgia militia, it seems reasonably certain that the rest of the forces which gathered at Fort Scott went via Fort Gaines and thus by the site of the breastwork just below Blakely. With available information it is not possible to say with certainty which of the units originally erected the stockade in lot 150. One is inclined to believe it was built by the federal troops that established Fort Scott because they cut the road from Fort Gaines to the site on Flint River and it seems likely they would have set up a way station in the form of a stockade while engaged in the task.

In the lottery to distribute Early County, it can be seen by the margin of the plat for lot 150 that Farrish Carter of Baldwin County was the "fortunate drawer" of the lot. This man eventually was to become an interesting and influential figure in Georgia life. As a wealthy planter, businessman, and industrialist he is reputed to have become the richest man in the state in his day. It is not amiss to mention him here because two of Georgia's interesting placenames—Cartersville in Bartow County, and Carters Quarters, on present U.S. 411, in southeast Murray County were named for him.

As mentioned, Andrew Jackson did not travel to Fort Scott via Fort Gaines and the breastwork at Blakely. He and his staff came via middle Georgia passing en route Vann's Ferry, that was mentioned in connection with the sketch on the Intrenchment creeks, thence by present Hawkinsville, thence across Flint River at or about the site of old Pindertown and from there southward to Fort Scott. For a long time his route west of Flint River was called Jackson's Trail, although it is very doubtful that he and his men had to cut the route, because the path was probably a well-known Indian way down the west side of the river. But be that as it may, the surveyor for District 15 of original Early County (now in upper Decatur) showed the "Jackson Trail" running along the Flint. Beside the river in the northeast corner of lot 267,[6] and near the path, he depicts a small stockade-like edifice marked "Camp." This spot may have been a stopping point for Jackson and his men. The shape of the structure shown supports this view, because it seems more like a breastwork than a camping place for Indian hunters or traders who travelled the route.

In numbers of instances one can find references in the old land records of Georgia to forts, intrenchments, stockades, blockhouses, and so on, but one of the most interesting spots which this writer has noticed in these documents is a place marked "Old Fortification" on the western boundary of lot 103 of District 8 of original Dooly County,[7] now a part of upper Wilcox. The place is above Abbeville, in a wooded section of the Ryals Mill District, G.M.D. 1177, approximately 3.25 miles east of a point on Georgia 11 or U.S. 129, and about 1.25 miles south of Cedar Creek. The spot is some two miles west of the Ocmulgee, and this is a curious feature because there are several good bluffs along the river in the general section and one would assume a fortification in the area would have been at one of these points.

The original plat surveyed in 1821 shows the "Old Fortification" just inside the western edge of lot 103, some 495 feet from the northwest corner. It is pertinent to add that in his field notes, the surveyor mentions the site as "Old Fortification"[8] and shows it as a circular form exactly on the boundary of lots 103 and 104, at the distance indicated from the northwest corner of the latter lot. It is important to note too that the structure was just inside of a swamp. This was a singular location since the plat shows a higher "pine rise" not far to the south. The surveyor does not show the fortification on his map of the district[9] but he does indicate a small branch or drain arising at the site, which suggests there may have been a spring there.

The plat does not show it, but not far from the fortification, in adjoining lot 104 to the west there was a trail running north and south. This path was actually a segment of the main Indian route leading up and down the west side of the Ocmulgee. It certainly had diverse connections to various parts of south Georgia and Florida and seemingly had some important links to the north. If the old fortification were really a stockade and not an Indian mound, one believes its erection was influenced by the trail. As already noted it was some distance back from the Ocmulgee and presumably could not have been concerned with any defensive purpose on that river. Nevertheless, judging by the original map of the area, it may have once been possible to approach fairly close to the fort from the river with canoes or poleboats, by means of a series of lagoons and creeks.

The writer has never had an opportunity to search for the remains of the fortification, and nothing is known of the nature of the site other than the geographic details that have been reported here.

For other students who may become interested in the place these possibilities for investigation are suggested: (1) The Old Fortification may have been an Indian mound. But if so, it will be of value to verify that fact. (2) The place may have been an outpost where General David Blackshear stationed a detail to watch the trail along the Ocmulgee while his troops were cutting the Blackshear Road southwestward from present Hawkinsville to the site of Fort Early on Flint River, in late 1814 and early 1815. (3) The old fortification may also have been a stockade to protect men and supplies that were being moved through today's Hawkinsville during the Jackson invasion of Florida in 1818. These movements took place down the Blackshear Road toward the Flint, but it may have been deemed necessary to watch the flanking trail up the Ocmulgee for troublesome Indians. (4) The site may simply have been a trading post. The fact that it was secluded in the edge of the swamp hints that such an operation might have been carried on there by unlicensed Indian traders who wanted to hide their surreptitious dealings from authorities. (5) It is possible the fort was merely a small stockade erected by white cattlemen who had come over the Ocmulgee from old Wilkinson County to range their cattle on Indian lands. Again the location of the place inside the swamp intimates that this could have been the case, because there were probably cane brakes in the low grounds of the river and expansive reed beds around the fringes of the swamp. (6) A really intriguing aspect of the site is the possibility that the fortification may have been erected by the Spaniards as a stopping point in travelling to and from the coast. This could have been the case since the surveyor in 1821 marked the place "old," and this word indicates the structure antedated the 1814-1815 or 1818 periods. The place may even have been a spot where DeSoto's men stopped for a while in 1540 while passing through this section. By consulting the official report of the United States Commission to study the DeSoto journey,[10] it will be seen the commission concluded the expedition first reached the Ocmulgee in the general area of the fortification. If DeSoto's army did not erect the place, it is possible that later Spaniards did so. It is known that they made trips into the interior, but they were secretive about such expeditions and there is little information about where and how they went. But if one examines a good map of Georgia, it will be seen that the fort site was strategically located in an area that could have served as a focal point for trails which reached the place from the south and north with a minimum of major stream crossings. And this would have been particularly true for routes leading from the areas of Brunswick (opposite the Spanish posts on St. Simons Island) and from St. Marks in Florida. It may be improbable but certainly not impossible that some day an old map or journal will turn up in the archives of Sevilla, Madrid, or Havana which will name and perhaps explain the reason for the Old Fortification.

—*GMNL* 14(1961): 32-34

NOTES

1. Map of District 28, Early County, survey of 1820, Robert Kennedy, D.S., Land Records of Georgia, Surveyor General Department, Atlanta.

2. District 28, Early County, Platbook FFF.

3. The writer wishes to express his appreciation to Mrs. Pat Bryant, Deputy Surveyor General at the Surveyor General Department, for the copies of this plat and the accompanying plat for lot 103 of District 8 of original Dooly County.

4. Letter dated Jan. 28, 1819, from the Adjutant and Inspector General's Office to the Secretary of War, Letter Book No. 5, from May 29, 1818, to Dec. 30, 1821, p. 173, War Records Division, National Archives.

The letter states the troops from the 4th Infantry first encamped on the site of Fort Scott in June of 1816 and started the fort in September.

5. *Ibid.*

6. District 15, Early County, survey of 1819, Clem Powers, D.S., lot 267. The "Camp" was just to the right of the present West Bainbridge-Newton road, a segment at this point of the old Jackson Trail.

7. District 8, Dooly County, survey of 1821, Zara Powers, D.S., Platbook QQQ, lot 103.

8. Field Notes, District 8, Dooly County, survey of 1821, Zara Powers, D.S.

9. Map of District 8, Dooly County, survey of 1821, Zara Powers, D.S.

10. *Final Report of the United States DeSoto Expedition Commission,* House Doc. 71, 76th Cong., 1st Sess. (Washington, D.C., 1939), see especially maps No. 2 and No. 10.

No. 83
Walnut Creek (Formerly the Oakchuncoolgau)

The particular Walnut Creek of this sketch is a large stream that rises in central Jones County, near Wayside, and flows south to join the Ocmulgee River on the east side at Macon. The stream has been known a long time by white people because it lay athwart the much-travelled and famous Lower Creek Trading Path, leading from Augusta via the Rock Landing on the Oconee and present Macon to the Creek Indians of Georgia and Alabama. But the waterway was not originally known as Walnut Creek. The John Stuart, or Joseph Purcell, map of Southeastern Indian country of the early 1770's refers to it as the "Oakehancoolga,"[1] and Colonel Benjamin Hawkins later mentioned it in 1797 as the "Oakchuncoolgau."[2] Two district surveyors of original Baldwin County in 1806 listed it as the "Okenchulga,"[3] "Okenchulgee,"[4] or "Okenchulgo."[5] Some district surveyors of Baldwin at the same period, however, gave the name of the stream as "Walnut Creek,"[6] thus showing that the present designation was coming into use by that date. The 1818 Eleazer Early map of Georgia continued the appellation as "Oakchancoolgau." By the 1820's the waterway was beginning to be commonly known as Walnut Creek and the H. S. Tanner map of Georgia and Alabama, published in 1825, lists it by that name. An official but undated manuscript map of Jones County prepared perhaps in the 1840's gives the appellation as "Walnut Ochangau Creek."[7] The garbled Indian version in the last listing intimates the aboriginal version was disappearing and people were no longer sure of the spelling of the name.

Oakchuncoolgau is an interesting expression to analyze because it offers a triple opportunity to delve into the intricacies of Indian placename derivations and at the same time learn a bit about medicinal practices of the Creeks and something about the origin of certain frontier terms which were used by backcountry white people.

The expression is of Muskogee or Creek origin but one can be certain the name has no connection with the Creek term *ahwa*, signifying walnut. Thus there is no relationship between the aboriginal Oakchuncoolgau and the later Walnut Creek, save for the fact that the whites came along and applied their name to a stream which the Indians were already calling Oakchuncoolgau.

The derivation of Oakchuncoolgau is involved but it seems certain the expression is derived from the Creek composite word

Okchànàtckiàlgi, from *okchànàtcki,* a green, slimy substance called "rock moss" that grows on rocks or shoally places in streams, plus *àlgi,* or "ulga." The latter form is a suffix which the Creeks usually employed to denote the plural number of most nouns or to signify the species, clan, or nationality of things or people. But the suffix was also used in a locative sense to indicate a place where something abounded or could be found. The intended meaning of the form depended on the connotation of the substantive to which it was attached.

In the case of Okchànàtckiàlgi the *àlgi* or "ulga" played this locative function, and since Oakchuncoolgau applied to a creek, one can assume the word *hàchi,* or "hatchee," meaning stream, was understood as a part of the name. Thus the entire expression signified in English stream where rock moss abounds. English-speaking people could have, if they had wished, simplified the name by making it Moss Creek or Mossy Creek. Indeed, on the Piedmont Plateau there are numbers of rocky streams called Moss or Mossy creeks and it is possible that some of these names are actual translations of Indian forms like Oakchuncoolgau. It was common practice for white people to translate Indian appellations which they found, and we continue using these translations, even down to this day.

There are still some points to make about the change of Okchànàtckiàlgi into Oakchuncoolgau. In their spoken language the Creeks often compacted their compound words by dropping vowels and slurring syllables. Okchànàtckiàlgi went through this process, so much so, that of the middle element *àtcki* only a *k* sound was retained to become the *c* of *coolgau* in the white man's version of the name. The *gau* of *coolgau* was employed by the whites to depict the hard *g* of *àlgi,* otherwise the form would have faced the risk of being mispronounced "ooljee."

The rock moss to which the Creek word *okchànàtcki* referred was also known to the frontier whites as salt grass and numbers of references can be found in old records to the latter expression. The vegetation was of economic importance because cattle liked the grass and would wade out into shoally spots of streams to eat it. Perhaps the moss actually does contain traces of salt and the animals craved it to supplement their diet of shoreside browse plants. In any case, salt grass is an English version of *okchànàtcki* because the first element of the Indian expression are clearly derived from the Creek word *okchànwä,* signifying salt. The whites supplied the word grass in the expression salt grass because the Muskogee term for grass, *paha,* is not an integral part of the composite word Oakchuncoolgau. And, to clarify a point that should be explained, neither does the Indian designation embody the Creek word *chato,* rocks or *asánwá,* moss for the rock moss derivation that was originally mentioned in giving the meaning of *okchánátcki.* Rock moss was, and still is, the colloquial name used in the Southeast for the slimy, stream-grown vegetation referred to.[8]

The Creek Indians eventually began to raise cattle and it is possible they gave the Oakchuncoolgau its name because their stock went there to eat salt grass. Perhaps the stream was so named, though, because deer and buffalo frequented the creek to eat the grass and the Indians learned they could find the animals along the stream in hunting. But Benjamin Hawkins offers interesting information which may explain how the waterway got its designation. He notes that "Oak-chon-utch-co" *(okchanatcki)* was one of the 14 physic plants used by the Creek medicine makers in preparing a sacred medicine which was drunk or rubbed on the joints by Muskogee men on the eighth and last day of the Busk or annual green corn festival of the Creeks.[9]

This usage of rock moss, of course, made the vegetation important in the eyes of the Indians and it is possible the red people, and especially the early Creeks living in Ocmulgee Old Town at the site of present Macon, originally named our Walnut Creek the Oakchuncoolgau because the stream was the customary source of their "Oak-chon-utch-co."

—GMNL 15(1962): 31-32

NOTES

1. John R. Swanton, *Early History of the Creek Indians and Their Neighbors,* Bureau of American Ethnology Bulletin 73, Plate 7.

The Special Collections Department of Emory University has recently received from the British Public Record Office, London, photostatic copies of two versions of this map from official manuscript copies in the PRO.

2. *Letters of Benjamin Hawkins, 1796-1806,* Collections of the Georgia Historical Society, Vol. 9 (Savannah, Ga., 1916), p. 89, entry for Feb. 23, 1797.

3. District 8, Baldwin County, survey of 1806, David Glenn, D.S., Platbook NN, lots 23, 24, 48, *passim,* Land Records of Georgia, Surveyor General Department, Atlanta.

4. *Ibid.,* lots 48, 77, 96, *passim.*

5. District 9, Baldwin County, survey of 1806, John L. Porter, D.S., Platbook PP, lots 3, 5, 23, 46, *passim.*

6. District 7, Baldwin County, survey of 1806, B. Smith, D.S., Platbook HH, lots 51, 53, 79, *passim;* and District 11, Baldwin County, survey of 1807, William Watson, D.S., Platbook PP, lots 88, 93, 107, *passim.*

7. Map of Jones County, in the official collection of Georgia counties, no author or date shown.

8. [One of the editorial readers, Professor Byrd Granger, Director of the American Place-Name Survey, finds the paragraph confusing but thinks it should be rewritten as follows: "In attempting to render the meaning of the Indian word *okchanatcki* in English, the whites added to the meaning 'salt' the word 'grass.' The Indian word derives simply from the Creek word *okchanwa,* signifying *salt.* Clearly the Indian placename has no trace of the Muskogee term for grass, which is *paha,* nor does *paha* occur in *Oakchuncoolgau,* a variant. 'Rock moss' was, and still is, the colloquial name used in the Southeast for the slimy, stream-grown vegetation referred to, yet nothing of that nature is included: the Creek word for rocks is *chato,* and for moss is *asanwa.* One must conclude that the original meaning given for Okchanatcki (rockmoss) is therefore in error." *FLU.*]

9. Benjamin Hawkins, *A Sketch of the Creek Country in the Years 1798 and 1799* (Americus, Ga.: Americus Book Co., 1938), pp. 72-73.

No. 84
Christmas Branch

In eastern Stewart County, commencing at the northwestern edge of Richland, there is an upper tributary of Hannahatchee Creek that bears the odd name of Christmas Branch. The unusual designation aroused curiosity as to the origin of such an interesting name and led to a bit of research on the subject. The answer was easily found in the early land records of Georgia. These documents show the label was first applied by John G. Scruggs, the district surveyor who laid off land District 24 of Lee County, now parts of Stewart and Webster. His notes show he reached the little stream while running a line on December 25, 1825, and since he had to supply a name for the waterway he marked it "Christmas Branch."[1] This version was later reproduced on the official plats of his survey of District 24 to perpetuate the name.[2]

It might be added there is a Christmas Bay in lower Echols County which extends over the Georgia line into adjoining Florida.[3] This portion of Florida was once claimed by Georgia and was actually surveyed in 1821 as a part of Appling County, Georgia.

The land records of the state show that District 13 of Appling (the section where Christmas Bay lies) was surveyed by Laird W. Harris, beginning April 10, 1821.[4] This date makes it unlikely that Harris applied the designation Christmas Bay, particularly in view of the fact that his notes simply mention the Bay as a "swamp."[5]

For the reader who is unfamiliar with colloquial Georgia geographic terms, the expression "bay" as used here does not apply to a body of water but pertains to a low, slashy timbered area of considerable size. There are numerous bays in the southern part of the state and some of them encompass thousands of acres. Many of the bays bear interesting titles which offer fascinating subjects for this placename series. Much information has already been gathered on the tabs and in due time sketches of them should appear here.[6]

—GMNL 15(1962): 32

NOTES

1. Field Notes for District 24, Lee County, survey of 1825-1826, John G. Scruggs, D.S., Land Records of Georgia, Surveyor General Department, Atlanta.
2. District 24, Lee County, Platbook TTTT, lots 72, 89, 104.
3. *Cypress Creek Quadrangle, Florida-Georgia* (U.S. Geological Survey, ed. 1955).
4. Field Notes for District 13, Appling County, survey of 1821, Laird W. Harris, D.S.
5. *Ibid.*
6. [The practice of naming a place on the date of discovery or some other significant event is well-attested. See Stewart, *American Place Names*, p. 97 (Christmas), p. 240 (King—the Three Magi), pp. 421-22 (San Antonio, San Diego, San Joaquin, San Pedro, San Saba). *FLU.*]

No. 85
Tallahassee Creek (Formerly the Osketochee)

Tallahassee Creek commences in the northwest corner of Dougherty County near the Terrell line and joins the west side of Kiokee Creek about a mile below the bridge on Georgia 234. The name is derived from the Muskogee Talwàahasihàchi, signifying Old Town Creek, from *talwa*, town, plus *ahasi*, old, plus *hachi*, stream. In accordance with an accepted rule employed by the Muskogees in making up compound words, they dropped the *wá* of *talwá* and converted the name into the more compact Talahasihachi, which white people changed to Tallahassee Creek. It will be noted the *háchi* was translated into the English form "creek" and not into the Anglicized "hatchee." The white people apparently followed no definite rule on this score. They often retained the Indian *háchi* as "hatchee," "hatchy," etc., of Muskogee names and at other times converted it into our expression creek or river.

The name of the Old Town community to which the designation Tallahassee refers is not known. Various records mention some large Indian settlements on the waters of the big Chickasawhatchee Creek of which the Tallahassee and Kiokee are tributaries, but little is known about these towns and their names, mainly because the Indian country travellers who wrote about the Creeks and listed their settlements never visited the places in the area of the Chickasawhatchee.

The early land records of Georgia throw no light on the name of the Old Town because curiously enough they do not refer to the creek as the Tallahassee but as the "Osketochy,"[1] "Oskeetochee,"[2] or "Osketochee."[3] These names, there can be little doubt, are derived from the Creek word *oskintacha*. Literally, the expression means rain stop, but freely in English it signifies rainbow. Perhaps the Old Town involved in the word Tallahassee was actually known as Rainbow Town. Such a possibility would not be far-fetched because numbers of Creek communities had unusual meanings when translated into English, like Dogwood Grove Town, Conch Shell Town, Buzzard Roost Town, Burnt Town, and so on.

The name Osketochee had hardly gotten recorded on the initial land plats of the survey covering northwest Dougherty before undergoing changes. An early copy of a map of district 2 of original Early where the stream lies lists the stream as the "Osteetoche."[4] Another official map of the district prepared in 1851 gives the designation as "Osteetchee";[5] while the 1870 Phillips map of Dougherty County marks the stream as "Asteechee Creek."[6] Following this recording the Osketochee and its mutations in spelling disappear from maps and the appellation Tallahassee Creek came into use.

—*GMNL* 15(1962): 32

NOTES

1. District 2, Early County (now Dougherty), survey of 1819, Grigsby Thomas, D.S., Platbook AAA, lot 57, Land Records of Georgia, Surveyor General Department, Atlanta.
2. *Ibid.*, lot 23.
3. *Ibid.*, lots 29 and 65.
4. "Map of District 2 of Early," certified by Carlton Wellborn, Surveyor General, *circa* 1825.
5. "Map of District No. 2 of County of Early," renewed in 1851 by James R. Butts, Surveyor General.
6. "Dougherty County," William Phillips, C.E., 1870.

No. 86
Five Mile Creek (Formerly the Saoxomoha)

Five Mile Creek (or, as some people call it, Five Mile Branch) arises in lower Sumter County to the west of Leslie and flows southwestward into Lee to join Muckalee Creek three miles to the east of Smithville. The name is interesting because it is said to stem from the length of the stream and not from its geographic location with respect to some given spot or town. There are numbers of streams in Georgia whose names embody a distance-indicating factor, like Two Mile Creek, Ten Mile Creek, Seventeen Mile Creek, and so on. But most of these waterways derive their appellations from the fact that they measure off the number of miles along some pioneer thoroughfare from a town or beginning point of significance. Five Mile Creek then is unusual because the name refers to its length and not to its position.

But the interesting thing about Five Mile Creek is the tab which it bore in Indian days before it was given its present-day title. When the area where the creek lies was being surveyed in 1827 after its acquisition from the Indians, an original surveyor labelled it variously as the "Soaxomoha,"[1] "Saoxamoha,"[2] "Saxomoha,"[3] "Suoxomaha,"[4] and "Saoxomoha."[5]

The word is of Creek origin and it affords a fine specimen for dissection to see how those Indians constructed their placenames. It also illustrates the difficulties which white transcribers faced when they tried to set down a strange expression from a language they did not understand.

Perhaps it is best to examine the word by first constructing a hypothetical model of the original Indian name and then discussing how it eventually came to be turned into Saoxomoha. The original expression was Sōkäsäsiimäha, a compound form that was derived in turn from *soka* (or maybe the dialecta *suki*), hog + the locative *sasi*, there or is there + *im*, his or its, + *aha* potato, meaning Hog Potato Creek, and referring to a kind of tuber that grew in low, moist places like the site of an old beaver dam. The expression *hachi* (or "hatchee") for stream or creek is not contained in the model but it was plainly understood in connection with the name since the Creeks usually employed the form as a suffix in speaking of streams. One can be sure the Indians did not actually use a moniker as long and as complicated as Sokasasiimaha. The English version, Saoxomoha, as reported by Surveyor Meriwether is evidence to support this conclusion. In compounding the word in the first instance the Creeks followed their customary practice of dropping syllables and vowels. Thus Sokasasiimaha was shortened to Soksamaha, a form which phonetically resembles the "Saoxomoha" of the surveyor. The white transcriber used an *x* in his word because *Sōksä* of the shortened Indian name sounded like "Saoxo" to him. He converted the *mäha* elements to "moha" because the broad *a* of the Indian term sounded like an *o*. The locative *sasi*, there, normally was treated as a suffix but in the word Saoxomoha, however, it served as an infix in that compounded form. It will be noted that only the letter *m* remained of the possessive pronoun *im*, his or its. In many Creek compound words the *i* of this element is retained and the *m* is the letter which is dropped. In the case of Sokasasiimaha, the presence of two *i*'s created an awkward situation that was corrected by eliminating the *si* of *sasi* and the *i* of *im*.

But to return to Hog Potato Creek, the equivalent of Soaxomoha(hatchee), one is puzzled about the real intent of the name. The Indians themselves ate the hog potato and the name may have been used because the red people went there to dig these tubers for their own food supply. On the other hand, it is quite possible the designation was applied simply because hogs frequented the little stream to root for the potatoes.

—*GMNL* 15(1962): 32-33

234 / Placenames of Georgia

NOTES

1. District 16, Lee County, survey of 1827, Thomas J. Meriwether, D.S., Platbook SSSS, lot 168, Land Records of Georgia, Surveyor General Department, Atlanta.
2. *Ibid.*, lot 209.
3. *Ibid.*, lot 201.
4. *Ibid.*, lot 202.
5. "Map of District 16 of 1st Section," (Lee County), survey of 1827, Thomas J. Meriwether, D.S. This version of the name was employed in the caption of the sketch because the surveyor used it on his original map and because it was also listed twice in Platbook SSSS showing District 16 of Lee. See lots 203 and 206.

No. 87
Alapaha River, Alabaha Creek, Little Alapaha River, Grand Bay Creek or Little River (Formerly the Alapahoochee), the Town of Alapaha, and the Indian Settlement of Alapaha Talofa

The Alapaha River commences to the southeast of Vienna in lower Dooly County and flows in a southerly direction to unite with the Suwannee in Hamilton County, Florida. On its way to this junction the Alapaha is joined on the west side, just below the Georgia line, by a sizable stream that is now known as Grand Bay Creek, or as Little River. The latter appellation is a partial translation of Alapahoochee, the original name as recorded by the first Georgia surveyor of the area. By reason of the Muskogee diminutive *oochee* affixed to the name, the designation signifies Little Alapaha, which was eventually turned into Little River, meaning of course the Little Alapaha River. Grand Bay Creek is a relatively new tab for the tributary and no doubt was substituted for Alapahoochee because it drains an extensive slashy area of northeast Lowndes County and southwest Lanier that is known as the Grand Bay. On the Florida side, Grand Bay Creek is marked as the "Apalahoochee River" on a map prepared by the U.S. Geological Survey.[1] This version is interesting since, as will be seen, one writer suggests Alapaha may be derived from the Creek word *apala*, signifying on the other side.[2] One early Georgia surveyor called the stream "Apoloochee,"[3] but this man also mentions it in the same source as the "Allappahoochee," which is close to various versions offered by the other Georgia surveyors of the area.

Farther down from the union with Grand Bay Creek or the Alapahoochee, the Alapaha is joined on the east by the Little Alapaha River. This stream (that was mentioned in the first Georgia surveys as Florida Creek) heads in a swampy area of lower Echols County and soon passes into Florida. Since only a small part of the waterway lies in this state it will not be discussed in detail.

Alabaha Creek, sometimes also marked Alabaha River, is a northbank tributary of the Great Satilla River. It joins the latter in Pierce County to the south of Blackshear. As will be shown, Alabaha is merely another form of Alapaha. One can be certain the two names had the same basic origin because the designations were alternately used in old documents.

But to return to the Alapaha River, the central theme of the sketch, the stream is unusual in several respects. It is about 130 miles long but has a comparatively small watershed for a stream of this length. Other waterways like the Withlacoochee and the Satilla crowd the Alapaha and capture waters that arise within a short distance of the latter stream. Perhaps the most unusual feature of the Alapaha, however, is the eccentricity of its flow. In times of heavy rains it rises and quickly overflows the low marginal swamps that border its course. In late summer it tends to dry up except for holes here and there; and in periods of extreme drought great stretches of it dry up completely leaving the white sandy bed to wind like the bleached skeleton of a great snake through the somber swamps along the channel. It is said the river loses its water in these instances through underground outlets. Since a considerable part of the stream passes through the Lime Sink Region of the Lower Coastal Plain, such subterranean drainage may well explain the disappearance of the water.

It is not known with certainty how long the Alapaha has borne its name. The designation is old and may be one of the oldest geographic appellations of Georgia and Florida. Dr. John R. Swanton was convinced that Alapaha is a Timucua Indian term that was borrowed by the later Creeks and in discussing the origin of the name he mentions as being in existence in 1655 a Spanish mission called Santa María de los Angeles de Arapaja.[4] He states the place was 70 leagues from St. Augustine[5] and this distance could have placed the mission in the general area where the Alapaha joins the Suwannee. Those who understand Spanish will quickly note the similarity of Arapaja and Alapaha, because the *ja* of the former sounds like the *ha* ending of Alapaha.

Unfortunately, however, until we know more about the Mission of Santa María de los Angeles de Arapaja and its location, one can not be sure the place had any relationship to the stream we call the Alapaha. The mission could have been 70 leagues from St. Augustine and still not near the Alapaha River.

With present available records it is necessary to move much farther along than 1655 to pick up the first direct references to the Alapaha. This is the case because the country where the river flows was long unknown to outsiders except perhaps to a few traders or Indian countrymen who did not report on the region. As far as the American settlers were concerned, the territory was screened on the east by the great Okefenokee, and apparently no one knew how far this swamp extended westward. Some early maps depict it as reaching nearly to Flint River.[6]

One of the first persons to traverse the area and make a positive reference to the Alapaha was Major Caleb Swan. In 1790 he listed the river as the "Alabaha" in a report made after his visit to the Creek Nation following the Treaty of New York with the Creeks.[7] The chiefs who attended this meeting were returned home by ship to the St. Marys, whence they travelled overland to their towns in western Georgia and Alabama. Major Swan was sent along to see the Indians home and to gather information about the Creeks and their country. From the St. Marys the group followed Kinnard's Path to Flint River; thus when Swan mentioned crossing the "Alabaha" he was certainly referring to the Alapaha River and not to the Alabaha Creek of Pierce County, because the latter stream is above the Great Satilla whereas Kinnard's Path ran to the south of that waterway.

Following the reference to the Alapaha by Swan in 1790, a considerable time elapsed before the river was mentioned again. The John Dutton map of Georgia, dated in 1814, shows a "Lappaha R."[8] but the stream is much out of place, since it is shown draining from a large unnamed swamp into the east side of lower Flint River. After this listing, one would expect to find the Alapaha on the noted 1818 map of Georgia published by Eleazer Early. That chart was prepared by Daniel Sturges, a former surveyor general of Georgia, but no mention is made of the river. In fact, the general area of the stream was left blank on the map as was the custom on most charts prepared before Sturges's day.

It was not till 1819 that people began to learn much about the Alapaha and Alabaha. In that year Georgia began surveying original Appling and Irwin counties where the streams lie.

This region was acquired from the Creeks in 1814 at the Treaty of Fort Jackson, but little effort had been made to open it for settlement because the section was generally regarded as a vast swampy and pine barren area that was not suited to farming and especially to cotton raising. Furthermore, although the Creeks had ceded the territory, parties of Indians continued to reside there and surveyors were reluctant to undertake surveying in the section for fear of them. Finally, in 1819, however, surveying got under way and by 1820 there were numerous plats and numbers of district land maps which mentioned the Alapaha and delineated its course in Irwin and Appling. By 1821 the surveys for lower Dooly were completed and made available to show the origin point and headwaters of the river.

When the surveyors encountered the Alapaha they apparently were familiar with the general location of the river since they all identified it and properly presented it to make the course continuous from one land district to another. Even though the surveyors knew of the stream, however, they were not sure of the way to spell its name. As a result, they rendered the designation in a variety of ways: Lopaha, Alopaha, Lappahaw, Allallehaw, Loppohaw, lop haw, Popaha, Lopahatchy, Allapauhau, Allopohaw, Allaphaw, Alloppehaw, Alapa hawchu, Alapa haw, Allappaha, Alla-pa-ha, and so on.[9]

These transcriptions are worth noting for several reasons. For one thing, they give inklings of the sound of the appellation as it was understood by old-timers. Some of the versions listed have spellings that are close to spoken forms presently used by people who live along the Alapaha. Furthermore, in the analysis of Indian names it is helpful to ferret out the early listings for a given name because some of the old renditions may furnish a much better idea of the true meaning of an expression than the polished up and often garbled form which eventually was adopted for use on present maps. And lastly, in these days when Indian names are neatly set down on charts under commonly accepted spellings, the early versions serve to remind us how difficult it was initially to capture aboriginal appellations and transcribe them before they evolved into the familiar forms we now know.

At the time the Irwin County surveyors were having trouble in the reduction of Alapaha to writing, the men laying off old Appling County were also having difficulties with Alabama Creek in present

Pierce County. They first listed the stream under tabs like: Elebahaw, Allabaha, The Allabaha, Elibahaw, Elebaw, Elabahow, Elebehaw, etc.[10]

These variants, of course, are identifiable with the present Alabaha, but an important point to note is that some of the Appling surveys also mark the Alabaha as "Alapaha"[11] or "Alapahau.[12] In the same period, one of the surveys listed a fringe of the Alapaha as "Allabahaw Swamp."[13] In this connection it will be remembered Major Swan mentioned the latter stream as the "Alabama."[14] There can be little doubt then the two names were the same except for the use of a *b* in one and a *p* in the other. It was fairly common for early whites to switch these cognates in recording the Indian names of Georgia.

To turn next to the pronunciation of Alapaha, it is safe to say the expression is commonly considered as one of the most puzzling placenames to be found in Georgia. Apparently many people about the state have little idea how the word is pronounced and one judges these individuals could have been easy victims for the wag who is reported to have said the pronunciation of Alapaha resembles the sound made in raising a rusty umbrella.

Actually there is no substance to this whimsical explanation, and the name is easy to pronounce in any of the several slightly different versions when one has some suggestions on how to go about saying it. Old people living along the river often refer to it as the "Loppyhaw." This form is of long standing because it is similar to some of the original listings of the word made by the surveyors. Other individuals living in the vicinity of the river, or in the present town of Alapaha in Berrien County, pronounce the name "A lop' pa haw," or as "Lop'pa haw." The *o* in these forms has the sound of *o* in words like lock or dock, and no doubt is used to represent a broad *a* that was found in the aboriginal word. This letter was very common in languages of the Southeastern Indians and it is reasonable to conclude it occurred in Alapaha. In fact, all four of the *a*'s in Alapaha were probably broad *a*'s in the original name.

It will be noted in two of the versions given above the initial *a* is slurred. The dropping of this letter at the beginning of an Indian placename was a fairly common occurrence. Perhaps the Indians themselves practiced this slurring and the white people are not to be entirely blamed for it.

Numbers of individuals pronounce Alapaha as "A lăp' pȧ hä. This variant appears to be a modern version and perhaps has come into use in an attempt to sound the word as it appears in print. The rendition is not particularly objectionable and it is possible it will eventually become the accepted pronunciation. For one thing, it involves the use of two *p*'s which are desirable in the word even though it is now written with only one *p*. Some of the old surveyors understood the name to have the two letters and they spelled it accordingly. The "hä" at the end of "A lăp′ pȧ hä" does not quite depict the sound of the syllable as it comes out in speech. The element in the aboriginal form may have carried the broad *a* or *ä*, but white people have long sounded the *ha* as a lusty "haw" and not like the word *ha* that is used as an exclamation.

The pronunciation of Alabaha parallels the form used for Alapaha. A seemingly modern version is "Labbyhaw." There may be old people who say "Elebbyhaw" or "Lebbyhaw," but one has not heard these last two forms.

The meaning of Alapaha and Alabaha has long been debated by placename students. William A. Read in his study of Florida names avoided a forthright treatment of the word by placing it in a category entitled "Florida names of dubious or unknown origin."[15] He does suggest, however, that the name might contain the Creek word *pahi* (or *paha*) signifying grass, or the expression *apala* meaning on the other side.[16] With respect to the latter conjecture, it will be recalled that a topographical sheet for Florida lists Grand Bay Creek of Georgia as the Apalahoochee. In one instance a Georgia surveyor used a form similar to this in his notes.[17] But the same man and the other surveyors of Irwin County also marked it as the Allappahoochee, Allapohoochee, Alapacoochee, etc.,[18] and designations similar to these were later long applied to the stream. If *apala* had any bearing on the designation, it is curious that the only name which might have indicated such an origin applied to a tributary and not to the main Alapaha.

Mr. J. Clarence Simpson in his report on Florida Indian names suggests that Alapaha may be derived from the Creek word *halpata*, alligator, since those saurians were once abundant on the stream.[19] Major Swan supports him on the presence of alligators in the river. He wrote that when he and the Creek chiefs reached the Alapaha the stream was badly swollen and the party had to wait several days for it to drop because they were afraid to cross the flooded river through fear of the large and fierce alligators that lived in the stream.[20]

It is doubtful that Alapaha is derived from *halpata*, or its related version *alpata*, because both words lack the key syllable of *lop* as found in Alapaha.

Dr. John R. Swanton, the eminent scholar of the Southern Indian tribes, offers the best explanation of the meaning of Alapaha. He states the word was quite certainly taken from the Timucua language by the Creeks and changed from Arapaja (or Arapaha).[21] The Creeks switched the *r* from the original word to an *l*, which was in accordance with Creek practice in adopting words containing the *r*. Swanton goes on to say Alapaha is derived from the Timucua *ara*, bear, and *paha*, house.[22] The complete form should not be construed literally but should be taken to mean something like Bear Park, Bear Home, Bear Den, Bear Lodge, Bear Range, Bear Heaven, and so on, and was probably applied because bears were numerous in the swamps of the Alapaha and the Alabama. In this connection it is interesting to add that Grand Bay Creek (formerly the Alapahoochee) drains a part of a large swampy area of southern Lowndes County,[23] and a section of this low area is now referred to as Bear Garden.[24]

Swanton does state the name may have been derived because some members of the Bear Clan (of the Timucuas) lived along the Alapaha.[25] This possibility is questioned because there is little evidence that Indian clan designations had any significant bearing on the aboriginal geographic names of this region. The clan relationships are sometimes reflected in recorded personal names of Indians, but not in placenames.

As has been noted there is a town as well as a river which bears the designation Alapaha. This place is in Berrien County, on the west side of the river, and at the juncture of U.S. 82 and 129. And interestingly enough, one of the early Georgia surveyors also found an Indian town on the river which he reported as "Alapahaw."[26] The surveyor was A. B. Shehee and he discovered the Indian settlement in 1819 when he was laying off District 16 of original Irwin County. In this survey, Shehee went much below today's Georgia-Florida line because at the time Georgia claimed her territory extended farther south than the present boundary. In his work, therefore, Shehee ran many lines and laid off numerous lots in what is now Hamilton County, Florida.

During the survey Shehee saw numbers of Indian trails in the district. One day he and an assistant decided to follow one of the more important routes to see where it led. They came out at an Indian settlement of 70 to 80 houses, situated on the west side of the Alapaha, at a point where paths converged to cross the river.[27]

Shehee noted there was an oval-shaped pond of deep water in the center of the place, with nearly perpendicular banks of 5 feet in height.[28] Most of the inhabitants were away, since the surveyors only saw a half-dozen women and one Negro man who fled when they approached. Shehee stated the settlement was a new town and added a woman at the place said it was called Alapahaw. She also said the head man was Micco (which merely means chief or king) and that he was a brother of Old Hoop.[29] The latter individual apparently was a person of some importance among the Indians at that period.

The town visited by Surveyor Shehee was also mentioned as "A-la-pa-ha talofa" by some Florida chiefs in a conference with Andrew Jackson at Pensacola in 1821,[30] but the location given was vague since the place was only noted as being somewhere between the Suwannee River and Miccosukee, a prominent town on Lake Miccosukee in today's Leon County, Florida. Shehee's location of Alapahaw was more specific. According to his account, it was in present Hamilton County, on the west side of the Alapaha at the lower side of Section 29, T2 N.R13 E. The site was to the northwest of today's Jasper, Florida, and was about one mile north of the bridge where U.S. 41 now crosses the Alapaha.

At the 1821 conference with General Jackson, the Seminole leaders said the chief of Alapaha Talofa was named Oakmulgee and that he had recently died.[31] They also mentioned that the people of the settlement were Upper Creeks.[32] The reference by Shehee to the chief being a brother of Old Hoop, however, suggests the people may have been Lower Creek and that they had removed to the Alapaha from the vicinity of present Lee County, Georgia. No leader called Hoop or Old Hoop could be found in the listings of Creek chiefs of the period, but there was a well-known headman called Hoponnie or Hoponny who lived till around 1818 in the Lee County section. He was an enemy of the whites and when Andrew Jackson and some of his troops passed through Lee in early 1818 for the invasion of Florida, Hoponnie and his followers are believed to have taken off for Florida. Perhaps then, Chief Oakmulgee was this Hoponnie's brother and he left Lee County at the same time to found the New Town that Surveyor Shehee visited. The designation Oakmulgee supports this conjecture. A chief ordinarily would not bear this sort of name. It is possible the Seminole chiefs were trying to tell Jackson that the man was an Oakmulgee Indian and they literally did not mean his name was Oakmulgee. It is known that a band of Oakmulgees once lived in the Lee County area because Benjamin Hawkins mentions them as being there in 1797.[33] He adds they were remains of the people who once lived at the site of Oakmulgee Old Town,[34] located at present

Macon. These postulations and comments are of value because some of the Indians of the Lee County area certainly quit that section some years before it was finally ceded in 1826 and they had to go somewhere. Perhaps they went to the Alapaha and formed the town seen by Surveyor Shehee.[35]

—GMNL 15(1962): 95-98

NOTES

1. *Jennings Quadrangle, Florida-Georgia* (U.S. Geological Survey, 1956). There is conflict on various maps about the course and location of the lower part of Grand Bay Creek or the Apalahoochee River. Cartographers should work on the matter. Perhaps the difficulties about the course are caused by the stream's crossing a state line. The *Valdosta Ga.-Fla.* sheet, NH17-4 (1959) of the U.S. Geological Survey properly locates the stream.

2. William A. Read, *Florida Place Names of Indian Origin and Seminole Personal Names*, Louisiana State University Studies No. 11 (Baton Rouge, 1934), pp. 43-44.

3. Field Notes for District 11, Irwin County, survey of 1819, John H. Brodnax, D.S., Land Records of Georgia, Surveyor General Department, Atlanta.

4. John R. Swanton, *Early History of the Creek Indians and Their Neighbors*, Bureau of American Ethnology Bulletin 73, p. 322.

5. *Ibid.*, p. 324.

6. "A New and Accurate Map of the Province of Georgia in North America," *The Universal Magazine*, April, 1799; and Thomas Wright, "Map of Georgia and Florida," photostatic copy from an original MS in British Archives in the Emory University Library, Atlanta.

7. Major Caleb C. Swan, USA, "Position and State of Manners and Arts in the Creek or Muscogee Nation in 1791," in Henry R. Schoolcraft, *Information Respecting the History, Condition and Prospects of the Indian Tribes of the United States* (Philadelphia: Lippincott, 1855), 5: 253.

8. John Dutton, "The State of Georgia," 1814, from a photostat of a copy in the British Museum, London.

9. Taken from the field notes, platbooks, and district land maps for Districts 1, 2, 3, 5, 6, 10, 11, and 13 of original Irwin County, surveys beginning in 1819.

10. Field notes and platbooks for Districts 1, 2, 3, 4, 8, and 9 of original Appling County.

11. Field notes for District 5 of Appling County, survey of 1819, E. R. Young, D.S., lots 28, 29. He also refers to the stream as the "Allabahaw."

12. District 4 of Appling County, survey of 1819, John P. Blackmon, D.S., Platbook KKK, lot 88. In lot 47 of this source, it is also listed as "Alapaha."

13. Field notes for District Lines of Irwin County. This survey covered the courses of the guide lines for the subsequent laying off of individual districts.

14. Swan, "Creek or Muscogee Nation in 1791," p. 253.

15. Read, *Florida Place Names*, p. 43.

16. *Ibid.*, pp. 43-44.

17. Field Notes for District 11, Irwin County, by John Brodnax. He mentions it as "Apoloochee," but also lists the word as "Allapohoochee" and "Allopohoochee."

18. Field notes, platbooks, and land district maps for Districts 16, 11, 10, and 9 of original Irwin County.

19. J. Clarence Simpson, *A Provisional Gazetteer of Florida Place-names of Indian Derivation*, ed. Mark F. Boyd, Special Publication No. 1, Florida Geological Survey (Tallahassee, 1956), p. 22.

20. Swan, "Creek or Muscogee Nation in 1791," p. 253. The party waited five days before crossing.

21. John R. Swanton, review of Read's *Florida Place-names of Indian Origin* in *American Speech* 9 (Feb. 1934): 219.

22. *Ibid.*

23. See *Valdosta Ga.-Fla.* sheet, NH17-4 (U.S. Geological Survey, 1959).

24. *Clyattville Quadrangle, Ga.-Fla.* (U.S. Geological Survey, 1956). The Bear Garden now drains via Jumping Gulley into the Withlacoochee and not toward Grand Bay Creek. In periods of very heavy rains the "Garden" may have drained the other way.

25. In *American Speech* 9 (Feb. 1934): 219.

26. Letter, A. B. Shehee, Surveyor of District 16, Irwin County, to Gov. John Clark, dated Milledgeville, Ga., Nov. 24, 1819, original at the Surveyor General Department.

27. *Ibid.*

28. *Ibid.*

29. *Ibid.* [The annotator of our copy notes that Simpson in his *Florida Place-Names* says this town was later called Micco Town. *FLU.*]

30. Extract of a talk held by Gen. Jackson with three chiefs of the Florida Indians, at Pensacola, Sept. 18, 1821, *American State Papers*, II. Indian Affairs 2: 413.

31. *Ibid.*

32. *Ibid.*

33. *Letters of Benjamin Hawkins, 1796-1806*, Collections of the Georgia Historical Society, Vol. 9 (Savannah, 1916), p. 173.

34. *Ibid.*

35. [Read, *IJAL* 16 (1950): 203, accepts Swanton's derivation of Alapaha and the bear-clan theory. Goff clearly did not know Read's work on Georgian stream names. Could the Bear House have been a ritual dwelling, such as that described in Frank G. Speck's *The Celestial Bear Comes Down to Earth* (Reading, Pa., 1945), p. 38? See John R. Swanton, *Myths and Tales of the Southeastern Indians*, Bulletin of the Bureau of American Ethnology 88 (Washington, D.C., 1929), pp. 190-93. *FLU.*]

No. 88
Yahoola Creek

Yahoola Creek arises in upper Lumpkin County, on the lower slopes of the Blue Ridge, and flows southward to join the right side of Chestatee River to the south of Dahlonega. Since the creek lies in the area of the gold-mining activities that took place in the Dahlonega section, it has long been a stream of considerable prominence. But even before the gold rush, the waterway was well known for the Cherokee families that dwelt along it. Among these were the Wards, who were kinsmen of the famous Nancy Ward. Ward Creek which joins the Yahoola to the northeast of Dahlonega commemorates this Cherokee family. Yahoola Creek is said to have derived its name from an individual called Yahula, who lived on the stream prior to the Revolution and who became a mythical figure among the Cherokees. James Mooney tells of the traditions about Yahula and states the spot were he lived was known to the Indians as Yahula-i or Yahula place.[1] The site was located about 10 miles above Dahlonega toward the head of the creek.[2]

Mooney notes the name Yahula is common among the Cherokees but he seemed to think the word was of Creek origin and not Cherokee.[3] He based this view on the resemblance of Yahula to the Muskogee word *yoholo,* which referred to the song or cry that was used at the opening of the noted black drink ceremony of the Creeks at the commencement of their council meetings. He might have added that Yoholo was also a ceremonial title for the individual who was appointed to bear the drink to the assembled chiefs and to utter the black drink cry at the beginning of those meetings.

Mooney does not offer an opinion to explain why or how the Creek word *yoholo* might have been transplanted to the Dahlonega area. At one time there may have been Creeks who lived high up on the Chattahoochee and its tributaries, like the Chestatee, but at the time Yahula is said to have dwelt on the stream that bears his name, the section was regarded as Cherokee territory.

One doubts that Yahoola was derived from the Creek word and it is probably mere chance that the name resembles the Muskogee term *yoholo.* Many versions of Yahoola Creek can be found in old records and in most instances they are closer to *yahula* than to *yoholo:* Yewhoola, Yehola, Yuhuler, Yohooler, Uhuler, Uhoola, Yoohoolah, and so on.

More than likely one thinks, Yahoola is derived from the Cherokee word *yahula* signifying doodle bug. Mooney acknowledges that this could have been the origin of the expression, although he notes the term could also have referred to a variety of hickory.[4] Yahoola probably meant doodle bug because the Cherokees often named people after some sort of insect. In the last years of the Cherokees in Georgia, for example, there were numbers of people bearing names like Cricket, Long Boy Wasp, Mellow Bug, Weavel, Bugg or Leoyah, Grasshopper, Snail, The Snale, Lightening Bug, Grubworm, Fly, Roach, Skin Worm or Utterah, Housebug, Spider, and so on. Such designations were much more common than were names which related to some kind of tree like a hickory.

The white people of today may regard these insect names of the Cherokees as unusual, and there may be some individuals who dislike seeing Yahoola rendered as Doodle Bug, but apparently there was nothing scornful or derogatory about such designations in the eyes of the Indians—the insect names were merely a phase of the Cherokees' system of applying personal names. The correctness of this conclusion is implicit in the name of Yahula or Yahoola, an esteemed individual among those Indians. It is certain they would not have called him Yahula if the expression were a disparaging moniker.[5]

—*GMNL* 15(1962): 98-99

NOTES

1. James Mooney, *Myths of the Cherokee*, Nineteenth Annual Report of the Bureau of American Ethnology (n.p., n.d.), Pt. 1, p. 347.
2. *Ibid.*, p. 348.
3. *Ibid.*, pp. 482 and 574.
4. *Ibid.*
5. [Read, *IJAL* 16 (1950): 207, uses Mooney and Swanton's mythical explanations, and mentions that Creek *yaholo* could have been a male deity. He also allows the possibility of "hickory" or "doodlebug," or of an Indian trader carried away by ghostly spirits. Explanations seem to be legion. *FLU.*]

No. 89
The Milksick Coves

A recent issue of the *Emory University Quarterly* contains a hitherto unpublished story by Charles Egbert Craddock (Mary Noailles Murfree) entitled "When Old Baldy Spoke."[1] The scene of the piece is in the mountains of east Tennessee and the story treats among other things a "milksick pen." This structure had been erected to fence off an area where grazing cattle could contract an ailment known as the milksickness. In old records various references can be found to this affliction. Any person apparently who drank the milk or ate the meat of an affected animal ran a risk of being made violently ill or even of dying.

The accounts are not based on some old folktale or superstition. There was a milksickness disease—not to be confused with milk fever—and its origin is a mystery. It has long been believed that the disease is caused by cows' eating a certain plant (or plants) and to minimize risk on this score it was once a common practice to fence areas where the trouble-causing vegetation was thought to grow to keep cattle out of such places. The name of the plant is not known, but it may be a *Eupatorium,* perhaps *Eupatorium urticaefolium* Reichard. The latter, which is also called white snake root, is said to be poisonous to cattle.

The milksickness seems to be mainly confined to the mountain regions of the South and one can hear more about the disease in those areas than elsewhere. Interestingly enough, Georgia has at least three placenames that stem from this affliction and these are the milksick coves. Two of the coves are in Towns County—one on the north side of the Blue Ridge, at the head of Cynth Creek, to the southeast of Presley on Georgia 17 and 75;[2] and the other on the Georgia–North Carolina line, to the north of Sassafras Knob, at the head of Davenport Branch that drains into Giesky Creek in North Carolina.[3]

Another Milksick Cove is in Rabun County, on the eastern slope of the Blue Ridge, some two and a half miles due east of Mountain City.[4] The cove is at the head of Tuckaluge Creek, that flows southward into Warwoman Creek.

In the North Carolina mountains, not far from the Georgia line, there are other milksick places. One of these is a Milksick Cove, off Licklog Creek, a tributary of Lake Chatuge;[5] and another is Milk Sick Knob on the line of Macon and Clay counties.[6]

—*GMNL* 15(1962): 99

NOTES

1. Charles Egbert Craddock, "When Old Baldy Spoke," ed. William B. Dillingham, *Emory University Quarterly* 18 (Summer 1962): 93ff.

2. *Osborn Quadrangle, Ga.-N.C.* (Maps and Surveys Division, Tennessee Valley Authority, ed. 1943).

3. *Ibid.*

4. *Rabun Bald Quadrangle, Ga.-N.C.* (Maps and Surveys Division, Tennessee Valley Authority, ed. 1947).

5. *Shooting Creek, Quadrangle, N.C.* (Maps and Surveys Division, Tennessee Valley Authority, ed. 1957).

6. *Rainbow Springs Quadrangle, N.C.* (Maps and Surveys Division, Tennessee Valley Authority, ed. 1957). All of the above maps are available through the U.S. Geological Survey. [For milksickness see the word *milk sick* in *A Dictionary of Americanisms* (Chicago, 1951), 2: 1055. Several plants are involved, among them "Water Hemlock" and *Eupatorium ageratoides.* North Georgia had an epidemic in 1898, and the disease is reputed to have caused the death of Abraham Lincoln's mother. *FLU.*]

No. 90
Pears or Perry Creek

The subject of this sketch is a small stream that begins on the slopes of Doogan Mountain, to the east of Cisco in upper Murray County, and flows westward on a curving course to join the left side of Conasauga River about a mile below the Tennessee line. Some present-day maps show the waterway as Pears Creek[1] while others list it as Perry Creek.[2] The latter version stems from the Cherokee days when the stream was called Perry's Creek. The name was derived from a man called Sol Perry or Perry Spaniard, who resided on the south side of the creek, immediately west of the old trace leading from Spring Place to McNairs. The last site was located above the Georgia line, in present Polk County, Tennessee, on our U.S. 411. The Georgia surveys for original Cherokee County show Sol Perry's house in lot 15 of District 10, 3rd Section and depict his fields and clearings a short way off in the lower part of the same lot and in the upper part of adjoining lot 22.[3] The Spring Place–McNairs road mentioned above passed through the western end of the fields.[4] The home and clearings were a mile and a half to the southwest of present Tennga, on U.S. 411, in northern Murray County.

In the appraisals of Cherokee property and improvements prior to the removal of those Indians, Perry was mentioned in 1836 as "Perry (Spaniard)."[5] The next year he was referred to as "Perry Spaniard" in a listing of Cherokees who had voluntarily enrolled for emigration to the West.[6] The Cherokee census of 1835 provides columns for indicating the blood relations of persons living in the Nation at that time, but this document does not mention a Sol Perry. In view of the references to him as Perry Spaniard, however, it seems certain he was part Spanish because the census names other Perrys in the same general locality, who are given as mixed Spanish and Cherokee. One group of these was the Robin Perry family that resided on Sugar Creek, across the Conasauga, and to the west of Sol Perry's home. Robin's family consisted of two fullbloods and seven mixed Spanish.[7] Another group was the Liddy Perry family of three part-Spanish members who were listed in the census as being on the Conasauga.[8]

The property appraisal reports refer to her as Lydia Perry and place her on Sugar Creek.[9] The original survey field notes mention her as "Mrs. Berry" and indicate she lived on the Conasauga and had a field in lot 98 of District 10.[10]

Since Perry is a surname it seems reasonable to conclude that the original name of these part-Spanish Cherokees was Pérez and not Perry. It was easy and perhaps logical to Anglicize Pérez to Perry, because when properly pronounced the former word sounds very much like Perry. Many English-speaking people are prone to mispronounce the name by turning it into "Pay rezz." Actually the word is accented on the first syllable and is pronounced "Payress." It would have been easy then for the Cherokees and the backcountry whites to turn this form into either Pears or Perry and one believes the little creek derived its designation in this roundabout fashion.

The progenitor of this Cherokee family, whoever he was and however he spelled his name, belonged in an interesting category of individuals who were referred to as "Indian Countrymen." Over the years there were many such white men among the Indians, and always in reading about them one is moved to wonder why they took refuge with the red people. They were mostly English, Scotch, or Irish, but there was also a sprinkling of Germans, French, Dutch, and Spaniards. The latter were usually found among the Creeks who were neighbors of the Spanish in Florida, but there were also Spaniards living with the Cherokees, and at the time of the removal of the tribe several persons of Spanish origin were residing among them. They had travelled a long way to reach the Cherokees and it is intriguing to speculate on why they were there.

—*GMNL* 15(1962): 99-100

NOTES

1. *General Highway Map of Murray County, Georgia* (State Highway Department of Georgia, ed. 1953); and *Chattahoochee National Forest, Georgia* (U.S. Forest Service, ed. 1954).
2. *Dalton Quadrangle, Ga.-Tenn.* (U.S. Geological Survey, ed. 1938); and *Cohutta Mountain Quadrangle, Ga.-Tenn.* (U.S. Geological Survey, ed. 1911).
3. Field Notes for District 10, 3rd Section of Cherokee County, survey of 1832, F. A. Brown, D.S., and platbook for the same survey, Land Records of Georgia, Surveyor General Department, Atlanta.
4. District 10, 3rd Section, Cherokee County, platbook.
5. "Valuations of Cherokee property and improvements in Murray County, Georgia in 1836 by Agents Young and Macmillan," Record Group 75, Records of the Bureau of Indian Affairs, National Archives.
6. "Heads of Cherokee families who enrolled for emigration and have received advances under the Treaty of 1835, Jan. 1837," list no. 68, Record Group 75, *ibid.*
7. "Census of Cherokees in the Limits of Georgia in 1835—the Henderson roll," p. 59, Record Group 75, *ibid.* The two "fullbloods" must have referred to the Spanish father and the Cherokee mother, with seven children being counted as mixed bloods.
8. *Ibid.*, p. 60.
9. "Valuations of Cherokee property."
10. Field Notes, District 10, 3rd Section, Cherokee County.

No. 91
Pine Log Creek, Pine Log Mountain, and the Former Cherokee Town of Pine Log in Bartow County

Pine Log Creek is the central theme of this sketch but for locational reasons it is best to begin the discussion with Pine Log Mountain.[1] This eminence extends from Beasley Gap on Georgia 140 in western Cherokee County southwestward into neighboring Bartow. Some two miles west of its lower tip, lying parallel and to the east of U.S. 411, there is a lesser rise known as Little Pine Log Mountain. The larger formation with an altitude of some 2,300 feet above sea level, is the most southerly, relatively high mountain in Georgia. It is considerably higher than that of such prominent mid-state elevations as Stone Mountain in DeKalb, Kennesaw and Lost Mountain in Cobb, Tally Mountain in Haralson, or Pine Mountain in the central western part of the state. But in contrast to the latter places, Pine Log Mountain is not particularly well known to the public. It stands much above its immediate surroundings but the ridges, hills, and small mountains about its base so effectively screen the Pine Log it is difficult to secure a good nearby view of it from most of the roads that pass through the section.

There are other Pine Log creeks in Georgia but the waterway involved here is a considerable stream that arises at the northeast edge of Pine Log Mountain and flows northwestward across parts of Cherokee, Bartow, and Gordon counties to unite with Salacoa Creek, thence to join the Coosawattee River in the last county named. The waterway is unusual in that it has two upper tributaries named Little Pine Log Creek. One of these (which is also called Sugar Hill Creek) commences at the southern end of the mountain, in the saddle between it and Little Pine Log Mountain, and reaches the main stream just below the bridge on U.S. 411. The other Little Pine Log Creek arises in east central Bartow and joins the big Pine Log to the southeast of Sonoraville in Gordon County. This last tributary flows on a winding course through a hilly region, but at one place located to the northwest of the present community of Pine Log just west of U.S. 411, the margins widen to form a lovely little valley. Here was the former home of Corra Harris, the novelist.

In the discussion of these streams, it is interesting to note that while there are two Little Pine Log creeks, the main waterway is customarily not referred to as *Big* Pine Log. And too, although there is a Little Pine Log Mountain, the main elevation is not spoken of as *Big* Pine Log Mountain unless there is a need to differentiate between the two formations.

A noted Cherokee settlement called Pine Log Town once stood in a little valley on the upper part of the main creek. The official map for District 23, 2nd Section of original Cherokee County based on the survey of 1832 shows the location of the town.[2] The place was not far inside eastern Bartow County from the Cherokee line, on the north side of today's Georgia 140 (the old Pine Log Trail), and something over three miles to the east of the present-day community of Pine Log on the Louisville and Nashville Railroad and 140.

The valley which Pine Log Town occupied is an attractive place with fertile fields. It is approximately a mile long and something over a half-mile wide at the widest place. Except for the outlet of the creek in the northwest corner, the valley is entirely surrounded by a ring of small mountains with a backdrop of the big Pine Log to the south. When the Cherokee Indians started moving into this section of Georgia during or immediately following the Revolution, it is easy to believe as a mountain-loving people that they were much pleased with the Pine Log site, because it no doubt reminded them of their native valleys which they had abandoned in upper South Carolina, northeast Georgia, or east Tennessee to migrate to the region which was to become northwest Georgia. Prior to these migrations, that latter area had been occupied by the Creeks.

It is not known when the Cherokees settled the Pine Log Town, but the time was prior to 1785. The place was in existence by that date because Chesecotetona or the Yellow Bird of Pine Log signed the noted 1785 Treaty of Hopewell in behalf of the town.[3] This chief certainly resided at the Pine Log under discussion because Colonel Marinus Willett visited the settlement in 1790 and noted that Yellow Bird was the headman of the community at that date.[4]

Colonel Benjamin Hawkins also stopped at Pine Log, in late 1796, on his way to take up duties as Indian agent among the Creeks. He gives an account of the place in a journal that appears in the first part of his letters.[5] He observed that the people grew cotton,[6] and it is interesting to note this crop is still being raised at the old site. Hawkins also examined a split cane basket made by an Indian woman of the settlement and commented on the expertness of the workmanship.[7] But most important of all, Colonel Hawkins gives the Cherokee name of the town as "Notetsenchansie."[8] The word literally signifies pine footlog place, and thus discloses that the Pine Log occurring in the names of the creeks and mountains discussed is actually a translated Indian expression. At the time Hawkins transcribed the appellation, however, he was not very familiar with the Cherokee language and garbled the name. James Mooney gives a more precise version of it as Náts asûñ tlûñyî, from *na'tsi*, pine, plus *asŭñtlun*, a footlog or bridge, plus the locative *yî* signifying place.[9]

In the analysis of the name it is important to know that the expression Pine Log actually referred to a crossing place on a stream. Without the original meaning from authoritative sources one could not have been sure of the matter. The English form of the name did not necessarily signify a footlog. It could have referred to a pine log or stump that marked a turning point or dividing place on a wilderness trail. Such spots were at times indicated by expressions like Chopped Oak, Skinned Chestnut, or Burnt Hickory.

The site of the crossing which gave rise to the name is a matter of speculation with present information. It may have been on Pine Log Creek, near the present bridge where U.S. 411 now crosses. An important Cherokee route known as the Tennessee Road or as the Sally Hughes Trail[10] went over the stream at about that point.

More than likely, though, one thinks the pine log crossing was more closely connected with the site of the town than with a trail crossing located several miles away. This conclusion is implied in the close relationship of the name with the community. Since Pine Log Creek passed through the middle of the settlement, it is possible there was a footlog over the stream between the two sections of the town. The creek at the site is not very large or deep at the ordinary stage, but its upper watershed is comparatively large and steep-sided from the mountains about. In times of sudden heavy rain the stream could rise quickly and be dangerous to cross. In such periods it is easy to believe a safe footlog crossing between the two parts of the town would have been useful to the inhabitants and that this facility was provided in a felled pine log, thus giving rise to the name.

At the time Colonel Hawkins travelled past Pine Log Town, he was a newcomer to the Indian country and was not experienced in keeping his course straight.[11] In reading his account of the journey in question some students have concluded from the bearings given that the Colonel visited another Pine Log settlement and not the town which has been discussed in this sketch. The possible second place, so the reasoning goes, was somewhere to the west of our Canton, on the north side of the present Allatoona Reservoir, and probably on Stamp Creek in eastern Bartow County. Hawkins's description of the trip would seem to place a Pine Log in the area mentioned, but one can be certain the place he actually visited was the Pine Log Town which has been described. In the place he met a prominent Cherokee woman named Mrs. Gagg.[12] Her husband was Thomas Gegg, Gagg, or Gogg, a longtime Indian countryman and trader who resided at Pine Log. On his trip in 1790, Colonel Willett met Gagg or Gogg and employed him as a guide for a period.[13] There can be no doubt Willett visited the Pine Log Town on Pine Log Creek, and it seems equally clear that Hawkins went to the same place since he met Mrs. Gagg who resided there. The point is worth mentioning because there is a chance some one may be tempted to locate a Pine Log settlement that did not exist.

In the beginning, mention was made of other Pine Log creeks in Georgia. One such stream arises above Ballard Mountain in northeast Union County and flows into Clay County, North Carolina.[14] In former years, one source reported the present Young Cane Creek of Union as a Pine Log Creek.[15]

In the early years of Georgia when travel conditions were primitive there were numbers of Pine Log crossing places on various streams. One of these 200 years ago was on lower Briar Creek, 14 miles above the mouth,[16] in present Screven County. This Pine Log may have been the crossing place for the noted Old River trail, which was opened in 1736-1737 at the direction of Oglethorpe to link Savannah and Augusta. The trace was the first long white man's thoroughfare of Georgia.[17] Another prominent Pine Log was on the Ogeechee River, at Fenns Bridge, to the east of Sandersville, where Zachariah Fenn opened the first bridge on the upper Ogeechee, about 1784. The Pine Log crossing before the erection of the bridge was on the Chickasaw Path leading from the Oconee to the settlements of those Indians on the Savannah River, in today's lower Richmond County. And still another Pine Log was on the upper St. Marys River, upstream from the present town of Moniac in Charlton County. This crossing was on the Miccosukee Path that swerved southward around the Okefenokee swamp on its way to Traders Hill and Colerain on the St. Marys, located below Folkston and near today's bridge on U.S. No. 1. A present-day name that seemingly perpetuates a much older designation is found in Pine Log Bridge over Yellow River in Rockdale County.

—*GMNL* 16 (1963): 45-47

NOTES

1. Some helpful maps showing the area of the creeks and mountains under discussion are: the county highway maps prepared for Cherokee and Bartow counties by the State Highway Board of Georgia; and the following topographical sheets issued by the U.S. Geological Survey: *Cartersville Sheet* (ed. 1896, reprinted 1939); *Waleska Quadrangle* (ed. 1950); *Adairsville Quadrangle* (ed. 1944); and the *Calhoun Quadrangle* (ed. 1951).
2. Map of District 23, 2nd Section, Cherokee County, survey of 1832, James H. Warren, D.S., Land Records of Georgia, Surveyor General Department, Atlanta.
3. Richard Peters, ed., *The Public Statutes at Large of the United States of America*, Vol. 7, Indian Treaties, pp. 18-21(20), Nov. 28, 1785. The site of this treaty was at Hopewell, the home of Gen. Andrew Pickens, on the Keowee or Seneca River, in present Oconee County, S.C. The Treaty of Hopewell was the first treaty between the United States and the Cherokee Nation.
4. William M. Willett, ed., *A Narrative of the Military Actions of Colonel Marinus Willett* (New York, 1831), ch. 9, entry for April 23, 1790.
5. *Letters of Benjamin Hawkins, 1796-1806*, Collections of the Georgia Historical Society, Vol. 9 (Savannah, 1916), p. 20, entry for Nov. 30, 1796.
6. *Ibid.*
7. *Ibid.*

8. *Ibid.*

9. James Mooney, *Myths of the Cherokee*, Nineteenth Annual Report of the Bureau of American Ethnology (n.p., n.d.), pt. 1, p. 527. Although the name could be translated into bridge as well as footlog, it is virtually certain to have referred to the latter facility in the case of the Bartow County place. It is highly improbable there was a real bridge at the place as early as 1785, when the site was first mentioned.

10. So-called because it led southward to a ferry on the Etowah which was maintained by a Cherokee woman named Sally Hughes. The site was downstream from the present bridge on U.S. 41. Below the Etowah the route connected southward with the Sandtown Road, eastward with a route to Standing Peachtree and northeastward with the noted Hightower Trail that had connections all the way to Augusta.

11. See *Letters of Benjamin Hawkins*, pp. 17-20, entries for Nov. 28 through Dec. 1, 1796.

12. *Ibid.*, p. 20.

13. Willett, *Narrative of Military Actions*, ch. 9, entries for April 23-27, 1790.

14. *Gumlog Quadrangle, Ga.-N.C.* (Maps and Surveys Division, Tennessee Valley Authority, ed. 1942).

15. James F. Smith, *The Cherokee Land Lottery* (New York: Harpers, 1838), map of District 9, 1st Section of original Cherokee County, between pp. 30 and 31.

16. Allen D. Candler, ed., *The Colonial Records of Georgia* (Atlanta: Franklin, 1904-1916), 9: 191, July, 1764.

17. The footlog was in approximately the right place to have been the crossing for the Old River Road or trace on Briar Creek. A prior reference, dated in 1762, however, mentions the route crossing Briar Creek as the "Pine Log Path." See Candler, ed., *Colonial Records of Georgia*, 8: 769, petition of John Caspar Greiner. The early route ran close to the Savannah River. As a result it had to cross tributary streams of the river where all the creeks were wide. It is possible most of the waterways were spanned by felling long, limb-free pines at most of the crossings, thus giving rise to the name Pine Log Path as an alternate to the name "the River Road."

No. 92
Marbury Creek

Marbury Creek commences in central Barrow County to the west of Winder and flows southeastward to join the Apalachee River at the extreme northwest corner of Oconee County. This stream bears the name of two worthy early citizens of Georgia—the venerable Colonel Leonard Marbury of Columbia County, and his son, Captain Horatio Marbury. The latter, who served as secretary of state for Georgia from 1799 to 1811, is best remembered for the noted *Digest* of the laws of Georgia which he prepared in collaboration with William H. Crawford.[1] It is not known if the creek was named for the father or the son. Probably it was named for both of them since the two were original owners of property on the waterway at the same period. They acquired this land and numerous other holdings in old Franklin County when that area was opened to settlers in 1784, after its cession by the Cherokees in the 1783 Treaty of Augusta. Plats for lands owned by the Marburys on the creek are recorded in the state's land records. These documents dated in 1785 show and name "Marbury's Creek" running across the properties.[2]

It is doubtful if either of the Marburys ever actually lived on the waterway which bears their name, since their holdings there were merely two of many tracts they owned. This probably explains why there has long been confusion about the spelling of Marbury Creek. In the first years it was properly listed as Marbury's Creek, but following that period the designation began to be distorted into forms like Marberry's Creek, Marbries Creek, and so on. On some present-day maps the name has become Marburg Creek. A number of Georgia's pioneer appellations have been thus garbled over the years and it would seem for the sake of accuracy that these names should be restored to their correct forms on today's maps and charts of the state. A good name to begin with in their restoration is Marbury Creek.

—*GMNL* 16(1963): 47-48

NOTES

1. Horatio Marbury and William H. Crawford, *Digest of the Laws of the State of Georgia* (Savannah, 1802).
2. Land of Leonard Marbury, 1150 acres, Franklin County, survey of 1785, Platbook A, p. 385, and property of Horatio Marbury, 4025 acres, Franklin County, survey of 1785, Platbook R, p. 440, Land Records of Georgia, Surveyor General Department, Atlanta.

No. 93
Haynes Creek (and Cornish Creek)

The origins of certain placenames are often difficult to determine but on occasion with enough patient inquiring an explanation for an elusive tab will sometimes turn up. This situation came about in the case of Haynes Creek, which arises at the western edge of Grayson in Gwinnett County and flows southward into Rockdale to unite with the Yellow River at the Newton-Rockdale line. On its course it is joined on the east by Little Haynes Creek that commences on the Walton-Gwinnett boundary, near Loganville. The origin of the name Haynes in connection with these streams was long an enigma. The district land maps, plats, and field notes of the original surveyors of the area in 1819 and the early 1820's show or name the two waterways but these sources offer no inkling to indicate how the Haynes creeks got the name.

A fellow student of Indian matters apparently found the answer recently in some unpublished correspondence which he turned up in the Federal Record Center at East Point, Georgia, and which he kindly made available to the writer.[1] One of these documents was a letter, dated July 11, 1810, at Fort Hawkins,[2] by Lieutenant Daniel Appling to Captain Thomas A. Smith, commanding the U.S. Rifle Regiment at Fort Hawkins. The letter is a report by Lieutenant Appling of the results of an expedition by a detachment of federal troops which he led that had been ordered to drive trespassing white settlers from Indian lands located to the west of the High Shoals of Apalachee River where present Walton and Morgan counties now corner. According to the report, Appling and his men went about their task in a diligent and thorough manner. They destroyed salt logs, cow pens, and houses of the "intruders" (as the squatters were called), burnt fences, and cut down acres of green corn. One piece of property that received attention was the pierhead of a gin that belonged to Thomas Haynes. This structure was "in the waters of Ocmulgee." Since Haynes Creek (via the Yellow River) is an upper tributary of the Ocmulgee, it seems reasonable to conclude that this gin, or beginnings of a gin, was on the creek and that it had been installed by Thomas Haynes, who gave his name to the stream. This conclusion is supported by the fact that when official surveyors came some 10 years later to survey the section after it had been ceded by the Indians, Haynes Creek already bore its name.

It is mere conjecture to speculate on the location of this gin, but as good a guess as any would be that it was on Little Haynes Creek, at the site of the later old Princeton Mill. This was a good place for a water-powered gin, and also it was at the crossing point of the Hightower Trail, the best-known trace of the region in question.

Lieutenant Appling mentions the names of the individuals whose property had been destroyed and states these people were the only trespassers that he could find or hear of. But perhaps he missed some intruders, and among them there may have been a man named Cornish who gave name to Cornish Creek, that parallels the course of Haynes Creek but enters the Alcovy instead of the Yellow River. This appellation was also listed by the first surveyors, a fact which plainly indicates the name was in use before they arrived to lay off the area where the stream lies. Maybe Cornish was one of the trespassers but escaped detection by the soldiers. But be that as it may, Cornish Creek is one of the elusive names previously mentioned, and it will be interesting to see if some day an old document will also turn up to throw light on the origin of the name.

Interestingly enough, it should be noted that Lieutenant Appling's report was attached to a hitherto unreported letter of Colonel Benjamin Hawkins, dated October 19, 1810, at the Creek Agency on Flint River[3] and addressed to William B. Bulloch, U.S. Attorney for the Georgia District. Hawkins reviewed the problem of white people trespassing on Indian lands and stated the Creek chiefs were complaining about the matter. He asked that a Colonel Easley of the High Shoals be prosecuted for being the leader in the settlements beyond the Indian boundary.[4]

—GMNL 16(1963): 48

NOTES

1. The writer wishes to express his appreciation to Mr. Marion R. Hemperley of East Point for photostatic copies of the documents mentioned in the sketch.

2. Fort Hawkins was located on the east side of the Ocmulgee, in present east Macon.

3. The Creek Agency which was established by Col. Hawkins and served as his headquarters for years was on the east side of Flint River, below the bridge on Ga. 128, and some 7 miles west of Roberta in Crawford County.

4. [Cornish Creek may be taken from a man's name, or it may have been bestowed by someone with Cornish sympathies. The personal name is common; see P. H. Reaney, *A Dictionary of British Surnames* (London: Routledge and Kegan Paul, 1958), p. 78, and compare Cornwallis. Has the personal name been attested for Georgia? *FLU.*]

No. 94
The Red Hills Region (and an Early Description of Parts of Macon, Peach, Crawford, and Bibb Counties)

The region which geologists and geographers call the Red Hills or the Southern Red Hills, begins in eastern Houston County and curves southwestward across parts of a dozen counties to pass out of Georgia into Alabama in upper Clay County, to the north of Fort Gaines. On the top, the Red Hills mostly tend to be level or gently rolling, but around the edges of the formation where there is evidence of erosion the sides have a red appearance which plainly indicates how the ridge received its name. The expression Red Hills seems to be a simple matter-of-fact descriptive title; and so it is, but the Creek Indians had already applied the name to the hills before the first white people entered the region to settle it. Colonel Benjamin Hawkins makes this clear in his letters. On a journey in early 1797 he crossed the hills and referred to them as "Ecimna Chate (red hills)." On this trip he was travelling from the Indian-country home of Timothy Barnard, located on the west side of Flint River, about a mile below today's Oglethorpe, to Ford Fidius on the east side of the Oconee, downstream and opposite present Milledgeville. In the account of the journey Hawkins not only refers to the Red Hills, but also he recorded for the first time some interesting information about the area of the state which eventually became Macon, Peach, Crawford, and Bibb counties. For instance, he mentions a deposit of fossilized oyster shells on Flint River, above Montezuma, and refers to the establishment of a dairy in the Indian country. This operation must have been the very first dairy in all of western Georgia. Hawkins also comments on some fine peach trees which he saw growing at the site of our Montezuma in a section that was later to become famous as a peach-raising region.

To bring out these interesting points as well as the origin of the name of the Red Hills, it was decided to reproduce here and annotate the account given by Hawkins during two days of his trip. This period covered the travel from Barnard's place to a camping site on Tobesofkee Creek in today's western Bibb County.

From present Montezuma northward Hawkins followed a trail that coincided closely with the course of our Georgia 49. At a point 8 miles above town, however, instead of turning eastward along No. 49, he continued north, and above Spring Creek of upper Macon County he climbed the Red Hills and reached the later site of a home which

Dr. John D. Wade of Marshallville states is known as the old Nathan Bryan place. This house is located three miles northwest of Marshallville on the road from that place to Nakomis in extreme lower Crawford County. The Bryan house was built on the road which subsequently developed on the trail followed by Hawkins and it is traditionally reported as having served as an inn on that road.

From the site of the Bryan place Hawkins climbed a little higher up the ridge to pass over the Ecimna Chate, travelling close along the course of the Marshallville-Nakomis road and spent the night of February 21 on a small stream located immediately south of Nakomis and on the lower side of present Georgia 96, the Fort Valley-Reynolds road.

The course of the first part of the trip across Crawford County on the following day is open to question because the original and official surveys of the area do not show any Indian trails that would help identify the route Hawkins travelled. From his description of the trip, though, it can be reasonably concluded that his party bore northward on or close along the course of the present road leading from Nakomis past Zenith, Gaillard, and Horns (on U.S. 341, to the south of Roberta). From the latter site the travellers veered northeast on a little dirt road for some miles, and then on a way that does not now exist, they continued to join the horse path mentioned by Hawkins some three miles to the east of present Knoxville, in Crawford County. The trail intersected was the noted Lower Creek Trading Path, or Old Horse Path, leading westward from Augusta to the Creek Indians of western Georgia and Alabama. This particular stretch of the early thoroughfare later became a segment of the Federal Road that was opened in 1805 across the Creek country. Mostly at present, however, where Hawkins joined the route, it is referred to as the old Knoxville-Macon Road.

Hawkins and his party turned east on the trading path, and if they continued on the part which subsequently became the Federal Road, they veered left from the later Knoxville-Macon route to cross Echeconnee Creek below the mouth of Sweetwater Creek and passed into today's Bibb County. Some miles farther along, to the southeast of Lizella, they entered the course of today's U.S. 80 and soon reached a ford on Tobesofkee Creek, located near the present bridge on No. 80. The party crossed the creek, turned upstream a short distance and stopped for the night of February 22 at an old Indian camp. The travellers apparently were pleased to find this ready-made camping site, but the modern reader should also note that Hawkins commented the stop was made at a site where there was a brake of "Winter Cane." This type of cane, a waist-high variety, remained green all winter, and its presence at the camping place indicated the group would be able to graze their horses in the brake. One can be certain the availability of this forage was as important to Hawkins's party as a filling station would be to present-day travellers.

The remainder of Hawkins's trip to Fort Fidius is interesting, but it bears no relationship to the Red Hills section, hence will not be traced here.

The excerpt for the account of the trip for February 21 and 22, 1797, follows:[1] (21st February)

I sat out this day for Fort Fidins,[2] Mr. Barnard and his son, Homanhidge, accompanied me; we X the river at Mr. Barnard's and take up it N. Go one mile X a small reedy creek,[3] here on the north side Mr. Barnard has begun to establish a dairy,[4] the situation is fine for it,[5] the ground high, an excellent spring surrounded with evergreens; and here two Mr. Barnard's sons, Falope and Yuccohpee, have begun an establishment for themselves. They were here with their father's negroes, at work clearing a field, and preparing logs of pine for their houses. The land good for corn, to the river swamp, and that and the swamp of the small creek good for rice. There is a margin on this river of oak, pine and hard shelled hickory, adjoining the swamp, and then back of this pine barron,[6] the good land but a small strip. Continue on ¾ of a mile, come to a plantation of Mr. Barnard's; here some fine peach trees, the lands pretty good on the creek; here lives Tenpoeje,[8] another son and his Cusetta wife, they were both of them clearing land with a small black boy. He has just finished a dwelling house, mostly the labour of his own hands. We gave him some garden seeds and I promised to assist him with tools.[9] X a creek at the plantation 30 feet over,[10] and continue on over some land pretty good for corn, the timber a mixture, oak, pine and some hard shelled hickory, here and there some long moss.[11] Most of the oakes, the scrub, very crooked, with many limbs and all of them with a green broad leaved fern moss. In 8 miles X a branch runing to the right,[12] this is a branch of the creek I crossed at Tunpanejies,[13] and the path has been on the ridge which divides its waters from the hollows making into the river. This is a small branch, but covered with reeds.[14] Continue on 2 miles and there 2 very steep heads of bottoms close to the left,[15] and from the first is distant view of the lands on the other side of the river; here I saw an Indian encampment. One woman at the camp, without any other food than hickory nuts. There were several others but all of them out gathering these nuts,[16] and I am informed they frequently take to the woods at this season, when there is a great hickory masst,[17] and fatten on them and the cold potatoe uccollewauhohah.[18] I saw under all the oakes great quantities of acorns. Continue on 2 miles farther and come to some reed patches,[19] continue over the flat and cross a small creek runing to the left,[20] abounding with reed, and rise up a steep hill,[21] and have a very extensive view of a bed of reeds to the left,[22] nearly ¾ of a mile through; continue on this ridge and soon arrive at Ecimna Chate (*red hills*),[23] from these there is an extensive view S. W.[24] and the bed of reeds continuing in that direction to the river, and appear surrounded with hills covered with pine, amidst them is distinctly marked the margin X the river, forming a vain[25] wandering through the piney view, of growth usual on the swamp lands. 2 miles farther, passing over wavering pine barron, come to the side of a large bed of reeds on the left, as extensive as those before described; continue on near a mile and X a small branch making into the bed, and this well stored with reeds.[26] Continue on 4 miles farther and encamp on a small reedy creek runing to the left.[27]

I saw this day the yellow jasmine, the plumb, may cherry,[28] strawberry and sassafras in bloom. I have not any where seen less sign of game, although we have guns and dogs, we have not been able to get any thing.[29] The ridge on this side the creek[30] extends to the river and there forms a bluff 80 feet high, at the lower part of which, near low water mark, is a bed of oyster shells.[31]

We sat out this morning early and continue our course, one mile, leave the path which go's to the Uche village,[32] and go through the woods, one mile and enter the Uchee path[33] continue on, take a small path to the left to facilitate the crossing of the beaver dam,[34] the direct path being the nearest, but the passage of the creek nearly impracticable when the season is wet. In 5 miles X the beaver dam,[35] and in 5 miles enter the old horse path[36] our course now E.N.E.; continue on 5 miles and X a small branch,[37] here we breakfast.[38] The first 2 miles pine barron, the trees large,[39] the path in sight of the reedy bottoms which make into the river.[40] The remainder of the way through broken pine barron, in several places the trees dwarf pine and black jack.[41] Resume our journey, in 2 ½ miles X a small creek stored with reed; in 1 & ½ farther X a small branch,[42] and in one mile X Itchocunnah (deer trap),[43] 40 feet over, runing to the right; the whole of these 5 miles through a pine forest. This creek has its name from being covered with moss on its rocky bed, and the deer resorting to it, where they are killed by the hunters. Continue on one mile, X a small creek runing to the right, the hillsides steep, the growth poplar, oak, hickory and dogwood, the creek stored with reed; one mile farther another small branch of the like discription, and in 2 miles, X Horse Rosemerry, a small creek runing to the right; this is so named by the packhorsemen from the quantity of the rosemerry which grows near its borders.[44] Continue on 2 miles farther over flat piney sloshy[45] land, passing some fine reedy glades to the right, arrive at Tobosaufkee,[46] 60 feet over, runing to the right. There is a little creek within a few yards of Tobosaufkee, the land is broken and stoney, and there are on the left of the path, and within view of the creek, some large rocks; X the creek, left the path and went up it 200 yards and encamped near a small branch, the north side of which was well stored with winter cane,[47] still higher up, ¼ mile, is a small creek stored with small cane, the lands broken & gravelly, but rich, the growth a mixture of oak, pine and small hickory. At this camp the Indians have left a very convenient camp standing; it had been used during the winter's hunt; on a small beech at the mouth of the branch are marked the initials of my name and the date.[48]

—GMNL 16(1963): 48-52

NOTES

1. *Letters of Benjamin Hawkins, 1796-1806,* Collections of the Georgia Historical Society, Vol 9 (Savannah, 1916), pp. 86-88.

2. The spelling of "Fidins" is a transcription error; the correct word is Fidius. It was located at the site mentioned in the introductory statement to the sketch.

3. The present Spring Creek on the lower side of Montezuma.

4. Except for domestic use Barnard would have had no outlet for fresh milk from his dairy. If he proposed to make cheese, however, he would have had a good market because that product as a preserved food was commonly used by wilderness travellers.

5. The dairy establishment was somewhere about the present Montezuma filtering plant on the south side of town, below Beaver Creek.

6. The section to the east of Montezuma is now considered good farming country. Those now living there will find it hard to believe the area was ever labelled "pine barron."

7. The stream mentioned here is now called Beaver Creek, which reaches Flint River at Montezuma. The main part of Montezuma is on the north side of the creek.

8. Refers to the son who became known as Timpoochee Barnard. He later served with United States forces on several occasions and became a major.

9. Part of Hawkins's duties as Indian agent involved persuading the Creeks to learn new agricultural methods. Here we find him active in that task.

10. The stream is Beaver Creek, and the crossing was at the southeast edge of Montezuma.

11. "Long Moss" refers to the vegetation which nowadays is usually called Spanish moss.

12. This branch arises below Ga. 127 and reaches Beaver Creek downstream from Trebor Station on the Central of Georgia.

13. Refers again to Timpoochee Barnard. The versions of his name used by Hawkins were probably Uchee because Timpoochee's mother was an Uchee woman. The Creeks and white people could not correctly pronounce the name and turned it into Timpoochee.

14. "Reeds" means the short cane that is variously called "reed cane", "switch cane," etc. It was very important as a browse plant in the wilderness days, and Col. Hawkins frequently mentioned it in his writings.

15. One of these "heads" apparently is the draw now followed by Ga. 127 down to the ferry on Flint River.

16. On several occasions in his accounts of wilderness travel, Hawkins mentioned Indian women gathering nuts. The Indians not only ate the nuts, they also extracted an edible oil from the kernels or pulverized the meats into a milk.

17. "Hickory Mast" relates to hickory nuts, but the word mast also applied to a variety of nuts and seeds that were found on the forest floor—like acorns, chinquapins, beechnuts, pine mast, etc.

18. The Indian word given is garbled. It should have been *okliwahaha*, from *okliwaha*, bog, plus *aha*, potato. The expression refers to a variety of edible tuber which the Indians gathered in the boggy areas of abandoned beaver ponds.

19. These reed patches, or beds of reed cane, were on the south side of Spring Creek in upper Macon County. The later plats of surveys for District 8 of original Houston County (of which Macon is a part) show extensive reed patches beside the trail which Hawkins followed. See illustration of the plat for lot 114 from District 8 of Houston, survey of 1821, A. G. Raiford, D.S., Platbook UUU, Land Records of Georgia, Department of Archives and History, Atlanta.

20. This stream is Spring Creek, that arises to the north of Marshallville and flows west to join Flint River. Two streams which Hawkins mentioned in the account are now called Spring Creek—one on the lower side of Montezuma and the other the waterway mentioned above.

21. This "steep hill" was a southern slope of the Red Hills, and the route up it which Hawkins followed can be identified with the path shown on lot 10 of original District 8 of Houston County, based on the survey of 1821 in Platbook UUU. The trail led up the hill past the later site of the old Bryan home. In Louise Frederick Hays, *History of Macon County, Georgia*, p. 419, Mrs. Hays indicated this place may be the oldest house in Macon County. It was built in the 1820's and is said to have served as an inn on the road that subsequently developed along the antecedent Indian trail and another thoroughfare that was opened to Bryan's ferry on Flint River. Four generations of Bryans lived at the home until it was sold in 1928—letter dated April 3, 1963, from Col. Bert N. Bryan, USA-Retired. The house still stands but is now unoccupied. The route followed by Hawkins and the subsequent road has now become a deep gully that runs down the hill from the house toward Spring Creek.

22. From the top of the hill, looking southwestward, one can still appreciate the extensive view mentioned by Hawkins, although the great reed beds referred to have now disappeared. Hawkins wrote of looking "left," but the path curved and he was looking southward.

23. "Ecimna Chate" literally means hills red. In the Creek language the adjective was placed after the noun, as is commonly the case, for example, in the French and Spanish tongues.

24. The top of the Red Hills does afford a fine view to the south and southwest but curiously Hawkins does not mention the scene to the north, up the Flint River Valley. The latter vista today is one of the singular scenes of Georgia because one can "look up" to the Piedmont Plateau from the Coastal Plain. In most areas of the state the change from one of these regions to the other is so imperceptible one cannot easily tell where the Plain stops and the Plateau begins. Hawkins's view of the Piedmont to the north was perhaps obscured by trees growing on top of the Red Hills.

25. "Vain" means the defined course or borders of the river winding through the swamp.

26. Instead of "well stored," today we would say well stocked.

27. The party camped on the small stream that arises to the northeast of Nakomis and reaches Flint River just below Ga. 96, the Reynolds-Fort Valley road. The camp was on the side of the creek, immediately south of Nakomis and the present highway.

264 / Placenames of Georgia

28. Dr. A. E. Baker of Emory University states the "May cherry," notably referred to as *Amelanchier*, is also known as the shad bush or Serviceberry.

29. Contrary to beliefs of modern individuals, wild game was often scarce along wilderness trails and numbers of writings such as the comment made by Hawkins attest to that fact.

30. This paragraph is by way of summary of the day's travel and refers to the section covered from Beaver Creek at Montezuma.

31. This comment refers to the bed of fossilized shells that is sometimes mentioned as the "Lanier deposit," because it is on the east side of the Flint, opposite the old site of Lanier, the first county seat of Macon County, which was located near the ferry crossing on Ga. 127.

32. The settlement mentioned was the Uchee village of Patsiliga, located on the west side of Flint River, at the mouth of Patsiliga Creek, and immediately above the Central of Georgia Railroad, to the east of Reynolds, in Taylor County.

33. Refers to the main Uchee path that led eastward from Patsiliga village to Oakmulgee Old Fields at the present site of Macon.

34. Relates to Beaver Creek of middle and lower Crawford County. A long study of Georgia land records makes it clear the extensive beaver colonies living in this creek constituted the largest beaver area mentioned in those documents. See John H. Goff, "The Beaverdam Creeks," below, pp. 370-79.

35. Means beaverdams on the Beaverdam Creek mentioned in the preceding note. This stream is now sometimes called Spring Creek or Avera Creek, but on early maps it is referred to as Beaver Creek and most citizens of the area remember it by that name.

36. The old horse path mentioned was the main line of the noted Lower Creek Trading Path, one of the longest and most historic Indian routes of America. It led from Augusta via Shoals of Ogeechee, the Rock Landing on the Oconee and present Macon to Creek Indian towns in western Georgia and Alabama. It also had connections from the latter places to the Chickasaws and Choctaws of present Mississippi.

37. This branch is a tributary of upper Sweetwater Creek, in eastern Crawford.

38. "Breakfast" here means lunch in present-day terminology. Hawkins uses the expression numbers of times in this sense in his writings. It is the equivalent of the French *déjeuner*, breakfast, in contrast to the *petit déjeuner*, little breakfast, for the early morning meal.

39. Modern people are prone to think of a pine barren as having had only scrubby trees, but this statement indicates the pines noted were fine, tall specimens.

40. This part is a resume of the day's trip thus far. He is referring to the area of Crawford County traversed and "the river" means the Flint.

41. Dwarf pines and black jacks (oaks) signified the particular areas in question had inferior soil. Hawkins makes many references to the trees he observed in his travels. The varying trees denoted varying qualities of soil fertility. Lands with white oaks, dogwoods, and hickories were considered as having the best soils.

42. The stream mentioned here probably is the small branch that enters Sweetwater Creek at the Martha Johnson Girl Scout Camp in eastern Crawford. The old Lower Creek trail passed just below this establishment.

43. See Sketch No. 16, above.

44. This stream arose near the juncture of present Tidwell Road and U.S. 80 in Bibb County and flowed to Tobesofkee Creek. References to Horse Rosemerry can be found in several accounts dealing with travel on Indian country trails. The plant was horse mint, a species of *Monarda*.

45. "Sloshy" here may be interpreted as our slashy, an expression that refers to a flat, spongy area where shallow water stands for a part of the year and especially in the winter.
46. See above, Sketch No. 14, "Tobesofkee and Rocky Creeks."
47. This vegetation, as noted in the prefatory statement, was important as a browse plant for the horses of wilderness travellers because the cane remained green all winter.
48. Hawkins apparently made a practice of carving his initials on a tree at camping places. The markings later helped him identify such spots. In several instances in his writings, he mentions stops at sites where he had previously cut marks.

No. 95
Sweetwater Creek (of Crawford County)

There are numbers of Sweetwater creeks in Georgia, but the stream mentioned in the preceding sketch about the Red Hills merits a particular discussion because there are good grounds to indicate it bears one of the oldest recorded names of interior Georgia. The creek arises to the northeast of Knoxville at the edge of U.S. 80, in Crawford County and flows eastward to join Echeconnee Creek below the bridge on No. 80 and not far above the site where the famous Lower Creek Trading Path crossed the latter waterway. This Sweetwater most likely was the stream of that name mentioned by William Bartram on a trip through the Indian country in the company of a party of Indian traders with a train of 60 horses. The group camped by the creek on the night of July 4, 1776, according to Bartram's reckoning. But surely he was mistaken in the date by a whole year, and this error is brought out in the recent edition of Bartram's *Travels* which was edited by Francis Harper. The latter corrects the year by moving it back to 1775,[1] and in doing so clears up a chronological question that must have puzzled many a reader of prior editions of the Bartram book.

Harper, however, identifies the present Culpepper Creek, that arises to the northward of Knoxville and flows via Beaver Creek to the Flint, as the Sweetwater mentioned by Bartram.[2] This identification rests on a Sweetwater Creek in the general area that is shown on a map cited by Harper,[3] and also on the fact that Culpepper Creek is 20 miles from Rocky Creek in Bibb County, where the botanist and his companions spent the night prior to the stop on Sweetwater Creek.

There was another Sweetwater in the area and Benjamin Hawkins noted it about 1801 in his "Viatory."[4] This stream is today's Mathews Creek, located some three miles west of the Culpepper near Knoxville. Harper dismisses our Sweetwater as a "modern" stream, meaning apparently a creek with a comparatively new name. In fact, though, the designation has long been in use, since the original and official surveys of the area, made in 1821,[5] show and name the stream, together with the route of the 1805 Federal Road which developed along the course of a substantial segment of the noted trading path followed by Bartram.

Our Mathews Creek, the former Sweetwater mentioned by Hawkins, does not seem to be the stream noted by Bartram because it is located a good three miles farther than the party travelled. With the long pack train, this extra distance would have been tedious and Bartram would probably have noted it. It is very unlikely that Culpepper Creek was the waterway involved, because at the old crossing point on the former trading path it has boggy margins and is not at all like the Sweetwater of Bartram which he described as a "beautiful large brook." Furthermore, the Culpepper seemingly has always been boggy. It was a head stream of the Beaver Creek system that contained the largest complex of beaver colonies which are shown in the early land records of Georgia.[6] Culpepper Creek actually was one of these beaver streams because Colonel Hawkins mentioned it as such in 1797.[7]

With this background then, and in view of the fact that the trading path skirted the full length of Sweetwater Creek, it seems very likely it was the stream referred to by Bartram and that his party stopped somewhere near its head, at a place about four miles east of Knoxville. This site is only some 17 miles from Rocky Creek but en route the travellers had to ford some big creeks and go over so many hills the botanist could easily have concluded the group went 20 miles. Another bit of information which seems to confirm the stopping place indicated can be found in Colonel Hawkins's "Viatory." On a trip eastward on the trading path in 1800, at a point some three and a half to four miles east of Culpepper Creek, and at or near the probable camping site of Bartram on Sweetwater Creek, the Colonel noted a place called "Co, hau thluc ulgee." This expression in the Muskogee language plainly signifies Big Canebrake, from *koha*, cane, plus the augmentative *hláko* or "thlucco," big, plus *álgi* or "ulgee," a locative suffix which here indicates where something abounds, meaning in this instance, of course, where plenty of cane was found. Since

Bartram's group had a large number of horses that had to be rested and fed, it is likely a camp was made at a place where the animals could graze on cane. Hawkins's big cane brake, then, provided the place, because in the wilderness days cane was the only browse plant of importance in Georgia.

—*GMNL* 16(1963): 52-53

NOTES

1. Francis Harper, ed., *The Travels of William Bartram* (New Haven: Yale University Press, 1958), p. 380, Commentary on Part II.
2. *Ibid.*, p. 397.
3. Tracing of Joseph Purcell's map of the Indian country which appears as Plate 7 in John R. Swanton, *Early History of the Creek Indians and Their Neighbors*, Bureau of American Ethnology Bulletin 73 (Washington, D.C., 1922). The Special Collection Department of the Emory University Library has a photostat of the original MS of this chart in the Public Record Office, London.
4. "A Viatory or Journal of distances and observations," MS in the Library of Congress. The date of the entry is not certain, but it was probably in early 1801, because it comes after notes on a similar trip dated June, 1800.
5. District 3, Houston County (now Crawford), survey of 1821, Paul McCormick, D.S., Platbook TTT, lots 39, 56, 71, 73, 89, and 101, Land Records of Georgia, Surveyor General Department, Atlanta. The Sweetwater is shown joining Echeconnee Creek.
6. John H. Goff, "The Beaverdam Creeks," see pp. 370-79 below.
7. Hawkins's "Viatory," revised entry of June, 1800. He marked Culpepper Creek as "intach Cooche." This Muskogee name means Little Beaverdam, from *intachki*, a dam across water, plus *uchi* or "oochee," little. The former expression applied to beaverdams.

No. 96
The Big Savannah, Savannah District, Savannah School, Dougherty, Palmers Creek, Russells Creek (Originally Child Toaters Creek), Proctors Creek, Bags Branch, Baggs Creek, Wicked Creek, Toto Creek, Dukes Creek (and the Former Cherokee Town of Tensawattee)

Many travellers driving along U.S. 19 in lower Dawson County have no doubt often noticed the fine bottomlands which stretch away from the highway up and down the north or right side of the Etowah River. These pretty fields extend about seven miles, beginning a mile or so to the east of Georgia 53, upstream from U.S. 19 and curving downward along the river, gradually widening as they go, to the course of the former Dawsonville-Barrettsville Road, located about a mile to the west of No. 19.

In the Cherokee days this attractive locality was known as the *Big Savannah* and numbers of references to it under that English designation can be found in old records. Since the area had a considerable settlement of Indians, it is reasonable to conclude the expression is a translated version of the Cherokee name for the place. No listing of the aboriginal form, however, could be located and to derive the approximate native name it was necessary to make a literal translation of Big Savannah into Cherokee. This reconstructed version is Ayuhwasi-egwa-hi from *ayuhwasi* ("eye-yuh-wah'-see"),[1] savannah, plus *egwa* ("eggwah"), big or great, plus the conventional Cherokee locative *hi* ("hee"), place. This literal rendition may have been abbreviated or slurred a bit in actual use, but even so, the expression would have been complicated for the early white people to record and it is easy to see why they resorted to their own simpler *Big Savannah*, which can be found in documents.

The first white traveller to visit the Big Savannah and make a definite reference to the area was Colonel Benjamin Hawkins, who passed through the place in 1796 on his way to the Creek country to take up his duties as Indian agent. He did not mention the area as the *Big Savannah*, but did describe it as a "Large and beautiful savanna" and noted that the western end, the part near our U.S. 19, had the richest vale of land he had seen.[2] Hawkins's comments are important because they provide a documentary basis to explain how the term savannah came to be used in connection with the place. In pioneer terminology a *savannah* was a moist, open, meadow-like area where grass or reed cane grew in abundance. In a forested region like early Georgia, such sites were once prized spots for grazing stock and were much used for that purpose by both Indians and whites.

No doubt there was a heavy growth of cane in the original Big Savannah because in his short description of the place Colonel Hawkins mentions this vegetation four times.[3] The canebrakes have long since given way to the fields that have been mentioned, but before the bottoms could be converted to farming it was necessary to ditch and drain parts of the area. Interestingly enough, some of this draining began while the Cherokees were still here, because one claimant for reimbursement for improvements made prior to removal of the Indians asked payment for 249 rods of ditching which he had opened on his place in the Big Savannah.[4] The necessity for drainage confirms indirectly that the section was once an area of canebrakes because cane flourished in places with a low, moist soil such as that found in the Savannah.

It might be noted in passing that one can now see ditches in the fields of the old Savannah and perhaps unknown to present owners, it is possible that the basic patterns for some of these drains date back to Cherokee years.

The Big Savannah continued under that name for many years after the departure of the Cherokees. For a period around 1874, the locality had a post office bearing the name,[5] but by 1890 this designation had been changed to *Dougherty*, and people then began to drop the word Big from the original name to retain only the Savannah part. Except perhaps for some old persons aroundabout, it is doubtful if many people now remember the former full name of the community. The two best reminders of the appellation are found in the surrounding Georgia Militia District No. 931 which is called the *Savannah District*;[6] and in a school, church, and cemetery site at Dougherty, on Georgia 53, that is known as *Savannah* or *Savannah School*.

There was an important Cherokee settlement or town connected with the Big Savannah that is mentioned in various sources as Tensawattee, Tinsawattee, Tinswatte, Tensawatie, Tensaw Watee, Tansaw-Wattee, Tenswattee, Tensau water, Tennessewater, and so on. The name is especially interesting because it means *Tennessee Old Town*, with the word town being understood as a part of the intended meaning of the Indian form. But the reason for a place with this name situated so far down in Cherokee country is a mystery. Those Indians were comparative newcomers to the area and indeed, when Benjamin Hawkins passed through the Big Savannah in 1796, he noted a site called *Newtown*,[7] and this place was probably the beginning of Tensawattee because the Colonel did not mention another settlement in connection with the Savannah.

The use of New with the town listed by Hawkins reflected a conventional placenaming practice. When people of one site remove to another, it is fairly common to adopt the designation of their older settlement along with the word New to differentiate the two places. The Cherokees followed this practice, as is exemplified in New Echota in contrast to their noted town of Echota in east Tennessee. But in the case of *Tensawattee,* as evidenced by the form *wattee,* from *weti* ("watee"), old, the Cherokees who founded the town did not follow the usual procedure. The reason for this choice is not known, but perhaps to identify themselves as the transplanted nucleus of a completely abandoned settlement in another location, they adopted the modifier *weti,* old, to signify that they were members of a former place called Tensa.

There were several early Tensa places that could have supplied the name for *Tensawattee,* but the best-known site, and one in which the residents were under pressure to quit, was a settlement known as Tanasi, Tunasee, Tensee, or Tennessee, located on the Little Tennessee River in Monroe County, Tennessee. This town (which furnished the name for the river and state) by the 1780's was dangerously situated near the northern boundary of the Cherokees. The Indians of the section were intermittently engaged in fighting the Tennesseans, and it is reasonable to think the people of the settlement decided to quit the troubled area and move way down into Georgia where at least the white people were not regularly engaged in raiding, burning, and otherwise harassing Cherokee towns. Since the site on the Little Tennessee was actually abandoned, it seems likely the citizens, or some of them, did move to Georgia and adopt the name *Tensawattee* to identify themselves as being from the Tennessee town mentioned.

It is important to note that the designations *Tensawattee* and *Big Savannah* were sometimes used interchangeably. For instance, numbers of Cherokees can be found listed as residents of Big Savannah, but when these same individuals were rounded up for removal to the West in 1838, they were reported as being from Tensawattee. It is to be doubted, however, that the two names were precisely identical. Very probably, *Big Savannah* was the name for the whole settlement, stretching along the Etowah, while *Tensawattee* was the designation for the central meeting place of the community.

The exact location of the Tensawattee town is not certain. An original Georgia survey of the area, made in 1832 while the Indians were still there, labels present Mill Creek as *Tensawattee Creek.*[8] Mill Creek, which flows across the old Savannah to reach the *Etowah,* is the first stream to the east of U.S. 19. The survey suggests that Tensawattee was located on our Mill Creek and it may well have been. But if so, it was probably situated about a half-mile back from the river where the land rises from the Savannah proper, and near the present C. I. Thompson home. The bottoms themselves were too low to be a desirable site for a town.

Hawkins supports this approximate location in his reference to Newtown, because he only travelled a mile after noting the place before he quit the Savannah by recrossing the Etowah.[9]

Despite these comments, however, on the basis of present-day conditions, a better location for a town was two miles farther east than Tensawattee or Mill Creek, at today's Dougherty or Savannah School. This site was elevated, offered a fine view of the bottoms, and was situated in about the middle of the Big Savannah. Furthermore, various records show a number of prominent Cherokees actually resided in the immediate vicinity of Dougherty.

Sometime in the 1820's the Baptists established a missionary station at Tensawattee under the stewardship of the Reverend and Mrs. Duncan Bryant.[10] The church did not remain long at the site, however, before it was removed to Hickory Log Town, near today's Canton.

In addition to Tensawattee Creek, several other sizable streams flowed across the Big Savannah to the Etowah, and with one exception these tributaries bear names which date back to the Indian days. The designation of present Palmers Creek which joins the river immediately above Dougherty was derived from Silas Palmour, an Indian countryman who early settled on the stream and married Sarah Dougherty, part Cherokee. He accumulated substantial property and was the man who opened the drainage ditches that were mentioned.

Present Russells Creek was not named in the 1832 surveys, although the designation has long been in use and was drawn from a site called *Russell's Mill* that was once located on the waterway. The stream was listed as *"Child Toaters"* or *"Child Toters Creek"* on the first survey and was named for a prominent fullblood who lived at the Big Savannah.[11]

Toto Creek, a small western tributary of the Chestatee, in Dawson County, located immediately below the bridge on Georgia 136, is probably a remnant of *Child Toter's* name that has become garbled over the years through a misunderstanding of that singular Indian moniker. The Toter element of the name was properly Carrier, but the frontier whites virtually always rendered it as Toter or Toater. The expression was a Cherokee rank, title, or denomination whose significance is now forgotten. There were once numbers of well-known Carriers or Toters among the Georgia Indians: Flax Toater, Bear Toter, Beaver Toter, Arrow Toter, and so on. Since Child Toter, a prominent, well-to-do Cherokee resided in the Big Savannah, not far from Toto Creek, it is easy to believe he once lived or farmed land beside the latter stream and left his name on it to be corrupted into Toto.

Farther eastward, toward the head of the Savannah is Proctors Creek. It was named for John Proctor, a part Cherokee who lived beside the stream and owned a mill on it.[12]

Many Cherokees are recorded as residents of Tensawattee or of the Big Savannah. Some interesting individuals were Skyuke, Gal Catcher, Tucco, Drowning Bear or Yonahguskee, Boiled Corn, Rock, Ooloconah Stee Sheh Grits, Big Bean, Chickanaila, a woman, and numbers of mixed bloods with English surnames, like Downing, Vann, Willis, Crittenden, Ledbetter, and Nelms.

People living about the village of Dougherty say that name was in use at the site when the first white settlers arrived to take up lots they had drawn in the lottery to distribute the area. This tradition is supported by documentary evidence because Cherokees called *Dougherty* were listed as living in the area much before removal of the Indians. The best known of these individuals and the man who most likely furnished the name for the hamlet was James Dougherty, Sr., who long resided at the place.[13] He and his wife died there in 1837, a year before the Indians were sent West.[14]

Here and there in the Cherokee Nation there were also other Indians named Dougherty. No evidence could be turned up to show that they were descendants of Cornelius Dougherty, a trader who is reputed to be the earliest English-speaking man to reside among the Cherokees. He went to the Indian country before Georgia was founded and lived on the upper Hiwassee River, somewhere about the Georgia–North Carolina line.[15]

The names of certain Tensawattee citizens suggest that they may have moved to the Big Savannah from former Georgia Cherokee areas which had been ceded to the whites and left their names behind them. The Bag or Bagg family is an example.[16] They probably once lived on Baggs Creek, an extreme upper tributary of the Chestatee in

Lumpkin County and had to leave the stream when the section was ceded in 1819.

At least three Bags were connected with the Big Savannah or Tensawattee. One of them lived in the Savannah proper at lot 535 of District 13, North.[17] Another resided to the north on the west side of the Etowah in lot 180, at a stream called *Bags Creek* on the first survey.[18] Later this designation became Blastigam Creek. A third Bag called Charles Bagg dwelt on the east side of the Etowah in lot 267 of the 13th District.[19] It is assumed that the nearby Bags Branch which was so prominent in the gold-mining days was named for this Indian.[20]

Ned Wicked, a resident of the Big Savannah, perhaps removed from Wickeds Creek, a west-bank affluent of the Chattahoochee, in Hall County,[21] to the northeast of the present South Bend Church site. The significance of "wicked" as a name is not known, but very probably it was an old Cherokee war title because there were numbers of Wickeds among those Indians. The present Cherokees of Oklahoma have mostly turned the tab into Wicket or Wickett.

Cossalowa Duke, a fullblood who lived at the lower end of the Big Savannah, provides an inkling to explain how Dukes Creek in White County may have received its name. The waterway was reported as *Dukes Creek* in 1820 by two original surveyors and the fact shows the designation was well established at the date.[22] Cossalowa's name at least confirms there were people called Duke among the Cherokees.

The time when the Cherokees had to quit their pretty valley finally came. Some Indians over the years had voluntarily departed for the West, but most of the Big Savannah inhabitants remained in their community until they were forced to leave. In the summer of 1838 they were rounded up, probably at Dahlonega or Fort Buffington,[23] the nearest concentration points, and taken to Ross's Landing (Chattanooga), where on June 17, 1838, they were consolidated with some other Cherokees to form a party of 762 for migration to "Arkansas" (now Oklahoma) under the direction of a Captain G. S. Drane.[24] Presumably the group went by water, because they made a relatively quick trip, arriving at Flint in the Cherokee Nation West on September 7, 1838.[25]

The party suffered a tragic loss of lives on the way. Indeed, on the basis of emigration rolls now in the National Archives, the band experienced the heaviest losses of any single group that travelled the Trail of Tears. Of the 762 people, 146 died between June 17 and September 7, 1838.[26] Of the approximate 178 people from Tensawattee, around 40 died while only two births were reported during the trek. Moses Dougherty lost 3 members of his family of 5; Red Bird lost 2 out of 6, but had one birth; Little Bean lost 2 out of 7; Child Toater saw 4 out of 10 die; Toonowee 2 out of 6; and Humming Bird had 2 die in his family of 6.[27] The families of Bresh Picker, Ah See Na Bagg, Walking Starr, Samuel Downing, Polly Sanders, Buzzard Hen, Ski Yah took Lakey, and Charley Bagg lost 1 individual each.[28] Some families fortunately had no deaths reported for the trip. Among these were Thomas Sanders, Tooniah Sanders, Jessey Buzzard, Wah wa nah Stee or Pott, Cunnuck, Dirt Jug, Johnson Sanders, and John and Thomas Wind.[29] There are others on the roll that arrived safely and some families who lost members, but the manuscript roll is mutilated in places and it is not possible to make out their complete names.

The emigration roll does not give an explanation why the migrating party had so many deaths although it does indicate that many children were among those who died. The trip was made in less than three months during a favorable season. Apparently there was some sort of outbreak or epidemic which the Cherokees and accompanying white officers were helpless in combating.

Several trails served the Big Savannah area but only two need be mentioned here. One was the War Hill Road that led eastward via today's Gainesville to the frontiers of Georgia,[30] approximately along a part of the course of present Georgia 53. Another was the Downing or Downing Ferry Road[31] that skirted the full length of the area, running mainly along the first high ground that rises along the north side of the Savannah. The route followed this course because the bottoms were too low for a trail and especially for vehicles. The Downing Road connected eastward to Leathers Ford on the Chestatee, at the head of the present Lake Lanier pool. It forded the Etowah at the bridge site on our Georgia 136, thence westward along the Big Savannah, passing a little above Dougherty. Toward the western end it curved down across the bottoms to recross the Etowah at a ford upstream several hundred yards from the old Barrettsville bridge site. It led on past Barrettsville and from there to Hightower crossroads in western Forsyth County where it crossed the noted 1805 Federal Road leading from Georgia across the Cherokee Nation to Tennessee.[32] The Downing Road continued west, running just below Canton, to cross the Etowah again at Downing Ferry, later Fields Bridge, and near the site of the bridge on Georgia 20, at the upper end of the present Allatoona Reservoir. This ferry was the facility which caused the early way to be known as the *Downing Ferry Road.* The thoroughfare led on past the Cartersville and Rome areas into Alabama as the *Alabama Road.*

The Downing Ferry Road was a vehicular way, but before achieving this status, significant stretches of it once served as the main east-west trail across the lower Cherokee country. Indians and traders as far away as Guntersville and Browns Valley, on the Tennessee River, in north Alabama used the route as a path to reach the trading post at Oconee Station in Oconee County, South Carolina.

In the Cartersville section the principal path from the Cherokees to the Muskogees forked southwestward from this important east-west route. Benjamin Hawkins was on his way to reach this connecting trail to the Creeks when he passed through the Big Savannah in 1796.

Except for some slight relocations and an abandoned stretch here and there, much of the old Downing Ferry route continues in use, although the name *Downing Road* seemingly has long since been forgotten in the Big Savannah area. A few people remember it as the Rome Road, but some years ago there were old-timers who recalled it as the Old Alabama Road.

The original 1832 map depicts Tensawattee Creek and a stretch of the Downing Road.[33] The route is shown dropping from its elevated course to the old Savannah. It intersected and ran along the course of our U.S. 19 for a short strip (at the first jog above the bridge over the Etowah), thence continued across the Savannah to the fording place above the Barrettsville bridge site.

A deeply worn, abandoned section of the former trail is located to the east of U.S. 19. The present-day road was moved years ago from this gullied stretch and located immediately to the right or south.

There is one final point which should be noted in the details about the Big Savannah and Tensawattee: oddly enough none of the old documents referring to the place mentions the headman of the community. There surely must have been a chief or chiefs at the place but no specific reference to them could be found in the records consulted and one is left in the dark about their identities. Silas Palmour can be ruled from consideration because he was a white man. Since

James Dougherty, Child Toater, and John Proctor are the most-mentioned individuals of the Savannah, one thinks these men were the leaders of the settlement and that one of them was probably the principal headman.[34]

—GMNL 16(1963): 88-92

NOTES

1. *Ayuhwasi* is still retained in the name of the Hiwassee River and in the town of Hiawassee. These forms contain a so-called Cockney *h* that was once used in connection with the river's designation. See above, Sketch No. 27.

2. *Letters of Benjamin Hawkins, 1796-1806*, Collections of the Georgia Historical Society, Vol. 9 (Savannah, 1916), pp. 17-18, entry for Nov. 28, 1796.

3. *Ibid.* Cane was an important browse plant for wilderness travellers and Hawkins frequently mentioned it in notes of his travels.

4. Valuation of the property of Silas Palmour, a white man at Big Savannah, Lumpkin (now Dawson) County, in 1836 by Agents Hutchins, Shaw and Kellogg, pursuant to the Treaty of 1835, Records of the Bureau of Indian Affairs, Record Group 75, National Archives.

5. *United States Official Postal Guide*, No. 1, Oct. 1874, Dawson County, Ga. The name is listed as "Big Savanna."

6. For the outlines of the Savannah District, or G.M.D. 931, and the former Big Savannah area, see *General Highway Map Dawson County Georgia* (State Highway Department of Georgia, ed. 1952).

7. *Letters of Benjamin Hawkins*, p. 18.

8. Map showing the south half of District 13, 1st Section of Cherokee County, survey of 1832, Walter Nunnelee, D.S., Land Records of Georgia, Surveyor General Department, Atlanta.

9. *Letters of Benjamin Hawkins*, p. 18.

10. Emmet Starr, *Early History of the Cherokees* (n.p., 1917), p. 76; and Adiel Sherwood, *A Gazetteer of the State of Georgia*, 1st ed. (Charleston, 1827), p. 105.

11. Map of the north half of District 13, 1st Section, Cherokee County, survey of 1832, Charles Smith, D.S., and Smith's field notes for the same area. The map lists the name as ".'Child Toater" while the notes give it as "Child Toter."

12. Map, south half, District 13, 1st Section, Cherokee County. The field notes of Surveyor Nunnelee for this district show Proctor lived in lot 533, on the west side of the creek, where the Downing Road mentioned in the text crossed the stream.

13. Heirs of James Dougherty, Sr. *v.* U.S. Docket 119, "1st Cherokee Commission under the 7th article Treaty of 1835" [to hear and pass on complaints about reservations and valuations of Indian properties], Record Group 75, National Archives.

14. *Ibid.*

15. See above, Sketch No. 26.

16. Despite the appearance of this name, it may have been pronounced "Bog" or "Bogg."

17. Field notes, District 13, 1st Section north, Cherokee County, survey of 1832, Charles Smith, D.S.

18. *Ibid.*
19. *Ibid.*
20. *Ibid.* The surveyor notes there were valuable gold lots on "Bags Br." in lots 233, 232, 207, and 208. These tracts were near 267 where Charles Bag lived.
21. Plats for District 10, Hall County, survey of 1820, William Triplett, D.S., Platbook NNN, lots 165 and 167 where the creek enters the Chattahoochee.
22. District 3, Habersham County (now White), survey of 1820, Arch'd. C. McKinley, D.S., Platbook NNN, lots 30, 31, 32, 60, 68, *passim;* and District 5, Habersham, survey of 1820, William Evans, D.S., lots 32 and 34.
23. See above, Sketch No. 59.
24. Cherokee Emigration Records, "Muster Roll No. 5, party directed by Capt. G. S. Drane," Record Group 75, National Archives.
25. *Ibid.*
26. *Ibid.*
27. *Ibid.*
28. *Ibid.*
29. *Ibid.*
30. War Hill was an early stockade site on the western fringe of old Franklin County, on the upper waters of the Oconee River.
31. One source also refers to the eastern end of this route as "Goodmans Road." See map, north half, District 13, 1st Section, Cherokee County, survey of 1832, Charles Smith, D.S. Its better known name, however, as indicated, was Downing or Downing Ferry Road.
32. See "Retracing the Old Federal Road," below, pp. 349-60.
33. Map, south half, District 13, 1st Section, Cherokee County, survey of 1832, Charles Smith, D.S.
34. [Because of the fame of Savannah, Georgia, one might assume that the typographic name is a local word. It is from Spanish *zavena,* treeless plain, said by Oviedo to be a Carib word, and appears as early as 1555 in explorer's accounts (Eden, *Decades;* see *Oxford English Dictionary*). The Savannah tribe may have taken its name from the terrain, though the closeness to their other name, Shawnee, suggests a kind of folk-etymological reinforcement. See Frederick W. Hodge, *Handbook of American Indians North of Mexico,* Bulletin of Bureau of American Ethnology 30 (Washington, D.C., 1910), II, 532. Read, *IJAL* 15 (1949): 132, doubts the Spanish-Carib (Arawak) etymon for the Georgia Indians; he cites Hodge and goes beyond him. *FLU.*]

No. 97
Betty Creek, Mud or Estatoah Creek, (and the Former Cherokee Settlement of Eastertoy)

Old maps and original plats depicting wilderness areas of Georgia show a substantial number of streams bearing the names of women. Most of these designations remain with us as a category of enigmatic names whose origins are difficult to explain. It is always a matter of satisfaction, then, when a derivation can be found for any of these appellations. One name which can be explained is Betty, Bettys, or Little Bettys Creek in Rabun County. This stream arises in Macon County, North Carolina, on the slopes where the Blue Ridge and Nantahala Mountain diverge,[1] and flows into Georgia, across Rabun, to join the Little Tennessee River in front of the Rabun Gap–Nacoochee School and immediately to the south of Dillard.

On the map showing the survey on the Georgia–North Carolina line in 1819 the stream is mentioned as Valley Creek.[2] But in the official survey for District 2 of Rabun made a few months later it was labelled Little Betty's Creek, or Fork[3] and it has borne a version of this designation ever since. The tab was puzzling because the use of the word Little in connection with the name implies there should also have been a Big Betty's Creek somewhere in the vicinity. This was not the case, however, because the creek was not called *Little Betty's* to differentiate it from a larger stream. It was named for a Cherokee widow known as Little Betty who once resided in the area and claimed a reservation on the stream. According to the Cherokee treaty of 1819 which allowed each Indian to select a reserve of 640 acres, provided he agreed to become a citizen of the United States,[4] Little Betty applied to the Cherokee Indian agent for such a reservation where she lived, at Eastertoy on the headwaters of the Little Tennessee River.[5] Since the site filed for was in Georgia, and the federal government was committed to have the Cherokees removed from this state, the Indians living in the area of Georgia ceded by the 1819 treaty were not allowed to remain on reserves they had claimed.

Little Betty eventually brought suit for the value of the reservation before the Indian Claims Commission and won her case, with $2,345 being set aside to cover the claim after the property had been appraised.[6] It was in this suit that she identified the site of her residence and the location of Eastertoy as being in Rabun County, Georgia.[7] Her statement, coupled with the use of *Little Betty's Creek* by the original surveyors of Rabun in 1819, makes it certain then that the Indian woman left her name on the stream.

Several other applicants for reservations listed themselves as residents of Eastertoy and thus confirm there was a settlement of this name in Rabun. The designation is of special interest to students of the Indians because early listings of Cherokee towns do not show a settlement of this name in what is now Rabun County. There were two places with a similar name located in other parts of the Cherokee

Country. These communities have been variously recorded as *Estatowih, Estatoie, Estotowee, Estatohe*, etc. Charles Royce spells the name *"Estatoe"* and locates one of the early towns on the Tugalo, below the junction of the Chattooga and the Tallulah rivers.[8] He places the other settlement in present Pickens County, South Carolina.[9]

Since no early Estatoe is mentioned in connection with Rabun County, it seems reasonable to think the people of Eastertoy probably removed from one of the older places when the settlement where they once resided was ceded to the whites, and brought along the name with them to the Rabun area.

The exact site of the town of Eastertoy is not known but most likely it centered about present Dillard, which is located on a fine rise that overlooks the beautiful bottoms along Betty Creek and the Little Tennessee. Old people around Dillard used to say they had always heard that Indians were living at the site when the first white people arrived to take up properties they had won in the land lotteries. Further evidence that the place was at Dillard can be found in the fact that Mud Creek which is also known as *Estatoah*, or as *Estatoah Falls Creek*, enters the right side of the Little Tennessee on the northeast side of Dillard.

One final note should be added about Little Betty: in her claim she stated there were 18 members of her family.[10] One has been unable to learn what name those Cherokees subsequently used.[11]

GMNL 16(1963): 92-93

NOTES

1. For a good map of the Bettys or Betty Creek area, see *Dillard Quadrangle, Ga.-N.C.* (Maps and Surveys Division, Tennessee Valley Authority, ed. 1946); and *Walhalla Sheet* (U.S. Geological Survey, ed. 1892).

2. Manuscript map of the Georgia-North Carolina boundary, as surveyed by a Joint Commission in 1819, Land Records of Georgia, Surveyor General Department, Atlanta.

3. Field Notes, District 2, Rabun County, survey of 1820, Hiram Glazier, D.S., pp. 12, 15, 18, *passim;* and Platbook OOO, lots 147, 158, 161, *passim,* both in Land Records of Georgia.

4. Charles J. Kappler, *Laws and Treaties,* Senate Doc. 319, 58th Cong., 2nd Sess. Vol. II (Treaties), Art. 2, p. 178.

5. "Cherokee Reservations Treaty of July 8, 1817 No. 1" (a register of reservations beginning with the treaty of 1817), No. 307, dated Sept. 19, 1819, "Little Betty (a widow) at Eastertoy," Records of the Office of Indian Affairs, Record Group 75, National Archives.

280 / Placenames of Georgia

6. Little Betty v. United States, Claim 114, before the "1st Cherokee Claims Commission under 7th Article Treaty 1835," Record Group 75.
7. *Ibid.*
8. Charles C. Royce, *The Cherokee Nation of Indians,* Fifth Annual Report of the Bureau of American Ethnology (Washington, D.C., 1887), accompanying map, "Territorial Limits of the Cherokee Nation of Indians."
9. *Ibid.*
10. Little Betty v. United States.
11. [Eastertoy as a folk-etymology for Estatoah is likely. Goff ventures no explanation for the Indian form. Since *isti* means people in Muskogee-Hitchiti (see No. 81, Eastahatchee) and *towah* or *italwa* mean town (Read, *IJAL* 16 [1950]: 205 on Etowah), a rough-and-ready etymon is at hand. *FLU.*]

No. 98
Rossville

Rossville in extreme northern Walker County and located immediately to the south of Chattanooga, Tennessee, has been much in the news of late due to the celebrations there incident to the restoration of the Chief John Ross house around which the town developed. Interesting additional information about this place and the home of the noted Cherokee leader can be found in the land records of Georgia. A platbook among these documents, based on the original survey of the Rossville area in 1832, contains a plat which names Rossville and depicts the Ross home in lot 9 of District 9, 4th Section of original Cherokee County of which Walker is now a part.[1] The little chart is unique because it depicts in the embryo stage a community that eventually was to develop into a city. The land map for District 9 shows there were two other buildings at the site of the home, in addition to the residence shown on the plat.[2]

The drawing of the Ross house is merely a sketch but, except for outside chimneys at the ends of the structure, it is a reasonable depiction of the place as it was known in later years. In the recent restoration of the house, the structure was moved about 100 yards from the original site to a pool formed by a spring that is said to have been the source of water for the Ross family. The little stream shown on the left center of the plat is seemingly the brooklet that drained from the spring. It will be noted there was an "Impr," that is, a clearing for fields, of 14 acres on the area of lot 9. But the fertility of the land was not rated highly by the surveyor because it is marked "3d O&H," meaning third quality oak and hickory land.

It will also be seen that Rossville was located beside the noted Federal Road, connecting Georgia and Tennessee across the Cherokee country. This thoroughfare was the first vehicular route of Georgia west of the Chattahoochee. It was formally opened in 1805 pursuant to a treaty with the Cherokees in that year. The road began at the southeast boundary of the Cherokees, approximately the present Hall-Jackson County line, and led northwestward toward Tennessee.[3] Near present Ramhurst, in Murray County, it forked with one prong leading northward toward Knoxville and the other continuing northwestward past Rossville toward Nashville. The latter branch became an important "movers" or emigrants route to west Tennessee and north Alabama. And no doubt the presence of the road caused the first post office in northwest Georgia to be opened at Rossville in 1819.

The left margin of the plat showing Rossville discloses that James Jones of the Rick District of Laurens County was the "fortunate drawer" who won lot 9 in the 1832 lottery to distribute the area of District 9.

—*GMNL* 16(1963): 93-94

NOTES

1. 4th Section, Cherokee County, survey of 1832, Platbook (pages not numbered) showing Districts 8, 9, and 10, Land Records of Georgia, Surveyor General Department, Atlanta.

2. Map of District 9, 4th Section, Cherokee County, survey of 1832, Thomas G. McFarland, D.S.

3. For more details of the Federal trace, see "Retracing the Old Federal Road," pp. 349-60 below.

No. 99
Spring Bluff

Recent news reports about a large rocket plant under construction in Camden County have occasionally mentioned nearby Spring Bluff, a small place on U.S. 17, located on the south side of Little Satilla River, at the first significant rise in the river's bank after passing the low coastal marshes about the stream's mouth. Spring Bluff has borne its name for at least 200 years, and the designation antedates the time in which Georgia had a clear right to occupy the area to the south of the Altamaha. The site was mentioned in early 1763 on a plat for land granted by South Carolina to William Hazard of that province.[1] The property involved was a 3,000-acre tract at the head of Little St. Tilly about three miles to the west of a mineral spring known by the name of *Spring Bluff.* A plotting of this tract with subsequent grants made by South Carolina at the same period makes it certain our Spring Bluff was the place referred to.

The reader may perhaps be surprised to learn of the Carolina authorities making grants to their citizens in an area that is commonly thought of as having been a part of Georgia since the foundation of the colony. It should be recalled, however, that Georgia was created from territory falling within the historic boundaries of Carolina as provided in Charles II's grants to the Lords Proprietors in 1663 and 1665, and that the southern limits of the new colony were confined to the Altamaha River. When the danger of the Spaniards was removed after the acquisition of Florida by the British in 1763, South Carolina claimed the territory below the Altamaha belonged to her and began to make large grants of land to the south of that river. Governor James Wright of Georgia vigorously protested these grants with the result that in George III's Proclamation of 1763 the section between the Altamaha and St. Marys was added to the Province of Georgia.[2]

In his new commission to Governor Wright in January 1764, the King modified the 1732 Charter of Georgia by extending the boundaries of the Province to the St. Marys.[3]

—*GMNL* 16(1963): 94

NOTES

1. Land of Captain William Hazard, survey of May 14, 1763, Platbook 15, p. 375, Land Records of South Carolina, Department of Archives, Columbia.
2. Book of "Proclamations, 1754-1794," pp. 85ff., Department of Archives and History, Atlanta.
3. "Commission Book B," p. 140, Department of Archives and History.

No. 100
Sardis or Sardins Creek (Formerly Sartains Creek)

As has been noted in previous sketches, placenames sometimes go through changes due to a misinterpretation or misconstruction of the expressions. A good example of such a shift can be found in Sardis Creek that arises on the Johnson-Jefferson line, at the old Sunbury Road, and runs southwestwardly across northwest Emanuel County to join the Little Ohoopee River immediately above a noted frontier spot called *the Cowford*. Sardis Creek was originally *Sartains Creek* and was named for James Sartain, who acquired property along the stream as early as 1794.[1] The original name seems simple enough, but for some reason over the years people had trouble in rendering it and began changing it into forms like Sertains,[2] Sartian, Sartium, Sartins, Sardins, and finally into Sardis. The last version appeared on a map of Johnson County issued in 1908.[3]

—*GMNL* 16(1963): 94

NOTES

1. Grant of 200 acres in original Montgomery County, 1798, Platbook CC, p. 430; and grants of two 1,000-acre lots in the same county, 1794, Platbook CC, p. 431, Land Records of Georgia, Surveyor General Department, Atlanta.

2. Land of John Blake, survey of 1798, Platbook XX, p. 98. This version reflects a remnant of British speech wherein a written *e* may come out in speech as broad *a*, e.g., clerk into "clark." The best-known such form that still remains with us is varsity, a shortened version of university. Since the surveyor who laid off Blake's land was not certain of the spelling of Sartains Creek, he substituted an *e* for the first *a*.

3. Roger D. Flippen, *Map of Johnson County* (Atlanta: Hudgins, 1908). [Sardis, the derived name, is Biblical—one of the Seven Cities to which Jesus orders John to send his Book of Revelation (1:11, 3:1-14). Sardis was urged to repent though it contains a saving remnant worthy of white raiment. Of the other six only Smyrna appears in Georgia (Cobb County); it is far enough away to militate against a theory of systematic naming. *FLU.*]

No. 101
Spoil Cane Creek

Spoil Cane Creek heads at the south side of Unicoi Gap on the Blue Ridge at the White-Towns line and flows nearly due south to join the upper Chattahoochee River above Robertstown in White County. The stream has long borne its odd title because the original surveyor of the area mentioned it as *Spoil'd Cane Creek* in his survey of 1820.[1] It is not known with certainty how the *Spoil Cane* got its name but with a knowledge of the importance of cane, and especially of "reed" or switch cane as a forage plant in early years, coupled with the importance of Unicoi Gap as a passage over the Blue Ridge, one can make a good guess about the origin. The creek was followed for its full length by the noted Unicoi Road that began on the Tugalo to the east of Toccoa and ran to Nine Mile Creek, to the south of Maryville in East Tennessee. This thoroughfare, which was opened as a turnpike after 1813 by a company of Cherokees and white men, was the first vehicular way over the middle Blue Ridge. Prior to its opening as a road, though, the route was one of the most important trading paths leading from Charleston and Augusta to the Valley towns and Overhill settlements of the Cherokees.[2] Thus for a long period there was a great deal of travelling by packhorse trains and horsemen up and down Spoil Cane Creek. Since grass was scarce in the wilderness country and corn rarely available for stock feed, early people largely depended on cane as food for their animals on nightly stops along a trail; and because reed or winter cane grew on virtually every stream in Georgia, travellers could usually count on the availability of the vegetation wherever they camped. The traffic up the narrow defiles of Spoil Cane, however, was so heavy, it is reasonable to conclude the supply of cane along it was very early "spoiled", i.e., overgrazed or used up.

More than likely, the designation *Spoil'd Cane* was a well-understood, precautionary expression which warned travellers to expect little forage for their animals if they proposed to stop along the stream for the night on the long, tedious climb up to the gap.

Although the original surveyor marked the creek *"Spoil'd Cane"* on his surveys,[3] plats, and district map, he no doubt intended this form to be an abbreviation for spoiled cane. On present maps the appellation is listed as *Spoil Cane* or *Spoilcane*. The slight shift from the old version to the new has been a common practice in American English: ice tea for iced tea is an example that is familiar to everyone.

The successor route to the Unicoi Road and the old path is our Georgia 75 which follows a segment of the original course on the lower reaches of the Spoil Cane, but switches to a cut on the side of the mountain toward the upper end of the creek to get an easier approach to the pass. From the edge of No. 75, just short of the Unicoi Gap, one can look down on the very head of Spoil Cane Creek and the remnants of the earlier thoroughfare. A glimpse at the former course leaves the thought it could only be known as a road through courtesy or charity.

—*GMNL* 16(1963): 94-95

NOTES

1. Plat for District 5, Habersham County, survey of 1820, William Evans, D.S., Platbook NNN, lots 7, 8, 11, *passim*, Land Records of Georgia, Surveyor General Department, Atlanta.
2. For a discussion of major trading paths across the Blue Ridge, see Sketches 27 and 28, above, on Hiwassee and the Hiwassee Trail.
3. Field Notes, District 5, Habersham County, survey of 1820, William Evans, D.S.

No. 102
Fodder Creek

Fodder Creek is the main western tributary of the upper Hiwassee River in Towns County. It arises on the slopes of Brasstown Bald and reaches the river at the head of the Chatuge Reservoir, to the south of the town of Hiawassee. The first surveyors along the stream in 1832[1] labelled it *"Fodders Creek"* and that possessive form plainly indicates it was named for a person, most likely an Indian called *Fodder* (or Saluwaugah in the Cherokee version), since there were several Indians named Fodder who lived at various places in the Cherokee country of Georgia before the removal of the Indians in 1838.[2] It is not known why these people bore such a name, but probably the tab was applied because they followed the practice of white people by topping their corn at the end of summer to save the cured blades as forage. But whatever the reason for the moniker, it fell into a sizable category of Cherokee personal names that carried an economic connotation like Tobacco, Hemp, Waggon, Fense [sic] Maker, Bean, Cross Cut, Melting Ladle [for melting lead for bullets], Drawing Knife, Coffee, Skillet, Potatoe, Bridgemaker, Goodmoney, and so on in an interesting variety.

—*GMNL* 16(1963): 95

NOTES

1. Field Notes for District 17, 1st Section, Cherokee County, survey of 1832, Samuel Torrence, D.S.; and Field Notes, District 18, 1st Section, Cherokee County, survey of 1832, Joseph Byers, D.S., Land Records of Georgia, Surveyor General Department, Atlanta.

2. The Cherokee census of 1835 shows there were also Indians named Fodder on Valley River in North Carolina and at Ooltewah in Tennessee.

No. 103
Sopes Creek and Soap Creek

Sopes Creek arises within the northern limits of Marietta and flows southeastward to join the Chattahoochee about two miles below the Johnson Ferry Bridge. Although *Sopes Creek* appears on present-day maps under that spelling and the United States Geographic Board has approved the version,[1] it is plain the designation is a backwoods remnant of the original name which was properly *Soaps Creek*, according to the surveyors who laid off the area of the stream in the first official surveys of 1832.[2]

The creek and some neighboring streams in Cobb County like *Noses*, *Nickajack*, and *Rottenwood* creeks were named for Cherokees who once resided on those waterways; but by the time of the 1832 surveys mentioned, all Cherokees living as far down as Buzzard Roost Island (where the southern boundary of present Cobb County reaches the Chattahoochee) were supposed to have removed above a line running westward into Alabama from the Shallowford (located just below Roswell and the bridge on U.S. 19) along the divide between the waters of the Etowah, Tallapoosa, and Chattahoochee. This boundary was known as the Coffee Line, and was named for General John Coffee who had recommended it in 1829 to President Andrew Jackson as the southern limit of the Cherokees after being sent to Georgia to investigate a dispute between the state and those Indians over the location of the boundary. When the President approved Coffee's recommendation in early 1830, all Cherokees residing below the line were ordered to remove north of it and the Indian agent was directed to see that this was done.

Numbers of the Cherokees of the lower Cobb County area then migrated to the middle Etowah River region or to tributaries of that stretch of the stream because their names can be found in the area subsequent to 1830. Apparently the Soap who furnished the name for *Sopes Creek* was in their group since the Cherokee census of 1835 mentions an Old Soap on the waters of Sharp Mountain Creek[3] that arises in central Pickens and unites with the *Etowah* in Cherokee County, to the south of Ball Ground. A later valuation report of Cherokee properties made subsequent to the Cherokee treaty of 1835 places him in the same locality[4] and there is little doubt that he resided on present Soap Creek of Cherokee County which is an upper tributary of the Sharp Mountain.[5] The use of "old" in connection with Soap's name implies he was an Indian of some standing, although not necessarily a chief. It seems reasonable to conclude this man was the individual who also once lived on Sopes Creek in Cobb County and that he gave name to both streams. It merits saying again that the official survey, census, and valuation reports mention the Indian's name as Soap and not as Sope, the present-day version. The former designation was not unusual among the Cherokees of Georgia. As pointed out in the preceding sketch on Fodder Creek, originally *Fodders Creek*, a personal name with an economic connotation was fairly common with those Indians.

There is a Soap Creek, a tributary of the Savannah, in Lincoln County. This waterway has one of the oldest names on the upper Savannah. It was recorded as early as 1757,[6] and has been mentioned many times subsequent to that date in records or on maps. Occasionally it can be found as Sope but mostly it is listed as Soap. So far as could be learned it has never been referred to in the possessive as Sopes or Soaps. The origin and significance of the name could not be determined.

—*GMNL* 16(1963): 95-96

NOTES

1. "Decision List No. 6103," *Decisions on Names in the United States* (United States Board on Geographic Names, 1962), p. 20.

2. Field notes, plats, and land district map for District 16, 2nd Section, Cherokee County, survey of 1832, J. F. Cleveland, D.S.; and District 17, 2nd Section, Cherokee County, survey of 1832, Hugh M. D. King, D.S., Land Records of Georgia, Surveyor General Department, Atlanta.

3. "Census of Cherokees in the limits of Georgia in 1835," census of Cherokee Indians known as the "Henderson Roll." Records of the Bureau of Indian Affairs, Record Group 75, National Archives.

4. Valuations in Cobb, Cherokee, and Gilmer counties in 1836, Appraisal No. 91, by Agents Yancey and Worley, Record Group 75.

5. Soap Creek joins Bluff Creek about a mile above the mouth of the latter on Sharp Mountain Creek—see *Tate Quadrangle, Georgia* (U.S. Geological Survey, ed. 1928).

6. Allen D. Candler, ed., *Colonial Records of Georgia* (Atlanta: Franklin, 1906-1916); 9: 652, petition of Samuel Chew for 200 acres at Soap Creek 40 miles above Augusta, Nov. 1757. This petition was approved but it is not clear that Chew actually settled at the place. The area above Little River in which Soap Creek lies was not ceded to Georgia until 1773 at the Treaty of Augusta.

No. 104
Fulsams Creek (Formerly Folsoms Creek)

Fulsams Creek commences at the edge of Georgia 22 in northeast Hancock County and runs southeastward to enter the *Ogeechee River* two miles below Mayfield. The stream is of interest because its name serves as a reminder that Georgia frontier families sometimes suffered in real life Indian depredations that were as harrowing as the episodes which appear on our Westerns. The creek was named for a Captain Benjamin Fulsam, or Folsom, who came to Georgia from North Carolina in 1773 with his wife, one son, and three daughters.[1] He secured in the recently opened New Purchase territory a small grant of 100 acres, located on the east side of the *Ogeechee*, opposite the mouth of the waterway that was to bear his name.[2] Folsom made the tragic mistake of crossing over the river and establishing another farm on what was then Indian territory.[3] This sort of intrusion was risky but fairly common in the early years. He made substantial improvements at the site by clearing and fencing 30 acres and by erecting a house and other structures.

In September of 1777, a party of Creek Indians descended on the place and devastated it. They killed Folsom, burned all the buildings, destroyed the fencing, and ruined 30 acres of corn standing in the fields.[4] Mrs. Folsom and the children and some farm hands managed to escape and left the Indians to round up and drive away all of the hogs, cattle, and workstock. Their escape may not have been happenso. During the period in question, British agents were stirring up the Creeks against the Americans, and it is possible some Tory with the raiding party was humane enough to restrain the Indians from killing the widow and the children.

John Folsom, the son, later stated he and his mother did not return to the site until after the "American War."[5] This visit was probably made in 1783 after the area had been ceded by the Treaty of Augusta in that year. The Folsoms continued to reside for a period in the general area, but apparently they never again lived at the site of the attack.

—*GMNL* 16(1963): 96

NOTES

1. "Journal of the Augusta Land Court, December 7, 1773, Records of the Court of Land Commissioner, Appointed by Governor Wright to Issue the Ceded Lands—1773 to 1775," original in the Department of Archives and History, Atlanta.

2. *Ibid.* The grant was 3 miles below the "Upper Trading Road" (the Upper Creek Trading Path or Oakfuskee Path). This trail crossed the Ogeechee at a present mill site a mile above Mayfield—see John H. Goff, "The Path to Oakfuskee," *Georgia Historical Quarterly* 39 (March 1955): 1ff. At 3 miles below the path, the Folsom tract was at and opposite the mouth of our Fulsams Creek.

3. Two statements filed years later in connection with a claim of Folsom's son John against the Creeks (by men who were familiar with the details of the raid) show the Folsom farm was on the west side of the Ogeechee, in Hancock County: Deposition of Jessey Kelley, Wilkes County, July 25, 1835, "Indian Depredations," Vol. II, pt. 3, p. 969, Department of Archives and History, Atlanta; and statement of David Cooper, Hamilton (Harris County), May 10, 1835, *ibid.*, pt. 2, pp. 52-53. Kelley stated the incident occurred in Sept. of 1777, and that the site was at the mouth of "Folsoms Creek" on the west side of the Ogeechee.

4. Kelley Deposition.

5. John Folsom's claim, 1835, "Indian Depredations," pt. 3, p. 970.

No. 105
Black Creek (Formerly the Weelustie) and Iric Creek

Black Creek is a two-pronged stream which heads in south central Bulloch County and flows down into Bryan to enter the Great Ogeechee to the west of Meldrim. The creek is interesting because it is one of the few comparatively small waterways in the older part of Georgia which bears an Indian or translated Indian name. The rivers of that section mostly have Indians designations but not the lesser waterways. Black Creek was originally called the *Weelustie*,[1] from the Muskogee wiwa ("weewŭh"), water, plus *lasti* ("lustie"), black. This aboriginal form did not remain in use long, because even before the Revolution people were referring to the stream as *Black Creek,* and it is significant to note they did not use the word water in this translated form.

Black Creek has darker waters than upcountry people are accustomed to see, but its stream could not be termed a decided black and it ordinarily would not be considered nearly as black, for example, as the St. Marys River or other coastal waterways. The point is of significance here, because if we could ever know how the creek got its name, we might be surprised to learn that *Weelustie* was really a symbolic designation which was intended to signify West Creek or West Water, i.e., West Fork, and that the expression had nothing to do with the color of the stream. It is known the Creeks sometimes used colors for directions and black was a label for west.

The two major prongs of Black Creek are now called *Upper Black Creek* and *Lower Black Creek,* but in post-Revolutionary years these branches were referred to as *First Black Creek* and *Second Black Creek.*[2] This designation of waterways by numbers is an interesting place-naming practice which is still followed in Georgia, and the custom furnishes an opportunity for a future sketch on the subject.

Black Creek has many tributaries with interesting names, but one stream in particular which should be singled out is Iric Creek that begins above Arcola on U.S. 80 in Bulloch County and joins Upper Black Creek to the south of Stilson. This stream was named for Adam Eirick, who petitioned the provincial authorities in 1768 for a headright grant of 500 acres on the north side of Black Creek at a tributary that would later bear his name.[3] Governor James Wright formally signed the grant a few months later.[4]

In a prior petition, Eirick had asked for 500 acres at Eatton's Gardens on the Ogeechee.[5] In this request he stated he had been in the province five years, that he had a wife, two children, and five negroes, but no land had been granted him. The tract asked for in this instance proved to have been surveyed for some one else, so Eirick switched his petition to a request for land on Black Creek.[6]

Iric Creek is of more than passing interest since Eirick was one of the earliest settlers west of the Ogeechee, above the mouth of the Cannoochee. For his day he was a far-out pioneer, near the boundary line established between Georgia and the Creeks at the Treaty of Augusta in 1763. The Indians became disgruntled with the subsequent running of this line and it was not finally laid off and marked till 1768. In the Black Creek area the boundary ran from the lower end of Paramore Hill in our Jenkins County to a point to the east of Jesup, thence to the St. Marys River. Eirick got his grant about the time it was safe to move into the new area.

—*GMNL* 16(1963): 96-97

NOTES

1. Samuel Savery, D.S. "Sketch [map] of the Boundary Line between the Province of Georgia and the Creek Nation," 1769, Public Record Office, London.
2. Bulloch County, survey of 1797, Platbook BB, p. 44; survey of 1813, Platbook WW, p. 423; survey of 1819, Platbook AC, p. 315; survey of 1846, Platbook AF, p. 42; survey of 1851, Platbook AH, p. 104, Land Records of Georgia, Surveyor General Department, Atlanta.
3. Allen D. Candler, ed., *Colonial Records of Georgia* (Atlanta: Franklin, 1904-1916), 10: 652, Dec. 6, 1768.
4. *Ibid.*, p. 751, April 13, 1769, in St. Philips Parish.
5. *Ibid.*, p. 477, May 3, 1768.
6. *Ibid.*, p. 652.

No. 106
Cowpen Creek (Originally Jones Cowpen Creek)

Cowpen Creek begins in northern Washington County at the Hancock line and joins the Little Ogeechee River[1] near the latter's mouth on the Great Ogeechee, to the northeast of Warthen. There is nothing particularly notable about Cowpen Creek except to state that it was originally called *Jones Cowpen Creek* and that it bears one of the oldest English placenames west of the Ogeechee. Presumably it was named for a squatter or Indian countryman named Jones who set up a cowpen on it long before the area where it flows was opened to settlers by the 1783 Treaty of Augusta with the Creeks. Two maps dated in 1763 name *Jones Cowpen Creek* but they err by showing it draining westward toward Buffalo Creek and the Oconee instead of southeastward to the Ogeechee.[2]

Several early land plats, however, confirm that our Cowpen Creek was identical with Jones Cowpen Creek. For example, Squire Arthur Fort, a pioneer leading citizen of the upper Ogeechee area, exercised his right to a Revolutionary bounty of 287½ acres by asking for land on the southside of the Little Ogeechee where it joins the main river. The plat for his property shows Jones Cowpen Creek crossing the land to join the Little Ogeechee.[3] The Jones in the name has long since been dropped. Even the 1818 Eleazer Early map of Georgia shows the stream as *Cowpen Creek.*[4]

—*GMNL* 16(1963): 97

NOTES

1. There are two Little Ogeechee rivers and an Ogeechee Creek in addition to the Great Ogeechee River. The larger of the Little Ogeechees arises in Effingham County and reaches the sea in Chatham, at a point to the east of the mouth of Great Ogeechee. The Little Ogeechee to which Cowpen Creek is tributary commences near Sparta and joins the big river in northeast Washington County. Ogeechee Creek arises in central Screven and reaches the Great Ogeechee in the southwest corner of that county.

2. Henry Yonge and W. G. DeBrahm, "A map of the Sea Coast of Georgia & the inland parts thereof . . . ," 1763, photostatic copy in the William L. Clements Library, Ann Arbor, Mich.; and Thomas Wright, "A Map of Georgia and Florida," MS, C.O.700/North American Colonies/Georgia 13, Public Record Office, London.

3. Washington County, survey of 1784, Platbook B, p. 188, Land Records of Georgia, Surveyor General Department, Atlanta.

4. [Compare the Revolutionary battle at Cowpens, South Carolina; see Stewart, *Names on the Land,* p. 169. *FLU.*]

No. 107
Alecks Creek, Aleck Island, Doctortown, Doctors Creek, Old Doc Slough, Sansavilla Bluffs, the Williamsburg Reserve, the Dead Town of St. Savilla or Williamsburg, Fort Defense, Williams Fort (and the Indian Settlements of Santa Sevilla and St. Iagos Town)

Alecks, Alex, or Ellis[1] Creek arises to the southwest of Mt. Pleasant on U.S. 25-341, in Wayne County and flows northward to reach the Altamaha River at the upper end of the Sansavilla Bluffs, about six miles directly north of Mt. Pleasant. The stream's name belongs to a category of interesting appellations pertaining to Georgia's geography and history. The little creek was named for a Lower Creek chief called Alleck or Captain Alleck who once resided near its mouth on the Altamaha and gave up his place following boundary adjustments between the Creek Indians and the English subsequent to the noted treaty of 1763 at Augusta. As will be seen shortly, there are good grounds for believing he removed to the site of our Doctortown and gave rise to that unusual name, because the Doctor element of the designation is a translated version of the Creek Indian word Alleck.

Alleck had an unusual career in his relations with the white people which is not exactly comparable with that of any other Indian in Georgia's history. Seemingly he came to the colony as a youth and spent most of his life living within the settlements or along the margins of the province.[2] His main residence was at a cowpen and farm on Alecks Creek at the Altamaha.[3] There is evidence, however, to show he was granted an island in the Midway District.[4] He is mentioned most often as a stock-raiser, but he also engaged in some farming since he had "plantations."[5] It is significant to note that during his stay in or along the frontier of the colony, Alleck resided far from the principal Lower Creek towns that were situated to the west on the waters of the Flint and Chattahoochee rivers. In his stay here he left his name on more places than any other person in Georgia's history.

The Alleck or Captain Alleck of this sketch should not be confused with another chief bearing the same name and rank who lived on the Chattahoochee. Benjamin Hawkins refers to the latter Indian as Captain Ellick and says he was an old Cusseta chief who had married three Uchee women. In 1729 this man quit the Cussetas, moved down river, and founded the noted Uchee town on the west side of the Chattahoochee[6] below the mouth of Uchee Creek in present Russell County, Alabama. Since Captain Ellick established the Uchee town in 1729, it seems very unlikely that he was identical with the Captain Alleck who was residing years later on the Altamaha and who had lived in or on the edge of the colony since his youth.

The Alleck of this sketch was outwardly friendly to the white people, and he gave helpful information on Indian matters to governors John Reynolds, Henry Ellis, and James Wright. He was especially useful to Wright in negotiating boundary line matters with the Creeks. But Alleck was no Tomochichi. There is substantial evidence to show he was a self-serving, devious fellow.

Alleck had received or assumed his title of Captain Alleck by 1749.[7] And although he was once denounced as a liar, renegade, a fake warrior despite his title of captain, and a man without influence among the Indians,[8] he was certainly a chief, and as such he played a leading part in three important Indian treaties. At the famous 1763 Congress in Augusta (which was attended by the governors of Georgia, South Carolina, North Carolina, the lieutenant-governor of Virginia, and John Stuart, British Superintendent of Indian Affairs) Alleck was a principal spokesman for the Creeks in negotiations to establish a boundary line between the whites and the Indians.[9] Later when uncertainty arose about the direction of this line from the Ogeechee to the St. Marys, Alleck was empowered by the Creek chiefs assembled for the treaty of Picolata, Florida, in 1765, to agree upon a course for the line with Governor Wright.[10] The two met in early 1766 and reached an agreement which Wright labelled a "Treaty."[11] When the boundary was eventually run in 1768, however, there were some further changes made in the course which were favorable to the whites and Alleck very probably had a part in arranging the shifts.

After the 1766 agreement with Wright, Alleck gave up his place near the mouth of Alecks Creek because the promulgated boundary was due to pass to the west of his home leaving the site on the colony's side. In 1766, after the chief had quit his place, and two years before the boundary line was finally run, Winwood McIntosh applied to the provincial authorities to purchase 500 acres at Alleck's former site.[12] The petition was approved and a plat for the land was prepared.[13] No bearings are shown for the lines of the survey, but the plat does show an old house and "Capt. Alus Field," near the Altamaha. Alleck's name is misspelled but Miss McIntosh's petition makes it certain she wanted to buy the chief's former place, which was located just above the Sansavilla Bluffs.

Alleck demanded payment from the province for his property and was given a runaway slave which he had apprehended. The authorities settled the matter by paying the owner of the slave 60 pounds.[14]

At the same time Alleck also asked for 30 head of cattle which he claimed Governor Henry Ellis had promised him for services to the colony.[15] These duties apparently concerned reports which Alleck had made about schemes of the Bosomworth's to get control of certain lands and islands that had been reserved by early treaties for the Indians as a whole.

Some references to Alleck connect him with the Indian town of Santa Sevilla, which was on the Sansavilla Bluffs that have been mentioned.[16] The settlement apparently stretched along these rises, although the main part was probably toward the upper end near Alecks Creek. But be that as it may, Alleck's name was also concerned with the other end of the bluffs, since immediately below this part there is even now a rise in the Altamaha swamp called Aleck Island.[17] The place is not actually an island but is an elevated area fronting toward the river and nearly surrounded by a boggy section. A small stream called Aleck Island Creek drains along the lower edge of the rise.

It seems virtually certain the island derived its name from Alleck because of his connection with the Santa Sevilla settlement and his cattle-raising activities. The area of the island was probably a good range territory in early years. Alleck made no claim for payment for the island, however, subsequent to the treaty of 1763. By the time he began to aid Governor Wright in adjusting the boundary line, the area below the Altamaha had been added to Georgia by the king, and through the efforts of Oglethorpe, the Creeks had long since given the whites the right to claim lands as high up the coastal rivers as the tide flows. Since tidal effects reach the Sansavilla Bluffs and Aleck Island is below that section, the province was under no obligation to pay the Indians for it.

This point suggests an interesting possible feature of the place which Alleck gave up and Miss McIntosh bought from the colony. The Alecks Creek area and the site of the Indian's home is not far above the vanishing point of the tide on the Altamaha. Alleck probably was shrewd enough to select a place above the tidal influence point, but only high enough to be within Indian lands, pursuant to the agreement with Oglethorpe.

Governor Wright and Indian Agent Stuart mentioned a headman named St. Jago and another called the Doctor.[18] St. Jago (properly Iago or Santiago), like Alleck, was another chief who lived in or on the fringe of the colony, and Governor Wright had made use of him in dealings with the Creeks. For a period, he resided at a settlement called Iago's Town, which was located at the head of some branches of the Ogeechee in present northeast Bulloch County.[19]

St. Iago, or Santiago, is Spanish and the name hints the chief may once have resided in Florida, and deserted to the English. If his Indian tab has been recorded, it could not be located or identified and thus there is no suggestion from an aboriginal name about the tribe or band to which he belonged. He probably was not a real Creek since he lived so far from the main settlements of that nation. Iago's town had 20-30 families[20] and the people apparently had quit the settlement by 1768 when the boundary line of 1763 was finally run. Surveyor Savery referred to the town but marked it "Now called Cavenah's Place."[21] It is not known where the settlement moved, but Santiago was around in 1772 because he is mentioned in a trading account entry during that year as "Sainte Iagua."[22]

Wright and Stuart's reference to an Indian called the Doctor is virtually certain to have meant Alleck. The two men asked the Creek chiefs to come down and finish running the boundary line and if they could not do so, to empower St. Iago and the Doctor to supervise the laying off of the line. Governor Wright had previously had the cooperation of St. Iago and Alleck on the boundary matter and it seems clear he wanted their help again. He and Stuart merely switched the name from Alleck to the Doctor.

The point is significant to the study because it seems plain that Aleck's name[23] is from the Muskogee word *alekcha* or *alikcha*, meaning doctor in English. The derivation in turn suggests how Doctortown, below U.S. 82, to the east of Jesup in Wayne County, received its unusual name. The place was first reported in 1768 as the Doctor's Town by the surveying party which went by the site while completing the 1763 treaty boundary between the Canoochee and the St. Marys.[24] The spot continued to be known as Doctor's Town for many years afterward, although in recent times it has been simplified into Doctortown.

The 1768 listing of Doctortown is significant because this date was only two years after Alleck had given up the place which Miss McIntosh bought. Alleck, of course, had to move somewhere and it seems reasonable to think he shifted to the site of Doctortown that was not far away from his former home on Alecks Creek, but which was still beyond the point where the projected colonial boundary line would cross the Altamaha. Alleck knew from his negotiations with Governor Wright where the line would go over the river. The Doctortown site provided a fine, elevated location, and it is easy to believe Alleck removed the relatively short distance to the spot and caused the place to become Doctor's Town, since the name Alleck was in fact a title signifying doctor.

There are some other place names in the area of Alecks Creek and Doctortown which also probably retain Alleck's name. One of these is a considerable stream in Long County called Doctors Creek that joins the north side of the Altamaha below Doctortown and not far above Alecks Creek. Doctors Creek is mentioned on numbers of early maps and plats, and since it lies in the general area where Alleck once lived, it is reasonable to think the stream retains an English version of Alleck's name.

About four miles above Doctortown, on the east side of the Altamaha, there is still another name that may stem from Alleck, the doctor. This is Old Doc Slough, a creek or drain coming out of the river swamp.

Despite a wide and low approach through the Altamaha swamp across from Doctortown, the place was a well-known crossing point in late colonial and post-Revolutionary years. Trails from the direction of Savannah led there; and on the west, or Doctortown side, the noted Alachua Path bore southward from the crossing through today's Wayne, Brantley, and Charlton counties to the St. Marys, thence to the Alachua Seminole towns centering in present Alachua County, Florida. Presumably there were trails that led westward from the Doctortown site to the Creek and Hitchitee settlements of southwest Georgia, but the names and courses of these probable routes are not known.

There is no available record of an early ferry at Doctortown, but importance of the place suggests there must have been some facility there to aid travellers and traders in getting over the broad and deep Altamaha. The surveyors who passed the place in 1768 mention no difficulty in crossing at Doctortown, which intimates there may have been at least a canoe ferriage available at the place.

Due to the prominence of Doctortown as a river crossing, the state established a stockade at the site in post-Revolutionary years to guard the passage against Indian incursions into white settlements on the east side of the Altamaha. The little post was called Fort Defense[25] and in 1794 it was under the command of Captain James Armstrong.[26]

Doctortown is one of the very few former Creek Indian town sites which retains its original name.[27] Most of the former places are now nameless fields or wooded spots. In some instances—like Macon, Albany, Fort Gaines, and Bainbridge—white people built towns on former red settlements but they changed the names of the places. In other cases, the whites ignored the sites of the Indian communities but borrowed the names of the places to apply elsewhere. Cusseta in Chattahoochee County is a good example of such a shift; it is miles away from the location of the former noted Lower Creek town of Cusseta, which was on the Chattahoochee, within the Benning Reservation.

The Sansavilla Bluffs which were mentioned bear one of the most interesting and most enigmatic geographic designations in Georgia. The bluffs extend along the river for almost three miles—from Aleck Island to Alecks Creek. The southeast end is called Lower Sansavilla, while the northwest tip which breaks at Alecks Creek is called Upper Sansavilla. The latter is the higher of the two places, but Lower Sansavilla comes to an elevated point directly on the river at a bend and permits a more commanding view up and down the Altamaha. In fact, the scene is one of the unique and unforgettable sights of Georgia.

The meaning and significance of Sansavilla has long baffled placename students. Over the years the expression has changed drastically in spelling. It is now written Sansavilla on most maps, but curiously enough, a common local[28] pronunciation is "Sensavilla." These forms bear little resemblance to the versions of the name as recorded in colonial documents where it is listed as Sevillo, St. Sevila, Saint Sevillies,[29] Santa Sevila, Sancta Sevilla, St. Sevelia, Sta. Sevilla, etc. None of the early renditions contains a Sensa as found in the local current version.

Often in analyzing place designations, one can usually depend on the early recorded forms to provide clues about the intended meanings of the original names. But this did not prove to be the case of Sansavilla. The Santa or Sancta suggest the appellation was of Spanish origin and bore the name of a saint. This conclusion appeared reasonable because the Spaniards were in the general area of the bluffs long before Georgia was founded, and it seems certain they were familiar with the imposing bluffs. But no record of a Spanish mission, fort, or settlement could be found in connection with Sansavilla, nor could any saint be found with a name that approximated Sevilla, Sevella, Sevela, etc.

For a time after the Revolution there was a white settlement called St. Savilla on the Upper Sansavilla Bluff where Alecks Creek joins the Altamaha.[30] In December, 1792, however, the place was incorporated as Williamsburg by William Williams, Farr Williams, John William Lambert, William Cook, and Roswell King, as commissioners.[31] The town was surveyed and laid out with named streets.

Initially it was assumed that Williamsburg derived its name from the Williamsburgh Reserve which was established in 1759 along the north side of the Altamaha, from Cathead Creek, near Darien, to the mouth of the Ohoopee River.[32] The reserve was set aside at the behest of some citizens of Williamsburgh, South Carolina, who promised to remove to this colony if land were held for them till March, 1760.[33] The extension of the reservation as high up as the Ohoopee was a long stretch that ran far beyond the point which had been cleared of Indian title. In fact, the area at Sansavilla above the high tide point was not ceded till the 1766 agreement of Alleck with Governor Wright resulted in the boundary being moved up, practically speaking, to a point opposite Doctortown. From that area up to Beards Creek the land was ceded in 1773, while the territory as far up as the Ohoopee was not ceded by the Indians till 1783.

Some people from South Carolina did receive grants in the Williamsburgh Reserve,[34] but they apparently had nothing to do with the later establishment of the town on the Sansavilla Bluffs. The place was founded on the land of William and Farr Williams and probably was named for them.[35] These men perhaps were the sons of Joseph Williams, who got a grant in the Sansavilla section in 1766.[36]

The Williamsburg area, being on the south side of the Altamaha, was dangerously exposed to Indian attacks. During the Indian troubles of the 1790's General James Jackson thought the site was so important he recommended that Regulars be stationed there.[37] Elsewhere at the same period he prepared a memorandum which notes the settlement already had three blockhouses and a stockade fort.[38] The latter structure was probably a fort on Captain William Williams land, which is mentioned as being in existence about 1788.[39] Williams was one of the original incorporators of Williamsburg, and the town was partially laid out on his land.

Williamsburg's life under that name was of short duration. By 1818 it had reverted to St. Sevilla because it is listed under that designation by the Eleazer Early map of that year. But St. Savilla itself eventually disappeared and the place became one of Georgia's so-called ghost towns. Today the former site is a serene, detached spot, situated in expansive pine woods. A fine old church, a house or two, and a recently established recreation place on the river are the only present structures in the vicinity. There is nothing now to intimate the place was ever concerned with marauding Indians, blockhouses, or streets.

Williamsburg and St. Savilla's fate brings to mind a curious feature of the Altamaha River. With the exception of Darien and Doctortown,[40] there has never been an enduring town on the banks of this large river. The stream is bordered by many wide and wild swamps, but at some places, and especially on the south side, the stream has several high and beautiful bluffs along its strand which would have made splendid sites for towns. Such places, however, never materialized.

Interestingly enough, there are now two Williamsburgs in Georgia. One of these is a mere spot, in Clinch County, on the west side of the Suwannee River, and nearly opposite the Lem Griffis fishing camp. The other place is a small town in lower Calhoun County, to the south of Morgan. In 1886 the site was known as Williamsburgh, but in time it became Williamsburg. The village has been in existence for a considerable period but despite much inquiry one has not been able to learn how the name came to be applied. It is said the place was originally established as a concentrating point for shipping saw logs. The experience in trying to ascertain how present Williamsburg and many other similar places got their names points up a singular feature of placename study: It is usually much easier to determine the meaning of an Indian appellation than it is to learn how an English-type name like Williamsburg came to be applied to a site.

—*GMNL* 17(1964): 55-60

NOTES

1. Local people about Alecks Creek commonly refer to it as Ellis Creek due to a misconception of the sound of the name. Numbers of reliable maps and documents properly refer to the stream as Alecks Creek.

2. Allen D. Candler, ed., *Colonial Records of Georgia* (Atlanta: Franklin, 1904-1916), 3: 566.

3. There are many references to Alleck in colonial documents, but most of the sources connect him with the area about Alecks Creek or the Sansavilla Bluffs and give the impression he had long resided in that section.

4. Candler, ed., *Colonial Records* 8: 467, 1761.

5. *Ibid.*, 14: 332.

6. Benjamin Hawkins, *A Sketch of the Creek Country in the Years 1798 and 1799*, Collections of the Georgia Historical Society, Vol. 3 (Savannah, 1848), p. 62.

7. Candler, ed., *Colonial Records* 6: 283.

8. Thomas Bosomworth to Gov. John Reynolds, Savannah, April 10, 1756, MS Vol. 27, Colonial Records of Georgia, pp. 389 and 400. The MS volumes of the Colonial Records, apart from volumes published under the editorship of Allen D. Candler, were assembled from unpublished Candler transcripts and other sources by the Georgia Department of Archives and History and are housed at that place.

9. MS Vol. 39, Colonial Records of Georgia, pp. 348 and 369.

10. Candler, ed., *Colonial Records* 10: 575.

11. *Ibid.*, 9: 666-67.

12. *Ibid.*, p. 520, June, 1766.

13. Winwood McIntosh, Spinster, 500 acres, St. Davids Parish, 1766, re-recorded, Platbook C, p. 224, Land Records of Georgia, Surveyor General Department, Atlanta.

14. Candler, ed., *Colonial Records* 14: 332 and 334-35.

15. *Ibid.*, p. 333.

16. *Ibid.*, p. 332; and MS Vol. 37, Colonial Records of Georgia, p. 344.

17. *Everett City, Ga., Quadrangle* (U.S. Geological Survey and Corps of Engineers, U.S. Army, ed. 1920, reprinted 1944).

18. Talk addressed to Creek Chiefs, Savannah, July 27, 1768, MS Vol. 37, Colonial Records of Georgia, pp. 347-51 (348) with map.

19. Samuel Savery, "Sketch of the Boundary Line between the Province of Georgia and the Creek Nation," 1769, original at the Public Record Office, London, copy in Special Collections Department of the Emory University Library. Savery was the surveyor who ran the line in 1768.

20. Talk of Gov. Wright to Creek Chiefs, Jan. 3, 1767, MS Vol. 37, Colonial Records of Georgia, p. 172. Wright referred to a report of Col. Edward Barnard whom he had sent with a company of Rangers to inspect the route of the 1763 boundary. Barnard mentioned an Indian town of 20-30 families on the south[west] side of the Ogeechee, and recommended to the Governor that the people be removed to prevent trouble with the whites. Wright asked the Creek chiefs to move the settlement. The place mentioned by Barnard could only have referred to Iago's Town, since the boundary line only passed two Indian communities—St. Iago's place and Doctortown.

21. Savery, "Sketch of the Boundary Line."

22. George Galphin's "Silver Bluff Account Books, 1767-1772," entry for July 1, 1772, Manuscript Collection, Georgia Historical Society, Savannah.

23. Many versions of Alleck's name are listed in the records: Ellick, Alec, Ellic, Alex, Elix, etc.

24. Savery, "Sketch of the Boundary Line."

25. Affidavit of Richard Roddenberry, June 19, 1796, MS in Department of Archives and History, Atlanta.

26. *Ibid.*

27. In contrast to the former Creek town sites, there are a number of communities in north Georgia that retain their old Cherokee designations, in either English or Indian forms.

28. One relatively recent map uses this version—see *Ludowici Quadrangle* (Corps of Engineers, U.S. Army, 1943 ed.).

29. "Sevillies" illustrates the once common practice of referring to an Indian settlement in the plural. Attapulgus seemingly is the only remaining Georgia placename that reflects the former custom.

30. Map showing southeast portion of post-Revolutionary Georgia, no title, no author, but *circa* 1787, MS in the Library of Congress.

31. Robert and George Watkins, *A Digest of the Laws of the State of Georgia* (Philadelphia: Aitken, 1800), pp. 468-69, Dec. 17, 1792.

32. Candler, ed., *Colonial Records* 8: 46-47, Council Meeting of May 9, 1759.

33. *Ibid.*

34. *Ibid.*, pp. 271-72, April, 1760.

35. Watkins, *Digest*, pp. 468-69.

36. Candler, ed., *Colonial Records* 9: 425 and 644.

37. Jackson to commanding officer at St. Savilla, Savannah, April 2, 1793, Lilla M. Hawes, ed., "The Letter Book of General James Jackson, 1788-1796," *Georgia Historical Quarterly* 37 (Sept. 1953): 225-26.

38. "Memo [draft] of a letter to be dated April 7, 1793," James Jackson Papers, Department of Archives and History, Atlanta. A Mrs. "Cooke" supplied the information about the fortifications. A William Cooke was one of the commissioners who founded Williamsburg.

39. Deposition of Prussia Cole and legatees of John Cole, April 16, 1821, "Indian Depredations, 1787-1825," Vol. II, pt. 3, pp. 770-71, Department of Archives and History.

40. Doctortown for many years was the site of a large sawmill and woodworking plant. These facilities have now closed, but a modern paper mill on the north side of the place apparently assures continuation of the town.

No. 108
Beards Bluff, Beards Creek, Fort James Bluff, Five Mile Creek, Ten Mile Creek, Boundaries of the Creek Land Cession of 1773, Oglethorpe Bluff(and Mount Venture)

Beards Bluff is located on the east side of the Altamaha opposite a small island and immediately below the mouth of Beards Creek which marks the northwest boundary of Long County. The reader can easily pinpoint the site on any good highway map because it is situated where Georgia 261, a presently unpaved road, deadends at the river after intersecting U.S. 25-301, to the south of Glennville.

Beards Bluff stretches along the Altamaha for about a quarter of a mile and rises some 10 feet above the normal level of the river. This elevation is not great, but it so happens the bluff is the termination of a natural terrace or levee that skirts the lower side of Beards Creek and spans the low, marginal swamps that extend back from the river. The levee sometimes overflows in spots, as in the case of the high waters of the spring of 1964, but ordinarily the little ridge is elevated enough to permit relatively easy access to the Altamaha and this access makes the rise the best natural approach to the river for many miles up and down the left bank of the stream. Elsewhere, except for the slight bluff at old Fort Barrington (above Darien) and for the high banks that begin upriver about the mouth of the Ohoopee, the east side of the Altamaha is generally characterized by networks of creeks, sloughs, bogs, and immense swamps that easily overflow.

The area directly across from Beards Bluff is low but immediately beyond it and upriver a bit there are some rises that are among the highest and most striking river bluffs in Georgia.

The comparatively easy approach to the river from the east coupled with the accessible high banks on the western side combined to make Beards Bluff a noted crossing point on the Altamaha in early years. There apparently was no ford at the place and travellers had to get over the river as best they could by swimming, floating across on rafts or logs, using hide-away canoes, and so on. But the same methods would also have had to be employed at most other crossings, which did not have the advantageous approaches offered by the Beards Bluff site.

The Indians used the Beards Bluffs crossing since several important trails converged there. This situation attracted traders and a man named William Clark is known to have maintained a post there in 1785.[1] Due to the accessibility of the place by both land and water, it seems reasonable to think there were other traders at the place long before that date, but they can not definitely be connected with the site because Beards Bluff was not known by that name till shortly before the Revolution. The designation of the place prior to that time is not known.

During the Revolution and for many years afterward it was necessary to watch Beards Bluff to prevent Indian incursions into white settlements. Even earlier, in fact, as will be seen, Oglethorpe directed this area of the Altamaha to be guarded against the Spaniards and their Indian supporters. In 1777 troops under a Lieutenant Bugg were sent to the spot.[2] On the way they were ambushed beside Beards Creek and forced to retreat with a loss of three men.[3] Captain Chesley Bostwick was then dispatched to the bluff with a company under orders to build a stockade there.[4]

This structure, if built, apparently fell into ruins. In 1784 Timothy Barnard wrote Indians claimed a fort was being built at Beards Bluff, a report he discounted as a rumor,[5] because Barnard was familiar with the place. He traded there for salt and other goods and a trail bearing his name led there from his home on Flint River,[6] below our Oglethorpe in present Macon County. The Indians did give trouble in the 1780's. In 1788, a group of whites from Liberty County pursued a party of 20 marauding warriors within two miles of the bluff and killed two of them.[7] The posse turned back but somewhere between Beards Bluff and the later Macon-Darien stage road, four miles from the river, the party was counter-attacked or ambushed and had a man killed.[8]

As a result of such troubles there was a fort at Beards Bluff at least by 1790. Through the generosity of friends, the Georgia Department of Archives and History has recently acquired original sketches showing the ground plan and elevations of the structure.[9] These sketches indicate that the fort faced "north," which would be east in present-day terminology relating to locations on banks of rivers.

On occasion one can see references to an Indian treaty held at Beards Bluff in 1795 between James Seagrove (Indian agent before Benjamin Hawkins took over that position in 1796) and some Creek chiefs. This "treaty" did not involve formal negotiations over a land cession but was primarily a conference with the chiefs about the return of stolen or runaway slaves.[10]

The exact derivations of the names Beards Bluff and Beards Creek are not known but the source apparently can be narrowed to one of three men called Beard who are mentioned in connection with the general area. One of these was Edmund Beard, who petitioned for a grant of land in 1768 at Dukes Pond in present northwest Jenkins County.[11] Edmund failed to take up the land in the allotted time and in 1772 it was granted to another man.[12] Dukes Pond was near a noted crossing on the Ogeechee that later became known as Triplets Ferry and which will be mentioned shortly. A trail led from this crossing southward to Beards Bluff and perhaps Beard drifted down this route and resided at the bluff or upon the creek and left his name on them. More likely though the places were named for either George or Matthew Beard who lived nearer by[13] in St. Johns Parish that later became Liberty County, the original county in which Beards Bluff stands.

In late 1796, pursuant to Article III of the Treaty of Colerain signed with the Creeks in that year,[14] United States troops began construction of a fort, upon Indian land, on the west side of the Altamaha, about a mile above Beards Bluff. The structure was completed in early 1797. It was called Fort James[15] and placed in charge of an Ensign Thomson with 25 men in the command.[16]

Although a trail led to a point directly opposite Beards Bluff, that west-bank site was not a good location for a fort because of danger from floods. The federal troops, therefore, moved upstream and built Fort James on a commanding height that borders on the river. The site is still remembered as Fort James Bluff.

Fort James was primarily established as a trading post and military station to guard the Beards Bluff crossing but probably it was also erected to prevent infiltrating white people from crossing the Altamaha to trespass on Indian lands.

Fort James was never of great importance. Some officers and soldiers who constructed it went on to build Fort Wilkinson on the Oconee, below Milledgeville. This place, which was also erected pursuant to the Treaty of Colerain,[17] became one of the famous frontier forts of Georgia with a subsequent important impact on the area where it stood. Fort James occupied a beautiful site but it had little influence on the ultimate growth of surrounding communities, and in fact is now a detached site considerably removed from any present-day town.

The precise location of Fort James is not certain. The original surveyor of the area in 1819-1820 failed to show or mention the place in his plats or field notes,[18] presumably because the former site did not fall directly on the course of a surveyed line.[19] An old pencilled notation on an early official map names and shows the fort in the northeast corner of lot 380 of District 3 of Appling (now a part of Wayne) County.[20] This indicated location is doubted. The original plat for lot 380 shows the "River Trail" and "Barnett's [Barnard's] Trail"[21] converging in the lower part of the lot, to the south of the purported site of Fort James.[22] Since these united trails passed the fort, and since they led on to the edge of the bluff, in adjoining fractional lot 381,[23] it is believed the fort was in that lot and not in No. 380.

Another official map dated in 1869,[24] shows Fort James opposite and down a bit from Beards Bluff in lot 337 of District 3. This location is incorrect since lot 337 is in a swamp across from the bluff. All reliable maps and documents mentioning Fort James refer to it as being above Beards Bluff and the retained name Fort James Bluff plainly indicates the site was upriver a short distance and not opposite the bluff.

Two interesting names that stem from the Fort James site and the approach to Beards Bluff on the west side are Five Mile Creek and Ten Mile Creek.[25] The former stream, which now serves as the boundary between Wayne and Appling, was five miles from Fort James Bluff, measured along the course of the former River Trail, while Ten Mile Creek in Appling County was that distance on the same route. Farther along, the original surveys also show a Fifteen Mile Creek in Appling.[26] This name has disappeared from present maps and apparently the little stream has become today's Bay Branch.

Running east and west across Turner and Irwin counties, there are strips of an early path that is remembered as the Ten Mile Trail.[27] It may have received the name because it was connected with a Ten Mile Creek in present south Pulaski County. Since the remnants of the old path in Irwin have an easterly bearing, however it seems more likely that the trail led toward the Ten Mile stream of Appling. The route may have been called Ten Mile instead of Five Mile (the nearer stream to Fort James) because there were trail forkings on Ten Mile and presumably travellers needed to know where the turns were located.

About six miles down the Altamaha from the Fort James locality, where the bluffs paralleling the river swing back to the edge of the stream after curving around the outer rim of a wide swamp, there is a beautiful and imposing rise bordering directly on the river which is known as Oglethorpe Bluff. The appellation has long been used. It is not mentioned in the field notes or plats of the original survey of 1819-1820, but it is shown on the Eleazer Early map of 1818.[28] A local version for the origin of the designation holds the site was named for Oglethorpe because the General once rode over the bluff into the river while being pursued by Seminoles. This story is far-fetched, of course. In fact, no documentary sources could be found to show Oglethorpe ever personally visited this part of the Altamaha.

But the age of the name suggests a relationship of Oglethorpe to the bluff that is not now clear. A possible connection can be found in an early colonial trading post of Jacob Matthews which was called Mount Venture and which Oglethorpe in 1741 directed to be used as a station to guard the middle Altamaha section against an invasion from Indians or Spaniards. The General assigned 20 rangers to the place and appointed Matthews a captain to command the detail.[29] Matthews in turn named William Francis his lieutenant.[30] Actual command devolved on the latter because Matthews became too ill to serve.[31] In 1742 while Francis was away in Frederica, a band of Yemassee Indians, presumably inspired by the Spaniards, surprised the post, massacred all of the occupants including Francis' wife and child,[32] and burned the place.[33] Oglethorpe wrote the destruction of the fort opened an access into the settlements and that he would strive to build a stronger place at the passage.[34] This statement indicates Mount Venture was situated at a well-known crossing that was regularly available for use. Such a condition would not apply to Oglethorpe Bluff, since the east side of the river opposite it is especially wide, swampy, and subject to overflow. Mount Venture, then, was probably at some other place and most likely, one thinks, at either Doctortown or the Fort James site. Maps which show and name Mount Venture are not helpful in determining its precise location. A 1763 chart by Yonge and DeBrahm depict it on the west bank of the Altamaha in a position which might have been either Doctortown or Oglethorpe Bluff.[35] Another map, however, shows the mount higher up the Altamaha at a place that could have been Fort James Bluff.[36] A third map prepared in 1748 places Mount Venture on the east side of the river in the vicinity of Beards Bluff.[37] This depiction is questioned. Yonge and DeBrahm were surveyors general of the province and it seems likely they were correct in showing the place on the west side of the Altamaha and closer to the site of today's Doctortown than to either of the other possible locations. Furthermore, as shown in the prior sketch No. 107, on Doctortown and related places, there was an important trail leading directly south from that locality into Florida. This route might well have been followed by Spaniards and their Indian allies to attack the English. The fact remains, though, that the Beards Bluff–Fort James site was a better crossing than either Doctortown or Oglethorpe Bluff, and Mount Venture may well have been located there. Seemingly the exact location of the place cannot be determined until more precise documentary references to it can be found. It does seem reasonably certain, however, that it was at one of the three places discussed, with available evidence pointing to either Doctortown or the Fort James Bluff as the most likely site.

A final matter of geographical and historical importance should be mentioned about Beards Bluff and Beards Creek. The mouth of the stream and the upper end of the bluff was a corner on the most abstrusely worded Indian land cession in Georgia's history. At the treaty of Augusta in 1773 the Creeks and Cherokees jointly ceded a very large section of upper Georgia that eventually became original

Wilkes County. At the same time the Creeks ceded a substantial area between the Ogeechee and the Altamaha that embodied parts of present Long, Liberty, Bulloch, Tattnall, Evans, Emanuel + Candler, Bryan, and Jenkins counties. The white commissioners and the Creek chiefs at the treaty probably understood well the courses of the cession because there was no subsequent dispute about the boundaries although viewed in present-day light the conveyance is notable for the vague description of the applicable boundary lines.

The text states the Lower Creeks ceded from the mouth of "Phinhotaway" (Penholoway) Creek[38] on the Altamaha, thence up river to an island opposite Barber Creek, thence across to Ogeechee River opposite to a road about four miles above Buckhead where a canoe ferry used to be kept.[39] Here description of the boundary ended but it can be safely assumed the line was supposed to turn down the Ogeechee to a point below our Scarboro, thence across country to the Altamaha on the course of a previous boundary that was run in 1768 pursuant to the treaty of Augusta in 1763. The route of this line will be traced shortly in more detail, but it is necessary to note here that it was originally expected that this 1763 line would run to the Sansavilla Bluffs. Later, however, after some additional negotiations by Governor Wright with the Creeks the destination at the Altamaha was moved upriver to a point opposite the mouth of Penholoway Creek. Ultimately though, due to some further arrangements by Wright with Captain Alleck (the central figure in names discussed in Sketch No. 107), the 1768 surveyor shifted the promulgated boundary northward and reached the river across from Doctortown and upstream some ten miles direct from the mouth of the Penholoway. Practically speaking, then, in the 1768 survey, the whites took over the intervening area between Penholoway Creek and Doctortown. For this reason the tracing of the boundaries of the 1773 cession can start opposite the latter place and not across from Penholoway Creek.

Beginning opposite Doctortown, the 1773 line led up the Altamaha to the island at the mouth of Beards Creek and opposite Beards Bluff. The drafters of the treaty were confused when they wrote Barber Creek instead of Beards Creek. The latter name apparently had only recently come into use and the authorities were not certain of the designation. Beards Creek is sure to have been the stream intended, because when original Washington County was created in 1783, from the Creek cession of that year, it extended down to the creek, as did Montgomery which was taken from Washington in 1793. Original Tattnall in turn was cut entirely from Montgomery in 1801 and its extreme southwest boundary has always been Beards Creek. Furthermore, despite contrary depiction by certain maps, original Liberty County extended to Beards Creek and it cornered at the mouth of the stream.[40]

The wording of the 1773 cession suggests the boundary was to run from the island at Barber Creek to the Ogeechee on a direct line, but actually it followed Beards Creek as evidenced by the fact original Washington and later Tattnall bordered on it. The course of the line between the head of Beards Creek and the stipulated point on the Ogeechee is conjectural since no evidence could be found to show it was ever surveyed. But the destination on the Ogeechee is known, and to reach that site it seems likely the boundary ran from the head of Beards Creek along the dividing ridge between the waters of the Canoochee and the Ohoopee to a point in the vicinity of Swainsboro where the line veered northeastward to reach the designated canoe ferry crossing mentioned in the treaty and which was in our Jenkins County. One suspects, but could not confirm with documentary sources, that the first settlers of the 1773 cession area considered the line as far as the head of Beards Creek as identical with an early trail that led from the canoe crossing on the Ogeechee to Beards Bluff.

Two rare post-Revolutionary plats disclose the 1773 boundary line reached the Ogeechee immediately below the mouth of the Deep Creek, in present western Jenkins County, at a place about a mile and a half below today's Herndon. The point is shown in a 1784 plat for land of James Pugh of Effingham County.[41] The place on the river reached by the western border of Pugh's property is marked "Old Indian Corner." The site is certain to have been the turning point for the 1773 line because no other Indian treaty prescribed a corner on this part of the Ogeechee.

As noted, Pugh's land was in Effingham County, whereas the adjoining property to the west, beyond the Old Indian Corner, was in Washington. This is shown on the plat for the adjacent land which was granted to James Hudson in 1784.[42] His plat names Deep Creek and immediately over the east boundary, on Pugh's side, at the Old Indian Corner, it shows "Triplets Ferry." This crossing became well known in post-Revolutionary years and there is little doubt it was the successor to the former canoe ferry crossing mentioned in the 1773 treaty.

The Indian corner, at old Triplets Ferry, is a bit over eight miles from Buckhead Creek that reaches the Ogeechee immediately to the west of Millen. It will be recalled the treaty mentions the canoe ferry crossing as being about four miles above Buckhead. There appears to be a discrepancy here, but this would not be the case if the treaty referred to the estimated distance of the canoe ferry upriver from the outer limits of the Buckhead settlement about the mouth of Buckhead Creek and not from the creek itself.

It should be recalled again that James Pugh's land was in original Effingham where that county bounded original Washington. The point merits repeating since geographers, cartographers, and historians have long been puzzled about the limits of original Effingham up the Ogeechee. It should be added too, that prior to the creation of Effingham in 1777, the old Indian corner on Pugh's land subsequent to the 1773 treaty also became the northern limit of St. Philips Parish. Following the treaty of that year, the boundary of the parish was automatically extended up the Ogeechee from its original location on the river near today's Scarboro, at the lower end of Paramore Hill that stretches along the east side of the river.[43]

To continue tracing the 1773 boundary, the line ran down the south side of the Ogeechee to a point opposite the lower end of an island located about three-quarters of a mile below the old Scarboro bridge site. Here the boundary intersected the line of the 1763 Creek cession as finally run in 1768 by surveyor Samuel Savery. Since the 1773 cession ceded lands to the west and north of this boundary as far as the Altamaha, the 1768 and 1773 boundaries became identical between the Ogeechee and the former river. Thus by tracing Savery's 1768 line to the Altamaha, it is possible to close the boundary of the 1773 cession.

There are published bearings for the 1768 survey by Savery but the figures are confused.[44] Savery's map, however, prepared subsequent to the survey and approved by the supervising commissioners gives a good description of the course.[45] Starting at the point below Scarboro, where the two boundaries joined, the Savery line ran southward parallel with the Ogeechee and about five miles back from the river until it crossed Black Creek[46] and Mill Creek in present upper Bryan County, near the Bulloch line. Then it veered southwest to reach the Canoochee just above the mouth of Savage Creek. The 1763 cession line had been marked thus far in 1766, but the Indians and white commissioners became involved in a dispute about the remainder of the course to the Altamaha. The Creek chiefs expected to continue to the mouth of Penholoway Creek, but the white commissioners at Governor Wright's request wanted to shift the line to the north to incorporate some goose ponds in today's Liberty County that had become important ranging areas for settlers' stock. By the time Savery took over the surveying in 1768 the matter of embodying the ponds had been adjusted with the Indians. Instead of continuing toward Penholoway Creek, Savery went up the Canoochee two miles and ran a line westward past the Hinesville area as far as upper Horse Creek near the present Liberty-Long boundary. Since this course cleared the goose ponds, Savery turned the boundary slightly southward, thence past the upper side of present Ludowici, thence close along the course of U.S. 82-25 to a point opposite the Indian settlement of Doctor's Town, at the site of our Doctortown on the Altamaha, in Wayne County. The 1773 line thus ended on the east side of the river opposite that place. Savery and his party dropped down the Altamaha a mile and a half and continued their 1768 line southward to the St. Marys. This survey, though, had no subsequent relation to the 1773 cession and need not be traced here.

—*GMNL* 18(1964): 60-66

NOTES

1. Letter of John Carr, Coweta, April 7, 1785, MS Vol. "Creek Indian Letters, 1705-1793," pt. 1, p. 70, Department of Archives and History, Atlanta.
2. Hugh McCall, *The History of Georgia* (Savannah, 1816), 2: 97.
3. *Ibid.*
4. *Ibid.*
5. Barnard to Maj. Patrick Carr, Flint River, April 13, 1784, MS Vol. "Letters of Timothy Barnard," pp. 29-31, Department of Archives and History, Atlanta.
6. Eleazer Early, "Map of the State of Georgia," 1818, drawn by Daniel Sturges.
7. Col. D. Stewart to Col. James Maxwell, Newport, Liberty County, Sept. 26, 1788, "Creek Indian Letters," pt. 1, pp. 181-82.
8. *Ibid.*
9. The sketches were acquired from a dealer. It is not known who kept them during the intervening years.
10. Claim of James Smith, Oct. 1, 1821, "Indian Depredations, 1787-1825," Vol. 2, pt. 2, pp. 610-11, Department of Archives and History, Atlanta.
11. Allen D. Candler, ed., *Colonial Records of Georgia* (Atlanta: Franklin, 1904-1916), 10: 618-19, petition of Oct. 4, 1768. Beard said he had been in the colony six months and asked for 100 acres.
12. *Ibid.*, 12: 166, petition of Rev. Timothy Lowten, Jan. 7, 1772. The original approval of Beard's petition was made contingent upon his taking out a grant in seven months. He failed to exercise this right.
13. *Ibid.*, p. 269, petition of George "Beaird" for some 300 acres, in St. Johns Parish, approved April 7, 1772; and Grant Book M, p. 158, grant of 200 acres to Matthew Beard in St. Johns, Aug. 2, 1774, Land Records of Georgia, Surveyor General Department, Atlanta.

14. Charles J. Kappler, *Indian Affairs, Laws and Treaties*, Senate Doc. 319, 58th Cong., 2nd Sess., Vol. II, pp. 46ff., Treaty of Colerain, June 29, 1796.

15. *Letters of Benjamin Hawkins, 1796-1806*, Collections of the Georgia Historical Society, Vol. 9 (Savannah, 1916), p. 65. In late colonial years, there was another Fort James, at the site of Dartmouth, later Petersburg, in the forks of the Broad and Savannah rivers.

16. *Ibid.*

17. Kappler, *Laws and Treaties*, Treaty of Colerain, Art. IV.

18. Plats for District 3, Appling County, Platbook JJJ; and field notes for the same district, survey of 1819-1820, Joshua Coffee, D.S., Land Records of Georgia.

19. The land lots for original Appling were 490 acres in size and were much larger than most Georgia lots. Surveyor Coffee could easily have missed the site and failed to mention it.

20. Map of District 3 of Appling redrawn in 1866 by N. C. Barnett. The restoration of the map indicates Surveyor John Coffee's original 1820 map of District 3 was damaged or lost prior to 1866.

21. The name was properly Barnard's Trail, for Timothy Barnard, the Indian countryman. For some reason this man's name was commonly written as Barnet or Barnett.

22. Plat for lot 380, Platbook JJJ.

23. Plat for fractional lot 381, *ibid.*

24. B. W. Frobel, original map of Appling County, 1869, *ibid.*; made by authority of the state.

25. Plats for District 3, Appling, *ibid.*

26. *Ibid.*

27. Elderly people in these counties remember this route, but published references to it are rare. John Ben Pate in his *History of Turner County* (Atlanta, 1933), p. 9, makes a brief comment on it.

28. "Map of the State of Georgia."

29. Candler, ed., *Colonial Records*, 5: 485, "Journal of the Earl of Egmont."

30. *Ibid.*, pp. 485-86.

31. *Ibid.*

32. *Ibid.*, p. 657.

33. Oglethorpe to the Duke of Newcastle, Frederica, Nov. 24, 1742, MS Vol. 35, Colonial Records of Georgia, p. 544, Department of Archives and History, Atlanta.

34. *Ibid.*

35. Henry Yonge and W. G. DeBrahm, "A Map of the Sea Coast of Georgia and the inland parts thereof . . . ," 1763, William L. Clements Library, Ann Arbor, Mich.

36. Map showing South Carolina, Georgia, and upper east Florida, *circa* 1780, in Land Records of Georgia. This map may have been prepared by DeBrahm.

37. Emanuel Bowen's map of the Georgia country, 1748, from Harris, *Voyages and Travels*, Vol. II, photocopy in the Ivan Allen Collection, Special Collections Department, Emory University Library.

38. For a discussion of Penholoway Creek, see Sketch No. 8, above. The name has become distorted over the years. It should be Fenholoway, since it signifies high crossing, referring to a high footlog crossing place.

39. Treaty of Augusta, June 1, 1773, MS Vol. 39, Colonial Records of Georgia, p. 498; and MS Vol. "Indian Treaties, 1705-1837," p. 72.

Beards Bluff / 313

40. The wording of the statute creating Liberty County is vague (see Marbury and Crawford, *Digest of the Laws of the State of Georgia, 1755-1800*, p. 6 and p. 151), but the extension of original Washington as far south as Beard's Creek makes it plain the stream was also the boundary of Liberty.
41. Platbook B, p. 207, Land Records of Georgia.
42. Washington County, survey of July 4, 1784, Platbook A, p. 331.
43. For a discussion of Paramores Hill, see Sketch No. 38, above.
44. See Charles C. Royce, *Indian Land Cessions in the United States*, 18th Annual Report of the Bureau of American Ethnology, pt. 2, p. 638.
45. Samuel Savery, D.S., "Sketch of the Boundary Line between the Province of Georgia and the Creek Nation, 1769," copy in the Special Collections Department of the Emory University Library.
46. For a discussion of Black Creek, see Sketch No. 105, above.

No. 109
Amicalola Creek, Amicalola Falls (and the Former Cherokee Community of Bread Town)

Amicalola Creek arises in northwest Dawson County, toward the western end of the Blue Ridge, and flows southward to join the Etowah River in the lower part of the same county. On its way it follows a winding course through a broken, hilly section. The upper east fork of the stream, called Little Amicalola Creek, begins on top of the Blue Ridge and then spills over its steep eastern front in a slow, bouncing descent of hundreds of feet to form the beautiful and noted Amicalola Falls. These feathery cascades gave rise to the name because Amicalola means tumbling water, from the Cherokee *amá*, water and *kalóla*, tumbling, rolling, or slow-moving.

In the present form Amicalola is an attractive word and is pronounced "Ammy ka lo' la", or "Ammy kuh lō lee'" by some of the people living around the stream and falls. It is doubted if any one today would want to change the present name, but it now differs substantially from the way pioneer surveyors and Indian country white men first heard it and spelled it. They recorded the expression as Ummah cololake, Umakeololake, Ahma co lo la, Armicalola, Armeca-cola, Armicalolo, Amuclalalah, and Amakalola. This last version was noted by an original surveyor of Cherokee County in 1832[1] and is correctly spelled for proper pronunciation if the word is sounded with broad *a*'s. It will be seen, however, from the other listings that this letter troubled the recorders of the name. Some of them sought to depict it with an *Ar,* while others turned the *a* into an *o* in middle or final syllables of their renditions.

Difficulties of the early white people with the broad *a* or *ä* in the name gave rise to our Amicalola. The chief trouble lay in failing to give the *ama* element of the tab its proper sound. It was pronounced "ahmah," with stress on last syllable. This sort of accentuation is difficult for English-speaking people. Instead of stressing the last syllable of a word like *ama,* we are prone to slur the second vowel into an obscure or uncertain letter. This tendency is plainly reflected in some of the early versions given above wherein *ama* is rendered as "armi," "arme," and "amu." These technicalities explain how Amakalola has come down to us as Amicalola, or "Ammy kalola."

It should be noted that our Amicalola Creek was labelled Amicalola "River" in virtually all of the early references to the stream. The waterway is actually a sizable creek and not a river in the common understanding of that term.

In the last years of the Cherokees here, they had a settlement on the Amicalola which was called Bread Town. This community was on the lower end of the creek, near its juncture with the Etowah, in southwest Dawson County. The site today is encompassed by the reservation of the Lockheed nuclear facility. One has not seen the Cherokee version of Bread Town in old records but most likely it was Gatú-yi, ("gah too' yee") from *gadu'* or *gatu'* bread, and the locative *yi,* place. The reason for the name is not known. It may have stemmed from fertile bottoms along the Etowah and lower Amicalola which permitted an abundant production of corn for bread.

In the final years of the Cherokees some Indians with interesting names lived at Bread Town or along the Amicalola.[2] Among these were Big Coat, Standing Wolf, King Fisher, Heaven (probably for heaving), Waker, Drawing Knife, Stealer, Buzzard, Red Bird, Sconti, Chickanailer, Snip or Cototota, Toyleesa or Beaver Toter, Paunch Lifter, Kullalutta, Blackbird, Kechuaga or Dick Termat, Augoonaneecher or Ground Hog, and Waununka or Short Arrow. The last man's Indian name embodied the word *uwani,* or "wanee," literally signifying hickory, but as evidenced by the English portion of his name, was no doubt intended for arrow, an old ritualistic designation with the Cherokees.[3]

—*GMNL* 18(1964): 66-67

NOTES

1. Map of District 5, Section 2, Cherokee County (now parts of Pickens and Dawson), survey of 1832, Abner Wise, D.S., Land Records of Georgia, Surveyor General Department, Atlanta.
2. As listed in the "Census of Cherokees in the limits of Georgia in 1835," the Henderson Roll, Record Group 75, Records of the Bureau of Indian Affairs, National Archives; and in "Valuations of Cherokee Improvements . . . made under the Treaty of 29 Dec 1835," Record Group 75.
3. [Read, *IJAL* 16 (1950): 203-204, confirms Goff's translation of Amicalola. *FLU.*].

No. 110
Sterling Creek

Any placename, no matter how unimportant it may appear, that has endured since Georgia's first days would merit a discussion in this series. One such appellation is Sterling Creek, a small stream that enters the "south" (west) side of the Ogeechee two miles below Richmond Hill in Bryan County.[1] The little waterway derives its name from two Scotch brothers, William and Hugh Sterling, who received in June, 1734, a 500-acre grant from General Oglethorpe along the Ogeechee at the creek.[2] The Sterlings were two of several Scots that received grants in the same area at the time, but the brothers were the only grantees that moved to their property and started developing it. As a result, for a short period, the Sterlings' place was the most southerly plantation in the English colonies along the Atlantic coast.[3]

The Sterlings became dissatisfied with the remoteness of their settlement and weary with the task of clearing the land. They became early proponents of slavery, but the colonial authorities would not permit the introduction of slaves. After several years the brothers gave up their place and drifted away, leaving their name behind them on Sterling Creek.

Early records mentioned a Sterling Swamp and a Sterling Hill in connection with the brothers' property. Presumably the swamp was the boggy area at the head of the creek. Sterling Hill most likely was the home site of the Scotchmen. Seemingly it was above the creek and not far removed from the spot where Henry Ford later erected his home named Richmond Hill.

This section of Bryan lies in the Coastal Flatwoods Region, one of the flattest parts of the state, but for some odd reason people of the area have long been fond of using the word Hill in their placenames: Sterling Hill, Richmond Hill, Rabbit Hill, Scratchy Hill, and so on.

The grants to the Sterlings and other Scots in what is now Bryan County refute the contention that Oglethorpe's treaty of 1733 with the Creek Indians limited the colony to the area between the Savannah and the Ogeechee. The General would certainly not have jeopardized the good relations which he established with the Creeks through that treaty by making large grants to white people beyond the Ogeechee unless he had a clear right under the agreement to do so.

—*GMNL* 18(1964): 67

NOTES

1. For the location of the creek, see *Limerick Quadrangle* (U.S. Corps of Engineers and the U.S. Geological Survey, ed. 1950).

2. Allen D. Candler, ed., "Journal of the Earl of Egmont," *Colonial Records of Georgia* (Atlanta: Franklin, 1904-1916), 5: 172-73. Another reference verifies that the settlement was at Sterling Creek by mentioning the stream and stating that the Sterlings' land was about five miles above Hardwick—see *Colonial Records,* 8: 370, petition of William Handley, 1760.

3. Candler, ed., *Colonial Records,* 5: 172. Egmont said the brothers were settled "50 miles Southward [by water] of any settlement in the Province." When the Sterlings first went to their place in June, 1734, they were in fact the most southerly settlers in any British colony on the Atlantic coast.

No. 111
Pocataligo

A designation which usually catches the eyes of placename lovers is Pocataligo, a village in northwest Madison County. The word sounds like "Pokey tally go" in the local pronunciation and this version apparently has given rise to two slightly different stories about the origin of the name. As one explanation has it, the expression stems from the advice which an old Negro gave on the way to make a balky mule go by saying "poke 'e tail 'e go." Another account however, had the man saying a sure method to make a closed-up turtle open his shell and move was to "poke 'e tail 'e go."

It could not be learned exactly when Pocataligo was first applied in Madison County, but it is virtually certain the above drolleries do not explain the origin of the name. More than likely Pocataligo is a Yemasee Indian word that was borrowed from an earlier place with the same name in Beaufort County of southern South Carolina where the tab had been in use since the first years of that colony as the designation of a principal Yemasee Indian town.[1]

Following a bloody war with the Carolinians in 1715, the Yemasees left that province and sought refuge among the Spaniards in Florida. The white people eventually moved into the former Yemasee country and adopted the designation Pocataligo that still remains in a town on U.S. 17, in today's upper Beaufort County. Nearby is Pocataligo River that dates from the Yemasee years and also retains the name of the former settlement which stood on the stream.

When the Yemasees quit South Carolina following the war in 1715, it is very unlikely that a band of them removed to the area of Madison County, Georgia, and took the word Pocataligo with them. No documents show any Yemasees in that section, and if they had tried to settle there, either the Creeks or the Cherokees would probably have driven them off. As stated, from what is known of the subsequent movements of the Yemasees, they went to Florida, where they mainly settled in the vicinity of St. Augustine. Thus it is improbable the Indians took the name to the Madison County section. Most likely the word was carried there in post-Revolutionary years by white settlers who emigrated from the South Carolina lowcountry to find a new home on the high, healthy region of the Georgia Piedmont.

An inkling that Carolina settlers moved to the area of Madison County from the Pocataligo River section can be found in the designation of Scull Shoal Creek in Madison, a stream which arises near our village of Pocataligo. Carolina land documents show an Edward Scull received a grant on Pocataligo River in 1732.[2] The surname is so unusual, it is easy to think some of Scull's descendants were among the presumed settlers who removed to what is now Madison County.

The present spelling of Pocataligo, in both Georgia and South Carolina, differs considerably from some of the initial recordings of the names. In early Carolina documents the Yemasee town is mentioned as "Po cot allago," "Pocotalligo," "Pocotallagua," etc.,[3] and old plats of that colony refer to the Pocataligo River as "Pocotuligo," "Pogotallago," "Pocotalago," "Pocotagle," "Pogataligo," "Pocotallago," "Pocotalaugo," and so on.[4]

With the present limited knowledge of the Yemasee tongue, it is not feasible to make a direct positive translation of the Pocataligo forms into English. Since Yemasee and the Creek tongues, however, belonged to the Muskogean linguistic stock and were thus similar in some respects, it has been possible to make meaningful translations of the name by using Creek. It is believed one of these derivations accurately conveys the original meaning of the name. In Creek Pocataligo perhaps signifies Big gathering place town, from *poga*, a gathering place or resort, and the first syllable of *talwa*, town, plus the augmentative suffix *hlako*, big. The last element was difficult for white people to pronounce and they often garbled it into forms like "thlucco," "thlocko," "laka," or "lika."[5] Another possible meaning for Pocataligo is big ball or ball play town, from *pokke*, ball or ball play, + the *tal* of *talwa*, + the suffix *hlako*.

In view of the importance of Pocataligo as the principal Yemasee town in Carolina, one favors the gathering-place version offered above.

Some students of Creek may insist the final element of Pocataligo was derived from the locative *liga*, place, or some kindred Yemasee form, and that the translation should have been either Gathering Place or Ball Place. This version should be rejected because the "lago," "lagua," and "laugo" endings in some of the early renditions of the name indicate the word terminated in *hlako*, or perhaps its Yemasee equivalent, and not in the locative *liga*.

One factor which may have a bearing on the derivations advanced for Pocataligo should be noted. The Pocataligo River once had a small tributary called the Pogasavo.[6] The tab obviously resembles the name of the river but no meanings for the *savo* element can be offered from the Creek language. Maybe it was a Yemasee form that signified little, branch, left fork, or some such meaning. The designation cannot be found on present maps and perhaps has long since been forgotten. In any case, the Pogasavo makes it all the more certain that the origin of Pocataligo had nothing to do with poking a stubborn mule or prodding a reluctant turtle to make them go.

—GMNL 18(1964): 67-68

NOTES

1. For a discussion of the Yemasee Indians in both South Carolina and Georgia, see John R. Swanton, *Early History of the Creek Indians and Their Neighbors*, Bureau of American Ethnology, Bulletin 73, pp. 80ff; and his *Indian Tribes of North America*, Bureau of American Ethnology, Bulletin 145 (Washington, D.C., 1952), pp. 114-16.
2. Plat for Edward Scull's land, survey of 1732, Platbook 1, p. 362, Land Records of South Carolina, Archives Department, Columbia.
3. "Journals of the Commissioners of the Indian Trade, 1710-1718," *Colonial Records of South Carolina*, pp. 8, 12, 25, 31, *passim*.
4. Platbook 1, pp. 90, 98, 144, 362, 508, *passim*, Land Records of South Carolina.
5. It will be noted there was an alternation of the letters *g*, *k*, and hard *c* in the various names mentioned in the sketch. The interchange of these letters in Indian names was common.
6. Land of Edward Scull, Platbook 1, p. 362, Land Records of South Carolina.

No. 112
Muckalee Creek and Some of Its Tributaries

Muckalee Creek is a fine, large stream which heads in Marion and Schley counties to drain across Sumter and Lee into Dougherty County where it joins Kinchafoonee Creek some three miles above the latter's mouth on Flint River at Albany. The name is derived from a Chehaw town which once stood beside the creek.[1] The Chehaw band of Indians belonged to the Hitchitee subtribe of the Creek Confederacy.

Muckalee is a unique Indian designation because it is one remaining Georgia placename which certainly embodies the Hitchitee word *okli*, *ulki*, or *okalee*, that is usually taken to mean people or town, but which on occasion may also be interpreted as signifying home, abode, retreat, or den. Another appellation which seemingly contains *okli* is Ochlawilla, as found in the names of two church sites in Brooks and Lowndes counties that are located near the Withlacoochee River. For a time one was convinced that Ochlawilla did in fact embody *okli*, but some recent evidence indicates the word may be derived from a garbled version of the Hitchitee name for the Withlacoochee.

Colonel Benjamin Hawkins, as in so many other instances involving Georgia Indian designations, was the first person to mention the Muckalee and offer an explanation for the name. He spelled it "Aumuc-cu-le" and stated it signified "pour upon me."[2] Seemingly he assumed the expression was derived from the Creek *okâlkâh,* pour, or by reason of the *okâ* element, pour water on. Albert Gatschet realized that Muckalee was not Creek but instead of properly attributing it to the Hitchitees, he wrote it was derived from the Cherokee word *amicalola*[3] (water descending or tumbling) as found in the designation of the noted falls and a creek in Dawson County. Gatschet was an able scholar and a pioneer student of the Indian languages of this area. He had a knowledge of Hitchitee and should have known better than to offer such an explanation for Muckalee since there is no relation between that word and *amicalola* save for a slight similarity in the English versions of the appellations. Furthermore, it is likely that Muckalee as a well-established name among the Hitchitees has been in use longer than Amicalola since the Creek treaty of 1739 at Coweta mentions a Chehaw place named Occullaveche which may reasonably be taken as a distorted version of Muckalee.

Muckalee plainly means something like my people or my town or perhaps my home, and is derived from the Hitchitee *am,* my + *okli, okalee,* or *ukli,* town, people, etc. In the Indian mind any of the translations probably signified the same thing. The comprehensive French expression *chez moi* conveys the meaning of Muckalee more succinctly than any of the English expressions.

Muckalee as now spelled is a slurred word, but its derivation and change into its present form can be seen in the varying listings of the name as recorded by the first official surveyors of original Lee County when that section was laid off in 1826-1827, after cession of the area by the Creeks. The surveyors' records give the name variously as "Amaculle," "Amacalle," "Mucalee," "Mucala," "Muckulle," "Mucklee," etc.[4] The last version if pronounced with an initial broad *a* would be nearly identical with Amokli, the original and correct name. One surveyor had trouble with the word and spelled it three different ways: "Amucale," "Amakullee," and "Muccallee."[5] The last name is close phonetically to the present word.

The above listings commencing with "Am" confirm that the name once began with the Hitchitee *am,* my. Elision of the initial *a* in placenames was a common practice in early years, and omission of the beginning *a* in Muckalee is of long standing because the tab was mentioned in 1797 as "McCullee."[6]

The Muckalee has numbers of tributaries with interesting names. Chief among these is Muckaloochee Creek that arises in western Sumter and joins the main stream to the north of Leesburg, in Lee County. The *oochee* ending in the name is the Creek diminutive suffix *uchi* which turns the expression into Little Muckalee in English. Interestingly enough, the upper west fork of Muckaloochee is now called Little Muckaloochee. People about the stream perhaps are unaware that the English modifier turns the full expression tautologically into "Little Muckalee little." On the 1827 surveys the Little Muckaloochee was listed as Hendricks Creek and was named for a member of the surveying party.[7] It was fairly common for a frontier surveyor in need of a label for an unknown stream to name it after one of his assistants. The east fork of upper Muckaloochee was originally marked Wolf Creek by the surveyor of that district.[8] Today this designation applies to another tributary to the west of Americus that is also called McMaths Mill Branch. The surveyor marked the latter stream Camp Creek,[9] perhaps because he maintained headquarters on it during the survey.

In addition to Muckaloochee and Little Muckaloochee there is also a Little Muckalee which joins the main stream to the north of Americus. On the first survey of the area this tributary was listed by one surveyor as the "Taulagee"[10] which can be taken as the Creek word *telogi*, signifying pea or wild peavines for a native browse plant of importance to stock-raisers. Today's Parkers Mill Creek of upper Sumter was once another Muckaloochee according to the original surveys.[11] Its tributary, the present Angelica Creek, may have borne the same name in Indian form as Notosahatchie, but if this were the case, the surveyor failed to catch the word, for he merely labelled the stream Creek. It seems reasonable to think the waterway was known as Notosahatchie, because roots of the Angelica plant were important to the Creeks in making one of their principal medicines or for adding to smoking tobacco. It was common for Indians to name a stream or site for a medicinal plant which could be found in such places.

Present Mill Creek, an east-bank affluent of the Muckalee located to the south of Americus, was called Tululgah in Indian days.[12] The word means where palmettoes abound, and approximately represented our expression Palmetto Branch. The plant is not now plentiful along Mill Creek, but the name clearly indicates it was once common on the stream. In the wilderness years, young palmetto shoots were eaten by stock when some better forage plants such as cane or peavines were not available. Furthermore, the Indians of lower Georgia used mature palmetto fronds to thatch their huts, and since Indians often named waterways for useful things that could be found along their banks, it seems clear why the Tululgah was so named.

Today's Philema Creek which joins Muckalee below Americus was marked as Beaverdam Creek on the first surveys.[13] It would be interesting to know how Philema came to replace Beaverdam as the designation for the stream. Philema was a Chehaw chief who distrusted the white people. Most references to him place him farther south in Lee County, on the lower Muckalee or at the old Pindertown on Flint River. Some references represent Philema as a rogue or villain, and seemingly he did engage in cattle-rustling and trouble-making for the whites, but part of the abuse directed at him probably stemmed from his reluctance to cede lands to the Americans. His name is still perpetuated in a little spot called Philema in Lee County. The name of both the creek and the place is locally pronounced "Flim' Mee".

On the west side of Muckalee, up from Philema Creek, there is a small stream named Bear Branch. The Indians called it the Oaheathla.[14] This expression does not embody the word for bear in either Hitchitee or Creek but the *heathla* element was derived from *huihli*, *weathlee*, or *weethly*, meaning standing. The *oa* part however, is so brief no satisfactory meaning can be offered for it to indicate the thing that was standing.

Farther down, in Lee County, the Muckalee is joined on the east by Five Mile Branch or Creek. This stream was called the Saoxomoha by the Indians. The name signifies Hog Potato and has already been sketched in this series.[15] And still lower down, also joining on the east is Fox Creek. This name was listed by the first surveyor.[16] It may be a translated word or it may have been named by the surveyor because he saw or killed a fox on the stream. After the Muckalee joins Kinchafoonee Creek, the united streams down to Flint River are sometimes referred to as the Muckafoonee. The moniker has been in use a considerable time, but it is a white man's coined or synthetic appellation that is meaningless in the Indian tongue since Muckalee means my town while Kinchafoonee signifies mortar bone or pestle, from *kicho* ("keecho"), pestle + *funi*, bone.

Although the aboriginal names mentioned were in a former Hitchitee area, the expressions given, with the exception of Muckalee, appear to be more Creek than Hitchitee. Another curiosity is the absence of the word *hachi*, or *hatchie*, stream, in connection with the names of the waterways. Since Muskogean peoples ordinarily used *hatchie* with their stream designations, a lack of the form in connection with the Muckalee and tributaries is noticeable. Perhaps the waterways had the Hitchitee version *hahchi* attached to them and the white surveyors failed to use the tab because they found it hard to pronounce and difficult to depict in English. This situation arose because the second *h* of *hahchi* (coming before another consonant, *ch*) took a gutteral sound which occurs in the Scotch or German tongues but not in English. Indeed, we have no adequate letter to represent the sound, and it is easy to believe the surveyors simply skipped the word, if they heard it in the names.

In conclusion, it should be noted there is now a place called Immokalee in Collier County, Florida, where some of the Seminoles live. The name contains an extra *m*, but it is from *im*, his + *okli*, or okalee, meaning His Town, or His People. Again, as in the case of *chez moi* for Muckalee, the French *chez lui* represents the meaning of Immokalee better than the English equivalents.

One final point should be made about Muckalee. The reader no doubt noticed resemblance of the original form Amokli to the "Okla" of present-day Oklahoma. The names are similar because Oklahoma is a Choctaw word meaning red people. Choctaw and the Hitchitee dialect of the Creeks are similar because both languages belong to the Muskogean linguistic stock.[17]

—GMNL 18(1964): 68-70

NOTES

1. Benjamin Hawkins, *A Sketch of the Creek Country in the Years 1798 and 1799*, Collections of the Georgia Historical Society, Vol. 3, pt. 1 (Savannah, 1848), p. 64; and *Letters of Benjamin Hawkins, 1796-1806*, Collections of the Georgia Historical Society, Vol. 9 (Savannah, 1916), p. 172. In the first source Hawkins stated the town was 9 miles up the Muckalee; in the second he noted it was 15 miles up the creek.

2. Hawkins, *Creek Country*, p. 64.

3. Albert S. Gatschet, *Towns and Villages of the Creek Confederacy in the XVIII and XIX Centuries*, Miscellaneous Collections of the Alabama Historical Society, Vol. 1 (1901), pp. 387-415 (392).

4. Plats, land maps, and field notes for Districts 1, 2, 13, 15, 16, 17, 26, 27, 30, and 31 of original Lee County, surveys of 1826-1827, Land Records of Georgia, Surveyor General Department, Atlanta.

5. Plats for District 26, Lee County, survey of 1826, David Dean, D.S., Platbook TTTT.

6. *Letters of Benjamin Hawkins*, affidavit of Robert Walton, dated Nov. 20, 1797, p. 245.

7. Field Notes for District 17, Lee County, survey of 1826, Felix P. Gibson, D.S. Jack Hendricks was listed as a chain carrier for the district.

8. *Ibid.* and Platbook SSSS, showing District 17 of Lee.

9. District 26, Lee County, Platbook TTTT.

10. *Ibid.*

11. District 27, Lee County, survey of 1826, Charles Evans, D.S., Platbook TTTT.
12. District 27, Lee County, continued in Platbook UUUU, lots 202 and 235.
13. Plats and map for District 16, Lee County, survey of 1827, Thomas J. Meriwether, D.S., lots 144, 145, 162, *passim.*
14. *Ibid.,* lot 78; and lot 93 at the mouth of the creek.
15. See Sketch No. 86, above.
16. Field Notes, District 13, Lee County, survey of 1826, W. Gaddy, D.S.
17. [Read, *IJAL,* 16 (1950): 205, accepts Hawkins' "pour upon me" for Muckalee and scores Gatschet as Goff does, but does not proceed with Goff to the *chez moi* meaning. *FLU.*]

No. 113
The Tobler Creeks and the Poor Robin Places

The origins of some of Georgia's most interesting placenames are so obscure, one is often tempted to follow mere hints in seeking possible meanings or derivations for such tabs. Take for instance the Tobler creeks. There are presently three streams of this name in the state and a fourth waterway that once bore the designation but which has now become distorted in spelling. The word Tobler is correctly pronounced "Tōbe ler," but here and there in the areas of the creeks the expression may be heard as "Tōbe ly." As will be seen shortly the appellation may have been derived from the surname of a South Carolina family of Swiss extraction.

It is not unusual to find a repetition of waterway names in Georgia, but the singular location of the Tobler creeks with respect to each other creates one of Georgia's geographic curiosities. All of the streams are direct tributaries of major rivers and in each instance the mouths of the creeks are situated east or west of each other on a slightly curving line that can be drawn westwardly across the state from the Savannah to Flint River.

One of the Tobler creeks arises in northwest Baldwin County and reaches the Oconee at the upper edge of Milledgeville. Another stream with the name originates in south Monroe County, near Bolingbroke, and joins the west side of the Ocmulgee to the south of Popes Ferry on Georgia 87. The third and largest of the Tobler creeks begins in Lamar County and flows across Upson to unite with Flint River about three miles above the bridge on U.S. 19-80. The lower part of the latter creek is sometimes labelled Swift Creek on charts, but its first recorded name was Tobler Creek and it appears under this designation on many maps.

All three of these Tobler creeks were listed on the original and official state surveys of the area in which they lie.[1] The fourth stream, a tributary of the Savannah River, is now called Jobley or Jobleys Creek. It heads to the north of Girard in Burke County and joins the river in the same county. The stream was first mentioned as Toblers Creek or Branch on early plats.[2] The area about the creek's mouth was also listed as Toblers Bottoms.[3] By late post-Revolutionary years the name began to undergo a change in spelling by being shifted to Toblar, Jobbler, Joblers, and finally to the present Jobleys. The switching of an initial t to a j (or sometimes to a ch), as occurred in this name was not uncommon in former years, although such changes were usually confined to Indian words.[4]

It is not known exactly why the Tobler creeks were so called, but their unusual location east and west of each other was not happen-so, because the three streams which retain the name were all linked by an Indian trail called Toms Path. This route with some important adjacent and connecting ways, has already been discussed in this series.[5] The eastern end of Toms Path is subject to some conjecture, but at and between the Oconee, Ocmulgee, and Flint rivers, the course of the trail is known. In each instance where the path crossed those rivers it went over at a shoally Fall Line fording place which was located at the mouth of one of the Tobler creeks.

East of the Oconee, from the mouth of Tobler Creek at Milledgeville, Toms Path is virtually certain to have led to Old Town, on the east side of the Ogeechee, below Louisville, in our Jefferson County. The path may have continued from Old Town to Jobleys Creek on the Savannah, but if it did, no evidence could be found to show that the route led there. The comment is important to the discussion because Jobleys Creek, a former Tobler Creek, may be the key to explain how all of the Tobler creeks received their names. Since Toms Path went by three of the streams, perhaps it also led or connected to the fourth. If the route did in fact run to Jobleys Creek, however, it veered from the most direct course to pass Old Town. A shorter way to the mouth of Jobleys was available via a connection of Toms Path. This spur was the noted Chickasaw Path that forked eastward from Toms Path in upper Washington County to the site of Fenns Bridge, on the Ogeechee, to the east of Sandersville. Thence the trail led to the area of present lower Richmond and upper Burke where the Chickasaws once resided. Somewhere about Waynesboro, there could well have been a fork that led on an easily travelled course the relatively short distance to the mouth of Jobleys Creek on the Savannah. This possible spur, plus a segment of the Chickasaw Path, plus a long stretch of Toms Path would have joined all of the Tobler creeks on a comparatively direct line.

A comment by Captain Daniel Pepper (commander of Fort Moore on the Carolina side of the Savannah below Augusta) intimates there may have been a reason for such a trail when he wrote Governor Lyttelton of South Carolina in 1757 that a William Tobler was selling liquor to Indian traders contrary to regulations.[6] This man was a member of a Swiss family that had migrated to South Carolina in the 1730's and settled in the Savannah River section from the area above Augusta down to the vicinity of Silver Bluff.[7] The latter place was not far from Jobleys Creek in Burke County. Perhaps the traders who bought Tobler's spirits crossed the Savannah at Jobleys Creek to escape detection by authorities. The place was a good site for a clandestine crossing because it was approximately half-way between Mount Pleasant (in present northeast Effingham County) and Augusta which Georgia had established as inspection points on the Savannah for regulating Indian trade.[8] No Georgia land records show a Tobler received a grant in the area of Toblers Bottoms and Jobleys Creek, but obviously from the expressions someone of the name was connected with the vicinity. Since there is no record of a good fording place on the Savannah at the creek, it is possible that William Tobler maintained a ferriage facility such as a canoe for traders to use in crossing the river at the site to get a supply of forbidden rum.

Illicit liquor traffic is traditionally a secretive matter, and we shall probably never know for certain, but there is a chance the Tobler creeks were all so named because they marked a surreptitious, rum-running route which unauthorized traders followed in going to and from Tobler's place. The conjecture is supported by the fact that while Toms Path and the Chickasaw Trail followed easy, natural courses, they mainly ran on ways that passed below or between the noted Upper and Lower Creek trading paths which were usually taken by licensed traders going to or from Augusta. Toms Path did cross the Lower Creek route to the east of the Oconee[9] but this transit presumably was easy to make without detection in the wilderness days. The point is worth making because traders were rewarded for informing on the forbidden activities of other individuals.

The Poor Robin places represent another set of similar but speculative names which can be found in connection with major rivers along a projected line across Georgia. The first and oldest of these sites, as far as records show, pertains to a cluster of Poor Robin designations on the Savannah River to the southeast of Sylvania, in Screven County. In a stretch of about three miles, there is a Poor Robin Lower Point, Poor Robin Lake (slough), and a Poor Robin Bluff and Landing. The last spot probably gave rise to the names in the first instance because it is referred to in Georgia colonial records.[10] Upriver from this bluff, about three-quarters of a mile, on the Carolina side, there is a Poor Robin Upper Point.

Southwestward from these places, on the west side of the Oconee, immediately below the mouth of Turkey Creek, in Laurens County, there is a Po' Robin Bluff. And again, to the southwest of this spot, on the west side of the Ocmulgee and about three miles above Abbeville in Wilcox County, there is another cluster of Poor Robin places: Poor Robin Spring, Poor Robin Lake, and a Poor Robin Landing.

These localities are not generally east and west of each other as were the Tobler creeks, but they will fall on a gently curving line projected southwestwardly from Poor Robin Landing on the Savannah to the Poor Robin sites near Abbeville.

The origin of the Poor Robin names is subject to as much speculation as the reasons for the Tobler creeks. The former monikers may stem from the old rivermen's language and had meanings that are now lost. But, if this were so, how did it happen the names were applied along the hypothetical common line across the state?

The Savannah River landing was referred to in some colonial documents as "Poor Robin's Bluff."[11] The possessive form suggests the locality was named for an individual. That person might have been a Creek chief named Robin who signed the 1733 treaty with Oglethorpe, and who is mentioned as having been bred among the English.[12] Perhaps the chief resided at the bluff and became known to the whites as Poor Robin. Later, when the area between Brier and Ebenezer creeks was eventually evacuated by the Indians,[13] the man perhaps removed to the Oconee, and then to the Ocmulgee, leaving his name behind after each shift. If this sequence of removals took place, though, how did Robin happen to settle southwestwardly close on the axis of a common line?

Land records for the area of the Ocmulgee Poor Robin places furnish a clue which may explain how those particular sites received their designations. An original plat shows a William Hill of Screven County was the first grantee of the lot which embodies the Poor Robin sites above Abbeville.[14] Hill may have brought the name from Screven to Wilcox although the document indicates he came from the western part of Screven and not from the Savannah River area of the Poor Robin cluster of names.

One suspects the Poor Robin places probably received their names because they were all once linked by an Indian trail, as were at least three of the Tobler creeks. No evidence of such a route could be established, however, save for the fact that an Indian path crossed the Ocmulgee,[15] on the east side of Abbeville and above the present bridge on U.S. 280. The trail is shown but not named on the original survey. It is commonly remembered in the community today as the Oswitchee or Switchers Trail. After settlement of the area by the whites a ferry called the Poor Robin Ferry was established at the former Indian crossing.[16] This name, of course, indicates a direct relationship between the designation Poor Robin and the former path, even though the present-day Poor Robin sites are some three miles above the old trail crossing.

The course of the Oswitchee Trail from the Abbeville and Poor Robin Ferry site is subject to conjecture. Westward it presumably led to the Lower Creek town of Oswitchee, located on the west side of the Chattahoochee, within the big bend of the river, in present Russell County, Alabama. The present-day village of Oswichee, on Alabama 165 in Russell County and located about two miles west of the former Indian town site, commemorates the name.

Eastward from Abbeville, the Oswitchee Trail is said to have run through Dodge County, but no evidence could be found to indicate if it went on by the Po' Robin Bluff in Laurens to the Poor Robin places on the Savannah.

—*GMNL* 18(1964): 71-72

NOTES

1. Land district maps and platbooks for the first official surveys of original Baldwin (1804-1805), Monroe (1821), and Houston (1821) counties, Land Records of Georgia, Surveyor General Department, Atlanta.

2. Land of James Gray, St. Georges Parish, survey of 1759, rerecording, Platbook C, p. 69; and land of William Royals, Burke County, 1786, Platbook I, p. 73.

3. Land of Joseph Perry, St. Georges Parish, survey of 1759, Platbook C, p. 418; and land of Jonathan Mulkey, St. Georges Parish, rerecorded plats, originally dated 1766 and 1767, Platbook C, p. 196.

4. An example can be found in Tulapocca, the former name of the present Apalachee River, which is mentioned in old records as Tulapocca, Julapocca, and Chulapocca.

5. See above, Sketch No. 78.

6. Daniel Pepper to William H. Lyttelton, Esq., March 30, 1757, "Indian Book, 1757-1760," Vol. 6, pp. 11-19 (14), South Carolina Archives Department, Columbia.

7. Appreciation is due Mr. F. M. Hutson, Archivist at the South Carolina Archives Department, and to Prof. Charles G. Cordle of Augusta for information about the early Toblers of South Carolina.

8. Mount Pleasant and Augusta were established as forts and inspection points for Indian trade on the Savannah under powers set forth in the first law enacted by the Trustees of the colony of Georgia. See Allen D. Candler, ed., *Colonial Records of Georgia* (Atlanta: Franklin, 1904-1916), 1: 31-42 (40), Jan. 9, 1734.

9. Two alternate but paralleling branches of Toms Path crossed the Lower Creek Path about the present Washington-Hancock line in northeast Washington, and in today's southeast Baldwin County. The Chickasaw Path mentioned was reached by either of the alternating ways of Toms Path.

10. Candler, ed., *Colonial Records*, 7: 436; 8: 337, 370; 9: 84, 177, 209, 229, and 625; 11: 93. The first reference, in Vol. 7, was dated 1756.

11. *Ibid.*, 8: 337 and 370. Both references dated 1760; and "Folder of Loose Colonial Warrants," warrant authorizing Yonge and DeBrahm to survey 100 acres at "poor Robin's bluff," July, 1760, Land Records of Georgia.

12. MS Vol. 39, Colonial Records of Georgia, Department of Archives and History, Atlanta, pp. 494-95. Taken from Oldmixon's *British Empire in America*.

13. Oglethorpe in the first years of the colony would not allow white people to settle along the Savannah between the mouth of Ebenezer Creek and the Brier. The area was reserved for Indians and was referred to as the "Uchee lands" or "Indian lands." Robin, the chief, may have been an Uchee.

14. District 1, Irwin (now part of Wilcox), survey of 1819, John White, D.S., Platbook GGG, lot 214, marginal entry. The plat notes Hill was from "District 180" of Screven. This was an error and should have been District 80, which is in Screven—180 was in Wilkes.

15. *Ibid.*, fractional lot 200.

16. MS map of Wilcox County, 1869, prepared on the authority of the state by B. W. Frobel, Land Records of Georgia.

No. 114
Ossabaw Island, Wassaw Island, Wassaw Sound, the Warsaw Places, and Cumberland Island, Formerly Wiso

Ossabaw is a large offshore island fronting the Atlantic and lying below the mouth of the Great Ogeechee and Ossabaw Sound, in extreme southern Chatham County. Wassaw Island, also in Chatham, lies to the northeast across Ossabaw Sound.[1] Beyond the latter island, at the mouth of Wilmington River and to the south of Tybee Island, is an inlet called Wassaw Sound. Both of the names Wassaw and Ossabaw antedate the founding of Georgia. One is not certain of the age of the former but Ossabaw is one of the oldest continually used appellations in the state. Along with a few other designations—like Sapelo and Ochlocknee—it ranks next to Aucilla,[2] Altamaha, Coosa, and Conasauga, which are the oldest recorded names because they were listed by the chroniclers of DeSoto in 1539 and 1540. Spaniards on the Georgia coast first mentioned Ossabaw and John R. Swanton indicates they were using their version of the name by the late sixteenth century.[3] To Spanish ears Ossabaw sounded like "Asopo,"[4] or "Asapo."[5]

After the English arrived and began to list the word, as was their wont with aboriginal names, they wrote it in a variety of ways: Ussybaw, Ossaba, Ossebau, Usebau, Osebaw, Ussawbah, Ussuybaw, Ussybaugh, etc., and interestingly enough, all of these versions are similar to present-day pronunciations which can be heard for our Ossabaw. Some of the first recordings spelled the name with the so-called Cockney *h:* Hussoope, Hosaba, Hassabaw, and so on. It was fairly common for the English settlers of Carolina and Georgia to use an initial *h* in placenames commencing with a vowel, like: "Hogechee," "Halatamahaw," or "Hoconee." During this period, however, there were some people who wrote the name as Ossabaw and that version remains as the established spelling. But fortunately among the diversity of early recordings listed above there are words which offer better clues to the meaning of Ossabaw than can be found in that retained expression.

Ossabaw is a Guale (wally) Indian word. Those people lived along the Georgia coast or on its offshore islands, and spoke a Muskogean dialect that resembles Creek. In the case of the word Ossabaw the similarity of the two tongues seems close enough for one to take the early versions reported by the English and use Creek to translate the name. It seems plain that Ossabaw is a compounded word which was originally Asiàpi ("ussy uppy"), or Asiàba (ussy ubba), signifying freely "yupon holly bushes place," with the last word being an implied part of the name. The first element of the aboriginal forms is from *àsi,* literally meaning leaves but by common understanding signifying leaves of the cassine or yupon holly, the *Ilex vomitoria.* We sometimes substitute words in this fashion ourselves, as in the case of weed for tobacco. *Asi* is pronounced "ussy," and this sound can clearly be found in some of the early English renditions of Ossabaw. The second element of Asiàpi reflects the Creek expression *àpi* for stems, stalks, plants, or bushes. The Spanish version of Ossabaw and two of the English listings show some early transcribers understood the name to contain the letter *p* instead of *b* which can be found in most English versions of Ossabaw. Perhaps in the Guale dialect *àba* was the equivalent of the Creek *àpi*, and the transcribers showed this in their "baw," "bau," "ba," "bah," and "baugh" endings.

But be these technical differences as they may, it seems certain that Ossabaw was so named to identify the island as an important source of the yupon holly. It was common for Indians of this region to name a stream or a particular area after some plant which could be found there and which was useful to them for its stems, bark, roots, or leaves. Yupon or cassine was prized by Muskogean peoples because they used the parched leaves of the plant to make their famous black drink that was drunk by warriors assembled for meetings in the town squares. On certain ceremonial occasions the drink was brewed strong to serve as an emetic for cleansing and purifying the users.

Wassaw Island is another name which reflects the Indians' propensity for naming a given place after some plant that was important to them. Wassaw is derived from the Creek word *wiso* ("wee' so"), meaning sassafras. Two early charts confirm this translation by referring to Wassaw Sound as "Wesso Sound."[6] It seems reasonable to conclude that this inlet, as an approach to the island, was named after the place, since other sounds, bays, and inlets down the coast reflected the designations of adjacent islands. It is not known if the Spaniards used the name Wassaw, or some related form. One early Spanish chart shows Wassaw Sound as "Barra de aguadulce" (Sweetwater Inlet or Bar),[7] but Swanton gives the Spanish name as "Bahia de la cruz" (Bay of the Cross).[8]

It should be noted that the back side of Wassaw Island is drained by a stream called Wassaw Creek; and across the intervening marshes between Wassaw Island and Skidaway, there is a Little Wassaw Island that rises in the marshes.

The distortion of Wassaw as a name dates from the earliest years of Georgia. From the beginning it has been spelled Wassa, Wassau, Wassaw, or Warsaw. The last form has been used on occasion for over 200 years but it represents an extreme case of garbling because the Creeks had no *r* in their language and, in fact, could not pronounce that letter.[9]

Warsaw has also been used in other parts of Georgia, and the name is still retained in at least two places: a spot on a country road northeast of Townsend in McIntosh County; and a village to the west of the Chattahoochee in extreme northeast Fulton County. The latter place has borne its name for a long time but apparently it is the successor to an earlier Warsaw that was established about two miles away in the early 1830's on the east side of the Chattahoochee, in Gwinnett County. The older community was at the eastern end of George Waters' ferry that connected over the Chattahoochee with the noted Alabama Road cross the Cherokee country. Waters was an Indian countryman with settlements on the west side of the river. A James Cleland originally from the Savannah area married one of Waters' girls and settled at Waters Ferry.[10] About this time the crossing became known as the Warsaw Ferry. Perhaps Cleland hailed from Wassaw Island near Savannah and decided to commemorate the place by applying the name on the Chattahoochee.

In his early account of Georgia, Francis Moore mentions an island formerly called "Wissoo," which was located to the south of Jekyll.[11] He goes on to identify the place as Cumberland and states the island was given that name by Oglethorpe at the request of Toonahowi to honor the Duke of Cumberland.[12] When the young Indian visited England, with his uncle Tomochichi, the Duke had given the boy a gold watch and he asked that the designation be changed from Wiso to Cumberland to honor his benefactor.[13]

—*GMNL* 18(1964): 72-73

NOTES

1. For the locations of these islands see *Ossabaw Island Quadrangle* (ed., 1945) and *Wassaw Sound Quadrangle* prepared by the Corps of Engineers, U.S. Army, and available through the U.S. Geological Survey.

2. See above, Sketch No. 12.

3. John R. Swanton, *Early History of the Creek Indians and Their Neighbors*, Bureau of American Ethnology, Bulletin 73, pp. 51 and 82.

4. *Ibid.*

5. "Mapa de la Ysla de la Florida," Spanish Ministry of War, author not shown, *circa* 1683, Library of Congress.

6. John Herbert, "A New Map of His Majestys Flourishing Province of South Carolina, 1725," from a certified true copy by George Hunter, Surveyor General of Carolina, 1741; and a map of the southeastern region of America transmitted by Col. William Bull of South Carolina to the Board of Trade, May, 1738.

7. "Mapa de la Ysla de la Florida."

8. Swanton, *Early History of the Creek Indians*, p. 51.

9. English transcribers of Indian names used the *ar* as found in Warsaw to denote that the letter *a* of the combination was broad. This sound was not used in pronouncing "Wesso" or Wiso.

10. List of valuations of Cherokee Improvements . . . made under the Treaty of Dec. 29, 1835, item 28, valuations made in 1836 by Agents Hutchins, Shaw and Kellogg, Record Group 75, Records of the Bureau of Indian Affairs, National Archives.

11. Francis Moore, "A Voyage to Georgia," *Collections of the Georgia Historical Society*, Vol. 1, p. 23.

12. *Ibid.*

13. [The folk-reworking of an Indian Wassaw to a Polish Warsaw is paralleled in Wisconsin, where the town of Wausau from Algonquin "far-away" is likewise made Polish, especially by non-residents from an *r*-less area like Massachusetts (on FLU's testimony). See also Stewart, *American Placenames*, p. 522 (s.v. *Warsaw*). *FLU.*]

No. 115
Suomi

Suomi is a small community located a mile below Chauncey on U.S. 23 in Dodge County. At a glance the word appears to be Indian, but actually it is the native and official name of the country which most of the world calls Finland. Except perhaps for philatelists who note the word Suomi on Finnish postage stamps, few people are familiar with the designation since gazetteers, geographies, and dictionaries usually refer to Suomi as Finland. The latter name, so the Finns say, was applied to them by the Swedes.

The Dodge County Suomi is locally pronounced "Sue oh' mee," and interestingly enough this form is virtually identical with the pronunciation used in Finland. Some American dictionaries depict the sound as "Swo' mē," but when Finns say the word one hears a "sue" or "soo" and not a "swo" sound as found in the English terms swollen or sworn.

Suomi and Finland mean the same thing because both expressions signify fen and refer to a low, moist ground or swampy land. These descriptive terms could well apply to parts of Finland but not to the area about our Dodge County Suomi. One must, therefore look elsewhere for a reason to explain why the name was applied here. The people of the community do not recall how the place received the name, but they generally agree it was first used in connection with a siding or station on the present Southern Railway line that runs nearby. When this road was originally constructed in post-Civil War years it was built to tap the great timber reserves between the Oconee and Ocmulgee. Large sawmills sprang up in the section, and since Finns are noted lumbermen, it seems likely some of them were brought here to work in these mills or to cut timber. These possible workers may well have named Suomi in honor of their former homeland.

—*GMNL* 18(1964): 73

Unnumbered Short Studies

Old Chattahoochee Town: An Early Muscogee Indian Settlement

Of the many Creek or Muscogee Indian appellations which the white man retained in this region, one of the most interesting and most pleasing was that of Chattahoochee. With the influence of Sidney Lanier's song to send the word lilting through the mind, we are prone to think of the term only as the euphonious title of a stream and forget that it originally was the name of a town which Swanton says was the oldest Muscogee settlement on the river that now perpetuates the name.[1] But curiously in contrast to most of the other notable Creek towns, no one seems to have located the precise site of Chattahoochee. The name in one spelling or another can be found on numbers of early maps but always in such a generalized fashion that students of Indian matters could not be certain of the location.

Fortunately Colonel Benjamin Hawkins provides the clue which solves this little problem. In his unpublished "Viatory,"[2] which was a log that he kept of his numerous excursions through the Indian country, he tells us with reasonable exactness about the location of Chattahoochee.

The particular trip in which he divulges this information involved a journey (presumably from his headquarters at Coweta Tallahassee, located some seven miles below Columbus, Georgia, on the Alabama side of the Chattahoochee) to Tennessee by way of Etowah, a Cherokee settlement.

He began the trip on October 5, 1798, and followed a course up the western side of the river. By the end of the second day he reached a camping site at what is now the upper side of the business section of West Point, Georgia; and interestingly enough for the readers who

335

may live in that area, he notes that the lands about the encampment were "bereft of trees by hurricanes."

On the morning of the seventh, after a short ride, he crossed "O, so, li, jee" Creek[3] and continued up the west bank of the river, passing en route the ruined town of Ocfuskeenene which was destroyed by a group of Georgians in 1793.[4] To this very day the place is referred to as the "old burnt Indian fort." He crossed Wehadkee Creek which he labels "Hoithle tigau"; by noon he had travelled 12 miles and nearly reached the high hill that runs westward from the Chattahoochee by Abbotsford in western Troup County.[5] He crossed this ridge and commented that the top was "paved with small white flintstone." Shortly he crossed "Hatche soof, kee," or Deep Creek, which is today's Whitewater.[6] By camping time he had covered another 10½ miles, making the total for the day as he calculated it from travelling time, 22½ miles. He had reached a spot near Owensbyville on the Troup–Heard county line. Again, it may be noted, he encamped at a place where a "hurricane" had "blowed down many trees."[7]

The next day, after less than an hour's travel, he reached an Indian village on the Chattahoochee called "Chau, ke thlucco," or Big Shoal.[8] The spot is easy to identify as today's Jackson Mill Shoals.[9] This stretch is upriver from Philpot's old ferry in the big bend of the river on the Heard–Troup line.[10]

Hawkins remarks that the "falls" (meaning shoals) here appeared fordable at several spots. And so they were. There is good evidence that one branch of the noted upper trading route from Charleston via Augusta to the Creeks, Choctaws, and Chickasaws crossed the Chattahoochee at this place and possibly the first trail used by the English-speaking whites for deeply penetrating the Indian country passed this way. Two early charts support this belief. One of these, the Bull Map of 1738, shows a trail from Charleston to the Chickasaws of what is now north Mississippi.[11] That path crossed the Chattahoochee just below the town of "Chatahuchee" at a point which easily could be Chaukethlucco. And although this map is dated 1738, Bull inscribed along the path: "The course Capt. Welch took in ye year 1698, since followed by ye traders." Another early English map, *circa* 1715, shows a similar trail leading past "Chattahuces" on the "River Cusitie."[12] It is reasonable to assume though that this path actually crossed at the Jackson Mill Shoals or Chaukethlucco, and not a little farther up at the area of Chattahoochee Town where the fording opportunites do not seem good.

From Chaukethlucco Hawkins continued his trip up the river, travelling close to the bank. He passed through some old fields and in about an hour reached "Luchaw, pogau" Creek. Elsewhere he spells the name "Loo-chau po-gau" and tells us the word means "The resort of terrapins."[13] This stream seemingly is today's Brush Creek.

In twenty-five minutes' travelling time above Brush Creek, he reached a fork in the trail and makes this comment in the "Viatory": "A path to our right to Chatto ho chee tal lauhassee, from whence that river has its name." Hawkins continued on his way to Tennessee seemingly without visiting the old site. This omission, however, is understandable because the town had been abandoned. But he was not far from the spot because as has been indicated, he was travelling (on this stretch of his journey) parallel with and close to the river.

In another place Hawkins stated that the name Chattahoochee is derived from *chatto*, a stone, and *ho che*, marked or flowered, from rocks of that description which could be found in the river at the site of the settlement.[14] The "Chatto ho chee tal lauhassee" which he mentioned in the "Viatory" means Chattahoochee Old Town.

On Hawkins's authority then, one is safe in concluding that the town was located on the west bank of the Chattahoochee, some four and a half or five miles below present Franklin, in Heard County, Georgia. The village was not large and could easily have been in any one of several narrow fields or "cuts" that fringe this section of the river. The site was not a particularly good one when compared to the locations of such noted Creek centers as Coweta, Oswichee, Oconee, Cusseta, Tallassee, New Yorka, Tuckabatchee, Uchee, and numbers of others. Seemingly Chattahoochee Town would flood when the river got on a rampage. Perhaps this factor was one reason for its abandonment.

It should be noted that Hawkins spells the name "Chatto ho chee" and in view of the explanation which he gives of the origin and meaning of the word, one would think that is the form we should have inherited. Anyone, however, who likes to work with old maps becomes aware of the fact that a sort of struggle went on between the early variations in the spellings of the names of numbers of important streams before the final forms that we now know were chosen. Thus in the case of the Chattahoochee we find there were several variants of the name. Some of the commonest were: Catahooche, Chattahuces, Chatahouchy, Chata Uchee, and Chatehoochie. The last form, if pronounced "Chatty hoochie," would really be close to the way the word is said by hundreds of people today. The French also had their names: Tchattaouchi and Chactas-Ou-Guy.

The term Chattahoochee, as a title for the river, conceivably might have been dropped in favor of some other name, since the stream is referred to as Great Flint, River Cusitie, presumably because it flowed past Cusseta,[15] and Apalachicoli. The last name endures as the name of the lower part of the stream. The French variously called the river, Rivière des Chattaux, Rivière des Caouita, and Rivière du Saint Esprit. But with that singular enduring quality which is often displayed by a placename, the original appellation held on in its various spellings until we finally formalized it as Chattahoochee. This tenacity lends support to Swanton's thesis that Chattahoochee Town was the oldest Muscogee settlement on the river.[16]

—*GMNL* 6(1953): 52-54

NOTES

1. John R. Swanton, *Early History of the Creek Indians and Their Neighbors*, Bureau of American Ethnology, Bulletin 73 (Washington, 1922), p. 226. He adds the place was possibly established to open trade with the Spanish.

2. Benjamin Hawkins, "A Viatory or Journal of distances and observations," original in the Library of Congress. The pages are not numbered, the various trips being set forth by appropriate headings and dates.

3. Hawkins spells this name in a way that permits its proper pronunciation. The present-day spelling of Osiliga is incorrect, because the word did not have a hard *g* sound. Old-timers now living in the vicinity of the stream pronounce the name as Hawkins wrote it.

4. Ocfuskeenene means Oakfuskee Trail, from the main stem of the upper trading path which crossed the Chattahoochee here at a shoally stretch now called Hell Gap. The village was at the back of the present Fletcher place, and below the mouth of Wehadkee Creek, in western Troup County.

5. The ridge ran back from the river, on the north side of and roughly parallel to the tracks of the Atlantic Coast Line Railroad.

6. The present name Whitewater Creek is interesting. Today's Wehadkee Creek means white water, from *wewa*, water, and *hátki or hutke*, white. Hawkins, in crossing that stream, however, called it "Hoithle, tigau," meaning War Ford, presumably referring to the Oakfuskee Trail ford that crossed at or near Ocfuskeenene Town. Somehow over the years there was a conversion of the names, with Hoithletiga becoming Wehadkee and Hatcheesofka becoming Whitewater.

7. Early wilderness travellers and surveyors occasionally made comments about the effects of tornadoes which they had seen. The results of such blows must have been tremendously devastating in primeval forests.

8. Chaukethlucco literally means Shoal Big. The Creeks usually put the modifier after the noun as a suffix.

9. Jackson's Mill no longer exists but the name is retained.

10. A useful map which covers the area under discussion is the *Wedowee Quadrangle* (U. S. Geological Survey, ed. April, 1902).

11. "Map of East and West Florida, South Carolina and Florida," transmitted by Col. Bull (President and Commander in Chief of South Carolina) to the Board of Trade, 1738, photostatic copy in the Library of Congress, original in the Library of the British Colonial Office.

12. "Map of North and South Carolina and Florida," 1715 (?), no author, original in the Colonial Office Library, London; photostatic copy consulted in Archer Butler Hulbert's *The Crown Collection of Photographs of American Maps*, Vol I, Series III, plate 13, copy in the Ayer Collection, Newberry Library, Chicago.

13. Benjamin Hawkins, *A Sketch of the Creek Country in 1798 and 1799*, Collections of the Georgia Historical Society, Vol. 3 (Savannah, 1848), p. 47. He was referring to a Tallapoosa River settlement of Creeks that had removed there from Luchapoga Creek. This name is perpetuated by Loachapoka, Alabama, a village in western Lee County.

14. *Ibid.*, p. 52.

15. The noted Creek town of Cusseta was located on the east bank of the Chattahoochee at the site of today's Lawson Field, Fort Benning's main airport.

16. [Dr. Goff and the editor visited Heard County twice in 1965 to observe more closely the route travelled by Hawkins. At that time Dr. Goff concluded that he was in error in locating Chattahoochee Old Town south of Franklin. It was probably somewhere near downtown Franklin, which is on a bluff overlooking, and on the east side of, the Chattahoochee River. For a complete annotation by the editor of Hawkin's travels through that section, see the *Georgia Historical Quarterly*, 56 (1972), 415-431. MRH.]

Hog Crawl Creek

The dividing line between Dooly and Macon counties, Georgia, is a stream with the distinctive though somewhat ungainly title of Hog Crawl Creek. That waterway has long borne this name, even back to the Indian days. Although it was marked "Beaver Creek" on the 1821 survey of original Dooly,[1] it was also labelled "Beaverdam or Hog Crawl Cr." on the plat for James Barnard's 805-acre reserve which straddled a portion of the stream and which was surveyed a little later.[2]

The designation Hog Crawl referred to a type of pen or enclosure, but one can be certain that Barnard did not invent the term, even though he was a member of a prominent Indian country stock-raising family.[3] Actually this unique appellation goes back to the earliest days of the state since several references can be found to hog crawls in the colonial records of Georgia. Noble Jones, for instance, in a communication to the Trustees, dated July 1, 1735, mentions a

"Hoggs Crawl" at a "fine Blough" on the Savannah River.[4] The bluff he referred to was downstream a mile or so from the later site of the famous old Ebenezer Church in Effingham County.[5]

The name cropped up again in May of 1765 when John Price petitioned the colonial authorities to grant him an island of Crooked River (in today's Camden County) for the purpose of "settling an Hog Crawl."[6] About the same time, John Fox requested a grant on the Main opposite Frederica at a place called "the Hog Crawl."[7] This location, which was near today's Brunswick, must have been fairly well-known, because in 1768 Jacob Moore asked for land on the north side of Turtle River at a place called "hogg Crawl Creek";[8] and in 1771, William Moore, presumably Jacob's kinsman, petitioned for 200 acres on the south side of the same stream.[9]

As noted, a crawl was a type of enclosure to hold hogs. But there is no good explanation to show why this designation was employed in preference to the simple word pen in referring to an installation to contain swine. Certainly early citizens were not in the least averse to using pen because that term can be found in numbers of Georgia's geographic names: Cowpen, Ox pen, Mulepen, Shuck Pen, and so on.

The singularity of hog crawl as a name, therefore, leaves the impression that this sort of structure differed from other pens. Presumably the pioneers' rail or pole pens for horses and cattle were not effective in holding the half-wild, self-reliant frontier hogs that were accustomed to roaming the woods in search of their own food. On the other hand, an enclosure made of posts or heavy pickets placed upright and close together in the fashion of a stockade would have been "hog tight," as we say today.

The most interesting thing about this enigmatic name, however, lies in the word crawl itself and the reason why the term came into use to denote a hog pen. Webster's *New International Dictionary of the English Language, The Shorter Oxford English Dictionary,* and *A Dictionary of American English* agree that the designation comes from the colonial Dutch word *kraal,* that in turn seemingly was derived from the Spanish or Portuguese *corral.* But how the name got into colonial English is a mystery. It may have been brought here from the West Indies, or more probably directly from Africa by slaves or slave-traders, because the dictionaries in discussing the word mention a crawl as an enclosure for slaves. Apparently the name was known in South Carolina before Georgia was founded. *A Dictionary of American English* notes it in connection with Carolina as early as 1682.[10]

—GMNL 7(1954): 38-40

NOTES

1. District 1 of Dooly County, surveys of 1821 and 1825, Platbook PPP, lots 38, 59, *passim*, Land Records of Georgia, Surveyor General Department, Atlanta. The 1821 survey for this district contained errors; it was re-surveyed in 1825 by E. L. Thomas, D.S. Plats from both surveys are in the source cited.

2. "Islands and Reserves," Platbook EEEE, p. 19. The plat shows no date for this property, but the survey for Buck Barnard's Reserve in the same platbook is dated 1828; cf. p. 46.

3. James Barnard was a grandson of Timothy Barnard, the noted Indian countryman who married an Uchee woman and lived on the west side of Flint River, a mile or so downstream from today's Oglethorpe.

4. Noble Jones to the Trustees, Savannah, July 1, 1735, MS Vol. 20, Colonial Records of Georgia, Department of Archives and History, pp. 421-28.

5. In connection with a stream as a possible mill site, Jones mentioned a creek that was 8 miles above Purrysburgh. The waterway involved would be today's Lockner Creek, a west-bank tributary of the Savannah River in Effingham County. He added it was 2 miles below "Hoggs Crawl" and four miles below "Ebenezer River."

6. Allen D. Candler, *Colonial Records of Georgia* (Atlanta: Franklin, 1904-1916), 9: 351.

7. *Ibid.*, pp. 362-63.

8. *Ibid.*, 10: 598.

9. *Ibid.*, 101: 421.

10. [The etymology of Hog Crawl is probably not from Colonial Dutch *kraal* but from the parent Spanish *corral*, which influenced both Dutch and early English (1660). Audubon (1838) also speaks of a Beaver "crawl," from the English verb crawl "to creep" (see *Dictionary of Americanisms*, 1: 430—not in the 4-vol. *Dictionary of American English* used by Goff). Hence there may be some causal relationship between the names Beaverdam Creek and Hog Crawl Creek. See Utley, "Hog Crawl Creek Again," *Names*, 21 (1973): 179-95. *FLU*]

The Creek Village of Cooccohapofe on Flint River

In his *Letters* (p. 173) Colonel Benjamin Hawkins mentions a Creek settlement on Flint River which he calls "Cooccohapofe." He shows it was five miles below the ford at the Old Horse Path (the noted Lower Creek Trading Path) and three miles above the town of "Padjeeligau." The latter place was an Uchee settlement situated at the mouth of today's Patsiliga Creek, to the east of Reynolds in Taylor County.

Dr. John R. Swanton also mentions "Cooccohapofe" in his *Early History of the Creek Indians and Their Neighbors* (p. 284) and in his *The Indian Tribes of North America* (p. 164), but in both of these sources he erred by locating the town at some undesignated site on the Chattahoochee River. This statement is to correct that slip and to bring out the fact that Cooccohapofe derived its name by reason of a location on the edge of an immense canebrake on Flint River.

It is difficult to pinpoint the site of Cooccohapofe by beginning at the Old Horse Path Ford above the place because one cannot be sure whether Hawkins computed his distance from the ford to the village by water or directly by land. But location of the settlement three miles above Padjeeligau makes the problem simple because the site of the latter is known. Measured off then from this place, Cooccohapofe was on the west side of Flint River in upper Taylor County, and about a mile and a half to the northeast of the crossroads at White Hill Church and Cemetery on Georgia 128. A little field road runs from the crossroads to or very near the spot where the village was located.

Except for the *cooc* part, Cooccohapofe is easy to interpret. It is from the Creek words *koha*, cane, plus *ápi*, stems or stalks, plus the locative form *ofi*, or ofa. The last element literally signifies in or among, but the Indian country whites sometimes translated it into expressions like ground, meaning a locality. The *cooc* seems to be garbled with the final *c* being unnecessary. The term may have been intended for the particle prefix *ko, ka, ku,* or *cu* that can occasionally be found in Creek words and placenames. Its meaning is obscure, but to make a guess, one thinks the *cooc* may have been something like the Anglo-Saxon *bi*, meaning near to, which has come over into English placenames as "by." If this conjecture is correct, Cooccohapofe meant By Canes Ground, i.e., town by the side of a canebrake.

In compounding Cooccohapofe (*kukohapofi*) from *ku* + *koha* + *ápi* + *ofi*, it will be noticed there was an elision of vowels. This practice was common in making up Creek placenames from several words. In the final name, only the *p* of *ápi* remained. Its obscure *á* gave way to the *a* of *koha* and its *i* was dropped in favor of the stong *o* of *ofi*.

Cooccohapofe undoubtedly received its name because it was located on the edge of a great canebrake that began just above the village site and extended down the Flint low grounds to a point below today's Montezuma. Colonel Hawkins and the early surveyors of the section make it plain that this brake was the largest such swamp reported for early Georgia. In connection with Cooccohapofe, Hawkins says it was three miles across at the settlement, and with respect to Padjeeligau he states the swamp was three miles "high," meaning apparently it extended upriver that far. He adds the canebrake on the Padjeeligau or west side of the Flint was a mile through. This last stretch is still a sizable brake and so far as the writer knows is the only place in Georgia where the long, fishing-pole type of cane still grows in considerable numbers.

People who live on Georgia 128 in the vicinity of White Hill Church crossroads say there is an Indian mound on the Flint—above the site of Cooccohapofe and to the east of Griffith Crossroads No. 128. But despite much walking one was unable to find the spot. The section is a wooded area a mile or so from the road, and an outsider who finds the mound will probably need local help to locate it.

It should be noted that Cooccohapofe was the only known Indian settlement located at or just below the Fall Line on Flint River. This situation is in singular contrast with similar locations on other major southward-flowing rivers of Georgia and especially so when compared to the vicinities of present Augusta, Milledgeville, Macon, and Columbus where there were important Indian settlements on the rivers that passed those places.

Interestingly enough, too, no white man's city sprang up at the lower edge of the Fall Line on the Flint, notwithstanding the fact that Colonel Hawkins proclaimed the area as one of the finest places he had seen and gave a potential city at the point a start by establishing the Creek Indian Agency there about 1800 (near the present bridge on Georgia 128), before Milledgeville was founded and years before Macon and Columbus were established. The situation offers promise as a good location for a city, and if the need should ever arise for a site to start such a place from scratch, the area of the Old Agency would merit serious consideration. On the Taylor County side of the locality, between Flint River and Georgia 137, there is a flat-topped ridge which would make a beautiful residential area, overlooking rolling hills to the north and affording a commanding view of the Flint River valley to the south, where Cooccohapofe once stood and the great cane swamp stretched away downstream.

—*GMNL* 14(1961): 34-35

An "Indian Fort" on Flint River

On a bluff at the western edge of the Flint River swamp and located 2.2 miles to the east of Reynolds in Taylor County, there is an earthern embankment that gives every evidence of being man-made. The structure is not an Indian mound, but a square of breastworks which measures about 3 feet in height and 30 feet along each side. The formation is in a dense thicket and cannot be easily found except by careful searching; but it is to the north of Georgia 96 and on the upper side of the Central of Georgia Railroad at the point where a deep cut of the railway and the swamp bluff corner. Anyone wishing to find the spot can walk along the railroad till this corner is reached, then scramble up the bank to the site. An easier approach would be to cross a wooden bridge that spans the western end of the railway cut, then follow a road eastwardly along the fields on the north side of the right of way until the turn at the bluff is encountered. One should be careful not to confuse a deep drainage ditch running parallel to the railroad with any part of the breastworks. This ditch apparently was dug by the Central of Georgia engineers to divert water that would otherwise run down the cut to the swamp and in so doing undermine the track bed.

People living near the breastworks on the bluff have long known the spot as an old "Indian fort." And in fact, the structure does stand at the lower side of a former Uchee Indian settlement which Benjamin Hawkins mentioned as "Padjeeligau."[1] This community occupied the fields which stretch upriver along the bluff from the "fort." The word means Pigeon Roost in the Muskogee language and Patsiliga Creek which reaches the Flint opposite the upper end of the former town perpetuates the name of the settlement.

But despite the location of the so-called fort at an old Indian site, it seems highly unlikely that the place was built by Indians because the red people of this section did not erect such fortifications. Very probably, one thinks, the raised banks were the foundations of a Confederate palisade or blockhouse which was put up to protect the railroad bridge during the War Between the States. The Confederates did build stockades at other river crossings and the remains on the Flint look very much like some of those places. Furthermore, by studying the Taylor County site one can see the place was located at a point which gave it a direct and commanding view of the nearby railroad crossing on the river.

Students of the Civil War period perhaps could ascertain if the place was a Confederate fortification from the Georgia Militia records of the war. The fort is not listed in the index to the *Records of the War of Rebellion*. The likelihood of the blockhouse being Confederate would be supported if a similar structure could be found on the east side of the river opposite the spot in Taylor County. This possible second place, however, might prove considerably harder to find than one would think. To gain an idea of the type of structure to look for, one should first find and examine the site that has been mentioned here.

—*GMNL* 16(1963): 53

NOTES

1. *Letters of Benjamin Hawkins, 1796-1806*, Collections of the Georgia Historical Society, Vol. 9 (Savannah, 1916), p. 171.

The General

Retracing the Old Federal Road

About a mile north of Flowery Branch, Georgia, where U.S. Highway 23 veers from the Southern Railway, is a place known locally as the Federal Crossing. At this spot a country road leads from the pavement over the railroad tracks and disappears in the hills and woods to the west. This nondescript little byway is a remnant of the Old Federal Road, an historic highway that once joined Georgia and Tennessee across the Cherokee Nation.[1] Eastward from the Federal Crossing, on the eastern boundary of the Cherokees, now the Hall-Jackson county line, it joined roads that in turn had connections leading from many parts of upper and lower Georgia via Jefferson and Athens. Westward across the Chattahoochee, this former thoroughfare was the first white man's road of northwest Georgia, a route for reaching such widely separated places as Knoxville and Nashville.

The road owes its name to the fact that the federal government took the initiative in securing from the Cherokees the right of a passageway across their lands to facilitate communication and travel between Tennessee and the lower Southeast. The Indians were much opposed to granting such privileges when first approached about the matter in 1801. But the government's chief representative among the Cherokees, Colonel Return J. Meigs, by intrigue and persistent persuasion, continued to press for rights to establish a road, and in 1803-1804 an informal agreement was reached with certain influential Indian leaders to open that part of the road which runs from east Tennessee to Georgia. At the Treaty of Tellico, Tennessee, in 1805 the Cherokees ceded important lands to the whites and granted the right to lay out another prong of the trace from the direction of Nashville to intersect the first road in Georgia. Some of the tribe, however, were so incensed at the concessions in this agreement that they assassinated Doublehead, one of the principal chiefs who negotiated it.

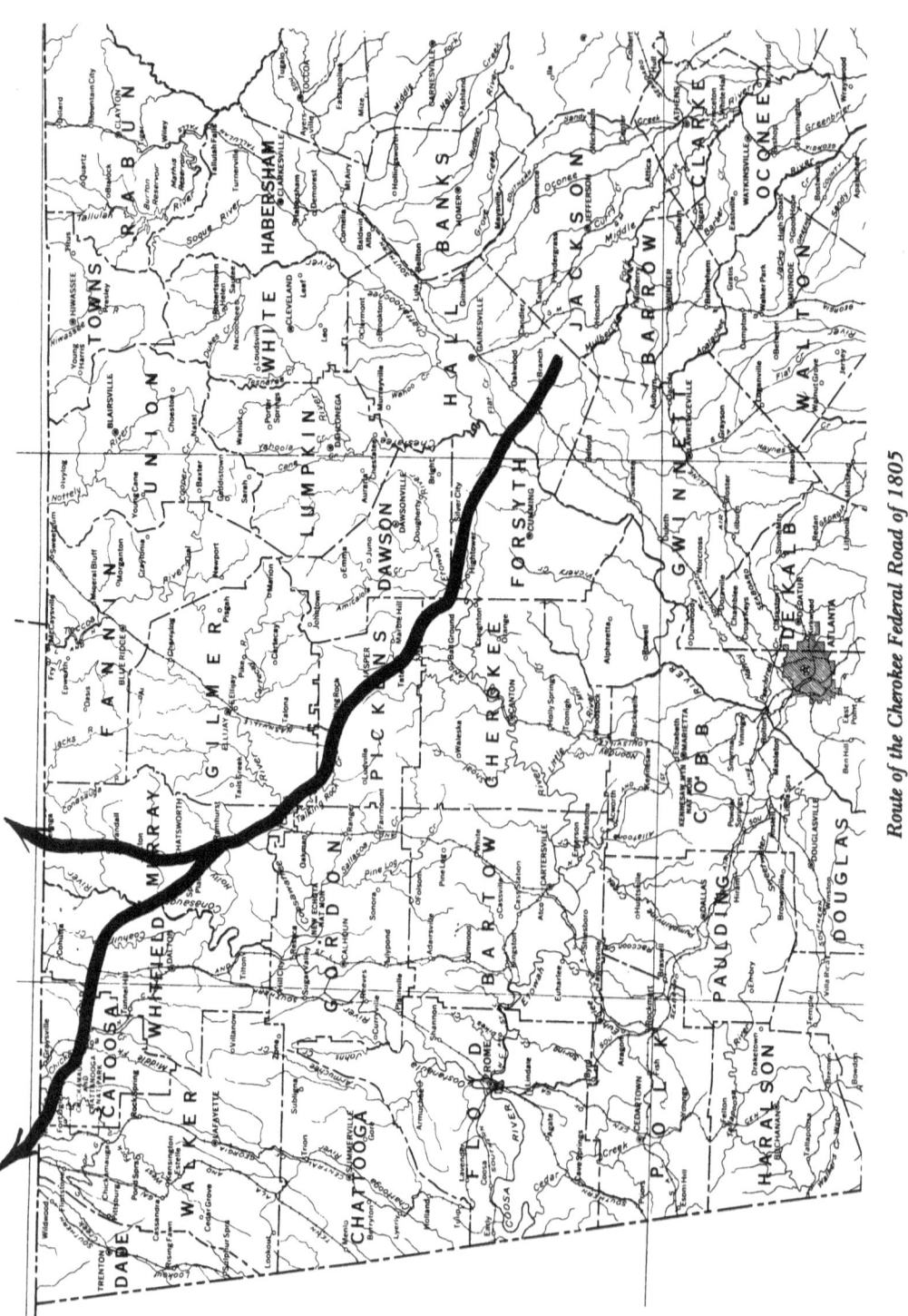

Route of the Cherokee Federal Road of 1805

But the road was never a federal thoroughfare as we today would understand that term. After gaining the privilege of establishing a road, the government left actual selection of a route and development of the highway to Tennessee and Georgia. And later, when the interest of these states flagged, the Cherokees apparently took over parts of the old route and allotted them to different persons to operate as toll roads. The attitude of the federal government toward this thoroughfare is in direct contrast to its position on the rights which it gained from the Creek Indians in 1805 to open a trace across their nation from what is now Macon, Georgia, to a point on the Alabama River not far above Mobile. In the latter case the government selected the route and used federal troops to cut the road.

But however the Old Federal Road across the Cherokee lands was opened and operated, it fulfilled well the functions for which it was planned. Very early it became an immigrant artery for reaching west Tennessee and the rich lands of the Tennessee River valley in northern Alabama. Its value in this respect caused it in time to become one of the so-called Alabama Roads. It developed military importance too, and in the war with the Creeks in 1813-1814, the Tennessee and Georgia authorities sent couriers by this route to exchange information on their plans for attacking the Indians. And later, in 1818, when Jackson passed through Georgia to fight the Seminoles in Florida, he went this way. As time passed, the old road became a noted stage route and a way over which Kentucky and Tennessee stockmen drove their animals to markets in Georgia and South Carolina. It became an important post route, with the earliest post offices in northwest Georgia being established along its course, the first at Rossville in 1819 and the second at Spring Place in 1819.

With the aid of an ordinary highway map it is easy to locate the key points served by the Old Federal Road. Beginning at the Federal Crossing on U.S. 23, it led to a ferry site on the Chattahoochee. The ferry, which has long since ceased operating, was first known as Vann's, later as Winn's and finally as Williams Ferry. Today where the old road now dead-ends on the east bank of the river, it is hard to believe that such a spot could ever have been of significance. But in frontier times the community bustled, with a stream of wayfarers funneling through the place. Over the hill from the site of the ferryman's house, in Booger Hollow, a gold stampede took place. And on the trail itself, just to the east of the ferry, a dubious legend says that the first diamond found in Georgia was picked up.

352 / Placenames of Georgia

To pursue the Federal Road farther one must now detour several miles via Browns Bridge and Oscarville in Forsyth County to the old ferrying point on the west bank of the Chattahoochee. From here, with the exception of a few missing sections which will be noted, the road runs its Y-shaped course unbroken toward Knoxville and Nashville.

There is scant evidence of the Federal Road at the ferry landing on the west side of the river, but a sunken stretch across the bottomlands indicates its former course. Several hundred yards from the bank, however it takes up again beyond the old Vann house. This structure, now the James F. Boyd residence, once served as a tavern and inn for the Cherokee or eastern end of the trace. It must be one of the rarest buildings in Georgia, because it is possibly the best-preserved example of an Indian-country hostelry remaining in the state. Originally constructed of logs, the house is now weatherboarded and painted and appears outwardly to be much like other pretty, well-kept farm homes. Inside, however, one quickly notes the frontier influence in the huge fireplaces of the kitchen, and in the former public room which now serves as a parlor. In the corner of the latter is a cubicle which was a dram shop in the old days. Mr. Boyd, whose family has owned the place since 1851, says that originally there was a hole cut through the logs for passing out drinks to travellers on the road, but this opening was covered when the house was remodeled. By narrow little stairs one ascends to the upper story, where cell-like sleeping quarters were provided for the guests. This part of the interesting old lodging has been left as it was when the inn was constructed nearly a century and a half ago.

At the top of the hill going westward from the tavern a small stretch of the Federal Road is missing, but a short ride back through Oscarville brings one around to Two Mile Creek, where it takes up again as present Georgia Highway 141 to Coal Mountain. There it passes over U.S. 19 and continues to the northwest corner of Forsyth County, where it originally crossed the Etowah River, just beyond Hightower Crossroads at the Frogtown Ford.

From here the route bears northwestward toward McConnell's Crossroads in northeast Cherokee County. At the top of the hill, beyond the Frogtown Ford, people living thereabouts say that in Cherokee days one of the Vann Indians was killed. This point brings out a human trait that often crops up in answers to inquiries along old roads. Instead of forgetting a killing or murder, people are prone to remember such an incident and will mention it years or even generations after it occurred. The recollection of such a tragedy tends to cling to a spot like some evil taint that not even time will dissipate.

The old trace passes Shiloh Church and on through Mica into Pickens County, following a fine high course that provides a magnificent panorama of the surrounding country. Shortly after entering Pickens, the highway leads past the noted old Four Mile Church, and a little farther on, Federal School, one of the few remaining places bearing a name which is derived from the former thoroughfare. Along here, too, is a well-preserved two-story log dwelling that must have witnessed much in the years it has stood on the federal trail.

The road next steeply ascends a high dome-shaped hill, from the top of which there is a splendid view of Sharptop, Grassy Knob (Mt. Oglethorpe), and other mountains of the Blue Ridge that stand out sharply to the north and east. For the early lowcountry visitor who was eager to view the mountains, this was the place.!

The Federal Road drops from the crest of this hill in sharp curves to strike the Tate-Dawsonville Highway just to the east of the bridge over Long Swamp Creek. Here in pioneer times was Daniels and across the creek was Harnages or Harnageville. Both places were stage stops.

Harnages in time became Tate, the noted marble-producing center. From there the old road bears northward and, as Georgia Highway 5, passes through Jasper to Talking Rock. About a half-mile beyond this point the federal trace turns left from the Ellijay road. Here was the site of Sanderstown, home of George Sanders, a prominent mixed-blood Indian leader. Here too was the site of Taloney or Carmel Missionary Station, where missionaries labored to carry out the Great Command among the Cherokees. They and others of their calling were ill-treated by the local whites, but that is a skeleton which might well be stored far back in the closet.

At this fork from the Ellijay road is one of the rare public markers which commemorate the old trace. It notes that the Federal Road follows the course of a trail that connected the ancient Indian town of Cisca in Tennessee with St. Augustine, Florida.

The Federal Road led on to Blaine, but today's highway does not entirely follow its route. It is easy to trace the latter, however, as one approaches the village, because it runs as a tree-bordered depression in a pasture to the left of the modern road.

Beyond Blaine the Federal Road coincides closely with Georgia 156, which has been under construction in the last year or two. It leads northwestward through a rugged, sparsely settled country, passing over Talking Rock Creek by a bridge, where there used to be a crossing called the Ball Creek Ford, and on toward Clipper Crossroads. From there it runs toward Berean School in southwest Gilmer County. At a white house on the left, the original route deserts No. 156 and cuts to the left directly across a mountain on a course that is difficult to follow in an ordinary car. This trying stretch is probably more like the original trail than other still-travelled sections. It leaves the impression that the thoroughfare was a road by courtesy only, when viewed with modern eyes.

By riding around near Berean School, the old road can be rejoined. Farther on at the foot of the mountain it suddenly comes out into the Coosawattee River Valley, near Carters Quarters, one of the loveliest parts of Georgia. The Federal Road does not cross Talking Rock Creek as does Georgia 156,[2] but turns right along the foot of the mountain and soon passes the edge of a great corn field, a notable spot because it contains the site of Coosawattee Old Town, a Cherokee settlement.

Along the edge of the field by the road is a remarkable stone fence, the likes of which can rarely be seen in Georgia. An inquiry of an old Negro as to its origin brought the response that it was built "way befo' my time in the dark days of slavery."

Farther along, the road crosses the Coosawattee on a narrow, old-fashioned concrete bridge. Travelers on the original federal trace forded the river just above, where the stream widens into swift but shallow shoals. Standing on the bridge gazing at the sparkling riffles, one could not avoid speculating on and trying to visualize the interesting characters and cavalcades that once splashed those waters: roistering frontier riflemen with bobbing coonskin caps, strings of packhorses, hurrying couriers, Old Hickory and his troop, wagons of hopeful immigrants, and shouting drovers, urging their reluctant animals into the swift stream. But this spot is a natural crossing, and even before there were drovers and emigrants, bands of painted savages must have forded here; perhaps, too, furtive English agents seeking to stir up trouble among the Cherokees against the revolting colonists slipped along here; and perhaps also, DeSoto and his army crossed at this spot, because he is thought to have visited this section.

At Coniston, two miles farther on, the old road strikes U.S. 411. Near here, in pioneer days, dwelt the long-lived and beloved preacher, Reverend William J. Cotter. In his *My Autobiography* he left one of the few writings which mention the Federal Road.

Near this place also, not far from a present large dairy barn, in frontier days was an interesting place named Bloodtown. Origin of the name is obscure, but the site was a noted spot where south-bound cattle drovers penned their stock at night for feeding and resting while en route to markets. Traces of Bloodtown have long since disappeared, but tales of the reveling and brawling which took place there persisted long.

Up the road a little farther, in front of a filling station which now marks Ramhurst, Georgia, on U.S. 411, the Old Federal Road branched. One fork, which will be followed later, turned left toward Chattanooga and Nashville. The other continued straight ahead, approximately along the course of U.S. 411, via present-day Chatsworth, Eton, and Cisco to Tennga on the Georgia-Tennessee line.

Just beyond Tennga, on a slight rise, to the left of and opposite the point where a road turns from U.S. 411, or Tennessee 33, to go into the village of Conasauga, are some metal-covered farm buildings. The Old Federal Road ran behind these structures through what is now a cotton patch. Out in the field, on the edge of the depression which marks the course of the trace, is a tiny cemetery surrounded by a stone wall and surmounted by several small peach trees. Inside are buried David McNair, a prominent Indian countryman who married into the Cherokee tribe, and his wife Delilah. The marble slab which covers their graves is the most poignant object along the Federal Road. Its lettering is chipped and blurred, but the inscription reads:

> Sacred
> To the memory of
> David and Delilah McNair
> who departed this life
> the former on the 15 of
> August 1836 the latter
> on the 31 of November 1838.
> Their children being natives
> of the Cherokee Nation, and
> having to go with their people
> to the West, leave this monument
> not only to tell their regard for
> their Parents [but?] to guard their
> sacred ashes [against?] the unhallowed
> intrusion of the white man.

This section is a beautiful region; little wonder that the Cherokees hated to leave it. The McNair children, being mixed bloods and apparently literate, were able to grave on stone the harsh feelings which hundreds of their less learned tribesmen must have felt but had to carry away to the West in their hearts.

From the site of McNairs, the Old Federal Road closely parallels U.S. 411 for a distance and then begins to pull eastward from it as a present-day backcountry road. It crossed the Ocoee River at Cates Old Ford and continued into Benton, Tennessee, where, in the words of one elderly informant, "It whupped by the Courthouse Square and kept a-going north, straight as an arr'r." And along here it does go nearly as straight as an arrow. From the beginning at Ramhurst to its northern end, this eastern fork of the Federal Road follows a remarkably straight course. Its directness is the more unusual because as it goes farther into Tennessee, it passes through a country that becomes more and more rugged. The road takes skillful advantage of little valleys, however, running between rows of serrated knobs along a level course which seems especially provided for it by nature.

The old trace crossed to the west of No. 411 at Benton and passed over the Hiwassee River near Columbus, below the mouth of Conasauga Creek. From there it leads on to Good Springs to the west of Etowah. Above this point a stretch of it is now missing, but the road takes up again at Mecky Pike, the first crossroads above Etowah, where it now runs to the east of U.S. 411, and then, as a poorly maintained crushed rock road, it leads past Nonaburg (or "Nonnyburg") to the east of Englewood. It continues still as a present-day route into Monroe County, Tennessee, past Nochee Creek and Rocky Spring to a little crossroads two miles east of Madisonville. This road junction is Old Tellico, county seat before the coming of the railroad. It was once a prominent intersection point for early thoroughfares, with various trails fanning out to the notable towns of the Overhill Cherokees along the Little Tennessee river to the north. The main stem of the Federal trace, however, led on to Niles Ferry on the Little Tennessee, just below the bridge where U.S. 411 now spans that stream. Here the Old Federal Road ends. By ferry it connected over the river with the noted Old Maryville Road and from there to Knoxville. Across the river and up a bit was the famous Tellico Block House which the Americans maintained for awhile among the Cherokees.[3] Upstream, just a short distance from where the old road ends, in a pretty wooded bend is the site of tragic Fort Loudon, where nearly two hundred years ago a besieged British garrison surrendered to the Cherokees with the understanding that it could withdraw to Carolina. Many of the soldiers were slaughtered, however, a day or two later while on the return home. A little farther up, the river valley widens into an area of beautiful pastures and meadows surrounded by rolling grassy hills. This section was the heart of the Overhill Cherokee country. Each pretty bend of the Little Tennessee here was the site of a Cherokee town or village. Chief among them all, several miles up from Niles Ferry, was Chota, the noted old capital of these Indians.

Back at Ramhurst, Georgia, the left branch of the Federal Road leads northwest by historic Spring Place in Murray County toward Chattanooga. No one living along its course now seems to remember it as a federal route; generally it is referred to as the Old Chattanoogee Road[4] although in rare instances a few old-timers recall it as the Georgia Road. The last is its oldest name, under which the government first sought a passageway through the Cherokee country.

At Spring Place the road bore to the left of the village and the majestic old Vann house that stands just north of that place. This was the home site of James Vann, an Indian country white man who was influential on the Indian side in opening the trace. The original ferry and the old inn back on the Chattahoochee were established and operated by him.

A stretch of the early trail is missing along here, but it takes up again at Free Hope Church Crossroads, northwest of Spring Place, and runs straight north to the Old Chattanooga Ford below the mouth of Mill Creek on Conasauga River. The ford is no longer used, but the former trace is still there. It leads northward through Whitfield County by Dawnville and on toward Prater Mill, where today's highway crosses Coahulla Creek. A mile or two below the mill, however, the Federal Road turned west to cross the Coahulla back of the Thompson place at lots 267 and 274 of the 11th District 3d Section of the original Cherokee County.

At the top of the hill beyond Prater Mill on the old Manis place, it rejoins the present-day road, Georgia 201. To retrace the dim former trace from this intersection back to its ford on Coahulla was a long jaunt afoot for a hot day, and the round trip called for rest. Then an old man happened along, and his curiosity, coupled with the attraction of another fellow comfortably stretched in the enticing shade, tempted him to sit and talk.

He was kindly and intelligent and remembered much about the route. Near us, back a bit on the original trace, he said, was a log house, a "public stop, whur travelling folks putt up at." He had helped tear down the structure and had found some long-hidden gold pieces in the chinking between the logs. The incident reminded him of a rich old man who had once lived up the road, who was fond of wearing a longtail coat ornamented with five-dollar gold pieces for buttons. When the man died he was buried in this coat, but some ghouls disinterred the body one night shortly after the burial and made off with the buttons. He rambled along from one tale to another and finally came to the incident of the stagecoach falling in the hole. (That was the third time this one had cropped out in the excursion along the old trace!) Many years ago, he recounted, a stagecoach travelling the Federal Road passed over a cavernous stretch that collapsed, plunging the vehicle, passengers, driver, and horses into a chasm. This incident made a great impression, and some old-timers on the route can relate the incident with as much vividness as though it had happened last year. Their knowledge of the event, however, must be at the very least third-hand, because the accident took place as early as 1829.

The old man's recountings pointed up the fact that a reservoir of stories, tall tales, and backwoodsy anecdotes surround the notable early roads and trails of this region. They seem to float over the old thoroughfares, waiting for some inquisitor to pluck them from the air and commit them to print. But the last generation to plod the roads in the days of the horse, and which had time on the relatively slow trips of those days to absorb these stories from older people, is going fast and there is not much time left to capture what they know.

From the Manis place the Federal Road runs with Georgia 201 to Varnell, Red Hill in pioneer days, and from there led west over Cohutta Ridge on a course so steep that the modern road was relocated to get a better grade. It continues westward into Catoosa County, and just to the east of Ringgold Gap joins U.S. 41. Along here in Indian days was Taylors, a noted public stop. Taylor's Ridge, running to the southwest from the gap, commemorates the name. The old highway passed a little below today's Ringgold, but soon falls into U.S. 41 again and turns northwestward. At Pine Grove Church Crossroads beyond Peavine Creek, it turns left from 41 and in the fashion of Roman military roads went straight over a steep ridge, leaving a person of nowadays wondering how old-timers and their draft animals had the wind power and stamina to use such a trail. On the far side of this hill the trace ran down a draw, locally known as the Narr'rs, and came out by what is now the Scruggs farm. Superficial evidence of the road now ends, and it is necessary to search afoot from here on to the Tennessee line for signs of its course. In front of the Scruggs residence, it ran through a bottom and pasture to West Chickamauga Creek, where it crossed at the Red House Ford, which was named for a distillery that used to be located on the west bank. During the War Between the States sharp fighting took place at this passage, which today at a casual glance seems nothing more than a depression by which stock go down to drink. Closer examination of the area, however, will disclose that it is the only natural crossing for a considerable distance up and down the stream, because at the ford a little island has choked the steep-banked and miry creek into a shoal.

A short distance beyond the creek the former trace passed in front of the old Mack Smith home. Viewed from a present-day nearby road the house sits at an odd angle. Actually it was built to face the Federal Road. This fact can be verified by lining up the gentle, grassy depression in front of the home with the Red House Ford and it will be seen that the declivity is the old highway.

The Federal Road led on across Spring Creek bottoms in what is now a large dairy pasture and mounted Missionary Ridge beyond, passing the Stancell place above Lake Winnepesaukat. It is now right at the Tennessee line, in the outskirts of Rossville. It is lost, however, in a maze of yards, alleys, and streets. But from here it went on to Ross's Landing, now Chattanooga, and from there around the tip of Lookout Mountain, over Raccoon Mountain and along the south side of the Tennessee River, to a crossing successively known as Lowrey's or Belcher's Ferry at the mouth of Battle Creek above South Pittsburg in Marion County, Tennessee. From there an early road turned down the west side of the Tennessee into Alabama, and this trail was the route followed by early emigrants from Georgia and the Carolinas into the area around Huntsville, which became Alabama's first capital. The main course of the Old Federal Road, however, continued northwestward in Tennessee, passing Monteagle, the head of Stone's River, and Murfreesboro, to Nashville.

In reconsidering the route of the Federal Road, familiarity with the present highway maze may make it difficult to understand why the old trace followed the course which it used. At first glance it appears to follow a circuitous path. As a matter of fact, however, it was a remarkably straight thoroughfare considering the days in which it was laid out, and this can be verified by laying a rule across a map between Chattanooga and Athens, Georgia. It will be seen that the edge of the rule coincides closely with the route followed by the western leg of the old trail. The branch from east Tennessee is not so direct because of the necessity of by-passing the rugged Blue Ridge. As noted, though, this fork, from Niles Ferry to Ramhurst, is unusual for its directness considering the country traversed.

On the whole, the route of the old road was selected with skill. It was planned to avoid excessive fordings, which early travellers dreaded because of the delays or dangers of high waters. When such passages were necessary, the road in nearly every instance led to spots where geological structures changed, in order to take advantage of the shoals which often characterize such locations. When the trace went straight over steep hills or followed high ridges, presumably such a course was followed to save distance or to stick to elevated, well-drained areas.

Following 1805, the road served as a leading thoroughfare for about 30 years. After the 1830's it gradually declined in importance as a through route, when new towns sprang up and the highway system grew and reshaped itself in other directions. Possibly some of the old road's decline, however, may be attributed, as one informant opined, to a desire of travellers to "git shet of them lung-bustin' hills." Even though the Federal Road lost its arterial character a century ago, it was never completely abandoned, since large segments yet serve the communities along its old course.

—*GMNL* 10(1957): 150-57, reprinted from *EUQ* 6(1950)

NOTES

1. The author first travelled a part of the Old Federal Road many years ago. He is grateful, however, to the Research Committee at Emory for a grant-in-aid which enabled him to trace this former thoroughfare and a number of other historic trails and highways across the South.

2. On the original surveys of Cherokee County, the early trail is shown crossing Talking Rock Creek and then crossing back before continuing as depicted in the text.

3. Negotiations with the Cherokees to establish the Federal Road were carried on here. Also the original Indian route which the Federal Road followed forded the Little Tennessee near the Block House.

4. One may smile at this pronounciation of Chattanooga, but the people who use this form say the word exactly as it was handed down to them as an Indian name.

Wolf Pens and Wolf Pits

The common occurrence of Wolf in the geographic names of Georgia serves as a reminder that this animal was once plentiful in the state. Apparently the Indians made little effort to kill wolves, but the early stock-raising whites became implacable enemies of these predators and sought to destroy them at every chance because of their destructive inroads into the settlers' cattle. The most effective methods for catching wolves involved traps called wolf pens and wolf pits. These devices were widely used, first in the older section along the coast and eventually across the state as the various areas were settled. No doubt these traps were mainly responsible for the ultimate extinction of wolves in the region. And, although those savage creatures have long since disappeared from these parts, we still retain here and there among Georgia's interesting placenames the terms Wolf Pit and Wolf Pen.

The last name is usually found in old records or on maps in connection with a stream or mountain, viz: Wolfpen Branch, an upper affluent of Lotts Creek in western Bulloch County; Wolfpen Branch in McIntosh; Wolfpen Branch in Bryan; Wolfpen Branch in Habersham; Wolfpen Mountain in Gilmer; Wolfpen Gap in lower Union; and Wolfpen Ridge on the line between Union and Towns counties.

The designation Wolf Pit, on the other hand, is more likely to be found in a community name, as in the Wolf Pit District of southern Stephens County; or, as the appellation of a specific place, like The Wolf Pit on upper Brushy Creek in Irwin, about three miles south of Ocilla. Other wolf pit sites are in western Bacon County and in the Bowen Mill District of Ben Hill, to the northeast of Fitzgerald. There were exceptions on this score, however, since northeast Bartow has a Wolf Pen District and Liberty County once had a Wolf Pit Branch.

There probably are numbers of other places in which names such as these are known locally although they do not appear on maps, because, as has been previously noted, wolf pits and pens were once much used. W. A. Covington, for instance, in his *History of Colquitt County*, says that county formerly had three or four pits for trapping wolves.

We have to depend largely on hearsay for information about the nature of these traps, since there is probably no one in the state now who is old enough to have seen one of the pits or pens in actual operation. Fortunately, however, there are numbers of elderly people who have heard older persons explain how the contrivances were used. Apparently there were different kinds of pens and at least two ways of operating a pit, one of which involved the use of a pen as well as a hole in the ground.

One type of pen was constructed of large saplings, and had the appearance of a miniature log cabin, except that it was flat across the top, being well-covered with small logs or sections of stout saplings. A U-shaped tunnel large enough to permit passage of a wolf was dug from the outside to the inside of the structure, where a piece of meat was placed as bait. A wolf would crawl through the hole to get the bait but would be unwilling to leave by the way he had entered, thus staying penned up until his captors arrived to kill him. It is hard to believe this sort of device could have been very effective in trapping wolves, although some old-timers say such pens were used in South Georgia. One would think that a wolf was too foxy to be caught by such means; or that small animals would have rendered the trap ineffective by eating the meat before a prospective wolf victim showed up.

A more logical type of wolf pen was constructed of strong saplings, much on the order of a common bird trap, that is, the sides of the pen would be gradually recessed as the structure rose, making a sort of pyramid. The top, however, would be left open. Such pens were about six feet high. When bait was placed inside, a wolf was easily tempted to climb the sloping outside to the open top and jump in. But once inside the slope of the sides was against him to prevent crawling out, and he was unable to leap straight up the necessary height to escape through the hole by which he had entered.

In thinking about the operation of the wolf pens, one wonders if the animals did not sometimes scratch out and get away. No old-timers mention floors being used with such structures. Possibly wolves did occasionally escape in this way, a contingency which perhaps encouraged the preparation of a wolf pit, a trap that was tedious to build, but which undoubtedly was effective in catching and holding the wolves.

One type of wolf pit involved digging a hole about 10 feet square and 6 to 8 feet deep. Such a pit was dug in firm soil around a deep-rooted tree which was left standing in the hole, with a small mass of surface roots and earth to form a sort of island in the middle of the hole. In digging the pit, care was taken to slope the sides outward from the top toward the bottom in order that the prospective victims would not be able to get a good foothold for climbing out.

This sort of pit was "set" by dragging a piece of meat about the area surrounding the hole to provide a scent leading up to the trap. The meat as bait would then be placed at the former base of the tree standing in the pit. Seemingly a wolf was not afraid to try leaping across the opening to the meat at the foot of the tree. But even if he landed by the bait, he was caught, because from a narrow clinging position, the animal could not spring back the distance to freedom on the outer edge of the pit. In trying to do so he fell short and dropped into the hole. It is said a whole pack of wolves could be caught at one time with a device of this type.

Another form of wolf pit was both a pen and a pit. This combination apparently explains why some sites of former wolf pits are referred to as both wolf pens and wolf pits.

This trap was made by digging a hole some 6 feet square and 6 to 8 feet deep, again with the sides sloping outward from top to bottom. A small pen in the form of a fence would then be erected around the hole. In the middle of the pit a stake as high as the hole was deep would be placed to hold the bait and support some light brush and leaves that would be spread over the opening to conceal the pit. In setting this trap the meat for bait would also be dragged around through the woods and then placed atop the stake. A wolf to get at the bait would jump over the pen or fence, but instead of landing to enjoy a feast would crash through the covering of brush into the pit to await his captors. The use of a stake with this sort of pit seemingly explains the origin of the name Wolf Stake Knob, a mountain on the line between Towns and Rabun counties.

—*GMNL* 6(1953): 87-89, 108

Ty Ty as a Geographic Name

The wag who said there is nothing unusual about the name Ty Ty[1] except that it is spelled with two capitals and two small letters understated the attractiveness of such a singular appellation. It is one geographic term of this state that is sure to catch the eye and set in train speculation as to its meaning. The wag was right, however, if he meant to imply that the designation Ty Ty is more common than is generally thought. Actually Georgia has long used this word, perhaps even back into colonial times, as a label for certain streams, swamps, thickets, galls, ponds, and lakes. The name is drawn from two members of the Cyrilla family: *Cyrilla racemiflora,* variously called ironwood, leatherwood, he-huckleberry, or white titi; and *Cliftonia monophylla,* also known as buckwheat tree or black titi. These plants, as shrubs or small trees, are found in the pineland regions of the coastal plains, growing as thickets in low wet places, or along the boggy fringes of streams.

The best known bearers of the name are the town of Ty Ty in western Tift County, and two Georgia Militia districts, one in the above county and another in Colquitt. These political entities in turn, however, draw their names from neighboring Ty Ty Creek, a stream which rises in Worth County, near Shingler, to the northeast of Sylvester, and flows southward through Tift and a part of Colquitt to join Warrior Creek, thence into Little River, a tributary of the Withlacoochee.

In addition to the foregoing use of the appellation, there is a Ty Ty Creek in western Sumter County, an affluent of the Kinchafoonee;[2] and a Ty Ty Branch, an Alapaha River tributary, in extreme eastern Lowndes.[3]

Formerly the name was employed in connection with other streams and spots, viz.:

1. Tyty or Tight eye Creek a rightbank tributary of Flint River which entered that stream about 7 miles above Oglethorpe in Macon County.[4]

2. Tye Tye Lake in Bibb County, below Macon and to the east of Stratton on the Southern Railway.[5]

3. Titi Swamp to the east of Bainbridge and near Open Pond Crossroads in eastern Decatur County.[6]

4. Titi Swamp in Bulloch County, on the left bank of Lott's Creek.[7] The name in this instance was found on an early land plat, dated 1799. This is the oldest recording of the term which could be located.

5. Ty Ty Crossing, a former point on the old Savannah and Southern Railroad in what is now the Camp Stewart area of upper Long County.[8]

6. Two neighboring "tieties" or swamps in Effingham County;[9] and

7. Ty Ty Pond at the old San Barnard hunting and camping site near Isabella in Worth County.[10]

Probably there are numbers of other spots to which the label Ty Ty has been applied locally, although these designations have not appeared on maps.

It is of interest to add that neighboring states have also used this appellation. Maps of those areas, for instance, have listed a Titi School, to the northwest of Pineland in Jasper County,[11] South Carolina; a Tietie Creek, an affluent of Yellow Water River, near today's Crestview, Florida,[12] a Tighteye Chute and a Tighteye Bar in Alabama on the river of that name, near Selma.[13]

Placename students have long debated the origin of Ty Ty or titi. It is commonly held that the word has an Indian background. Perhaps so, although there is little or no proof that such is the case. A check of available Muscogee and Choctaw dictionaries and word lists did not reveal any term or definition that seemed to have a bearing on the name. The designation, of course, might be traceable to the Uchees or Yemasees, because it can be found in early usage in areas that were once inhabited by those Indians. The word may be African in origin and this possibility should not be overlooked.

On the other hand, Dr. Roland Harper, referring to the inscrutable density of ty ty thickets, has suggested that the name may be derived from tighteye.[14] The writer favors this version of the word's origin because it is easy to believe that pioneer people would have delighted in coining a term like tighteye for a thick place that was difficult to see through. But more important still, this explanation has documentary support. In at least two instances, early Georgia surveyors in laying off wilderness lands applied the terms Tighteye, Tight Eye, and Tight-eye to watercourses which we came to know as Ty Ty creeks. These streams are the creeks of Sumter[15] and Macon[16] counties that have been previously mentioned. It should be noted that the surveyors employed the singular form in these spellings and not the plural.

In conclusion, it might be pointed out that there are little grounds for the complaint that botanical texts and references confuse the term by spelling it titi. This form is subject to being mispronounced "teetee," but otherwise texts follow a version of the name that was used in this area over a century and a half ago.[17]

NOTES

1. Ty Ty is now customarily written as two words. It is not uncommon, however, to see it spelled TyTy or Tyty.
2. Map of *Sumter County Georgia* (State Highway Board of Georgia, 1939.)
3. *Lowndes County Georgia* (State Highway Board of Georgia, 1939).
4. 1st District in the 2nd Section (or 1st District of original Muscogee [now Macon] County), W. P. Reid, D.S., survey of 1826, Platbook KKKK, Land Records of Georgia, Surveyor General Department, Atlanta.

As Ty Ty Creek the stream enters Flint River in land lot 86. It is labelled "tyty Cr." in lot 95, and "Tight eye" in lots 105 and 106.

The William Phillips "Map of Macon County," 1871, original in the Surveyor General Department, labels the stream "Tilys Creek."

5. B. W. Frobel, "Map of Bibb," 1869, original in the Land Records of Georgia.
6. Lot 57, 15th District of original Early (now Decatur) County, survey of 1819, Platbook DDD. By error this lot was entered with the lots of District 14 in the same volume. A note with the entry, however, indicates that lot 57 of the 15th District is meant. The spot in question is labelled "Gall or Titi Swamp."
7. Land of George Willis, Bulloch County, survey of March 19, 1799, Headrights Platbook I. I. p. 51.
8. *Glenville Quadrangle—Georgia*, topographical map (U.S. Geological Survey, ed. 1920). The spot is shown in Liberty County; it would be in today's Long.
9. Land of William Hester, Effingham County, survey of 1836, Headrights Platbook A.B., p. 163. It was not possible to locate the present area of these "tieties."
10. Mrs. Lillie Martin Grubbs, *History of Worth County, Georgia*, (Macon: Burke Co., 1934), p. 32.
11. *Pineland Quadrangle*, topographical map (U.S. Geological Survey, ed. 1919).
12. S. Augustus Mitchell, *Map of the States of Louisiana, Mississippi and Alabama* (Philadelphia, 1835).
13. Appendixes to the report of the Chief of Army Engineers, 1884, House Exec. Doc. 1, 48th Cong., 2nd Sess., Part 2, Appendix N19, p. 1201.
14. Roland Harper, "How Ty Ty Got Its Name," *Albany Herald*, May 23, 1953.
15. District 17 of original Lee (now a part of Sumter) County, Felix G. Gibson, D.S., survey of 1827, Platbook SSSS. The stream is labelled "Tight Eye" in lots 53 and 56; "Tight-eye" in lots 55, 58, 108, *passim;* and "Tighteye" in lots 52 and 109.
16. 1st District in the 2nd Section; (or District 1 of original Muscogee), lots 105 and 106.
17. [The *Dictionary of Americanisms*, 2: 1732, clearly connects *tight-eye* with "thicket" and *titi* with the shrub, but it does not commit itself to the Goff reversal of folk-etymology. The earliest citations in *DA* for *tight-eye* are 1905; for *titi* 1827. The plat books mentioned in Goff's notes 4 and 15 bring the date of *tight-eye* back to 1827, one more piece of evidence of the value of placename study for lexicographers and word-historians. See Goff on Gardi-Guardeye in Sketch No. 58, above. Byrd Granger remarks: "It seems to me that early surveyors might have created a folk etymology by writing down what they thought they heard. Texas chapparal, for instance, is as 'tight-eye' as anything, and New England briar country is no slouch, so that it seems to me, at any rate, that similar circumstances should bring up the same 'tight-eye' elsewhere, but so far as I know, it does not occur elsewhere." In other words, there had to be an Indian name in the district to beget the folk etymology. *FLU.*]

The Poley Bridge Creeks

Southwest of Lithonia, Georgia, in lower DeKalb County, there is a stream which bears the interesting title of Pole Bridge Creek. Although Georgia has long had streams of this name, earlier people usually gave a distinctive twist to the expression by making it "poley bridge." As the words imply, this designation was derived from the use of poles in constructing a bridge. The name, however, seems peculiar to Georgia, and especially to the old central eastern counties where the term goes back to Revolutionary days. With the possible exception of South Carolina,[1] if neighboring states use or once used the name, it does not appear on general maps of those areas.

A person seeing or hearing the expression Pole Bridge or Poley Bridge for the first time is likely to be puzzled. But other people, including surveyors, cartographers, and platbook clerks, have also been confused by the name because the term can be found locally in old records or on early maps under forms like: "Polley Bridge Creek,"[2] "Pooley Bridge Branch,"[3] "Pole Bridge Creek,"[4] "Polebirds Branch,"[5] and "Pooloy Bridge Creek."[6] One modern map labels such a stream "Polar Bridge Branch."[7] The same chart also lists a "Poorly Branch." Perhaps this last spelling was a phonetic spelling of poley, because poorly pronounced "po' ly" in our vernacular would come out poley.

When one seeks information from elderly people on the nature of a pole bridge, he finds differing views on the subject. These conflicting explanations are all plausible, but they leave an urbanite of nowadays uncertain as to what a poley bridge was *really* like. Perhaps there actually were several types of such bridges.

Certain old-timers, for instance, say the pioneers' poley bridge was nothing more than a strip of what is now commonly called a corduroy road, that is, a roadway formed by placing a layer of poles on the ground at right angles to the course, usually across a boggy or muddy stretch. These teeth-rattling structures were fairly common before the advent of the automobile, and even today they can be found in swampy areas where logging and lumber trucks operate. This sort of crossing, of course, would not be a bridge in the present understanding of that term.

Others claim a poley bridge was not a corduroy road but a simple device on the same principle. These informants say a pole bridge was constructed at a boggy spot or over a difficult branch by placing a pile of poles or saplings at the troublesome site, taking care to alternate the ends of the butts and the tips of the poles to prevent a vehicle skidding or sliding, as would be the case if the large ends of the poles were all placed on the same side with a slope toward the smaller tips at the other extremity of the saplings. Furthermore, this alternating of the tips and butts tended to lock the poles in place so they would not be washed away with a freshet. This sort of passage is common in Georgia today, in connection with field and wood roads.

Some informants insist that a poley bridge was a true bridge which frontiersmen made by using logs as stringers with saplings or poles placed close together as cross pieces for the flooring. Such a structure, they point out, could have been cheaply and easily built over a small stream at most any point.

Despite these explanations, however, the question can be raised whether pole bridges were designed for vehicular traffic. Usually the streams bearing the name were small creeks or branches that ordinarily would not have required a bridge for the passage of a wagon or cart. Furthermore, some of the old land plats which name pole bridge creeks do not depict a road crossing the streams, although it was customary for a surveyor to indicate such routes on the plats of properties he surveyed. And too, in at least two instances,[8] pole bridge creeks were reported by original surveyors in surveying wilderness lands which had been acquired from the Indians. There were some crude vehicular ways in the areas of these surveys, but they are not shown going over the streams in question. These points leave the impression that poley bridges were constructed for foot passage only.

There are informants who support their view by insisting that a pole bridge was merely a footlog with a handrail for balancing while crossing the log. Others say that such a bridge was made by felling or placing two parallel logs across a stream, then weaving a mesh of poles between them to form a relatively wide walkway. This explanation leaves the interesting implication that some pioneers were too giddy to cross a single footlog and needed a wider passage. It might also be added that of the types of pole bridges which are being discussed, this last structure is the only one that can not be found in use at the present time.

And finally, there are informants who say a real poley bridge was none of the devices that have been described above. They claim a pole bridge was made by placing several stout poles side by side, between sets of holding stakes at each end, to form a span over a small stream or across a low, wet place. The bridge could be laid with or without a handrail. These people point out that structures of this type are still fairly common in Georgia, and that this crossing is superior to a footlog in that it is wider and flatter. They also note that a series of poley bridges could be easily placed over a wide boggy spot in the same manner as one would construct a catwalk of planks. Such a structure could provide passage across a difficult site too wide for a footlog to span.

—*GMNL* 7(1954): 133-35

NOTES

1. There is a Pole Branch (a tributary of Fox Creek) in northwest Aiken County, S.C. Cf. *Warrenville Quadrangle* (U.S. Geological Survey, ed., 1928). This stream may have once been known as a pole bridge branch, because several of Georgia's former pole bridge streams are now simply called pole, poley, or poly branches without the word bridge.

2. Land of Alexander Berryhill, Richmond County, survey of 1787, Platbook L, p. 192, Land Records of Georgia, Surveyor General Department, Atlanta. This stream is seemingly the Polar Bridge Branch mentioned in the text and cited on the *Hephzibah* topographical sheet. See n. 7, below.

3. Land of Isaac Barker, Screven County, survey of 1796, Platbook BB, p. 408.

4. Lot 118, District 16 of original Henry County, Platbook CCCC, survey of 1821. This stream is now in southeast DeKalb County. The creek did not actually cross lot 118; the plat bore the notation that the lot was on the waters, meaning watershed, of "Pole Bridge Creek."

5. "Map of Bibb County," B. W. Frobel, 1869, original in Georgia Surveyor General Department. This stream, an east-bank tributary of present Rocky Creek, was in the area of today's West Macon.

6. Adiel Sherwood, *A Gazetteer of the State of Georgia* (Charleston, S.C., 1827), p. 87. He placed this creek in Morgan County, as a headwaters tributary of Little River.

7. *Hephzibah Sheet*, distributed by the U.S. Geological Survey, but prepared by the U.S. Army Engineers, 1948.

8. District 16 of original Henry County, survey of 1821, Platbook CCCC; and lot 260, District 4 of original Early County, survey of 1820, Platbook AAA. The Pole Bridge Creek in original Early did not retain that name. It was in today's northwest Calhoun County where it is now considered as the west prong of Pachitla Creek.

The Beaverdam Creeks

For general convenience and to meet the requirements of postal authorities, we avoid the repetition of names for towns, cities, and counties within a particular state. But in the naming of communities, rural church sites, crossroad points, and physical objects like mountains or streams we are prone to duplicate names. In Georgia, for instance this tendency is especially noticeable in stream naming. Thus there can be found here a surprising repetition of names like Cedar Creek, Camp Creek, Dry Creek, and so on. Chief among these manifold appellations, however, is a group that will be referred to in this article as the beaverdam creeks. This category embodies streams bearing labels like: Beaver Creek, Beaver Fork, Beaver Ruin, Beaver Run, Beaver Branch, and, of course, Beaverdam Creek.

Such names date back to the earliest days of Georgia. By 1829, according to Adiel Sherwood, the state had no less than twenty creeks and branches called Beaver Dam, with nearly every county of that period having a stream of this name.[1] In the intervening century and a quarter, some of the designations covered in Sherwood's count were changed; but in the meantime numbers of other streams in the beaverdam category were also added, until now Georgia has about forty water courses which reflect a beaver label. This number, coupled with the names that were once applied, seemingly makes the beaver creeks rank over the years as Georgia's leading geographic appellation.

The prevalence of this long-used tab serves to remind us of how plentiful beavers once were in the state. In fact, it is chiefly through these names that we know where those animals could be found in this section, because there is scant material in the literature of Georgia about beavers and relatively little information to indicate that the animals were once as abundant here as the names imply. Perhaps beavers were so commonplace in former years that few people ever thought of discussing them in detail while writing about Georgia. It might be added too, that despite the apparent abundance of beavers, the pelt of that animal seems not to have been very important here in the fur and skin trading of Indian days, certainly less so than in more northerly states. The beaver skin is mentioned in old trading house journals of this area but not nearly so often as the deer hide which was the staple of trade with red people.

The accompanying map names and locates the beaver creeks of

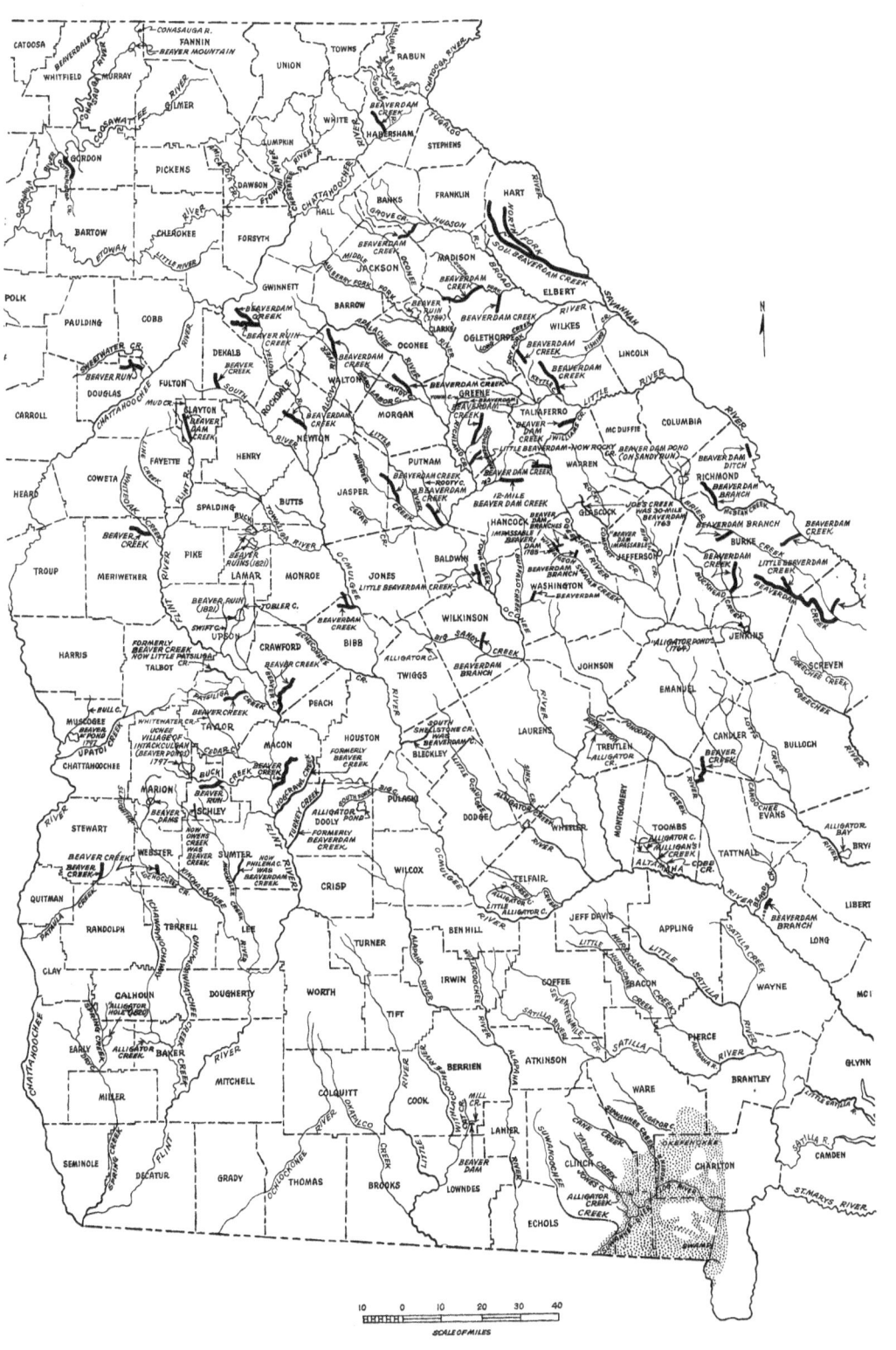

The Beaver Dam Creeks of Georgia

Georgia.[2] It will be noted that these streams were arranged in an interesting fashion, and that they were not uniformly distributed in all parts of the state. Instead of being widely scattered, the beaverdam streams tended to concentrate in a rough horse-shoe pattern or arc that spanned the middle part of the state from the central Savannah River area to southwest Georgia. Judging by the waterways that bear their names, therefore, the beavers favored the Piedmont region and certain sections of the Upper Coastal Plain as a habitat. They were not common in the upper and lower parts of the state, or along the coast. One source consulted does show a Beaver Creek on Wolf Island at the mouth of the Altamaha,[3] but local people say this label is a mistake; the stream properly should be Beacon Creek after a marker located near its mouth. The lack of beavers in the southern part of the state where alligators were found is easy to understand because the latter were deadly enemies of the beavers. But the general absence of beavers in the mountain counties is a puzzle which will be left for others to solve.

Perhaps biologists and geologists will find the pattern of beaver distribution of interest and will be able to explain why the animals favored the area of the rough arc across the state. And too, wild life and conservation specialists may be interested in the sections which were once preferred by the beavers.

Among the former beaverdam streams that now bear other names are the following:

1. South Shellstone Creek, of western Bleckley County, which enters main Shellstone, on the south side near its mouth on the Ocmulgee River.[4]

2. Hog Crawl Creek, on the line between Macon and Dooly counties.[5]

3. Turkey Creek, an east-bank tributary of Flint River in Dooly.[6]

4. Little Patsiliga Creek of southeast Talbot and upper Taylor counties.[7]

5. Rock Creek in the Liberty District of south Greene County.[8]

6. Doolittle Creek that heads in the East Lake Country Club area of southwest DeKalb County and flows southward into South River.[9]

7. Owens Creek, an east-bank tributary of Muckalee in southwest Schley County.[10]

8. Philema Creek, a left-bank affluent of Muckalee in south central Sumter.[11]

9. Long Branch or Davenport's Mill Creek that enters Bear, or Lochochee Creek to the east of Weston in Webster County.[12]

In addition to the above there are even earlier streams that have lost the word beaver in connection with their names. One of these was the 30-Mile Beaver Dam, which lay athwart the noted lower trading path from Augusta to the Creek Indians. Packhorsemen stopped beside the stream to camp, it being a long day's journey from Augusta. Yonge and DeBrahm name and depict the creek on their map of 1763, in what is now Warren, Glascock, and Jefferson counties, running southward into the Ogeechee, to the west of Rocky Comfort Creek.[13] This location, however, was a guess, because there is no large stream entering that river where they show it. Very probably Yonge and DeBrahm were referring to a stream now called Joe's Creek, which arises in southwest Warren and flows southward to enter Rocky Comfort on the west side, to the south of Gibson. A map of 1779 shows a Beaver Dam creek joining Rocky Comfort in this area.[14] Furthermore, a 1786 plat shows the stream as both Joe's Creek and as Beaver Dam.[15]

It would be interesting to know the origin of the name 30-Mile Beaver Dam. Ordinarily titles like Two Mile Creek, Ten Mile Creek, etc., derived their designations from the fact that they were a stated number of miles from some given spot. This creek was more than 30 miles from Augusta, although it was about 30 miles from the Rock Landing,[16] chief crossing point for the old trail on the Oconee. Perhaps this last distance gave rise to the name. It is possible, of course, that the expression referred to the length of the stream. In such a case, the prominence of the creek may have arisen from the difficulty of crossing it to avoid a long detour and not from the attractiveness of its banks as a camping site. The boggy nature of a beaver colony made such spots extremely difficult to cross.

Not far from the 30-Mile Beaver Dam Creek, in today's Hancock County, to the north of Sparta, was the 12-Mile Beaver Dam Creek.[17] This stream, a south-bank affluent of Shoulderbone Creek, still retains the name Beaverdam, but without the 12-Mile portion of its frontier tab. And interestingly enough, its early designation seems also to have been connected with another Indian traders' trail, because the noted Oakfuskee Path or main Upper Creek trading route, from Augusta to present Alabama, skirted the full length of the stream.

Among the former beaver waterways which lost their names were two small Beaver Dam branches of present northeast Washington County, in the area between Williamson Swamp Creek and the Ogeechee.[18] Each of these streams had one of the branches as a tributary.

Williamson Swamp itself was once an important home of beavers, because an early land plat showing an upper section of the stream is marked "Impassable beaver-dam on."[19] The area involved lay to the north of present Warthen in Washington County. Two other beaver creeks are shown in early surveys to the west of the above areas: one as an affluent of Lamar's Creek, to the southwest of Sandersville; and another in present southeast Baldwin County as a small east-bank tributary of the Oconee.[20]

It is of interest to find these particular beaver areas because they are inside the arc of the beaverdam pattern across the state, in a region that generally did not have many beaver streams according to old records.

In view of Georgia's profusion of Indian names, it is surprising that only one or two present Indian designations can be found which relate to beavers. One clear example in this category is Oothkalooga Creek which empties into the Oostanaula, below Calhoun, in Gordon County. According to Mooney, this name was derived from a Cherokee word which referred to places where there are beaver dams.[21]

In the area where the Creeks or Muscogee Indians lived there is only one term that may have pertained to beavers. This name is found in Ichawaynochaway Creek which heads in southern Stewart and Webster and flows southward to join Flint River below Newton. Since beaver in Muscogee has been variously rendered as *ichas, itchas, itch hasooka, Ets hasswah,* and *itch hásua,* there are grounds for assuming that Ichawaynochaway possibly concerned beavers. One can not be positive about the matter, however; that name may have referred to a male deer, since the Muscogee word for buck was *itchóonúnwaw.*

Curiously, the Creek term for beaverdam did not include the Indian word for beaver. Benjamin Hawkins makes this plain in referring to an Uchee Town called Intackculgau, which he translates as Beaver Ponds.[22] Elsewhere he spells the name "In-tuch-cul-gau" and states that the word is derived from "in-tuch-ke," a dam across water, plus "ul-gau," all, meaning beaver dams.[23] The settlement in question was on upper Opilthlucco, or Big Swamp Creek near today's Tazewell in Marion County. This stream is known today as Buck Creek.[24]

In another place Hawkins mentions a waterway called "Intachcoochee."[25] This word means Little Beaver Dams or Ponds, on the basis of his interpretation of the first name. The stream referred to seems to be present upper Culpepper Creek, of today's central Crawford County.

In their clan names the Creeks apparently used both the word for beaver and for beaverdam. For example, Gatschet says *Itch hásualgi* means beaver gens;[26] and that *Intatckalgi* refers to beaver dam people.[27] As noted, however, with the possible exception of Ichawaynochaway, none of these Muscogee forms remains among the Creek words that are retained today.

In a consideration of the names concerned with beavers, one appellation that deserves particular attention is Beaver Ruin. This unusual expression goes back to post-Revolutionary days and is apparently indigenous to the state. If other sections use, or once used the label, it does not appear on their general maps. The name, as applied here, referred to an extensive area which a colony of beavers had flooded and devastated with a network of dams. Such spots were characterized by expansive bogs and large numbers of deadened trees which had been destroyed by sheets of backed-up water. From the shadings that early surveyors put on maps and land plats to indicate the area of a beaver ruin we know that such developments reached incredible sizes. In some instances there were elongated ruins that extended for several miles up and down a creek, while there were others which spread from the main stream into the areas of tributary water courses.

Georgia had a number of Beaver Ruins, and even today retains the name in Beaver Ruin Creek, which heads on the east side of Norcross in Gwinnett County and flows eastward to join the Yellow River. This waterway has borne its title continuously since 1819, when the first surveyors of that section noted the name on their land plats and maps.[28]

One of the earliest Beaver Ruins is shown on a plat dated in 1784. It lay on the east side of the upper Middle Fork of Oconee River, at the juncture of several small tributaries of that stream.[29] Apparently the section involved was in today's Clarke County, to the west of Athens.

Another large Beaver Ruin was noted by original surveyors along what is now Little Buck Creek in present upper Lamar County, to the north of Liberty Hill. This stream, which was labelled "Beaver Ruin,"[30] and "Big Ruin" Creek,[31] had an enormous colony that extended virtually the entire length of the water course.

In the same general area, but to the south of Liberty Hill, Bonner's map shows another Beaver Ruin Creek, as a right-bank tributary of Towaliga.[32] The stream involved is the upper part of today's Little Towaliga Creek.

One of the most formidable Beaver Ruins was in today's Upson County on the headwaters of Tobler's Creek,[33] in the vicinity of the present Thomaston-Yatesville Road. It spread over parts of land lots 26, 27, 28, and 42 of District 10 of original Monroe County. These lots consisted of 202 ½ acres, and when it is noted that approximately two-thirds of lot 27 alone was shaded to indicate the area covered by devastation, one can appreciate the havoc which the beavers wrought. It might be of interest to add that much of the expanse which was covered by this ruin has now become fields and pastures.

Still another large section that was devastated by beavers but which is not actually labelled Beaver Ruin was found in District 7 of original Houston County,[34] now part of today's Crawford. From its great size, however, one is warranted in concluding that the area had the attributes of a ruin. In fact, this beaver colony, or series of colonies, was the most extensive that appears on original Georgia land surveys. Parts of it were indicated in lots 147, 165, 166, 176, 178, 187, 188, and 184 of the district; nearly half of lots 185 and 202 were shaded to show the extent of the development; while substantially the whole of lots 203, 204, 205, 207, 208, and 209 were shown as beaver swamp. The realm was so vast that it spread along the system of streams embodying Spring, Culpepper, Avera, and Beaver creeks of today's central and southern Crawford County. This great development was so extensive that early wilderness travellers made circuitous trips to by-pass it during wet weather. Benjamin Hawkins mentions such a detour when he journeyed this way in 1797.[35]

In addition to Beaver Ruins there were also Beaver Ponds. Perhaps the two designations were synonymous to the pioneers, since it is hard to envision a large pond that was not also accompanied by the devastation of a ruin. Anyhow, a plat for a 500-acre grant of 1784, in early Wilkes County, shows two beaver ponds that occupied a substantial portion of the land involved.[36]

In this instance we can be reasonably certain the grantee wanted the land for agricultural purposes, and that he proposed to get rid of the beavers. Seemingly early citizens soon learned that much of a beaver site could be turned into fields and pastures. In fact, they had a critical eye for such an opportunity, because Colonel Hawkins, in 1797, noted on the lower edge of today's Columbus a 40-acre beaver pond which he remarks was capable of being drained "at small expense of labour."[37] His comment points up the fact that beaver ponds were not deep. From observation of former beaverdam sites (and of actual beaver developments today) one is safe in concluding that ponds were usually shallow expanses of water which ranged from mere inches to only a few feet in depth.

It must have been relatively easy, therefore, to break the dams and let the water run out. The big task in reclaiming such a site involved disposing of the beavers to give the land a chance to dry. Those industrious animals were noted for their persistence; they would have been certain to work energetically to restore the broken structures unless killed or somehow driven away from the spot.

In conclusion, it might be noted that beavers have long since vanished from most of the streams which bear their names. But they have never entirely disappeared from Georgia, especially from the southwest part of the state. On Lanahassee Creek, for instance, along the edges of Webster and Marion counties,[38] there is a beaver colony which old-timers thereabouts say has endured since Indian days. In the same general area of the state there are also developments which are said to have grown from animals released by wild life people some 20 years ago. From reports, one gathers the original and planted colonies are thriving, so much so there are complaints that little beaver ruins are again being formed!

—*GMNL* 7(1954): 117-22

NOTES

1. Adiel Sherwood, *A Gazetteer of the State of Georgia*, 2nd ed. (Philadelphia: Martin and Boden, 1829), p. 77.

2. The map was prepared from numbers of sources, some of which are cited in connection with particular beaver areas in the text. The names for present-day streams are from the following: (1) current series of road maps for Georgia counties issued by the State Highway Board; (2) topographical sheets that have been prepared by the U.S. Geological Survey for parts of Georgia; and (3) *Geologic Map of Georgia*, 1939, prepared by the Georgia Division of Mines, Mining and Geology in cooperation with the U.S. Geological Survey. Among the early maps consulted were: (1) Eleazer Early, *Map of the State of Georgia*, 1818; (2) H. S. Tanner, *Georgia and Alabama;* and (3) S. Augustus Mitchell, *The Tourist's Pocket Map of the State of Georgia*, 1836. The beaver spot indicated along Lanahassee Creek in Marion County, southwest of Buena Vista, is only an approximation. Col. Hawkins mentions an Uchee settlement in that area called "Toc-co-gul-egan (tad pole)" which is believed to have been located between Lanahassee and Kinchafoonee, or just to the south of the former stream, on the Savell place. He says the site was near some beaverdams on branches of the Kinchafoonee. See Benjamin Hawkins, *A Sketch of the Creek Country, 1798-1799,* Collections of the Georgia Historical Society, Vol. 3, pt. 1 (Savannah, 1848), p. 63. The area on Lambert's Creek in Jefferson County is from the plat for Robert Cooper, survey of 1771, Platbook M, p. 23, Land Records of Georgia, Department of Archives and History, Atlanta; the site is labelled

378 / Placenames of Georgia

"Beaver dam Impassable." The beaver dam below Ray City is from the *Map of Berrien County, Georgia* (Atlanta: Hudgins, *ca.* 1910). The Alligator streams shown are from the modern maps cited above except the following: Alligator Hole on the east side of Spring Creek in Baker County is shown in lot 390, District 6 of original Early County, D. I. Blackburn, D.S., survey of 1820, Platbook BBB, Land Records of Georgia; Alligator Pond in Jenkins County is mentioned in a petition for land by William Murphree, dated Aug. 7, 1764, *Colonial Records of Georgia,* 9: 200.

3. *Darien Quadrangle—Georgia,* Zone B, topographical map (U.S. Geological Survey, 1921, reprint 1937).

4. Early, *Map of the State of Georgia.*

5. District 1, Dooly County, surveys of 1821 and 1825, Platbook PPP, lots 38, 59, 60, *passim;* and "Islands and Reserves," James Barnard's Reserve, *circa* 1825, Platbook EEEE, p. 19.

6. District 9, original Dooly County, survey of 1821, N. Parramore, D.S., Platbook QQQ, lots 64, 65, 73, *passim.* The south prong of this stream is now called Pennahatchee, which means Turkey Creek. Seemingly this name gave rise to the label Turkey Creek for the main stream.

7. District 14, original Muscogee County, survey of 1826, John Landrum, D.S., Platbook MMMM, lots 15, 16, 18, *passim;* William Phillips, map of Taylor County, 1871; originals in the Surveyor General Department.

8. Early, *Map of the State of Georgia.*

9. *Atlanta Sheet—Georgia,* topographical map (U.S. Geological Survey, ed. 1895).

10. District 30, original Lee (now part of Schley), survey of 1826, R. Whitehead, D.S., Platbook UUUU, lots 140, 141, 149, *passim.*

11. District 16, original Lee County (now part of Sumter), survey of 1827, Thos. J. Meriwether, D.S., Platbook SSSS, lots 144, 145, 161, 162, *passim.*

12. 18th District, original Lee County, survey of 1827, B. C. Lansdell, D.S., Platbook SSSS, lots 123, 134.

13. Henry Yonge and William DeBrahm, *A Map of the Sea Coast of Georgia and the inland parts thereof . . . ,* 1763, copy in the Clements Library, Ann Arbor, Mich.

14. *A New and Accurate Map of the Province of Georgia . . . ,* published in *Universal Magazine,* April, 1779, copy in the Ivan Allen Collection, Atlanta.

15. Land of Ignatius Few, Wilkes County, survey of 1786, Platbook H, p. 45.

16. The Rock Landing, main crossing point on the Oconee River for the Lower Creek Trading Path, was some four miles below Milledgeville, above the mouth of Buck Creek.

17. Land of Robert Middleton, Washington County, survey of 1784, Platbook F, p. 221; and property of Charles Burk, Greene County (now Hancock), survey of 1787, Platbook N, p. 170.

18. Grant of 15,000 acres to John and George Golphin (*sic*), Washington County, survey of 1784, Platbook A, p. 235.

19. Land of Jesse Millar, Washington County, survey of 1785, Platbook O, p. 140.

20. The "beaver dam" of Lamar's Creek is from a plat for Samuel Camp's land, Washington County, survey of 1786, Platbook O, p. 14. Its approximate location is shown on the accompanying map. The beaver creek waters on the east side of the Oconee, in present southeast Baldwin, were indicated on: land of Cornelius Dysart, Washington County, survey of 1786, Platbook O, p. 36; and land of Elijah Clarke, Washington County, survey of 1784, Platbook B, p. 12.

21. James Mooney, *Myths of the Cherokee,* Nineteenth Annual Report of the Bureau of American Ethnology (n.p., n.d.), pt. 1, p. 529 and p. 545. Mooney spells the name Oothcaloga and states that it is derived from *vý gilâ gĭ,* an abbreviated form of the Cherokee *tsuyú gilâ gĭ,* where there are dams, i.e., beaver dams.

22. Benjamin Hawkins, *Letters of Benjamin Hawkins, 1796-1806,* Collections of the Georgia Historical Society, Vol. 9 (Savannah, 1916), p. 171.

23. Benjamin Hawkins, *A Sketch of the Creek Country in the Years 1798 and 1799,* Collections of the Georgia Historical Society, Vol. 3, pt. 1 (Savannah, 1848), p. 62.

24. Buck Creek is not named for the male species of deer, but for Buckee Barnard (son of Timothy Barnard, the noted Indian countryman) who lived at present Montezuma, opposite the stream's mouth on the Flint River.

25. Benjamin Hawkins, "A Viatory or Journal of distances and observations," MS in the Library of Congress—trip to Fort Wilkinson, starting Flint River, 1800.

26. Albert S. Gatschet, *A Migration Legend of the Creek Indians* (Philadelphia: D. G. Brinton, 1884), 1: 155.

27. *Ibid.,* p. 21.

28. District 6, Gwinnett County, survey of 1819, Jos. T. Cunningham, D.S., Platbook MMM.

29. "College Land," 5,000 acres, survey of 1784, Platbook A, p. 151.

30. District 3, Monroe County (now part of Lamar), survey of 1821, John McCulloh, D.S., Platbook WWW, lots 27, 38, 58, 59, *passim.*

31. *Ibid.,* lot 39.

32. William G. Bonner, *Map of the State of Georgia* (Milledgeville, 1847).

33. Map of District 10 of Monroe (now part of Upson), survey of 1821, Allen W. Prior, D.S.

34. District 7 of Houston County (now part of Crawford), survey of 1821, John C. Love, D.S., Platbook UUU.

35. *Letters of Benjamin Hawkins,* p. 87, trip from Timothy Barnard's to Fort Fidius.

36. Land of James McClean, original Wilkes County, survey of 1784, Platbook A, p. 49.

37. *Letters of Benjamin Hawkins,* p. 54, trip of Jan. 4, 1797, to Cusseta Town.

38. There are two Lanahassee creeks in Marion County; one of them heads to the southwest of Buena Vista and enters Kinchafoonee near the Savell place (see n. 2, above); the other arises in south central Marion and flows into the Kinchafoonee to the southeast of Preston in Webster County.

The Buffalo in Georgia

When one is willing to take note of them, placenames often serve as reminders of some interesting but forgotten aspect of former times. Many cases could be offered to exemplify the possibilities of names in this respect; for instance, in Georgia the frequency with which the word buffalo can be found in connection with geographic appellations is a plain clue that the great bison was once fairly widely distributed here, even down toward the fringes of Florida. This suggestion may surprise the reader because from what we read one would be inclined to associate the buffalo entirely with the plains beyond the Mississippi.

Now, of course, the mere existence of buffalo names here does not necessarily prove that the animals once inhabited Georgia. But the places that bear the names are old, and the persistence with which the names have clung to maps over the long years strongly suggests that the creatures were here and that perhaps other information could be found to verify their presence in these parts.

The earliest indication of buffaloes in the section can be found in Garcilaso de la Vega's account of DeSoto's journey across Georgia in 1540. In writing of this area he tells of one scouting party which found some "cow horns" in an Indian village, and adds that on several occasions the Spaniards saw "fresh beef" among the natives. They naturally concluded that this meat was from domestic animals and importuned the Indians to tell them where they kept their cows. The redskins, though, were evasive and never gave satisfactory answers to the inquiries. It is reasonable to conclude in these instances that the beef and horns came from buffaloes because the red people of those days had no tame cattle.

No less a personage than General Oglethorpe is thought to be the first individual to mention the buffalo in connection with Georgia in English records. In a 1733 document entitled "A New and Accurate Account of the Provinces of South Carolina and Georgia," which is attributed to the General, he says the buffalo was among the game of those colonies. A few years later, Francis Moore in "A Voyage to Georgia Begun in the Year 1735," while writing of St. Simons, says there were no buffaloes on the island, but that large herds were to be found "on the Main," that is, the area around what is now Brunswick.

Some years later more positive evidence on the presence of buffaloes here can be found in the report of a "Ranger" who accompanied Oglethorpe on his famous trip across Georgia to treat with the Indians at Coweta Town, located on the west side of the Chattahoochee, a few miles below present-day Columbus. The Governor and his entourage began the wilderness part of this journey in July, 1739, setting out from Mt. Pleasant on the Savannah, in Effingham County. Immediately after crossing the Ogeechee, some Indian hunters attached to the party killed several buffaloes which proved to be "very good Eating." The scene of this hunt seems to have been what is now lower Jenkins County, because Oglethorpe probably was following a well-known traders' path from Charleston via Mt. Pleasant to the Creeks, and this route crossed the Ogeechee by a ford located at what we now call Paramore Hill, to the south of Millen.

A few days later, just west of the Oconee, the party saw several herds of buffalo of sixty or more and the hunters again killed two of the animals. If the group had continued on the familiar path (and it is reasonable to conclude that they did so), these herds were seen in lower Baldwin County, because that noted trail crossed the Oconee at the Rock Landing some four miles below the site of Milledgeville.

Two other interesting experiences of Oglethorpe further add to knowledge of the buffalo in Georgia. At the first treaty with the Indians in May of 1733, before some fifty headmen and warriors, Tomo-Chi-Chi gave the Governor a buffalo skin adorned with eagle feathers. This mark of esteem, said the Chief in making the presentation, symbolized the speed of the eagle and the strength of the buffalo. On another occasion, at a convention held at Savannah in 1735, the noted Creek Chief Chekilli delivered to Oglethorpe in the presence of colonial officials and some sixty Indians a young buffalo hide that had written on it in red and black characters a migration legend of the Creeks. This skin was taken to London and put on exhibit in the Georgia Office at Westminster.

There is little evidence indicating the size of the buffaloes which lived in this section, although the "Ranger" who accompanied Oglethorpe said that they were heavy beasts and that they could outrun and tire a horse. Possibly these bison as forest-dwellers were not as large as those that were found on the Western plains and which are said to have reached eighteen hundred or two thousand pounds in weight. But even if the largest animals of this area weighed only a thousand pounds they would have been bigger than the ordinary "horned cattle" which the first settlers raised.

The American bison were gregarious animals that preferred to run in droves. This habit explains why they always impressed early people as moving in large numbers. But in Georgia—as elsewhere—there was great diversity in the sizes of herds reported. In one instance, Thomas Spalding states that his grandfather, Colonel William McIntosh, often told him he had seen ten thousand buffaloes in a herd in the area between Darien and Sapelo River in what is now McIntosh County. The section mentioned undoubtedly was one of the chief buffalo habitats of the state, and even today large areas of it still are associated with the name buffalo. The number in his report seems entirely too large; probably the herds of sixty or upwards which Oglethorpe's party saw in 1739 near the Oconee were more representative of the droves which inhabited Georgia. The smaller numbers seem reasonable in view of the fact that grazing facilities of this area were more limited than the vast grasslands of mid-continental regions.

The buffalo was certainly of economic importance to the Indians of this section. We can be sure they used the meat, and apparently they employed the hides in making robes, covers, moccasins, and possibly shields. But oddly enough, there seems to have been no trade in buffalo skins with white people. There are some good records available about the business relations with the Indians of the area, but they make little or no mention of buffalo skins. The deer skin was by far the chief item of trade with Indians of the region, although pelts of a few fur-bearing animals like the beaver, "tyger" (panther), otter, and raccoon are sometimes mentioned. The absence of the buffalo skin in trade is a mystery in view of the fact that a considerable commerce eventually developed in the hides of the Western bison. Perhaps there was no demand in the European markets at this date for the thick heavy buffalo hide, whereas the lighter buckskin was eagerly sought. Possibly transportation difficulties and expense discouraged the movement of heavy buffalo hides. In the earliest days of trade the white traders in this region hired Indian "burdeners" to carry their peltries out of the wilderness, and this form of transport must have been relatively too costly for buffalo skins. Perhaps too, because of the great size of the bison, the Indians did not often bother to skin the huge animals entirely and were content to peel back just enough of the hide to reach choice meat portions of the carcass.

As yet there has been no listing of the actual places that perpetuate the name buffalo in Georgia. Two of the oldest localities bearing the designation are in McIntosh County: Buffalo Creek and Swamp, an upper tributary of Cathead Creek; and Buffalo Swamp, a wide, dense area along the Altamaha, to the west of Darien. These sections, which are not far apart, have seemingly borne their labels since the founding of Georgia, and they must have constituted a part of the grazing territories for the immense herd mentioned by Colonel William McIntosh.

To the south of the Altamaha there are two other large buffalo localities: Buffalo River (and Swamp) which heads on the northeast edge of Wayne County and flows across Glynn County to join the

Turtle River above Brunswick; and Buffalo Swamp that begins in Wayne, to the south of present-day Mt. Pleasant, and extends southward into upper Brantley. By means of an arm called Little Buffalo Swamp this section also drains across Glynn to the upper Turtle River. These early buffalo places probably were the main feeding grounds for the herds mentioned by Francis Moore.

Still another large Buffalo Creek and Swamp can be found on the west side of the Great Satilla in lower Brantley County. And for several miles down the Satilla from the point where it is joined by the creek there is a stretch called the Buffalo Reaches. This name, an old rivermen's term, may have been derived from the adjacent swamp, but there is a possibility that it arose because the bison once swam the river here in going from one grazing ground to another. A glance at a map will show that these buffalo places are near the St. Marys River and the Florida line.

One of the oldest and largest streams that perpetuates the name is Buffalo Creek, which heads in southwest Hancock County and flows in a southerly direction across Washington to join the Oconee River just to the west of the little town of Oconee. This waterway appears on some of the earliest maps that show the interior of Georgia, and since it lay athwart the main courses of the famous Lower Creek trading routes from Charleston and Augusta, it presumably has carried the name since English traders first passed that way around the turn of the eighteenth century. The stream is not far to the east of the area where Oglethorpe's party saw the herds of buffalo in Baldwin County.

In eastern Oglethorpe County, draining away to Long Creek, a tributary of Broad River, there is a small Buffalo Creek which is of special note because of its proximity to some famous buffalo licks. There are still other Buffalo Creeks: one of these, arising in lower Jackson County, to the southwest of Jefferson, enters the west side of the Middle Fork of the Oconee; and another heads on the lower outskirts of Carrollton and flows southwestward to join the Little Tallapoosa, just above the Old Victory Mills in Carroll County. These three streams indicate a wide distribution of the buffalo because they are relatively removed from the other places that have been mentioned.

Washington County in its earliest days had some interesting spots called Buffalo ponds. One of these places was well-known when the county was formed in 1784 because the Justices of the Peace were directed to hold the first court there. The exact location of the site is not certain now but it is believed to have been in the vicinity of present-day Warthen. In another instance, an early land plat for Washington County shows a Buffalo Pond to the northwest of Sandersville near the Chickasaw Path and not far from Buffalo Creek.

Above Mt. Vernon in Montgomery County is a site called Buffalo Church. The origin of the name is not known, although an old land plat for the general area shows a Red Buffalo Creek. The church is located on the upper side of a stream called Flat Creek, and that waterway may have once been the Red Buffalo stream; but more than likely, however, the surveyor got his names confused and should have written Red Bluff Creek, for a well-known tributary of the Oconee that lies to the north of the church site.

Two interesting points should be made about these buffalo places: first, with the exception of the creek in Carroll County, the names are found in the central section and in old southeast Georgia. There are no buffalo sites—on maps at least—in the northwestern and southwestern parts of the state. This situation is difficult to explain, especially in the case of the Cherokee country of upper Georgia. It is definitely known that those Indians were familiar with the buffalo because they used its meat as food. Nonetheless, in the very complete official surveys for the original Cherokee section there is no mention of a buffalo site. And too, the same thing can be said for the early surveys of southwest Georgia. It is reasonable to believe that the bison once ranged these areas, but the surveys were made so long after the disappearance of the animals from those parts that the surveyors did not note any places that retained the name in either Indian or English forms.

A second interesting point to note about the buffalo appellations is that the names are closely connected with streams and big swamps, a fact which plainly suggests that such localities were favored habitats of the creatures. This preference is easy to explain: undoubtedly the best feeding areas for the buffalo were the expansive canebrakes to be found in swamps and along the margins of waterways. From the records available about the use of cane by early settlers' stock we know this vegetation was by far the most abundant browsing food that could have been available in this section. There was grass, of course, but not nearly as much as one might think today, because early Georgia as a forested region did not have many spots where an abundance of grass could grow, except in occasional low, wet glades called *savannas* and in the open spaces to be found along the coastal margins or in the sandy pine regions.

One grass which the buffalo presumably ate is mentioned by Colonel Benjamin Hawkins. On a trip in 1797 from the Chattahoochee to the Oconee, at a point in present upper Taylor County, he noticed an herbage called "Buffalo grass," and gave its Muscogee Indian name as "So, we, nah." It would be interesting to know the botanical name of this particular plant, although it would certainly not be the same as that for the noted short buffalo grass of the plains, because the Creek "So, we, nah" or other *sowena* refers to a fibrous vegetation like hemp. William Bartram travelled almost identically the same route used by Hawkins, twenty years before the latter's journey, but unfortunately he did not mention the buffalo grass.

Probably the most historic of the buffalo places in Georgia was the Great Buffalo Lick, a noted spot in upper Georgia which was visited by game that came to lick a mineral deposit to be found at the site. Indian hunters frequented the locality to kill these animals, and the lick was so well-known that it served as one of the key points along the boundary line established between the Indians and the Georgians by the Treaty of Augusta in 1773.

William Bartram went along with the surveyors who laid off this line. He visited the Great Buffalo Lick and left the best description which we have of it. According to this account, the place covered an area of three or four acres and was distinguished by a white "fattish clay," said to be impregnated with "saline vapours," arising from fossil salts deep in the earth. Bartram tasted the clay but thought it sweetish instead of salty. Since no notable saline deposits or salt springs are known in the general area in which the site was located, modern geologists are inclined to believe the spot may have been a bed of primary kaolin.

Despite its former prominence, the location of the Great Buffalo Lick has been a matter of present-day disagreement. Some people hold that it was near Union Point in Greene County, while others insist it was to the east of that place, in the vicinity of Sunshine near the edge of Taliaferro County. Fortunately, a map among the Candler transcriptions of the colonial records of Georgia now in the Georgia Department of Archives and History settles the question. This chart, the original of which is in London, was prepared by Philip Yonge to show the area of the Indian land cession of the Treaty of 1773. Yonge was one of the surveyors in the party which Bartram accompanied. The map shows the actual trail which the group followed to reach the Great Buffalo Lick. Furthermore, it depicts another Buffalo Lick which Bartram did not mention. On the basis of this official document, the Great Buffalo Lick was on a divide above the extreme upper tips of the north fork of Little River and at the beginning of a south branch of Long Creek. This location places the lick in the Bowling Green District of present Oglethorpe County, to the south of Lexington and to the east of the village of Stephens.

The other Buffalo Lick shown was on the trail some seven miles to the southeast of the Great Lick, on the east side of the north fork of Little River. This location would place it west of Philomath in the southeast corner of Oglethorpe. No details are given about this lick, but it may have been known as the White Lick because a 1785 land plat for Wilkes County shows a "Whitelick path" crossing a branch of Kettle Creek not far from this Buffalo Lick.

In the same general area of these Buffalo licks the map also shows a Boggy Lick located on the upper east side of the Buffalo Creek of Oglethorpe County. Presumably this spot was also a buffalo lick although it did not bear the name.

One well-known characteristic of the bison was his love of rolling on the ground at certain favored places which pioneer people called buffalo wallows. These wallowing places could be either dry dusty depressions or wet mud holes. The latter sites were prepared by big bulls that rolled in a boggy spot and plowed the earth into a mucky state with their horns. Apparently the animals resorted to these muddy spots at times when vicious stinging flies were prevalent. By wallowing in the muck they caked themselves with a layer of mud which formed effective shields against their insect tormentors.

Georgia must have had buffalo wallows, but there is scant evidence to show that this was the case, although the buffalo ponds in Washington County may have been such places. Not far over the Georgia line, however, in Chambers County, Alabama, there was a big wallow, whose former location is well known to the people of that area. A little village and railroad station called Buffalo, up the hill from the spot, still commemorate the old site.

Frank Gilbert Roe in *The North American Buffalo* says in essence that people have made it a creed of believing that buffaloes were responsible for trails which in time became the highways of today. This belief is certainly prevalent in Georgia, and it is seemingly held by people who have no knowledge that the animals once actually lived here. It is difficult to say how the view became so general, because old records of this area do not attribute the origin of our early routes to the buffalo. Perhaps stories of buffalo ways in other sections like the paths to salt licks in Kentucky, or the so-called migration trails of the bison in the West, are responsible for this commonly held belief.

Now, when buffaloes did decide to move from one place to another, it is well known that they formed a single file. From this habit then no doubt a sizable herd of the great beasts could have quickly made a noticeable passage, especially in a big canebrake or swamp where openings were rare. And, if the animals habitually followed such a course over a long period of time going to licks, wallows, watering holes, or fresher browsing grounds, they would have formed permanent trails which would have been useful to the Indians and eventually, of course, to the white people.

Nonetheless, students of early trails in Georgia and the lower Southeast are prone to scoff at the idea that the wilderness routes found here were formed by buffaloes. This view is especially pronounced with respect to the great arterial trading paths that were sometimes hundreds of miles long and which tended to converge on various prominent trading centers like Augusta, the Forks of the Ocmulgee, and Trader Hill on the St. Marys River. They contend that it is hardly likely that buffaloes would have created such a neat radial pattern of trails leading to these particular points. Furthermore, it is argued, such routes virtually always led to the best fording sites on rivers and this was a result of human choice, exercised originally by Indians and later by white people, because buffaloes were good swimmers and when crossing rivers did not have to confine themselves to the shallow fords.

These views are certainly logical, but even so there is enough evidence to suggest that buffaloes actually did have some part in laying out the original wilderness paths of this area. In virtually every instance, some significant trail passed by, through, or very close to the Buffalo places that have been mentioned. For example, the Chickasaw path (a branch of the Lower Creek trading route) that ran from the Savannah River to Rock Landing on the Oconee led past Buffalo Creek and the Buffalo Pond in Washington County, and the noted Oakfuskee path to the Upper Creeks passed by the Buffalo Wallow in Chambers County, Alabama. Furthermore, the *Colonial Records of Georgia* mention a site on the lower Satilla River called the Buffalo Ford. Apparently the place was in the area of the Buffalo Creek in Brantley County. If the spot was toward the lower end of the Buffalo Reaches, at the site of the Burnt Fort crossing in Camden County, that buffalo fording place would have been on the main historic trail leading from Georgia into Florida. If, however, it was a little higher up on the

Satilla at a crossing near the mouth of Buffalo Creek, the ford would have been on a prominent trace leading from the coast by present-day Waycross to the Seminoles of southwest Georgia.

In addition to these indications, the Whitelick path on Kettle Creek in Wilkes County should be mentioned again—and also the definite trail which Bartram and the surveyors followed to pass the buffalo licks in Oglethorpe County.

It is not known how late the buffalo was still to be found in Georgia, but by the middle of the 1700's the animals were greatly diminished in numbers, and some people were concerned about their disappearance. In 1759 the provincial House of Commons passed an act to restrict the killing of deer, beavers, and buffaloes in certain areas. In 1763 The Mortar, a leading Creek chief, sent Governor Wright a "talk" which complained that the buffalo and other game were being driven off the land above Augusta by settlers and their stock. James Adair, an old Indian countryman, writing about 1761-1768, said buffaloes were then "scarce" in this region. William Bartram in his wide travels a few years after this period did not see any bison although he reports that they were once plentiful. One of the last references to living buffalo in Georgia pertains to the 1770's. Thomas Spalding later wrote that in that period his father maintained a string of trading houses from the Satilla to St. Marks and that he was regularly supplied with buffalo tongues to eat. This part of the animal was considered a delicacy, but one hopes that the last of the great creatures in these parts were not slaughtered solely for those mere morsels.

—*GR* 11(1957): 19-28

Some Old Road Names In Georgia

In these days when we do much travelling with the aid of efficient little touring maps on which most of the highways are carefully numbered, one is prone to forget that roads bear names as well as numbers. Georgia has a profusion of such road names. Mostly the designations are mere matter-of-fact tabs, like Albany Road, Macon Road, Elberton Road, and so on. But there is also a substantial group of unusual route names that rank high in Georgia's galaxy of fascinating geographic appellations. This essay will single out some of these unique names to indicate their range and diversity. It would be helpful to the reader to indicate with exactness the courses of the routes, but that task would be complicated without a special set of accompanying maps. The discussion, therefore, will be presented as a place-name sketch with a few comments about the origins of some of the ways to be listed.

In common with any significant body of geographic names, many of Georgia's old road designations are subject to division and subdivision into categories of kindred words. Sometimes, each of the routes in a given group will bear the same name, like, River Road, Pocket Road, Old Shell Road, and so on. On the other hand, while the import and significance of individual road names may differ with a given group, the implications of the terms plainly show that they belong in a common order. For example, titles like, Tobacco Road, Old Stave Road, Potash Road, Gold Diggers' Road, Egg and Butter Road, etc., are clearly of economic significance; while names like Shakerag Road, Fussville Road, Cocklebur Road, Bump Head Road, Nowhere Road, Dark Corner Road, and Red Bug Road are intended to be facetious.

The largest of these name groups by far encompasses the River roads, a designation which usually applies to routes that run up and down major streams on courses that are adjacent to and parallel with the waterways. Interestingly enough, however, ways leading from and to rivers may also be referred to as River roads. The little point is worth noting, because roads usually have dual names and a particular designation will depend on the direction and destination of the traveller. A route leading to a river would properly be a River road, while one leading away from the stream would ordinarily bear the title of the first important place or community in that direction. Nonetheless, in Georgia, a thoroughfare running either from or to a large stream may sometimes be known as a River road.

The expression River road is not especially distinctive, but some of the ways that fall into this category are among the most noted routes of Georgia. Chief among these is the Old River Road from Savannah to Augusta, which led up the west side of the Savannah River. This early way was "marked out" in 1736-1737 on the orders of General Oglethorpe and was the first long white man's thoroughfare of Georgia. Parts of it have been paved and have thus become segments of the modern road system. Other sections, however, are either abandoned completely or only remain as obscure little dirt byways.

At the time this Old River Road was opened, Oglethorpe commented that it connected at Augusta with a trail that the Cherokees had blazed from their country. He was speaking of a noted trace which early records mention as the Cherokee, or Upper Trading Path. Substantial parts of this aboriginal way eventually evolved into pioneer white men's traces that are yet remembered by the people along their courses. One of these is the Petersburg Road, leading from Augusta to the site of the former town of Petersburg, that is now inundated by the waters of Clark Hill Dam, but which was located in southeast Elbert County, between the forks of the Broad and Savannah rivers. Above Petersburg, another route which developed along a part of the Cherokee Path was the Red Hollow Road, that runs by Amandaville and Avalon to the area of Toccoa. It is not known when or how the road derived its name, or the location of the hollow that gave rise to the appellation.

At a point above Toccoa, the Red Hollow Road intersected the Unicoi Turnpike, leading northwestward to Tennessee. This route was the first vehicular way over the Blue Ridge in north central Georgia and was one of the earliest interstate toll roads in the nation. It was first planned in 1813 by a company of Cherokee chiefs and Indian country white men to run from east Tennessee to the head of poleboat navigation on the Tugalo, an upper tributary of the Savannah River, and was intended to be the shortest land-water route from Tennessee to the Atlantic seaboard. Beginning at Nine Mile Creek near Knoxville, it crossed extreme western North Carolina and led over the Blue Ridge in Georgia through the Unicoi Gap (that commemorates the name of the trace), thence through Nacoochee Valley, and then to a point on the Tugalo not far to the east of Toccoa.

At Toccoa there developed as a spur of the Cherokee Path (or Red Hollow Road) an interesting pioneer route called the Locust Stake Road. This trace bore northward through Stephens and Habersham counties to cross Tallulah River at a former ford located in front of the Samuel Dobbs summer home on Lake Rabun, thence by Clayton and through Rabun Gap to a locust stake or post on the Georgia–North Carolina line, above present Dillard. The old way derived its name from this marker on the boundary of the two states.

The Petersburg Road mentioned above belongs in a curious and interesting category of road names, because it leads toward a town that no longer exists. As noted, the site of Petersburg is now flooded, but even before this inundation the place had long since died, although the town at one time had a boat and ferry landings, streets, and some fifty houses. The name of the thoroughfare, however, has been continued over the long years. This persistence illustrates well the enduring tenacity of most old road names.

Another route that remains, although the town which gave rise to its name has long since ceased to exist, is the Old Sunbury Road. This thoroughfare was the longest post-Revolutionary road of Georgia. It began in Greensboro and led southward via Sparta, Swainsboro, Taylors Creek, and Midway Church on U.S. 17 to Sunbury, located on the Midway River in eastern Liberty County. Sunbury was once a prosperous and flourishing place, and during colonial years it was the second port of Georgia. In 1804, however, the community was visited by a tropical storm that crippled the site; and in 1824, another hurricane devastated the place so badly it dwindled to a village and finally became a dead town. Even so, back in the interior, from Washington County southward, the road to Sunbury is still remembered, although the people on the old course often garble the name by calling it Sunsberry or Sunburg Road.

There are a dozen or so of these old thoroughfares which lead to places that no longer exist. One route, with an interesting twist, is the Hard Money Road, that runs across lower Webster County into a town now called Weston. But before this last name was adopted in 1856, the place had been known for a considerable period as Hard Money. The distinctiveness of the road name lies in the fact that although the town changed, the designation of the highway did not.

It is not known how the village of Hard Money originally received its name, although one gathers that people were ashamed of the tab because it bore an avaricious connotation. Such appellations were common in the formative years of Georgia. In that period backcountry wags delighted in foisting whimsical monikers like Hard Money on little trading points where it was claimed people were cheated or denied credit in the stores. Thus there was an array of names like Hard Cash, Hard Bargain, Pay Up, Cheatum, Grab All, Trickem, and so on. Georgia still retains numbers of these amusing names, mostly in the designations of nondescript little crossroads that were once the sites of country stores. There must be, even now, a half-dozen Grab Alls, and equally as many Trickems.

The commemoration of former towns in the names of routes that lead to the sites of such places brings to mind another feature of old road names: there are two early ways which switched destinations during the passage of years, although after such shifts the changed ways continued to be known under their old names. One of these is the Peachtree Road, which is probably the best-known thoroughfare of Georgia. This route was originally opened in the Creek War of 1813-1814 as a military way for hauling supplies to the Chattahoochee, where in turn it was expected the goods would be moved downstream by boats to troops operating in areas contiguous to the middle section of the river. The road began at Hog Mountain in today's upper Gwinnett County, and ran in a southwesterly direction via Duluth, Norcross, and Brookhaven to present Buckhead. Instead of continuing southward, however, along today's Peachtree Road (and Peachtree Street) into the heart of Atlanta, the original old way turned at Buckhead along what is now Paces Ferry Road to Moores Mill Road, thence approximately down the course of the latter to the Indian community of Standing Peachtree at the mouth of Peachtree Creek on the Chattahoochee. With the removal of the Creeks from the area in the 1820's, the former Indian village, still under the name Standing Peachtree, changed to a little trading spot and post office of the white people. When the point which became Atlanta started developing to the east after the coming of the railroad, the route from Buckhead to Five Points became increasingly important, and finally this extension appropriated the name Peachtree Road. Actually the stretch was a connection of that road at Buckhead and not a segment of the original thoroughfare.

Another noted route that switched destinations is the Old Quaker Road. This thoroughfare was opened in 1769 by a colony of Quakers who settled around Wrightsboro in upper McDuffie County as a direct way from this settlement to Savannah. The route led southward across Brier Creek, thence via Waynesboro to the present juncture of U.S. 301 and Georgia 24, where it intersected an established trace to Savannah—a way which will be mentioned shortly as the King's Road, Middle Ground Road, and Old Savannah–Augusta Stage Road. As the years passed, Wrightsboro continued in existence, but with diminished importance. In time Warrenton sprang up to the southwest of it and began to grow. These developments led to a switching of the northern terminus of the Quaker Road from Wrightsboro to Warrenton. This shift occurred so long ago that people in the latter place firmly believe the road has always ended there. This could not have been the case, however, because when the Quaker Road was first opened, the site of Warrenton lay beyond the Georgia frontier, in Indian territory.

Among the most significant of Georgia's old road appellations are the names of the noted arterial emigrant routes across the state to the West. The leaders among these were two Federal roads. One of them led from the present Hall-Jackson County line northwestward across the Cherokee country toward Knoxville and Nashville, while another ran westward from what is now Macon across the Creek Nation to the Alabama River. The rights to open these Indian country ways were formally provided for in treaties of the federal government with the Cherokees and Creeks in 1805. Each of the traces became the first vehicular and post route of their respective areas of the state. Much of the former Cherokee Federal Road remains in daily use, but the Creek country way is largely abandoned and forgotten because it followed a sandy course which was difficult for vehicular traffic.

In addition to the Federal roads there were a half-dozen later emigrant ways to the West that became known as Alabama Roads, because their first general destination to the west was the territory or state of Alabama. Actually, however, the thoroughfares were the routes used by early "movers" into the whole area of the Old Southwest, since in Alabama there were connections into Mississippi, and from there to Arkansas, Louisiana, and eventually to Texas. Beginning in the 1820's, the great saga of the westward cotton expansion mainly took place along these thoroughfares.

With the exception of a route that sloped across northwest Georgia from Tennessee to Alabama and the Cherokee Federal Road which had a connection to that territory, the Alabama roads began in the middle of the state, on the western banks of the Ocmulgee or upper Chattahoochee, and ran westward on roughly paralleling courses that ranged up to forty miles or so apart. At the beginning points on these rivers the emigrant thoroughfares had a complexity of connections that led from Virginia, the Carolinas, and the older parts of Georgia. Most of the Alabama roads remain in use and are well-remembered by old folk who dwell along their courses. Curiously enough, though, people who live on one of the routes are prone to insist that their thoroughfare is *the* Old Alabama Road, and they seem unaware there are other ways bearing the same name.

As has been indicated, some road names can properly be assigned to an economic category. An interesting little subgroup that belongs in this division comprises the Wire roads. There are several routes in this grouping, and they derive their names from the fact that they were once followed by early telegraph lines. The most significant of these ways is the Creek country Federal Road of 1805, which was mentioned above as running west from Macon. In the middle of the last century, when a telegraph line from New York and Washington to

New Orleans was strung across Georgia, the facility passed through Macon and followed the Federal Road for a considerable distance westward out of that place, thus giving rise to the dual name Old Federal Wire Road under which the thoroughfare is now remembered by old people. Beyond Flint River, however, the Wire Road and the original Federal Road diverged. The former led on to Columbus as the Wire Road, whereas the latter veered southwestward to pass through the Fort Benning area and reach the Chattahoochee to the south of Columbus.

But there were other interesting road names with an economic implication. One of these was the Tobacco Road. This name was not a figment of Erskine Caldwell's imagination. There was, and still is, an actual route bearing that label. It began in the vicinity of Grovetown to the west of Augusta and led through the present Fort Gordon area toward a point on the Savannah River to the east of Gracewood in Richmond County. The Tobacco Road was a rolling road, i.e., it followed a high, dry course which permitted users to roll goods like tobacco along its course in oaken hogsheads. When such containers were turned on their sides and tongues or shafts attached to their ends, they could be pulled with draft animals just as a wagon is drawn.

One of the most intriguing names in the economic category is the Old Gold Diggers' Road of Lumpkin County. It seemingly began on the Chestatee River and led westward to a point on the upper side of Dahlonega, where it curved southward to the site of Auraria. Significant parts of it are now abandoned, but in the gold rush days around Dahlonega and Auraria, it was a connection by which gold-rushers from upper Georgia and the Carolinas reached those mining centers.

Another route name with an economic implication is Steam Mill Road. There are several such appellations in Georgia. One of the ways bearing the name runs east from Columbus to the site of a former mill in Muscogee County, on the upper side of Upatoi Creek. Another route with the title is in northwest Seminole County where there has long been a village called Steam Mill. Both of these names are old tabs, and they serve to remind us that steam mills were once exciting innovations in a community and marks of progress into a new age.

Some of the most intriguing (and naturally the oldest) road names are found in the areas of colonial Georgia, in the coastal region and along the Savannah River. Of particular interest in these sections were early routes known as King or King's Road. There were several thoroughfares bearing this designation, and the name is interesting because it carried about the same connotation in provincial days as our present "U.S. Highway." The most noted of the King roads ran from Savannah to Augusta through Springfield, Sylvania, and the present village of Shell Bluff in eastern Burke County. The route ran parallel with and to the west of the earlier Old Savannah–Augusta River Road that has been mentioned. After the Revolution the name King's Road apparently proved distasteful to the citizens because the way next became known as the Middle Ground Road. Eventually it evolved into the Old Savannah and Augusta Stage Road, and it is now remembered by most people under that designation. A probable King Road that still survives begins on U.S. 17, above Darien, and runs via Townsend to Ludowici. One cannot be positive that the expression is of royal origin, but the name is very old, and the route lies within former colonial territory.

A name that is comparable to King Road is Old Colony Road, a designation which elderly people in Evans and Liberty counties apply to a lower segment of the Sunbury route that has been mentioned. The section in question stretches from a point near Daisy in the former county to Taylors Creek in Liberty, via a present-day place called Willie.

During the Revolution there developed some interesting thoroughfares that were known as Tory roads and Rebel roads. There are several references to the Tory ways in Revolutionary records, but apparently people were willing to let the name sink into oblivion and it is not now possible to identify the routes which once bore this title. The Rebel roads are also frequently mentioned in old documents, and for a time it seemed that they too were lost. But in the last year, Mr. and Mrs. Leodel Coleman of Statesboro have been finding elderly informants who remember something about the course of a Rebel Road in Bulloch County. Actually the Rebel roads seem to have been parts or branches of one common route that had the approximate shape of an inverted Y. The thoroughfare apparently began in the middle Savannah River region, between Savannah and Augusta, and curved southward in an arc around British occupied areas about Savannah and along the coast. Below the mouth of the Canoochee River, one fork of the inverted Y led down the west side of the Ogeechee to the sea, while the other prong extended over the Altamaha River via Fort Barrington, and past Burnt Fort on the Satilla, to the St. Marys. The latter way was used by the Americans for the invasion of Florida during the Revolution.

This article began by contrasting in a fashion numbered highways and those that bear names. This point perhaps by implication may leave the thought that highway numbering is a new practice. Such is not the case, however. Virtually from the foundation of the American colonies it became common to mark the course of a route through the wilderness by cutting a selected number of chops, notches, or blazes on trees along the way. This marking was the pioneer equivalent of today's road numbering. A blaze was a smooth-cut gash on the trunk of a tree, while chops or notches were V-shaped indentations that were cut into the trunk. Anyone desiring to mark a route could select any given combination of these symbols. For instance, federal troops in this region customarily used three notches to indicate new military traces through the forest. About 1816, when some soldiers were sent from south Alabama via present Fort Gaines to establish Fort Scott on Flint River below Bainbridge, they marked the way with the customary three notches and thus opened a road bearing that name. This particular Three Notch Road and most marked ways eventually lost their early names, but interestingly enough Georgia still has two routes that commemorate the frontier method of numbering roads. One of these is the Old Five Notch Trail that runs up the west side of the Chattahoochee in Heard County; and another is the Old Two Chop Way of upper Bulloch County.

Some other categories of names which should be touched upon briefly are the Longstreets, the Plank roads, the Old Shell roads, the Smoky roads, and the Avenues. There were once several Longstreet roads, and at least two important old routes with this name still survive. One is in eastern Elbert County and the other is in northwest Bleckley. The expression did not refer to a paved street, but rather to a relatively heavily populated road with numbers of houses along the course. Georgia had at one time numbers of Plank roads, i.e., thoroughfares which were constructed by laying two rows of hewn logs on the ground as stringers with planking across from stringer to stringer to furnish a bridge-like route. The longest Plank Road led from Augusta to Louisville, but the best-remembered way with the name ran from the area of present Griffin across the northwest corner of Pike County to the Flat Shoals of Flint River. The route coincided with a segment of the earlier Oakfuskee Path, one of the most famous arterial Indian trading ways of the country. Shell roads, constructed with fossilized sea shells or oyster shells, were once common along the coast and on important offshore islands. They were probably the finest man-made routes of their day in the state. Both Shell roads and

Plank roads were usually chartered turnpikes that operated as toll roads. The expression Smoky Road is one of the most enigmatic road names in the state. No one seems to know the significance of the designation; or if people know, they are unwilling to tell the meaning. There are several Smoky roads; perhaps the two best-known ones are in western Fulton County and in southwest Coweta County. The name Avenue is a grandiloquent old Georgia road name that used to be applied to a long, straight thoroughfare cut through pine forests. The name was used in several instances, but the most prominent route with the name was Railroad Avenue, that ran straight from Brunswick northward to the Altamaha River.

In addition to road names that can be fitted into groups, there are many interesting appellations which are not subject to categorizing. One of these is the Bonny Clabber Road of lower Laurens County. The name involves a route leading to a former boat landing on the west side of the Oconee called the Bonny Clabber Bluff. The designation was originally Baunauclaughbauh, but so few people could pronounce that tongue-twisting moniker, the expression was simplified to Bonny Clabber.

Georgia people have long delighted in taking the name of a bird or animal and turning it into an interesting placename: Eagle Grove, Owl Rock, Crow Harbor, Hog Heaven Branch, Buzzard Flopper Creek, Alligator Congress, and so on in great variety. This proclivity has been extended into road-naming: there is a route called Snake Nation Road in upper Lowndes County.

One of the most distinctive route names of Georgia is the Hightower Trail, a former Indian trace which ran from the Apalachee River to the Etowah. A substantial part of the course is the present boundary line between DeKalb and Gwinnett counties. This name, one can be certain, is a corruption of the Indian word *itawa* which the white people also turned into the present Etowah. In the two instances in which the word Etowah occurred in the old Cherokee country of Georgia, the whites also converted the name to Hightower. The really interesting point about the appellation, though, is the fact that the initial *h* of Hightower is a Cockney *h* that was long ago stuck on the word, probably by early Indian traders. In the years when we were closer to the British, it was common to use an *h* before placenames beginning with a vowel: "Hocony" (Oconee); "Hohoopee" (Ohoopee); "Howgechu" (Ogeechee); "Hallatamaha" (Altamaha), and so on. The *h*'s were eventually dropped from such words, however, except in the cases of Hightower and Hiawassee. The latter word is of

Cherokee origin and should properly have been Ayuhwasi, meaning a meadow or savannah. The significance of *itawa*, or Etowah, is not known.

One old thoroughfare name that merits discussion is the Shakerag Road. The route leads west from Suwanee in Gwinnett County, across the Chattahoochee along the boundary between Fulton and Forsyth counties. A short distance west of the river it reaches a village that is properly called Sheltonville but which has long been known to the facetious-minded as Shakerag. The spot is not the only Shakerag in the state: there are some half-dozen other communities and spots in Georgia with the name, but the first locality mentioned seems to be the only such place that has a road with the same tab. Interestingly enough, we do not have very good documentary evidence to explain the significance of Shakerag. The omission is an unusual shortcoming in view of the fact that the name was once a popular pioneer whimsy. Failure of older people to leave us a written explanation of the term would be analogous to our neglecting to define the slang word scram, so that people a century from now would know what we meant by that term when they saw it in print. Now, scram was not picked at random for this comparison: from what one can learn in talking to some old people, Shakerag probably meant something like scram. Apparently the expression was applied to communities that prided themselves on being rough and tough; and any stranger who did not have business in such localities was liable to be chased away shaking his rag, i.e., with his shirttail flying. Numbers of other explanations have been offered for the name, but the one given seems to be the most logical on the basis of information from elderly citizens of various Shakerag sections. It might be noted that the informants in these instances were themselves amused with the backwoodsy old expression and seemed to enjoy talking about it.

There is one feature of road-naming that has not been mentioned, and this point involves antonymical expressions to be found in road names. Placename students quickly learn that in any substantial body of names there are nearly always some appellations with opposite meanings from others. Indeed, the searcher soon begins to watch for words with such contrary connotations. By way of illustrating the matter, the Welcome All Road of lower Fulton County has the opposite implication from Shakerag; while the Gratis Road in Walton County is exactly the reverse of the Grab All Road in upper Lincoln County. Sometimes the contrast between names is not so obvious. For example, a Lick Skillet Road (of which there are several) leads to a poor community; whereas, an Oakland Road (of which there are also several) leads to a relatively rich section, because Oakland signifies an area with superior soil.

In closing there are three intriguing names which should be noted. One is the old Laughing Gal Road to a little crossroads bearing that name in western Cherokee County; another is the Kissingbower Road that leads southward from U.S. 78 at the western fringe of Augusta. And lastly there is the Linger Longer Road which runs to a crossing called Linger Longer Bridge on Richland Creek in lower Greene County.

—*GMNL* 11 (1958): 98-102, reprinted from *EUQ* 14(1958): 30-42

The Devil's Half Acre

An individual who becomes involved in the fascinating subject of Georgia placenames is usually drawn to a comparison of our geographic appellations with those that can be found in the British Isles. Only a brief study in this direction is required, however, to disclose that there is not nearly as much kinship in the names and placenaming practices of the two regions as one might suppose. In fact, with certain particular exceptions and apart from the universal generic English or Anglicized geographic words like river, mountain, valley, sound, bight, island, and so on, there is little resemblance between the names of England and those of the United States. In the main our designations and methods of deriving them are our own, and if not actually Georgian in origin they are at least typical of the American scene. This is true even of borrowed words like Rome, Athens, Seville, Milan, Berlin, Vienna, and Bremen, because America is the only one of the relatively new nations that has shown a decided willingness to use the labels of well-known foreign cities.

But one of the placenaming customs which we did inherit from the British is the interesting practice of attaching the word devil to some peculiar, dangerous, or awesome natural formation or site. The English have long applied satanic names to such spots: Devil's Throat, Devil's Bellows, Devil's Kitchen, Devil's Cauldron, Devil's Beef Tub. The Americans obviously delighted in such terms and were glad to use some of those which the Englishmen had coined and also to add a proliferation of their own.

It should be emphasized that neither the English nor the Americans consider these names improper. They no more think of them as being profane than the expression devil's food cake; nor is the term devil in this usage regarded as being maledictory. The contrast in the implication of the word in these instances can well be illustrated by a note which an old Georgia surveyor scribbled on a plat depicting a fatiguing survey which he had just made of some land that was covered with thickets and an expansive canebrake. After giving the bearings and other details which customarily go on a land plat, he added with conformable nineteenth-century restraint: "This is a d——l of a place." The denunciatory significance of devil in this instance led the surveyor to constrain his language. Had he simply marked the area as Devil's Thicket or Devil's Canebrake, no one would have raised a question about the propriety of the wording.

Georgia has its share of devil sites, some of which apparently date from colonial days. Seemingly the oldest place that now bears the tab is the Devil's Branch, which rises near the Screven-Effingham line and flows southeastward to join The Runs, that in turn constitute the upper waters of historic Ebenezer Creek. The branch no doubt derived its designation from the narrow but dense swamp that fringes its banks. Apparently the area has always been tedious to penetrate. One early surveyor who was called upon to make a survey that embodied a part of the swamp left his impression of the place to posterity by depicting the land in the shape of a devil's head!

Devil's Branch is mentioned in some of the oldest provincial records of Georgia, but actually the name may outdate the colony because the stream lies on the course of an early arterial trading path from Charleston, via Fort Pallachucola and Old Mt. Pleasant on the Savannah River, to the territory of the Lower Creek Indians. Perhaps packhorsemen using this route long ago gave the waterway its droll title because of the difficulties of traversing the swamp.

As time passed, other streams received this sort of label. Among these is a Devil's Branch to the east of Allentown in Wilkinson County, and, in northwest Clinch County, at the head of Suwanoochee (Indian for Little Suwannee) Creek, there is a sizable area called Devil's Bay. A bay in this sense refers to a low, swampy wooded section that may sometimes cover hundreds of acres. Such places in wet weather are extremely difficult to penetrate or cross.

From the present-day point of view, perhaps the most aptly labelled diabolic places are the Devil's Elbows, to be found on the Savannah, Oconee, and St. Marys rivers. The word elbow is an old rivermen's term for any pronounced bend in a navigable stream, but Devil's Elbow had a special meaning and was reserved for sharp curves that were particularly dangerous to negotiate. Such places were characterized by V-shaped formations having a dagger-like tip of land on the inside turn and a deep pocket with an undercut bank on the opposite shore. In the early days it was a trying task for periaguas (large, flat-bottomed rowboats used on early Georgia streams for commercial purposes), keelboats, poleboats, rafts, and other vessels to round these elbows safely, as the inner point directed the full current into the outer curve. Any passing craft that allowed itself to be caught in this sweep was driven into the overhanging bank opposite the dagger. A hapless raft in such a situation was often broken up, while a boat ran the risk of striking the bank with sufficient violence to precipitate a cave-in and be overwhelmed by tottering trees and tons of earth. Boat hooks and poles were of little value for jamming the shore to fend the vessel away because their use might well occasion the very collapse that was dreaded. Little wonder that such spots were called Devil's Elbows!

The boatmen and raftsmen have long since disappeared from these parts, but in accordance with the usual enduring tenacity of placenames we still retain their designations for these once terrifying spots. One of the Devil's Elbows is on the Savannah in southeast Burke County, about two miles above the Screven line; another is on the Oconee, about three and a half miles by river above its mouth; and another is the second bend of the St. Marys River, immediately upstream from the town of St. Marys.

Another devil name which the rivermen left applied to an old spot called the Devil's Trash Pile situated on the Oconee River, below the mouth of Lotts Creek in Montgomery County. In the boatmen's vernacular, a trash pile consisted of a mass of floating logs, limbs, chunks, and other materials that gathered in a relatively deep and still bend where gentle eddies or circular currents tended to hold the debris in place and keep it from drifting downstream. These accumulations were not as dangerous for vessels and rafts as were the Devil's Elbows, but in conjunction with the contrary currents of the eddies they could make navigation difficult.

Perhaps the most distinctive of Georgia's demoniacal tabs is a place called the Devil's Drag Out, located just above Ammon's old ferry on the Great Satilla River to the northeast of Lulaton, in Brantley County. The origin of the expression is not known, but it is believed to be a loggers' name that referred to the difficulties of dragging logs out of the swamp to dump into the river for floating to sawmills on the lower Satilla.

Then there are Devil's Dens. Stephens County has two spots with the name: Devil's Den Creek, a tributary of Little Panther in the northern section, and a Devil's Den on the east side of the middle fork of Broad River in the southwest corner. And too, Decatur County claims a Devil's Den Springs just off Flint River in the southwest part of the county.

But not all of the devil sites were confined to waterways. Upper Greene County had a place called the Devil's Hop, Skip, and Jump, and even now, near Barwick, on the Brooks–Thomas county line, there is a forbidding sink hole called the Devil's Hopper.

Hell was as popular as the devil with the originators of placenames in Georgia. We have as many infernal locations as devilish ones. In general there is not much difference in the implications when either devil or hell is attached to a spot. Both terms can be found in connection with dangerous places or as designations for impenetrable thickets and dense swamps. The main distinction between the words seems to be that devil is reserved for awesome places like the sink hole near Barwick, or for unusual configurations like Devil's Elbow; whereas hell tends to appear more in perilous straight stretches of a stream that have dangerous shoals or rocks. The Big Hell Sluice and Little Hell Sluice on the upper Savannah, at Paris Island in Elbert County, and Hell's Shoals on the Altamaha, near the Tattnall–Toombs county line, are examples of such applications of the word.

One common feature of the devil and hell names lies in the fact that former boatmen invented most of the expressions which remain with us. Illustrative of this point are the Hell Gates which are located on the coast and along the rivers. One such place is in the Florida Passage, a sound between Ossabaw Island and the mainland of Bryan County. At certain times in this passage erratic currents rush with such force as to constitute a hazard to boats and make this spot one of the most dangerous on the entire inland waterway along the coast.

Below Burnt Fort, just inside Camden County, on the Great Satilla, there is a Hell's Gate; and on Flint River, a mile below the mouth of Ichawaynochaway Creek in Baker County, is an evil stretch known as Hell Gate Shoals. Both spots are characterized by tortuous boat channels and tricky currents that were long the terror of navigators. A pilot who lost control of his craft in one of these passages faced the danger of having his vessel capsized or wrecked.

On the Chattahoochee, in western Troup County below the mouth of Wehadkee Creek, there lies a shoally stretch of river with the unique title of Hell Gap. This designation was probably not a boatmen's term, since this portion of the Chattahoochee never had significant navigation. More than likely the name was originally applied by Indian traders because the main strand of the noted Oakfuskee trading path from Augusta to the Upper Creek Indians of Alabama forded the river at these rapids. Today, in watching the turbulent, racing waters at this former crossing, a modern observer can easily see how packhorsemen might well have applied a stygian label to such a place.

On the Savannah River in southeast Burke County, about a mile below the Devil's Elbow of that stream, there is a looping bend whose tip is called Little Hell Point. The turn in some respects is like one of the diabolic elbows, although in this instance the title does not seem to have been derived from the dangers of the point, but rather from a difficult stopping place on the opposite South Carolina shore named Little Hell Landing. It is understandable why boatmen dreaded to touch at this spot, because as the river sweeps around the bend it swings over in a shearing movement along the bank at the landing, making it a risky maneuver for a boat to approach the place. It so happened, however, that former shippers and receivers of freight along here wanted to use this particular landing since the road approach to it followed the only elevated course which was available for miles up and down the Carolina strand. One surmises that the patroons of early periaguas first gave Little Hell Landing its name, and that later steamboat pilots were quite willing to continue such a descriptive name.

The term little used in the hell titles undoubtedly had a special connotation: differentiating a hellish spot here on earth from the Big Hell, or real Purgatory.

In lower Long County and upper McIntosh, another Little Hell can be found along the east side of the Altamaha, as the title of a wild and somber swamp that stretches up and down the river. The locality has borne its name for at least a century and a half, and the denomination is just as appropriate today because the jungle has only been lightly touched by the hand of man.

On the edge of this Little Hell, just below the mouth of Penholoway Creek in Wayne County, the Altamaha has formed a big bend called Old Hell Bight. Possibly this interesting name was derived from the adjacent great swamp; but what is more likely, the tab is a rivermen's moniker which had its origin in the troublesome currents that swirled in the bight. If this is the case, it is a coincidence that these two hell names occur so close together.

Another area which might well have been a Little Hell, but which actually is known as Cow Hell, comprises a dense swamp along the east side of the Oconee, at the mouth of Buckeye Creek in upper Laurens County. The section is not shown on many maps but it is well known to the residents thereabouts who say the place was named for treacherous bogs which entrapped cattle that ventured into this bovine Hades.

Perhaps the reader on occasion has heard some person recount a tedious trip by saying that he had travelled all over Hell's Half Acre in going from one place to another. Well, Georgia has a real Hell's Half Acre in lower Burke County, above the Barkcamp Community and to the east of Magruder. The name is a metaphorical whimsey, since the tract is far larger than a mere half-acre. The designation, however, is quite descriptive of the place, and people in the vicinity insist that their Hell's Half Acre is so thick that a hunter's dog cannot go through the dense thickets which cover the area.

Thus far, it may seem that only middle and south Georgia have devil and hell places, and to a large extent this is true. North Georgia was either more reluctant to use such terms or had fewer sites that the titles fit. Rabun County, however, has two such places: Devil's Branch, a fork of Little Persimmon Creek in the western section, and a rugged pocket called Hell Hole Branch, a fork of Wildcat Creek, that in turn is a tributary of Tallulah River. In Walker County, a mile or so to the southwest of Estelle, is a narrow rough little valley called Devil's Cove; and in Oglethorpe, to the north of Crawford, where Grove Creek heads, there is an old place known as Devil's Pond.

One slightly different infernal name which should be singled out for mention is The River Styx in lower Charlton County, to the northeast of Moniac and along the southeastern fringe of the great Okefenokee Swamp. The designation embodies a densely forested section and some small branches that form the extreme eastern headwaters of the St. Marys River. People who live near the locality simply refer to the place as The Styx, but in so doing they unwittingly mislead outsiders, who assume they must mean The Sticks. It is logical to reach this conclusion as the little streams flow through a wild, uninhabited tract. However, The River Styx is the correct name for the region and seemingly it has borne this old tab for many years.

Some of the Plutonian names which once appeared on Georgia maps and land plats have long since been dropped. For instance, in the 1780's, Burke County had a Purgatory Creek, and at the same time Washington County had a Hell Creek. A century later a map showing northeast Screvèn depicts a point with the backwoodsy label of Haides. This place too has disappeared and is now forgotten unless some old people about the site happen to recall the word.

Placename students soon learn that there are sometimes antonyms for a given body of geographic appellations. Although the devil places seem to be an exception in this respect, Heaven is used as an antonym of the hell spots. The Americans, but not the English, employ the latter word in an unusual phase of naming. Here, for instance, when some area is ideally suited to the raising or subsistence of certain animals, we are prone to speak, though not in an irreverent sense, of such a section as a Heaven for those creatures. Thus, in Worth County, Georgia, to the east of Sylvester, there is a stream called Hog Heaven Branch; and in eastern Alabama, not far from the Georgia line is an area called Turkey Heaven Mountains; while in southern Washington along the Columbia River there is an extensive region known as the Horse Heaven Hills.

We have wandered over the state discussing the various devil and hell places without getting around to the expression which furnished the title of this article. Perhaps the deferment was proper since the subject concerns an appellation with a different implication from the other names that have been mentioned. This designation, which once applied to a crossroads in Putnam County, located ten miles southwest of Eatonton, originated about 1806. At that time a man purchased a half-acre of land at the road intersection and established a dram shop which became a "theatre of so much vice" that the distinctive name Devil's Half Acre was given the spot. After a great religious revival in 1827-1828, however, the vicinity turned quite moral again, and eventually the place became Stanfordville. But interestingly enough a modified and "cleaned up" version of the old name still hangs on: the community aroundabout continues to be known to this day as The Half Acre.

—*GMNL* 12(1959): 27-29, reprinted from *GR* 9(1955): 290-96

The Poor Mouthing Placenames

The people who lived during the first half of Georgia's span of history had the unique responsibility of providing most of the geographic names which are in use today. In fulfilling this duty, as any good map will amply show, those early citizens adopted a great variety and range of appellations. They continued a few names which the Spaniards left along the coast and, fortunately for the placename lovers of today, appropriated a diversity of fascinating Indian nomenclature. After the Revolution they began to manifest a preference for names of admired political and military leaders, a propensity which by no means was limited to popular American figures, as is demonstrated by names like Chatham, Burke, Camden, LaFayette, Pulaski, Bolivar, and Kossuth. By the end of the formative period a partiality for names of foreign cities and places had developed: Athens, Lisbon, Rome, Montevideo, Lodi, Ceylon, Egypt, etc. And all during this time, as the state expanded, there was growth in the number of old familiar church name sites: Ebenezer, Mount Tabor, Mars Hill, Bethlehem, Mount Pleasant, and so on. All of this time, too, the people were busy adding names, which, if not always Georgian in concept, were heavily imbued with the pioneer outlook and the influence of the American way of life.

Now, apart from conventional English geographic words like slope, hill, mountain, river, sound, ridge, etc., a curiously missing factor in this pattern of Georgia placenaming is a readily discernible influence from the British Isles. There are English, Scotch, Welsh, and Irish place appellations in use here, but not nearly as many as one might assume in view of the fact that Georgia is a daughter of Britain. We do, for instance, employ designations like Oxford, Birmingham, Chelsea, Donegal, Tyrone, Erin, and Scotland, but some of these adoptions came fairly late and their appropriation is quite analogous to such other borrowings as Seville, Bremen, Toledo, Berlin, Amsterdam, and Cairo. Indeed, the impact of the British on Georgia names is outwardly so tenuous that one has to study nomenclature closely to discover where kinships exist. But relationships *can* be found on detailed maps, and when one turns up groups of names which are similar in the two areas, the discovery becomes intriguing, since the expressions imply an affinity in the thought processes that motivated the British and the Americans in making up such names.

There are several groups of English appellations which evidence a bond between Georgia names and those used in other states, but two of these categories are especially significant because they can be closely linked to American designations which one might easily assume are pure examples of indigenous backwoods placenaming. The first of these groupings embodies monikers containing the words devil and hell. Both the British and the Americans were fond of such terms in their names, and this predilection has already been discussed in the *Georgia Review* in an article entitled "The Devil's Half Acre." The second category comprises names which obviously show that they were applied in the British Isles because the originators of the expressions lamented having to live or work at sites bearing designations like Poverty Bottom, Starve All Farm, Labour in Vain, Beggary, Hungry Down, Hungry Hill, Hungerford, Hungerton, Hungry Law, and Pinch Gut Hall. Expressions in this vein also appealed to the Georgians and other Americans and they willingly adopted such terms here.

It is not known what the British label their group of poverty designations, but in the Georgia vernacular the names reflect a phase of what is called "po' mouthing"; that is, such appellations were improvised because certain citizens, either seriously or facetiously, bemoaned their lot at having to dwell in areas where their labor was considered as unrewarding. And since most of the terms in Georgia stem from the years when agriculture was the chief means of livelihood, the words imply a poor regard for farming prospects in the localities where the names were applied. It might be added that there is still much poor mouthing, but nowadays seemingly the practice has mostly been transferred to urban scenes where glum-minded individuals deplore, or pretend to deplore, the woeful state of business. The pretended deprecations are most likely to be manifested when donations are being solicited for some civic project or when a committee from the church calls to ask for contributions. No doubt there was also a measure of pretence among old rural placenamers, although more than likely when they adopted a hard luck form which was not warranted by farming conditions, they were merely being facetious or satirical. Evidence of this possibility can be found in the fact that comparable communities bearing optimistic titles often adjoin or lie near areas which have been dubbed with pessimistic labels. For instance, in upper Fulton County there is a Hardscrabble section; while nearby are districts called Providence and Hopewell. So far as the modern observer can see, the three old communities are very similar in their general attributes.

In discussing the actual po' mouthing names in Georgia, perhaps it would be best to begin with some expressions that most closely resemble the British appellations and then turn to impecunious nomenclature which seemingly is expressed in more indigenous Georgia terms.

Some expressions that stem from the British are the poverty places. Georgia once had several areas which were so designated and even now has at least two such localities: a Poverty Hill in lower Jones County, to the northwest of Griswold; and a Poverty Creek that arises in southwest Lumpkin County and flows into Dawson to join Gab Creek in the latter county.

Then there are Hungry names. One of these is Hungry Valley, lying to the west of Dalton, in Whitfield County. Another is Hungry Hill in eastern Bryan County, on Georgia 63, below Richmond Hill. The name is old, but one gathers it may have originally been a satirical tab since the locality is in no sense a hill, but is situated in about the flattest of the Coastal Flatwoods. In southwest Carroll County, emptying into the Little Tallapoosa River, there is a Hungry Creek. This stream, however, does not bear a strict po' mouthing name, because the early surveyor who laid off this area in 1827 after its acquisition from the Indians originally recorded the tab. It is not known why he used the name. Perhaps he was not impressed with the area along the waterway and dubbed it Hungry on his maps and plats to tip off future land lot winners on the type of land they would draw in the lottery to distribute the section. Or, maybe the surveying party ran out of provisions in the fatiguing task of laying off a virgin territory, and under these straitened conditions adopted the tag. A similar name, which was possibly applied under the same conditions, is found in Hunger and Hardship Creek, that enters the Oconee at Dublin in Laurens County. Some people of the area, though, claim the designation is of Indian origin. Perhaps it is, although the title lacks the air of an Indian expression. More than likely, one believes, the creek was named by a weary and hungry surveying party, when the section was first laid off in 1804-1805.

The Pinch Gut which was mentioned in the British list has been widely used in America. Georgia once had a stream called Pinch Gut Creek in original Pulaski County. The name has long since been dropped from maps and the stream apparently is now the waterway called Joiner Creek in southeastern Dodge County.

To pass to the more home-improvised po' mouthing names, the Hardscrabble mentioned above seems to be such a word. The name is now perpetuated in an old route called the Hardscrabble Road, but originally it applied to a section in present northwest Fulton County. Some people of the community think the name arose because it was formerly a hardscrabble to get over the road in a wagon, while others say the name was coined because it was once difficult to make a living in the area. The last explanation finds support elsewhere, since Hardscrabble has been much used across America—in West Virginia, Indiana, Wisconsin, California, and other areas—as a po' mouthing word. With respect to the name in this sense, though, the reader should again be reminded that this droll tab, and others which will be mentioned, were probably improvised in attempts at rustic humor that was not necessarily founded on actual meager economic potentials of the sections which received such names. It should be added, too, that present-day citizens apparently do not object to the whimsical old expressions. Indeed, many people find the names humorous and seem to enjoy talking about them.

Some other poor mouthing expressions which seem more native to the scene are Hard Up, Hard Fortune, Pulltight, (i.e., pull the belt tight), Lickskillet, and Rabbit Hill. The first spot is a community in northeast Baker County. For a period the place was even a post office under the name Hardup. Hard Fortune appears in the name of a creek which arises to the south of Dearing and enters the east side of Headstall Creek, in McDuffie County. The appellation is of post-Revolutionary origin and today seems a bit stilted. But the name was quite descriptive in the pioneer way of thinking, and a present-day crossword puzzle expert would be hard put to suggest an expression which would carry exactly the same connotation. Such modern terms as Hard Luck Creek or Tough Luck Creek would certainly fall short of the implication which the old-timers wanted to convey with the words Hard Fortune. Pulltight is a locality to the east of the Big Slough, on the Decatur-Grady line. The name occurs again in Pulltight Hollow, that largely lies in Hamilton County, Tennessee, but which actually drains into extreme upper Dade County, Georgia. Another such whimsy is Lickskillet. The name has even been formalized by being retained in the official titles for two Georgia Militia districts, one in Cherokee County and another in Schley. There was once a third Lickskillet, in what is now western Fulton County, but the name was later changed to the more dignified Adamsville, a vicinity which has become a part of metropolitan Atlanta. Rabbit Hill is a locality in eastern Bryan County, below Richmond Hill and near the Hungry Hill which has been mentioned. No one knows when the name originated but people aroundabout say it arose because the residents had to rely on rabbit meat as a food in order to "get by." There must be substance in this explanation, since other states also use the word rabbit in their indigence expressions, and the same interpretation can be heard in those regions. Kentucky, for instance, has three Rabbit appellations: Rabbit Town, Rabbitsville, and Rabbit Hash. The last place, which was once a post office, connotes best the intended meanings of the three tabs.

In addition to names which can be identified as po' mouthing expressions there is a substantial list of monikers which possibly belong in that category. One cannot be certain of the classification and has to resort to speculation about the meanings because there is little documentary evidence to explain the old names, and elderly people often disagree on details of the origins. Blue John Creek, in Troup County, below LaGrange, is an interesting example of this class. Some citizens of the area concede they do not know the significance of the expression, while others state the stream was given its name because the water had the color of "blue John," a frontier expression that signified skimmed milk. The hue in turn, it is said, was caused by the waterway flowing past a deposit of bluish clay. This explanation may be correct, but the fact that people refer to the stream as *Old Blue John Creek*, is an inkling that there may have been another explanation. There is a chance that some backcountry wit who lived on the stream adopted the name because he claimed his family was forced to drink blue John as a regular diet.

It might be of interest to note that the British use Blue John as a placename but not in a sense that is subject to interpretation as a poor mouthing form. Their term, which applies to a spot in Derbyshire called Blue John Mine, derives from *bleu-jaune*, the French name for a beautiful amethystine spar that is found in the area.

If Blue John Creek is a po' mouthing expression, some possible kindred names are found in the Buttermilk places. Such tabs have long been used in Georgia, even in colonial years, because there was once a pre-Revolutionary place called Buttermilk Bluff on the St. Marys River in present Camden County. Buttermilk Sound, at the mouth of the Altamaha, is one old form that still remains. In the interior, there is a Buttermilk Shoals on the Ocmulgee near Hawkinsville, a Buttermilk Creek in lower Cobb and northeast Douglas counties, and a Buttermilk Bottoms in a section of Atlanta. The last name is commonly thought to be of po' mouthing origin, but there is disagreement about meanings of the other expressions. Some people think the terms originally had a poverty implication because residents of the localities had to depend on buttermilk to survive, while others insist the names were applied because glistening waters where the names are used had a whitish appearance like buttermilk.

Closely akin to Blue John Creek and the Buttermilk places as possible po' mouthing names is a spot called Bonny Clabber Bluff, located on the west bank of the Oconee River, in lower Laurens County. Some people in the area say the name is of Scotch or Welsh origin, but on its face it is an Anglicized Irish expression for sour buttermilk, sour clabber, or a kind of sour curdled milk. (According to informants in Laurens County, Bonny Clabber Bluff was originally Baunauclaughbaugh. If the name were Irish, it would have been derived from *bainne*, milk, plus *claba*, thick.) The Irish apparently are fond of the drink, especially with honey or molasses, but Americans seemingly have never cared for it. Perhaps in a way that is not now clear, Bonny Clabber was used in lieu of buttermilk as a poverty name for the bluff.

And still another name that resembles Blue John Creek is Poor Joe Branch, a tributary of Lime Creek, in eastern Sumter County. No explanation could be turned up about the origin of the tab; it may be a po' mouthing name, or it may simply have been applied to an individual called Poor Joe, who lived on the stream.

An additional possible po' mouthing name is found in the Crackers Neck section of lower Greene County. The locality is old and beginning in the 1830's once had a post office called Crackers Neck. Some people claim the name arose because crackers, who had a hard time making a living, resided in the community. But apparently no one knows exactly how the appellation came into being; it may possibly have been applied by outsiders, in which case it would not be a genuine po' mouthing label because the true poverty names were self-imposed.

Some possible po' mouthing names are doubtful because the places are not listed on maps and one can not be sure of the proper spelling of the words. For instance, in Towns County, to the east of Visage, there is a little spot called Barefoot or Bearfoot. If the coiners of the appellation intended the latter meaning, the word probably simply signified bear track. If, however, they really meant Barefoot, the word would reflect impecuniosity because it referred to a place where people had to go without shoes.

Uncertainties arise about some possible indigence names because the appellations are subject to alternate interpretations and at this date we do not know what the old-timers intended a particular expression to mean. For instance, consider the words scuffle and scrouge, as found in designations like Scrougetown, Scuffletown, Scuffleton, and Scuffle Bluff. In one sense Scrougetown might have referred to a place where people were crowded or pushed too close to each other. On the other hand, the term could have been used to denote a community were people complained they had a tight squeeze or scrouge in making ends meet. Scuffle meant to tussle, wrestle, or even brawl and a Scuffle place might have been a spot where people customarily gathered for scuffling as a pastime, thus giving rise to a tag like Scuffletown. Scuffle, however, also meant to struggle, and in an area where life was hard and people had to scuffle for a living, they might well have named such areas Scuffletown or Scuffleton.

To give examples of some of these places, there is a Scrougetown community in central Gilmer County; a Scuffletown in northeast McDuffie; and a Scuffleton in lower Effingham, near the Chatham County line. Scuffle Bluff is an old spot on the north side of the Ocmulgee River, in lower Telfair County.

One former Scuffle name in what is now Twiggs County had an interesting turn: in 1806 when the area was first being surveyed, the district surveyor dubbed the present Richland Creek, Scuffle Creek. His reason for this choice is purely a matter of conjecture. Perhaps he had to scuffle hard in running his lines along and across the stream; or perhaps he was not impressed by the potential of the area and simply tagged the stream with the term Scuffle to indicate his personal evaluation of the locality. But be that as it may, the later citizens apparently did not like the implications of the name and switched it to Richland Creek. The last expression is a plain antonym of a poor mouthing name.

One intriguing name which may have been intended as a straitened moniker is Tuckahoe. Georgia has had several localities by this name and at least two remain—one in Jefferson County, above Wrens, on the Old Quaker Road, and another in northeast Screven, between the forks of Briar Creek and the Savannah River.

Tuckahoe is an Algonquian Indian word which has spread along the Atlantic Coast from New York and New Jersey to Georgia. The expression originally applied to several varieties of truffle-like mushrooms and tubers that pioneers called Indian bread. In difficult times when food was scarce people were reduced to eating the substance. Perhaps, then, in the fashion of the poverty names, Tuckahoe got turned into a po' mouthing word. There is a possibility, though, that the term was merely a nickname for Virginians and was applied to areas where people from that state settled in Georgia.

There still remains an array of possible po' mouthing names, but space will only permit the listing of a selected few to indicate the diversity of the forms and the pervasiveness of their distribution: Flint Hill in southeast Floyd County; Rye Patch in Long; Briar Patch in Bulloch; Frog Pond in Emanuel; Dog Fennell in Evans; Ashbank in Putnam; Shanty Town in Dade; Dodo (now Brewton) in Laurens; and perhaps Pebble Hill in Ware County.

As has been seen above, streams were often dubbed with po' mouthing tags. This was natural because watercourses were important adjuncts to land holdings in pioneer times and given areas were usually identified in that period by their relationship to streams. Some additional possible po' mouthing forms that are reflected by waterway names are Mangy Branch in McDuffie County; Needy Creek in Rabun; Naked Creek in Walton; Trouble Creek in Oglethorpe; and Troublesome Creek in Spalding. Two probable names in this group, with a Cherokee background, are Big and Little Scarce Corn creeks in Pickens County.

There are numbers of Georgia names which bear such a close resemblance to po' mouthing words that placename students are sometimes led astray in interpreting them. The outstanding example in this respect is Hard Labor Creek that commences in central Walton and drains across Morgan to enter the Apalachee River to the eastward of Madison. The real significance of the name is not known, but one can be certain it was not a pioneer farmer's po' mouthing expression, but an Indian country name because the original surveyors of the area which is now Morgan and Walton encountered the expression and recorded it on their first maps and plats. The appellation was used in other wilderness regions in stream-naming, and one suspects it was a derisive Indian tab which poked fun at the white man's difficulties in fording creeks.

Rocky Comfort Creek, which arises in Warren and flows across Glascock to join the Ogeechee in lower Jefferson, is a name which might be mistaken for an ironical po' mouthing expression. No one knows when the appellation was first used, but it probably antedates the founding of Georgia. It may be a translated Indian term which was first used by early traders, since the stream lay athwart the two main trading routes from Charleston via present Augusta to the Creek Indians. On one of these trails (the famous Lower Creek Trading Path), near or along Rocky Comfort Creek, there was a noted camping spot called the Flat Rock. This favored and convenient place perhaps gave rise to the stream's name. But if this were the case, the expression had an opposite implication from a poverty tag.

Another non-po' mouthing form which should be mentioned is No Business Creek in present Gwinnett and DeKalb counties. The precise significance of the expression is not clear, but its usage transcends the period of permanent settlers because original surveyors found the tab when they laid off the section after its acquisition from the Creeks. The Vinegar Hill community of Walton County seems to bear an impecunious label, but more than likely, one believes, it is an Irish name that commemorates the battle of Vinegar Hill (near Enniscorthy, in Wexford) which was fought in 1798 between Irish rebels and the English. In Ireland the word may have originally carried a po' mouthing meaning but this was probably not the case in Georgia. Then, there are appellations like the Barren Hills section, above Villanow, on the boundary of Walker and Whitfield counties; and Dismal Knob, Dismal Gap, and Dismal Cove on the Blue Ridge at the Towns-Rabun line. These names are really descriptive terms for unpromising areas that were never suited to farming. They are not lamentational and are thus not true po' mouthing words. They are subject to misinterpretations, however, because in some states the words dismal and barren occur in poverty forms. In fact, the latter term, as used in the expression Pine Barren, found former po' mouthing usage in Georgia.

In addition to such names, there is another group of words which may be mistaken for po' mouthing names: Dark Corner; Grab All; Hard Cash; Barrel Head; Frog Bottom; Peckerwood District; Possum Trot; and so on. These monikers are very different from the po' mouthing order in their significance and origins. One can be virtually certain that all of them were disparaging expressions which were originally foisted by outsiders on the spots and areas where they apply. Dark Corner, for instance, meant benighted in pioneer terminology and was probably an expression that had to be used with a smile, if a fight were to be avoided. One can reasonably conclude that it would not have been voluntarily adopted by a community. A backcountryman might not object to his area being referred to as a Lickskillet district, but he would have resented its being called a Dark Corner. Grab All, Barrel Head, and Hard Cash were attached to little trading points where people complained they were cheated or denied credit in stores. Possum Trot is a waggish tab which was applied to remote, out-of-the-way places where possums formed trots, i.e., regular trails in coming and going. The name bore approximately the same connotation as our "hole-in-the-road." Georgia still retains numbers of Possum Trots, although it would be rare to find the name listed on a map.

Two relatively modern names which are easily mistaken for po' mouthing expressions are Po' Biddy Crossroads on U.S. 80 in Talbot County and a community bearing the droll title Scantville in western Carroll. The former arose from an incident in which a diner took the last piece of chicken at a dinner and caused another individual at the party to exclaim, "There goes the last of the po' biddy!" The Scantville section in Carroll is said to have derived its name from the practice of bootleggers thereabouts watering down their product. The measure of real liquor in the stuff was so scant, as the story goes, some wag called the area Scantville and the name has stuck.

In concluding, it should be emphasized that not all old-timers were pessimistic souls who bemoaned their lot through placenames. There were many sanguine individuals who collectively left Georgia a profusion of optimistic appellations. Indeed, the roll of such terms is fully as long as the roster of actual and possible poor mouthing names. And interestingly enough, the expressions are largely native to the American scene because the English make relatively little use of this type of name. It is not feasible here to mention and locate all of the cheerful nomenclature, but the following list will indicate that the forms were as diverse as the pessimistic group: Sweet Home, A I, Hopeful, New Hope, Grand Center, Ideal, Prosperity, Cornucopia, Magnet, Eureka, Excelsior, Good Hope, Zenith, Humming, Fancy Hill, Paradise, and so on in great variety. Some antonymical expressions were improvised to bear a precise opposite meaning to the bemoaning farmers' monikers. Among such words are Richland, Cotton Hill, Rich Hill, Blackacre, and Blackankle. The last expression denoted an area of deep, fertile, black soil. The name is still retained in Chatham, Upson, and Fannin counties.

—*GMNL* 12(1959)65-68, reprinted from *GR* 12(1958): 440-50

The Derivations of Creek Indian Placenames

Introduction

An Oklahoma informant of Creek descent replied in answer to an inquiry about the meanings of certain Indian placenames of Georgia that he could not identify and explain the words. He added the white people in the old Creek country where his ancestors lived had "butchered" Muskogee designations so badly the present-day Creeks are unable to recognize many of the names, much less interpret them. The respondent was an intelligent man who on occasion had willingly helped on translations and it was plain his comment was more rueful than critical. Perhaps he was judging the matter on the basis of the particular names submitted to him because they are among the most enigmatic appellations that can be found in the area of Georgia where the Creeks once resided. He had never been queried about simpler names whose meanings are clear; nor had he been asked about words that are plainly not of Creek origin. For example, it is known that Aucilla is the oldest recorded Indian name of Georgia since it was mentioned in 1539 by the chroniclers of DeSoto. The stream bearing the name lies in former Creek country but since the word was of Timucuan origin and not Muskogean, it would have been pointless to ask a modern Creek to explain such an appellation.

Nonetheless the Oklahoma man's remark about the "butchered" words does point out a situation which is recognized by students of aboriginal placenames—that our interesting Indian nomenclature, both Creek and Cherokee, is not always what it seems; that most such names are distorted to some degree; and that others were so poorly recorded in the first place, or have been changed so drastically with the passage of time, their original forms and intended meanings are not clear.

Composition of the Creek Federation

This article is an incursion into the field of Creek names to study the rudiments of that language to see how those Indians derived some of their placenames and why white people were prone to distort these appellations when they borrowed them from the red people. As a background for the discussion there should be a summary statement about the Creeks. At the time of the establishment of Georgia, they lived to the south of the Cherokees and claimed the territory stretching from the Savannah River and the Atlantic across Georgia and upper Florida to Alabama. There were two principal geographic divisions of the powerful tribe at that period: the Upper Creeks who lived from the upper Chattahoochee River area westward into Alabama, on the waters of the Tallapoosa, Coosa, and Alabama rivers; and the Lower Creeks whose main settlements were entered on the Chattahoochee from present Columbus southward. The Creeks were not a homogeneous people; actually the nation consisted of a confederation composed of different tribes, subtribes, and bands: Hitchitees, Alibamos, Uchees, Natchez, Chickasaws, Shawnees, Muskogees, and possibly some small remnants of former peoples that once lived in the region; like the Apalachicolas, Yemasees, and Timucuas. The dominant element of this confederacy were the martial Muskogees who governed the nation in a loose fashion and impressed many of their customs upon it. The expression Creek is often used as an alternate name for the Muskogees, and will be so employed here, but it is important to note that the former designation is actually a generalized, collective term which the real Muskogees did not use in speaking of themselves.

The Hitchitees represented another important element of the Creek coalition. At one time they lived from the middle Ocmulgee River southward, but at the time of the foundation of the province they mainly resided in southwest Georgia on the lower Flint and Chattahoochee. They were the forerunners of the Seminoles, after they began moving farther south into Florida. As Seminoles, however, and especially after the Creek War of 1813-1814, they received a large influx of the true Upper Creeks who fled their traditional homes on the Tallapoosa and Coosa rivers in Alabama.

The members of the Creek confederacy each had their own way of speaking but with several important exceptions their language was similar because it stemmed from a common linguistic stock, the Muskogean. Thus there were dialects among these peoples and the differences are reflected in the place nomenclature of Georgia. Dialectal variations are most noticeable in south Georgia where Hitchitees resided away from the main centers of the Muskogees.

In addition to speech differences among the several elements of the confederacy, there were curious men and women's dialects in use within certain groups. Except perhaps for "baby talk," that is not based on sex, we have no speech forms that are analogous to these peculiar vernaculars. Little is known about the nature of the idioms by sexes, except that they existed at one time. It is possible that some of our enigmatic names derive from these forgotten forms. If this is true, however, the white people have not necessarily "butchered" the words; their meanings have simply been lost to the present Creeks.

Some members of the Creek coalition, such as the Uchees and the Shawnees, did not speak a Muskogean tongue. The former used a gutteral speech that few other people ever learned, so much so that little is known about the real names of the Uchean settlements because these towns are mentioned in old records by their Muskogee designations and not by their Uchean labels. Except for certain stream names that are referred to as Uchee creeks, because those Indians are known to have resided on such waterways, we have no remaining placenames that can positively be identified as Uchee. The Ogeechee River is seemingly the most important place designation that belongs in the group of stream names because it was the River of the Uchees and is apparently a variant of the word Uchee. There are several Uchee creeks, in both Georgia and Alabama, and interestingly enough, old people who live about those streams pronounce them "Oochee," despite the fact that Indian scholars write the word as Yuchi and pronounce it "Yoochee."

The Shawnees who once lived in these parts were members of a migratory band that settled at various places among the Creeks. They were of Algonquian stock and their traditional home was much to the north, on the Cumberland and Ohio rivers. One group of these red gypsies resided for a while in the area of today's Augusta and there is substantial evidence to show that the Savannah—the River of the Shawnees—is named for them.

Before turning to the Creek words, it might be of interest to mention the Chickasaws. Their home was in north Mississippi, west Tennessee, and north Alabama, but at least two groups of them once resided temporarily in Georgia—one along the Savannah in the area of Augusta, and another below Upatoi Creek and near the Chattahoochee, within the present Fort Benning Reservation. The bands seemingly left several interesting placenames. One of these applies to Halloka Creek, in Chattahoochee County, and located in about the center of the fort's reservation, not far removed from the old Chickasaw village site. The expression means beloved and possibly referred to some sort of reserve such as a hunting ground which had been set aside by the Creeks for the use of the Chickasaws. Another probable Chickasaw name occurred in the aboriginal designation of Whitewater Creek in Taylor and Macon counties. Benjamin Hawkins states this stream was originally the Okauhutkee and that the name was Choctaw for whitewater. Now, the latter Indians lived in Mississippi, far from the area of the Okauhutkee. The name most likely was left by the Chickasaw group that lived in the Fort Benning area because the Chickasaw language was nearly identical with Choctaw. In southeast Richmond County near the Savannah River there is a place called Tahoma. The spot is near some former haunts of the Chickasaws. The name does not seem to be Creek, and since its last element *homa* is the Choctaw-Chickasaw word for red, one believes the appellation is an interesting word that harks back to the years in which the Chickasaws lived in the area.

As in the case of the Uchee streams, there are also one or two Chickasaw creeks in old east Georgia that are remainders of the stay of those Indians in the state. Also in southwest Georgia, heading in central Terrell County, there is a big stream called Chickasawhatchee Creek. It is doubtful, however, that this waterway derived its name from the Chickasaws because no records show any of those Indians in the area. The name is pronounced "Chick' sī hatchee" by old people and one early surveyor shows this form is of long standing by reporting the name in 1826 as "Chickasyhatchy." More than likely one thinks this name is Hitchitee, being derived from *chiki*, or *chickee*, house, i.e., council house, plus the locative, *sasi*, is there, plus *hahchi*, a stream, meaning Council House Creek. As will be seen later, *hahchi* is more difficult to pronounce than appears. Apparently by the process of assimilation the white people in this instance converted it to the easier and better-known Creek word *hachi*, or hatchee. The readers who are familiar with the Seminoles of Florida will recall that the present Seminole word for house is *chickee*.

English Authorities for Creek Placenames

To turn now to Muskogee names that are retained here, it should be mentioned that the appellations were originally recorded in our language by a variety of people: Indian traders, army officers, travellers, officials, missionaries, or surveyors. Some of these individuals had little first-hand knowledge of the language of the Creeks and had to depend on an assorted lot of Indian countrymen—guides, packhorsemen, escaped Tories, renegades, squatters, squaw men, and so on—as sources of information on the words that were reported. Most of these informants were probably backwoodsy fellows without the benefit of much schooling and were as likely to have butchered their own language as well as the Indian. It is only fair to note, though, in calling off the red people's expressions they sometimes added simple, incisive interpretations of the names. Such explanations are valuable for present-day students because they provide clues about the real meanings of a number of interesting names. One of the best transcribers of the appellations was Colonel Benjamin Hawkins, who long resided among the Creeks as Indian agent. He learned the language of the people, and was one of the first persons that attempted to write in Muskogee.

Transcribing Creek Vowel Sounds into English

In reporting on Creeks words and names, it is safe to say the early white transcribers were double victims of the difficulties of their own tongue and the intricacies of the Indian languages and dialects. The Creeks had at least eight vowel sounds and these had to be rendered with an array of English vowels that had a multiplicity of sounds. The results led to a switching about and alternation of vowels by the whites. The situation is well illustrated by the recordings for the word Upatoi, as found in the name of a large creek that enters the Chattahoochee below Columbus. This term is now spelled Upatoi and pronounced "Yoo' pa toy." In early records it was variously reported as Au-put-tau-e, Euphautaus, Opatoy, Opatahway, Upatoy, Uptois and Epitoy. Albert Gatschet, the Creek scholar, gives the word as "Apata-i" and states that it signifies a sheet-like covering. One strongly suspects, however, it meant something like farthest out, on the fringe, or perhaps last, and was so named because the Creek village of Upatoy at the forks of the stream that bears the name was the easternmost settlement of Muskogees in its day. The stream called Utoy Creek in western Fulton County seems to be the same word in garbled form and received its designation because the town of Buzzard Roost located where the creek reaches the Chattahoochee was the last Creek community in its time, going upstream, on the east side of the river.

One Creek vowel which troubled the English-speaking people was the broad *a* or *ä* that occurs in words like father and psalm. The Muskogees made extensive use of the letter and the white recorders of names were uncertain about the way to render it to make sure the letter would be recognized. As a result they often switched the *ä* to *au*, *aw*, *ar*, *ah*, or even to an *o* (like that in lock and dock), and such forms can be found in many of the early recordings of Creek placenames. The changes had some practical value because otherwise a person might miss the sound of a word and fail to understand it. For instance, the Indian name of the present Harrel Mill Creek in Webster County was reported by the original surveyor of the area in 1826 as Archibookta. The last part of the name may be garbled but the expression appears to be the Creek word *achitohto,* meaning corn crib, from *achi,* corn, plus *tohto,* crib. *Achi,* standing alone, is easy for an English-speaking person to mispronounce. One might easily call it 'aitchy," or even "ake" or "aiky" because of its resemblance to our word ache, as in headache. By rendering the word as *archi,* the surveyor sought to approximate its sound which was "ä' chĭ."

Some Creek words containing the *a* have long since seen the letter evolve into the *a* of fat and hat. An interesting example can be found in Chattahoochee. This name was originally "Chä' tō hochi," meaning flowered rocks, or rocks with designs running through them. Over the years it has been changed to Chattahoochee, which is pronounced "Chattyhoochee" by hundreds of people.

Another example can be found in Patsiliga Creek in Taylor County. This name is from *pächi,* pigeon, plus the locative *līga,* signifying, in this instance, a roosting place. The *pachi* was rendered as "parchee," "padjee," or "pahchee," but it long ago evolved into "patsi," with an *a* like that in *pat.* Apparently there is a common thought process which governs language change in this sort of word because in south Alabama, much removed from Taylor County, Georgia, another Pachiliga Creek evolved into Patsiliga, just as in this state.

Only a few of the retained placenames keep their original *ä*'s. Altamaha and Alapaha, if they can be considered as true Creek names, retain the letter in a slightly modified form. Perhaps the remaining word that comes closest to the original letter is Wahoo which occurs in the names of several streams and spots in the state. The expression signifies winged elm, *Ulmus alata,* and was once spelled in a variety of ways: Wawhoo, Warhoo, Waughoo, etc. Eventually, though, the expression became formalized under its present spelling with an *ä* that maintains its original sound.

Another Muskogee *a* which troubled the old name transcribers was the obscure *a* that has the sound of *u* in words like jut and nut. This letter is common in both English and Creek and is a true *a.* We use it frequently in words like diadem, sofa, and aghast. The Indian name transcribers probably knew this, but did not know how to differentiate this *a* from others except by changing it to *u,* or *uh,* or even into other vowels. Today when it is necessary to distinguish the letter with precision we do so by writing it as an italicized *a* with a dot over it, thus, *à*. The old-timers did not hit on so simple a device and thus left us Indian names that have become distorted through misunderstanding of the vowel. A good illustration can be found in the name of Wehadkee Creek, which arises in east Alabama and enters the Chattahoochee above West Point. The word signifies whitewater, from *wĭwà,* or *wēwà,* water, plus *hàtkĭ* ("hut' kee"), white. For a long time, however, the last element has been written hadkee or hatkee, with an *a* like that in hat.

The most important place word by far that originally had the obscure *à* and is now mispronounced is found in hatchee, hatchie, and hachee. The correct Muskogee equivalent of these words was *hàchi,* pronounced "hutchee." The expression means stream but we usually translate it as Creek and pronounce it to rhyme with catch. The expression is important because the Creeks customarily used it in connection with stream names. Their practice in this respect was in striking contrast with the custom of the Cherokees who did not employ their word for stream in naming waterways.

By converting *hàchi* into hatchee, the English-speaking people created a bit of confusion about the word *hachi,* that means tail. The matter is worth mentioning because there was a noted post-Revolutionary Creek chief known to the whites as the Bird Tail King. He resided in today's southwest Chattahoochee County, in the Fort Benning area, and his name translated back into Creek comes out as Fushachimiko from *fuswà,* bird + *hachi,* tail + *miko,* chief. Interestingly enough, the present Pruitt Creek in southeast Randolph County was once listed as Fushatchee Creek but one does not know if the name was intended to mean Bird Tail's Creek or Bird Creek. Since an early English name for the stream was Claybank Creek, it is possible that *fus* of Fushatchee was a garbled form of *foki,* or "fookee," meaning clay, earth or dirt and the name had no connection at all with *fuswà,* bird.

Despite the persistence of the early whites in making *hàchi* into hatchee, they were consistent in converting the *à* of some words to *u.* This was the case with *làsti,* meaning black, which was written lustie or lustee. Seemingly this uniformity stemmed from the fact that *làsti* would not be very meaningful, whereas all the whites understood hatchee. An interesting example of a name that once contained *làsti* can be found in the present Black Creek of Bulloch and Bryan counties. This stream was originally Wilàstihàchi, or water black stream. It next became Weelustee, and eventually was converted to Black Creek.

Another obscure *à* that often got shifted to a *u* was the *à* of the Creek augumentative suffix *thlàko*, meaning big, which was commonly rendered as *thlucco*. The form occurred in Hatcheethlucco, or Big Creek, an obsolete name of Upatoi Creek. Sometimes the *à* of the word was also changed to an *o* or even an *i*, making the expression into *thlocco*, *thlocko*, or *lika*. The latter version was found in Upelikee, (or Big Swamp), the Indian name for the main head stream of Chickasawhatchee Creek in Terrell County. The town of Opelika, Alabama, perpetuates the same appellation in slightly different form.

In addition to difficulties with the letter *a*, the old-timers had troubles distinguishing between the Creek *o*'s and *u*'s. This is known to be the case because on occasion one transcriber would list a word with an *o* while another man would record the same letter as a *u*. It must be said, however, the Indians themselves also made alternative use of these two vowels. An interesting name in which the letters were switched can be found in Chokeeliga Creek in northwest Lee County. The expression means Council House-stands-there Creek from *chuko*, council house, and locative *liga*. The *u* of *chuko* got changed to *o* and the appellation has come down to us Chokee. Chokee Creek in lower Sumter and northeast Lee County is the same name, without the suffix *liga*.

Most Georgia placenames of Creek origin are usually easy to pronounce, even by people who are not familiar with the words. Their pronunciations may not accord with a scientific rendering of the appellations, but at least they will be close to the original versions reported by the early whites. There are, though, several important exceptions in this respect since some expressions do not have the sounds called for in the spellings of the words. Two good examples can be found in Towaliga, the name of a large west-bank tributary of the Ocmulgee River in northeast Monroe County; and in Sowhatchee Creek, an affluent of the Chattahoochee in lower Early County. The *ow* in these designations has a long *i* sound, and not the value of *ow* in words like tower and power. Thus, in the spoken versions Towaliga becomes "Tī' lī' ga," or "Tī' lī' gee"; and Sowhatchee in Early County becomes "Sī' hatchee." An explanation for the pronunciation of the former seems easy—the original expression was probably *tiwaliga*, meaning scalp place, and had the long *i* instead of an *o* in the first place. "Sihatchee" for Sowhatchee is difficult to explain. The name was long spelled Sawhatchee, and was derived from the Hitchitee *sawi*, raccoon, and *hahchi*, stream or creek. The mystery of the evolution of the name is heightened by the fact that *sawi* was probably pronounced *shawi* by the Hitchitees, since those Indians often sounded an initial *s* as *sh*, just as we say "shure" for sure, or "shumack" for sumac.

With respect to the Georgia county called Coweta, that name is commonly pronounced "Kou eeta," the first element sounded as cow. Even so, if one listens closely when the name is used, he will at times hear it as "Kī-eeta."

In his *Creek Country*, Colonel Benjamin Hawkins mentions one of these *ow* names that gives a good clue to the meaning of *Kiokee*, a baffling appellation that occurs several times in Georgia waterway names. In writing about present Mill Creek, an Alabama tributary that joins the west side of the Chattahoochee at today's Columbus, Hawkins gave the Indian name of the stream as "O-cow-ocuh-hat-che or falls creek." The *Cow-ocuh* elements of this designation are close phonetically to Kioka. Validity of the comparison is strengthened by the fact that an original surveyor reported the present Kiokee Creek of Dougherty County as Okiokee.

The oldest recorded Kiokee Creek (or Falls Creek) is a Columbia County tributary of the Savannah. The name is of more than passing interest because it was one of the first small-stream Indian designations to be retained by Georgians. This point can be verified easily by examining a good map showing the oldest areas of the state. It will be seen there are big streams with Indian names—Canoochee, Ohoopee, Altamaha, etc., but few small waterways and sites with aboriginal designations in those sections. The Georgians did not begin to adopt Creek Indian appellations to any appreciable extent until they got the lands beyond the Oconee.

Creek Consonant Sounds into English

The Creek consonants, of course, were fully as important as vowels in setting down placenames and the old transcribers found this to be the case in numbers of instances. Space will not permit a treatment of all the complexities involved in converting the Indian consonants to writing but several phases of the problems involved should be discussed. One of these concerns the *r*. The old Creeks did not use the letter, and in fact could not pronounce it. Thus, when one sees a purported Muskogee placename spelled with an *r* he can be sure the word has been garbled. Most such distortions apparently were made in an attempt to depict the broad *a* with an *ar*, as found in the designation of Coloparchee Creek in Monroe and Bibb counties. The meaning of the word is not certain because of the *r* but one strongly suspects it was from Kolopäkinhàchi, signifying Seven Creek, because it was the seventh stream that had to be crossed in travelling the noted Toms Path from Flint River to the Ocmulgee. The full Indian name could easily have been converted into the present form by retaining the *ä* of pakin as an "ar" and the *chi* of *hàchi* as "chee," after eliding other elements of the native word. Such changes were not great as far as the compounding of Creek words was concerned.

Since the early Creeks could not pronounce the *r*, they had trouble with the letter when they encountered it in an English word. One can be virtually certain this difficulty gave rise to the name of an old spot called Canoy, located on the east side of Kinchafoonee Creek, to the northwest of Leesburg. The name is one of the interesting place words of Georgia because it marks the site of Jack Kennard's settlement in Indian days. Kennard was a prominent mixed-blood leader who was friendly to the Americans. The Indians could not pronounce this chief's name and converted it to Canoy. The statement is supported by the fact that the Kennards finally called themselves Canards, and were beginning the use of this surname before they moved West.

The Muskogees always pronounced *g* hard, as in Ocmulgee, Towaligee, and Muscogee. The *gee* of these words rhymes with the *Gi* of Gillespie and not with the *gee* of gee whiz, or the *jee* of jeep. In many Creek names it is common to find the hard *c*, *k*, and *g* alternating with each other. Our word Muscogee depicts such shifts. The Muskogees referred to themselves as Màskoki or Màskogi, but we preferred to use Muscogee, which phonetically is very close to the other forms.

In setting down Creek words the old recorders of names often transposed *b*'s and *p*'s. We sometimes do the same thing, as evidenced by the use of "Gipson" for Gibson. Two remaining Indian names that contain these alternate letters are Alapaha River in central south Georgia and Alabaha Creek in Pierce County. The meaning of the name is not known; it has generally been considered a Timucua name, but there is some evidence that it was Muskogee or Hitchitee.

The letters *t* and *d* were frequently interchanged in Creek names. A case in hand is found in the Wehadkee Creek that was discussed.

The *d* of the retained name was a *t* in the original and correct form, *wihátki*.

A consonantal dipthong that offered a great deal of trouble in recording Creek names is the combination *ch*. The symbol was complicated because it is also a complex letter in English. We say it in a variety of ways: with a conventional *ch* sound as in chop, as an *sh* in chute and machine, as a *k* in character and epoch; and as a *qu* in choir. In a simple word like church we even have two *ch* sounds, the last of which is a *tch*. Sometimes the *ch* is silent, as in schism and yacht; and sometimes the sound occurs in a word that does not contain a *ch*, as in the case of righteous that uses a *t* to express the sound. Indeed, few languages have such a variety of *ch* sounds as English, and this fact handicapped the early transcribers of Indian names because the Creeks also had some difficult *ch*'s. One of these was a letter which had a *sh* or *sch* sound as found in Chemolly, the former name of Beech Creek which joins Flint River, on the east, at the upper side of the old Creek Agency Reserve in western Crawford County. There is evidence too, that the name Senoia, a town in Coweta County, once began with this *ch - sh* sound.

One *ch* that frequently occurred and was actually properly reported was the *ch* that is found in *ēcho*—(pronounced "eacho"), the Creek word for deer. The letter in this instance has the value of the *ch* in choke, but when we see *echo* written down, we are likely to mispronounce it as "ekko" because of our word echo. The old-timers knew this, of course, and sometimes rendered the word as *itcho, itchee, echee*, etc. An interesting reminder of *echo* can be found in Echeconnee Creek of Bibb, Crawford, and Monroe. The name is from *echo*, deer + *conna*, trap, and was so called because the Indians hid on the banks of the stream to shoot deer that were attracted to shoally areas of the creek to eat a greenish, slimy vegetation called rock moss or salt grass.

The most difficult *ch* sound of all, however, arose in connection with a peculiar *h* that took a guttural *ch* sound when the former letter immediately preceded another consonant. The English language does not have a character to represent the singular letter but the sound is found in German words like *ich*, or in the *ch* of the Scotch *loch*, or in the Spanish *jota* or *j* of words like *bajar* or *dejar*. Americans generally have pronounced the letter as a *k*, as in "Lock" Lomond, or changed it to some other form. Sometimes the letter was left with a conventional *h* sound. In the case of the Hitchitee names for Chickasawhatchee and Sowhatchee creeks, for instance, it will be recalled the original appellations ended with *hahchi* and not *hàchi* or *hatchee.* Since the second *h* of *hahchi* occurs before a *c*, it properly must receive the guttural *ch* sound. The letter was particularly hard to pronounce in this instance because it came close after the initial *h* in the word. The white people could not well have pronounced *hahchi* as "hakchi," so by assimilation they converted the word to the more familiar Creek *hàchi,* or "hatchee," thus leaving Chickasawhatchee and Sowhatchee as hybrid names, half Hitchitee and half Muskogee. There was still another Creek *ch* that was difficult to bring over into English, and it occurred in Chulapocca, the obsolete name of the Apalachee River. Sometimes the word can be found as Tulapocca and on other occasions as Julapocca. Maybe this *ch* had a *dj* sound in it like that in George; or perhaps a *ch* sound as called for by the *t* in the word question. The exact meaning of Chulapocca is not known; it may have signified pine trunk or stem, or maybe fox ball, whatever that would have meant. In any case, one believes the name was dropped from use because of the uncertain *ch.* A remaining important appellation that now contains a *ch* is Ochlockonee, the designation of a river in south Georgia. The word originally was from the Hitchitee *ōkilägni,* signifying water yellow. Old people living about the stream now call it "Oaklocknee," although the substitution of a *ch* for the *k* in the present spelling leads outsiders to mispronounce the name with an "okk" or "otch" sound. Incidentally, *Ochlockonee* does not necessarily mean yellow water in the sense of muddy water; it might have been intended to signify north, because the Creeks sometimes employed symbolic color words to indicate direction and yellow was used for north. It may not be mere happen-so that the three largest Indian "water yellow" streams of Georgia flowed from north to south.

A consonant that should be singled out for mention is an initial *h* which was once used by white people before Indian placenames or other words beginning with a vowel: "Haltamahaw," "Hoconee," "Hohoopee," "Hogeechee," etc. In the early years when we were closer to the British, it was common to find *h* used in this fashion just as it is now so employed in the Cockney speech of London. Indeed, usage of the letter still continues here in a few words, like the colloquial "hit" and "hain't" for it and ain't. In most placenames, however, the *h* has long since been dropped. The outstanding exception can be found in the Cherokee name Hiawassee, or Hiwassee, in north Georgia. This word was originally *ayuhwasi,* a meadow or savannah, but someone long ago added an initial *h* to it and the letter has remained as an accepted part of the spelling. Another example can be found in Hightower, an Anglicized, colloquial form of Itawa, or Etowah. In the old Creek country there is one name which may retain one of these Cockney-like aitches and this is Hodchodkee Creek in Stewart and Quitman counties. The name is from *aha*, potato + *chutki*, or "chotkee," small. The expression refers to a variety of Indian potato and not to the size of the stream. Now *aha* was sometimes rendered by the whites as "auhau," "auhaw," or "hauhaw." The last form unquestionably contains the early initial *h* of the white Indian countrymen. If the *Hod* of "Hodchodkee" is derived from the second syllable of "auhau" or "hauhaw," the name does not begin with the Cockney-type *h* because that syllable was derived from the *ha* of *aha*. But, if on the other hand, the *Hod* is from the first element of "hauhaw," Hodchodkee undoubtedly retains the former initial aitch and would be as a consequence one of the unique placenames of Georgia. One is prone to think the word actually retains the first element of "hauhaw," because in compounding Creek words, it was the second syllable and not the first of the initial form which was commonly elided.

At the time people added initial aitches where they did not belong, they also dropped them where they should have been retained. The Cockneys of London follow the same practice today by saying "Harab" for Arab or "harrows" for arrows. But in pronouncing words like Harry or Herbert, they say "'Arry" or "'Erbert." Georgia probably has one of these old dropped-aitch words in Ichabuckler Creek in southwest Stewart County. In pronouncing this name the local people call it "Itcheebuckluh." This pronunciation is important since it brings out the fact that the *a* in the name is sounded as a "ee," while the final *er* becomes "uh." The last point is also significant because Ichabuckler could not be a true Creek word, if it contained an *r*. Now, if "Itcheebuckluh" is taken apart and examined, the "Itchee" element might be a corrupted form that could have been intended to mean one of several things: deer, beaver, gun, or bow. But these derivations do not match up with "buckler." If the name is put together again and pronounced easily and rapidly with an initial *H*, it sounds very much like Hïchïpàkwà, the Creek word for pipe, i.e., a tobacco pipe. *Hichi* is the Muskogee word for tobacco, but on occasion it can be found in old records as "'itchee," without a beginning *h*. The *pàkwà* elements of Hichipàkwà are pronounced "puckwuh," and this sound could easily have become the "buckluh" of Ichabuckler. One does not have to worry over the switching about of the *p* of *pàk* and the *b* in *buck* because as has been noted *p*'s and *b*'s alternated in Creek names.

Of all the Creek vowels or consonants which the white people tried to pronounce or write down, the most difficult letter was a peculiar voiceless *l* which we do not have in English. The letter is hard to sound correctly even with much practice and it is doubtful if many white people ever mastered it. The el is important here because it was widely used by the Creeks and originally occurred in such attractive names as Withlacoochee, Willacoochee, Lannahassee, and possibly in Cohelee, the designation of a Creek in Early County. The letter was also found in the Indian names for Stone Mountain, Standing Peachtree, the St. Marys River, Tally Mountain in Haralson County, in Standing Boy Creek in Harris and Muscogee, in Big Potato Creek of Upson, and so on. Perhaps the aboriginal appellations of these sites and streams were not retained because the white pioneers could not pronounce the vexatious *l* which was found in the Indian names.

The Creek voiceless *l* was not a totally new sound in the realm of languages. The Anglo-Saxons used it in numbers of words like *hlinc*, which we retain in link, as in golf link, in *hleap*, that became leap, and in *hlaf*, which evolved into loaf, or even into our word lady, from *hlafdæge*, loaf server. The Welsh employ the letter regularly in their speech in a *ll* form such as found in the personal names Lloyd and Llewelyn. The French have a devoiced *l* that occurs in words like *meuble*, furniture, and *peuple*, people. The letter only partially resembles the Creek el, however. The presence of the French *l* toward the end of a word makes it easier to say than the Indian form which can be found at the beginning or in the middle of words as well as at the end. Apparently, though, Americans do no better with *peuple* or *meuble* than with the Indian words; they are prone to pronounce the former expressions as "purp' " and "murb' " and forget about the *l.*

Before going farther with the peculiar Creek *l*, it might be well to digress a bit into the field of phonetics to indicate the character of the voiceless letter to show the difficulties it caused with the aboriginal names. Our English *l* has a definitely voiced sound, that is, in saying it we set up vibrations in the vocal cords of the larynx. The nature of the sound can be noticed by experimenting a bit. Take some words, such as lot, lack, or Opelika, a placename that now contains a voiced *l* but which originally had the voiceless form. In pronouncing the els in these words the voiced vibrations given the letter *l* can be felt by squeezing the fingers lightly on the larynx, or by pressing the index fingers against the openings of the ears, or by pressing the palm of the hand on top of the head as the letter is uttered. The problem in sounding the Creek voiceless *l* was to say the letter as an el, without giving it voice. This is a difficult task as the reader will quickly learn.

The best way apparently for Americans to sound the voiceless *l* is to say it with the help of a preceding *h*. This can be done, by way of illustration and for practice, by placing the tip of the tongue against the fore palate at the gum line of the teeth, in the usual position to sound an *l*, and then pronouncing words like Llewelyn and Lloyd as if they were spelled "Hlewelyn" and "Hloyd." If the tongue tip is held in place, the preceding *h* causes the *l* to be aspirated and not voiced, with the breath escaping laterally along the edges of the tongue. If the reader wants to attempt a real Creek word (that was probably converted to an English name because of its voiceless el) let him try Hlonotiskahàchi, which means Flint River and was the old Muskogee name for that noted stream.

The voiceless *l* is a surd letter, because in English orthography there is no character to represent the sound. People who have been confronted with the el in transcribing Creek words used various devices to depict it: *cl, kl, ll, 'l, tl, lt, hl, thr,* and *thl.* Some present-day students of Creek show the letter with a notch on the stem of the *l,* like a lower case representation of £, the symbol of the British pound sterling. In the International Phonetic Association's symbols it is shown as ɬ. In the Loughridge and Hodge Muskogee dictionary the letter is represented by *r.* Apparently this symbol was used because the Creeks did not have a true *r* and the English had no satisfactory way of indicating the difficult *l.* The *r* of the dictionary was designed to represent a sound that is totally different from the English *r,* but familiarity with the letter in its conventional use has tended to confuse white people when they use the dictionary.

As far as the Indian country transcribers were concerned, the commonest symbol used to depict the voiceless *l* was the *thl,* as found in our Withlacoochee River. The name means Little River, from *wiwà,* water + *thlàko,* big + *uchi* (or "oochee"), little. The rendering of *thlàko* with the much-used *thl* resulted in a change in the word that makes it very different from its native form. For one thing the *thl* caused the word to take on the sound of our "with," when in fact this sound did not exist in the original, where the *wi* was pronounced "wee" and the *th* had no value at all except to signify that the *la* element, a remnant of *thlàko,* carried a voiceless *l.*

Willacoochee, another Georgia stream name, is identical in origin with Withlacoochee. Early land records in which the rivers are mentioned make this identification certain. The only difference between the names rests in the way the voiceless *l* was depicted in the two words. Both names are pretty and few now would want to change them to the awkward-looking Wihlàkuchi for the sake of scientific linguistics. But it might be added that Withlacoochee and Willacoochee illustrate better than any other Georgia Indian names how many geographic appellations have been dressed up to give them a pleasing appeal. Such furbishing, however, must have been a factor in causing the Oklahoma informant to complain that Creek words had been "butchered" here.

Compounded Names

The greater part of Creek placenames are compound forms that were made up with elements of two or more words. In some instances, except for the ever-present garbling of the spellings, these elements are kept intact in a designation. For instance, the name of the great Okeefenokee Swamp retains the full words that originally went to make it up—*oki*, water, plus *finoke*, or "finoka," trembling or quivering. Numbers of other designations, however, are not so simple because they have undergone considerable slurring and elision. It is difficult to say in many instances who was responsible for the changes—the whites or the red people. It is certain that Indians compacted some forms and dropped letters and syllables in doing so. For example, when white people introduced the horse, the Creeks had no word for the creature. They were reluctant to borrow a name and even if they had tried to use horse they could not have pronounced it because of the *r*. So they made up their own label by calling the animal *echothlàko*, big deer. This word was slurred into '*cholako* and can be found in various forms, such as "chelocko" or "cholucko."

The Creeks had some general rules about the dropping of syllables in compounding names. For example, words ending in *wà* usually had this syllable omitted when a word containing it was to be the first element in a compounded form. Thus, when the term *pinawà*, turkey, was to be combined with *hàchi* to make Turkey Creek, the Indians elided the *wà* and made the name Pinahàchi. The present Pennahatchee Creek of Dooly County was formed in this manner. In similar fashion, Tallahassee Creek in Dougherty County derived its name from *tàilwà*, town + *ahasi*, old, for some former settlement on the stream.

Prefixes, Infixes, and Suffixes

In their speech the Creeks resorted to wide use of prefixes, infixes, and suffixes to make their language flexible and versatile and some of these forms are returned in our placenames. For instance, in its beginning element *Oc*, the Ocmulgee River reflects the interesting prefix *äk* which has both locational and directional connotations. The name means in, or down in + *mulgis*, bubbling or boiling. The full expression has been translated numbers of times as signifying boiling water. And by implication Ocmulgee probably was intended to have that meaning, but it plainly does not contain the word for water. Another name carrying the same prefix can be found in Oakfuskee Creek, that reaches Flint River to the west of Concord in Pike County. This name is from *ak*, or "oak," and *faski*, a point, meaning down in a point of land.[1] This name, however, probably did not arise from a bend in the Flint, but because the little creek was skirted by the famous Oakfuskee Path that led from Augusta to Oakfuskee Town on the Tallapoosa, in Alabama, which was situated in a point or bend of that river.

The Muskogees employed both augmentative and diminutive suffixes. The former was represented by *thláko*, or *hláko*, big or large; and the latter by *uchi*, little or small. The last form was sometimes also rendered as *ochi*, but it has become conventionalized as *oochee* in place names. Thus Suwanoochee Creek in Clinch and Echols counties is so labelled to distinguish it from the Suwanee River to which it is tributary; while Muckaloochee Creek of Sumter and Lee denotes a stream that is smaller than the bigger Muckalee Creek in the same area. *Oochee* was not confined to streams and placenames. The term had wide usage in differentiating between big and small things and between old and young things or people. For example, *waka* meant cow, while *wakuchi* meant calf. The present Wacoochee Creek, a west-bank tributary that enters the Chattahoochee, opposite southwest Harris County, signifies Calf Creek.

Except for Withlacoochee and Willacoochee and possibly for Okapilco Creek in Colquitt and Brooks counties, the *thláko* form does not now appear in significant Georgia names although it was once used in numbers of expressions that have been changed. The present Buck Creek that reaches Flint River opposite Montezuma experienced such a shift. The Indians called the stream Opilthlucco, that was contracted from *opilwá*, swamp, and *thláko*, big. The obsolete Upelikee

[1] See Introduction on "oak."

Creek of Terrell County that has been mentioned had the same origin. The former Opilthlucco Creek was renamed Buck Creek for Buckee Barnard, a son of Timothy Barnard, the noted Indian countryman. Another appellation that disappeared was Chahkithlàko, or "Chaukeethluco," on the west side of the Chattahoochee, in lower Heard County. The word meant Big Shoal and applied to an Upper Creek village located beside a shoally place in the river. The site later became known as Jackson's Mill Shoals. It will be noted that the second *h* of Chahkithlàko came before the consonant *k* and as a result should have received a guttural *ch* sound. It is obvious from "*Chaukeethlucco*," though, that the letter was omitted entirely in the English recording.

It is interesting to add that *chobi*, the Hitchitee equivalent of *thlàko*, remains in Cemochechobee, the name of a creek that enters the Chattahoochee just above Fort Gaines. The word means Big Sandy from the Hitchitee *sumochi*, sand + *chobi*, big.

One important suffix which the Creeks used was *honànwà*. The term signified male and was affixed to the generic name of an animate species to denote a masculine creature. Thus *echo* meant deer, while *echohonànwà* signified buck. The form is found in Ichawaynochaway Creek in southwest Georgia, which means Buck Sleeping (Place) Creek from *echohonànwà*, buck + *nochawà*, sleeping, which by implication was a locative form signifying that buck deer slept or hid along the stream. The present Buck Creek that enters the Oconee on the east side some miles below Milledgeville originally bore an Indian name that is identifiable with today's Ichawaynochaway.

By the use of suffixes the Creeks could expand the scope of their language in a manner that engenders admiration. The greatest efficiency in this respect was attained with the form *àlgi*, or "ulga," that commonly appears in old recordings as *ulgaw*, *ulcah*, etc. The form could have infinite implications, depending on the connotation of the substantive to which it was affixed. Thus when an English-speaking person understood the noun, he could nearly always grasp the full implications of a name or word terminating with the versatile suffix. One could write a dissertation on the uses of the expression, but in summary form *àlgi* had these diverse functions: (1) to denote all, entire or whole; (2) to indicate that something abounded in a given area or stream; (3) to serve as a collective form to indicate a clan, grove, species, group, or nationals of a particular tribe or country; and (4) to form the plurals of most nouns.

To illustrate the function of the suffix in a specific instance, take the Indian name of the present Lime Spring Pond Creek that enters the south side of Kinchafoonee Creek in southeast Webster County. The former designation of the stream was Tallulga. This word literally would be interpreted as abounding in palmettoes, from *tala*, palmetto + the collective, plural-forming *álgi*. The pioneer whites who knew Creek, one can be virtually certain, would not have thought of the stream in the terms of such an unwieldy moniker. They no doubt simply construed the name as Palmetto Creek, or maybe as Palmetto Flats Creek. Not far from the Tallulga, also in Webster County, there was a tributary of Lochochee Creek which the first surveyor of the area in 1826 marked as the "Asanalka." This word is from *ásanawá*, moss, i.e., Spanish moss + *álgi* in the garbled form of *alka*. There can be little doubt that the early whites would have interpreted this name as Mossy Creek, or maybe if they felt a bit poetic about it, as Mossy Dell Creek.

At least two remaining Indian names retain *álgi*, or "ulga." One of these is Attapulgus, that signifies Dogwood Grove, from *atap' ha*, dogwood + *álgi* to signify grove. The designation applied to a settlement that was once located in Decatur County, Georgia, near the Florida line, but which later removed into the latter state. The *s* is a white man's contribution to the name and it dates back to the years in which a given Indian band or town was referred to by white people in the plural—like Cussetas, Cowetas, Eufaulees, etc. Attapulgus is the only remaining placename in Georgia that perpetuates this practice. The village of Schatulga in eastern Muskogee County also retains the ulga. The name signifies crawfishes, or crawfish place.

Some students of Muskogee refer to affirmative suffixes as postpositives. The expression is well taken, but it should be noted there was at least one important post-negative. This word was *siko* or *sigo* and when affixed to a noun it gave the expression a negative meaning that could be variously interpreted as no, not, incorrect, unlike, less, without, not having, minus, and so on, with the intended meaning depending on the sense of the expression containing the affixed *siko*. Thus *oski* means rain, and *oskisigo* signifies no rain or without rain, but in our way of thinking the latter form simply connoted dry spell or drought. A common Creek word that contained the negative form was the war title *fiksiko*, or "fixico," from *fiki*, heart + *siko*, signifying heartless, no heart, or merciless in war. A well-known individual whose name contained the suffix was Emisteseegoe, a principal Creek chief who negotiated with Governor James Wright about affairs of the

Indians and whites. His name was from *im*, his + *isti*, people (probably meaning men or warriors) + *siko*, without or not having. One ventures to guess the expression was a war name given for some outstanding accomplishment and that it may have signified something like alone or single-handed.

Siko does not remain as a placename in Georgia, but in the Indian years the red people were afraid of the Okefenokee Swamp because they believed it was inhabited by "Immortals" or supernatural beings called Este Fatchasicko. This awe-inspiring name seems innocuous enough when translated literally since it means simply incorrect or not right people, from *isti*, people + *fáchi*, right, honest or correct + *siko*, to negate or reverse the positive nature of the preceding elements of the expression. The white Indian countrymen could probably have captured the real meaning of the name by turning the incorrect people or Immortals into plain "boogers" or "hants."

Creek Words for European Names

The early Muskogees were a proud people who stubbornly refused, with surprisingly few exceptions, to borrow words from any other language. Like the Greeks, they had a name for nearly everything that affected their lives. In the long years they were neighbors to the English, French, and Spaniards, they did not adopt more than a half-dozen words from the whites. Chief among these was the Spanish *vaca*, for cow which the Creeks turned into *waka*. But why they should have appropriated this particular word is a puzzle because when the horse, goat, sheep, and the hog were introduced among them they devised their own names for those animals. The horse, as has been noted, became *echothláko*, big deer, while the goat became *echohata*, bleating deer, and the sheep was simply called *yápifiká*, or horn twisted. In the case of the hog, the Creeks switched their word *suka*, opossum, to the animal and then proceeded to differentiate between possum and hog by labelling the former *sukahátki*, or white hog.

The gun and the bullet were striking innovations for the Muskogees but they developed names for the objects by the simple expedient of substituting their word bow for gun and their term arrow for bullet. When they had to differentiate between a gun and a bow they called the latter a crooked or bent gun; while real arrows were distinguished from real bullets by labelling the former long bullets. These applications may strike us as unusual but in a fashion we have shifted the meanings of significant words in a similar manner. For instance, great steam and diesel vessels "sail" the seas; while the expression "manufacture" has become symbolic of large-scale industry, although the word basically refers to production by hand.

The Muskogees also refused to borrow any appreciable number of words from neighboring tribes. The *tiwa* element of Towaliga is a rare exception. The term means scalp, but it is not known why (or from whom) the word was borrowed because the Creeks had their own form for scalp. *Panola*, or *ponola*, for cotton is a loan expression which the Muskogees seemingly borrowed from the Choctaws. They might have adopted the word *oki* for water from the Hitchitees since *oki*, or "okee," can be found in Muskogee names, even though the latter had their own word *wiwa*, signifying water. More than likely *oki* was a proto-Muskogean word that descended to all peoples using Muskogean languages.

Since this essay began by mentioning the "butchering" of Indian names, it might not be amiss in closing to say the Creeks were also guilty of mutilating English designations. By way of examples, Washington, D.C., became Wacena, and in the Creek tongue Georgia came out as Chacha. The people of this colony or state, though, were usually not called Chachàlgi, or Georgians; for the most part they and all Americans were referred to as Vajinulgee, which literally means Virginians, from *Vajin*, Virginia + *àlgi*, or "ulgee," to denote nationality, clan, or tribe. In this instance the form was the equivalent of our *-ians*. The most unusual name, perhaps, which the Creeks garbled can be found in New Yaucau, the designation of a small settlement that was located on the east bank of the Chattahoochee River, in present upper Heard County, near or opposite the mouth of Pink Creek. Now, interestingly enough, Pink Creek was originally known as Punk Creek, and probably derived this name from a village called Punk Knot, or Tukpafka. According to Benjamin Hawkins the people of the town quit the Chattahoochee about the time of the Revolution and removed to the Tallapoosa River in Alabama to settle at a point opposite the site where the battle of Horse Shoe Bend was later fought. Hawkins also states the village ultimately changed its name from Punk Knot (Tukpafka) to New York. Presumably this shift was made to honor New York City by reason of the noted treaty which was held with the Creeks at that place in 1790. But, be that as it may, the Indians could not pronounce their adopted name and twisted it into various forms that are hardly recognizable. New Yaucau is a common version, and when the Creeks removed to the West they took along the name and eventually formalized it as Nuyaka. It is a mystery why the designation was carried to Heard County, Georgia. But very probably some of the people moved back to the old site on the Chattahoochee after their Alabama settlement was destroyed in the Creek War of 1813-1814 and some 700 of their tribesmen were killed across the river in the Horse Shoe Bend fight. If the assumptions made here are correct, and New Yaucau actually was derived from New York, the appellation is distinctive and in a class by itself because it represents the only instance in these parts of a white man's appellation being borrowed by the Creeks for one of their towns. Otherwise, as the reader knows, the name borrowing always worked the other way around.

GMNL 14(1961): 63-70

Pronunciations of Georgia Placenames
Part I

In view of Georgia's profusion of geographic names it is easy to appreciate that we have numbers of appellations with unusual pronunciations. There are too many of these distinctive words to treat in a single essay and the present discussion of them will be limited to selected expressions and especially to some Georgia names that are pronounced differently from versions of the same tabs that are used in other areas.

Take for instance, our town of Bremen in Haralson County. This place is reliably reported to be named for the German port city of Bremen, which is pronounced "Bray men" by the Germans and "Bremmen" by English-speaking people generally. The citizens of the Georgia Bremen, however, call their place "Breemen." To the south of our Bremen, in western Carroll County, there is a town called Bowdon. This name is pronounced "Bo' dun," the first element rhyming with how, or now.

One Georgia pronunciation which always attracts attention is found in Vienna, the county seat of Dooly County. This place is called "Vye en'" whereas the noted capital of Austria for which it was named is "Vē' en a." It should be noted, though, that "Vē en' a" is the designation in international terminology. Actually the Austrians spell their city Wien and pronounce it "Vēn." The Americans make use of the form in their words wienner, or wiennie, a kind of small sausage that originated in Vienna.

The people of Cairo, in Grady County, speak of their town as "Kā ro," although the Egyptian city for which it was named is "Kye ro." In southern Illinois there is also another Cairo, and it is said the citizens of that city prefer to have the place known as "Kye ro," but the fact remains that it is commonly referred to by many Americans as "Kā ro," the same version that is used for the Georgia community.

One of the most unusual pronunciations of Georgia can be found in a local version of Albany, the flourishing city in the southwestern part of the state. Many Georgians use a conventional pronunciation for the place by calling it "All' ba ny." But old-timers living in the area give the name an interesting shift by switching the accent and turning the word into "All ben' ny" or into "All bain' ny."

The common pronunciation of "Loo' i ville," used in connection with a prominent city like Louisville, Kentucky, apparently influences the pronunciation of many people for the Georgia town of Louisville, the county seat of Jefferson, and once the capital of Georgia. This place is properly called "Loo' is ville," as if it were written Lewisville.

One of Georgia's places with a singular pronunciation is Clyo, a railroad station and post office in eastern Effingham County. The name is unusual because of both its sound and spelling. There are numbers of places called Clio around the country, and, in fact, our neighbors Alabama, Florida, and South Carolina each have a Clio, but only Georgia seems to have a Clyo. The word is pronounced "Kleye yo," and this version suggests that it was derived from the Greek *kleio*, the proclaimer, from *kleiein*, to proclaim, to tell of, or to make famous, while the Clio places of other states were most likely named directly for Clio the Muse of History.

The designations of most of Georgia's 159 counties are easy to pronounce correctly save for a half-dozen or so names that offer difficulties for some individuals even when they were born and reared in the state. Perhaps the most unusual of these names is borne by Taliaferro County, in central east Georgia. This name is pronounced "Tol' i ver." Schley County in southwest Georgia bears a deceptive name for the uninformed who are tempted into calling it "Slay." The designation is a family surname and is correctly pronounced "Sly." Houston County of central Georgia in the spoken version becomes "House tun." Many people mispronounce the name because they know the city in Texas and the county in southeast Alabama are referred to as "Hus tun" or "Hewes tun." Chatham County, the mother county of the state, is pronounced "Chattum." People have difficulty with the word because there is no guiding rule in the English language for pronouncing names like Chatham, Latham, Statham, and so on. Dougherty County in Southwest Georgia is difficult for some individuals, but the name sounds approximately like "Dority."

Georgians, like most Americans, have a strong proclivity for borrowing Spanish names, and this state has adopted an array of such appellations. Virtually all of these borrowed words have been Anglicized, and in some instances have become so garbled a Spaniard would surely not understand them. An interesting loan expression in this group is Rincon, a place in southeast Effingham County. The word signifies nook, corner, or retreat and is pronounced "Rink' on" in Georgia. In Spanish the expression is "Rin con'" (Reen cone'), with the accent on the last syllable.

In common with numbers of other states, Georgia has, in northeast Bartow County, a place called Bolivar which honors the famous South American patriot Simon Bolivar. In Spanish this name is pronounced "Bo lee' var." In Georgia, however, and in other areas of the United States, the word has turned into "Bol' i ver."

The noted Spanish city of Seville has many namesakes in various parts of the world. Among these is a Georgia village, located on U.S. 280, in western Wilcox County, to the east of Cordele. Now, dictionaries give the pronunciation of Seville as "Sev' il" or as "Se vil'," but the people of the Georgia community give their word an unusual twist by making it "See ville," with the stress being equally distributed between both syllables.

Curiously enough, none of the above versions is precisely correct, because Seville in the first instance is an Anglicized version of the real Spanish name of the city, which is Sevilla or "Say veel' yah."

Americans love the Spanish name Buena Vista, not only because of its meaning, good view or fine view, but also because the appellation commemorates one of the notable battles of the Mexican War. Georgia's Buena Vista, the county seat of Marion, is pronounced "Bū' na Vista," while the true Spanish version sounds like "Bway' na Veesta."

One of the most baffling names of Georgia, even to natives of the state, is Ludowici, the principal town of Long County, in southeast Georgia. This word, of German-Italian origin, is pronounced "Loo' do wee' cee."

To the south from Ludowici, in upper Wayne County, there is a place called Gardi. This name is pronounced "Guard-eye," and the latter form exactly recalls the origin of the moniker because the town was named after a nearby dense swamp called Guard-eye where people had to guard their eyes in pushing through the thick place. In the earliest years the name was written as Guard-eye.

Philema, a little railroad station in eastern Lee County, has an odd pronunciation that is not in accordance with its written form. The place is called "Flimmee," and was named after a former Chehaw Chief called Fullemy who resided in the area.

Most Indian names of Georgia are fairly easy to pronounce in the forms that have evolved over the years and now appear on maps. There are, however, some unusual versions whose pronunciations do not accord with their written forms. The best example of this can be found in Tugalo River, an upper tributary of the Savannah, that skirts the northeast boundary of Georgia. There is an inclination to say the word as "Tugg' a lo," but actually it is "Too' ga lo," and there is good evidence that it was originally "Too' goo loo."

The Towaliga River, a west-bank tributary of the Ocmulgee, in Monroe, Butts, and Henry counties, has several slightly different pronunciations, none of which an outsider would be likely to hit upon. The best of these versions, perhaps, is "Tye lye' gee." The *gee* of the last syllable has a hard *g* sound and resembles the *gee* in geese or in Ocmulgee. Upatoi, a stream and village in eastern Muscogee County, becomes "Yoo' pa toy"; while Sowhatchee or Sawhatchee Creek in Early County becomes "Sye hatchy." Chatuge, a reservoir lake in upper Georgia on the North Carolina line, is correctly pronounced "Cha too' gee," with another *gee* like that in geese. More and more it seems the word is being pronounced "Cha tuj'" with a sound similar to that in refuge. It is possible the name may finally become, "Cha tuj."

In concluding, it should be noted there is another important Indian name that is being shifted away from its original and correct form. This word is Okefenokee, the designation of the great swamp in southeast Georgia. Apparently in both Georgia and Florida more and more people are rendering this beautiful, eye-catching word as "Oakfenoak." Due to the prominence of, and interest in the swamp, this mutation should be discouraged and an effort should be made to retain the full and proper pronunciation which is "O' kee fee no' kee." Incidentally, the name is commonly given as signifying land of trembling earth, when as a simple fact the expression means trembling water from *oki*, water, plus *finoki*, trembling, quivering, or shaking. The name is from the Hitchitee language, but apparently the Creeks adopted and continued the appellation.

Pronunciations of Georgia Placenames
Part II

Placename students quickly become aware of the fact that there may be more than one pronunciation for certain geographic names in Georgia. In such instances there are usually only two forms for a given appellation—one, a formal rendition that sounds a term according to its spelling on maps; and second, a local, spoken version which is used by people living in the area where the name applies. Sometimes these colloquial pronunciations are mere rusticisms, but often, and especially with Indian expressions, they are closer to the original names than are the polished-up renditions that now appear on maps. Take for example, Osiligee or Osiliga Creek, that enters the Chattahoochee on the right side, just above West Point. Old-timers about pronounce this name as "Ossilijee" (with a long *i* in the penultimate syllable) and in so saying it they come close to the original form first reported by Colonel Benjamin Hawkins in 1798 when he listed the stream as the "O, so, li, jee." The present-day Osiliga apparently was adopted for maps in the mistaken belief that the word contained a hard *g* instead of a *j*, and that this *g* needed to be emphasized by ending the name with an *a* instead of its original "ee."

This tampering with the endings of names, and particularly with Indian words, explains numbers of the dual pronunciations which were mentioned above as being used in this state. For instance, although the two Chattooga rivers and Chattooga County are formally listed by that spelling on charts, old people in the county and the vicinity of the rivers pronounce the name as "Chat too gee," with a *gee* like that found in Muscogee, Ocmulgee, and Ogeechee. Their version may seem a bit backwoodsy, but actually they sound the name very close to the original Indian expression, which was "Cha tu' gi," with a hard *g* such as found in words like Gillespie or Gilbert.

Similar names that have such dual pronunciations are Chickamauga, which applies to a large creek in northwest Georgia and to another smaller stream of the same name in White County; and Conasauga, the designation of a considerable river in the northwestern part of the state. Locally these names respectively are pronounced by many as "Chickymawgee" and "Connysawgee." With the exception of the *y* in the second syllables of each expression, these colloquial versions are similar to the Cherokees' Chikamagi and Kanasagi. The substitution of a *y* or *i* sound for a second-syllable unaccented *a* as found in "Chickymawgee" is fairly common in the provincial versions of Georgia Indian names. Thus Chattahoochee is locally pronounced "Chattyhoochee" by literally hundreds of people. A very important exception is found in Altamaha, the designation of one of the state's largest rivers and which can be counted among the oldest names of Georgia because it was mentioned by some of DeSoto's chroniclers in 1540. The word is pronounced "All' ta ma haw'," with the stress falling on the first and last syllables. The "haw" part merits particular noting because there is a tendency on the part of some people to pronounce the final syllable like the exclamation *ha* or *hah*.

Readers who have long been interested in placenames no doubt recall that Altamaha was once spelled Alatamahaw or Alatamaha with an additional *a*, and that this letter was not finally dropped until about a century and a quarter ago. It is to be doubted the added *a* ever played much of a part in the sound of the word, and in fact it may have been silent, because there are appellations containing a silent or scarcely audible letter. For example, Tuckaseeking, an old place on the Savannah River, in upper Effingham County, to the north of Clyo, is pronounced "Tuck' see king." And on the opposite shore in South Carolina, there is another old site called Pallachucola. This name is locally pronounced "Pal lo chook' la," without the letter *o* and with an initial syllable that sounds like "pal," as in "my pal." It is not too much of a digression to go over the river for this name since Pallachucola was once a gateway into Georgia, because the lowest fording point on the Savannah was at the place and one of the earliest land approaches to the colony crossed there.

In addition to names with dual pronunciations, there are some designations that are pronounced in three different ways. One of the most important of these is Screven as found in the county of that name in southeast Georgia. As some people say this word, it sounds like "Skreven" to rhyme with seven. On the other hand, there are those who call it "Skreeven" to resemble Steven. The citizens of Screven County, however, pronounce the name as "Skriven" to rhyme with driven. Mr. Clyde Hollingsworth of Sylvania, the able historian of Screven County, indicates the latter form is the correct pronunciation of the name.

Since the essay has touched upon the subject of a county name, there is an opportunity to add notes on the pronunciations of other counties. Charlton County, in the extreme southeast corner, is pronounced "Charl' tun," with a *ch* like that in Charles and not with an *sh* sound as found in Charlotte. Virtually all Georgians know how to pronounce the established version of DeKalb County, which is "De Kalb'," with the "al" factor having the same sound as found in cal, sal, or gal. Newcomers to the state, however, sometimes have trouble with the expression and may call it "DeKolb."

In the first of the series, it was pointed out that Georgia has many Spanish names, nearly all of which have been more or less changed from their true Spanish forms in our spoken language. An interesting example is Villa Rica in northern Carroll County, near the site of an early gold strike. In Spanish the expression is "Veel' ya Ree' ka," but in Georgia the Villa becomes "Villa," like "fill er," while the Rica form has a subtle, intermediate sound somewhere between the Spanish "Reeka" and the English "Ricka."

Another interesting Spanish tab listed on maps is Montevideo, the name of an old community on the Elbert-Hart line, to the south of Hartwell. It is not known when or why the appellation was adopted, but it has been in use for a long time and presumably was adopted from the noted city of Montevideo, in Uruguay, South America. In Spanish the word is pronounced "Mon tay vee day' o." Americans have long had trouble with the expression and have tended to say it as "Moan tee viddy oh." The Georgia pronunciation for its place resembles the latter form, but with added twists. Here the name is pronounced "Mount' vide eo" or "Mont' vid eo."

Newcomers to Georgia are often uncertain about the pronunciations of the names of a substantial number of Georgia towns, seemingly because they are completely unfamiliar with the appellations or because they have heard other or different versions of the names elsewhere. For instance, they may refer to Canton, the county seat of Cherokee, as "Can ton'," whereas the accepted form in Georgia is pronounced "Can' tun." Other names in this group are: Cordele in Crisp County, which is called "Cor deal" and not "Cor dell"; Tennille in Washington County becomes "Tenn' il," and Warthen in the northern part of the same county is properly pronounced "Wer then." Relee in northern Coffee County is not "R. E. Lee" or "Reelly" but "Reelee." Vidette in western Burke is "Vye dette"; and Vidalia in upper Toombs is "Vye dale yuh." The pronunciations of the last two names are consistent with the Georgia version of Vienna, as explained in the first article of this series.

Both newcomers and many natives are also mystified at the proper pronunciations of certain names in the state. Some designations in this category are Manor in western Ware that sounds like "May' nuh"; and Braganza in the same county which is "Bra gan' zer." Not far from the latter, in western Brantley County, is a town called Schlatterville. This word is pronounced "Slaughterville," and is unique by reason of the comparatively large ratio of consonants to vowels found in the appellation. It will be noted Schlatterville uses four consonants before reaching the first vowel in the expression.

An interesting name that also belongs in the above group is Attapulgus in southeast Decatur County. This designation is pronounced "At' ta pul' gus" or sometimes "Atty pul' gus." The letter *u* in both the last and penultimate syllables has the sound of "uh" as found in the *u* of nut, jut, etc. The name is derived from a nearby stream called Attapulgus Creek which in turn was derived from a Lower Creek or Seminole village called Ataphulga (from *atapha*, dogwood, plus *ulgi*, or "ulga," signifying grove) which originally stood on the creek or one of its branches, at the present Georgia-Florida line. The early white people added the *s* to the name by referring to the inhabitants of the settlement as the Attapulgas. This practice was common on the part of the whites and thus many Indian communities were referred to in this plural manner: Oconees, Cussetas, Eufaulas, Chehaws, and so on. Interestingly enough, however, Attapulgus is the only remaining placename that commemorates the former practice. One might argue that Tallokas in Brooks County is such a word but no evidence could be found to show there was an Indian town by that designation and one concludes the name very probably had some other origin to explain its plural form.

And finally, one distinctive Georgia name that should be mentioned in this sketch on pronunciations is Ypsilanti, which applies to a little crossroads community in upper Talbot County, to the northeast of Talbotton. The name is locally pronounced "Ipp' see lan' tee," which is quite close to the pronunciation given by dictionaries. One would have guessed that the Talbot citizens would have given the strange name an unusual turn as has commonly been the case in Georgia where foreign words were concerned.

Ypsilanti was named for the noted Greek revolutionary leader Demetrios Ypsilanti who fought the Turks to free his people, and for this reason the expression belongs in the same category of names as the Bolivar of Bartow County which was mentioned in the previous article. When the Georgians and other Americans were younger peoples and closer to their own struggle for independence they were quite willing to commemorate with placenames the revolutionary heroes of other countries. But today this would not be the case and it is unthinkable that people here would want to name a site for anyone like Lenin, Hitler, Mao Tse-tung, or Castro.

Pronunciations of Georgia Placenames
Part III

By running the eye down a time schedule or along a map showing a main railway line leading from any of the state's principal cities, one can usually find a group of Georgia placenames with interesting pronunciations. For instance, on the Seaboard Airline Railroad running eastward from Atlanta toward Richmond, in Gwinnett County, there is a station called Luxomni. This word is pronounced "Lucks ahm' nee" and signifies All Light from the Latin *lux*, ("Lukes"), plus *omni* ("ohm' nee"), all. Farther along, on the same line, there is another village known as Gloster. The expression is a family surname, but it is pronounced "Gloss' ter," or to be more precise phonetically in the Georgia speech, "Gloss' tuh." The sound is virtually identical with the pronunciation employed for Gloucester, a designation used for cities or towns in Virginia, Massachusetts, and other states.

And even farther along, still in Gwinnett County, there is another place that bears the unusual title of Dacula. The term is a coined name and is subject to two slightly different pronunciations. Some people call it "Day cue' la," while others pronounce it "Day coo' la." Individuals who have not heard the word are inclined to say it as "Dack' oo la."

Next along the line is Winder. A newcomer to the state could hardly be blamed for mispronouncing this name by saying it with a *win* such as found in "window." Actually the appellation is a surname and is pronounced "Wine duh."

Another name along the Seaboard, to the east of Winder, is Statham. The word is pronounced "Stay' tum," without a *th* sound.

And lastly along the Seaboard, in Madison County, there is a station (at Carlton) called Berkeley. The place is pronounced "Berk' ly," and is interesting because it offers an opportunity to contrast the Georgia way of saying certain names with British pronunciations of the same expressions. An Englishman most likely would pronounce Berkeley as "Bark' ly." Also, in county names like Effingham and

Habersham, a Britisher would clip these words and pronounce the last syllables lightly as "hum" and "shum." Georgians, and Americans generally, on the other hand, place greater stress on the endings and sound more clearly the "am" of the words.

Three other Georgia appellations to contrast with the English pronunciations of the same expressions are Barwick, on the Brooks-Thomas county line; Warwick, on the east side of Flint River in extreme upper Worth County; and Norwich, a former siding on the Atlantic Coast Line, near Mauk, in western Taylor County. The British omit the letter w in such names and pronounce Barwick as "Barick," Warwick as "Worick," and Norwich as "Noridge," with only a light stress on the last parts of the words, whereas we pronounce all of these designations as they appear on their faces: "Bar' wick," "War' wick," and "Nor' witch." Barwick and Warwick apparently are derived from Georgia family names, but even so they resemble English places with the same spellings.

The Mauk mentioned above as near the former site of Norwich is pronounced both "Mawk" and "Mock." Most people apparently use the former, but one suspects "Mock" is closer to the original version of the word.

In the preceding essays of this series on pronunciations attention was given to some of the many Spanish words that can be found among Georgia's placenames. A few interesting additions for the list are Aragon, near Rockmart in Polk County; Toledo in Charlton; Alamo, the county seat of Wheeler; and Pavo, if the term is a true Spanish term, in northeast Thomas County.

In Georgia the pronunciation of Aragon sounds like "Arrow' gun" or "Arrer' gun," with the accent on the first element, whereas the Spanish word is "A rä gōn'," with broad a's, a long o, and an accent on the last syllable. Toledo is "Toe lay' do" in Spain but here it becomes "Toe lee' do," a form that is used elsewhere in the United States, as in Toledo, Ohio.

In Georgia, Alamo is pronounced "Al' a mo," with an al like that in Albert, and this sound is the conventional American pronunciation in saying the name of the noted site in Texas. In Spanish, the initial letter is a broad a and the l shifts to the second syllable, turning the name into "Ah' la mo." Pavo here is pronounced "Pay' vo." In Latin and Spanish it is "Pah' vo." If the word is from the former language, it signifies peacock. If it is of Spanish origin, it means turkey. Curiously enough, the Spanish name illustrates the confusion which exists in the world's major languages about the designation of the turkey. The creature is a native of the New World, but this origin is not clearly indicated in those languages. In fact, a variety of misleading misnomers for the bird can be found in the various idioms. Our own "turkey" and the adoption by the Spaniards of the Latin *pavo*, for peacock, illustrates the point. Any one of several American Indian languages had good names for the turkey, but none of these was ever adopted by the white people. The Creek Indians called it *pinawa*, as found in Pennahatchee Creek of Dooly County, but now it is highly unlikely that the designation of the turkey would ever be switched to a word like *pinawa* merely to provide a truly aboriginal name for the fowl.

On occasion, newcomers to the state have trouble with certain Georgia names, and sometimes with easy-appearing words. Take for instance, Concord, which occurs in the designation of numbers of church sites, little crossroads places, and in a small town in Pike County. The pronunciation here ranges from a dignified "Con cord" to the rustic "Con cawd." In some other regions of the country, and especially in New England, the name is pronounced "Kon' kerd" with a sound that is very similar to "conquered."

Another name that troubles the newly arrived is borne by Rabun County, in the northeast corner of the state. This word, which honors a former governor of Georgia, is pronounced "Ray' bun" and not "Rabb' un."

A group of names around Georgia with interesting pronunciations are: Adel in Cook County, which is pronounced "A dell'" or "Ay dell'"; Avera in upper Jefferson that sounds like "Avery"; Surrency in Appling County which rhymes with "currency"; and Mussella in upper Crawford that is pronounced "Muzzella," with a long *u* like that found in muse. In nearby Bibb County, however, Lizella is not "Lizz ella" but "Lye zella." One of the most unusual pronunciations is found in Machen, a small place in northeast Jasper County, above Monticello. In the speech of the people around-about this word is sounded as if it were "matchin." And finally, a noted old place dating back to colonial years, in extreme upper Screven County, near the Savannah River and the Burke line, is an early post office site called Mobleys Pond. The first element of the expression does not sound like the word mob, a crowd or throng, but is pronounced like a long *o* to rhyme with "mobe." Thus the full name becomes "Mobe' leys Pond."

—*GM* 6, No. 1(1962-1963): 13-15; No. 2, 14-15, 27; and No. 3, 12-13

The Rising Fawns

This essay primarily involves the personal names of Cherokee Indians who once lived in Georgia, but the discussion will be facilitated if there is an introductory sketch to show the area of the state in which those Indians lived before they finally left for the West in 1838. In the years prior to that date the Cherokees had ceded all of their early and original territory of northeast Georgia, and for the most part removed to the area lying north of the Blue Ridge and west of the Chattahoochee, as far down as a line running from Buzzard Roost Island (at the southeast corner of Cobb County) to a point on the Alabama boundary in upper Haralson County. The section above the Blue Ridge was old Cherokee country, but the people who moved into the region beyond the Chattahoochee were relative newcomers to that territory. The general area had been regarded as Creek, but beginning about the time of the Revolution, the latter tribe permitted the Cherokees to begin settling there because of pressures exerted on them from the east by the white people. These pressures were intensified after the war, and more and more Cherokees immigrated to the new section until by the 1820's they were living down to the southern boundary mentioned above. Georgia protested the occupancy so far southward, claiming the section had been Creek and belonged to her through cessions by those Indians. Andrew Jackson ended the dispute in 1830 by approving a new southern limit for the Cherokees to begin considerably above Buzzard Roost Island at a ford on the Chattahoochee, located below the bridge on U.S. 19, thence to run westward to Alabama. The United States agent was directed to remove all Cherokees above this new boundary, which became known as the Coffee Line, because it had been recommended to the President by General John Coffee.

The Indians multiplied in Georgia, and by the time of the Cherokee census of 1835, 8,946 Cherokees, or more than half of the tribe living east of the Mississippi, were residing in this state, and mainly in the comparatively new section lying west of the Chattahoochee. The remainder of the nation dwelt in adjacent areas of North Carolina, Tennessee, and Alabama.

From old records and various other sources one can learn the names of scores of the Georgia Cherokees. It is easy to determine the general area in which most of these people lived, and in certain instances the actual sites where some of them resided. They bore a fascinating array of personal names, titles, and odd monikers. Many of the designations can be found in English form, but these versions have curious meanings whose import is not always understood, and indeed may never be known because even modern Cherokees are mystified by many of them.

Interestingly enough, in areas where the Cherokees lived, numbers of their personal names have been left on the streams and sites where they once resided to become a part of the place nomenclature of Georgia. The most distinctive of these remnant names is Rising Fawn, the designation of a town on U.S. 11 in Dade County. The Cherokee version of the name has variously been recorded as Kunnateetah, Kinnetehee, Kenotetah, and Agi-na-gi-li (this version is the one used by James Mooney, the Cherokee scholar). These forms lack the lilt of the English expression and they do not translate literally into Rising Fawn, since the words merely signify Young he is rising. Nonetheless because of the Cherokee method of constructing many compound words from syllables or portions of other terms, the name in this instance was properly understood as embodying the word fawn, because it was derived from the second element of *ahwi-agina*, deer-young, signifying fawn in Cherokee. The Indian country whites took the intended meaning and turned it into Rising Fawn, thus displaying a latent flair for changing an Indian name into a pleasing English expression when they chose to exert themselves. Too frequently, as will be seen, they were content to translate names into literal, matter-of-fact forms, like Bullhead, Crawfish, Rottenwood, Old Bear Guts, Auger Hole, Noisy, Gone to Mill, or Pigeon on the Roost.

In the vicinity of the town of Rising Fawn one can hear a romantic, fanciful account which relates that the name was derived from a pretty Indian princess called Rising Fawn who once lived in the area. Other than the display of a pervasive talent for thinking up Indian maiden stories about placenames, there is no substance to this tale. One can be sure the appellation is very much a masculine name which long appeared in early records in connection with prominent men, some of whom were chieftains.

The real significance of Rising Fawn as a name is not known, but probably the expression stems from the ancient ceremonial title of some functionary whose duties have now been forgotten. But be that as it may, in the 1830's there were a half-dozen Cherokees called Rising Fawn in Georgia and as many more living in areas contiguous to this state. The Rising Fawn who furnished the name for the town lived on upper Lookout Creek, near the site of the place that bears his name.

Two of the Georgia Rising Fawns had the word Old used in connection with the English version of their names. The term had differing implications in a name, depending upon its particular application. Sometimes the whites used the expression in a jocular or even derogatory sense, as in Old Totterhair, Old Crying Buffalo, or Old Mealy Mouth. On occasion though, the word could be taken to mean senior, to differentiate a father from a son; but at times the use of old implied deference to a venerable individual of repute. One of the Old Rising Fawns lived on Little River in present Cherokee County, and another was a resident of Lost Town Valley in the western part of the same county. This place is a secluded, mountain-ringed cove on the south side of Pine Log Mountain, and it was once the home of several well-known Indians. One of these was Old Settingdown, who probably supplied the name for Settingdown Creek in Forsyth County, and another was a chief called Amahuskasata, or Dreadful Water. Presumably these men and others who resided in Lost Town Valley selected the place to live because they felt at home there. Prior to moving into northwest Georgia most of the Cherokees had dwelt for generations in mountain areas of the Carolinas, Tennessee, and extreme northeast Georgia. When they removed to the new section in Georgia, the old Indians and fullbloods seemingly sought out detached places for their homes and left the young Indians and mixed bloods to settle in more open regions such as found in Cobb, Bartow, Gordon, and Murray counties.

Among the Cherokees living in Georgia there was a substantial list of people bearing the names of noted chiefs and personages: Black Fox, Kennesaw, Noonday, Nickajack, Double Head, White Path, Lying Fish, Chulio, Cunsena, Cabin Smith, Earbob, Broom, Willeo, Dirt Seller, Bushy Head, and Wahatchie, all of whom left their names or titles in the geographic appellations of Georgia. Wahatchie can be found twice in connection with streams—a Wauhatchie Creek in Elbert County where the early Cherokees resided, and in a waterway of the same name in Dade. Because it embodies the form *hatchie*, which resembles the Muscogee expression for stream, the name has often been mistaken for a Creek term. One can be certain, though, the word is Cherokee in origin, from *waya-tsi* or *wayachie*, signifying mighty or terrible wolf.

Some of the men listed above, like Cabin Smith, Dirt Seller, White Path, and Kennesaw, were the actual individuals who caused their names to become prominent through tribal activities. There were other Indians here, however, who used the names of chiefs or leaders, but were not the first individuals who originally bore those designations. In their desire to emulate the white man by adopting his customs, it seems likely that numbers of these names were borrowed by the Cherokees in order to have a surname in the fashion of the whites. Since some Indians actually were descendants of noted personages, they apparently took over the tabs of such relatives in order to have a family name of prominence. This practice, though, was counter to the traditions of the tribe, because the early Cherokees were of matrilineal descent and did not receive the father's name.

In addition to adoptions of designations, it seems clear that some surnames were foisted on the Indians by white people who did not understand Cherokee naming practices and followed their own custom by applying first names and surnames to the Indians. In any case, one noted surname that remains with us is found in Conesena Creek, a tributary of the Etowah in Bartow County. This stream derives its name from a family called Cunsena that once lived at its mouth. The word literally signifies dragging, but its full intended meaning is Dragging Canoe, from Tsi-yu-gunsini (*tsiyu*, poplar, i.e., a dugout canoe made from a poplar log, plus *gunsini*, dragging or pulling). The name first applied to a noted fighting chief called Dragging Canoe who was a leader of the Lower Cherokee towns on the Tennessee. The Tennesseans destroyed these places in 1794 and the chief is supposed to have been killed at the time. Seemingly some of his descendants removed to the Etowah, and caused his name to be applied to the Conesena Creek where they resided.

Old Dragging Canoe was an implacable enemy of the Americans, and he must smile from his warriors' bourn at the irony of his name being perpetuated among the people he fought so bitterly.

The early Cherokees were warlike. They battled neighboring tribes, and from 1760 to 1794 were almost continuously embroiled in fighting the white people, first the English and later the Americans. The Indians who migrated into northwest Georgia, however, turned peaceful enough, and they dwelt here for over a generation without conflict. Even so, they were close to their belligerent years, and there were many men among them who bore names or titles that reflected martial accomplishments. Among these were War Club, Fought, Standbefore, Gut Sticker, Sharp, Wicked, The Tough, Still, Old Knockum, Cut-Throat, Scalp, Ketchum (perhaps for Dagugiskee, a slave catcher, i.e., a captive-taker), Skyuga, Hider, Watch, and so on in profusion.

Two war titles of especial interest were Fool and Killer. The first rank at a glance appears a bit preposterous, but it was a label of distinction, because, even though it was derived from *oolskuntney* or *ooscuntena*, for fool, as a title it signified foolhardy, reckless, or brave. Indeed, we employ the word in the same sense in expressions like Fighting Fool or Flying Fool. The native version of Fool was more difficult to depict in English than appears, and the white transcribers garbled it into a variety of forms: Scantee, Scantakee, Scunti, Secondi, and Scontie. One could not verify the origins, but it is possible that Skitt and Skut as found in Skitt Mountain in Hall County and Skut Knob of Towns, are also versions of this designation.

The Cherokees made extensive use of the suffix *tihi* or *tehee*, killer, in their war names, and the title was affixed to a variety of designations: Chickasawkiller, Pathkiller, Nightkiller, Niggerkiller, Overkiller, Whitemankiller, and Mankiller. The last name was subject to widely different interpretations, and seemingly only the Cherokees knew how to construe it in a given instance. As a war title it referred to one who had killed an enemy; but again it could signify murderer; and in another usage applied to a baleful spirit who could bewitch and kill.

Whitemankiller's name in Cherokee was Unega-tihi. The expression simply means Whitekiller, but the white people easily grasped the intended meaning of the title and supplied the word man in their version of the name.

A noted chief called The Glass, who lived in extreme northwest Georgia on the Tenneseee line, was really a killer, because he was known to the Cherokees as Tagwatihi, or Catawbakiller. Due to a resemblance of the former name, however, to the word *adaketi*, meaning looking glass or mirror, the white people misinterpreted the title by translating it into Glass.

The commonest killer rank among the old Cherokees (which still finds expression in the long-adopted surnames of the Oklahoma Indians) was made by affixing *tihi* to an appropriate numeral. Thus there were Cherokees called Twokiller, Threekiller, Fourkiller, and so on. One of these titles remains here in Fourkiller Creek of upper Fulton County, above Roswell. A crossroads called Sutalee in western Cherokee County also commemorates the rank. The name means Six, but one can be virtually certain the original form was Sutalitihi, or Sixkiller.

Closely akin to, or maybe even a part of the war names, were Cherokee personal designations containing the words bullet, arrow, short arrow, or long arrow. The exact implications of the words in a name are not always clear, but apparently at times the expressions were interchangeable. Thus an Indian named Bullet could also be thought of as Short Arrow, while one known as Long Arrow could also be called Long Bullet. These alternations took place because when bullets were introduced among the Indians they had no name for them, and since they were projectiles, they were labelled short arrows, while real arrows were spoken of as long arrows because of the shafts.

Another arrow form which had no relation to the above expressions was *uwani*. The word signifies hickory, because arrow shafts were made of that wood. When applied to a person, however, the name meant arrow, and was an old, ritualistic designation. There were once numbers of Owanes, Wanies, or Wannahs among the Georgia Cherokees.

Georgia has one remaining placename that stems from the bullet-arrow group, Long Bullet Creek, a west-bank tributary of the Hiwassee River, in upper Towns County.

Like most American Indians the Cherokees were superstitious and were firm believers in the existence of spirits, ghosts, witches, hants, boogers, and even of some leprechaun-like figures that were called little people. Skena, from *asgina* or *eskina*, "ghost," as found in our Skeenah Creek of Fannin County, is the only remaining placename here which reflects these former superstitions.

To overcome the tricks and injuries attempted by supernatural beings, or to heal the sick, forecast events, and so on, the Cherokees had a body of healers, doctors, medicine makers, wizards, conjurors, and prophets. Apparently none of the titles of these interesting individuals remain in our placenames, unless it be in the case of Toonigh, a village in Cherokee County. The Indian word was *tuni*, but the whites spelled it in a variety of ways and pronounced it "too ni." The western Cherokees retain the expression, but now say it is a given name for girls. In Georgia, though, there was a Tooni in virtually every community, and the title applied to both men and women, a fact which suggests they may have been some sort of curers or healers. One important man who bore the title was Toonowee, a lesser chief who lived on the waters of Toccoa River, in Fannin County. Toonowee Mountain, located near his home, and which sounds like "Tooni" or "Toonigh" in pronunciation, perpetuates his name.

The names of numbers of women can be found among the listings of Cherokees: Go-luckee, Taunny, Auley, Nasa, Allucha, etc., but the labels are hard to decipher, because there are few functional titles connected with them to aid in identifying the words, as is often the case with men's names. One tab in the list is Sukey, but this designation apparently meant "Miss," or at least was used in that sense by the white Indian countrymen. Some Cherokee women had both Indian and English names: Alleka, or Jenny; Sokena, or Susan; Echauteh, or Anny; Wahti, or Betsey; and so on. These expressions were dual forms, however, and the Indian names did not literally translate into the English versions.

There were a few prominent Cherokee women, and some of them left their imprint on us. One of these was Sally Hughes, who lived on the Etowah to the south of Cartersville and operated an early ferry on that river, thus causing her place to become a focal point for Indian-country travel. Another prominent woman was the Widow Fool (perhaps the wife of Fool, a fighting chief in Tennessee), who lived in the vicinity of Rome and operated a ferry at the site. And still another woman of note was Old Nancy, who lived on Nancys Creek in Bartow County. One strongly suspects that she originally dwelt at Nancy Town on Nancytown Creek in Habersham County. She may even have removed from there to the Standing Peachtree community and left her name on the Nancys Creek of upper Fulton County before moving on to our Bartow County.

The most distinctive woman's name of all, however, can be found in Warwoman Creek to the east of Clayton, in Rabun County and in the original Cherokee territory. The name was an honored title among the Indians. It was their custom to take a woman along on war parties, mainly to cook and sew, but when one proved her mettle on several expeditions she was given the designation of War Woman. It is doubtful if we shall ever know how Warwoman Creek got its name, because it has borne the tab for over 200 years, but it may have been named for a valiant War Woman who gave a good account of herself in some unknown battle in the narrow defiles along the stream.

One of the most unusual groups of Cherokee names involved expressions that outwardly seem to represent the names of women but which actually applied to men. In this category were designations like: Mad Woman, Good Woman, Gal Ketcher, Woman Holder, Girl Killer, Little Woman, Crying Woman, and Laughing Gal. The man with the last name lived on Shoal Creek, near its mouth on the Etowah, in western Cherokee County. Not far from the site where he resided there is even now a crossroads called Laughing Gal.

The Cherokees had four groups of enigmatic names that merit note. These were the Eaters, the Lifters, the Carriers or Toaters, and the "in the water" characters. There were numbers of individuals with names that fell in the first category: Gourdeater, Coon Eater, Peach Eater, Head Eater, and Crane Eater. A man bearing the last designation lived on a tributary of the Coosawattee River, in Gordon County, that is yet called Crane Eater Creek. The Western Cherokees still use names belonging to this group, although somewhere along the way they added a new one as Tick Eater. If this moniker were once applied in these parts it could not be found in old records.

There were fewer Lifters than Eaters but their names were interesting: Otter Lifter, a noted Chickamauga chief, Turkey Lifter, Pigeon Lifter, and Paunch Lifter, who resided on Amicalola River in Dawson County. Taking up the Cur, a citizen of Sallacoa Creek, was perhaps another Lifter whose name was rendered in different English words.

Paunch Lifter's name brings to mind a famous Overhill Cherokee chief in East Tennessee who was known to the whites as Hanging Maw, because of his sagging stomach. Georgia also had some pudgy Cherokees, but instead of referring rhetorically to one of these fellows as Hanging Maw, or even as Tubby or Pot Belly, the local whites dubbed him with the inelegant label of Guts. In fairness, though, it should be noted the Indian countrymen did evidence a bit of deference to the opposite sex when they nicknamed a fat, rotund woman Maw.

There was a substantial list of Carriers, although in backcountry speech the whites nearly always rendered the name as Toater, or Toter. Among the Indians in this group were Beaver Toater, Flax Toter, Hemp Toter, Hogtoater, Arrow Toater, Turkey Toater, and Old Toater. No good explanation can be found for these names, though one early source states the title Fire Carrier applied to a conjuror. James Mooney indicates that this sort of Carrier (or Toater) was a spirit that went about at night, and that the word fire in the name may have referred to the Will of the Wisp. Toto Creek, a tributary of the Chestatee in southeast Dawson County, most likely is a Toater name. A well-known Cherokee called Child Toater lived on the Etowah, not far to the west of the creek, and it is easy to believe he owned property on it and left his name in the garbled Toto.

For reasons that are not understood the Cherokees made frequent use of the expression *amayi*, in the water, in connection with personal names. Thus there were people called Feather in the Water, Killing in the Water, Deer in the Water, Brush in the Water, and Log in the Water. So far as could be learned there are no remaining placenames in Georgia that perpetuate the "in the water" designations.

The Cherokees made extensive use of the names of birds, animals, and insects in their naming of persons. Curiously enough, though, they sometimes lacked a generic name for a given species within these groups. For example a black fox was *inali* and a red fox was *chula*. The former does not embody the word for black nor the latter the term for red. Neither expression contains a form which indicates the two creatures belonged to a common family. The same situation applied to owls. Each species of these birds bore a specific name that did not reflect kinship with other owls.

Chief among the animal appellations were names containing the word *yanuh* or bear: Bear Meat, Bear Paw, Bear at Home, Bear Conjuror, Yonakiller, and Yonaguska or Drowning Bear. Yonaguska was an important designation with the Cherokees, and several Indians with the name lived in Georgia. One of them left his imprint on us in Drowning Bear Creek, below Dalton in Whitfield County. The English version of the name is easy to misconstrue, because on its face it does not convey the intended meaning. Mooney in his analysis of the name says Yonaguska signifies "Bear drowns him," meaning the bear was doing the drowning and not being drowned himself.

Two other Bear names in the original Cherokee country of the state are Unawatti Creek, or Old Bear Creek, in Franklin County, and Mount Yonah in White.

There were numbers of Cherokees carrying the name of some insect: Spider, Cricket, Fly, Grasshopper, Wasp, Grubworm, Snail, etc. One unusual moniker in the group was Housebug, the name of a family living in Cedartown Valley. In Oklahoma some of their descendants later changed the name to Houseberg, but even so the expression is only a thinly disguised version of bedbug. One probable place name remaining from the insect appellations is Yahoola Creek in Lumpkin County. The term signifies doodlebug.

Both the Cherokees and the Indian country whites were callous in applying names to afflicted persons. They thought little of calling such people by names like Club Foot, Bend About, Lame Robin, Bead-eye, Ugly, Crooked Leg, Slimshanks, Soar-eyed Nancy, Cross-eyed Wat, Blinkey, Partridge-nose, and One-eyed Jenny.

Cherokees called Roman Nose, Long Nose, or simply Nose apparently did not belong in this afflicted group. Seemingly these designations represented a title or nickname for an individual who on the occasion of a play or charade put on a mask with a long leather nose. But be that as it may, one Indian called Nose resided on the stream in Cobb County which is remembered as Noses Creek. When the Coffee Line was established, he removed above it to a branch of Stamp Creek in Bartow that also became known as Noses Creek.

In contrast to most Indians, who were regarded as a taciturn lot, the Cherokees were relatively jocular and fun-loving. This proclivity no doubt caused them to apply humorous names to people: Allbones, Sour John, Dusty Belly, Dunbean, Whaca, Canoe Buster, Innasent George, Lazy Will, Nimble Will, All hollow through, Isickle, Stomp About, Scrape Shins, Buzzard, and Bull Frog. The last name was applied to a man with a hoarse voice. *Suli* or *soolee*, buzzard, was a nickname for a slow, dull fellow. The best-known individual of the category was a chief called The Breath, who was so named for his long-winded talkativeness: our windbag more nearly expresses the intended meaning of the label.

The drollest tab in this group, however, was Bear out run Him, who lived on Chickamauga Creek, in our Catoosa County, at the Tennessee line. The name as given is a dressed-up version for official records and it may be incorrectly rendered. When this Indian was first mentioned he was listed as Bar Outrunna by a field agent who was making evaluations of Cherokee properties. As these notes were being transcribed for a formal report, some prim purist put down the name as Bear out run Him and in so doing may have changed the sex involved. There is no inkling about the origin of the name, but the Cherokees were fond of pantomimes and parodies, and they thought such presentations were hilariously funny. Perhaps Bear out run Him (or Her, as the case might be) got his name as an actor in one of these affairs. However it was, though, the bear seemingly was the victor in the scene or event that gave rise to the name, because if pursued, he "out run" the pursuer; or, if he was doing the pursuing, he overtook the one that was caught.

The recording of Bar Outrunna is a reminder that numbers of Cherokee names were listed in the rustic terminology of white frontiersmen. Among such listings were Bresh Picker and Setting Turkle. Few people today say "bresh" for brush, but there are still those among us who use "turkle" for turtle. Another name was borne by an Indian family called Crap Grass or Crab Grass. In more formal listings, the name was given as Crop Grass. The appellation merits mentioning because the latter version was the original and correct form for the vexatious vegetation which we now call crabgrass. It is interesting to see that we retain the colloquial term and not the proper expression. And still another name in this backwoodsy group is Sope, as found in Sopes Creek in Cobb County. The latter name is in use today, on official maps, even though one can be positive that the Indian who furnished the designation was correctly known as Soap, and that he lived on the creek in question before the Coffee Line was established. After that boundary was set, he removed above it and settled on a stream in upper Cherokee County that is properly remembered as Soap Creek.

In the last years of the Cherokees here some of them dropped their Indian designations and borrowed the names of important white personages and places. Among these were King George, Washington, James Madison, Henry Clay, and Ignatius A. Few. One man who lived on Armuchee Creek took over the name of Philadelphia, perhaps because the Cherokees attended a treaty there in 1794 and he may have been a delegate. Philadelphia had nineteen members in his family, and one wonders what name those individuals eventually used.

Over the years many white men settled in the Cherokee Nation and married there. Among these individuals were men called Timson, Vann, Ragsdale, Buffington, Cordery, Harnage, Seabolt, Kell, Landrum, Ross, Adair, Baldridge, Rolston, Pettit, McLemore, Dougherty, Ward, Lavender, Proctor, and Taylor. By examining any good map showing the former Cherokee section of Georgia, one can find most of these names in the place terminology of the area.

There are still other classes of Cherokee appellations and a long list of personal names which have not been mentioned. Space will not permit a discussion of these, but there is one final category of names and one interesting title which should not be omitted here. This last group embodied unusual given names which were applied to Cherokees when they began to use names in the fashion of the whites. Some interesting expressions were "Meridian" Running Water, "Leaf" Dougherty, "Pheasant" June Bug, "Blowgun" Thomas, "Wagon" Crabgrass, "Early" Cordery, "Laugh to te tea" Graves, "Cricket" Sixkiller, "Mistaken" Grits, and "Try" Rogers. The latter lived on the Chattahoochee, in our Forsyth County, and was a kinsman of the late Will Rogers. Rogers Bridge over the Chattahoochee in Forsyth County still commemorates the Rogers name, because the family once maintained a ferry at the crossing.

And finally, the last title to be mentioned applied to Tucooyeskee, who ranked as the First Duck of Ducktown, located on the upper

Chattooga River in lower Walker County. Tucooyeskee very probably signified flint and was the man's personal name. One ventures to state that First Duck was a title which indicated he ranked as the headman of his community.

—*GR* (1963): 160-173, reprinted from *EUQ* 11(1963): 160-173

The Hurricane Placenames in Georgia

If one examines the placenames on reasonably well-detailed maps of Georgia he will be impressed by the frequency with which the word hurricane appears in the geographic nomenclature of the state. These appellations for the most part stem from the formative years and go back to the time in which people used the word hurricane to designate the violent wind storms that are now referred to as tornadoes or cyclones. The name hurricane occurs so often across Georgia that it can be ranked numerically with other widely used designations, like Beaverdam Creek, Caney Creek, Rocky Branch, and the ubiquitous piney places, such as Pine Grove, Pine Level, etc. In all, there must be some forty Hurricane streams, areas, or sites in the state. In other years, the number was even larger before some places which once bore the tab had their names changed.

With the exception of the coastal region and the southeast corner, the Hurricane places are fairly well distributed over Georgia, although there is a tendency toward concentration in a broad, east-west band across the center of the state. A few Hurricane creeks can be found in the southeastern section, but this number proportionally is small for such a large area. By way of contrast, in Dade County alone, in the northwest corner, there are two Hurricane creeks. One might easily conclude by reason of the present-day usage and understanding of the term hurricane that the places containing the word would be concentrated along the sea front. But this is not the case and apparently has always been so. The *Colonial Records of Georgia* make scant mention of the term hurricane in connection with the coastal section, and it would be rare to find the word on an old plat of property in that section, whereas in other parts of the state it is fairly common to see the name on early plats and on official district land maps which were prepared by the original surveyors, who were responsible for initially recording most of the Hurricane placenames that can be found today because they frequently noted the effects and paths of the storms in their field notes and on their maps. They were especially prone to mark streams in tornadic areas as Hurricane creeks. This readiness is easily understandable when viewed in the light of the tasks which a pioneer surveyor faced in laying off a wilderness area. He was customarily directed by the surveyor general to note all creeks in his surveys and since he often did not know the names of the lesser streams encountered he had to make up designations for them as he went along. Apparently most surveyors were matter of fact about this obligation because they were prone to adopt commonplace appellations like Cane Creek, Mud Creek, Sandy Creek, Turkey Creek, and so on, to leave a proliferation of such prosaic names across Georgia maps. But one can be sure there were special reasons for applying Hurricane names, especially to water courses. Streams, because of meanders and thick marginal swamps, were usually difficult to lay off in any case, but when such places had been visited by a tornado the fallen trees enhanced the surveying into a wearisome and time-consuming job that had to be performed without added pay. Little wonder then that surveyors who encountered such spots marked them as Hurricane places on maps and plats.

The courses of hurricanes were also noted and indicated by surveyors to inform prospective owners of newly surveyed areas that the properties had been visited by tornadoes. The notations "Hurricane Path," "Traces of a Hurricane," or simply "Hurricane" on a plat were quite as informative to an old-timer as were other comments about the features of a given parcel of land that might be listed on a plat of that property, like "Bay Gall," "Salt Marsh," "River Swamp," "2nd quality oak and hickory land," "Impassable Beaver-dam on," etc.

Interestingly enough, would-be owners of hurricane-devastated areas seemingly reacted in different ways to evidence of tornadoes on prospective property. Farmers apparently did not care much one way or the other since prostrate timber simplified the job of clearing the land. It was easy to burn the logs and limbs, although the task of filling in holes left by upturned root systems of fallen trees must have occasioned much hard work.

People who wanted land for the timber on it were among those who objected to the destruction of a hurricane on the property. This attitude is exemplified in the position of Elisha Butler who petitioned the Provincial Council in 1767 for the right to purchase 1,000 acres of timberland in St. Philips Parish to start a sawmill. The request was granted, but Butler was soon before the council again with another petition asking permission to rearrange the lines of the property, because on surveying the original tract, it was found that 300 acres had been "stript of Timber" by a hurricane. Lumbermen objected to trees from hurricane areas because the fallen trunks were too shattered for use. Even standing trees that had withstood a blow often had their texture so strained they developed the "shakes" and were not suited for sawing into lumber.

Pioneer surveyors were not the only early citizens to comment on traces of hurricanes. The blows were tremendously devastating in primeval forests, and the accounts of several travellers contain comments on the havoc, because prostrate trees athwart trails occasioned much tedious weaving among the fallen trunks to get clear of the damaged area.

Colonel Benjamin Hawkins is one of the best sources of information on hurricane traces in virgin forests. In performing his duties as Indian agent he travelled far and wide in the Southeast and left numbers of comments about the effects of tornadoes. On one trip, during the fall of 1798, in his unpublished "Viatory" (now in the Library of Congress), he noted the remains of five different hurricanes within the distance of a mile. The site involved was just over the Chattahoochee in Alabama, and a few miles below today's West Point, Georgia. On the same date he encamped on the upper side of what is now West Point and reported the lands were bereft of trees by hurricanes. The next day he camped on the west side of the Chattahoochee in present lower Heard County and noted a hurricane "had blowed down many trees" in the area. On the return from this trip a month later he mentions the remains of a hurricane a few miles below the Little Tallapoosa River in today's Carroll County. In his *Letters* Hawkins remarked in more detail on the same place in a prior account dated in 1796. He stated that repeated gusts of wind had blown down or torn to pieces a great many trees over a distance of 12 miles. Some of the blows he added had taken place many years past, some a few years before, and some during the year of the trip.

These particular comments by Hawkins pertain to the fringe and western side of Georgia, but eastward from this area, in a band across the middle part of the state, from the Chattahoochee to the Savannah, there was a sort of hurricane belt in the early years. The original surveyors mention hurricane places in this zone and, as will be seen shortly, there is documentary evidence to show that the greatest tornado reported in old records swept all the way across Georgia within this band.

Hawkins's comment on the remains of hurricanes along a 12-mile stretch brings to mind the length of early tornado paths. There were several blows of this approximate length mentioned in the old land records of Georgia. One of particular interest is the former hurricane course that was once used to mark off the boundary between Jefferson and present Emanuel counties. Another long track was reported in 1819 by Joel Walker, the surveyor of District 5 of original Early County, that is now a part of lower Clay. The devastation of this storm began at the southwest edge of what is now the town of Bluffton and blew on a kidney-shaped course northeastwardly along the east side of present U.S. 27 toward northwest Calhoun County. It passed out of District 5 into District 4, but unfortunately the surveyor of the latter district did not mention or trace the storm on his plats, so its full length is not known. Judging by the intensity of the swath as depicted on the plats for District 5, however, it was going strong when it left that area. The tornado probably continued on across northwest Calhoun toward Carnegie in Randolph County. But this latter area was Indian country at the time of the Early County surveys, and when it was eventually surveyed some seven years later there was no mention of the hurricane's course in the Randolph plats.

Georgia has witnessed many tornadoes in its long years and surely one of the greatest, if not actually the greatest storm that has visited the state in historical times, was the mighty hurricane of April, 1804. There are records to show that this tornado passed all the way across the state from west to east. The official surveys of original Baldwin County depict the course of the big blow with precision, even to a slight eccentric side movement of the wind in District 11, at a point to the north of today's Gray. The hurricane entered old Baldwin near the mouth of Falling Creek on the Ocmulgee to the west of Wayside in present Jones County, and passed across the 30-mile span between the Ocmulgee and Oconee to the area of Milledgeville. Its path near Falling Creek was narrow and concentrated, but gradually it expanded to a band nearly two miles wide in the section just to the north of Milledgeville. The cyclone completely destroyed the timber over many land lots of $202\frac{1}{2}$ acres each and partially damaged the trees in numerous other lots. There is no record of the lives lost in the Baldwin County sector of the storm, because the affected area was largely uninhabited, having only recently been ceded by the Indians and surveyed preparatory to distribution to permanent white settlers through a land lottery.

The course of the storm as shown by the surveyors of Baldwin County apparently was a segment of a much greater track. This particular part of the blow was reported in detail because the surveyors happened to make their surveys a short time after the disturbance and were able to observe and report on the effects of the devastation. Mrs. Virginia Hill Wilhoit wrote about the same tornado or a phase of it in her "History of Warren County," that is now deposited in the Georgia Department of Archives and History. She states the storm passed across Warren and Richmond counties to leave Georgia above Augusta. She adds the path could be followed for many years and was remembered as The Old Hurricane. There is a difference in the date of the cyclone, however, as given by Mrs. Wilhoit and the Baldwin County surveyors. The latter all show the day as April 5, 1804, whereas the history states the time was April 4. Since it is certain the storm blew from west to east, perhaps there was a mistake about the latter date. It is possible, though, weather conditions were so out of balance at the particular period that two different tornadoes occurred on successive days.

In writing about the cyclone of 1875, another great storm that swept the state, J. T. Henderson says in *The Commonwealth of Georgia* (1885) that this tornado entered Georgia in Harris County and passed near Milledgeville, Sparta, and Camak to leave the state a little above Augusta. He adds it followed a course that was close to the track of the 1804 hurricane. Many years after the great 1804 blow, a commission appointed to run the Georgia-Alabama boundary mentions the effects of that storm in its report and correspondence. The survey of the line began in July of 1826, on the west side of the Chattahoochee, below Columbus, and led to Nickajack Town on the Tennessee River. When the surveying party reached a point not far below today's West Point, Georgia, and opposite to northwest Harris County (in the same general area where Benjamin Hawkins saw traces of five different hurricanes in 1798) they noted signs of a great tornado. The chairman of the commission wrote Governor Troup that these remains were vestiges of the storm that had visited Sparta in 1804. Presumably he was also referring to the same tornado that struck Baldwin County.

Farther along, at a point near Texas in Heard County, the group encountered a big hurricane path that was three-quarters of a mile wide. Edward Lloyd Thomas, the chief surveyor of the commission, was of the opinion that this last track was a part of the storm which visited Milledgeville and Augusta in 1804. Thomas was one of the state's outstanding surveyors. He was well acquainted with Georgia, and his views on the entering point of the tornado merit attention.

On the Georgia side of the Chattahoochee, opposite the tornado signs below West Point, the surveyor of the twentieth district of Muscogee County (now in Harris) mentions evidence of an "old hurricane" in the field notes of his 1827 survey. He did not seek, however, to connect the destruction with the 1804 tornado. It is possible, of course, that these remains were a part of the earlier storms noted by Hawkins in 1798.

The big blow of 1804 resulted in the creation of several placenames and especially of some Hurricane creeks and branches that lay in the path or along the edges of the tornado. Perhaps the most interesting name that seemingly stemmed from this storm was Howell Cobb's Hurricane Plantation in Baldwin County.

The last name brings to mind the fact that while many of the hurricane placenames are found in connection with waterways, all of the appellations by no means are borne by streams. For instance, there is a Hurricane District in western Coweta County; a Hurricane Grove in Habersham; and a Hurricane Bridge Church in Jenkins.

Some of the hurricane names are connected with streams but not for reasons that have been noted here. For example, the Hurricane Shoals on the North Fork of the Oconee River, in upper Jackson County, have borne their label since post-Revolutionary years. It is commonly understood that the name was applied to the site because of the roaring, tempestuous waters at the shoals and not because a storm once swept the place. The Hurricane Falls, one of the five great cascades making up the original Tallulah Falls, received the name for thundering waters that formerly flowed over the drop. All of these falls, once a scenic marvel of Georgia, have been stilled by a present-day power dam and reservoir.

One former hurricane place created an amusing situation. When Jefferson County was formed in 1796, the creating law provided among other things that the boundary should run south along the Sunbury Road (now the Jefferson-Johnson line) to the path of a Hurricane, thence eastward along its course to Williamson Swamp Creek. With the passage of time, after Nature's healing hand had time to restore the trees, the boundary along the storm's track became nebulous for property holders in the area. In 1810 the uncertainty was corrected in an act which provided that a new line should be substituted for the old hurricane course, to begin at the head of Rocky

Creek on the Sunbury Road, thence down the stream to Williamson Swamp. This boundary is now the line between Jefferson and Emanuel counties.

The Rocky Creek mentioned follows, or closely parallels, the course of the hurricane that was originally used for the boundary. This situation leaves the interesting thought that it might be possible to study aerial photographs of the area and still detect some evidence of the old storm path. The destructiveness of tremendous hurricanes was so great it is easy to believe they may have upset ecological conditions sufficiently along their swaths to leave some sort of evidence of the storms even at this date. Perhaps the route of the great tornado across Baldwin County would offer a better possibility for such an aerial study than would the segment of the former Jefferson line.

In view of the pervasiveness of the hurricane places and the profusion of Indian names in Georgia, it would be strange indeed if the state did not have some aboriginal designations that concerned hurricanes. There was at least one redman's name that stemmed from tornadoes and there were probably several other such appellations.

One former Indian hurricane place which is known to have existed was a Creek settlement called Hotalihuyana. The name was derived from the Muskogee *hotali* (pronounced "hoe tullee"), meaning wind and *huyana* ("hoo yahna"), meaning passing. The Indian country whites took the intended meaning of the expression and converted it into Hurricane Town. The settlement was on the west bank of Flint River, some five miles below Albany.

In his *Letters* Colonel Hawkins indicates there was another Indian hurricane community higher up the Flint from the first place. He lists the second site as Tullewhoquanau or Tucane Town. The last form is undoubtedly an incorrect transcription or a misprint, and the former is most likely a garbled version of Hotalihuyana. Since the *tali* elements of the last word are pronounced "tullee," Hawkins seemingly slurred the first syllable of *hotali* and wrote the rest as "tulle." This probable Hurricane Town was located above Albany, somewhere near present Philema in Lee County.

Hawkins also mentions in the *Letters* a Flint River tributary called "Ittoopunnauulgau." This stream seems to have been the present Sweetwater Creek that marks the boundary between Macon and Sumter counties. The version given by the Colonel was poorly rendered, but it apparently meant Trees Zigzagged from the Muskogee *ito* ("ee toe"), meaning tree, timber or wood, and *opanana* ("oh puh nah nuh"), zigzagged or crossed, plus the plural-forming suffix *algi* ("uhl-gee"). The latter form not only converted *ito,* tree, into trees, but also by implication it had a locative connotation. It is reasonable to conclude that the name referred to a place where prostrate, zigzagged timber such as might be found in the path of a destructive tornado could be found and that the area in the white man's way of thinking was actually a hurricane creek.

The next tributary of the Flint downstream from the Trees Zigzagged waterway was listed by Colonel Hawkins as "Crooked Wood Creek." It was some fifteen miles below the former and is identifiable with present Line Creek of Sumter County. Now, the first part of this name might have been a literal translation of the Creek word *itokutaksi* ("ee toe koo tock see") for crooked or bent wood, but it could also have been an English version of *itopanana,* a form that is very close phonetically to Hawkins's Ittoopunnauulgau. The main difference between the two names is lack of the plural indicator *ulgau* on the former word. Very likely, one believes, the Crooked Wood Creek was a hurricane place, with the literal English name being used to prevent confusion of the stream with the neighboring Ittoopunnauulgau.

Even more interesting than these obsolete Indian names is the present Tobannee Creek that reaches the Chattahoochee just below Georgetown in Quitman County. The first surveyor who mentioned the stream in 1827 listed it as "To-be-na-nie." The William Phillips manuscript map of Quitman in 1871 gives the word as "Tobe-Nahnee." One may not see the resemblance at first glance, but all three of the above versions are close to Hawkins's Ittoopunnauulgau, a fact that makes it reasonably certain the two names meant the same thing and signified hurricane creek. The main difference between the two appellations is the lack of an *ulgau* at the end of Tobannee. Otherwise the *To* ("toe") element of the latter is merely a slurred form of *ito,* or "itto," signifying tree or timber, while the *bannee* portion of the present-day name is identifiable with the *punnau* of Hawkins's word. The latter commences with a *p* and the former with a *b.* But this is a slight change, because the white people often switched these cognates in recording Indian names. Indeed, we sometimes make such changes in our own idiom. For instance, it is fairly common to hear someone say "babtize" for baptize, or "Gipson" for Gibson.

Another name which may have referred to a hurricane place is Tallokas, the designation of a community in Brooks County. The word is difficult to translate with certainty, and especially so because of the final *s* on the expression. The Creeks ordinarily did not use placenames terminating in that letter, a fact which implies that some white person who did not understand the structure of Muskogee names stuck the *s* on the designation. The word may well be from *teloki,* or *teloga* ("tee loh ga"), peas or wild pea-vines. But it also may be from *taloki* ("tah loh kee") signifying raincrow. On the other hand, the *Tallo* element of Tallokas intimates the designation may have signified palmettoes. If the expression is from the Hitchitee tongue and not the Creek, the name could be from *talaki* ("tah lah kee") prostrate or lying. This derivation, however, is not helpful because there is no indication of the thing or object that was prostrate. If the original expression were *ahitalaki* ("ah hee tah lah kee"), it would have meant tree (or trees) prostrate and might have referred to a hurricane effect. The same designation, though, could as readily have pertained to a footlog and not to trees knocked down in a tornado. In short, one can not yet be sure of the meaning of the interesting name Tallokas.

So far as could be discovered there are no native hurricane names remaining in the old Cherokee country of Georgia. This lack is noticeable since those Indians had a diverse and relatively rich language. Furthermore, some of the actual English hurricane places are in former Cherokee territory, so we know the storms occurred there. It is possible that some of these names are translations from the Indian. Cherokee was a difficult tongue for white people and the latter often converted placenames of that tribe into easy English forms.

In a list of Cherokee terms prepared for Thomas Jefferson by Benjamin Hawkins, the word "Ca, too, se" is given as signifying wind. This listing implies that perhaps Catoosa County derived its name from the expression, especially in view of the fact that the county has a large stream Hurricane Creek, which has borne its designation since Indian days and in view of the further fact that old people pronounce the name of the county as "Ca, too, see." It is not known where or how Hawkins got his word because the usual Cherokee expression for wind is *unauli* and the name for hurricane is *akalugi.* Furthermore, it seems probable that Catoosa County derived its designation from the Cherokee *gatusi* ("Gah too see"), signifying hill, small mountain, or high place and that the name has no connection whatever with a word for windstorm or hurricane.

We have wandered to and fro across Georgia, discussing the hurricane places and the effects of such storms without mentioning the origin of the word hurricane and how it came to be used here. Perhaps before closing, it would be helpful to touch upon the derivation of the term. It was borrowed through the Spaniards from the Carib Indians who lived around the fringe of the Caribbean and apparently from the Tainos who inhabited the Greater Antilles and the Bahamas, areas which are seasonally beset by howling sea storms. The Indians called such a blow *huracan,* signifying evil spirit. The early Spaniards, being from the temperate zone and unfamiliar with this type of storm, borrowed the name for it, converted the word to *huracán* and passed it on to other Europeans as the designation of a violent windstorm of destructive force. One might think that the geographical propinquity would have caused American colonists to be the first people to introduce the expression into the English language. Actually, however, the name was initially taken to England before any of the colonies were founded and was well established in use by 1650. Numbers of early English writers used the word: Eden, Hakluyt, Raleigh, Addison, and others. Shakespeare mentions it as "hurricanoes" in *King Lear.*

When the English colonists began settling the lower Southeast, they experienced vicious wind storms that on occasion appeared from nowhere during the warm months to devastate settlements and smash swaths through great forests. These newcomers, with an upper temperate zone background, knew about storms, gales, and squalls, and about thunder, lightning, and rain, but they were unfamiliar with the new type of storm and lacked a name for it. This led them to use the Spanish-Indian designation, which had already become known to Englishmen. And interestingly enough, they applied the expression to inland blows even though the original designation stemmed from tropically spawned tempests that periodically visited coastal margins.

It might be added that although the spelling of hurricane has now been formalized, the Americans have long had trouble pronouncing this borrowed expression. Over the years it has variously been written here as "harrcane," "hericane," "horicon," "hurrycane," and so on. As late as 1870 it was spelled "harricon" in a Georgia act concerning a change in the Jackson-Banks county line. In the spoken language, even now, there are people who say "hur'cane" and "harry kin."

Despite the once wide application of the word hurricane in the interior of Georgia and neighboring areas, the inlanders gradually quit using the expression for violent windstorms, although they continued to retain most placenames that originally contained the tab. The designation has been virtually discontinued as a hinterland term, so much so that people now are prone to think of a hurricane only as a coastal storm of tropical origin. This conception, of course, takes the word back to its original application, but it makes people forget the once common interior usage of the name and leaves them puzzled about some of their geographic nomenclature.

The evolution in the application of hurricane was desirable, however, and is an interesting example of language change, because in the earlier years there was no suitable term for differentiating between the great coastal storms and the destructive inland disturbances that are now called tornadoes.

The expression tornado, like *huracán*, or hurricane, is also a loan word from the Spaniards. The term was introduced to England shortly after the adoption of hurricane, but it did not begin to find much usage in America until about the time of the Revolution. Georgians were employing the word by the early 1800's, because one of the surveyors of old Baldwin County mentioned the great blow of 1804 as a "tornado or hurricane."

Various dictionaries state tornado is derived from the Spanish word *tronada*, a thunderstorm. Seemingly this derivation can be attributed to the *Oxford English Dictionary*, although that source does not positively state the expression is derived from *tronada*. This suggested origin is all the more unusual because tornadoes, in this area at least, are not necessarily always accompanied by thunder and lightning, although they are characterized by roaring, whirling winds. Eric Partridge in his book on word origins says the term is from the past participle of the Spanish *tornar*, meaning to return, come back again, to put into circular motion, or simply to wind. In view of the modern knowledge of the movements of tornadic winds, Partridge's explanation is easy to accept.

As time passed, Georgians and other Americans began to use cyclone as well as tornado for the havoc-making blows. Meteorologists apparently do not approve of the use of the former term as an alternate for tornado, but nonetheless around Georgia and in many other areas, people commonly understand the two words to mean the same thing. In addition to cyclone and tornado, the expression twister in relatively recent years has also been used as a name for this type of storm. The last tab evidently is a loan word which was borrowed from some other area of the country, perhaps from mid-continental regions.

Interestingly enough, to return finally to placenaming, tornado has never been used much in geographic designations. Only a few states have employed the word in this respect. Cyclone, on the other hand, has been widely adopted across the country. By 1890, there were seven post offices called Cyclone in the nation. One of these was in Screven County, Georgia. The place ceased to be a post office years ago, but the community is still referred to as the Cyclone District. In the 1890's there was a spot called Cyclonetta on the Georgia Southern and Florida (Southern Railway), located above Tifton and below Inaha. This moniker was a coined word, of course, but it represented a type of appellation which the former placename makers loved to think up. Cyclonetta has long since disappeared from maps and has been forgotten unless some old folk around-about happen to remember the site.

—*GR* 18(1964): 224-235

Our Changing Placenames

Geographic names are persistent things and once a given designation has been applied to a site, valley, stream, mountain, or area it has usually continued permanently in use. The spelling or sound of some appellations may be modified with the passage of time but the basic forms will tend to endure either on maps or in the minds of people. But there are scores upon scores of placenames and it is understandable that some of them would shift over the years. The number of changed and changing words, however, is relatively so small this short essay can easily indicate some of the more important switches.

The need for making some changes arose immediately after the foundation of the colony when the English were faced with the question of what to do with the well-established Spanish or Spanish-Indian names of islands along the coast. Two of these were changed to the present English forms of Jekyll and Cumberland, while other major islands were left with Anglicized versions of the names which the Spaniards had used. Thus San Simon became Saint Simons; Santa Catarina, Saint Catherines; Sapala, Sapelo; and so on.

In the same period there must also have been much changing of aboriginal names in the areas of the original colony, because by consulting any good map showing the first sections of settlement, one can see there are comparatively few Indian names applying to lesser streams and physical objects. The early settlers retained the appellations of large waterways like Savannah, Ogeechee, Canoochee, Alatamahaw, Satilla, and so on but not the tabs of smaller streams. The latter must also have borne Indian labels but the newcomers did not adopt them, and used instead their own designations which mainly endure to this day.

When faced with the selection of a name for the St. Marys River, the Georgians had the choice of using the Spanish Santa María or the Indian Thlathlothlakuphka as against the adoption of a new English designation for the stream. They chose Santa María and converted it to St. Marys to become one of the attractive placenames of the state. Fortunately they had the good judgment not to retain Thlathlothlakuphka since that formidable moniker is not only difficult to pronounce, but also it is reported to have the fulsome meaning of Rotten Fish River.

As time passed and as the state expanded to its present limits, a profusion of placenames reflecting various facets of Georgia life were ultimately added. In time, oddly enough, there was a greater willingness to adapt a variety of Indian appellations. This development was all the more unusual because as the settlers moved farther westward and northward their conflicts with the red people became more and more bitter, a fact which leads one to think the whites might have decided to ignore all Indian tabs.

As indicated, most of the names eventually adopted are still with us. If some of them have been stricken from maps, they are not necessarily forgotten because people living in areas where they once applied usually remember them. This is true even for old Jacksonboro (in upper Screven County) upon which Lorenzo Dow cast a spell and consigned to oblivion. The town did disappear but the name is still remembered by citizens aroundabout.

Some appellations were dropped from use in one place only to be taken up and applied at another site. An interesting and persistent example can be found in Georgetown. A community bearing this label was established in colonial years on the west side of the Ogeechee, below Richmond Hill, in present Bryan County. Later this designation was changed to Hardwick, but in post-Revolutionary years another Georgetown was founded on the east side of the Ogeechee in today's Glascock County, to the northwest of Mitchell. This place in time became a so-called ghost town but the name Georgetown was next adopted for the seat of Quitman County, where it has continued for over a century. Incidentally, the early Hardwick also eventually died, but the name was moved to a point south of Milledgeville.

Some appellations were changed because the words were also used elsewhere in the state and the postal authorities in a given instance would only recognize one of the places as a post office. This situation happened in the case of the two Dublins—one, the present well-known town in Laurens County, and another Dublin in southeast Butts. The former site was chosen as a post office over the Butts community, but citizens of the latter assuaged their desires for an Irish name by switching to Cork. Interestingly enough, they still retain Dublin as the name of their Militia district.

Originally Randolph County, which had been named for John Randolph, was changed in 1812 to Jasper because the Georgians disagreed with the policies of the Virginian. Eventually this irritation passed, and the name was again bestowed on present Randolph County when it was created in 1828. Another county name was permanently revoked in 1861 when Georgia switched Cass County to Bartow because the citizens became angry with Lewis Cass, for whom the county was originally named. But even prior to this date Kinchafoonee County was changed to Webster. When the county was formed in 1853 the people adopted the designation Kinchafoonee, after a neighboring big stream called Kinchafoonee Creek. The new name became a source of amusement, so much so the citizens decided to swap the appellation in 1856 for the safe and sound Webster, for Daniel Webster. There is nothing particularly humorous about Kinchafoonee as Indian names go, but wags tended to make it so and embarrassed the Webster people. It is quite possible the chief teasers and wits in this matter hailed from counties bearing Indian designations like Muscogee, Catoosa, and Chattooga.

The shift of Kinchafoonee County to Webster brings to mind some abrupt changes in the designations of towns. Usually the names of cities and communities have been quite tenacious. But over the years, for one reason or another, there have been some decided shifts. For example, Hard Money in Webster County was switched to Weston because early merchants at the place decided the former moniker carried a stingy, selfish connotation, a conclusion no doubt entirely correct.

Two other town names that were drastically changed are Harmony Grove that became Commerce, and Jug Tavern which was shifted to Winder. As far as changes in names of major places go, Atlanta holds the record. The community was first known as Whitehall, then as Terminus, next as Marthasville, and finally in 1845, after the railroad station was opened, as Atlanta.

Over the years some names have been changed because people lost sight of the original designations and their meanings with the passage of time. An interesting example in this category is St. Augustine Creek, a tributary of the Savannah River, in upper Chatham County. This stream was originally named for Walter Augustin or Augustine, who received a grant of land on it in 1735. In time people forgot this origin and began to refer to the waterway as St. Augustine, probably because of the resemblance of the name to the famous town in Florida. The shift began over a century ago, and the name has now apparently become confirmed as St. Augustine Creek even on official charts, despite the fact that the original designation was one of the earliest English geographic names of Georgia.

Other names switched through a lack of understanding of the tabs is Stocking Branch in Burke County, originally Stalkinghead; and Gray Coat Branch in Jefferson, initially Great Coat.

Another very unusual appellation in this group is Ty Ty Creek, a large stream in Worth, Tift, and Colquitt counties. There has been much argument about the origin of this word and its namesake, the town of Ty Ty in Tift, but there can be little doubt it stems from the pioneer expression tight-eye, applied to thickets of titi bushes which grow around the fringes of low, wet places on the Coastal Plain. The name seemingly was first used by early surveyors, because titi thickets were difficult to see through in making sightings along courses being surveyed.

A name that probably went through similar changes is found in Toto Creek, a tributary of the Chestatee River, in lower Dawson County. This word seems to be a corruption of Child Toter, the name of a prominent Cherokee who is known to have lived not far away on the Etowah River. He could easily have also had property on Toto Creek, and since Child Toter was sometimes simply called Toater it was easy for his name to be turned to Toto.[1]

Nearly all of the Indian names borrowed from tribes living here have been changed to some degree, and numbers of them substantially so. As will be seen shortly, shifting in this category is still going on. Most of the switched designations have long since become the established way of writing the words, thus Tallulah for Tarura, Cataula for Ketal, Muckalee for Amokali, Kinchafoonee for Kitchofuni, Withlacoochee for Wihlakuchi, and so on in great variety.

The reader no doubt knows we have a substantial body of placenames that are translations from Indian languages in use here, and especially from the Cherokee tongue. That idiom was difficult for white people, who usually only retained the most euphonious forms and translated the other retentions into easy English expressions like

Pine Log, Hothouse Creek, Cedartown, Spring Place, Turniptown, etc.[2] Expressions were also borrowed from the Creeks and translated: Big Potato Creek in Upson County, Black Creek in Bulloch, and Spring Creek, a large tributary of Flint River in southwest Georgia.

It should be noted that most of these changes from Indian words were made in the formative years. Once the translations were adopted the resulting nomenclature has mainly continued in use without further modification.

There are some placenames changing right under our eyes. A good example can be found in the designation Donegal that applies here and there to a number of little places across the state. It was seemingly adopted by Scotch-Irish or Irish people who lived in the communities. In Ireland the expression is pronounced "Do nay gaul," but here it can be heard as "Donnygal" and some wags are even calling it "Dinny gal."

In Talbot County there is a big stream known as Lazer Creek. The waterway has borne this label since Indian days, but more and more it is referred to as "Liza" or "Lizer" Creek. Perhaps in time it will become formalized under one of the latter versions.

In print, the Ohoopee River of southeast Georgia appears in that form, but in the area where the stream lies virtually everyone verbally refers to it as the "Hoopee." Indeed, the natives aroundabout can immediately spot an outsider when they hear him saying "Oh hoopee." It seems reasonable to think the word may some day become Hoopee.

The Ogeechee River is also frequently spoken without the *o*, or with an *o* barely audible. When the full name of the stream Great Ogeechee, however, is used one can plainly hear the *o*. In passing, it might be noted that Great is a classic example of the enduring quality of placenames. When the designation was first adopted at the beginning of Georgia, Great was the equivalent of our Big, as in Big Lotts Creek, Big Sandy, Big Road, etc. Because of their retention of the old form both the Great Ogeechee and the Great Satilla occupy a unique place in the list of Georgia's geographic nomenclature.

Some of the finest Indian names are undergoing present-day changes. For example, Okeewalkee Creek in Laurens and Wheeler counties is now appearing on some maps as Ochwalkee Creek. This latter version confuses people not familiar with the name, because they do not know how to sound the *och* element. Instead of pronouncing it correctly as "oak," they are prone to say "otch," or "ohtch," or "ohsh." These forms merely garble an otherwise pretty name.

Furthermore, in the area of the Okeewalkee there are people who shorten the name to "Walkee." This form not only mutilates an attractive word, it also reveals a lack of understanding of the meaning of the designation. Most likely it signifies a slash in our language, from *oki*, water, and *waki*, lying, referring to a wet, spongy place where shallow sheets of water stand at certain seasons. Thus, if people simply call the stream Walkee, they are omitting a key element in the name.

The present spelling of the Ochlocknee River in South Georgia poses the same sort of problem as found in Ochwalkee. In the original Hitchitee this name was Oki lagni, which sounded like "oaky locknee," and meant water yellow. Old people now living along the stream call it the Oaklocknee and thus very nearly retain the original sound. The power of the printed word is such, however, that if we keep on with the Ochlocknee, one of the oldest geographic names of Georgia may eventually become distorted through use of the *och* element on maps.

In southwest Georgia, the big west-bank tributary of the Flint called Ichawaynochaway is now commonly referred to as the "Nochaway." The full name signifies Buck-sleeping [place] Creek, from *echohonanwa*, male deer, plus *nochawa*, sleeping, with an implied locative connotation to signify place. Thus, when people merely use Nochaway in referring to the stream they miss the real meaning of the appellation. It would be better to translate the name into Buck Creek and let it stand at that. In fact, this was exactly the step taken by the first white people of what is now Baldwin County for the stream called Buck Creek, located on the east side of the Oconee, about four miles below Milledgeville. This waterway was another Ichawaynochaway in the Indian years.

If Nochaway eventually displaces Ichawaynochaway, as seems possible, the change may well pose some interesting arguments among future placename scholars. Two centuries from now there may be students who stoutly maintain the original name meant something like Camp Creek because the word *nochawa* signified sleeping and must have referred to a camping or sleeping place. And the truth would never be known unless some diligent researcher in musty records came up with the Ichaway, or Buck part, to confound the other scholars.

Cemochechobee Creek that enters the Chattahoochee on the upper side of Fort Gaines is still another name that is being shortened in the spoken form to Chobee Creek. The full name is Hitchitee and signifies Big Sand or Sandy Creek, from *samochi*, sand, plus the adjective *chobi*, big. When the stream is merely referred to as the Chobee, the users of the expression are plainly selecting the modifier and forgetting the substantive of the designation.[3]

One changing placename that apparently has already received official status is Sopes Creek, a tributary of the Chattahoochee in Cobb County. Now, admittedly this version of the name can be found in old records, but it is clearly a bumpkins' form that was once set down by people who could not spell. There are reliable documents to show the correct name of the stream was Soaps Creek and that it was so called after a Cherokee named Soap who once resided on the waterway. Furthermore, there is good reason to believe this Indian removed from our Cobb County to a stream in present north Cherokee County that even now is remembered as Soap or Soaps Creek.

An engaging phase of placename study which students usually watch for are antonymous designations, and expressions that run counter to the meanings and trends of a given body of names. Due to the nature of our changing placenames one will not find antonyms in that category, but there are appellations that were once changed and now have been or are being shifted back to their original forms. An interesting example can be found in the Pine Barren Road of western Chatham County. This version of that route is the correct designation but for years the old thoroughfare was also known by the pioneer label of Pine Bon Road. In recent years, however, road signs have been posted along the way under the wording Pine Barren and these markers have thus revived the original name.

The Bon of Pine Bon was a backwoodsy version of Barren, which was pronounced Barr'n, just as pioneer people also used "narr' " for narrow, "arr' " for arrow, "wheelbar' " for wheelbarrow, and so on. Since people of this region do not always sound the letter *r*, Barr'n was softened to "Bahn," and then to "Bon."

Another name that is being restored to its original version is Four Killer Creek in upper Fulton County. This stream was originally named after a Cherokee called Four Killer who lived at the head of the stream. Killer is an ancient Cherokee title that was awarded to a brave who had killed enemies, along with a numerical rating that indicated the number of kills on his record. Thus there were Indians named Two Killer, Four Killer, Six Killer, and so on. Due to our colloquial pronunciation of Four as "Fo'," people seemingly began to construe the word as meaning foe and turned the name of the stream into Foe Killer Creek. After considerable debate and some acrimony in recent years the expression is being switched back to its original and correct form of Four Killer.

And finally, of late there have been attempts to call back the Indian version of Flint River which was given up long ago by both the English and the Florida Spanish because they could not pronounce the first syllable of the name, which began with a voiceless ell, a surd letter that exists in neither English nor Spanish.[4] The first whites rendered the word as Thlonotisca, Clonoteeskaw, etc., but such versions fell short of capturing the true sound. Finally the people translated the word as Flint River and let it go at that until efforts began in fairly recent years to revive it as Thlonotisca or Thronoteeska. These forms are pleasing enough on their faces, but they do not correctly represent the appellation. Thronoteeska, perhaps the prettier of the two words, is most at fault since the original Indian word had neither a *th* nor an *r* sound. In fact the Creek Indians did not have an *r* in their language and experienced as much difficulty pronouncing that letter as we had with their vexatious voiceless ell.

—*Unpublished, from the Dr. John H. Goff Collection, Georgia Surveyor General Department, Atlanta.*

NOTES

1. ["Child Toter" suggests a folk etymology at a very early stage. What might the Cherokee term have been? *FLU.*]
2. [The process is usually known as folk etymology, based on misunderstanding of sound and sense rather than on "euphony," a subjective term not favored by linguists. *FLU.*]
3. [Read, *IJAL* 15 (1949): 129, confirms The Sandy Creek etymology, using Swanton as authority. *FLU.*]
4. [Though the sound is common in Welsh: Lloyd, Llewellyn, etc. *FLU.*]

Index

Index

Adams, Gen. David, 52
Adams Station, Lee Co., 120
Adel, Cook Co., 123, 447
Adsboro, Morgan Co., 119
Ahapioka, 42
Ahapioka Creek, Talbot and Taylor Cos., 42
Aiwassee: *See* Hiwassee
Alabaha Creek, Pierce Co., 235, 425
Alabama Road, 45, 145, 275
Alabama Roads, 393
Alachua Path, 297: *See also* Alachua Trail
Alachua Trail, 18, 19: *See also* Alachua Path
Alaga, Houston Co., Ala., 118
Alamo, Wheeler Co., 446
Alapaha, Berrien Co., 240
Alapaha River, 234, 235, 425
Alapahatalofa Town, 241
Alapahaw Town, 241
Alapahoochee River, Dooly Co., 234
Albany, Dougherty Co., 438
Aleck Island, Altamaha River, 295
Alecks Creek, Wayne Co., 293
Alleck, Captain, 293
Alligator Congress, 397
Altamaha River, 442
Amandaville, 390
Americus—Preston Road, Sumter Co., 36
Amicalola, 313
Amicalola Creek, Dawson Co., 313
Ammon's Old Ferry, Great Satilla River, 401
Angelica Creek, Sumter Co., 321
Annawaika, DeKalb Co., Ala., 215
Anneewakee Creek, Douglas Co., 214, 215
Apalachee River, 34
Apalachee Town, 32
Apatai: *See* Upatoi
Aragon, Polk Co., 446
Archibookta, 421
Archibookta Creek, Webster Co., 421

Arcola, Bulloch Co., 117
Ashbank, Putnam Co., 413
Assille: *See* Aucilla
Atlanta, 472
Attapulgus, 434
Attapulgus, Decatur Co., 22, 23, 24, 444
Auchumpkee Creek, 201
Aucilla, 31, 33
Aucilla River, Thomas Co., 31
Aupiogee, 42
Aupiogee Creek, 41
Auputtaue: *See* Upatoi
Ausmac, Decatur Co., 119
Aussilly: *See* Aucilla
Avera, Jefferson Co., 447

Bad Creek, Rabun Co., 46
Bad Prong Creek, Candler Co., 47
Baggs Creek, Lumpkin Co., 272
Bags Creek, Dawson Co., 273
Baldridge, 57
Baldridge Creek, Forsyth Co., 57
Ball Creek, Pickens Co., 57
Ball Creek Ford, Pickens Co., 57, 353
Ball Flat Community, Cherokee Co., Ala., 57
Ball Ground, 55
Ball Ground, Cherokee Co., 56
Ball Ground, Murray Co., 56
Ball Ground District, Cherokee Co., 57
Ball Ground District, Murray Co., 56
Ball Play, 55
Ball Play Creek, 56
Ball Play Creek, Etowah Co., Ala., 57
Ball Play Creek, Fannin Co., 56
Ball Play Creek, Lumpkin Co., 56
Ball Play Creek, Monroe Co., Tenn., 56
Ball Play Crossroads, Etowah Co., Ala., 57
Ball Ridge Creek, Forsyth Co., 57
Baunauclaughbauh, 397
Barber Creek, Long Co., 307
Barbour Island, McIntosh Co., 186

482 / Index

Barbour Island River, McIntosh Co., 186
Barefoot, Towns Co., 75
Barkcamp Community, Burke Co., 404
Barkcamp Creek, Burke Co., 6
Barkcamp Crossroads, Burke Co., 6
Barkcamp District, Burke Co., 6
Barkcamp District, Hall Co., 6, 7
Barnards Trail, Wayne Co., 305, 312
Barnes Trail, 37
Barren Hills, Walker and Whitfield Cos., 414
Barrettsville, Dawson Co., 105, 274
Bartow County, 472
Barwick, Brooks and Thomas Cos., 446
Bay Branch, Appling Co., 306
Bear Branch, 322
Beards Bluff, Long Co., 302, 303, 304
Beards Bluff Fort, Long Co., 304
Beards Creek, Long Co., 303, 308
Bearfoot, Towns Co., 75
Bear Skull, 171
Beaver Creek, Baldwin Co., 183
Beaver Creek, Dooly and Macon Cos., 339
Beaverdam Creek, 101
Beaverdam Creek, Dooly and Macon Cos., 339
Beaverdam Creek, Hancock Co., 373
Beaverdam Creek, Sumter Co., 332
Beaver Ruin, Lamar Co., 375
Beaver Ruin, Upson Co., 376
Beaver Ruin Creek, Gwinnett Co., 375
Beaver Ruin Creek, Lamar Co., 375
Beech Creek, Crawford Co., 426
Bel Air, Richmond Co., 87
Bell Creek, Towns Co., 63
Berkley, Madison Co., 445
Bidawee, McDuffie Co., 125
Big Attapulgee Creek: *See* Big Attapulgus Creek
Big Attapulgus Creek, Decatur Co., 21
Big Bend, Charlton Co., 139
Big Creek, Early Co., 181
Big Creek, Fulton Co., 94
Big Hell Sluice, Savannah River, 402
Big Savannah, Dawson Co., 66, 268, 273, 286
Big Scare Corn Creek, Pickens Co., 413
Big Shoals Road, 201
Big Survey: route of, 20, 110, 310
Big Swamp Creek, Marion Co., 374
Blackankle, Chatham Co., 415
Blackankle, Fannin Co., 415
Blackankle, Upson Co., 415
Black Creek, Bulloch Co., 290

Blaine, 353
Blastigam Creek, Dawson Co., 273
Bloodtown, 355
Bloody Branch, Charlton Co., 133
Bloody Creek, Franklin Co., 134
Blue John Creek, Troup Co., 410
Boggy Lick, Oglethorpe Co., 396
Bolivar, Bartow Co., 104, 439
Bon Air, Richmond Co., 87
Bonds Trail, 36, 37
Bonner, Dr. James C., 184
Bonny Clabber Bluff, Oconee River, 397, 411
Bonny Clabber Road, Laurens Co., 397
Booger Hollow, 351
Booths Ferry, Ocmulgee River, 201
Booths Road, 201
Bovard, Rabun Co., 74, 179
Braganza, Ware Co., 443
Brasstown, 59
Bread Town, Dawson Co., 314
Breastworks Branch, Early Co., 221, 222
Bremen, Haralson Co., 437
Brewton, Laurens Co., 413
Briar Patch, Bulloch Co., 413
Brushy Creek, 29
Buck Creek, 101
Buck Creek, Baldwin Co., 183
Buck Creek, Macon Co., 432, 433
Buck Creek, Marion Co., 374
Buckeye Creek, Laurens Co., 404
Buckhead, 171
Buena Vista, Marion Co., 439
Buffalo, Chambers Co., Ala., 386
Buffalo Church, Montgomery Co., 384
Buffalo Creek, Brantley Co., 383
Buffalo Creek, Carroll Co., 383
Buffalo Creek, Hancock and Washington Cos., 383
Buffalo Creek, Jackson Co., 383
Buffalo Creek, McIntosh Co., 382
Buffalo Creek, Oglethorpe Co., 383
Buffalo Ford, Satilla River, 397
Buffalo Lick, Great, 385
Buffalo Pond, Washington Co., 383
Buffalo Reaches, 383
Buffalo River, Wayne and Glynn Cos., 382
Buffalo Swamp, McIntosh Co., 382
Buffalo Swamp, Wayne and Brantley Cos., 383
Buffalo Wallow, Chambers Co., Ala., 387
Bump Head Road, 389
Burnt Fort, Charlton Co., 133
Buttermilk Bluff, Camden Co., 410

Buttermilk Bottoms, Fulton Co., 410
Buttermilk Creek, Cobb and Douglas Cos., 410
Buttermilk Shoals, Ocmulgee River, 410
Buttermilk Sound, Altamaha River, 410
Buzzard Flopper Creek, 397
Buzzard Flopper Creek, Cherokee Co., 160
Buzzard Mountain, 77
Buzzard Roost Ford, Flint River, 204
Buzzard Roost Island, Chattahoochee River, location of, 53, 286
Buzzard Roost Town, Taylor Co., 205
Buzzard Roost Trail, 203

Cahelee Creek, Early Co., 181: *See also* Cohelee Creek
Cahellahatchee Creek, Fla., 182
Cairo, Grady Co., 438
Calhouns Ferry, Flint River, 203
Caney Creek, 46
Caney Creek, Fulton Co., 94
Canoochee, 48
Canouchee Path, 110
Canoy, Lee Co.: *See* Kennard, Jack
Canton, Cherokee Co., 443
Capitol Road, 110
Captolo, Screven Co., 124
Carmel Missionary Station, 353
Carter, Farrish, 222
Carters Quarters, Murray Co., 222
Cartersville, Bartow Co., 222
Cass County, 472
Cataula, Harris Co., 175
Cataula District, Harris Co., 175
Cat Creek, 29
Cates Old Ford, Oconee River, Tenn., 356
Catoosa, 147
Catoosa County, 467
Catoosa Springs, Catoosa Co., 147
Catoosa Springs Branch, Catoosa Co., 147
Cedar Creek, Fulton Co., 94
Cement, 178
Cemochechobee Creek, 433, 475
Cemochechobee Creek, Clay Co., 475
Centralhatchee, Heard Co., 51, 122
Champion Creek, Washington Co., 198
Charlton County, 442
Chatham County, 438
Chattahoochee, 337
Chattahoochee Old Town, 337, 339
Chattahoochee River, 442
Chattooga, 59

Chattooga Church Crossroads, Walker Co., 58
Chattooga Cliffs, Jackson Co., N.C., 60
Chattooga County, 58, 441
Chattooga Ridge, S.C., 60
Chattooga Ridge, Jackson Co., N.C., 60, 61
Chattooga River, 441
Chattooga River, Jackson Co., N.C. and northeastern Ga., 58
Chattooga River, Walker Co., Ga. and Cherokee Co., Ala., 58
Chattooga Town, 58, 59
Chattooga Town, Tenn., 61
Chattoogaville, Chattooga Co., 58
Chatuge Reservoir, 58, 440
Chaukeethlucco, Ocmulgee River, 206
Chaukethlucco Town, 336
Cheatum, 391
Chechero Creek, Rabun Co., 179
Chechero District, Rabun Co., 74
Chehaw Creek, Putnam Co., 199
Chehaw Path, 199
Chekilli, 95
Chelsea, Chattooga Co., 61
Chemolly Creek, Crawford Co., 426
Chenchat, Walker Co., 117
Cherokee Killer, 95
Cherokee Upper Trading Path, 390
Chicherohe Town, Rabun Co., 74
Chickamauga Creek, 441
Chickasawhatchee Creek, Dougherty Co., 231
Chickasawhatchee Creek, Terrell Co., 419
Chickasaw Killer, 94
Chickasaw Path, 198, 253, 325
Child Toters Creek, Dawson Co., 271
Chissehulcuh Creek, 174
Chokeeliga Creek, Lee Co., 423
Chota Town, Tenn., 357
Christmas Branch, Stewart Co., 229
Christmas Bay, Echols Co., 229
Chusethlocco Creek, 170
Cliponreka, Bulloch Co., 124
Clipper Crossroads, 353
Clopine, Peach Co., 124
Clyo, Effingham Co., 438
Cocklebur Road, 389
Coffee Line, 287, 448
Cohelee Creek, Early Co., 429: *See also* Cahelee Creek
Coinston, 354
Coley Station, 4
Coloparchee Creek, Monroe and Bibb Cos., 425

Commerce, 107, 472
Conasauga River, 441
Concord, 447
Concord Crossroads, Sumter Co., 36
Conesena Creek, Bartow Co., 451
Connochee: See Canoochee
Cooccohapofe, 342
Cooccohapofe Town, 342
Coosawattee Old Town, 354
Cordele, Crisp Co., 443
Cork, Butts Co., 472
Cotton River, Henry Co., 166
Coweta Falls Road, 203
Cowford, Ohoopee River, 283
Cow Head, 171
Cow Hell Swamp, Laurens Co., 404
Cowpen Creek, Washington Co., 291, 292
Cox, McIntosh Co., 189
Crackers Neck, Greene Co., 411
Crane Eater Creek, Gordon Co., 455
Cranes Old Ford, 74
Creek Confederation, 416
Crittingtons Creek, Rabun Co., 180
Crooked Wood Creek, Sumter Co., 466
Crossville Road, Fulton Co., 145
Culpepper Creek, Crawford Co., 265, 374
Cumberland Island, 332
Cusseta Town, 11, 154, 206
Cut Cane, 59
Cuttingbone Creek, Rabun Co., 179, 180
Cyclone, Screven Co., 469
Cyclone District, Screven Co., 470
Cyclonetta, Tift Co., 470

Dacula, Gwinnett Co., 445
Daniels Stage Stop, 353
Dark Corner Road, 389
Dark Entry Road, Camden Co., 5
Davenport's Mill Creek, Webster Co., 372
Dawnville, 357
Deep Creek, Jenkins Co., 309
DeKalb County, 443
Deli Laing-Kat, Decatur Co., 178
Derisoes Creek, Washington Co., 198
Devils Bay, Clinch Co., 400
Devils Branch, Effingham Co., 400
Devils Branch, Rabun Co., 404
Devils Branch, Wilkinson Co., 400
Devils Cove, Walker Co., 47, 404
Devils Den, Stephens Co., 402
Devils Den Creek, Stephens Co., 402
Devils Den Springs, Decatur Co., 402
Devils Drag Out, Great Satilla River, 401, 402

Devils Elbow, 401
Devils Elbow, Oconee River, 401
Devils Elbow, St. Marys River, 401
Devils Elbow, Savannah River, 401
Devils Half Acre, Putnam Co., 405
Devils Hop, Skip, and Jump, Greene Co., 402
Devils Hopper, Brooks and Thomas Cos., 402
Devils Pond, Oglethorpe Co., 404
Devils Trash Pile, Oconee River, 401
Dillard-Keener Gap Highway, 77
Dirtseller, 59
Dismal Cove, Towns and Rabun Cos., 414
Dismal Gap, Towns and Rabun Cos., 414
Dismal Knob, Towns and Rabun Cos., 414
Dividings, Rabun Co., 73
Doctors Creek, Long Co., 297
Doctortown, Wayne Co., 296
Dodo, Laurens Co., 413
Dog Fennell, Evans Co., 413
Donegal, 474
Doolittle Creek, DeKalb Co., 372
Dougherty, Cornelius, 65
Dougherty, Dawson Co., 66, 269, 272
Dougherty County, 439
Downing, James, 94
Downing, William, 94
Downing Branch, Cherokee Co., 142
Downing Ferry, Etowah River, 275
Downing Ferry Road, 274
Drowning Bear Creek, Whitfield Co., 456
Dry Creek, 46
Dry Creek, Early Co., 221
Dublin, Butts Co., 472
Dublin Militia District, Butts Co., 472
Dukes Creek, White Co., 273

Eagle Grove, 397
Eastahatchee Creek, Decatur Co., 220
Eastanola River: See Oostanaula River
Eastanollee, 49
Eastanollee Creek, Stephens and Franklin Cos., 49
Eastertoy Town, 279
Echeconnee, 43, 44
Echeconnee Creek, 37, 38, 426
Echo Rock Creek, 102
Ecunhutkenene, 202
Edwards Station—Bodsford Road, Lee Co., 36
Effingham County, 445
Egg and Butter Road, 389

Egypt, Effingham Co., 115
Egypt Hollow, Dade Co., 115
Elko, Houston Co., 117
Ellen N, Fulton Co., 118
Ellick, Captain, 293
Estatoah Creek, Rabun Co., 279
Estatoah Falls Creek, Rabun Co., 279
Estatoe Town, 279
Estelle, Walker Co., 47
Etowah River, 64, 398
Evergreen Church Crossroads, Bleckley Co., 4

Falling Creek, 96
Fancy Bluff, Glynn Co., 131
Fancy Bluff Creek, Glynn Co., 131
Fancy Hall, Bryan Co., 131
Fancy Hill, Murray Co., 131
Fashion, Murray Co., 132
Federal Crossing, 349
Federal Road, Cherokee, 102, 251, 280, 349, 351, 360
Federal Road, Creek, 393
Federal School, Pickens Co., 353
Fenholoway River, Taylor Co., Fla., 21
Fenn, Zachariah, 253
Fenns Bridge, Ogeechee River, 253
FDR, Seminole Co., 120
Ficklins Mill, 202
Fields Bridge, Etowah River, 275
Fifteen Mile Creek, Appling Co., 306
Finhalloway Creek: *See* Penholoway Creek
First Black Creek, 290
Fishing Creek, Jones and Baldwin Cos., 191
Fishing Creek Valley, 199
Five Killer, 93
Five Mile Creek, Lee Co., 232, 322
Five Mile Creek, Wayne and Appling Cos., 306
Five Notch Trail, 396
Five Points, Taylor Co., 202
Flat Creek, Berrien Co., 97
Flat Creek, Clay Co., 96
Flat Creek, Dawson Co., 97
Flat Creek, Emanuel Co., 97
Flat Creek, Fannin Co., 96
Flat Creek, Fayette Co., 96
Flat Creek, Gilmer Co., 96
Flat Creek, Hall Co., 97
Flat Creek, Houston Co., 97
Flat Creek, Meriwether—Troup Cos., 97
Flat Creek, Miller Co., 96
Flat Creek, Montgomery Co., 97
Flat Creek, Rabun Co., 97

Flat Creek, Spalding Co., 96
Flat Creek, Twiggs Co., 97
Flat Creek, Walton Co., 96
Flat Creek, White Co., 97
Flat Creeks, 97
Flat Rock, 414
Flat Shoals, Pike Co., 97, 192
Flat Shoals Creek, 97
Flat Shoals Creeks, 97
Flexatile, Bartow Co., 123
Flint Hill, Floyd Co., 413
Flint River, 477
Fodder Creek, Towns Co., 285
Folsom, Capt. Benjamin, 289
Folsoms Creek, Hancock Co., 288
Fort Barrington, 303
Fort Barrow, Tenn., 157
Fort Buffington, Cherokee Co., 157, 273
Fort Defence, 297
Fort Fidius, Baldwin Co., 191
Fort James, 305
Fort James Bluff, 305
Fort Loudon, Tenn., 356
Fort Scott, 222
Fort Scott Road, 222
Fort Wilkinson, Baldwin Co., 191, 305
Four Killer Creek, Fulton Co., 93, 452
Four Mile Church, Pickens Co., 353
Four Mile Creek, Forsyth Co., 102
Fowlstown, Decatur Co., 21, 25
Fox Creek, Lee Co., 322
Fredonia, 116, 124
Free Hope Church Crossroads, 357
Frog Pond, Emanuel Co., 413
Frogtown Ford, Etowah River, 352
Fruitland, 178
Fulsams Creek, Hancock Co., 288

Gab Creek, Dawson Co., 408
Gagg, Thomas, 252
Galphinton, Jefferson Co., 197, 210
Gardi, Wayne Co., 155, 439
Garrison Road, 206
Georgetown, Bryan Co., 471
Georgetown, Glascock Co., 471
Georgetown, Quitman Co., 471
Georgia Road, 357
Ghost Hole Ford, Charlton Co., 134
Gloster, Gwinnett Co., 445
Goat Town, Washington Co., 128
Goddards Old Ford, Chattahoochee River, 102
Gold Diggers Road, 389, 394
Golden Grove, 2

486 / Index

Golden Grove Bend and Bar, Toombs Co., 1, 3
Golden Grove Creek, Oglethorpe Co., 1
Golden Hill District, Banks Co., 2
Gopher Town, Seminole Co., 128
Go' Town, Seminole Co., 128
Grab All, 391
Grab All Road, Lincoln Co., 398
Grand Bay Creek, Dooly Co., 234
Gratis Road, Walton Co., 398
Gray Coat Branch, Jefferson Co., 16, 473
Grays Ferry, Flint River, 204
Grays Ferry Road, Taylor Co., 202
Great Coat Branch, Jefferson Co., 16, 473
Grove, Banks Co., 2
Grove Creek, Banks Co., 2
Grove Creek, Oglethorpe Co., 1
Grovetown, Richmond Co., 87
Gualdaquini, 162
Guard Jam Bluff, Laurens Co., 156
Guinekelokee, 60
Guinekelokee River, Rabun Co., 60
Gun Merchant, 101

Habersham County, 446
Hachasofkee, 40
Hachasofkee Creek, Heard and Troup Cos., 41
Hachasofkee Creek, Talbot and Taylor Cos., 40, 42
Haides, Screven Co., 405
Halloca Creek, Chattahoochee Co., 153, 418
Hammock Grove, Crawford Co., 201
Hanging Maw, 101
Hannahatchee Creek, Stewart Co., 229
Happy Hollow, McDuffie Co., 125
Hard Bargain, 391
Hard Cash, 391
Hard Fortune Creek, McDuffie Co., 409
Hard Labor Creek, Walton and Morgan Cos., 413
Hard Money, Webster Co., 391, 472
Hard Money Road, 391
Hardscrabble, Fulton Co., 407, 409
Hardscrabble Road, Fulton Co., 409
Hardup, Baker Co., 409
Hardwick, Bryan Co., 471
Harmony Grove, 107, 472
Harnages Stage Stop, 353
Harnageville: *See* Harnages Stage Stop
Harpers Lake, McIntosh Co., 189
Harrel Mill Creek, Webster Co., 421
Harris Island, Flint River, 203
Hatchasaufka Creek: *See* Hachasofkee Cr.

Hatcheethlucco, 422
Hatcheethlucco Creek, Muscogee Co., 11, 422
Hat Creek, 13
Haynes Creek, Gwinnett and Rockdale Cos., 256
Heia Wassea: *See* Hiwassee
Heiferhorn Creek, Muscogee Co., 171
Hell Creek, Washington Co., 405
Hell Gap, Chattahoochee River, 403
Hell Gate, Bryan Co., 402
Hell Gate Shoals, Flint River, 402
Hell Hole Branch, Rabun Co., 404
Hells Gate, Great Satilla River, 402
Hell's Half Acre, Burke Co., 47, 404
Hells Shoals, Altamaha River, 402
Hemptown Creek, Fannin Co., 56
Hendricks Creek, 321
Hiawassee, 67
Hiawassee, Towns Co., 67
Hickory Grove Crossroads, Crawford Co., 202
Hickory Log Town, Cherokee Co., 271
Hightower Creek, Towns Co., 64, 65
Hightower Crossroads, Forsyth Co., 64, 352
Hightower District, Lumpkin Co., 64
Hightower River, 64
Hightower Trail, 64, 67, 130, 150, 254, 397
Highwassee: *See* Hiwassee
Hiwassee, 67, 68, 69
Hiwassee Creek, Rabun Co., 70
Hiwassee Gap, Rabun and Towns Cos., 70
Hiwassee River, Towns Co., 67
Hiwassee Town, N.C., 68
Hiwassee Town, Polk Co., Tenn., 68
Hiwassee Trail, 75, 78
Hodchodkee Creek, Stewart and Quitman Cos., 428
Hog Crawl, Glynn Co., 340
Hog Crawl Creek, Dooly and Macon Cos., 339
Hoggs Crawl Bluff, Effingham Co., 340
Hog Heaven Branch, 397
Hog Heaven Branch, Worth Co., 405
Hog Jaw, 171
Holly Creek, Murray Co., 137
Hominy Creek, Carroll Co., 41
Hootens Ferry, Flint River, 204
Hootenville, 205
Hootenville District, 205
Hopeulikit, Bulloch Co., 125
Hopewell, Fulton Co., 407

Hopewell Crossroads, Crawford Co., 201
Hopewell Road, Crawford Co., 201
Horse Heaven Hills, Washington State, 405
Horse Shoe Bend, Tallapoosa Co., Ala., 52
Hotalihuyana, 465
House Creek, Harris Co., 177
Houston County, 438
Howard Mountain, 77
Hunger and Hardship Creek, Laurens Co., 408
Hungry Creek, Carroll Co., 408
Hungry Hill, Bryan Co., 408
Hungry Valley, Whitfield Co., 408
Hurricane, 467
Hurricane Creek, Catoosa Co., 148, 467
Hywassee: *See* Hiwassee

Iago's Town, Bulloch Co., 296
Ichabuckler Creek, Stewart Co., 428
Ichawaynochaway Creek, 433, 475
Ichiconna Creek: *See* Echeconnee Creek
Ichoconno Creek: *See* Echeconnee Creek
Imlac, Meriwether Co., 124
Immokalee, Collier Co., Fla., 323
Inaha, 470
Indian Bluff, Jenkins Co., 109
Indian Fort, Taylor Co., 344
Indian Toms Path, 207
Intachcoochee Creek, Crawford Co., 374
Intackculgau Town, 374
Intrenchment Creek, Fulton and DeKalb Cos., 216, 217
Iric Creek, Bulloch Co., 290
Iron Hill, Baldwin Co., 129
Iron Hill, Bartow Co., 129
Iron Hill, McDuffie Co., 129
Islands Ford, Flint River, 201, 202
Itatchee Uscaw Town, 170
Itchocunnau Creek: *See* Echeconnee Creek
Ittoopunnauulgau, 465
Iwassee: *See* Hiwassee

Jackson, General Andrew, 52, 241
Jacksonboro, Screven Co., 471
Jacksons Mill Shoals, Heard Co., 433
Jacksons Trail, 223
Jasper County, 472
Jeffersonton, Camden Co., 5
Jekyll Island, Glynn Co., 161, 162
Jenkins Branch, Putnam Co., 199
Jerry Branch, Rabun Co., 77
Jobleys Creek, Burke Co., 325

Joes Creek, Warren and Glascock Cos., 373
Joiner Creek, Dodge Co., 408
Jolly, Pike Co., 131, 132
Jones Cowpen Creek, Washington Co., 291
Jug Tavern, 107, 472

Katalee, 44
Katalee Creek, Harris Co., 44
Keener Gap, 77
Kennard, Jack, 424
Kennards Settlement, Lee Co., 36
Ketalee, Harris Co., 175
Kinchafoonee, 121
Kinchafoonee County, 472
Kinchafoonee Creek, Lee Co., 36
Kings Road, 392
Kiokee Creek, Columbia Co., 424
Kiokee Creek, Dougherty Co., 231
Kissingbower Road, Richmond Co., 399

Laingkat, Decatur Co., 178
Lake Shangri-La, Clayton Co., 125
Lamars Trail, 197
Larkins Path, 209
Latchokowae Path: *See* Alachua Trail
Laughing Gal, Cherokee Co., 454
Laughing Gal Road, Cherokee Co., 399
Lazer Creek, Harris and Talbot Cos., 107
Level Creek, 96
Lewis Creek, McIntosh Co., 189
Lewis Lagoon, McIntosh Co., 189
Lickskillett, Fulton Co., 409
Lickskillett District, Cherokee Co., 409
Lickskillett District, Schley Co., 409
Lick Skillett Road, 398
Lime Spring Pond Creek, Webster Co., 434
Line Creek, Sumter Co., 446
Linger Longer Bridge, Richland Creek, 399
Linger Longer Road, Greene Co., 399
Little Alapaha River, Echols Co., 235
Little Amicalola Creek, Dawson Co., 313
Little Attapulgee Creek: *See* Little Attapulgus Creek
Little Attapulgus Creek, Decatur Co., 21
Little Bettys Creek, Rabun Co., 278
Little Big Creek, 28
Little Buffalo Swamp, Glynn Co., 383
Little Carpenter, 101
Little Hell, Altamaha River, 403
Little Hell Landing, Savannah River, 403
Little Hell Point, Savannah River, 403

488 / Index

Little Hell Sluice, Savannah River, 402
Little Haynes Creek, Walton Co., 256
Little Intrenchment Creek, Hall Co., 216, 217
Little Muckalee Creek, Sumter Co., 321
Little Muckaloochee Creek, 321
Little Ogeechee River, Hancock and Washington Cos., 292
Little Ogeechee River, Effingham Co., 292
Little Patsiliga Creek, Talbot and Taylor Cos., 372
Little Persimmon Creek, Rabun Co., 404
Little Pine Log Creek, Bartow Co., 250
Little Pine Log Creek, Gordon Co., 250
Little Pine Log Mountain, Cherokee Co., 249
Little Ridge Creek, Forsyth Co., 57
Little River, Cherokee Co., 29
Little River, Dooly Co., 234
Little River, Turner Co., 29
Little Scare Corn Creek, Pickens Co., 413
Little Tennessee River, 77
Little Tobesofkee Creek, 38
Little Tobesofkee Creek, Monroe Co., 38
Little Towaliga Creek, Lamar Co., 90
Little Wassaw Island, Chatham Co., 331
Lizella, Bibb Co., 447
Lizer Creek, Harris and Talbot Cos., 107
Locust Stake Road, 74, 79, 390
Long Branch, Webster Co., 372
Long Bullet Creek, Towns Co., 453
Longstreet, Bleckley Co., 4
Longstreet, Elbert Co., 4
Longstreet Road, Bleckley Co., 396
Longstreet Road, Elbert Co., 396
Long Swamp Creek, Pickens Co., 105, 196
Long Swamp Town, Pickens Co., 105, 106
Lordamercy Cove, Union and White Cos., 47
Lost Branch, Fannin Co., 159
Lost Creek, Mitchell and Thomas Cos., 159
Lost Gordonia, 190
Lost Mountain, Cobb Co., 159
Lost Town Creek, Cherokee Co., 158
Louisville, Jefferson Co., 438
Louisville—Savannah Road, 110, 111
Lower Black Creek, 290
Lower Cherokee towns on the Tennessee River, 451
Lower Creek Trading Path, 183, 195
Lower Sansaville Bluff, 298

Lower Trading Path, 37
Lowes, Harris Co., 45
Ludowici, Long Co., 439
Lumber City, 178
Luxomni, Gwinnett Co., 445

McConnells Crossroads, Cherokee Co., 352
MacFishery Landing, Wayne Co., 19
Machen, Jasper Co., 447
McIntosh Trail, 165
McMaths Mill Branch, Sumter Co., 321
McNair, David, 355
Macon—Darien Stage Road, 304
Mad Bear, 101
Magruder, Burke Co., 47, 404
Mangy Branch, McDuffie Co., 413
Manor, Ware Co., 443
Marbury Creek, Barrow Co., 254
Mars Hill Church, Oconee Co., 26
Mars Hill Church, School, and Crossroads, Dooly Co., 26
Mars Hill Church and Cemetery, Calhoun Co., 26
Mars Hill Church and Crossroads, Forsyth Co., 26
Mars Hill Church and Road Fork, Cobb Co., 26
Mars Hill District, Oconee Co., 26
Mars Hill Factory, Oconee Co., 26
Marthasville, 472
Mathews Creek, Crawford Co., 265
Mauk, Taylor Co., 446
Mecky Pike, Tenn., 356
Merry Hill Spring Branch, 131
Mica, Cherokee Co., 353
Miccosukee Path, 253
Midday Creek, 102
Middle Cherokee Trading Path, 102
Middle Ground Road, 392
Midville—Birdsville Road, Burke Co., 6
Milksick Cove, N.C., 246
Milksick Cove, Rabun Co., 246
Milksick Cove, Towns Co., 246
Milksick Knob, Macon and Clay Cos., N.C., 246
Mill Creek, Dawson Co., 270
Mill Creek, Russell Co., Ala., 424
Mill Creek, Sumter Co., 321
Milledgeville—Hawkinsville Road, 4
Miller Creek, Heard Co., 51
Millers Branch, Laurens Co., 127
Mobleys Pond, Screven Co., 447
Montevideo, Elbert and Hart Cos., 443
Montpelier, Monroe Co., 200

Morris Hill Church, Decatur Co., 27
Mountain Creek, Harris Co., 177
Mount Venture, 306, 307
Mount Yonah, 99
Muckafoonee Creek, Dougherty Co., 121, 322
Muckalee, 121
Muckalee Creek, Marion and Dougherty Cos., 319
Muckaloochee Creek, Lee Co., 320, 432
Muckaloochee Creek, Sumter Co., 321
Mud Creek, Rabun Co., 279
Mulberry Creek, Harris Co., 44, 175
Mulberry Grove, Harris Co., 44, 175
Mule Creek, 29
Mule Jaw, 171
Mussella, Crawford Co., 447

Naked Creek, Walton Co., 413
Nancys Creek, Bartow Co., 454
Nancys Creek, Fulton Co., 454
Nancy Town, Habersham Co., 454
Nancytown Creek, Habersham Co., 454
Needy Creek, Rabun Co., 413
Newquacaw: *See* New-Yau-Cau
New-Yau-Cau, 52
New Yaucau Town, Heard Co., 436
New-Yau-Cau Town, Tallapoosa Co., Ala., 50, 52
New Yauger: *See* New-Yau-Cau
New York: *See* New-Yau-Cau
Neyami, Lee Co., 36, 119, 120
Nickajack Creek, Cobb Co., 286
Niles Ferry, Little Tennessee River, 356
Niuyaka: *See* New-Yau-Cau
No Business Creek, Gwinnett and DeKalb Cos., 149, 414
No Business Creek, Morgan Co., Ala., 150
No Man's Friend Pond, Cook Co., 47
Nonaburg, Tenn., 356
Noonday, 59
Noonday Creek, 102
Norwich, Taylor Co., 446
Noses Creek, Bartow Co., 457
Noses Creek, Cobb Co., 457
Nowhere Road, 389
Nuoquaco: *See* New-Yau-Cau

Oak Cane Branch, Jenkins Co., 9
Oakchuncoolgau, 227
Oakchuncoolgau Creek, Jones and Bibb Cos., 226
Oakfuskee Creek, Pike Co., 192, 431

Oakfuskee Path, 92, 192
Oakfuskee Town, 193
Oakfuskee Trail, 92, 192
Oakland Road, 399
Obaldaquini, 162
Ocains Branch, Jenkins Co., 9
Ocfuskeenene Town, 338
Ochee Finnau, 200
Ocheese Towns, Ocmulgee River, 196
Ochillee Creek, Marion Co., 152
Ochlawilla, Brooks Co., 122
Ochlocknee River, 176, 475
Ochwalkee Creek, Laurens and Wheeler Cos., 474
Ocilla: *See* Aucilla
Ocmulgee Old Town, 228
Ocmulgee River, 432
Oconee Old Town, 183
Oconee River, 183
Ocowocuhhatche Creek, Russell Co., Ala., 424
Odessa, Wayne Co., 19
Ogeechee Creek, Screven Co., 292
Ogeechee River, 474
Ogeechee Trail, 110
Oglethorpe, James, 380
Oglethorpe Bluff, Altamaha River, 306
Ohoopee, 121
Ohoopee River, Johnson and Emanuel Cos., 474
Okauhutkee Creek, Marion and Taylor Cos., 419
Okeewalkee Creek, Laurens and Wheeler Cos., 474
Okefenokee, 140, 431, 440
Okefenokee Swamp, 140, 440
Old Chattanooga Ford, Conasauga River, 357
Old Chattanoogee Road, 357
Old Colony Road, 395
Old Doc Slough, Wayne Co., 297
Old Fort, Tenn., 157
Old Fortification, Wilcox Co., 223, 224
Old Hell Bight, Altamaha River, 403, 404
Old Horse Path, 195
Old House Creek, Harris Co., 177
Old Indian Corner, Jenkins Co., 309
Old Maryville Road, Tenn., 356
Old River Trail, 253
Old Shell Road, 389
Old Stave Road, 389
Old Toms Path, 207
Old Town, Jefferson Co., 197
One Killer, 93

490 / Index

Ooseoochee, 35
Oostanaula, 49
Oostanaula River, 49
Opelika, Ala., 423
Opilthlucco Creek, Macon Co., 423
Oredell, Polk Co., 123
Oseilla: See Aucilla
Osiligee Creek, Ala., 441
Osilla: See Aucilla
Osketochee Creek, Dougherty Co., 230
Ospo, 162
Ossabaw Island, Chatham Co., 329, 330
Ossahatchie, 45
Ossahatchie, Harris Co., 45
Oswitchee Town, 33, 35
Oswitchee Trail, 328
Oustanalee River: See Oostanaula River
Overflow Creek, Rabun Co., 60
Owassa: See Hiwassee
Owens Creek, Schley Co., 372
Owens Old Ferry, Camden Co., 5
Owl Rock, 397

Padjeeligau Town, 341
Pallachucola, S.C., 442
Palmers Creek, Dawson Co., 271
Panhandle, Clayton Co., 139
Panhandle, Taylor Co., 139
Panhandle, Warren Co., 139
Panola, 166
Panola, DeKalb Co., 165, 436
Panola Road, DeKalb Co., 165
Panola Shoals, DeKalb Co., 165, 166
Paradox Church Crossroads, Sumter Co., 36
Paramore Hill, Jenkins Co., 109, 110
Parkers Mill Creek, Sumter Co., 321
Pass Over, Rabun Co., 77
Pataula Creek, 98
Path Killer, 94
Patsiliga Creek, 202
Pavo, Thomas Co., 446
Pay Up, 391
Peabottom Cove, Union Co., 62
Peachtree Road, 392
Pea Ridge, Marion Co., 61
Pea River, Ala., 61
Pears Creek, Murray Co., 247
Peavine Creek, Walker and Catoosa Cos., 61, 62
Peavine Ridge, Walker and Catoosa Cos., 62
Pebble Hill, Ware Co., 413
Pecan City, 178
Penholoway, 19

Penholoway Creek, Wayne Co., 17
Penhoopee, Emanuel Co., 121
Pennahatchee, 20, 99
Pennahatchee Creek, Dooly Co., 20, 99, 122
Perry, Lydia, 248
Perry, Sol, 247
Perry, Spaniard: See Sol Perry
Perry Creek, Murray Co., 247
Persico, Meriwether Co., 124
Petersburg, Elbert Co., 390
Petersburg Road, 80, 390
Phaenehalloway Creek: See Penholoway Creek
Philema, 322
Philema, Lee Co., 322, 440
Philema Creek, Sumter Co., 322, 372
Phinhotoway Creek: See Penholoway Creek
Pinch Gut Creek, Dodge Co., 408
Pindertown, Lee Co., 36
Pine Barren Road, Chatham Co., 476
Pine Barrens, 82, 84, 86, 88
Pine Bon Road, Chatham Co., 476
Pine Bowery, 87
Pine Grove Church Crossroads, Catoosa Co., 358
Pine Head, 87
Pine Level, 46
Pine Log, 251
Pine Log, Bartow Co., 250
Pine Log, Charlton Co., 253
Pine Log, Screven Co., 253
Pine Log, Washington Co., 253
Pine Log Bridge, Rockdale Co., 253
Pine Log Creek, Cherokee Co., 250
Pine Log Creek, Union Co., 252
Pine Log Mountain, Cherokee and Bartow Cos., 158, 249
Pine Log Path, 254
Pine Log Town, Bartow Co., 250, 251
Pine Rest, 87
Pine Retreat, 87
Pine Ridge, 87, 101
Pine Creek, Heard Co., 51, 436
Plains, Sumter Co., 35
Plains of Dura, Sumter Co., 35
Plank Road, 396
Plumorchard Creek, Rabun Co., 70
Po' Biddy Crossroads, Talbot Co., 104, 114, 415
Pocataligo, Beaufort Co., S.C., 317
Pocataligo, Madison Co., 316, 317
Pocket Road, 389
Pole Boat, 156

Pole Branch, Aiken Co., S.C., 369
Pole Bridge Creek, DeKalb Co., 367
Poor Joe Branch, Sumter Co., 411
Poor Robin, 327
Poor Robin Bluff, Screven Co., 327
Poor Robin Ferry, Ocmulgee River, 328
Poor Robin Lake, Screven Co., 327
Poor Robin Lake, Wilcox Co., 327
Poor Robin Landing, Screven Co., 327
Poor Robin Landing, Wilcox Co., 327
Poor Robin Lower Point, Screven Co., 327
Poor Robin Spring, Wilcox Co., 327
Poor Robin Upper Point, S.C., 327
Popes Ferry, Ocmulgee River, 200
Popes Road, 200
Poplar Springs, 46
Poplar Springs, Liberty Co., 1
Po' Robin Bluff, Laurens Co., 327
Posco, Polk Co., 124
Possum Snout, 171
Possumtrot Branch, Walker Co., 138
Potash Road, 389
Poverty Creek, Lumpkin and Dawson Cos., 408
Prairy Creek, Henry Co., 167
Prattsburg, Talbot Co., 104
Princeton Mill, 256
Proctors Creek, Dawson Co., 272
Proverty Hill, Jones Co., 408
Providence, Fulton Co., 407
Pulltight, Decatur and Grady Cos., 409
Pulltight Hollow, Dade Co., 409
Punk Creek, Heard Co., 51, 436
Punk Knot Town, Heard Co., 436
Purgatory Creek, Burke Co., 405

Quaker Road, 392
Quanasee Town, 63, 65
Quebec, Schley Co., 36

Rabbit Hash, Kentucky, 410
Rabbit Hill, Bryan Co., 409, 410
Rabbitsville, Kentucky, 410
Rabbit Town, Kentucky, 410
Rabun County, 447
Racepath Trail, 74
Randolph County, 472
Rebel Road, 305
Red Bud, Bartow Co., 135
Red Bug Road, 389
Red Cap Swamp, 13
Red Hill, 358
Red Hills, 258
Red Hollow Road, 80, 390

Red House Ford, West Chickamauga Creek, 359
Reeves Creek, Henry Co., 167
Reeves Island and Shoals, Flint River, 202
Reka, Bryan Co., 118
Relee, Coffee Co., 443
Richland Creek, Twiggs Co., 412
Rickman Creek, Rabun Co., 77
Rincon, Effingham Co., 112, 439
Rising Fawn, Dade Co., 55, 449
River Road, 389
River Styx, Charlton Co., 404
River Trail, Wayne Co., 305
Roaring Creek, Muscogee Co., 174
Rockalo, Heard Co., 123
Rock Creek, Greene Co., 372
Rock Landing, Baldwin Co., 183
Rock Landing, Laurens Co., 184
Rock Landing Path, 184
Rockmart, Polk Co., 123, 178
Rocky Comfort Creek, Warren and Jefferson Cos., 413
Rocky Creek, 39
Rogers Bridge, Forsyth Co., 458
Rome Road, 275
Rossville, Walker Co., 280, 351
Rottenwood Creek, Cobb Co., 51, 286
Rouge Road, 130
Rough Creek, Murray and Fannin Cos., 47
Russells Creek, Dawson Co., 271
Rye Patch, Long Co., 413

Saco, Mitchell Co., 124
Saddle Gap, Rabun Co., 74
Sahara, 87
St. Augustine Creek, Chatham Co., 473
St. Catherines Island, 470
St. Clair, Burke Co., 13
St. Jago, 296
St. Marys River, 471
St. Sevilla, Wayne Co., 299
Saint Simons Island, 470
Salacoa, 135
Salacoa Creek, Cherokee and Gordon Cos., 136
Salacoa Town, 135
Salacoa Valley, Cherokee Co., 135
Sally Hughes, 454
Sally Hughes Ferry, Etowah River, 254
Sally Hughes Trail, 252
Salubrity, Fla., 87
Sam Thomas Path, 208
Sanborn Creek, Decatur Co., 220

Sand Creek, 101
Sanderstown, 353
Sandtown Road, 254
Sandy Springs, 101
Sansavilla, 298
Sansavilla Bluffs, 298
San Simon Island, 470
Santa Catarine Island, 470
Santa Maria River, 471
Santa Sevilla Town, 295
Santiago, 296
Saoxomoha Creek, Sumter and Lee Cos., 232, 233
Sardis Creek, Emanuel Co., 283
Sartains Creek, Emanuel Co., 283
Satolah, Rabun Co., 144
Savannah—Augusta Stage Road, 392
Savannah District, Dawson Co., 269
Savannah Ford, Polk Co., Tenn., 68
Sawhatchee Creek, Early Co.: *See* Sowhatchee Creek
Scantville, Carroll Co., 415
Schatulga, Muscogee Co., 155
Schlatterville, Brantley Co., 444
Schley County, 438
Scott Creek, Rabun Co., 63
Screven County, 442
Scrougetown, Gilmer Co., 412
Scuffle Bluff, Telfair Co., 412
Scuffle Creek, Twiggs Co., 412
Scuffleton, Effingham Co., 412
Scuffletown, McDuffie Co., 412
Sculls Bluff, Jenkins Co., 109
Sculls Creek, Jenkins Co., 109
Scull Shoal Creek, Madison Co., 111, 317
Second Black Creek, 390
Seventeen Mile Creek, 232
Seville, Wilcox Co., 439
Shakerag, Fulton Co., 398
Shake Rag Branch, Towns Co., 65
Shakerag Road, 52, 389, 398
Shanty Town, Dade Co., 413
Shawnee Indians, 418
Shell Creek, Decatur Co., 220
Shell Road, 396
Shoal Creek, Cherokee Co., 158
Shut-In Creek, Cherokee Co., 158
Silco, Camden Co., 169
Sillycook Mountain, White Co., 151
Sixes, 143
Sixes Branch, Cherokee Co., 142
Sixes Creek, Cherokee Co., 143
Sixes District, Cherokee Co., 142, 143
Sixes Gold Mine, Cherokee Co., 142, 143
Sixes Old Town, Cherokee Co., 143

Sixes Trail, 144
Six Killer, 93, 144
Six Mile Creek, Forsyth Co., 102
Skeenah Creek, Fannin Co., 453
Skitt Mountain, Hall Co., 452
Skut Knob, Towns Co., 452
Slab Camp Creek, Oconee Co., 9
Slosh-Eye Trail, 36
Slygo, Dade Co., 124
Smoky Road, Coweta Co., 397
Smoky Road, Fulton Co., 397
Smuteyes Trail, 203
Snake Nation Road, Lowndes Co., 397
Soap Creek, Cherokee Co., 458
Soap Creek, Lincoln Co., 287
Soaps Creek, Cobb Co., 286
Social Circle, Bulloch Co., 130
Social Circle, Walton Co., 130
Social Hill, Fulton Co., 131
Society Hill Church, Crawford Co., 131
Sofkee, 41
Sofkee, Bibb Co., 37
Sofkee Creek, Grady Co., 40
Sofkeehatchee Creek, Carroll Co., 41
Sonoraville, Gordon Co., 250
Sopes Creek, Cobb Co., 286, 458
South Fork of Ocmulgee River, 168
South River, 168
South Shellstone Creek, Bleckley Co., 372
Sowhatchee Creek, Early Co., 45, 440
Spanish Pete, 94
Spoil Cane Creek, White Co., 284
Spring Bluff, Camden Co., 282
Spring Place, 351
Stalking Head Branch, Burke Co., 13, 14
Stalkinghead Creek, Jasper Co., 15
Stalkney Head Branch, Burke Co., 14
Standing Boy Creek, Harris and Muscogee Cos., 170, 171
Standing Peachtree Road, 254
Stanfordville, Putnam Co., 405
Starkville, Lee Co., 37
Statham, 445
Steam Mill Road, 394
Sterling Creek, Bryan Co., 315
Sterling Hill, Bryan Co., 315
Sterling Swamp, Bryan Co., 315
Stevens Pottery, 178
Sticcoa Creek, Rabun Co., 63
Stitchihatchie Creek, Dodge and Laurens Cos., 126
Stocking Creek, Burke Co., 13
Stocking Head Branch, Candler Co., 14
Stop, 143

Index / 493

Strawns Road, DeKalb Co., 165
Subligna, Chattooga Co., 119
Sugar Hill Creek, Bartow Co., 250
Sulenojuhnene Ford, Flint River, 203
Sumach Creek, Murray Co., 137
Summertown, Emanuel Co., 87
Summerville, S.C., 87
Sunbury, Liberty Co., 131
Sunbury Road, 391
Suomi, Dodge Co., 333
Surrency, Appling Co., 447
Sutallee, Cherokee Co., 143, 452
Suwanee Trail, Fulton and Forsyth Cos., 52
Suwanoochee Creek, Clinch and Echols Cos., 432
Swan, Major Caleb, 236
Sweetwater Creek, Crawford Co., 265
Sweetwater Creek, Macon and Sumter Cos., 465
Sweetwater Iron Works, McDuffie Co., 125
Swift Creek, Lamar Co., 324

Tahoma, Richmond Co., 419
Taiwalagaw River: *See* Towaliga River
Taliaferro County, 438
Talking Rock Creek, 101
Tallahassee Creek, Dougherty Co., 230, 431
Tallokas, Brooks Co., 444
Tallulah River, Rabun Co., 63
Tallulga Creek, Webster Co., 434
Taloney Missionary Station, 353
Taphulgee: *See* Attapulgus
Tarboro, 178
Tate, 353
Taylors Ridge, Catoosa Co., 358
Taylors Stage Stop, Catoosa Co., 358
Tearbritches Creek, Murray and Fannin Cos., 47
Tellauguehatche River, 61
Teloga, 61
Teloga Creek, Chattooga Co., 61
Telogia Creek, Liberty Co., Fla., 61
Ten Mile Creek, 232
Ten Mile Creek, Appling Co., 306
Ten Mile Creek, Pulaski Co., 306
Ten Mile Trail, Turner and Irwin Cos., 306
Tennessee Road, 252
Tennga, Murray Co., 118
Tennille, Washington Co., 443
Tensawattee, 269
Tensawattee Creek, Dawson Co., 271

Tensawattee Mission, Dawson Co., 271
Tensawattee Town, 270
Terminus, 472
The Runs Creek, Effingham Co., 400
Thirty Mile Beaver Dam Creek, 373
Thlathlothlakuphka, 471
Thoms Ford, Oconee River, 208
Three Killer, 93
Three Notch Road, 396
Thronoteeska, 477
Tickeehatchee Creek, Dodge and Laurens Cos., 126
Tietie Creek, Fla., 365
Tieties, Effingham Co., 364
Tiger, Rabun Co., 74
Tight Eye: *See* Ty Ty
Tighteye Bar, Ala., 365
Tighteye Chute, Ala., 365
Timpson Creek, 78
Timson Creek, 78
Tired Creek, Grady Co., 40
Titi School, Jasper Co., S.C., 365
Titi Swamp, Bulloch Co., 364
Titi Swamp, Decatur Co., 364
Tobacco Road, 389, 394
Tobannee Creek, Quitman Co., 466
Tobesofkee Creek, Monroe and Bibb Cos., 37, 38, 40
Tobler Creek, Baldwin Co., 193, 324
Tobler Creek, Burke Co., 325, 326
Tobler Creek, Lamar Co., 324
Tobler Creek, Monroe Co., 193, 324
Tobosochte Creek, 38
Tobosophskee Creek, 38
Toledo, Charlton Co., 446
Tom Coward Gap, Rabun Co., 75
Toms Ford, Oconee River, 208
Toms Path, 195, 196, 207, 208
Toms Shoals, Ocmulgee River, 193, 199
Toms Shoals, Oconee River, 193
Toonigh, Cherokee Co., 453
Toonowee Mountain, Fannin Co., 453
Tophulga: *See* Attapulgus
Topkegalga: *See* Attapulgus
Toqua Creek, Monroe Co., Tenn., 56
Tory Road, 395
Toto Creek, Dawson Co., 271, 455, 473
Towalaga, 90, 91
Towaliga District, Butts Co., 92
Towaliga River, 90, 440
Towaliga Town, 92
Traders Hill, 178
Travellers Rest, 36
Treaty of Augusta, 1773, 308
Treaty of Tellico, Tenn., 1805, 349

494 / Index

Trices Ferry, Flint River, 203
Trickem, 391
Triplets Ferry, Jenkins Co., 309
Trouble Creek, Oglethorpe Co., 47, 413
Troublesome Creek, Echols Co., 47
Troublesome Creek, Oglethorpe Co., 47
Troublesome Creek, Spalding Co., 47, 413
Tuckahoe, Jefferson Co., 412
Tuckahoe, Screven Co., 412
Tuckaseeking, Effingham Co., 442
Tugalo River, 440
Tukpafka Town, 50, 51
Tulapocca River, 32, 427
Tululgah Creek, Sumter Co., 321
Tumbling Creek, 96
Tuphulga: *See* Attapulgus
Turkey Creek, 46
Turkey Creek, Dooly Co., 99, 372
Turkey Heaven Mountains, Ala., 405
Turkey Town, Etowah Co., Ala., 57
Tuskega Killer, 94
Tuskio-Micco Path, 206, 306
Tussahaw Creek, Henry and Butts Cos., 103
Tussekiah Mico, 12
Twelve Mile Beaver Dam Creek, Hancock Co., 373
Two Chop Way, 396
Two Killer, 93
Two Mile Creek, Forsyth Co., 102, 352
Tye Tye Lake, Bibb Co., 364
Ty Ty, 365
Ty Ty, Tift Co., 364
Ty Ty Branch, Lowndes Co., 364
Ty Ty Crossing, Long Co., 364
Tyty Creek, Macon Co., 364
Ty Ty Creek, Sumter Co., 364
Ty Ty Creek, Worth Co., 364, 473
Ty Ty District, Colquitt Co., 364
Ty Ty District, Tift Co., 364
Ty Ty Pond, Worth Co., 364

Uchee Indians, 418
Ulcohatchee Creek, 201
Uluftey River, Rabun Co., 63
Unawatti Creek, Franklin Co., 95, 99, 456
Unicoi Road, 284: *See also* Unicoi Turnpike
Unicoi Trail, 76
Unicoi Turnpike, 290: *See also* Unicoi Road
Union School Crossroads, Candler Co., 14

Upatoi Creek, Muscogee Co., 11, 420, 422, 440
Upatoi Town, 11, 12, 206
Upatoi Trail, 203
Upelikee Creek, Terrell Co., 423
Upper Black Creek, 290
Upper Creek Trading Path, 92, 192
Upper Sandersville Road, 198
Upper Sansavilla Bluff, 298
Upton Creek, Henry Co., 167
Useless Bay, Clinch Co., 48
Ustanali River: *See* Oostanaula River
Utoy Creek, Fulton Co., 420

Vann House, Forsyth Co., 352
Vanns Ferry, Chattahoochee River, 102, 217, 351
Varnell, 358
Vickery Creek, Fulton Co., 94
Vidalia, Toombs Co., 443
Vidette, Burke Co., 443
Vienna, Dooly Co, 437
Villanow, Walker Co., 123
Villa Rica, Carroll Co., 443
Vinegar Hill, Walton Co., 414
Visage, Towns Co., 75, 411

Wacoochee Creek, Ala., 432
Wahoo, 187
Wahoo, Lumpkin Co., 186
Wahoo Creek, Coweta Co., 187
Wahoo Creek, White and Hall Cos., 186
Wahoo District, Lumpkin Co., 187
Wahoo Island, McIntosh Co., 186
Wales, Levin, 129
Waleska, Cherokee Co., 159
Wallers Ferry, Ocmulgee River, 200
Wallers Road, 200
Walnut Creek, Jones and Bibb Cos., 226
Walthourville, 87
Ward, Nancy, 244
Ward Creek, Lumpkin Co., 244
Warrior Creek, 29
Warrior King of the Cussetas, 12
Warsaw, Fulton Co., 332
Warsaw, McIntosh Co., 332
Warsaw Ferry, Chattahoochee River, 332
Warthen, Washington Co., 443
Warwick, Worth Co., 446
Warwoman, 59
Warwoman Creek, Rabun Co., 74, 454
Warwoman Road, Rabun Co., 74
Wassaw Creek, Chatham Co., 331
Wassaw Island, Chatham Co., 330, 331
Wassaw Sound, Chatham Co., 330

Waters Ferry, Chattahoochee River, 332
Wauhatchie Creek, Dade Co., 450
Wauhatchie Creek, Elbert Co., 450
Wawhoo Island, McIntosh Co.: *See* Wahoo Island, McIntosh Co.
Webster County, 472
Weethlakutchee River, 28
Wehadkee Creek, Ala., 422
Welakochee River: *See* Withlacoochee River
Welcome All Road, Fulton Co., 398
Welustie Creek, Bulloch and Bryan Cos., 290
West Chattooga River, Rabun Co., 60
Weston, Webster Co., 391, 472
White Ground Path, 202
Whitehall, 472
Whitelick Path, 386
White Man Killer, 94
White Path, 59
Whitewater Creek, Heard and Troup Cos., 41
Whitewater Creek, Taylor and Macon Cos., 419
Whitley Branch, Laurens Co., 127
Wickeds Creek, Hall Co., 273
Widow Fool, 454
Willacoochee River, 27, 29
Williamsburg, Calhoun Co., 300
Williamsburg, Clinch Co., 300
Williamsburg, Wayne Co., 299
Williams Ferry, Chattahoochee River, 351
Williamson Swamp Creek, 198
Willie, Liberty Co., 395

Winder, Barrow Co., 107, 445, 472
Winns Ferry, Chattahoochee River, 217, 351
Wire Road, 394
Wissoo Island, 332
Willockoche River: *See* Withlacoochee River
Withlacoochee River, 27, 29, 430
Wolf Creek, 321
Wolf Creek, Sumter Co., 321
Wolfpen Branch, Bulloch Co., 361
Wolfpen Branch, Habersham Co., 361
Wolfpen Branch, McIntosh Co., 361
Wolf Pen District, Bartow Co., 361
Wolfpen Gap, Union Co., 361
Wolfpen Ridge, Union and Towns Cos., 361
Wolf Pit, Bacon Co., 361
Wolf Pit, Ben Hill Co., 361
Wolf Pit, Irwin Co., 361
Wolf Pit Branch, Liberty Co., 361
Wolf Pit District, Stephens Co., 361
Worse Creek, Rabun Co., 46

Yahoola Creek, Lumpkin Co., 243, 244, 456
Yellow Dirt Creek, Heard Co., 54
Yellow Land Creek, Heard Co., 54
Yellow River, 168
Yonah Mountain, White Co., 59, 151
Yonewatleh, 99
Young Cane Creek, Union Co., 252
Young Deer, 59
Young Deer Creek, Forsyth Co., 102
Ypsilanti, Talbot Co., 104, 444

www.ingramcontent.com/pod-product-compliance
Lightning Source LLC
Chambersburg PA
CBHW020633300426
44112CB00007B/95